Areas of the United States

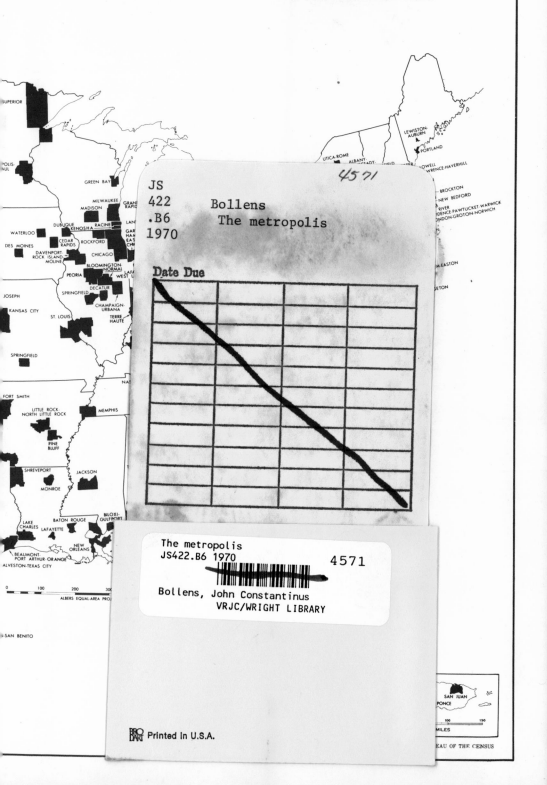

Printed in U.S.A.

THE
METROPOLIS

HARPER & ROW, PUBLISHERS   New York, Evanston, and London

THE METROPOLIS

ITS PEOPLE, POLITICS, AND ECONOMIC LIFE

SECOND EDITION

JOHN C. BOLLENS
UNIVERSITY OF CALIFORNIA, LOS ANGELES
HENRY J. SCHMANDT
UNIVERSITY OF WISCONSIN, MILWAUKEE

PICTURE CREDITS

Title page. Monkmeyer Press Photos. **Chapter openings: pages: 1.** The Port of New York Authority; **27.** American Industrial Development Council; **47.** Ford Foundation; **71.** Greater Vancouver Chamber of Commerce; **100.** American Airlines; **126.** The New York Times; **162.** US Public Health Service; **196.** United Press International; **226.** Ford Foundation; **251.** The Metropolitan Water District of Southern California; **279.** Sam Falk from The New York Times; **312.** The Metropolitan Water District of Southern California; **349.** US Department of Transportation; **373.** Ford Foundation; **396.** Japanese National Tourist Organization; **427.** John T. Hill

THE METROPOLIS: Its People, Politics, and Economic Life, Second Edition

Copyright © 1965, 1970 by John C. Bollens and Henry J. Schmandt

LIBRARY OF CONGRESS CATALOG CARD NUMBER: 77-96227

CONTENTS

Preface   **ix**

1 Nature and Dimensions of the Metropolitan Community   **1**

Defining Metropolitan Areas   2
Metropolis as Community   6
Metropolitan Characteristics   8
Urban and Metropolitan Growth   17
Metropolitan Variations   20
Metropolitan Territory   22
Metropolis in Perspective   23

2 The Metropolis as a Subject of Study   **27**

The Evolution of Metropolitan Research   28
Models   32
The Metropolis as a System   40
The Road Ahead   46

3 The Social Anatomy of the Metropolis   **47**

Spatial Pattern   48
Social Areas   51
Ethnic Structure   60
Age Structure   67
Some Implications of Social Geography   69

4 The Metropolitan Economy   **71**

Economic Types   73

v

Economic Structure 78
The Metropolis as a Labor Market 85
The Central Business District 90
The Economic Pattern and the Government 97

5 Government in the Metropolis **100**

Governments in Abundance 101
The Complexity of Government 102
The Original Governmental System 107
Evolution of the Governmental Pattern 109
Local Governmental Adjustments in the
    Metropolitan Age 113
The States and the Nation 118
Structure and Political Environment 123
Government in Perspective 125

6 Power, Politics, and Participation **126**

The Pattern of Influence 127
The Formal Decision-Makers 133
The Parapolitical Structure 135
The Individual as Civic Participant 146
Participation in Suburbia 155
The "Alienated" Urbanite 158
The Metropolitan Network 160

7 The Service Challenge **162**

Local Versus Area-Wide Functions 163
Transportation 167
Water Supply 176
Sewage Disposal 179
Air Pollution 181
Fire Protection 184
Police 186
Parks and Recreation 192

8 Social and Economic Dilemmas **196**

The Web of Problems 197
The "Deteriorating" City 200
The Problem of Race 210
Urban Education 218
The Good Life 224

9 The Planning Challenge   226

The Traditional Approach   228
The Tools of Planning   229
The Changing Character of Planning   234
Planning and Citizen Involvement   239
Planning the Metropolis   242
The Planning Outlook   249

10 The Fiscal Crisis   251

The Fiscal Dilemma   252
The Growing Public Sector   253
Revenue Patterns   255
Expenditure Patterns   267
Determinants of Fiscal Behavior   273
The Quest for Solutions   275
The Intergovernmental Road   277

11 The One-Government Approach   279

Municipal Expansion: The Halcyon and
    Dormant Years   280
The Annexation Renaissance   284
Annexation and the Urban Fringe   291
City-County Consolidation   297
School District Consolidation   307
Neighborhood Decentralization:
    Counterpoise to Bigness   309
The One-Government Approach: The Future   310

12 The Two-Level Approach   312

Metropolitan Districts   313
Comprehensive Urban County Plan   324
Metropolitan Miami: Comprehensive
    Urban County Government   327
Federation   335
Metropolitan Toronto: Federation in Action   339
The Two-Level Approach: The Future   346

13 The Cooperative Approach   349

The Growth of Cooperation   351
Interlocal Agreements: Scope and Characteristics   352
Cooperation in Metropolitan Philadelphia   356

Cooperation in Los Angeles County   358
Metropolitan Councils of Governments   364
The Cooperative Approach: The Future   369

14 The Politics of Reform   **373**

Barriers to Change   374
Who Gets Involved   376
The Issues   383
Voter Response   386
The Politics of Cooperation   391
The Path of Reorganization   393

15 The Metropolitan World   **396**

The Population Explosion   399
Social Organization   401
Comparative Urban Studies   403
London   404
Ibadan   409
Tokyo   415
São Paulo   420
Metropolitan Communities in a World Setting   425

16 The Image of the Future   **427**

The Existing System   429
Emerging Trends   431
The Present and Future   436
The Good Metropolis   444

A Commentary on Bibliography   **447**

Index of Names   **465**

Index of Subjects   **473**

PREFACE

DRAMATIC DEVELOPMENTS HAVE TAKEN PLACE IN THE METROPOLITAN WORLD since the first edition of this book appeared just five years ago. We were time and again reminded of this fact as we proceeded with the task of thorough revision. This brief period has been one of acute social ferment marked by the newly found activism of the urban disadvantaged, civil disturbances and even violent riots, the rise of the black power movement, and the conflicts generated by attempts to carry out the citizen participation policies of the national government. Congress has enacted significant legislation in efforts to ease tensions and achieve a greater measure of social, economic, and political equality for the deprived segments of the society. Meanwhile, the prestigious National Advisory Commission on Civil Disorders has condemned white racism as the root cause of many of the nation's social problems and has warned of the increasing polarization of blacks and whites. Taken as a whole, the events of recent years, shocking and disturbing as some of them have been, compellingly demonstrate the need for stepping up the pace of urban social change if domestic peace and order are to be assured. The present volume gives attention to these developments.

The metropolis is a complex phenomenon of many facets. It may be seen as a governmental system, a social organism, an economic unit, a collection of people and buildings, or simply a geographical area. For the political scientist, one set of dimensions seems to predominate; for the sociologist another; and for the planner, the geographer, the economist, the philosopher, and the artist, still others. What the observer or scholar looks for in the urban community depends largely on his point of vantage, his individual interests and tastes, and his objectives.

Our purpose here, as in the original edition, has been to present a balanced, multidimensional view of the metropolis, with emphasis on process and behavior as well as on form and structure. In doing so, we have been concerned with many of its major phases: social characteristics and trends, economic developments, physical and land-use considerations, government and politics, and citizen roles. We have also been concerned with the kinds of problems produced by metropolitan growth and functioning and with the various attempts to solve these difficulties. This focus on the "larger" community and its affairs leads to a more realistic portrayal of contemporary urban life than a compartmentalized treatment of the local community.

The approach throughout has been based on the conception of the metropolis as a dynamic system of interacting relationships among people, organizations, and institutions. The selection of material and fields of emphasis, although governed by this conception, has been eclectic and the treatment general. However, we have sought to utilize as fully as possible the growing number of empirical investigations into urban phenomena and the relevant theory that has emerged. For this purpose we have relied on the literature of political science, sociology, economics, and other related disciplines, and on our own research. The result is an up-to-date analysis of the metropolis that we hope will be of interest and value to students, persons in the social sciences, planning, and other fields, and to governmental personnel and other civic-minded citizens.

We are indebted to the many scholars who have written so ably and perceptively on various aspects of the metropolitan community. We have also profited from the insights of practitioners in the field, both public officials and private leaders, who have been confronted with the mounting challenges of growth. In addition, comments and suggestions from readers of the first edition have been valuable to us in preparing this revision.

JOHN C. BOLLENS
HENRY J. SCHMANDT

THE
METROPOLIS

1 /
NATURE AND DIMENSIONS OF THE METROPOLITAN COMMUNITY

THROUGHOUT THE ENGLISH-SPEAKING WORLD, THE TERM "METROPOLIS" AND its derivative *metropolitan* have become symbolic of the modern era. In a sense, the use of *metropolitan* in the name of the world's largest insurance company and of New York City's exciting new baseball team captures something of the significance and meaning of the word. To the contemporary American, it represents bigness, complexity, and dynamism. It is the verbal expression of one of the great phenomena and challenges of our time, the growth and mounting importance of densely settled developments that house most of the nation's populace and contain its most pressing and critical domestic problems. We call these settlements "metropolitan areas."

Metropolitan areas not only encompass most of the people and most of the jobs in the United States, but they also contain most of the public and private financial resources and most of the talent. They are the primary centers of industry, commerce, labor, and government; they are the major centers of education, art, music, drama, and entertainment.

1

They provide ways of life and ideas that pervade the entire nation. They are magnets of hope, both economic and social, for millions of people. As such, they pay a price in problems and difficulties, some social or economic, some governmental. Some of these problems involve deficiencies of public services or gross inequities in financing them; others concern the capacity of people of different racial, ethnic, educational, and social backgrounds to get along with one another. Still others involve the ability of newcomers and the metropolitan community to adjust adequately to each other, and the competence of metropolitan areas to prosper in the face of continued growth.

DEFINING METROPOLITAN AREAS

No precise and universally accepted definition of the *metropolis* exists. Most observers agree that it cannot be defined solely in terms of law, physical geography, or size, or by a combination of these three elements. The metropolis, as is well recognized, does not designate a legally definable entity as a municipality or county does, although metropolitan boundaries might conceivably be coterminous with the territory of a governmental unit. When people speak of Philadelphia, Chicago, or Seattle, they often mean the sociological or economic city, the larger community that extends out beyond the legal limits of the major municipality and embraces the adjacent population and governments.

The term *metropolis* and its derivatives—*metropolitan community* and *metropolitan area*—are used interchangeably and in several different ways. Originally *metropolis* (from the Greek, meaning mother or parent city) referred to the classical city-states of the ancients. Later the word came to be applied to all large urban settlements such as Paris, London, and New York. Within the past century it has acquired a more technical meaning as social scientists have used it as a category or concept to organize and order their data. The SMSA (standard metropolitan statistical area) is the best-known example of this latter application.

Definition Currently Used by the Census Bureau

The standard metropolitan statistical area is defined by the Bureau of the Budget with the advice of a committee of representatives from various federal statistical agencies. According to this definition, each SMSA must contain at least one city of not less than 50,000 population, or two contiguous cities constituting, for general economic and social purposes, a single community with a combined minimum population of 50,000. In general, then, the SMSA will include the entire county in which this central city is located, as well as adjacent counties that meet two criteria: they are *metropolitan in character*, and they are *economically and socially integrated* with the county containing the central city. (An adjacent county either adjoins the county containing the largest city or adjoins an intermediate county economically and socially integrated with the central county.)

To satisfy the criteria of metropolitan character an adjacent county must have at least 75 percent of its labor force engaged in nonagricultural work. In addition, it must meet at least one of three other conditions:

1. It must have not less than half its population living in minor civil divisions with a density of at least 150 persons per square mile, in an unbroken chain of minor civil divisions from a central city in the area. (Minor civil divisions are the primary divisions of a county, such as townships and election precincts.)

2. Its number of nonagricultural workers must equal at least 10 percent of the number of such workers employed in the central county, or it must be the place of employment of at least 10,000 nonagricultural workers.

3. Its nonagricultural labor force must equal 10 percent or more of the number of nonagricultural workers living in the central county, or the county must be the place of residence of a nonagricultural labor force of 10,000 or more.

To meet the test of integration, a neighboring county must satisfy either of two criteria. First, at least 15 percent of the workers living in the county work in the central county. Second, at least 15 percent of those working in the county live in the central county. Other measures of integration are applied only when the results of these two are inconclusive. They include average monthly telephone calls per subscriber from the county to the central county, audited newspaper circulation reports, extent of use by residents of the county of charge accounts in central city retail stores, delivery service practices of such stores, official traffic counts, the extent of public transportation facilities in operation between the county and the central city, and the extent to which local planning groups and other civic organizations operate jointly.[1]

The SMSA, which was initially developed in 1949 without *statistical* in the term, is the latest in a series of metropolitan definitions prepared by the national government. All of them have included the concept of a central city, although the figure has varied from 50,000 to 200,000. The SMSA term, however, was the first to employ the concept of an entire

[1] In New England, the minimum population requirement of 50,000 holds for the central city, but the units comprising a metropolitan area are cities and towns rather than counties. Thus, a New England metropolitan area consists of a central city (or cities), plus adjacent cities and towns having a population density of at least 100 persons per square mile.

county or a combination of counties.[2] This approach was adopted so that all federal statistical agencies could use common political boundaries in collecting and publishing metropolitan data for a variety of purposes. The current definition, like its predecessors, has received general acceptance. This is due in part to the fact that federal agencies, particularly the Bureau of the Census, are the major fact-collecting organizations and principal sources of comparable information about urban areas.

Criticisms of the Federal Definition

The national government's existing definition must be viewed, at best, as furnishing only an approximation of the territorial limits of these entities. And the definition has not gone without criticism. One complaint is that use of the entire county at times exaggerates the amount of metropolitan territory. This is very evident in the case of San Bernardino County, California, a central county of a metropolitan area; it stretches some 180 miles from the eastern border of Los Angeles County to the Nevada and Arizona state lines and consists mostly of sparsely populated or uninhabited desert land. In fact, one can drive from Los Angeles to the gambling and entertainment mecca of Las Vegas over many miles of open desert country in San Bernardino County and Clark County, Nevada (and on certain stretches of highway at speeds that defy even gamblers' odds), without ever having been out of a standard metropolitan statistical area! It should be pointed out, however, that the entire county concept distorts chiefly in terms of territory rather than population.

A second common criticism of the definition, made by William A. Robson, a noted British political scientist, and others, is that a population minimum of 50,000 for a central city is too low and robs the word *metropolitan* of any sociological or political significance. Robson urges that in a country as large and highly developed as the United States only areas with a central city of at least 300,000 and a total population of not less than 400,000 should be included. But many experts do not agree with this more rigorous definition. For instance, an international urban research unit at the University of California, Berkeley, in devising a definition of the metropolitan area for use in international comparisons, decided upon a minimum population of 50,000 for the central city (or continuous urban area) and a total population of not less than 100,000.[3]

---

[2] The concept of the urbanized area is also employed by the Bureau of the Census. In this definition the central city and only the surrounding densely settled area or fringe are included while county lines and other governmental boundaries are ignored. However, use of this definition compounds the difficulty of collecting data for comparative purposes.

[3] William A. Robson (ed.), *Great Cities of the World*, 2nd ed. (New York: Macmillan, 1957), p. 31; International Urban Research, *The World's Metropolitan Areas* (Berkeley and Los Angeles: University of California Press, 1959), pp. 26–27.

A third criticism points to the instability of metropolitan boundaries and denies that precise spatial limits can be located. Those who hold this view maintain that the dimensions of a community vary according to the function under scrutiny. Rejecting the notion that areal limits can be drawn by applying any single criterion, they suggest that a community has many boundaries. If the work-residence pattern is the basis, one set of boundaries emerges; if the retail trade area is plotted, another is evident; and if the daily communication network is outlined, there is a third. Fixing the limits of the metropolis for governmental and public service functions presents similar difficulties. The metropolis may embrace one area for purposes of water supply, another for air pollution, another for transportation, and still another for planning. In one case the municipality may constitute an adequate area for administrative or political control; in others it may be the county or even a far broader region.

Finally, some scholars go so far as to question the continuing validity of the traditional concept of the metropolis. Planners John Friedmann and John Miller, for example, believe that developments now under way will produce within a generation a new and broader ecological unit in the United States, which they call "the urban field." It has become increasingly possible, they point out, to interpret the spatial structure of this nation in ways that emphasize a pattern consisting of metropolitan areas and the intermetropolitan periphery; the latter includes, except for thinly populated portions of the American interior, all territory intervening among metropolitan areas. They foresee in the immediate decades ahead a new scale of urban living that will penetrate deeply into the periphery and transcend the long-established relations of dominance and dependence.

According to Friedmann and Miller, the urban field represents "a fusion of metropolitan spaces and nonmetropolitan peripheral spaces centered on core areas (SMSAs) of at least 300,000 people and extending outwards from these core areas for a distance equivalent to a two-hours drive over modern throughway systems (approximately 100 miles with present technology)."[4] About 90 percent of the national population is presently located within the boundaries of this system, while less than 35 percent of the total land area is included (Figure 1). Important consequences of the development of urban fields, they note, will be a wider life space, a wider choice of living environments, and a wider community of interests; moreover, the urban fields represent the environmental setting most consistent with the aims of a wealthy leisure society and this geographical spread will help to reverse the steady deterioration of the peripheries.

[4] John Friedmann and John Miller, "The Urban Field," *Journal of the American Institute of Planners*, XXXI (November, 1965), 314.

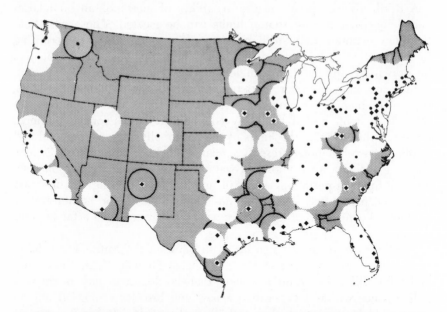

FIGURE 1   **The Urban Fields. Diagrammatic only. The white circles indicate
present urban fields; the dark rings, potential urban fields. The solid
dots are core areas; the diamonds, SMSAs of 200,000–300,000. From**
John Friedmann and John Miller, "The Urban Field," Journal of the
American Institute of Planners, **XXXI (November, 1965), 314.**

METROPOLIS AS COMMUNITY

The metropolitan area is frequently referred to in writings on urbanism
as a community. The first official recognition of this new phenomenon
occurred in a special census report published in 1886. Singling out New
York City as an example, the report called attention to the regional
ramifications of the area and stated that it seemed ". . . proper, in
treating of the vast population occupying the cities of New York, Brook-
lyn, Jersey City, Newark and Hoboken, to consider them not only as
constituting five different municipalities, but as one great metropolitan
community."[5] Also, at about this time pioneers in the study of American
municipal government, Frank J. Goodnow and others, began to refer to
the metropolis in their writings; and by 1920 political scientists were
describing the metropolitan area as an organic and economic unit. "The
simple fact is," one of them noted, "that the city and suburbs are in

[5] U.S. Bureau of the Census, *Tenth Census of the United States, Social Statistics
of Cities* (Washington: 1886), Part I, pp. 531–532.

reality one community, and no amount of political casuistry can alter that fact."[6]

Community is an ambiguous term with many meanings and connotations. Neighborhoods, suburban municipalities, and central cities, as well as the monastery and the beehive, are spoken of as communities. The sociologically oriented individual associates the term in a general way with a social group located within certain spatial or territorial limits and organized to satisfy some functional need. The politically minded person thinks of the term as applying to an organized governmental unit such as a city. But *community* used for the purpose of denoting an easily distinguishable entity has now lost much of its meaning. Some of the newer studies, for example, tend to de-emphasize it as a geographical unit populated by individuals and look upon it as a collection of small and informal social units possessing overlapping memberships that spontaneously generate or foster order in the society. These and similar usages sometimes create confusion, particularly when the fact is overlooked that community, like many other concepts in social science, can be viewed from different aspects and employed for different purposes.

A Combination of Two Definitions

Despite the broad and varied application of *community* and the difficulties of exact definition, a meaning of particular relevance to metropolitan areas can be determined. It is largely a combination of two core definitions that emerge from the literature. One refers to the modes of relationship in which the individuals and families involved share common values and objectives and closely identify themselves with the aggregate population; the other indicates a spatially defined social unit that has functional significance and reflects the interdependence of individuals and groups.

Community in the first-mentioned or classical sense is more applicable to the primary groupings of the past—the village or feudal manor—and seemingly to the early New England town. A community of this kind, as sociologist Scott Greer has pointed out,

disappears under urban conditions; it has no hold over the individual, for its functions are preempted by large specialized organizations in the interest of rational control, while the individual is highly mobile and is isolated in the local area only when he chooses to be. As the functional bases for interaction disappear, communion goes with them.[7]

[6] Chester C. Maxey, *An Outline of Municipal Government* (New York: Doubleday, 1924), p. 120.
[7] "Individual Participation in Mass Society," in Roland Young (ed.), *Approaches to the Study of Politics* (Evanston: Northwestern University Press, 1958), p. 338.

The second meaning relates essentially to the interdependence that arises among groups as a consequence of large-scale specialization. Here the need for social goods—economic production, employment, public and private services, and the whole network of mutually sustaining activities—requires constant interaction and communication among the residents of an area. The strong sense of communion and shared values characteristic of the first meaning may no longer be present, but the high degree of interdependence in daily activities which the urban system imposes on the aggregation creates a social group with strong ties of mutual interest and concern. These ties are coterminous with—in fact they help to fix—the territorial boundaries of the social collectivity or community.

This operational view coincides with the thinking of most contemporary social scientists who tend to regard the metropolis as a mosaic of subareas whose inhabitants are highly interdependent on a daily basis in terms of needs, communication, and commutation to and from work. The last characteristic was stressed by R. D. McKenzie in his famous classic, *The Metropolitan Community*. He stated that the term *metropolitan area* signifies "the territory in which the daily economic and social activities of the local population are carried on through a common system of local institutions. It is essentially the commutation area of the central city."[8] So also a member of the University of Pennsylvania's Institute for Urban Studies commented more recently, "The metropolitan region is not simply an area in which circulation reaches a higher density; it is an area in which a certain type of circulation, the journey to work, is of paramount importance and binds the entire region together."[9]

METROPOLITAN CHARACTERISTICS

Large cities have existed for over 5000 years, but the metropolis, in the current sense of the term, is a relatively recent phenomenon, dating from less than a century ago. Classical Rome might boast of almost a half million inhabitants at one time—but the Rome of the ancients would not be considered a metropolitan community according to modern concepts discussed later in this chapter. On the other hand, of the 230 urban centers in the United States called metropolitan areas, the great majority has less than 1 million people. Some of the latter may be metropolitan communities only in a very specialized sense and mainly

[8] (New York: McGraw-Hill, 1933), p. 84.
[9] Britton Harris, "The Economic Aspects of the Metropolitan Region," *University of Pennsylvania Law Review*, 105 (February, 1957), 469. The place-of-work question, which was included for the first time in a federal survey in the 1960 Census of Population, makes work-residence data readily available to the researcher.

for purposes of statistical tabulation. Vast differences, both qualitative and quantitative, exist among metropolitan areas. Metropolitan New York, for example, bears little resemblance to Metropolitan Lewiston (Maine). Nevertheless, many modern urban communities of vastly different scale have certain common characteristics that distinguish them from the population concentrations of the past and lead us to identify them as metropolitan.

Interdependence

The interdependence of the parts of the metropolis is pointed to as its key attribute in virtually all current writing on the subject. A moment's reflection should convince even the most skeptical that, regardless of whether this element is the primary factor in defining metropolitan areas, it is indeed a most significant and crucial characteristic. Residential suburbs must rely on other sections of the area for their daily supplies: food, clothing, newspapers, entertainment, hospitalization, and the host of other needs typical of the modern household. They must also depend on other portions of the area, some of them as far distant as thirty or forty miles, for the employment opportunities necessary to support many of their inhabitants. This dependence on the remainder of the community is precisely what enables such suburbs to specialize in residential development.

Conversely, the central city must rely on the outlying residential areas for a substantial portion of its labor force, including middle and top management. Downtown merchants in all urban centers still look to the entire area for their customers. In New York City several million persons daily pour into Manhattan to work, man the executive suites, conduct business, shop, or be entertained. In other SMSAs across the nation, the pattern is the same; only the scale is smaller. The people of the metropolis, in short, share a common spatial area for their daily activities. Within this area, although its limits may be imprecisely defined, an intricate web of business and social interrelationships exists and a high degree of communication and interchange among residents, groups, and firms continually takes place.

The close interrelations within a metropolitan area are reflected in many ways other than the work-residence pattern and the territorial division of labor. They are evidenced by the numerous private and semipublic organizations which cross local municipal or city governmental boundaries: the community chest, professional and trade organizations, labor unions, social clubs, and the many other groups that are established and operate on an area-wide basis. They are demonstrated by the privately owned utilities—telephone, electric, gas—which are organized to serve the entire metropolis. They are manifested in the social and cultural fabric of the larger community: the prestigious country club that draws its membership from a wide area; the symphony that is supported by central city dweller and suburbanite alike; the urban university that serves the higher educational aspirations of the metropolis; the medical facility that ministers to the specialized health needs of the total population; the civic center that symbolizes the hopes and achievements of the area.

This interdependence is so obvious, so taken for granted, that its significance and implications are commonly overlooked by the metropolitan resident. It is difficult for the average person to identify himself or his primary self-interests with a mosaic of diverse neighborhoods and governmental entities covering many square miles. He may have a vague idea of the interdependence but he seldom relates it to governmental organization and the need for coordinating public policy in matters affecting the metropolis as a whole. The residential suburb can zone out lower-income workers or the central city neighborhood can practice racial segregation with little thought as to how damaging these policies are to the total community. Suburban residents can insist on noninvolvement with the social problems of the core city as though escape from their consequences is possible; this reaction is simply to deny the realities.

Decentralization

The first great expansion of civilization occurred when large numbers of people came together in concentrations that became the large preindustrial cities of the past. In this movement the city served as a container or magnet attracting people of the hinterlands into a centralized urban culture. Security, religious worship, and greater economic and social opportunities were among the factors that drew the isolated villager within the protective walls of the town. Until well into the nineteenth century most cities were territorially small, highly compact, and largely self-contained. They stood in visible relation and in stark contrast to their surrounding rural environs. Residents of even the largest city could travel on foot from one section or neighborhood to any other within a relatively short time. Market place, temple, work, and kinsfolk were within easy walking distance. Industry was confined to the home or small workshop around which revolved family, religious, and economic activities—all localized in a definable residential district.

In modern times the movement to the urban centers has been greatly accelerated, but now, unlike the compact container of the past, "the city has burst open and scattered its complex organs and organizations over the entire landscape."[10] Under the pressure generated by a rising population the metropolis has expanded territorially, engulfing the

[10] Lewis Mumford, *The City in History* (New York: Harcourt, Brace & World, 1961), p. 3.

agricultural villages and small urban settlements in its path. The resulting scene is familiar to everyone. Long ribbons of development with
their gasoline stations, barbecue stands, automobile graveyards, neon
signs, and motels stretch out into the countryside while residential subdivisions play leapfrog with the land, spawning in the process new
centers of local government and commerce. Historian Oscar Handlin
describes it this way:

> Seen from above, the modern city edges imperceptibly out of its setting.
> There are no clear boundaries. Just now the white trace of the superhighway
> passes through cultivated fields; now it is lost in an asphalt maze of streets
> and buildings. As one drives in from the airport or looks out from the train
> window, clumps of suburban housing, industrial complexes, and occasional
> green spaces flash by; it is hard to tell where city begins and country ends.[11]

Gertrude Stein expressed it somewhat differently after a visit to one
of our typical sprawling metropolises when she was asked how she liked
it there. Her response was, "There?—There is no there there."

Jean Gottmann, a French geographer, has summarized the even greater
metamorphosis that is taking place in some areas. Writing of "megalopolis," the vast urbanized complex that stretches along the northeastern
seaboard of the United States from southern New Hampshire to northern
Virginia (Figure 2), he observes:

> In this area, then, we must abandon the idea of the city as a tightly settled
> and organized unit in which people, activities, and riches are crowded into
> a very small area clearly separated from its nonurban surroundings. Every city in
> this region spreads out far and wide around its original nucleus; it grows amidst
> an irregularly colloidal mixture of rural and suburban landscapes; it melts on
> broad fronts with other mixtures, of somewhat similar though different texture,
> belonging to the suburban neighborhoods of other cities.[12]

Projections by the Urban Land Institute for the year 2000 stretch
Gottmann's Atlantic Seaboard megalopolis to include the Lower Great
Lakes region (Figure 3). Two other vast regions are also expected to
develop by that year—California (Southern and Bay Area–Central
regions) and the Florida Peninsula (East and West coasts and the Central
Zone). Together, these three regions will comprise one-twelfth of the
land area of the continental United States and three-fifths of its population.[13]

[11] Oscar Handlin and John Burchard (eds.), *The Historian and the City* (Cambridge: M.I.T. Press and Harvard University Press, 1963), p. 1.
[12] Jean Gottmann, *Megalopolis: The Urbanized Northeastern Seaboard of the
United States* (New York: Twentieth Century Fund, 1961), p. 5.
[13] Jerome P. Pickard, *Dimensions of Metropolitanism*, Research Monograph 14
(Washington: Urban Land Institute, 1967), pp. 21–23.

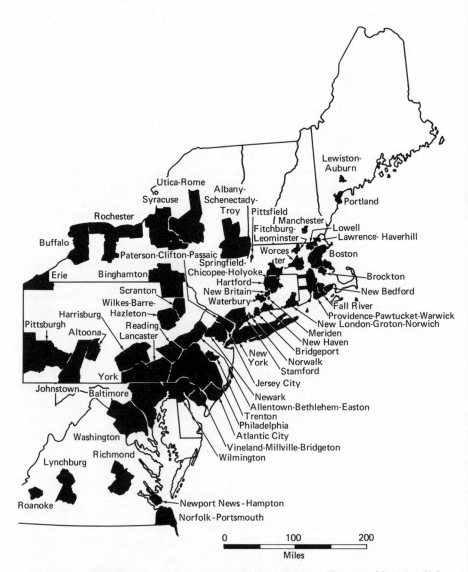

FIGURE 2   **Megalopolis of the Eastern United States. Map provided by U.S. Bureau of the Census: Standard Metropolitan Statistical Areas as Defined by the Bureau of the Budget to January 15, 1968.**

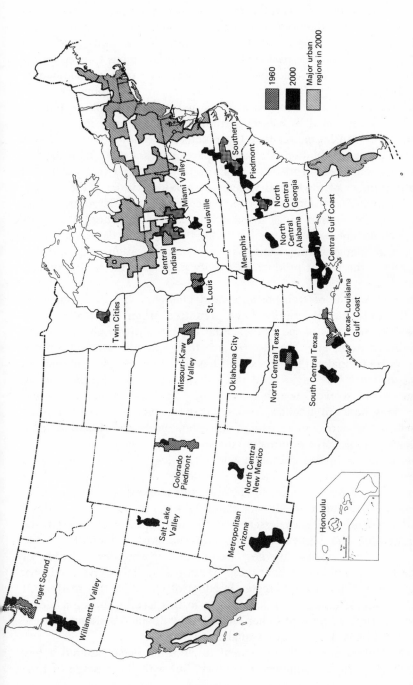

FIGURE 3   Urban Regions in the Year 2000. From Jerome P. Pickard, Dimensions of Metropolitanism, Research Monograph 14, copyright 1968. Reprinted by permission of the Urban Land Institute, 1200–18th Street, Washington, D.C. 20036.

The combination of centralization and deconcentration—the movement of people into the urban centers and the continuous decentralization within these areas—has resulted largely from the scientific and technological advances of the past century. Mechanization has spurred on the shift from farm to city and freed us from reliance on a predominantly agricultural economy. Since the early days of the Republic, American cities have grown faster than rural areas as surplus agricultural populations have been joined by migrants from foreign countries in the larger centers. The transformation that the nineteenth century witnessed was truly an "urban" revolution. Unlike the past, it meant more than the rise of an occasional New York City or Boston or a modest increase in the size and number of towns and villages. It heralded, instead, the appearance of genuine "urbanization" or the concentration of a large proportion of the population into areas of relatively limited territorial size. This change could not have occurred without the fantastic developments in public health, engineering, transportation, communication, and, most importantly, in the rise of productive activity made possible by the power-operated factory.

The new modes of transportation and communication that emerged from the Industrial Revolution have permitted urban dwellers to settle far beyond the walls of the citadel. First the interurban railway and the horse-drawn tram, later the electric streetcar, and still later the private automobile eliminated the necessity of having home and place of work in close proximity. No longer need the factory be located within walking distance of the worker's hearth or the trolley line. Now a man can spend his working hours in a central business district office or a soot-begrimed plant near the core and retreat in the evenings to the sanctuary of a residential suburb or a semirustic villa many miles away.

The advances in transportation and technology have also influenced factory location. Originally, industry was tied to the waterways and later to the railroads for its access to supplies and markets. (As late as 1910 there were more miles of railroads than highways in the United States.) This dependence has been lessened as the development of motor truck transportation, the highway system, and the greater mobility of the labor force have opened up new locational opportunities. A study of Milwaukee County shows how these developments have given industry in one metropolitan area a greater freedom of choice in this matter. Of the 218 plants selecting an industrial site in this locality during a recent ten-year period, 76 percent either chose sites without rail siding or were not using sidings if they were available.[14]

In the United States the movement to suburbia began around a few large cities in the late nineteenth century, but with the passage of time

[14] See N. J. Stefaniak, *Industrial Location in Milwaukee County* (Milwaukee: City of Milwaukee Office of Industrial Development Coordinator, 1959).

the outward thrust of urban population also became characteristic of smaller places.[15] Most cities of 50,000 and over now exhibit patterns of expansion and diffusion similar to those formerly found only around the larger municipalities. For example, in the 1950–1960 period most of the forty-four urban areas of less than 100,000 population that acquired metropolitan status showed an average growth rate of more than 40 percent in their suburban rings.

The decentralization of metropolitan areas, moreover, is not simply an hegira from the core city. Important as this factor is in accounting for ring growth, a portion of this increase is also due to migration from other areas. With high mobility among the managerial ranks of business and industry, the "organization man" frequently moves from the suburb of one metropolis to a similar community in another. White-collar workers in the child-rearing stage who move for one reason or another often follow a similar pattern. Natural increase is a further significant factor since many new suburbanites are young couples beginning the family cycle.

Governmental Fragmentation

The spread of population outward from the core has brought with it a corresponding decentralization of the governmental pattern. When the first great migration waves struck the urban centers, the increased population was absorbed within the cities. Later, as the original boundaries became inadequate to accommodate the newcomers, the corporate limits of the city were expanded by annexing adjacent areas. By the end of the nineteenth century, however, the outward movement had started to outrun the ability of the core city to enlarge its legal boundaries. With the diffusion of population all over the landscape, the metropolis began to look more and more like a formless agglomeration of people and enterprise. New units of local government—cities, towns, villages, school districts, and a wide variety of other special districts—multiplied with astonishing rapidity in the outlying areas. Today, governmental fragmentation is recognized as a major characteristic of the American metropolis.

Specialization

The concentration of people in urban centers, together with technological advancements, has made possible a high degree of specialization. This feature of metropolitanization is reflected in land use as well as commercial and industrial pursuits. With the assistance of planning and zoning, sections of the metropolis have been set aside for various purposes: residential sites, industrial parks, regional shopping centers, and

[15] Leo F. Schnore, "The Growth of Metropolitan Suburbs," *American Sociological Review,* 22 (April, 1957), 165.

many others. Some suburbs are entirely residential; a much smaller but still significant number are predominantly industrial; and still others contain varied combinations of factories, shops, and homes. Even within the central city, increased specialization of neighborhoods has been under way for a half century or more, stimulated in recent years by urban renewal and redevelopment efforts.

Decentralization and specialization have been made possible by size and technology. The motor vehicle and paved road and new methods of communication have linked the city and its environs in a closer functional relationship. The institutional division of labor which formerly characterized the compact city has been extended to include a wide range of outlying settlement. New subcenters closely linked to the core city have sprung up. These subcenters are seldom complete in their service structure but depend on the core for the more specialized and integrating functions.[16] Yet while they are subject to the dominance or influence of the metropolitan center, they in turn exert a significant influence in their more limited areas. The resulting decentralization of activity has brought urban communities into a new kind of relationship, one marked by a high degree of interdependence between the center and outlying areas and among the latter themselves.

Not only have new subcenters been created by the population "explosion," but the conquering of space by the automobile, telephone, radio, and television has also drawn long-established and formerly semi-independent communities into the orbit of the core city and forged vital links between them and other parts of the metropolitan area. Enveloped in the course of time have been settlements, some almost as old as the central city and formerly serving as local trading posts for the adjacent farm areas; industrial satellites which had been established on railroads and waterways some distance from the core; and wealthy residential suburbs peopled by the railroad commuters at the turn of the present century. Virtually without exception, these various territorial segments are under different local public jurisdictions, but this in no way affects the basic interdependence in daily activities that exists among them; it merely makes the process of governing them more difficult.

In summary, no definitive list of criteria for metropolitanism exists. Population size, interdependence, decentralization, governmental fragmentation, and specialization are the most frequently attributed characteristics. If the definition of a metropolitan area employed by the Bureau of the Census (the SMSA definition) is accepted without an understanding of its proper use, any city in an area not previously recognized as metropolitan automatically upon attaining a population of 50,000 becomes part of a metropolis. It would, however, be naive to assume that an area of slightly over 50,000 inhabitants exhibits the same

16 McKenzie, *The Metropolitan Community*, chap. 6.

characteristics as one of 5 million. It would be equally naive to believe that by studying the former we would be examining a microcosm or miniature replica of the latter. Size is, of course, a concomitant of metropolitanization, but the point at which an urban area becomes metropolitan cannot be defined merely by numbers of people.

URBAN AND METROPOLITAN GROWTH

There is a very basic reason for the increasing concern about metropolitan problems. We in the United States are in the midst, both nationally and internationally, of a continuing and seemingly unending period of urban and metropolitan growth. This is an irrefutable fact despite changes in the definitions of "urban" and "metropolitan" over the years and despite the more stringent definitions applied in a number of other nations.

Until relatively recent years, the United States has been a predominantly rural nation. From 1790, when there were only twenty-four urban places of 2500 or more and urban residents made up only about one-twentieth of our population, until the start of the present century, we grew steadily, although at times very slowly, more urban. In the current century, the rate of urbanization was particularly rapid during the first three decades. Nevertheless, the census of 1920 was the first to reveal that more than half of the American people lived in urban areas. Urbanization came to a virtual halt during the depressed economic conditions of the 1930s, but it accelerated again during the 1940s and has continued to increase since then. In 1960, at the time of the decennial count, 69.9 percent of the nation's population was recorded as urban. And urban growth is continuing.[17]

From Urban to Metropolitan

The transformation of the United States from an urban to a metropolitan nation came much more quickly than the change from rural to urban. In fact, it occurred so suddenly that, as Victor Jones, a veteran scholar in the field has wisely observed, the people of the United States became metropolitan before realizing their change from rural to urban.[18] The rapidity of this development is evident from the fact that the Census Bureau first took cognizance of the metropolitan phenomenon in a report

[17] According to the Census Bureau, the urban areas of the United States consist for the most part of cities and other incorporated places that possess at least 2500 inhabitants. In addition, under this definition, densely settled or heavily populated unincorporated areas are also regarded as urban territory. In this book, we often use the words *metropolitan* and *urban* synonomously to avoid monotonous repetition.

[18] Victor Jones, "American Local Government in a Changing Federalism," *American Review*, II (May, 1962), 108.

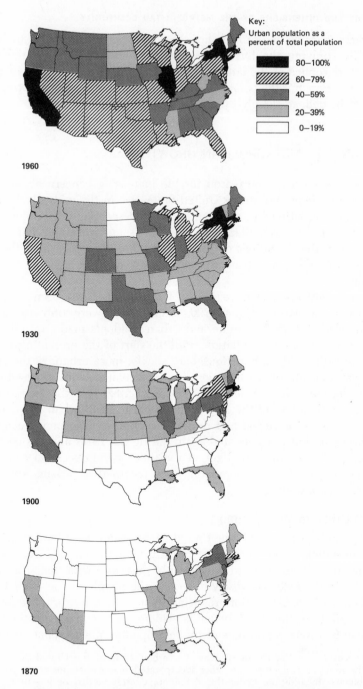

FIGURE 4   **The Growth of Urbanization by States, 1870–1960. From John R. Borchert,** The Urbanization of the Upper Midwest: 1930–1960, **Upper Midwest Economic Study, Urban Report no. 2, February, 1963, p. 2.**

on social statistics of cities in 1886. It was not until the census of 1910, however, that the pioneering official attempt to define the term was made and certain metropolitan aspects of the population were separately analyzed for the first time. The recentness of 1910 stands in marked contrast to the ancientness of 1790, the time of the first census and the first official defining of "urban."

The metropolitan growth of the United States has increased without interruption, but at different rates, during all of the present century. In 1900, the metropolitan population constituted a small minority—less than one-third of the American people. Forty years later, the minority became the majority; within the short span of four decades America had become primarily metropolitan. The population increase in metropolitan areas for the decade ending in 1960 exceeded the total population living in all such complexes in 1900. By 1960, according to the census, 62.8 percent of the national total, or 112,885,178 inhabitants, resided in metropolitan areas. They are still expanding and are expected to continue to do so. A census study estimated about two-thirds of the population to be metropolitan in 1965, and the National Planning Association, in making projections up to 1975, foresaw a further gain.[19]

During all of the current century the metropolitan population has been increasing faster than the rate for the rest of the nation. The disparity was very wide in the 1950s when the metropolitan population grew at nearly five times the nonmetropolitan rate. Since 1960 there has been a decided narrowing of the difference, but metropolitan complexes are still growing about 60 percent faster. The same growth trend is apparent in the number of metropolitan areas. The total has now reached 230, an increase of more than one-third in the past two decades, a gain largely attributable to formerly nonmetropolitan areas growing into metropolitan status.

Rampant metropolitan growth has not gone unchallenged. In some quarters the problems of urban ghettos are being tied to the problems of the continuing, although recently slowing, depopulation of the nation's rural areas, and there has been agitation for a rural renaissance. A national policy encouraging the economic and social renewal of farm areas and small towns has been called for. Rural America, it is argued, has space but not the opportunity for growth while urban America has the opportunity but no space for the millions who inhabit it. Those who advocate the renewal of rural areas see advantages in redressing population imbalance, effecting economies by reducing the costs of concentration,

---

[19] U.S. Bureau of the Census, *Estimates of the Population of Standard Metropolitan Statistical Areas: July 1, 1965,* Current Population Reports, Population Estimates, Series P-25, no. 371 (Washington: 1967), p. 1; National Planning Association, Center for Economic Projections, *Economic and Demographic Projections for Two Hundred and Twenty-Four Metropolitan Areas,* Vol. III (Washington: 1967), p. S-768.

and halting sprawl in favor of more orderly urban development.[20]

In recent years many federal programs have begun to supply increasing aid to depressed rural areas. Legislation such as the Rural Water Systems and Sanitation Act, the Appalachian Regional Development Act, the Manpower Training and Development Act, and the Food and Agriculture Act provide much needed assistance. In a⸳dition to the Department of Agriculture, which administers many rural assistance programs, other federal departments—Commerce; Labor; Health, Education, and Welfare; Transportation; and Housing and Urban Development—are increasingly investigating the needs of rural America. There is, however, no overall federal policy that thoroughly recognizes and acts upon the problems which have been created by the flight of young people from farm areas into expanding metropolises.

METROPOLITAN VARIATIONS

Although metropolitanism is a national development, its extent and nature vary among regions, states, and individual areas. The Northeast, consisting of the states from Maine through New Jersey and Pennsylvania, is the most highly urbanized region; metropolitan residents make up about four-fifths of its population. The West, composed of the Mountain and Pacific states, stands second, with about three-fourths of its people metropolitan. The North Central region (from Michigan and Ohio west through the tier of states extending from North Dakota through Kansas) is third, with a metropolitan population of approximately 65 percent.

The South, here defined to include Texas, Oklahoma, and Arkansas as well as the "old South," is the least metropolitan; slightly more than one-half of its inhabitants lives in such complexes. The extremes in regional differences are lessening in recent years, due to the slow metropolitan growth in New England and the rapid increase in the South, which has been second only to the expansion rate of the West.

Interstate metropolitan differences are also appreciable. SMSAs are located in forty-seven states and the District of Columbia. (There are also three in the Commonwealth of Puerto Rico but they generally are excluded from consideration in this book.) Only Alaska, Vermont, and Wyoming have no metropolitan areas.[21] The range in number of SMSAs

[20] See, for example, U.S. Department of Agriculture, *Agriculture/2000* (Washington: 1967); Advisory Commission on Intergovernmental Relations, *Urban and Rural America: Policies for Future Growth* (Washington: 1968); and John A. Baker, "Unlimited Alternative to City Problems," *Public Management*, 50 (July, 1968), 168–169.

[21] A congressman from Wyoming, in a resolution presented in 1968, pleaded for each state to have at least one area recognized as an SMSA, even though not satisfying the federally established criteria.

among the states is wide, from one to twenty-three. Six states have 10 or more. Texas leads by far with 23, followed by California and Ohio with 14, Pennsylvania with 12, and Massachusetts and Michigan with 10 each. At the other extreme are nine that have only one apiece. They are Delaware, Hawaii, Idaho, Maryland, New Hampshire, New Mexico, North Dakota, Rhode Island, and South Dakota.

The metropolitan proportion of the population of individual states is a more precise measure of interstate variations than is the number of areas. Twenty-six states are at least 50 percent metropolitan. Some have a very intense degree of metropolitan development; for instance, five— California, Rhode Island, New York, Massachusetts, and Hawaii—are above the 80 percent mark. On the other hand, in four states with metropolitan areas—North Dakota, South Dakota, Idaho, and Mississippi— the portion of population that is metropolitan is less than 20 percent of the total. The range extends from California with about nine-tenths of its people metropolitan to North Dakota with about one-tenth (excluding, of course, the three states which have no SMSAs and thus have no degree of metropolitanism).

Contrasts Among Metropolitan Areas

In addition to important regional and state variations, metropolitan areas differ greatly among themselves, a fact well illustrated by several demographic characteristics. Population size is a good example. Such areas vary from the New York Standard Metropolitan Statistical Area with an estimated total of 11,366,000 to those of less than 100,000. (It can be argued that the range is even greater. The New York interstate metropolitan area, called the New York Standard Consolidated Area by the Bureau of the Budget, is believed by many people to reflect more realistically the limits of the New York metropolitan area; it has an estimated population of 15,821,000.[22]) Only a few areas, such as Los Angeles— Long Beach, Chicago, Philadelphia, and Detroit, have more than 3 million inhabitants. Most have less than 500,000 and many possess fewer than 250,000.

Rate of population change is another variant. Rates differ greatly, and estimates for 1960–1965 demonstrate this fact. In this short period, ten metropolitan areas increased in population by one-fourth or more; they were led by the Las Vegas area, which experienced a growth of more than 80 percent. In contrast, a number of metropolitan areas in scattered locations (in Indiana, Louisiana, Minnesota, and Pennsylvania, among others) had fewer people in 1965 than five years earlier.

[22] In recognition of the importance of obtaining very inclusive statistics for New York–Northeastern New Jersey and Chicago–Northwestern Indiana, the Bureau of the Budget designates these two locations as standard consolidated areas. Their territory is specified in footnotes to Table 1. The New York and Chicago SMSAs are defined by the bureau as intrastate.

One other general characteristic of the population also shows important variations among SMSAs. There is a distinct division among them as to which portion, central city or suburban, houses the majority of the residents. In most metropolitan areas, the majority of the people lives in the central city (or cities). But the proportion of SMSAs where the suburbs are the more populous section has been constantly increasing. The shifting balance is even more evident when the relative percentages of the metropolitan population are considered. Reinforcing a long-time trend of faster growth, the suburbs in the 1960s drew ahead of the population total of the central cities (Figure 5). The contrasts in the distri-

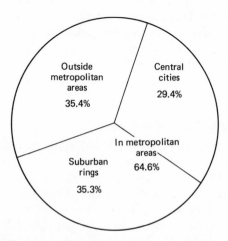

FIGURE 5 **Population Distribution by Metropolitan–Nonmetropolitan Residence for the United States, 1968. From U.S. Bureau of the Census, "Trends in Social and Economic Conditions in Metropolitan Areas,"** Current Population Reports, **Series P-23, no. 27.**

bution of residents are astounding in some metropolitan regions. In the San Antonio area, for example, less than one-fifth lives in the suburbs. The exact opposite is true in the Johnstown, Pennsylvania, area; there, fewer than one-fifth lives in the central city.

METROPOLITAN TERRITORY

Metropolitan growth in the United States is further shown in the total amount of territory such areas embrace. SMSAs contain approximately 365,000 square miles, an increase of about three-fourths over the 1950 total. This gain is due both to the emergence of new metropolises and to the territorial expansion of a number of older ones. Despite this considerable growth in total territory, the metropolitan areas together contain only about 10 percent of the nation's land. Obviously the population density of SMSAs is comparatively high—more than six times that of the United States in general.

Many Intracounty

Many metropolitan areas, 115 or exactly one-half of them, are located in a single county. It should be pointed out, however, that the areas of counties differ in the various parts of the country; those in the western states, for example, are much larger than those in the North Central region.

Intercounty metropolitan areas are also common. They contain from two to eight counties if the standard metropolitan statistical area definition is used exclusively, or they range from two to thirteen counties if the New York Standard Consolidated Area is included. None of these intercounty metropolitan areas is located within the boundaries of a single general-purpose local government.

Interstate and International Areas

Many intercounty metropolitan areas are also interstate in territory. There are thirty such areas when the SMSA definition is employed. There are thirty-two if the New York and Chicago standard consolidated areas are included (and certainly it is realistic to regard these two as interstate). Of the thirty-two, seven have more than one million people. The territory of some other metropolitan areas borders but does not cross state lines; these areas are interstate in impact, although not in territory.

Five metropolitan areas of the United States are in fact international in territorial extent since they adjoin substantial urban settlements located in other nations. They are the Detroit, Michigan–Windsor, Canada area; the San Diego, California–Tijuana, Mexico area; the Buffalo–Niagara Falls, New York–Fort Erie–Niagara Falls, Canada area; the El Paso, Texas–Ciudad Juarez, Mexico area; and the Laredo, Texas–Nuevo Laredo, Mexico area. In the first three instances the largest city is in the United States; in the latter two it is in Mexico. In addition, certain other metropolitan areas border international bodies of water, such as the Great Lakes, thus involving them in decisions of international importance.

METROPOLIS IN PERSPECTIVE

Whether praised or damned, the metropolis plays a major role in the lives of an ever-growing number of Americans. A giant producer and consumer of goods as well as a center of culture and urbanity, it helps to satisfy many of the deep-seated needs and desires of mankind. At the same time it creates vast public and private problems that challenge

TABLE 1   Interstate Metropolitan Areas

Metropolitan Area	States Possessing Part of Territory[a]	Number of Counties Included	1965 Estimated Population
New York–Northeastern New Jersey[b]	New York, New Jersey	13[c]	15,821,000
Chicago–Northwestern Indiana[d]	Illinois, Indiana	8	7,284,000
Philadelphia	Pennsylvania, New Jersey	8	4,664,000
Washington	D.C., Maryland, Virginia	6	2,408,000
St. Louis	Missouri, Illinois	6	2,249,000
Cincinnati	Ohio, Kentucky, Indiana	7	1,347,000
Kansas City	Missouri, Kansas	6	1,183,000
Portland	Oregon, Washington	4	897,000
Providence-Pawtucket	Rhode Island, Massachusetts	8	816,148[e]
Louisville	Kentucky, Indiana	3	771,000
Memphis	Tennessee, Arkansas	2	740,000
Toledo	Ohio, Michigan	3	657,000
Omaha	Nebraska, Iowa	3	516,000
Allentown-Bethlehem-Easton	Pennsylvania, New Jersey	3	515,000
Springfield-Chicopee-Holyoke	Massachusetts, Connecticut	4	493,999[e]
Wilmington	Delaware, New Jersey, Maryland	3	468,000
Davenport–Rock Island–Moline	Iowa, Illinois	3	339,000
Binghamton	New York, Pennsylvania	3	297,000
Chattanooga	Tennessee, Georgia	2	292,000
Duluth-Superior	Minnesota, Wisconsin	2	267,000
Huntington-Ashland	West Virginia, Kentucky, Ohio	4	260,000
Columbus	Georgia, Alabama	3	260,000
Augusta	Georgia, South Carolina	2	237,000
Evansville	Indiana, Kentucky	3	223,000
Wheeling	West Virginia, Ohio	3	188,000
Lawrence-Haverhill	Massachusetts, New Hampshire	2	187,601[e]
Steubenville-Weirton	Ohio, West Virginia	3	170,000
Fort Smith	Arkansas, Oklahoma	4	154,000
Fall River	Massachusetts, Rhode Island	2	138,156[e]
Sioux City	Iowa, Nebraska	2	114,000
Fargo-Moorhead	North Dakota, Minnesota	2	110,000
Texarkana	Texas, Arkansas	2	100,000

[a] The state containing the central city (or the more populous one when there are two such cities) is listed first.

[b] This is a standard consolidated area, which consists of four standard metropolitan statistical areas (New York, Newark, Jersey City, and Paterson-Clifton-Passaic) and Middlesex and Somerset counties, New Jersey.

[c] Counting New York City as a single county area.

[d] This is a standard consolidated area, which consists of two standard metropolitan statistical areas (Chicago and Gary–Hammond–East Chicago).

[e] 1960 official population.

SOURCE: Adapted from *Standard Metropolitan Statistical Areas*, Executive Office of the President, Bureau of the Budget (Washington: 1967).

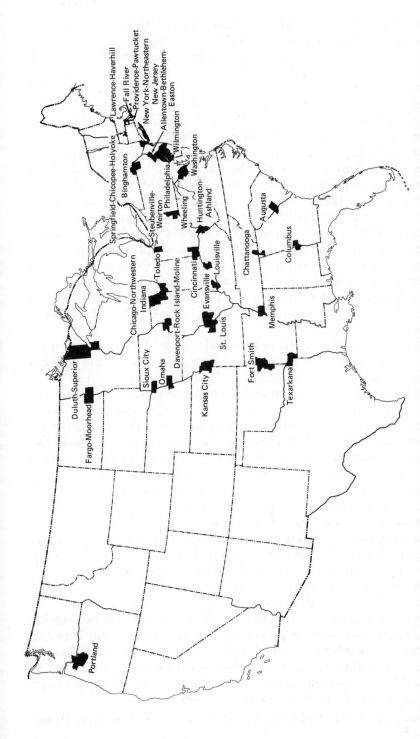

FIGURE 6 Interstate Metropolitan Areas, 1968. Adapted from U.S. Bureau of the Census Map: Standard Metropolitan Statistical Areas as Defined by the Bureau of the Budget to January 15, 1968.

the ingenuity of urban America. Dynamic technological, social, political, and economic forces are at work within this complex phenomenon and shape its character, physical form, and institutions. As the crossroads and assembly point for a continuously increasing flow of people, goods, and capital, the metropolis is the modern version of the preindustrial cities which flourished along the great trade routes of Europe and Asia. But now the abacus has given way to the electronic computer and the merchant prince to the organization man.

Variety of choice in all aspects of living and working has come to be regarded by many students of urban affairs as the basic goal of the metropolitan community. Dean John Burchard of the Massachusetts Institute of Technology once put it simply when he said that the only real excuse for the metropolis is that it provides a population large enough to satisfy many diverse interests. It must have enough people, he remarked, so that a particular kind of sausage or special cheese can be found in some store. Participants in a recent symposium viewed it in somewhat more formal terms as "creating fundamental opportunities for high incomes, a greater variety and a wider choice of modes of living, a way of life that could be more stimulating, more enlightened, and more conducive to innovations."[23]

These observations express in a general way the functional role of the metropolitan community in modern society. This role is one of many facets. It relates to the concentration of people and industry that makes possible both a widening variety of consumer goods and a reduction in the costs of producing them. It refers to the social and cultural opportunities that only a large urban complex can offer: the library, theater, art museum, and music hall. It involves the communications network that permits interpersonal contacts among large numbers of people in business and social transactions. And most important, it encompasses the means—the educational, experiential, and employment opportunities—that enable the individual to participate as an active producer and consumer of urban goods and urban culture.

The metropolis represents an accumulation of the human and material resources that make possible the accomplishment of goals undreamed of in a simpler and smaller-scale society. By bringing together a variety of personal skills and capital, it fosters specialization and a wide diversity of economic and social activities. It serves as the producer of goods and services and as a market place not alone for its own population but for a larger hinterland. It performs a less tangible but still important function as a symbol of an area's culture, its industrial and commercial might, and its distinctive position in the broader national and international scene. The metropolitan community of today is a way of life, one might even say a civilization. It is the city "writ large."

[23] Kevin Lynch and Lloyd Rodwin, "A World of Cities," *Daedalus,* 90 (Winter, 1961), 6.

2 / THE METROPOLIS AS A SUBJECT OF STUDY

EACH OF US SEES A COMMUNITY AND ITS QUALITIES DIFFERENTLY. TO SOME, New York City may be the acme of culture and sophistication; to others, an overcrowded and unfriendly Leviathan. Carl Sandburg once described Chicago as:

> Strong, husky, brawling
> City of the big shoulders
> Laughing the stormy, husky, brawling
> laughter of youth.

But some years later the *Chicago Daily News* saw it as:

> Sedate, sedentary, complacent
> City of the big waistline
> That is Chicago today.

In his daily round of working, making a home for his family, and recreating, the urban dweller senses some of the special qualities which

27

seem to mark the city or metropolis as a whole. He inevitably attempts to identify and structure this environment, to grasp it sensuously, to give it mental image. He builds up, as Anselm Strauss, a social psychologist, puts it, "a set of associations which prepare him to accept and appreciate a shorthand symbolic characterization of the place."[1]

The social scientist does not enjoy the license of the poet nor the image-making freedom of the citizen-observer. In his role as a scientist, he must seek to discover causal relations among the many variables or dimensions of community life that will enable him to explain urban phenomena. In this work he continuously faces the problem of how to formulate general (and empirically verifiable) statements about metropolitan areas which will be widely applicable despite areal differences in size and other characteristics. He can, of course, limit the statements to relationships which are so general that they apply to all such areas, but this procedure offers little analytical help since it obscures their important quantitative and qualitative differences. It is not likely, for example, that Metropolitan New York is a Metropolitan Abilene, Texas, projected onto a cinematic screen or that a small metropolis of 50,000 will play the political game in the same manner as one of 5,000,000. Nor is it likely that a socially and racially homogeneous community will behave in the same fashion or be confronted with the same spectrum of problems as one of social and racial diversity, even though they are similar in size. A more adequate framework of analysis than impressionistic assumptions is called for if generalizations about metropolitan areas are to achieve greater meaning and accuracy.

THE EVOLUTION OF METROPOLITAN RESEARCH

Metropolitan research in contrast to that relating to the individual locality is of relatively recent vintage. Although pioneers in the study of American municipal government around the turn of the present century referred briefly to the metropolis in their writings, it was not until the 1920s that social scientists began to regard this phenomenon as a subject worthy of serious study. The initial impetus grew out of the municipal reform movement of the early part of the century in which political scientists had been active participants. As local units began to multiply outside the central city during the post-World War I years, many who had been concerned with municipal reorganization shifted their attention to the governmental problem of the larger area. In doing

[1] *Images of the American City* (New York: Free Press, 1961), pp. 5–6. See also Kevin Lynch, *The Image of the City* (Cambridge: M.I.T. Press and Harvard University Press, 1960).

so, they brought with them a reformist orientation that was to dominate the work of political scientists in the metropolitan field for the next several decades.[2]

During this period, urban political scientists focused their attention largely on the matter of structural reorganization of the metropolitan governmental pattern. Within the framework provided by the philosophy and assumptions of administrative management, they sought to document a case, first for total amalgamation of local units and, when this remedy proved impossible of achievement, for some type of milder solution such as functional consolidation. The studies of particular metropolitan areas which emerged during these years followed a strikingly similar pattern. After identifying service deficiencies and directing attention to the uneconomical or inefficient mode of operation under existing arrangements, they prescribed remedies involving reconstruction of the organizational pattern.

While urban political science was engrossed in the problems of administrative reform, urban sociology was engaged in studies of a more basic nature. Sociological research in the early 1900s, like that of political science, had been normative and prescriptive in character and advocated social amelioration. However, with the publication of Robert E. Park's classic paper on the city in 1916,[3] attention was directed to the need for systematic urban research and theory formulation. The approach developed by Park and his colleagues at the University of Chicago represented efforts to adapt ecological concepts borrowed from biology to the organism of the city and its environs.

Ecological theory did not long enjoy a monopoly in the urban field. With the publication of the Lynds' study of Middletown (Muncie, Indiana) in 1929,[4] an increasing number of sociologists began to inquire into the relationships between the daily life of urbanites and the social structure of their community. Investigation of the concepts of social change, institutional organizations and functions, and social stratification

[2] For a critique of the resulting research see Alan R. Richards, "Local Government Research: A Partial Evaluation," *Public Administration Review*, XIV (Autumn, 1954), 271–277; Robert T. Daland, "Political Science and the Study of Urbanism," *American Political Science Review*, LX (June, 1957), 491–509; Wallace S. Sayre and Nelson W. Polsby, "American Political Science and the Study of Urbanization," in Philip M. Hauser and Leo F. Schnore (eds.), *The Study of Urbanization* (New York: Wiley, 1965), pp. 115–156; Henry J. Schmandt, "Toward Comparability in Metropolitan Research," in Thomas R. Dye (ed.), *Comparative Research in Community Politics* (Athens: University of Georgia, 1966), pp. 6–40; and H. Paul Friesema, "The Metropolis and the Maze of Local Government," *Urban Affairs Quarterly*, II (December, 1966), 68–90.

[3] "The City: Suggestions for the Investigation of Human Behavior in the Urban Environment," *American Journal of Sociology*, XX (March, 1916), 577–612.

[4] Robert S. Lynd and Helen M. Lynd, *Middletown* (New York: Harcourt, Brace & World, 1929).

became common. Although these early studies dealt with individual cities or villages, usually of small size, they laid the basis for later research into the larger metropolitan community.

In the 1950s metropolitan research took a new turn as foundation and other private funds became available to those working in the urban field. This assistance enabled a number of large-scale surveys to be carried out in such areas as Cleveland, Dayton, New York, and St. Louis. The resulting research sought to probe into the metropolitan community on a much broader and more systematic basis than preceding efforts. In these endeavors, political scientists, economists, sociologists, and geographers collaborated. Studies of governmental arrangements and services, while pursued, became secondary to more basic inquiries into the leadership pattern of the metropolis, its economic base and political and social interests, and the perceptions and attitudes of its citizens. Researchers were concerned with the state of the metropolitan community and did not avoid policy positions and recommendations, but they approached their subject with a commitment to rigorous empirical investigation.

By the end of the 1950s a further development had occurred in urban and metropolitan research, with the emphasis shifting from studies designed to provide policy guidance to inquiries aimed primarily at enhancing knowledge about how the system actually functions. The role of detached observer and analyst was stressed, and heavy criticism was leveled at those who continued to write in a prescriptive vein. Most characteristic of this decade were the power structure studies which predominated among both urban sociologists and urban political scientists, with something of a running battle being waged between the two disciplines.[5] These efforts, as in the case of the earlier community studies of the Middletown variety, concentrated mainly on the smaller communities to the neglect of the metropolis. This was also the time when many political scientists tended to discard governmental organization as a major dimension of the metropolitan problem. In fact, it appeared in some instances that in their reaction against the earlier bias for reorganizing the local government pattern, they were proceeding as though they were trying to make a case for political fragmentation.[6]

[5] Power structure studies are discussed in Chapter 6.

[6] This de-emphasis of governmental form has been balanced in more recent years by empirical studies which attempt to relate structure to various other factors of community life. See, for example, Leo F. Schnore and Robert R. Alford, "Forms of Government and Socioeconomic Characteristics of Suburbs," *Administrative Science Quarterly*, 8 (June, 1963), 1–17; Thomas R. Dye, "Urban Political Integration: Conditions Associated with Annexation in American Cities," *Midwest Journal of Political Science*, VIII (November, 1964), 430–446; Raymond Wolfinger and John Field, "Political Ethos and the Structure of City Government," *American Political Science Review*, LX (June, 1966), 306–326; and Robert L. Lineberry and Edmund P. Fowler, "Reformism and Public Policies in American Cities," *American Political Science Review*, LXI (September, 1967), 701–716.

The decade of the 1960s witnessed increased activity in the urban and metropolitan field not only among political scientists but among those in the other social disciplines as well. Political sociologists, among them Herbert Gans and Scott Greer, geographers including Jean Gottmann and Harold Mayer, social ecologists represented by Leo Schnore and Otis Dudley Duncan, economists such as Werner Hirsch and Wilbur Thompson, and planner-scholars of the caliber of William Wheaton and John Dyckman, all conducted numerous inquiries into various aspects of the metropolis. They sought causal relationships among its key variables. Their research, characterized by an increasing use of quantitative techniques, was of exceptional caliber. It contributed in important ways to the understanding we now have of metropolitan functioning.[7]

The current scene is marked by a continuing interest in basic research and a renewed emphasis on applied or problem-oriented research. The abrupt change in the political and social climate of the nation, as manifested in the civil rights struggle and the bitter and unprecedented protests against American involvement in the Vietnam war, has shaken the tranquillity of many social scientists. Having failed to foresee the eruption of the "social revolution" in the mid-1960s and finding themselves confronted with such new phenomena and concepts as black power, creative disorder, crisis precipitation, and maximum feasible participation of the poor, they have found it necessary to reassess their research assumptions and priorities. As recent developments in urban America have so forcefully reminded them, the new demands and challenges confronting the population centers of every region call for both political leadership of high quality and scholarship relevant to the critical needs and problems of the time.

The present chapter examines several conceptual schemes (or research frameworks) and some of the methodology which urban scholars employ in their study of urban and metropolitan communities. The purpose here is not to describe the scientific method or to examine in detail how metropolitan areas may be systematically studied. It is simply to provide guidelines and reference points, some conceptual ways of looking at these communities. Passing acquaintance with theory formulation and the methodological tools of modern scholarship will not transform an individual into a social scientist nor magically endow him with greater perceptive powers. It may, however, make him a more careful observer and give him greater appreciation of the complexity of the field and the need for examining the metropolis in the light of general concepts and underlying forces.

[7] For an overview of urban research, see Hauser and Schnore (eds.), *The Study of Urbanization.*

MODELS

The objective of the social scientist is to formulate what is essential for understanding and prediction in the field of social, economic, and political behavior. To this end he, like his colleagues in the physical sciences, seeks simplicity and order in the world of reality. Confronted with an infinite amount of data, he endeavors to develop a theoretical framework or conceptual scheme to guide him in selecting what is critical and significant from this huge stockpile. Patiently and painstakingly, he strives to determine how he can reduce his data to manageable form, how he can find order in its untold variety, what methods and research tools he can most profitably employ. To assist in this task of conceptualization and analysis, he often attempts to construct models or representations of the real system he is studying.

The term "model" is today a fashionable symbol in social science research. Borrowed from the vocabulary of technology (with its miniature replicas of airplanes, automobiles, and buildings), the word is loosely used to include everything from sets of simple propositions to highly sophisticated mathematical formulas. Basically, however, a model rests on analogy. The flow of water through a network of pipes, for instance, might be taken as an analogue of the flow of communications through a large bureaucratic organization. The value of conceptualizing the process in this way is not difficult to see. By examining the first, or the more simple and familiar, the researcher may obtain ideas about the operations of the second, or the more complex and unfamiliar. In other words, one system may serve as a model for another wholly unrelated system if the study of the former is useful for an understanding of the latter. This may be either because the first is less complex or because it has already been carefully investigated and its operations analyzed.

Models may also be used to simulate activity in the real world. Flight simulators are employed to check out commercial airline pilots on emergency procedures, mathematical traffic models translated into computer language are utilized to simulate the flow of traffic in a city or metropolitan area, and efforts have been made to simulate the dynamics of land use planning. It is conceivable, to cite one of many possibilities, that a mathematic model could be constructed to describe the fiscal operations of a municipality so that the impact of an increase or decrease of expenditures in one category of costs on other categories could be ascertained. This procedure has distinct advantages since the variables in the model can readily be manipulated to determine the effects of change—a form of experimentation that would not be possible or feasible with the subject matter itself. In this way the entire array of costs could be rearranged until an acceptable mix was attained.[8] Such information would be invaluable to city officials for policy-making purposes.

The International Relations Model

Several students of the contemporary urban scene have suggested that the relations among local governmental units in metropolitan areas can best be described by a theory of international politics. Victor Jones called attention to this possibility some years ago when he observed that the analogy between metropolitan organization and international organization "can serve to remind us that we are dealing with local units of government that are tough organizations with many political and legal protections against annihilation or absorption by another government."[9] He also noted that a study of experiences at the international level might lead to a form of metropolitan reorganization that would enable local governments to function more satisfactorily. More recently, political scientist Matthew Holden has attempted to show in some detail how the international model might be used to impose a measure of intellectual rationality upon the study of metropolitan political behavior.[10]

Certainly the governmental structure of the metropolis resembles the international system. Most metropolitan areas are administered by a host of local units, each with jurisdiction over a territorial segment of the whole, each enjoying legal autonomy, and each wary of the intentions of the other. Their actions in many ways are analogous to those of national states. They compete with one another for scarce resources (taxes, industry); they bargain for needed supplies and facilities (water, sewers); they seek to expand their sphere of control (through annexation and consolidation); and they form coalitions for defensive purposes (such as suburban leagues of municipalities). As they interact with each other, they develop an awareness of the problems which grow out of their coexistence and come to recognize the need for creating institutional devices to regulate relations among themselves. In Jones' words, "If local governments in metropolitan areas act toward each other as if they were national states, we should not be surprised to recognize among proposals for reorganizing them counterparts of world government, world federation, functional organization, and bilateral and multilateral compacts."[11] Illustrations of this analogy are readily found in the proposals

---

[8] See in this connection, Melville C. Branch, "Simulation, Mathematical Models, and Comprehensive Planning," Urban Affairs Quarterly, I (March, 1966), 15–38.

[9] "The Organization of a Metropolitan Region," University of Pennsylvania Law Review, 105 (February, 1957), 539.

[10] "The Governance of the Metropolis as a Problem in Diplomacy," Journal of Politics, 26 (August, 1964), 627–647. See also Philip E. Jacob and James V. Toscano (eds.), The Integration of Political Communities (Philadelphia: Lippincott, 1963).

[11] Jones, "The Organization of a Metropolitan Region," p. 539.

for consolidation of governments, local federal systems, and functional consolidation, and in the creation of intergovernmental representative bodies such as the Association of Bay Area Governments (ABAG) in the San Francisco Bay area, the Mid-Willamette Valley (Salem, Oregon, area) Council of Governments, the Metropolitan Washington (D.C.) Council of Governments, and the New York Metropolitan Regional Council.

The potential use of the international relations model as an analytical device merits serious attention. Research and theory-formulation in the international field are well advanced over those at the local level. If advantage can be taken of this work and if it can be made applicable to the metropolitan complex, the cause of urban scholarship would be considerably advanced. At the least, it would be possible to derive a set of propositions from international relations theory that could be empirically tested in the operations of metropolitan area governments. Holden takes this approach in exploring the possibilities of the model. Portraying the two systems—metropolitan and supranational—as analogous, he develops his inquiry around four groups of questions:

1. What substantive matters make it necessary for governments to interact with each other?

2. How nearly equal are the participating governments in status, power, and resources?

3. Do conflicts among the governments tend to be prolonged or are they settled in relatively short order?

4. What procedures are employed in the interaction situations among the governments?

With these questions as his focal points, he then attempts to relate propositions from the literature of international relations to the behavior of metropolitan area governments.

An illustration of this approach might be helpful. Holden refers to studies of how consensus is arrived at and integrative mechanisms are developed among national states. His purpose is to determine whether experiences on the international plane have relevance at the metropolitan level. Referring to the current emphasis on intergovernmental consultation (as typified in area-wide councils of public officials), he notes that this approach calls for the strategy of first seeking to achieve procedural consensus among the parties—getting them to become more responsive to each other—before tackling issues. The pertinent question here is whether such consultations actually lead to genuine consensus, and, if so, to what degree it will be translatable into substantive policy. As Holden points out, this is precisely the question to which several researchers have addressed themselves in the international field.[12]

[12] See, for example, Ernst B. Haas, *Consensus Formation in the Council of Europe* (Berkeley and Los Angeles: University of California Press, 1960). Haas also speaks of

Although Holden's efforts are only exploratory, they suggest that the governmental structures and political processes of metropolitan areas bear some analytical similarity to those at the supranational level. To the extent that they do, the international model can provide a useful analogue for conceptualizing the microcosmic world of the metropolis. We know, of course, that basic differences exist between the two systems as they do between most models and reality. Unlike national states, local governments are creatures of a higher level of political authority. As such, they are circumscribed in their behavior by constitutional and statutory provisions which define their powers and responsibilities, including the kinds of arrangements, if any, that they can enter into with each other. In addition, they have little control over such crucial elements as economic growth and population expansion. Many of the important decisions affecting their well-being and future are made at the state and national levels—tax allocations, welfare, redevelopment and housing policies, and highway locations, to mention but a few. Hence, the range of significant subject matter about which they can bargain among themselves is relatively narrow. Moreover, they have apparently felt little compulsion to interact extensively with each other even within this limited sphere. As Wallace Sayre and Herbert Kaufman concluded about New York:

> The haphazard character of the relationships between New York City and its neighbors has resulted from their relative independence of each other in the past with respect to all but a few governmental functions. Only occasionally did problems reach a state sufficiently acute to force them to pay close attention to each other and to try to influence each other's actions.[13]

This scene is in decided contrast to that at the international level where interaction among units is continual and negotiation constant.

To point out such differences is not to deny the relevance or usefulness of international relations theory for the study of metropolitan area government; it is to suggest several factors that must be taken into account when seeking to apply it. For despite the differences, the analogy between the two systems appears to be sufficiently strong to warrant full exploration of the model's possibilities. Whatever insight or clues, however small, that might possibly be gained from its application to metropolitan political behavior would be well worth the effort.

---

a "spill-over" theory which holds that once any agreement is made, the propensity of the parties to make further pacts is enhanced. Thus nations which begin by shipping coal and steel to each other may eventually be willing to enter into mutual defense treaties. Similarly, local units which contract with each other for police radio services may later be willing to execute agreements on more basic issues such as joint planning and zoning administration.

[13] *Governing New York City* (New York: Russell Sage Foundation, 1960), p. 596.

The Economic Model

Unlike the international relations approach which is based essentially on political interaction, the economic or municipal-services model rests on the analogue of the market place. It assumes that a process similar to choice and allocation in the private sector of the economy underlies the operation of the numerous governments that comprise the metropolis. Within this framework, the local units are viewed as competing for the trade of citizen consumers.

Attempts to apply economic models to the study of political behavior are of recent origin. The efforts in the main have been directed toward constructing a theory of government similar to the theory of markets. As formulated by one economist, the strategies of political parties to maximize voter support is likened to the efforts of individuals to maximize their satisfactions or returns in the private market place.[14] Or as conceived by others, the decision-making process of individuals in matters of politics is analogous to the determination of the terms of trade in an exchange of goods.[15] Voters theoretically cast their ballots for those candidates who will benefit them most. So also, they support those public policies which presumably bring them the greatest returns. The economic approach, in short, assumes man to be a utility maximizer in his political as well as in his market activity.

As applied to the metropolitan scene, the so-called municipal-services market model has received most attention. Basically, this approach equates the decentralized governmental structure of an urban community to a "quasi-market" situation.[16] It postulates that the various agencies producing public goods constitute a municipal-services industry which can be expected to exhibit patterns of conduct similar to those of private firms. By providing different bundles or levels of services, the local governments present the citizen consumer with a range of alternate choices. If, for instance, he wants high quality education for his children, he can live in that unit which operates a first-rate school system. Or if he is extremely tax conscious and opposed to expanding the public sector, he can choose a community where tax rates are comparatively low and services minimal. Implicit in this model, as in economic theory generally,

[14] Anthony Downs, *An Economic Theory of Democracy* (New York: Harper & Row, 1957).

[15] James M. Buchanan and Gordon Tullock, *The Calculus of Consent* (Ann Arbor: University of Michigan Press, 1962).

[16] Discussion of this model is based largely on Charles M. Tiebout, "A Pure Theory of Local Expenditures," *The Journal of Political Economy*, LXIV (October, 1956), 416–424; Vincent Ostrom, Charles Tiebout, and Robert Warren, "The Organization of Government in Metropolitan Areas: A Theoretical Inquiry," *American Political Science Review*, LV (December, 1961), 831–842; and Robert Warren, "A Municipal Services Market Model of Metropolitan Organization," *Journal of the American Institute of Planners*, XXX (August, 1964), 193–204.

is the assumption that both the producers (the governmental units) and the consumers (the residents) will act in their own interests to maximize their own values or satisfactions. The public agencies will behave so as to preserve the "establishment," retain and extend their power and influence, and enhance their prestige; the citizens in turn will select the producer that appears to best satisfy their preference patterns at the lowest cost.

Carrying the analogy further, public agencies, like private industries, are forced to compete over the service levels offered in relation to the taxes charged. This competitive situation ideally exists where a number of local units are located in close proximity to each other and where information about the performance of each is publicly available. In such cases, the resident-consumers are presented with the opportunity to compare performance and judge the relative efficiency of the producers. Theoretically, also, competition under such circumstances would motivate desirable self-regulatory tendencies on the part of local agencies, lead to greater responsiveness to citizen demands, and result in a sorting out and allocating of services between metropolitan-wide and local production in the interest of efficiency. It would furthermore provide residents of a typical metropolitan area possessing many local governments with a greater range of choice than would be available under a monolithic governmental structure.

The analogy between differentiated products in the private market place and differentiated political units in a metropolitan area involves, as economist Wilbur Thompson points out, monopolistic and not pure competition. For if the latter were applicable, the most efficient producer would ultimately drive his less efficient rivals out of the market, a situation that obviously has not occurred in the case of local government. What exists in this connection is, if anything, more analogous to monopolistic or imperfect competition in which products of a similar nature offered by each seller are different from those offered by other vendors in ways deemed significant by buyers. Many consumers, in other words, choose a foreign car over a domestic, or the more prestigious over the less well-known (whether shaving cream or place of residence) without regard to utilitarian efficiency criteria. This kind of purchasing is a mark of an affluent society. Thus many metropolitan dwellers choose, in effect, to devote part of their rising incomes to the luxury of buying small local government in disregard of the least-cost principle.[17]

The validity of the municipal-services model presupposes certain basic conditions: (1) the existence of several producers of similar public goods in the metropolitan area; (2) sufficient differentiation of their products to provide a basis for choice; and (3) awareness by the citizen consumer

[17] *A Preface to Urban Economics* (Baltimore: Johns Hopkins Press, 1965), pp. 259–263.

of the various alternatives and their costs to him. This last condition is the one which causes the most difficulty. The concept of the market place assumes that the buyer is familiar with the range of choices open to him and the price of each. As a rational man he then weighs the alternatives and selects the one which he believes will benefit him most. This kind of knowledge is seldom possessed by the consumer of goods in the public sector of the community. Numerous studies show that he knows relatively little about the operations and cost of the various local governments serving a metropolitan area. Under such circumstances, his choice process is not likely to resemble that of "economic man."

An element of uncertainty, moreover, is present in virtually all governmental transactions. Here, unlike the selection among private goods, no one-to-one correspondence exists between individual choice and the final outcome. When a consumer decides to purchase a Ford in preference to other makes of cars, he knows exactly what he will receive and how much he will pay for it. When he votes for a local official because he wants a better bundle of public services, he has no certainty that his candidate will be elected or, if elected, that he will carry out the promised policies. Similarly, while he recognizes that every public proposal has a cost-benefit ratio, he cannot possibly estimate his own share in the benefits or costs as he can in comparable market choices. (And if he does not exercise his choice, it will be made for him by others.)

The municipal services model has also come under attack for various other reasons. One is that contiguous units of local government cannot avoid heavy spillover effects that result in freeloading in some places (a common complaint of the central city against suburban residents who use its facilities) and overpayment in others. Another is that racial segregation circumscribes freedom of choice for a significant minority of the population even though some in this group possess the necessary economic means. A third, and more serious charge, is that the model tends to make efficiency in production the prime element in the polity while efficiency in social control simply drops out of the picture. This emphasis not only minimizes the political content of urban governmental operations but it also disregards the fact that such problems as race relations and poverty are hardly reducible to the adjustment of the market.[18]

The economic model seeks to provide an analytical framework for exploring metropolitan organization. It proceeds by conceptualizing a local government system in which the production of public goods is decentralized and choice is available to the citizens. This conception, despite the drawbacks noted, provides a point of departure for reevaluating traditional assumptions about the nature and development of public organization in metropolitan areas, the diversity of values that exist among

[18] Norton Long, among others, stresses this point. See his "Citizenship or Consumership in Metropolitan Areas," *Journal of the American Institute of Planners,* XXXI (February, 1965), 2–6.

their residents, and the patterns of conduct to be expected in a decentralized decision-making system. It also focuses attention on the question of whether the bargaining and adjustments among local units which are formally independent of one another and guided by their own interests can handle the problems of the wider area. These are questions of import; and if the economic analogue can contribute in any way to a better understanding of them, it will have served a useful purpose.

The "Games" Model

A third model, suggested by Norton Long, views community politics as a set of games and man as a "game-playing animal." This concept follows the tradition in political science which stresses the competitive nature of politics (as the international diplomacy and economic market models also do). In this formulation, individuals and groups are treated as contestants or claimants and public policy decisions are viewed as the outcome of conflict or competition. Emphasis is placed on the distribution of power, the resources which the various actors have at their command and the skill with which they use them, and bargaining and negotiation. Sayre and Kaufman in their study of the New York city government provide an excellent example of this approach. As they explicitly state, the city's political system is "vigorously and incessantly competitive. The stakes of the city's politics are large, the contestants are numerous and determined, the rules of the competition are enforced against each other by the competitors themselves. . . ."[19]

Long sees the metropolis as a territorial system of games in which local governments interact with each other and with other groups and organizations in the community. Sharing a common spatial field and collaborating for different and particular ends, the players in one game, such as government, make use of the players in another, such as business or labor, and are in turn made use of by them. Each is, in effect, competing with the others for the rewards the society has to offer. As Long explains it:

Thus, a particular highway grid may be the result of a bureaucratic department of public works game in which are combined, though separate, a professional highway engineer game with its purposes and critical elite onlookers; a departmental bureaucracy; a set of contending politicians seeking to use the highways for political capital, patronage and the like; a banking game concerned with bonds, taxes, and the effect of the highways on real estate; newspapermen interested in headlines, scoops, and the effect of highways on the papers' circulation; contractors eager to make money by building roads; ecclesiastics concerned with the effect of highways on their parishes and on the fortunes of the contractors who support their churchly ambitions; labor leaders interested in union contracts. . . .[20]

[19] Sayre and Kaufman, *Governing New York City*, pp. 709–710.
[20] "The Local Community as an Ecology of Games," *American Journal of Sociology*, XLIV (November, 1958), 253.

Long's conceptualization, as that of others who use the game analogy, remains at a highly abstract level and scarcely moves from metaphor toward theory. The problems of operationalizing such a framework and reducing it to workable terms raises serious questions about its usefulness in empirical research. Yet one may argue that the approach, by identifying and tracing the network of community games, offers the possibility of providing explanations for the behavior of the participants, predictions of social value distributions, and a framework for the construction of empirical theory of more modest proportions.[21]

THE METROPOLIS AS A SYSTEM

The metropolis is often referred to as a political (or social or economic) system. Those who conceptualize it in this way advocate the use of systems analysis as the desirable research approach. Economist James L. Green, for example, in urging the use of this approach to the study of metropolitan government maintains that those public services which are area-wide in nature and impact "can be combined into a total systems concept."[22] And sociologist Robert Gutman, in more ambitious terms, calls for a research program that sets forth "a concept of the metropolis as a social system, focusing on values, norms, and organizational structures in different areas, and on the processes through which these values, norms, and organizational structures are related."[23] Other supporters of systems theory suggest the application to urban problems of the concepts and techniques which have revolutionized policy-making in the Pentagon and sent astronauts to the moon.

The term *system,* as anyone who examines the literature will soon discover, has multiple usages. As someone once quipped, "There are more versions of the systems approach than there are shades of blond in a chorus line." We commonly speak of the heating system of a house or the sewer system of a municipality with some knowledge of what these designations mean. We also refer to the political system of a community, and in this case we employ the term in a broadly descriptive sense with only a vague understanding of its meaning and empirical content. The reason for this difference in comprehension is not difficult to surmise. In the first instance we are dealing with "physical" systems whose components are concrete entities, and in the second with "analytic" systems

[21] For one of the few attempts to incorporate empirical elements into the games theory approach, see Paul A. Smith, "The Games of Community Politics," *Midwest Journal of Political Science,* IX (February, 1965), 37–60.

[22] *Metropolitan Economic Republics* (Athens: University of Georgia Press, 1965), p. 141.

[23] "Urban Studies as a Field of Research," *American Behavioral Scientist,* 6 (February, 1963), 15.

that are intellectual constructs composed of aspects or attributes of concrete entities.[24]

The Meaning of System

Simply stated, a system consists of a set of elements or parts which interact with each other to constitute an identifiable whole. If, therefore, the concept is to be used as the nub of an analytic framework, the elements of the particular system under study must first be identified and the relations among them ascertained. This task presents no real difficulty in the case of a physical system (either mechanical or biological). The components of a heating system—furnace, pipes, blower, thermostat, and other necessary parts—can readily be identified and their interactions observed and measured. The task is far more complex, however, when we are dealing with an analytic system such as an urban polity or governmental system. Here we are faced not only with the problem of identifying the components and determining how they relate to each other, but also with establishing the boundaries which set this entity apart (for analytical purposes) from other aspects of the overall community system. It is little wonder that the designation is employed so loosely at times as to be almost without meaning.

The application of the term *system* to the metropolis is similarly vague. Yet implicit in its use, from the viewpoint of social science, is the concept of an ordered and more or less stable pattern of relations and interactions among individuals and institutions that result in the governance of the community. The international diplomacy and municipal services models are helpful here by way of illustration since they essentially involve systems. As proponents of the service model have explained, the various local governmental units in a metropolitan area may be said to function as a system to the extent they "take each other into account in competitive relationships, enter into various contractual and cooperative undertakings, or have recourse to central mechanisms to resolve conflicts."[25] In this conceptualization the local units represent the elements of the system, and emphasis is placed on the relations and interactions among these components rather than on their internal characteristics and operations.

A similar suggestion has been made as to the usefulness of the systems approach in the study of international affairs.[26] Such a strategy would

[24] For a general discussion of the systems approach in social science, see H. V. Wiseman, *Political Systems: Some Sociological Approaches* (New York: Frederick A. Praeger, 1966); and Oran R. Young, *Systems of Political Science* (Englewood Cliffs, N.J.: Prentice-Hall, 1967).

[25] Ostrom, Tiebout, and Warren, "The Organization of Government in Metropolitan Areas: A Theoretical Inquiry," p. 842.

[26] Anatol Rapoport, "Some System Approaches to Political Theory," in David Easton (ed.), *Varieties of Political Theory* (Englewood Cliffs, N.J.: Prentice-Hall, 1966), pp. 129–141.

single out the politically organized bodies, the nation states, as the elements and would concentrate on analyzing the relations among them. Identifying governmental units or nation states as the components of a system obviously involves no difficulty. The critical problem, however, is the formulation of indexes to determine and measure the interrelationships among these units. For there is little point in conceptualizing metropolitan or international governmental behavior as a system unless the connection between the elements or parts can be demonstrated.

The "Engineering" Concept

Granted the existence of a metropolitan system, however defined, the question of how it is to be studied still remains. Here is where systems analysis enters the picture, but the scene is blurred rather than sharply defined. When engineers and management consultants speak of systems analysis they have one concept in mind; when social scientists use the same terminology, they have another; and within each group there are many shades of distinction. The underlying principles may be the same, but the orientation and operation of these principles are differently conceived, depending on the background and objectives of the users.

On the engineering side, a methodology or systemic approach to problem solving has been developing over the past decade or two, with the most impressive work taking place in the areas of military and space research. Solutions to such complex problems as putting a man on the moon or developing intercontinental missile striking power require the cooperation of scientists from many fields and the bridging of many disciplines. As described by one scientist-engineer, systems analysis concentrates on the design of the whole as distinct from the design and production of the parts. The approach

insists upon looking at the problem in its entirety, taking into account all the facets, and seeking to understand how they interact with one another and how the best solution will bring these factors into proper relationship. . . . It starts by insisting on a clear understanding of exactly what the problem is, the goals that will lead to a solution, and the criteria for evaluating alternative avenues. As the end result, the approach seeks to work out a detailed description of a combination of men and machines with such concomitant flow of materiel, assignment of function, and pattern of information flow that the whole system represents a compatible and most satisfactory ensemble for achieving the performance desired.[27]

Or as a management consultant explained: "By systems analysis, urban governments faced with the problem of performing a multitude of complex, interrelated, and almost equally important functions, within budgetary limits, can examine the interplay and causal relations among

[27] Simon Ramo, "The Systems Approach: Automated Common Sense," *Nation's Cities*, 6 (March, 1968), 15.

these functions."[28] In this way, they will be in a position to select the program mix most likely to achieve the desired objectives.

These statements describe generally what is meant when we read about efforts or proposals to apply systems analysis in the solution of urban or metropolitan problems. One of the most widely publicized attempts in this regard occurred in 1965 when the state of California let contracts to five aerospace companies for the study of mass transportation, waste disposal management, and several other critical problems.[29] The small number of experiments of this nature thus far made have involved essentially physical or environmental matters such as those mentioned. Discussions have taken place about the possible applicability of the approach to urban social issues but it is unlikely that any major breakthrough along these lines will occur in the near future.

Functionalism

Social scientists have been less interested in systems theory as a problem-solving device than as a method or framework for studying social and political phenomena. Their efforts have centered on various forms of analysis derived from general systems theory, particularly functionalism (also referred to as structural-functionalism) and input-output analysis. The principal architect of the first is Talcott Parsons, a sociologist; the chief theoretician of the latter is David Easton, a political scientist.

According to Parsons, human behavior in the various realms of life can be usefully studied as the operation of a social system (defined by him as a network of interrelated roles) analogous in structure and functioning to physical or biological systems. The structure, in this formulation, consists of the mechanisms, institutions, roles, and patterns of action by or through which the purposes of the system are fulfilled. The functions refer to the basic requirements or operational conditions which must be carried out if a society or community is to continue as a going concern. Parsons identifies four broad categories of these requisites: (1) pattern-maintenance (preservation of the critical or essential features and norms of the system); (2) adaptation (the ability of the system to adjust to changes in its environment); (3) integration (coordination of the different components and operations of the system); and (4) goal attainment (capacity of the system to achieve its goals).[30]

[28] John Diebold, "Impacts on Urban Governmental Functions of Developments in Science and Technology," in Stephen B. Sweeney and James C. Charlesworth (eds.), *Governing Urban Society: New Scientific Approaches* (Philadelphia: The American Academy of Political and Social Science, 1967), p. 89.

[29] Harold R. Watt, "California Aerospace Experience," in *The Outlook for Technological Changes and Employment: Studies Prepared for the National Commission on Technology, Automation, and Economic Progress*, Vol. V (Washington: U. S. Government Printing Office, 1966).

[30] Parsons' theories are set forth in his *The Social System* (New York: Free Press, 1951), and *Essays in Sociological Theory: Pure and Applied* (New York: Free Press, 1959).

During recent years an increasing number of political scientists have endeavored to utilize adapted versions of functionalism in their research. This tendency has been most evident in studies of the political systems of developing nations.[31] Such efforts require a framework of analysis which takes account of the fact that in many non-Western societies the role played by formal governmental structures, such as political parties and legislative bodies, is often not as important as that of other institutions and processes. The functions of government, in other words, may be met in diverse ways. As one political scientist has said: "Government can exist without formal structure. It may be found in kinship systems, religious bodies, or other organizations that we are not accustomed to thinking of as government but that, in fact, are carrying out the functions of government."[32] The functional approach appeals to those studying non-Western societies precisely because it provides them with an analytical schema that directs attention to other instruments of social life which may be performing a political role.

These observations bear some relevance for urban research. If we conceive of metropolitan government as an integrated political unit with area-wide jurisdiction, few metropolises can be said to have a governmental system. If, on the other hand, we approach the question of metropolitan government by thinking of the functions which must be performed to keep a politically fragmented community operative, we are then led to look for the structures through which these functions are carried out. Viewed in this way, it is conceivable that a metropolitan governmental system may, in fact, exist where no formal area-wide structure has been established but where the functional prerequisites are being performed through other instrumentalities.

One of the few examples of the use of functional analysis in the field of urban politics is Harold Kaplan's study of the Municipality of Metropolitan Toronto.[33] Kaplan, a political scientist, describes the widely cited metropolitan governmental system of that area in functional terms and examines how, by what means, and with what success it performs its integrative and adaptive functions and meets its environmental demands. Political scientist Robert O. Warren's analysis of the governmental pattern of Los Angeles County also utilizes what is basically a functional approach, although his study is not specifically cast in these terms.[34] Warren

[31] See, for example, Gabriel A. Almond and James S. Coleman (eds.), *The Politics of the Developing Areas* (Princeton: Princeton University Press, 1960); and Fred W. Riggs, *Administration in Developing Countries* (Boston: Houghton Mifflin, 1964).

[32] David E. Apter, *The Politics of Modernization* (Chicago: University of Chicago Press, 1965), p. 17.

[33] *Urban Political Systems: A Functional Analysis of Metro Toronto* (New York: Columbia University Press, 1967).

[34] *Government in Metropolitan Regions: A Reappraisal of Fractionated Political Organization* (Davis: University of California Institute of Governmental Affairs, 1966).

documents over time the response of the governmental sector to the changing public needs and demands of the Los Angeles area and shows how these responses have managed to maintain, what is for all intents and purposes, a metropolitan governmental system composed of many politically autonomous parts. These two examples illustrate how functionalism can be useful as a method of research by directing attention to features of the metropolitan system and relations among its parts which might otherwise escape attention.

Input-Output Analysis

Input-output analysis has its roots in functionalism but its focus and emphasis are different.[35] We simply call attention here to this approach for its intrinsic interest and possibilities and not for its use since no effort has as yet been made to apply it to concrete political situations. One can perhaps best visualize the nature of input-output analysis by reference to an industrial production system. The input into such a system consists of raw or semi-processed material, labor, capital goods, and scientific know-how; the output is the finished product. The way in which inputs are transformed into outputs is known as the conversion process. Relating these concepts to the sphere of government, the political system is seen as a huge conversion operation in which inputs of demands and supports are processed and outputs of decisions and implementing actions produced. This process in its totality enables the governmental system to respond to the stresses arising from the social and physical environment in which it is embedded and to persist without the loss or destruction of its fundamental characteristics.

Economists, as we shall see in Chapter 4, frequently use a form of input-output analysis in examining the economic base of a region or metropolitan area. This technique enables them to ascertain the relationship among the various categories of economic activity by quantitative measurements. Thus it is possible, for example, to predict the impact that a given input of demand in one sector of an area's economy will have on the remaining sectors of the structure. The task confronting the urban political scientist or sociologist is far more complex since he must attempt to discover and measure the relationships between a host of social and political variables, many of which are not susceptible to quantification. An additional difficulty arises in metropolitan research since the problem of relating input to output in an area-wide political system is compounded by the fragmented nature of the governmental structure. Demands are made on, and policy emanates from, the many individual units of govern-

[35] See David Easton's careful formulation and comprehensive treatment of input-output analysis in his *A Framework for Political Analysis* (Englewood Cliffs, N.J.: Prentice-Hall, 1965); and *A Systems Analysis of Political Life* (New York: Wiley, 1965).

ment which make up the system. How these inputs and outputs can be conceptually and methodologically aggregated for purposes of metropolitan analysis presents a formidable challenge to the researcher.

It is highly unlikely that the concept of a metropolitan system will be developed in the near future to the point where it can be given empirical content. Systems analysis, whether of the functionalist or input-output variety, remains at too abstract a level to serve this purpose. Its chief value lies in suggesting the framework of analysis that a social scientist needs if he is to ask the significant questions and select the critical features of metropolitan life for study. This, however, is an important function of the approach and one not to be lightly valued.

THE ROAD AHEAD

It is apparent from the discussion in this chapter that no universally acceptable models or frameworks of analysis have been developed in the urban-metropolitan field. It is also evident that none is likely to be found in the immediate future because of the vast complexity of the phenomena involved. Yet, as this treatment of models and systems analysis demonstrates, urban research, as all scientific inquiry, must proceed on the basis of some conceptual scheme, some methodological strategy, and some theoretical assumptions, however rudimentary they may be.

Metropolitan and urban research will endeavor to serve two functions in the future as it has in the past: (1) provide a knowledge and understanding of urban problems that will be of assistance to policymakers; and (2) contribute to the broader theoretical concerns of the various social science disciplines, concerns which are relevant to progress in problem-solving. In serving these purposes, those engaged in studying metropolitan areas are not likely to follow any single path or direction. Models will be devised to suit the needs of the particular researcher, theory will be formulated to explain various aspects of urban life, systems analysis will increase in favor, and quantification and simulation techniques will be increasingly resorted to as high speed computers become more widely available. The future, if existing trends are any indication, will witness far greater interest in urban-metropolitan research and a far greater allocation of intellectual and financial resources to these efforts than the past has seen.

3 /
THE
SOCIAL
ANATOMY
OF THE
METROPOLIS

THE METROPOLITAN COMMUNITY IS AT ONCE A TERRITORIAL UNIT OF FLUID boundaries and a network of human relationships which may be called its social structure. This structure is vastly more complicated than that of the rural village or Sinclair Lewis' Zenith. Heterogeneous, constantly changing, fragmented, it presents a mosaic of social worlds arranged spatially in an often confused and seemingly incompatible pattern. "The other side of the tracks" is an expression well known to many small-town dwellers. But in the large population centers there are many "sides of the track." Numerous neighborhoods and suburban groupings of varying social, ethnic, and economic characteristics are scattered throughout the metropolitan complex. The luxury apartment casts its shadow on the tenement houses of workers. The Negro ghetto is ringed by a wall of white neighborhoods. The industrial suburb lies adjacent to the village enclave of the wealthy. Cheap souvenir stalls and penny arcades intermingle with the fashionable department stores and quality gift shops in the central business district. The contrast is sharp, the variety infinite.

It would be difficult to find a simple set of concepts or variables to describe the anatomy of a metropolis. If one were to draw a social profile of such an area, he would undoubtedly concentrate on such dimensions as educational level, income and occupational patterns, ethnic and religious composition, age structure, extent of home ownership, life styles, and population stability. These and similar variables provide a basis for comparing the social attributes of one metropolis with those of another.[1] In the present chapter we will examine several of the more important of these characteristics, with particular reference to their spatial distribution throughout metropolitan areas and to the implications this distribution has for the functioning of urban society. First, however, we will look briefly at the spatial forms within which this social geography has developed.

SPATIAL PATTERN

Cruising in an airplane over a large urban agglomeration, the traveler is inevitably impressed by the varied pattern of land use which stretches out below him. Clusters of large apartment buildings, concentrations of single-family residences, geometrically arranged subdivisions, open spaces, and industrial and commercial areas, all blend together—sometimes incongruously as though mixed by chance—into a vast web of human settlement. Ecologists have advanced various theories of urban growth to explain these spatial patterns. The four most commonly referred to are concentric or gradient zones, sector, star-shape, and multiple nuclei (Figure 7). The forms of growth which they represent are ideal types and thus are not likely to be found in their pure state in any existing metropolis.

According to the first, a metropolitan area tends to resemble a series of concentric zones or gradients, with persons of lower socioeconomic status living closer to the central business district.[2] Growth proceeds as the result of pressure from the center which causes one zone to expand into the next. At the core is the central business district and the adjacent industrial areas. Surrounding it is a transitional zone usually marked by deterioration and blight. (It is within this hypothetical circle that many of today's urban redevelopment projects are taking place.) This area in turn is followed by successive zones of predominantly residential housing

[1] Profiles of this nature are developed for 644 American cities in Jeffrey K. Hadden and Edgar F. Borgatta, *American Cities: Their Social Characteristics* (Chicago: Rand McNally, 1965), pp. 76–100.

[2] See Ernest W. Burgess, "Urban Areas," in T. V. Smith and Leonard D. White (eds.), *Chicago: An Experiment in Social Science Research* (Chicago: University of Chicago Press, 1929), pp. 113–138.

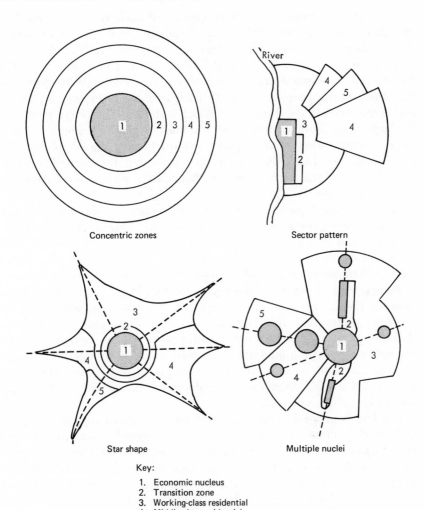

Concentric zones

Sector pattern

Star shape

Multiple nuclei

Key:
1. Economic nucleus
2. Transition zone
3. Working-class residential
4. Middle-class residential
5. Upper-middle and upper-class residential
– – Major traffic arteries

FIGURE 7   Urban Configurations.

that increases in value with distance from the core. Despite much criticism, the gradient concept remains the principal theory of urban growth.

The sector concept is a modification of the concentric zone pattern.[3]

[3] For a discussion of this theory, see Homer Hoyt, "The Structure of American Cities in the Post-War Era," *American Journal of Sociology*, XLVIII (January, 1943), 476–477.

Questioning the symmetry or homogeneity of such zones, it holds that growth occurs in sectors which extend radially from the center toward the periphery of the area. Thus a high-rent apartment neighborhood may develop on one side of the central business district or core zone and a low income residential area inhabited by a racial minority group on the other. In the process of growth each is likely to expand across the concentric zones in the direction in which it started. The Negro ghettos in the large cities illustrate this trend. Confined largely to a single sector of the community, they tend to push outward toward the periphery until in areas like St. Louis they extend in narrow but broadening corridors from the core of the central city to its boundaries, with some spillage into the adjacent suburbs.

The star-shaped pattern is a further refinement of the sector theory. It views urban growth as a linear development along the main radials—the roads and transportation arteries that converge on the central core. Examples of this pattern can be observed at the fringes of growing metropolitan areas where long finger-like appendages or tongues of settlement extend out along the highways with large vacant spaces lying between them. This type of development was first noticeable along the streetcar routes and the railroad commuter lines that provided the connecting links between center and periphery. Its vestiges are still evident in the existing land use characteristics of most large urban areas. However, with the passage of time, development of the intervening land has created a high degree of circumferential movement and made the pattern less distinguishable.

The fourth method of analyzing the spatial pattern rejects the notion that the community is uni-centered, as the concentric zonal theory leads one to assume. Pointing out that many phenomena of urban life occur in clusters, it denies that the round of daily life revolves mainly about a single center. As a leading ecologist points out, "Modern forms of communication and transportation have brought into being a sharply etched multi-centered community pattern. Formerly semi-independent communities scattered over the hinterland about a market center were drawn into close contact with one another as well as with the major center, differentiated as to function, and transformed into units in an extensive though highly sensitive local territorial division of labor."[4] Within the principal nucleus—the core or central business district—are concentrated the home or regional offices of business and industry, financial institutions, major governmental agencies, legal and other specialized professional services, the theater and other cultural facilities, and the shopping point for style merchandise and comparative buying. Clustered about the core throughout the metropolitan area is a constellation of subcenters: neigh-

[4] Amos Hawley, *Human Ecology* (New York: Ronald, 1950), p. 270.

borhood and regional shopping centers, suburban central business districts, outlying industrial concentrations, and local governmental bureaucracies.

SOCIAL AREAS

The relationship between the physical form and the social anatomy of metropolitan areas becomes evident when we observe how widely individuals and families of different socioeconomic rank, life style, and ethnic background are distributed in space. Just as sections of a metropolis are identified with particular industrial and commercial activities, so also are entire neighborhoods given over to socially differentiated groups. This social specialization, like that of services and economic opportunities, increases the degree of interdependence among the various geographical sectors of an urban community and necessitates integrating mechanisms for maintaining the harmonious and efficient operation of the whole. A neighborhood or suburb of corporate executives, for example, cannot exist without complementary neighborhoods or suburbs of workers.

We tend to speak of metropolitan areas as though they were all cut from the same cloth, but it is well to remind ourselves of the obvious at this point. No two of these agglomerations are identical in their social geography. Each has its own distinctive characteristics and its own contour of settlement. Each is composed of a set of neighborhoods or subcommunities of different values, life styles, and social attributes. One may have many neighborhoods of ethnic and nonwhite groups; another, only a few. In one, the suburbs may be entirely residential; in another, they may contain a substantial number of industrial satellites. In some, the wealthier portion of the population may be found outside the central city; in others, within its borders.

Discussion of metropolitan areas are often premised on a simple dichotomous pattern of social geography in which disparities between central city and suburbs are overemphasized and variations among SMSAs largely ignored. Thus we hear the central city commonly characterized as the home of the underprivileged, undereducated, unskilled, and nonwhite, while the suburbs are presented as the place of residence of the well-to-do, nonethnic, and stable members of the society. This widely accepted stereotype is substantiated in part when the metropolitan areas of the nation are considered as a whole. Significant differences between central city and urban fringe were revealed by a Census Bureau analysis which used a multiple-item socioeconomic scale combining measures of occupation, education, and income (see Table 2).

Proportionately more persons with high status scores were found in the suburbs with the most striking disparities occurring at the two ends of the scale. As the table shows, almost 23 percent of the urban fringe residents fall within the highest status category and less than 4 percent in the lowest, while comparable figures for the central cities are approximately 14 percent and 9 percent.

TABLE 2   **Socioeconomic Status Index for Urbanized Areas Based on Measures of Occupation, Education, and Income**

Place of Residence and Color	Percentage of Population with Status Scores of:			
	80–99	50–79	20–49	0–19
Total				
Central cities	13.7	42.4	35.2	8.6
Urban fringe	22.8	50.1	23.4	3.7
White				
Central cities	16.0	46.8	31.1	6.1
Urban fringe	23.7	51.3	22.0	3.0
Nonwhite				
Central cities	3.0	21.9	54.5	20.6
Urban fringe	3.6	25.2	52.7	18.4

SOURCE: Bureau of the Census, *Current Population Reports, Technical Studies,* Series P-23, No. 12, July 31, 1964. The urban fringe is that portion of the urbanized area (which is the SMSA excluding its sparsely settled parts) outside the central city.

These statistics, however, must be viewed in proper context. They deal with aggregates and not with individual population characteristics or individual SMSAs. They do show substantial disparities between central cities and suburbs but they also show that the boundary which separates these two geographical segments of the metropolis does not constitute a wall between the "haves" and the "have-nots"; or between the white-collar and blue-collar neighborhoods. Over one-fourth of suburban residents, as indicated in Table 2, are in the lower two status categories and over one-half the central city population is in the two highest categories. A survey of AFL-CIO members made by the organization's Committee on Political Education (COPE) in 1967 found that almost half of those polled lived outside the central city, and of those under 40 years of age nearly three-quarters were suburbanites. In short, the suburbia of today is not the exclusive domain of the country club set; increasingly it is being populated by the large middle range of American society: blue-collar workers, clerks, salesmen, and others in related occupations.

These general impressions of intracity and intrasuburban differentials can readily be verified by an examination of census data and existing studies. For example, the 1960 Census of Housing shows that the average value of owner-occupied housing units (generally a good indicator of wealth or socioeconomic status) ranges from $7500 in one Milwaukee city census tract to $38,000 in another. The same wide variance is found among suburbs in the Philadelphia area, with the residential market value per household ranging from less than $6000 in one community to well over $24,000 in another.[5]

Neither central cities nor their urbanized ring, in other words, presents a uniform social landscape; each contains a mosaic of social worlds. Manhattan has its Park Avenue as well as its Harlem; Chicago has its "Gold Coast" along with its slum tenements; and Boston has its Beacon Hill together with its Roxbury. In terms of suburbs, one would be hard put to find points of similarity between such fringe cities as the university-oriented community of Evanston and the blue-collar stronghold of Cicero in the Chicago SMSA, or between the predominantly Negro suburb of Compton and the fashionable enclave of Beverly Hills in the Los Angeles metropolis.

Sample surveys, moreover, have found no meaningful nationwide distinction in the political attitudes and activities of central city and suburban residents.[6] All parts of a given SMSA share a common social, political, and economic environment that is reflected in the attitudinal patterns and behavior of its residents. The blue-collar resident of the central city is likely to hold the same social and political attitudes as his suburban counterpart, and the same is true for the businessman, the physician, and the bank clerk. When differences do occur among central city and suburban residents of the same social rank, they usually pertain to intrametropolitan issues such as area-wide governmental reorganization, the location of public facilities, or changes in the local tax system.

To illustrate the extent and character of the central city-suburban differences and similarities, we have selected three studies for closer examination: one by the Metropolitan St. Louis Survey, another by Leo Schnore, and a third by the Advisory Commission on Intergovernmental Relations.

Social Area Analysis as Applied to St. Louis

Social area analysis is a method that has been widely utilized to study and describe the social geography of a community. This mode of investigation employs three indexes or basic forms of social differentiation:

[5] Oliver P. Williams, Harold Herman, Charles S. Liebman, and Thomas R. Dye, *Suburban Differences and Metropolitan Policies: A Philadelphia Story* (Philadelphia: University of Pennsylvania Press, 1965), p. 57.

[6] Joseph Zikmund, "A Comparison of Political Attitudes and Activity Patterns in Central City and Suburbs," *Public Opinion Quarterly*, XXXI (Spring, 1967), 69–75.

social rank, urbanization, and segregation. Using data organized by census tracts, the first measures the socioeconomic status of the neighborhood as a whole; the second, its life style; and the third, its proportion of Negroes and other segregated populations.[7]

Social rank is a composite index of level of education and kind of occupation. At the low end of the scale are neighborhoods composed predominantly of unskilled laborers and factory workers and of adults with no more than an eighth-grade education. At the other extreme are neighborhoods of business executives, professional personnel, and white-collar workers with high school or college education.

The second index, urbanization, is based on the kind of family and home typical of a particular neighborhood. This index has three components: (1) the ratio of children under five years of age to women of childbearing age (fertility ratio); (2) the proportion of women with jobs outside the home; and (3) the proportion of dwelling units that are single-family and detached. The highly "urban" neighborhood, according to this yardstick, is one of rooming houses and apartment dwellings, of single men and women, and of childless couples with both husband and wife working. The low "urban" area is familistic and is marked by single-family residences, young couples with small children, and few wives in the labor force.

The third index is based on the ethnic composition of the community—the proportion of Negroes and other segregated populations in the neighborhoods compared to the proportion of these populations in the total city or metropolis. Its function is to identify sections of the urban area where there are heavy concentrations of nonwhite or ethnic groups.

An analysis of the St. Louis area using these measurements shows the fallacy of too readily accepting the city-suburban stereotype. Although the central city was found to contain more neighborhoods of low social rank, high urbanization, and high segregation than its suburbs, it was also found to include many sections that resembled its ring counterparts (Figures 8 and 9). The conclusions of the study are of interest since similar observations are applicable to a majority of the nation's SMSAs.

1. The governmental boundary between the central city and its suburbs is nowhere a social boundary between a rural or semirural county and urban city, nor a line between the urban "poor" and the suburban "prosperous." Instead, the St. Louis city limits run through neighborhoods that are essentially similar in social rank on either side of the boundary.

2. Middle-rank neighborhoods contain approximately 70 percent of the population in the city of St. Louis and the suburban county.

3. The neighborhoods in which the other 30 percent resides differ

[7] These indexes are explained in detail in Eshref Shevky and Wendell Bell, *Social Area Analysis* (Stanford: Stanford University Press, 1954).

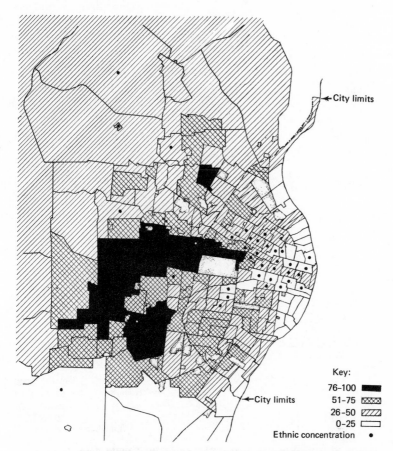

←City limits

Key:

76-100

51-75

26-50

0-25

Ethnic concentration •

←City limits

FIGURE 8   Occupation–Education Index, St. Louis City–County Area,
            1950. From Background for Action, Metropolitan St. Louis
            Survey, 1957, p. 12.

greatly between the central city and the suburbs. Those in the former,
which are located primarily in the central portion, are of very low social
rank while those in the latter are high on the occupation scale.

    4. A more consistent difference between the two areas is observable
when life style of the neighborhood populations is considered. The
suburbs tend to be child- and family-centered, regardless of social rank.
The central city is more urban in its characteristics, with more neighborhoods that have apartment dwellers, few children, and many women
working outside the home.

    5. The segregated populations are mostly in the central city. In St.
Louis they are usually Negro, with a few small enclaves of Italians and

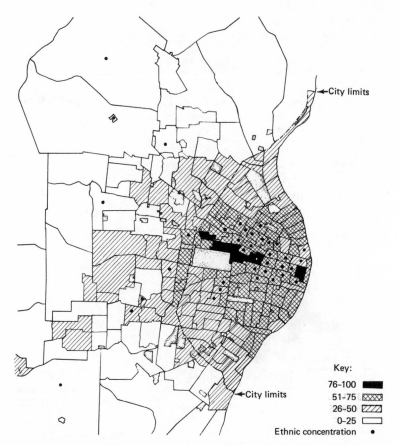

FIGURE 9   Urbanization Index, St. Louis City–County Area, 1950. From
Background for Action, **Metropolitan St. Louis Survey, 1957,**
p. 13.

eastern Europeans. They are found in the older neighborhoods of low
social rank. A few small settlements of Negroes are located in various
parts of the suburbs, but most of them are of long standing and came
into existence before modern means of transportation to accommodate
the household and garden workers of the wealthy commuters.[8]

As the St. Louis study shows, the social heterogeneity of the central
city is duplicated to a significant extent in the urban fringe. The popular
image of an homogeneous suburbia is based upon selected upper middle-
class suburbs, the familiar targets of novelists and commentators.
Whether in the central city or the surrounding ring, families of similar

[8] John C. Bollens (ed.), *Exploring the Metropolitan Community* (Berkeley and
Los Angeles: University of California Press, 1961), pp. 17–18.

TABLE 3   City-Suburban Differentials in Socioeconomic Status, by Size of
Urbanized Area, 1960

	Percentage of Urbanized Areas in Which Suburbs Rank Higher			
Size of Urbanized Area	MEDIAN FAMILY INCOME	PERCENT COMPLETING HIGH SCHOOL	PERCENT WHITE COLLAR	NUMBER OF AREAS
1,000,000 and over	100.0	100.0	87.5	16
500,000–1,000,000	100.0	100.0	86.4	22
250,000–500,000	79.3	75.9	55.2	29
150,000–250,000	72.1	62.8	48.8	43
100,000–150,000	70.3	64.9	40.5	37
50,000–100,000	56.6	49.1	30.2	53

SOURCE: Leo F. Schnore, "The Socio-Economic Status of Cities and Suburbs," *American Sociological Review*, 28 (February, 1963), 78.

socioeconomic characteristics are attracted to common neighborhoods. The same forces which make for socioeconomic homogeneity in the former operate with equal facility in the latter. People who identify with a particular status level usually desire to live with their "own kind" in an area or neighborhood possessing an identification with that status. For many families, of course, the choice of home and location is narrowly circumscribed by their fiscal resources. For some, the Negro in particular, it is often less a matter of choice than of enforced segregation.

City-Suburban Comparisons

When overall comparisons are made between central cities and their suburbs, significant disparities are found, as we have indicated, but they are neither as universal as generally assumed nor do they all run in the same direction. In a study of 200 SMSAs, Leo Schnore compared core cities and their urbanized rings on the basis of income, education, and occupation.[9] His findings demonstrate that the popular view of city-suburban differentials in social status is derived mainly from the experience of the larger metropolitan complexes. They show that although no city of more than 500,000 exceeds its suburbs on two of the three variables and only a few on the third, a clear reversal of this pattern takes place as one moves down the population scale (see Table 3). In the 53 smallest urbanized areas, those of 50,000 to 100,000, 23 central cities have larger median family incomes than their suburban rings; 27 of them have a higher ratio of persons 25 years old or over who completed

[9] Leo F. Schnore, "The Socio-Economic Status of Cities and Suburbs," *American Sociological Review*, 28 (February, 1963), 76–85.

high school; and 37 have a higher percentage of employed people in white-collar occupations.

The study also found that age of the area (measured by the number of decades that have passed since the central city first reached 50,000 inhabitants) is an important determinant of city-suburban differentials. The common conclusion that high-status persons live in the suburbs tends to be true of urbanized areas having very old core cities, but it is progressively less often true of the newer urban strongholds (Table 4). In the older areas, suburban fringes consistently register higher median family

TABLE 4   City-Suburban Income, Educational, and Occupational Differentials in SMSAs, 1960, by Age of Area

Census Year in Which Central City First Reached 50,000	Median Family Income		Percent Who Completed High School		Percent Employed in White-Collar Occupations	
	CITY HIGHER	SUBURBAN FRINGE HIGHER	CITY HIGHER	SUBURBAN FRINGE HIGHER	CITY HIGHER	SUBURBAN FRINGE HIGHER
1800–1860	0	14	0	14	0	14
1870–1880	0	17	0	17	0	17
1890–1900	5	31	9	27	15	21
1910–1920	12	36	12	36	22	26
1930–1940	9	23	14	18	22	10
1950–1960	26	27	28	25	40	13

SOURCE: Adapted from Leo F. Schnore, "The Socio-Economic Status of Cities and Suburbs," American Sociological Review, 28 (February, 1963), 80.

incomes, higher educational rank, and a larger proportion of white-collar workers. On the other hand, in areas which have reached metropolitan status in recent decades, the central cities themselves contain populations that are higher in socioeconomic rank than their adjacent suburbs. Age and population size of an area are closely related; but statistical analysis showed that even when size is held constant, age of the SMSA continues to exert a substantial influence upon the direction of social differentials between central cities and suburbs.

Schnore speculates that two factors help to account for much of the observed differences based on age. First, the housing structures of the older areas, particularly in the inner core, are often obsolescent and blighted and have come to be occupied by groups that have strictly limited housing choices. Today these neighborhoods serve largely as ports of entry for the new migrants: the displaced farmers, the "Okies" and "hillbillies," and the racial minorities. New residential developments in these older SMSAs have been concentrated in outlying zones and are occupied by those who can afford home ownership. In contrast, the housing in the central cities of the newer urban areas is not so old or obsolete as to lose its attraction to potential home owners of the expanding middle class.

As a second factor, Schnore suggests that the pressures of alternative land uses—particularly non-residential—are less intense in the newer cities than they were in the older urban centers at comparable stages in the past. The automobile and the truck, together with improved means of communication, have decreased the pressure of industrial and commercial land uses pushing outward from the core. Now these uses are more likely to be leap-frogging the interior residential zones for new industrial parks and shopping centers at the outer periphery. As a consequence, central residential zones in new cities "may be less likely to undergo the 'succession' or 'sequent occupance' of progressively lower status groups experienced by neighborhoods in the older cities."[10]

Metropolitan Socioeconomic Disparities

An extensive analysis conducted under the auspices of the Advisory Commission on Intergovernmental Relations provides further evidence that generalizations about socioeconomic disparities between city and suburb must be accepted with caution. In the words of the Commission, "very few generalizations about central city-suburban population differences are applicable to most metropolitan areas. The extent and direction of disparities vary enormously, especially with respect to the nonwhite population."[11] The study found that while racial disparities are large everywhere, most of the other major elements of the dichotomy, such as education, income, employment, and housing, fit the stereotype only in the largest metropolitan areas and those located in the Northeast.

The Commission's analysis indicates that for a majority of metropolitan areas there is less than a 10 percent difference between central cities and suburbs in their respective proportions of such socioeconomic indicators as undereducated adults, high school dropouts, and families with low income. In fact, in the smaller SMSAs a greater concentration of families with incomes under $3000 is found outside the central city and a greater percentage of those with incomes over $10,000 in the core municipality. Both sections of the metropolis, in other words, accommodate a diversity of economic and social characteristics, with a wide range of housing values in each. However, where the nonwhites are most

10 Schnore, "The Socio-Economic Status of Cities and Suburbs," p. 81.

11 Advisory Commission on Intergovernmental Relations, *Metropolitan Social and Economic Disparities: Implications For Intergovernmental Relations in Central Cities and Suburbs* (Washington: January, 1965), p. 23.

numerous, the other city-suburban differentials are accentuated, a not unexpected result in view of the low socioeconomic status of many in this category.

The Commission study, like the others, demonstrates that city-suburban disparities differ substantially from region to region and from metropolis to metropolis. It shows that the stereotype portraying the flight of white, middle-class families from low income, ethnic-dominated cities to the miniature republics of suburbia is generally appropriate only for the larger SMSAs. Since these are the areas, however, which contain a major portion of the nation's urban population and face the most critical and massive problems, the disparities within them are of serious concern to all Americans. At the same time, the emphasis on the large SMSAs should not obscure the importance of the more numerous small and medium-sized metropolitan areas which do not conform to the popular stereotype. For unless the national diversity in urban population patterns is clearly recognized, the need for tailoring policy and problem-solving techniques to specific kinds of metropolitan areas may be overlooked or simply ignored.[12]

ETHNIC STRUCTURE

Inscribed at the base of the Statue of Liberty in New York Harbor are the lines:

> . . . Give me your tired, your poor,
> Your huddled masses yearning to breathe free,
> The wretched refuse of your teeming shore,
> Send these, the homeless, tempest-tost to me:
> I lift my lamp beside the golden door.

The invitation, no longer open except on a highly restrictive scale, was eagerly accepted. As a result, generation after generation of Americans have been confronted with the task of assimilating strangers. In the half century following the Civil War, 25 million immigrants—over a million during each of six separate years shortly after 1900—came to the shores of the new Canaan. The early arrivals had been mostly from northern and western Europe, but in the several decades before World War I, settlers of Italian, Polish, and other southern and eastern European stock predominated.

---

[12] See in this connection, Marjorie Cahn Brazer, "Economic and Social Disparities Between Central Cities and Their Suburbs," *Land Economics,* XLIII (August, 1967), 294–302.

The Foreign Born

The majority of those who sought homes in the promised land, particularly the later migrants, settled in the cities. In 1960, there were approximately 9.3 million foreign-born whites in the United States, 87 percent of whom resided in urban areas.[13] Almost half of the total (48 percent) were concentrated in the northeastern states, 90 percent of them in urban areas. The South contained the smallest number, with less than 10 percent of the foreign-born whites residing there; and of these, seven of every ten were urban dwellers. The North Central states had 24 percent and the West 18 percent of the total, with about eight of every ten in both regions living in urban areas.

The number and importance of ethnic groups vary from city to city, with the largest concentrations outside the South. In urban centers such as Boston, New York, San Francisco, Minneapolis, Los Angeles, St. Louis, Milwaukee, Chicago, and Detroit, many different nationalities are represented. Some one group may predominate—in San Francisco, the Italians; in Minneapolis, the Swedes; in Los Angeles, the Mexican-Americans; in St. Louis and Milwaukee, the Germans; in Chicago and Detroit, the Polish—but for the most part the pattern is one of ethnic diversity. As the National Resources Committee noted in 1937:

Never before in the history of the world have great groups of people so diverse in social background been thrown together in such close contacts as in the cities of America. The typical American city, therefore, does not consist of a homogeneous body of citizens, but of human beings with the most diverse cultural backgrounds, often speaking different languages, following a great variety of customs, habituated to different modes and standards of living, and sharing only in varying degrees the tastes, the beliefs, and the ideals of their native fellow city dwellers.[14]

Although the process of assimilation has reduced the number and importance of the ethnic colonies and has woven them into the fabric of the large American city, some of them still maintain their distinctive cultures and traditions. The "New Polands," "Little Italys," and "Chinatowns" bear witness to the continued social reality of the culturally heterogeneous metropolis. And more recently the Negro and Spanish (or Puerto Rican and Mexican-American) Harlems have been added to the ethnic enclaves.

[13] The Bureau of the Census defines as urban residents all persons living in incorporated and unincorporated places of 2500 or more and in other densely settled unincorporated areas.

[14] National Resources Committee, *Our Cities: Their Role in the National Economy* (Washington: 1937), p. 10.

The New Migration

The number of foreign born in the United States grew continuously until World War I but since then has steadily declined. The immigration acts of the 1920s slowed the flow of "foreigners," but by this time the new migration within the United States had begun: from South to North and West, from farm to city. Although the principal participants in the new movement were Negroes, many rural whites at the bottom of the socio-economic scale also packed up their meager belongings and headed for the centers of industrial activity. During World War I, Mexicans also began to move into West Coast cities; and by World War II, Puerto Ricans were migrating to New York City in large numbers.

Contrary to the impression held by some, the scale of Negro migration has been relatively small compared to the earlier waves of European immigrants. From 1910 to 1960, the net Negro out-migration from the South was less than 5 million. Even during the first six years of the 1960 census period, the 613,000 blacks who left the South were vastly outnumbered by the 1.8 million immigrants from abroad. The heaviest movement of Negroes has taken place out of the rural areas of Mississippi, Alabama, and South Carolina into the metropolitan centers of the North and West. This shift has radically changed the geographical distribution of the nation's Negro population. At the turn of the present century, almost 90 percent of the blacks were concentrated in the South, mostly on farms; by 1968 this figure had dropped to about 53 percent.

Rapid changes in the racial composition of urban areas have been taking place as a result of the new migration. In 1960, 70 percent of all SMSAs in the nation had a higher percentage of nonwhite population than they had ten years earlier.[15] In the northeastern region all metropolitan areas showed higher proportions; and in the North Central and western states, all but eleven of the eighty-eight SMSAs registered similar increases. The opposite was true in the South. There, about six of every ten metropolitan areas had lower proportions of nonwhites in 1960 than in the previous decennial census year. However, of the nine southern SMSAs with populations over 500,000, seven showed increases in the proportion of nonwhites.[16] Samplings indicate that this same trend continued throughout the 1960s.

Intra-Area Distribution Patterns

The central cities of the SMSAs have been the main recipients of the black migration. From 1950 to 1968 the Negro residents of these munic-

---

[15] The designation "nonwhite" used by the Bureau of the Census includes Negroes, American Indians, and such far eastern nationality groups as Japanese, Chinese, and Koreans. Negroes account for approximately 92 percent of this group. Since the 1930 census, Mexican-Americans have been placed in the "white" category.

[16] Leo F. Schnore and Harry Sharp, "Racial Changes in Metropolitan Areas, 1950–1960," *Social Forces,* 41 (March, 1963), 247–253.

ipalities grew from 6.5 million to almost 12 million, the result of in-migration and natural increase. During the same period the white population showed no gain; in recent years it has steadily declined in numbers (Table 5). These developments have led to dramatic changes in the proportion of blacks in the central cities of the large SMSAs. By 1965, Negroes constituted two-thirds of the population of the District of Columbia and over one-third that of Baltimore, St. Louis, Cleveland, and Detroit (Table 6).[17] In contrast to this buildup of blacks in the core cities, the suburbs have remained predominantly white (approximately 95 percent). Negro suburbanites increased by only 1.4 million during the eighteen-year period from 1950 to 1968 while the number of whites rose from 34.8 million to 65.9 million.

TABLE 5   Population Change by Location, Inside and Outside SMSAs, 1950–1968 (in millions)

	Negro			White		
	1950	1960	1968	1950	1960	1968
United States	15.0	18.4	22.0	135.2	158.7	174.0
Metropolitan areas	8.4	11.9	15.2	80.3	99.4	111.3
Central cities	6.5	9.5	11.9	45.5	47.6	45.5
Urban fringe	1.9	2.4	3.3	34.8	51.8	65.9
Nonmetropolitan	6.7	6.5	6.9	54.8	59.3	62.7

SOURCE: U.S. Bureau of the Census, "Trends in Social and Economic Conditions in Metropolitan Areas," *Current Population Reports*, Series P-23, no. 27 (Washington: February 7, 1969), p. 2.

Not only has the city-suburban racial dichotomy become sharper, but the growth of the Negro population in urban places has been accompanied by an increasingly rigid pattern of residential segregation within the core cities themselves. This phenomenon is universal in American cities, regardless of regional location and irrespective of whether the black population is large or small. In contrast to the earlier pattern for European immigrant groups, segregation has remained at a high level despite the social and economic advances made by blacks in recent years. It is also high in comparison to that of Puerto Ricans and Mexican-Americans even though these groups are less well off in terms of economic measures than Negroes. As Karl and Alma Taeuber concluded in their extensive statistical study of racial residential patterns:

Negroes are more segregated residentially than are Orientals, Mexican-Americans, Puerto Ricans, or any nationality group. In fact Negroes are by

[17] Census Bureau figures indicate that the rate of growth of the Negro population in the central cities may have declined between 1966 and 1968 while increasing in the suburbs. However, because of the very high sampling variability, further observations are required before this trend can be confirmed.

TABLE 6   Percentage of Negroes in Central Cities
of Twelve Largest SMSAs, 1950–1965

City	1950	1960	1965[a]
New York	10	14	18
Los Angeles	9	14	17
Chicago	14	23	28
Philadelphia	18	26	31
Detroit	16	29	34
San Francisco	6	10	12
Boston	5	9	13
Pittsburgh	12	17	20
St. Louis	18	29	36
Washington, D.C.	35	54	66
Cleveland	16	29	34
Baltimore	24	35	38

[a] 1965 figures are estimates except for Cleveland
where a special census was made.
SOURCE: Bureau of the Census and Bureau of Labor
Statistics, *Social and Economic Condition of Negroes
in the United States* (Washington: October, 1967),
p. 11.

far the most residentially segregated urban minority in recent American history. This is evident in the virtually complete exclusion of Negro residents
from most new suburban developments of the past 50 years as well as in the
block-by-block expansion of Negro residential areas in the central portions of
many large cities.[18]

A segregation index devised by the Taeubers showed that an average of
over 86 percent of all Negroes in the 207 largest cities of the United
States would have to move from the blocks where they now live to other
blocks to create an unsegregated population distribution. Examination
of the census tract map of St. Louis classified by type of racial change
(Figure 10) graphically illustrates the typical pattern of segregation
which has developed in American cities.

According to the classification scheme used by the Taeubers, tracts
designated "succession" are those in which the nonwhite population
numbered 250 or more in 1940 and increased during the next ten years
while the white population declined. In those referred to as "invasion,"
whites dropped while nonwhites increased from fewer than 250 in 1940
to more than 250 in 1950. In "growing" tracts (not shown for St. Louis), the

[18] Karl E. Taeuber and Alma F. Taeuber, *Negroes in Cities* (Chicago: Aldine,
1965), p. 68.

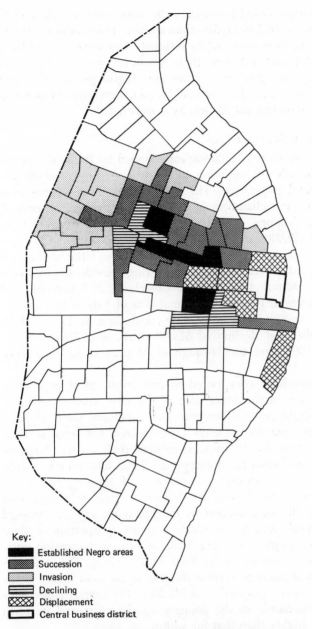

Key:

■ Established Negro areas
▨ Succession
▦ Invasion
▤ Declining
▧ Displacement
▢ Central business district

FIGURE 10 **St. Louis Census Tracts with 250 or More Nonwhites in 1960 Classified by Type of Racial Change, 1950–1960. Reprinted from Karl E. and Alma F. Taeuber,** Negroes in Cities **(Chicago: Aldine Publishing Company, 1965), p. 263. Copyright © 1965 by Karl E. and Alma F. Taeuber.**

nonwhite population increased faster than the white, and in "declining" tracts nonwhites decreased less rapidly than whites. "Displacement" tracts are those in which an increase in white residents was accompanied by a decrease in nonwhites, such as frequently occurs in urban renewal areas. A classification of this type gives us a more meaningful picture of racial change in an urban area than the commonly used enumeration of percentage changes in the nonwhite population by census tract.

Population Decline in Central Cities

Along with losses in white population experienced by the large central cities—the result largely of migration to suburbia—many of them are also declining in total population. The 1960 census figures came as a shock to the officials and chambers of commerce of many core cities.[19] St. Louis city had dropped over 100,000 during the period; Detroit, 180,000; Cleveland, 39,000; and Washington, D.C., 38,000. At the same time, the population gains for the SMSAs in which these cities are located had shown striking gains because of suburban ring growth: the St. Louis area, 19.8 percent; Detroit, 24.7 percent; Cleveland, 22.6 percent; and Washington, 36.7 percent. Population estimates as of July, 1966, indicate that the trend has continued for some cities, including St. Louis which experienced a further net decline of 52,000. Also, San Francisco lost 27,000, Baltimore 5000, and the borough of Manhattan in New York City 163,000.

A variety of causes have contributed to this result. Most population losses are taking place in the inner core of the city where homes are oldest and where blight and obsolescence have rendered many of them uninhabitable. Urban renewal projects have cleared out large sections in many of these areas and in the process reduced their density. Expressway construction and industrial development have also removed land from residential use and stricter enforcement of housing codes has eliminated some overcrowding in older structures. Another contributing factor, discussed in the next section, is the changing age structure of the metropolis. Central cities are acquiring a greater proportion of older people and childless couples as young white families in increasing numbers seek suburban environments for their child rearing. One countervailing factor which is likely to reverse the tide in the near future is the continuing increase in the proportion of blacks in the central cities. This population is predominantly in the younger age brackets and its birth rate is substantially higher than that for whites.

---

[19] There is strong evidence that the 1960 census undercounted the number of Negroes living in the large urban centers. Presumably some families residing in overcrowded quarters in violation of housing codes feared action by city authorities. Even if such an undercount occurred, however, the population loss in these cities was still substantial.

AGE STRUCTURE

The age structure of a population reflects trends in fertility, mortality, and migration. This structure has considerable social and political significance. A community of predominantly young married couples in the childbearing stage will place different demands on its governments than will a community of retired workers. Each group has different sets of educational, recreational, health, and welfare needs. The young family wants good schools and playgrounds for its children and modern roads to speed the breadwinner to his place of work. The elderly couple has specialized health and leisure requirements that differ from those of young people.

Two Comparisons

The proportion of the population in the economically productive age range is another socially important aspect of the age structure. A community with a large percentage of its residents below 15 and above 65 years of age has greater service needs and less economic potential than a similar area with a high proportion of its residents in the 15-to-64 age bracket. The local governmental budgets of St. Petersburg, Florida, a popular haven of "senior" citizens, reflect a different emphasis than that of the Levittowns of New York and Pennsylvania with their armies of young families. Comparisons of the age-sex pyramids of Pinellas County, Florida, which includes St. Petersburg, and of Levittown, New York, as shown in Figure 11, illustrate this difference. In the Florida retire-

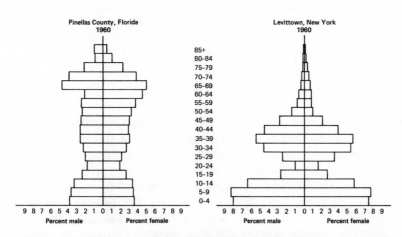

FIGURE 11   **Age—Sex Pyramids for Pinellas County, Florida, and Levittown, New York, 1960. From U.S. Bureau of the Census,** U.S. Census of Population: 1960, General Population Characteristics.

ment colony only about 20 percent of the population is under 15 years of age and almost 30 percent is 65 or over; the comparable figures for Levittown are approximately 44 percent and 3 percent.

A second comparison, made in Figure 12, also reveals how urban places of different types vary greatly in their age structure. Here, the age distribution pattern is plotted for three Wisconsin cities: Milwaukee, a central city of a major metropolitan area; Brookfield, a relatively new

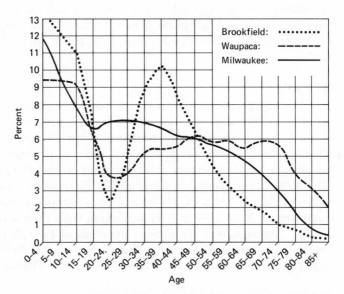

FIGURE 12   **Age Distribution for Brookfield, Waupaca, and Milwaukee, Wisconsin, 1960. From Glenn V. Fuguitt,** The Changing Age Structure of Wisconsin's Population, **The University of Wisconsin, Department of Rural Sociology, Population Series no. 3, April 1962, p. 15.**

suburb in the Milwaukee SMSA; and Waupaca, a nonmetropolitan city of approximately 4000 in the northwestern part of the state. Brookfield, typical in many ways of the new and rapidly growing suburban communities, has a high concentration of young children and adults in their middle years, but a marked deficiency of older children, young adults, and elderly people. Almost 40 percent of the population is under 15 years of age and less than 4 percent over 65. The situation is quite different in Waupaca, a rural community that showed virtually no population change during the last ten-year census period. Twenty percent of its residents are over 65 years of age and 27 percent under 15. Only 32 percent are in the 15-to-45 age bracket compared to 41 percent in Milwaukee and 44 percent in Brookfield. Milwaukee's age pattern occupies a somewhat intermediate position between the other two places. It has fewer young children and more elderly residents than Brookfield but more young people and fewer older citizens than Waupaca. It also has a greater percentage of residents in the young working years (15 to 30) than the other two, a proportion that is steadily increasing with the influx of nonwhites who are predominantly in the lower age categories.

The national pattern resembles the Wisconsin examples. In large urban areas the suburban communities generally have a higher proportion of children and fewer older people than the central city. Both the core and ring, however, have an increasing proportion of children under 14 and adults over 65, the result of higher fertility and lower mortality rates. The age structure of rural communities, on the other hand, is increasing principally in the higher age categories. Young adults are seeking better opportunities in the metropolitan areas while retired farmers are migrating to the villages or the "pensioner" colonies of the South and Far West where warmer climates help ease the infirmities of old age.

SOME IMPLICATIONS OF SOCIAL GEOGRAPHY

The rapid technological and social changes of the last half century have created a predominantly urban America in which the metropolis is the new frontier. With the passing of the old agricultural order, new vistas and new avenues of opportunity have been opened to a continuously growing society. Urban populations of today find themselves in a process of lively change. Social rank is moving upward, real income is rising, education is becoming more widespread, and ways of living are changing. The opportunities of the new order, however, have not been made equally available to all segments of the society. Gross inequalities in educational and economic opportunities continue to exist, racial discrimination remains an unsolved problem, and social conflict is becoming more pervasive and intensive. These developments find reflection in one fashion or another in the social anatomy of metropolitan communities.

The social geography of urban areas has important implications both as to the general functioning of such collectivities and as to the problems they face. Dysfunctional as well as functional consequences result from a spatial distribution in which metropolitan dwellers of similar income, occupation, life styles, and color tend to reside in the same neighborhoods. Spatial homogeneity, while it may provide a source of social identification for individuals and groups, also gives rise to divergent localized interests and demands that may be deleterious to the effective operation of the larger community. Specialization, whether social or economic, implies interdependence and the need for coordinated action to sustain the total system. Such coordination becomes extremely difficult if differentiation among the subcommunities is too sharp. The problem is compounded when this specialization is institutionalized within politically autonomous suburbs rather than neighborhoods within a single governmental entity. In such instances, the social values and interests of the spatially bounded subareas can be expressed directly through official public policies such as exclusionary zoning.

The most crucial aspect of social geography today relates to the spatial distribution of the Negro population within the metropolis. The growing concentration of blacks in the large central cities, combined with the exodus of white families to suburbia, will enable Negroes to achieve political control in many communities within the next decade or two. Such control will provide a solid basis for Negro leadership and involvement in local government and in other public and semipublic institutions of the core city. This development in turn may lead to efforts on the part of the whites to dilute Negro political strength at the local level through some form of metropolitan government or, what is more likely, it may result in further attempts by the white majority to isolate themselves and their activities spatially beyond the legal limits of the central city. Whatever the course, "the rise of black cities with Negro public administrators wielding power is certain," as an official of the NAACP expressed it, "to have the profoundest consequences for the future development of Negro life in America."[20]

The social pattern of contemporary metropolitan society reflects both great strength and severe weaknesses. The vigor and dynamism which characterize the intensive activity and fantastic technological developments of urban aggregations exist alongside the destructive social forces which precipitate violent outbursts, such as those we have recently witnessed in the ghettos of many of our cities, and which threaten the disruption of the entire social order. Contemporary developments not only impose new demands on the agencies of social control: from the family, through the voluntary associations, to the duly constituted units and agencies of public authority. They also call for a reassessment of local as well as national goals and values and a determined commitment to extend the benefits and opportunities of the society to all segments of the populace. The nature of the response by our various public and private institutions to these needs and pressures is crucially important in determining the kind of metropolitan environment in which most Americans now live and will live in the future.

[20] Herbert Hill, "Demographic Change and Racial Ghettos: The Crisis of American Cities," *Journal of Urban Law*, 44 (Winter, 1966), 236.

4 / THE METROPOLITAN ECONOMY

THE METROPOLIS IS NOT MERELY THE PLACE OF RESIDENCE FOR TWO-thirds of the nation's people; it is also the "workshop of American civilization." Vast aggregations of industrial might, scientific and technical skills, and human resources are concentrated within SMSAs which dominate the economy. These areas produce and consume the preponderant share of American economic wealth. They contain over 65 percent of the nation's labor force, serve as headquarters for most of its large corporate organizations, account for more than 70 percent of its taxable assessed valuation, and enjoy a consistently higher per capita income than the remainder of the country. They also encompass within their territorial limits the majority of the nation's financial institutions and its wholesale and retail establishments. As seats of human activity and organization, they offer the greatest number and variety of opportunities for work and leisure and provide the means for producing and marketing the widest possible range of goods and services.

The characteristics of modern urbanism are largely a result of the changes brought about by industrialization. These changes, such as mass production of goods and increasing specialization, are familiar to all Americans. What is not always recognized is the fact that economic forces are prime determinants of the ecological and physical structures of cities. Directly or indirectly, these factors influence the pattern of living as well as the social and governmental institutions of metropolitan complexes. Changes in the mode of production or of economic organization inevitably find reflection in metropolitan life.

Technological advances, for example, can revolutionize even the spatial pattern of the community. Witness the automobile; in a half century it has transformed closely textured cities into sprawling metropolitan areas and has permitted a radical change in life style, from urban to suburban, for many millions of families. The age of technological discovery, moreover, is still in its infancy. Further and probably even more startling transformations can be expected in the future as the peacetime uses of nuclear energy and other scientific resources are exploited.

Surprising as it may seem, economists have only in recent years discovered the metropolis as a unit worthy of analysis. In fact, the first textbook devoted specifically to urban economics did not make its appearance until 1965.[1] Much of the knowledge we have of local labor markets, intra-area industrial location, metropolitan growth processes, and urban redevelopment is derived from the works of geographers and planners, rather than economists. During the last decade, however, comprehensive economic studies of metropolitan areas—New York, Pittsburgh, and St. Louis, among others—have begun to appear with greater frequency. So also have a growing number of economists started to direct their attention to empirical and theoretical inquiry into the economics of metropolitan areas and urban regions.

Given the present state of research, it would be difficult to identify with certitude the critical economic variables that largely determine the form and functioning of the metropolis. Even if this could be done, it would be impossible to do justice to the economic dimensions of urban life within the confines of a general treatise on metropolitan areas. The most we can hope to do here is to focus on some of the more obvious factors and point out their linkages to the other institutional features of the urban community. Thus in the present chapter we concentrate on the economic structure of SMSAs, viewing them as individual local labor markets which are primary units of employment and income generation for their inhabitants. In a subsequent chapter, we examine the public financial structure of such areas, an economic aspect of vital importance since the American system looks to government at all levels—local as well as state and national—to redress, at least to some extent, the inequality which free enterprise inevitably produces in the society.

[1] Wilbur R. Thompson, *A Preface to Urban Economics* (Baltimore: Johns Hopkins Press, 1965).

ECONOMIC TYPES

Although we commonly speak of metropolitan areas (and metropolitan economies) as though they were all alike, this convenient designation should not cause us to gloss over the wide differences which exist among them. In the words of one observer, metropolitan areas "come in an assortment more varied than the wines of France, often with nothing more in common than conformity to the minimum standards of size and density set by the Bureau of the Census."[2] Size, age, economic structure, and demographic features are some of the more evident distinguishing variables but others of less obvious nature, such as cultural and leadership characteristics, are also of importance.

These differences point up the need for classifying metropolitan areas in order to facilitate their study and analysis. One long-recognized approach to classification involves the economic base or productive specialization of the community. As a report of the National Resources Committee in 1937 maintained:

. . . cities must be distinguished according to the principal function they serve. Whatever uniformities there may be found in the life of urbanites, it will make some difference whether the city in which they live is an industrial, a commercial, or residential city; a capital, an educational center, or a resort; whether it depends upon mines, oil wells, timber, a port, a river, or railroad; and whether its economic base is unitary or multiple, balanced or unbalanced.[3]

Many attempts have been made, both here and abroad, to construct a typology on the basis of economic function. Efforts in the United States date from 1905 when W. D. Tower, a geographer, developed a classification of cities according to their economic specialization.[4] It was not until recent decades, however, that the first systematic categorization of urban areas according to empirically derived criteria appeared. Two of the pioneers in these endeavors were W. F. Ogburn, a sociologist, and Chauncy Harris, a geographer. Both used census data on occupation and employment to group cities into such categories as manufacturing, retailing, mining, and educational.[5] Harris' classification in particular drew considerable attention and became the subject of subsequent

[2] Benjamin Chinitz, *City and Suburb: The Economics of Metropolitan Growth* (Englewood Cliffs, N.J.: Prentice-Hall, 1964), pp. 12–13.

[3] *Our Cities: Their Role in the National Economy* (Washington, 1937), p. 8.

[4] "The Geography of American Cities," *Bulletin of the American Geographical Society*, XXXVII (1905), 577–588.

[5] William F. Ogburn, *Social Characteristics of Cities* (Chicago: International City Managers' Association, 1937); Chauncy D. Harris, "A Functional Classification of Cities in the United States," *Geographical Review*, XXXIII (January, 1943), 86–99.

revisions by a number of scholars including Grace Kneedler and Victor Jones.[6]

The latest revision of the Harris typology appeared in the *Municipal Year Book* of 1967 (Table 7). The classification, made by geographer Richard Forstall, groups each of the nation's cities of over 10,000 population and each of its SMSAs according to dominant function. Seven major categories are recognized: manufacturing, industrial, diversified-manufacturing, diversified-retailing, retailing, dormitory, and specialized. Many large midwestern cities—including Chicago, Cleveland, Detroit, Milwaukee, and St. Louis—and well over 40 percent of the nation's SMSAs fall into the manufacturing class. Communities in the industrial grouping are confined almost entirely to the relatively small urban places such as Dubuque, Iowa, and Cadillac, Michigan. The number of cities in this category, presently seventy-four, has declined steadily in recent decades.

More than half of the cities over 500,000 population—among them Boston, Dallas, Los Angeles, and New York—are subsumed under the diversified-manufacturing classification. Urban communities seldom grow large without substantial manufacturing activity, and as they increase in size, they tend to become more diversified and to strike a closer balance among the various economic activities. Cities and SMSAs in this and the other manufacturing-oriented categories are highly concentrated in the Northeast and Midwest with moderate concentrations in the Southeast and in the two largest west coast urban areas, Los Angeles and San Francisco.

Communities typed as diversified-retailing include only four over 500,000 population: New Orleans, Phoenix, San Francisco, and San Antonio. "Retailing" cities, such as Aberdeen, South Dakota, are located principally in the less industrialized regions of the country and among the smaller urban places. Dormitory cities, found in the suburbs of virtually every SMSA, have large net commuting outflows of workers and little local employment. A good example of a specialized city is Rochester, Minnesota, the home of the Mayo Clinic, where employment in hospitals and related services exceeds that in either manufacturing or retailing. Champaign, Illinois, where a state university is the prevailing industry, provides another example. The largest city in this category is Washington, D.C., with its high percentage of government workers.

Multidimensional Classification

A classification of urban places based on a single dimension, such as dominant economic function, reveals some interesting configurations and points to aspects worthy of further inquiry. It also has the advantage of

[6] Grace Kneedler, "Economic Classification of Cities," *Municipal Year Book: 1945* (Chicago: International City Managers' Association, 1945), pp. 30–38; Victor Jones, Richard L. Forstall, and Andrew Collver, "Economic and Social Characteristics of Urban Places," *Municipal Year Book: 1963*, pp. 49–57.

simplicity, yet this advantage is also its weakness since every sizable community is multifunctional even though a single activity may dominate. Unless it can be shown that the selected activity accounts for a substantial portion of the variation in behavior between communities, the utility of a unidimensional classification is severely limited.

The recognized drawbacks of single dimension typologies have led to efforts to construct classifications based on more than one variable. An approach in this direction has been to develop occupational profiles or patterns of occupation distribution. (Figure 13 is an illustration of a less complex profile showing how cities vary in occupational characteristics.) Using the total number of employed workers as a base, the percentage

TABLE 7   Functional Classification of Cities by Region, 1963

Economic Function	North- east	North Central	South	West	Total	SMSAs
Manufacturing	245	201	90	33	569	98
Industrial	28	30	10	6	74	7
Diversified-manufacturing	61	63	85	25	234	62
Diversified-retailing	34	55	103	57	249	43
Retailing	16	36	74	71	197	7
Dormitory	156	133	53	62	404	0
Specialized: total	20	29	38	35	122	9
Wholesaling	5	2	5	6	18	0
Services	0	0	2	3	5	0
Mining	0	3	4	3	10	2
Transportation	1	1	2	2	6	0
Resort	0	0	1	2	3	2
Government	1	1	4	2	8	1
Armed Forces	7	2	6	4	19	2
Professional	0	0	0	2	2	0
Hospital	0	1	0	0	1	0
Education	6	19	14	11	50	2

Manufacturing: 50 percent or more of employment in manufacturing and less than 30 percent in retail trade.

Industrial: 50 percent or more of employment in manufacturing and more than 30 percent in retail trade.

Diversified-manufacturing: Manufacturing employment greater than retail but less than 50 percent of aggregate.

Diversified-retailing: Retailing employment greater than manufacturing but latter constitutes at least 20 percent of total.

Retailing: Less than 20 percent of employment in manufacturing.

Dormitory: No significant local employment.

Specialized: Single activity provides main economic support for community.

SOURCE: Richard L. Forstall, "Economic Classification of Places over 10,000," *Muncipal Year Book: 1967* (Chicago: International City Managers' Association, 1967), p. 40.

of employees in each major occupational category is calculated. An occupational score is then arrived at for each urban place by determining the deviation of each occupational group from the mean for communities of the same size group.[7]

Profiles are valuable since they provide a graphic method of locating the salient dimensions of cities and metropolitan areas *vis-à-vis* each other. It is obvious, however, that the more variables a researcher uses

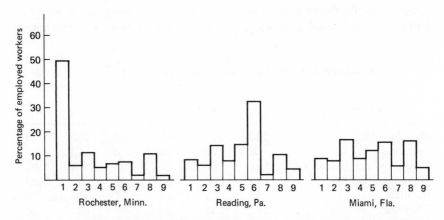

FIGURE 13   **Occupational Profiles of Three Cities. The numbers represent (1) professional, technical, and kindred workers; (2) managers, officials, and proprietors, excluding farm; (3) clerical and kindred workers; (4) sales workers; (5) craftsmen, foremen, and kindred workers; (6) operatives and kindred workers; (7) private household workers; (8) service workers, except private household; and (9) laborers, except farm and mine. From Raymond E. Murphy,** The American City: An Urban Geography **(New York: McGraw-Hill, 1966), p. 128.**

in attempting to construct a typology, the more complex the process becomes because of all the possible combinations of such characteristics. One way of dealing with this problem is through the use of factor analysis. This statistical process involves the clustering of those dimensions which are highly intercorrelated but not related to variables in other clusters. It is based upon the assumption, fundamental to all science, that a large and complex set of phenomena can be organized and understood in terms of a smaller set of concepts.

A number of recent studies have used the factor-analytic approach for purposes of classification. One of the more impressive of these efforts

[7] For an example of this method, see Paul Bates Gillen, *The Distribution Of Occupations As a City Yardstick* (New York: King's Crown Press, 1951).

was undertaken by Christen Jonassen, a sociologist.[8] After devising quantitative measurements for eighty-two dimensions of Ohio counties, Jonassen resorted to factor analysis to order the relationship among this large set of variables and to reduce them to a lesser number that would explain the differences between one county system and another. This method extracted seven factors or clusters into which the eighty-two variables grouped. Jonassen called these urbanism, welfare, influx, poverty, magnicomplexity, educational effort, and proletarianism. Instead of attempting to classify or differentiate among the counties on the basis of eighty-two dimensions, he could now speak in terms of seven factors which presumably subsumed all the other variables. As he observed, the combinations involved in the interrelationships of the many factors are like the parts of a jigsaw puzzle of thousands of pieces which fit together to present a meaningful picture of community systems.

A similar but more ambitious use of factor analysis was made by sociologists Jeffrey K. Hadden and Edgar F. Borgatta in attempting to classify all American cities over 25,000 population and all urbanized areas and SMSAs.[9] The sixty-five variables that they employed reduced themselves to eight clusters which they identified as socio-economic status level, nonwhite, age composition, educational center, residential mobility, population density, foreign-born concentration, and total population. The authors also used a broad array of economic specialization variables but found only a minimal relationship between these and the social factors utilized. This finding prompted them to argue that such economic factors as the amount of wholesale or retail involvement are closely related to total population size and hence are directly subsumed under this latter factor. It also led them to suggest that the primary method of classification of urban places should be based on the social characteristics of their populations rather than on their economic specialization. Perhaps because they sensed this possibility, economists have eschewed efforts to develop urban typologies.

Utility of Urban Classifications

There are many ways of classifying urban communities, including population size, density, regional location, age, and occupational structure. Classification, despite the way it is sometimes treated, is not an end in itself; it is a means of enlarging our understanding about whatever complex matter we may be studying. Little is gained, for example, by categorizing urban places by size or economic specialization unless this in-

[8] Christen T. Jonassen, "Functional Unities in Eighty-Eight Community Systems," *American Sociological Review*, 26 (June, 1961), 399–407. For a later application of this approach, see Charles M. Bonjean, Harley L. Browning, and Lewis F. Carter, "Toward Comparative Community Research: A Factor Analysis of United States Counties," *Sociological Quarterly*, 10 (Spring, 1969), 157–176.

[9] *American Cities: Their Social Characteristics* (Chicago: Rand McNally, 1965).

formation will enable us to predict other distinctive traits associated with communities in each of the devised classes. It may be interesting to know how many cities fall within a certain size category or how many rely on resort trade for their livelihood, but this kind of knowledge without further application has little scientific relevancy.

Those engaged in developing urban classifications often justify their efforts by claiming that such typologies are useful for comparative purposes or for studying the relationships between communal types and political and other social variables. Actually, however, few attempts have been made to relate urban classification schemes, economic or otherwise, to other phenomena; and those which have moved in this direction have been unable to show significant associations. The conclusions of the Hadden-Borgatta study are revealing in this regard. As the authors state:

One of the relatively clear outcomes from our analyses is that cities do not differ in distinct qualitative categories that correspond to types. Cities do not cluster in the form of one unique type as compared to another unique type. Rather, in the variables that we have examined cities tend to be distributed, and usually the distribution involves a gradient of differences.[10]

The various efforts at classification which have been made, in short, cast doubt on the possibility of devising a meaningful economic or other typology of urban places based on a single variable or a small set of factors. This does not imply the nonutility of classification schemes; it simply points to their limitations and the unlikelihood of discovering a typology which will serve all research needs. As Jonassen aptly noted: "It would seem that in any case the basis of classification for communities should be the one most significant and meaningful for the user."[11] Such an approach means that the combination of factors selected to use in establishing categories would differ according to the particular problem or purpose of the classifier.

ECONOMIC STRUCTURE

How does a metropolitan community provide a living for its residents? What particular types of economic activities characterize its operations? What products does it manufacture for its own residents and what goods does it export outside the region? How and to what extent do these activities conform to the pattern in other communities or in the nation

[10] *American Cities: Their Social Characteristics,* p. 71.

[11] *The Measurement of Community Dimensions and Elements* (Columbus: Ohio State University Center for Educational Administration, 1959), p. 68.

as a whole? Questions of this nature refer to the economic structure or productive pattern of an area. This structure may be highly diversified as it is when there are many types of industry and business in a community, or it may be relatively narrow as it is when a single industry, such as aircraft manufacturing, or a single group of businesses, such as those serving a tourist trade, dominate the economic life of the area.

Growth Determinants

Aside from such basic factors as geographical location, the most important single determinant of future growth in any metropolitan area or region is the level of production and expansion in the national economy. A rise or decline in the rate of production for the country as a whole will be reflected in varying degrees among its parts. When the nation surges ahead economically, most of the regions evidence substantial growth; when the nation lags, so do the regions. The reason is clear: the country in large measure has become a single, highly interdependent economic unit. Major industries produce for a national market; securities and money markets have become predominantly nationwide in scope; and psychological attitudes of both business decision-makers and consumers are transmitted throughout the economy.

Changes in the national picture, however, do not affect all areas in the same way. Some grow at a faster rate than others and some even decline. The Fort Lauderdale, Florida, SMSA, for example, tripled in population during the 1950–1960 decade while the Pittsburgh metropolitan area remained almost at a standstill and the St. Joseph, Missouri, SMSA declined (as did nine others). Technological advances, the development of product substitutes, and changes in merchandising practices are among the factors that have greater impact on one community than another. Similarly, increases in income may have differential effects on urban economies. Consumers with rising per capita income increase their expenditures more on automobiles and color television sets than on food and tobacco. The latter, unlike most durable goods and luxury items, respond little if at all to higher incomes. Economists refer to this phenomenon as "income elasticity of demand," or the ratio of the percent change in spending on a product to the percent change in disposable income. Areas whose industrial mix is oriented toward the production of goods most susceptible to elasticity of demand are generally in the most favorable long-run positions (although they may be hardest hit in periods of recession).[12]

The basic forces shaping the growth and economic structure of an SMSA can be the object of local or metropolitan policy only to the extent they are amenable to control from within the area. When these forces are not so responsive, an urban community can seek only to pro-

[12] See Thompson, *A Preface to Urban Economics*, pp. 31–33.

mote the best adjustment to them and to insulate itself as much as possible from the adverse effects of potential changes in the national economy. A metropolis or region might, to cite one example, stimulate growth by upgrading its labor pool through education and training, but it could do little more than adjust to changes in the national or international demand for products which comprise its export base.[13] The economic future of any metropolis is conditioned, in other words, by broad national trends—shifts in population, markets, and tastes—which do not originate within the area. To combat or resist these external forces is an exercise in futility; to utilize the new opportunities which they provide is the most rational course. For this latter purpose, a metropolitan community must have a sophisticated understanding of its economic structure, be able to identify its capabilities, and know what it will need if it is to exploit available opportunities and take advantage of technical progress.

Basic and Nonbasic Industries

In analyzing a community's structure and dimensions as a producer of goods and services, economists divide urban economic activities into the two broad categories of basic and nonbasic. The first includes the exporting industries or those that bring money into the community from outside. The second covers the nonexporting industries or those that produce goods and services for consumption by people residing within the metropolitan complex. According to this distinction, automobile and steel manufacturing are basic activities since most of the output is destined for external markets. Conversely, the retail trade and service industries are considered nonbasic since their output is primarily for the satisfaction of local demands. The level of nonbasic activity is closely related to that of the basic industries. Any substantial reduction or layoff of workers in the factories and plants will be reflected in the sales of such retail or service establishments as furniture and clothing stores.

The ascribed importance of specialized production for external markets has prompted some scholars to classify businesses which engage principally in this type of activity as "city-forming," implying that such industries provide the major sources of urban growth and the prime reason for the existence of cities as centers of economic enterprise. When this categorization is used, the nonbasic activities are referred to as "city-serving." The general assumption underlying these various methods of classification (basic-nonbasic, export-import, city forming-city serving) is that most metropolitan areas are self-sufficient with respect to one set of industries and at the same time are specialized producers of certain

---

[13] See in this connection, Edgar M. Hoover, "Pittsburgh Takes Stock of Itself," in Benjamin Chinitz (ed.), *City And Suburb: The Economics of Metropolitan Growth*, pp. 53–65.

types of output beyond their own needs. The revenues derived from external sales of these latter products enable the community to finance the importation of goods and services in which it is deficient. If the community has little to export, it must depend on its own restricted resources to supply its needs. In such case it resembles the farm family which produces little to sell on the market and therefore finds itself compelled to live on its own limited range of goods.

This depiction of the urban area as heavily dependent on external trade casts the export sector in the key role relative to the economic well-being and growth of metropolitan communities. Not all scholars, however, are willing to accept the proposition that the so-called basic activities are more important to a local area than those of a nonbasic character. Some, particularly planner Hans Blumenfeld, even argue that it is really the local service sector which is basic since its efficiency is critical to the operation of export firms. In their view, the high development of business, personal, and governmental services, together with other ancillary activities, enables a metropolis to sustain, expand, and when necessary replace primary industries which may be lost to the uncertainties of the market. As Blumenfeld puts the case, it is the nonbasic industries that ". . . constitute the real and lasting strength of the metropolitan economy. As long as they continue to function efficiently, the metropolis will always be able to substitute new 'export' industries for any that may be destroyed by the vicissitudes of economic life."[14]

Whatever the merits of this position, several facts should be noted concerning the basic-nonbasic pattern. First, a community improves its balance of payment ratio when it produces goods which it previously imported. The effect of this production is the same as a corresponding increase in its exports. Second, the basic-nonbasic ratio in employment is highest in the small urban areas and lowest in the largest. As a community increases in size and becomes more metropolitan in character the percentage of persons employed in basic activities decreases while the proportion furnishing goods and services needed locally rises. In short, the larger the community, the greater the variety and differentiation of its activities and the more its inhabitants live, to use Blumenfeld's expression, "by taking in each other's washing." Third, as local business services become more varied and improve in quality, they inevitably replace similar services previously imported from larger and more highly developed neighboring areas. The net effect is for the the local economy to increase its degree of self-sufficiency in this sector also.

All relatively large SMSAs now exhibit some activity in each major nonagricultural group of industries, and the overall trend is toward a greater uniformity of industrial structures among the various regions. Each

[14] "The Economic Base of the Metropolis: Critical Remarks on the 'Basic-Nonbasic' Concept," *Journal of the American Institute of Planners*, 21 (Fall, 1955), 131.

major area tends, as industrial location studies show, to develop its own manufacturing complex for the satisfaction of its own needs. This movement toward regional self-sufficiency is stimulated by the growing availability of basic industrial needs—from rare skills to service facilities—in more parts of the country.

Employment Base Method

One method of identifying the basic industries in a community is to compare the structure of local employment with that prevailing nationally. This approach rests on the premises that (1) the country as a whole is relatively self-sufficient and therefore serves as a model for measuring the extent of local self-sufficiency; (2) the output per worker in each industry category is approximately the same in each community; and (3) the extent to which the employment pattern in the community deviates from the national average provides a basis for determining what proportion of the area's various industrial categories is above or below its local requirements. Thus, if 20 percent of the local labor force is engaged in the manufacture of chemicals and drugs in comparison to a national average of 2 percent, we would conclude that the large bulk of its production in this sector is exported. We would assume, in other words, that only about 2 percent of the community's work force was required to supply the chemical and drug needs of its own residents and that the remaining 18 percent was producing for outside markets. The reverse is equally true. If we discovered that less than 1 percent of the local labor force is engaged in food processing as against a national figure of 5 percent, we could justifiably conclude that the area imported a large portion of its food products.[15]

Table 8 illustrates the application of the employment base method to four major sectors of the economy: durable goods manufacturing, nondurable goods manufacturing, personal services, and government or public administration. The percentage of the labor force employed in the four sectors is given for six selected SMSAs and comparisons made with national averages. As the compilation shows, Pittsburgh is far above the national mean in durable goods manufacturing but well below it in nondurable goods production. In the first instance it is a large exporter and in the second an importer. New York exhibits the reverse pattern, standing below the national average in durables but above it in nondurable manufacturing. Such results are hardly surprising since Pittsburgh's economic structure is built principally on steel while New York's manufacturing is oriented more toward printing, publishing, and the production of wearing apparel. In contrast to these two SMSAs, Philadelphia has a more

[15] For an application of the employment base method, see Ezra Solomon and Zarko G. Bilbija, *Metropolitan Chicago: An Economic Analysis* (New York: Free Press, 1959).

TABLE 8 **Percentage of Labor Force Employed in Selected Economic Activities in Six SMSAs**

SMSA	Durable Goods	Nondurable Goods	Personal Service	Public Adminis- tration
Pittsburgh	30.4	6.6	4.4	3.6
New York	10.2	15.6	5.8	4.7
Philadelphia	17.5	17.5	5.1	4.9
Washington, D.C.	2.8	4.7	6.9	26.9
Sacramento	9.7	6.7	5.9	19.1
Miami	5.4	6.1	11.8	4.4
United States	15.2	11.9	6.0	5.0

SOURCE: *County and City Data Book, 1962* (Washington: 1962).

balanced pattern, with approximately the same percentage of its workers employed in each of the two categories.

Unlike Pittsburgh, New York, or Philadelphia, the other three SMSAs have only a relatively small proportion of their employed residents engaged in either durable or nondurable production. Two of the three, Washington, D.C., and Sacramento, California, are principally exporters of public administration, the first for the nation, the second for an individual state. Compared to a national mean of 5 percent, almost 27 percent of Washington's labor force and 19 percent of Sacramento's are in government service. Miami presents still another picture. Its principal economic activities revolve around the tourist trade, a fact shown by the 11.8 percent of its employment pool (double the national average) that is engaged in personal services such as the operation of hotels. It is evident from these examples that the degree of specialization in an SMSA is inversely related to the national economic structure. The higher the degree of specialization in an area, the more the area will deviate from the national pattern, as the example of Pittsburgh illustrates.

Input-Output Analysis

The use of employment statistics provides a simple means of describing the economic base of a metropolitan area and a framework for observing changes and trends within it. This type of analysis, however, has certain limitations, and some economists have been highly critical of it.[16] Most important, they note that it does not spell out the interrelationships among the various segments of the local structure nor does it indicate to

[16] On this point, see the collection of articles dealing with economic base techniques in Ralph W. Pfouts (ed.), *The Techniques of Urban Economic Analysis* (West Trenton, N.J.: Chandler Davis, 1960).

what extent increases or decreases in one sector of the economy affect other sectors. If, for example, a 10 percent increase in steel production is anticipated in the area, how will other local industries, including government, be affected? To provide data of this kind, a more complex, as well as more costly, method of investigation has been put to use in metropolitan economic studies. Known as input-output analysis, this approach is concerned essentially with interindustry relations. Its objective is to calculate the demands which various sectors of the economy place on others in carrying out a given program of production.

Input-output analysis is based on the concept that to produce outputs or goods, such as automobiles and radios, a set of inputs, such as labor and raw or semiprocessed material, is needed.[17] If increased activity occurs in a particular industry, additional inputs will be required to meet the new demand. Some of them will be secured locally and some outside the region. Those obtained locally will generate activity in other industries and businesses in the community. Thus, new sales by a manufacturing firm will cause increased employment and increased payrolls in the local economy. These in turn will stimulate additional purchases from retail firms and additional buying by the retailers from wholesalers. By tracing this pattern of activity, the total impact of the change on the economy of the area and on each individual sector can be predicted.

Several recent metropolitan surveys, including one in Dayton, Ohio, have utilized input-output analysis in examining the local economic structure.[18] The Dayton study, on the basis of information obtained from consumers and business firms, outlined the effects of a change in output by one sector upon its purchases from other sectors of the local metropolitan economy. It showed, for example, how an increase of $1 in manufacturing sales would ultimately produce locally an additional 35 cents in retail sales, 49 cents in the receipts of other businesses, 68 cents in wages, and approximately three cents for local government in the form of taxes. Part of these increases would occur within the city of Dayton and part in the rest of the county.

The Dayton figures demonstrate well the sensitivity of one sector of the metropolitan economy to changes in another. They also furnish additional evidence of the high degree of economic interdependence among the geographic divisions of an SMSA, showing the extent to which business and household incomes in one political subdivision are directly affected by the fortunes of industrial enterprises situated in other local government enclaves within the metropolitan area. As the study observed, "It makes very little difference where the initial change arises; it will

[17] A discussion of the nature, execution, and uses of economic base studies is contained in Charles M. Tiebout, *The Community Economic Base Study* (New York: Committee for Economic Development, 1962).

[18] *Metropolitan Challenge* (Dayton: Metropolitan Community Studies, 1959), chap. 13.

ultimately affect incomes in both Dayton and other parts of the county in approximately the same way."[19]

THE METROPOLIS AS A LABOR MARKET

The metropolis can be viewed in economic terms as an instrument for the creation of wealth and the provision of want-satisfying goods and services. Essentially it is a local labor market, a fact emphasized by R. D. McKenzie and other social ecologists who define the territorial boundaries of the metropolitan community by place of residence–place of work criteria. In an advanced urban society, the economic structure will be characterized by an extensive division of labor and a high degree of occupational differentiation. A great variety of job opportunities is required for large numbers of people to reside together at reasonable standards of living. In the sizable metropolises these opportunities, similar to the social groupings we observed earlier, are widely distributed in space. The lion's share of jobs may still be based in the central cities but the continued dispersion of industrial and commercial activities in suburbia is bringing about major revisions in the classic pattern.

Occupational Pattern

More than 74 million Americans, including approximately eight million nonwhites, are in the civilian labor force. This total represents an increase of over seven million since 1960 and almost 30 million since 1940. In excess of 75 percent of those employed are urban dwellers, the predominant majority of whom live in metropolitan areas. The significance of this concentration is indicated by personal income tax returns which show that residents in the 100 largest SMSAs account for two-thirds of the nation's salaries and wages and over 70 percent of its dividend income.

Important changes have taken place during the last several decades not only in the size of the labor force but also in the distribution of the workers among the occupational categories and among the various economic sectors or industry groupings. Upward occupational mobility has characterized American society during the present century as automation and other technological developments have increased the need for professional and skilled personnel and progressively lessened the demand for the unskilled. Since 1940 the percentage of professional workers among employed males has almost doubled while the proportion of laborers has declined 40 percent. Similarly, the percentage of employed women who work as household servants (which does not include housewives, although many women may argue otherwise) has been reduced by well over one-half while the proportion of those in clerical and sales work has grown by one-fourth. These trends are further reflected in the growth of the na-

[19] *Ibid.*, p. 156.

tion's labor force from 1960 to 1967, when the rate of increase of white collar workers was one-third higher than that of blue collar employees. Just as the industrial labor force caught up with and passed agricultural employment around the turn of the present century, so by the middle 1950s the number employed in white collar occupations had crossed the divide and leaped ahead of the blue collar figure.[20]

Occupational opportunity and mobility, however, are not enjoyed equally by all segments of society. Unemployment rates in the poorest sections of the larger cities are more than double those of the remaining neighborhoods. Unemployment among Negroes, moreover, is twice as high as that of whites. The black teenager, in particular, is affected; almost one of every three of them is jobless (Table 9). Not only do dwellers

TABLE 9   White and Negro Unemployment Rates in Central Cities for Selected Groups

	White	Negro	Ratio: Negro to White
1968			
Both sexes, 16 years and over	3.5%	7.8%	2.2
Both sexes, 16 to 19 years	12.3	30.4	2.5
Male, 20 years and over	2.5	6.0	2.4
Male, married, wife present	1.8	4.5	2.5
Female, 20 years and over	3.5	5.9	1.7
1960			
Both sexes, 16 years and over	4.9	10.7	2.2
Both sexes, 16 to 19 years	9.8	22.7	2.3
Male, 20 years and over	4.8	9.9	2.1
Male, married, wife present	3.4	7.5	2.2
Female, 20 years and over	4.3	10.1	2.3

SOURCE: U.S. Bureau of the Census, "Trends in Social and Economic Conditions in Metropolitan Areas," *Current Population Reports*, Series P-23, no. 27 (Washington: February 7, 1969), p. 31.

in poverty neighborhoods have a higher incidence of unemployment but they are also more likely to have menial low-paying jobs when working. One-half the employed workers in such areas are in unskilled, semiskilled, and service jobs compared to 35 percent for the nation as a whole; and the lowest end of the occupational scale is disproportionately weighted with Negroes.[21]

[20] Arnold R. Weber, "Labor Market Perspectives of the New City," in Chinitz (ed.), *City and Suburb: The Economics of Metropolitan Growth*, p. 69.
[21] U.S. Department of Labor, *Manpower Report of the President* (Washington: April, 1968).

In addition to shifts within occupational categories, major changes have been occurring in the distributional pattern of employment by industrial groupings. The most far-reaching of these is the continued decline in the number of farm workers: from 5.4 million in 1960 to 3.9 million in 1966. The decrease was greatest in the South, an indication that the economy there is moving toward the pattern prevailing elsewhere in the nation. The loss also indicates that a minimum level of employment in farm production is fast being reached, a situation which is significantly reducing the scale of farm-to-city migration. Along with the dramatic decline in agricultural employment are the less widely known changes in the non-agricultural sectors. As Figure 14 illustrates, the percentage of employees engaged in manufacturing has declined almost 10 percent since 1919 while the proportion of those in the trade, government, and service categories has increased substantially. The last-named group comprising a wide complex of functions such as finance, advertising, medical care, and repairs has been the fastest growing segment of the economy in recent decades. Since 1947 the annual growth rate of employment in this sector has tripled that for employment in the nation as a whole. One reason for

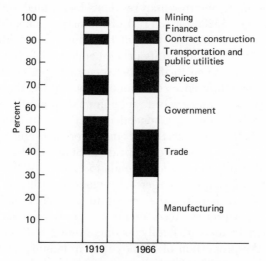

FIGURE 14   **Percent Distribution of Employees on Nonagricultural Payrolls by Major Divisions, 1919 and 1966. From U.S. Department of Labor, Bureau of Labor Statistics,** Employment and Earnings Statistics for the United States, 1909–1967 **(Washington: October, 1967).**

the higher rate is the fact that the services industry—and the same is true of the trade and government groupings—has been less affected by technological progress than the others, particularly agriculture, manufacturing, and mining. More importantly, however, this growth is characteristic of a society enjoying a high rate of productivity and rising standards of living. As personal income increases, the demand for consumer services and consumer goods mounts. Women have more to spend at apparel and beauty shops; people have the means to travel more extensively and to devote their leisure time to expensive recreational activities; local taxpayers are willing to support a broader range of governmental services; and so on. The wealthier a metropolitan area becomes, the more these kinds of demands are reflected in the composition and distribution of its labor force and in the budgets of its local governmental units.

Income

Closely related to the character of a metropolitan labor market and its wage structure is the level of income enjoyed by residents of the area. Per capita or per family income is one of the principal measures of performance of an economy, whether local, state, or national. We can appreciate this fact when we compare SMSAs with nonmetropolitan areas. In 1964, for example, metropolitan residents had a median family income of $7290 as against $5208 for the rest of the nation. This difference is not a matter of surprise since the bulk of the country's wealth and income-producing facilities is found in its urban communities. Income variances, however, are not confined to those between metropolitan and nonmetropolitan areas; wide differences exist among the SMSAs themselves. As the 1960 census revealed, there was a range in median family income extending from $8745 in Stamford, Connecticut, to $2952 in Laredo, Texas.

Two factors help to explain the income differential among metropolitan areas: population size and regional location. Statistics drawn from census data show that urban income level tends to increase with size of population. As a community grows larger it becomes more highly industrialized and in the process acquires the means to provide broader and better employment opportunities. According to one study, as much as 30 percent of the variation in median family income among SMSAs is statistically explained by the proportion of employment in manufacturing. The large urban area also provides better opportunity for holding a second job ("moonlighting") and for the employment of married women; both factors have contributed to the sharp increase in family income in recent years.

The second variable, regional location, is independent of population size in accounting for metropolitan income differentials. Median family income in 1964 was $7698 in the western SMSAs compared to $6510 in the southern metropolises and $7290 for the nation's metropolitan areas as a whole. Since income levels are related to the degree of industrialization,

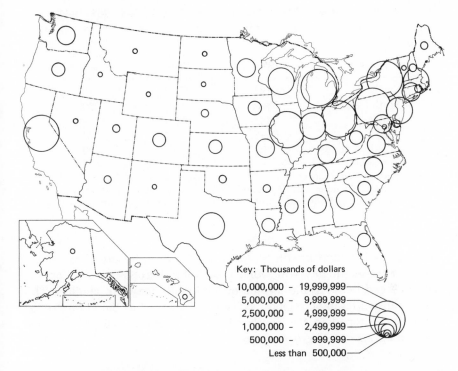

FIGURE 15   **Value Added by Manufacture by States, 1963. From U.S. Bureau of the Census,** Census of Manufactures: 1963, **Vol. I, p. 40.**

the South's position at the bottom of the income scale is to be expected. Until recent decades the industrial might of the country was concentrated almost exclusively in the northeast and North Central regions. As late as 1963 not a single southern metropolis was among the top fifteen SMSAs ranked according to value added by manufacturing and only six were in the first fifty.[22]

Since World War II the South has been making significant gains in industrial expansion and has been moving closer to the income level of the rest of the nation. From 1958 to 1963 it led all sections of the country in the proportionate growth of its productive activity, showing an increase of 45 percent in value added by manufacture. This figure was well above the national average of 36 percent and was approached only by the 43 percent increase in the western states. The growth in the South's economy was accompanied by a corresponding rise in income. During the period from 1959 to 1964 median family income in southern SMSAs increased far more rapidly than in the other regions (Table 10).

[22] U.S. Bureau of the Census, *Census of Manufactures: 1963,* Vol. I, p. 43.

TABLE 10   Median Family Income in SMSAs by Region, 1959–1964

Region	1959	1964	Percentage Increase, 1959–1964
Northeast	$6191	$7354	19
North Central	5892	7618	29
South	4465	6510	46
West	6348	7698	21
United States	5660	7290	29

SOURCE FOR TABLES 10 AND 11: U.S. Bureau of Census, "Income in 1964 of Families and Unrelated Individuals by Metropolitan-Non-metropolitan Residence," *Current Population Reports* (Washington: 1966).

One serious impediment still faced by the South in its efforts to achieve greater income equality with other geographical sections is the continuing wide gap between the income of white and nonwhite families. This gap is substantial in all regions, as Table 11 shows, but the most striking difference is found in the South where the sharpest occupational discrimination against Negroes occurs.

TABLE 11   Median Family Income in SMSAs by Race, 1964

Region	White	Nonwhite	Nonwhite Income as Percentage of White Income
Northeast	$7575	$4938	65
North Central	7891	5185	66
South	7031	3742	53
West	7827	6198	79
United States	7603	4671	61

THE CENTRAL BUSINESS DISTRICT

A major topic of concern whenever the economy of metropolitan areas is discussed is the fate of the central business district. As several observers have expressed it, "The CBD is on trial." To many urban planners the future of the metropolis depends on the future of downtown. They regard this core as the heart and soul of the metropolitan community, the focal point around which the activities of the entire area revolve. There can be no prosperous periphery, in their view, without a successful downtown. Destroy or let this hub deteriorate, and the metropolitan area will be sapped of strength and vigor. This view, although widely accepted, is sharply disputed by some observers. Maintaining that the CBD has ceased to serve a useful purpose, the dissidents question the wisdom of spending millions of dollars each year to pump new vitality into what they regard as an obsolete and outmoded appendage. In their eyes, attempts to save the downtown are economically unsound and unrealistic; let its fate be determined by the free play of the market place. Those who take this position would have the community free itself from its long-standing commitment to the preservation of the CBD and devote its resources to the development of alternatives. Others take a more moderate stand and while acknowledging the crucial importance of the downtown section criticize the failure of city planners and administrators to recognize its changing role and to act accordingly.

Regardless of who is right or wrong in this controversy, metropolitan areas—particularly the central cities—have a large stake in their downtown core. Despite any obsolescence, the CBD represents a huge investment of community wealth and an important source of tax revenue for local government. Within its territorial confines is the area's highest concentration of office buildings, department stores, specialty shops, hotels, financial institutions, and governmental agencies. The density of its daytime population greatly exceeds that in any other section of the community. Its land values are by far the highest in the area. It is the center of the community's transportation and communications network. A map of any large metropolitan area shows how the expressways, major streets, and mass transit lines gravitate toward the downtown center. By almost any test we apply, it would be difficult to ignore the significance of the CBD to the life, economy, and government of the metropolis.

Changing Characteristics

The character and functions of the CBD have changed materially over time. Until about a half century ago, the downtown was an area of multiple uses—residential, commercial, industrial, and institutional. With the passage of time, overcrowding and obsolescence led first to the decline in residential use and later in manufacturing and wholesaling use. The arrival of the motor vehicle gave the dweller in this core area the mobility to flee from the center and at the same time it broadened the locational freedom of industrial establishments. New methods of fabrication and new techniques for handling materials and goods outmoded the old multi-story factory and warehouse buildings and created a demand for single-story space. The high cost of downtown land together with the difficulty of assembling sufficiently large parcels to meet the new space requirements discouraged manufacturing expansion in the core. On the periphery land was far cheaper, traffic and congestion were much less, and the problem of getting the worker to and from his job had been solved by the motor vehicle.

The story is the same in virtually all the large metropolitan areas. In Chicago, a pronounced movement of both old and new firms from the central city to the northwest suburbs has taken place. In Boston, the traveler along Route 128 can see the huge complex of electronics industries which form a circumferential arch around the city. In St. Louis, he can observe the numerous industrial parks and giant manufacturing establishments such as McDonnell Aircraft, Chrysler, and Monsanto Chemical which dot the suburban landscape. Because of this exodus, central cities have been losing manufacturing jobs to the suburbs in substantial quantity and at a higher rate than they have been replaced. From 1958 to 1963, the number of such jobs declined absolutely in the core municipalities of nine of the ten largest SMSAs (Table 12). Only the District of Columbia showed a slight increase but this gain is of little significance since manufacturing constitutes only a small portion of the city's economic base. The city of Detroit, on the other hand, lost approximately 13,000 manufacturing jobs while the suburbs gained 40,000. Similarly, Chicago lost over 60,000 such jobs while the rest of the metropolitan area showed an increase of almost 65,000.

A trend, resembling that in manufacturing, has also been taking place

TABLE 12   **Number of Manufacturing Jobs in Central Cities of Ten Largest SMSAs, 1958 and 1963**

	Number Employed in Central City, 1958	Number Employed in Central City, 1963	Percent Gain or Loss, 1958 to 1963
New York	998,620	927,413	− 7.7
Los Angeles	299,596	280,221	− 6.9
Chicago	569,356	508,797	−11.9
Philadelphia	298,521	264,893	−12.7
Detroit	213,480	200,586	− 6.4
San Francisco	65,299	60,639	− 7.7
Boston	90,215	82,512	− 9.3
Pittsburgh	99,330	81,707	−21.6
Washington	21,287	22,147	4.0
St. Louis	146,770	129,069	−13.7

SOURCE: U.S. Bureau of the Census, *1963 Census of Manufactures*, Vol. III, *Area Statistics* (Washington: 1965).

in retail trade. While industrial location is determined by such factors as space requirements, access to transportation facilities, and economy and efficiency in operation, the retail trade pattern is shaped by considerations of convenience for the consumer. As population moves outward from the center, the shops and stores follow. Prior to 1920 over 90 percent of retail sales were made in the central business districts. By 1968, this figure for the large metropolitan areas had dropped to an average of less than 50 percent. In all twenty-five of the nation's largest SMSAs, the core city's share of the retail market showed a loss between the 1954 and 1963 censuses of business. For many of them, the decline represented an absolute loss as well. A Bureau of the Census analysis of CBDs in 109 major cities in 1958 showed that the volume of retail sales in fifty of them had decreased during the preceding four-year period, in some cases as high as 20 percent and in one instance as high as 30 percent.[23]

Retail employment in the central city has been similarly affected. Philadelphia, for example, contained 62 percent of the population and 79 percent of the retail jobs in the SMSA in 1930; in 1960, it contained 46 percent of the metropolitan area's residents and 51 percent of its retail jobs. Huge shopping centers are now a common sight on the metropolitan periphery. Established downtown department stores have opened outlying branches; major grocery chains have been quick to tap the growing market; and discount houses have emerged on the suburban scene to offer a new form of competition to the merchandising traditionalists. Convenient to the suburban housewife and equipped with ample parking facilities, the new centers are luring shoppers away not only from the core city CBD but also from the business districts of outlying neighborhoods and of the older ring municipalities. These smaller commercial concentrations are especially vulnerable since they have neither the free off-street parking of the new shopping centers nor the wide selection of merchandise of the CBD.

The seriousness of this problem for the central city cannot be shrugged off, but the picture is not one of unmitigated bleakness. Even though the city is losing retail trade and manufacturing to suburbia, it has advantages which no other section of the area can offer. The concentration of office buildings, financial institutions, department stores, and related service facilities within its CBD provides a business environment that would be difficult to duplicate anywhere else in the metropolitan community. Because of these features, certain activities continue to remain within the special province of the core city despite the changing character of urban society and the forces of obsolescence.

Frank Lloyd Wright once proposed the construction of a single mile-high building in the downtown area to house what he identified as the

23 U.S. Bureau of the Census, *1958 Census of Business*, Vol. I, *Retail Trade*, p. 13.

primary functions of the central city: banking and prostitution. We need not accede to Mr. Wright's architectural fantasy nor agree with his delineation of the core city's role to see that what is involved here is the bringing together of certain specialized activities in a central location. These activities, moreover, are metropolitan-oriented and not merely neighborhood-oriented. The banking facilities of the CBD, for example, serve the major needs of business and industry regardless of their location in the SMSA. The same observation also applies to the downtown department store since its clientele is area-wide. In contrast, the branches which banks and department stores establish in suburbia can rarely, if ever, lay claim to serving the whole metropolis.

Advantages of the CBD

The CBD, and the central city in general, offer unique advantages in three functional areas by (1) furnishing specialized and comparative shopping; (2) providing office facilities for the so-called "confrontation" industries, which are the occupations and activities that depend on face-to-face contact for the conduct of business; and (3) servicing the small businesses and industries that seek the economies which concentration offers.

SPECIALIZED AND COMPARATIVE SHOPPING   Until the last few decades, the downtown area of the core city served as the main shopping center for the entire metropolis. In more recent years this function has been badly eroded by the spatial decentralization of retail trade. Whatever viability the CBD now retains in the retail sector is due largely to the opportunities it offers for comparative shopping. Its large aggregation of department stores and specialty shops enables it to provide a depth and variety of merchandise and a range of choice in brand, style, quality, and price that is economically unfeasible to furnish elsewhere. Large numbers of customers are needed to support activity of this type and only the downtown, as the pivotal gathering point of masses of people, satisfies this requirement.

It has been evident for some time that the CBD cannot compete with the outlying centers in standardized goods. The suburban housewife simply will not make the long trip downtown for items that she can readily purchase in her neighborhood or regional shopping district. Only when she wishes to broaden her range of choice or obtain specialized products is she willing to undergo this inconvenience. The development of larger regional centers on the periphery, a tendency that now is emerging, will lessen the advantage of the CBD, even for comparative shopping. On the other hand, the downtown stores can still count on a large clientele of office workers, government employees, and others who are brought into the CBD for purposes other than shopping. A local clientele of some size is also being created in the larger SMSAs as a result of the new luxury apartments which are appearing in or near the core on land made available largely by urban redevelopment projects.

"CONFRONTATION" INDUSTRIES Aside from retailing activities, the core city still remains the preferred location for the "confrontation" industries. Financial institutions and business offices, particularly corporate headquarters, tend to group themselves in highly cohesive clusters in the city center. For them the dominant locational need is one of speedy and direct communication. The telephone or letter provides no substitute for the advantages that the managerial élite find in dealing directly with their business associates. As economist Raymond Vernon points out, "The process of negotiation and conferring oftentimes involves subtleties of emphasis and expression too elusive to be imparted by letter, telephone, and even perhaps by closed circuit television."[24] The large office establishments, moreover, attract to the CBD a host of other activities with which they have linkages. Advertising agencies, accounting firms, office suppliers, and similar service-providing enterprises find it helpful and convenient to be located near the doorsteps of their major clients and customers.

In the past, a downtown location made it easier for a firm with large office needs to recruit clerical personnel. Young women have long held most of the office jobs involving repetitive work. With an employment force of this nature, a location at the hub of the mass transit network was at one time highly advantageous. Today, with automobile commuting commonplace even among young women, this factor has lost much of its appeal. Other features, however, continue to make downtown the preferred place of employment for young female office workers. The opportunities for lunch-hour shopping, for after-hours recreation and entertainment, and for meeting people—including eligible bachelors—are unexcelled in the region.

SMALL PLANTS AND BUSINESSES The third group of enterprises for which the CBD and its adjacent areas offer locational advantages are the small plants and businesses which produce mainly nonstandard products and are dependent on economies obtainable through the use of "external" facilities or services. The New York Metropolitan Region Study called attention to this feature in noting that size of establishment is closely related to affinity for the central districts. It found that more than half of the New York area's employment in industries having sixty or less workers per plant was in the central city. Because of the limited scale of their operations, these enterprises have to rely on services which their larger competitors provide for themselves. Through clustering, the small plants attempt to overcome the handicap of size by securing externally the

[24] *The Changing Economic Function of the Central City* (New York: Committee for Economic Development, 1959), p. 30.

economies which the large companies enjoy internally. Thus, as the New York study observed:

> To avoid stockpiling their materials in disproportionately large numbers, they [small plants] have clung close to the center of the urban cluster where they can get materials on short notice; to meet the problems of labor force variations or machine breakdowns, they have chosen locations where they can recruit workers for brief periods or on short notice. They have chosen loft space, short run in commitment and flexible in size, in preference to the separate factory building away from the urban center. In sum, the denser areas of the New York Metropolitan Region are acting as a common pool for space, materials, and labor, meeting the inherent uncertainties of the small plants which occupy these areas.[25]

The attractiveness of the core to small industry is, however, diminishing. Clustering can take place in suburbia as well as the CBD if proper facilities become available. The New York study showed, for example, that in recent years Manhattan has suffered an absolute decline in the number of small plants. The study attributed this loss to the spread of external economies to the outlying areas. Rentable manufacturing space is now being offered to smaller plants and businesses in suburban industrial parks, while repairmen and subcontractors are found in increasing numbers throughout the area. At the same time, sewage disposal, water, fire and police protection, and adequate trucking service are becoming available on the periphery. As a result of these developments, "The early city monopolies—their ability uniquely to provide an environment in which small plants may settle—are being broken. And in time small plants will have amost as wide a geographical choice as their larger competitors in selecting a site for their activities in the Region."[26]

The Future of the CBD

It is evident that the CBD is going through a period of change and adjustment, and the same may be said of the central city as a whole. The CBD's future will depend heavily on its ability to adapt to the new circumstances and to capitalize on those activities which it alone can do, or which it can do better than the remainder of the area. This adaptation may require, as some urban specialists contend, the further enhancement of the CBD's economic efficiency by a displacement of less intensive activities with those of a more specialized nature. Or it may require, as planner and developer Victor Gruen has suggested for Fort Worth, physical changes in which the main downtown streets are made pedestrian malls, with parking garages on the periphery and moving sidewalks to

[25] Edgar M. Hoover and Raymond Vernon, *Anatomy of a Metropolis* (New York: Doubleday, 1962), pp. 48–49.
[26] *Ibid.*, pp. 50–51.

bring shoppers and office workers from their cars to the center of activity.

Of more serious concern in assessing the strength and potential of the central city are the social by-products of economic structural changes. As many types of jobs, particularly manufacturing, move out into the periphery, the cities are becoming more specialized in those functions which require professional, technical, and clerical skills. And as this development occurs, employment opportunities within the central city are diminished for core area dwellers, many of whom lack the requisite qualifications for the specialized positions. Increasingly, such dwellers find that the only job opportunities available to them are in the suburbs where manufacturing plants have continued to redeploy. They must thus pay a price in terms of transportation costs that they can ill afford. Job seeking is also discouraged by the increased physical distance from place of residence to place of potential work. As a result, the core area resident is often stranded, thus raising the unemployment rate and welfare costs which must be borne in large part by the central city.[27]

THE ECONOMIC PATTERN AND THE GOVERNMENT

The relationship between the economic and social structures of metropolitan areas is generally recognized, at least in vague fashion, by most people. What is often overlooked, however, is that the economic structure, like the social structure, also bears an important relationship to the governmental and political system of the metropolis. As scholars from classical times to the present have pointed out, government and economics cannot be divorced. The urban community, for example, is a workshop and a producer of wealth. The economic activity it generates takes place within an institutional or governmental framework and this framework is naturally of concern to the economic side of urban existence.

On the one hand, industry and business depend on local government for such essential services as water supply, sewage disposal, police and fire protection, roads, schools, and zoning. On the other hand, the character and trend of economic activity affect and, in a sense, even determine the operations of the governmental system. No public body can intelligently plan its service expansion, capital improvement programs, or land use patterns without a knowledge of the community's economic structure and its potential. An area that is expanding in the direction of heavy industry will have a different set of service needs and land use requirements than one which is developing into an electronic research center. A static or declining community will require different governmental treatment than one experiencing explosive growth. Similarly, a large, heterogeneous

[27] See in this connection Arnold R. Weber, "Labor Market Perspectives of the New City," pp. 73-74.

SMSA will have needs that vary from those of a smaller, homogeneous one. In short, the ability of a metropolitan governmental system to meet the current requirements and to anticipate the direction of change in its economic structure is a critical aspect of the contemporary urban scene.

Many other interconnections could be cited. By way of illustration, one which has important consequences for the administration and financing of government is the daily movement of people throughout the area, a result largely of the wide spatial distribution of jobs and economic activities. The population in some sections of the metropolis, the central business district in particular, increases manyfold during the daytime and then drops sharply at night as workers and shoppers disperse homeward over the countryside. To accommodate this movement, public services in the locations of daytime concentration must be greatly expanded over the requirements of the resident population. Should the pattern of economic activity change so that the downtown or other sections of heavy concentration cease to attract large daytime populations, the impact on local government would be substantial. Not only would the large capital investment in roads and public utilities in these sections be jeopardized and the tax base eroded, but the community would also be faced with the huge task of redesigning its transportation network and its service facilities.

In addition to these fairly obvious relations, the economic pattern has a more indirect and subtle effect on local government. Sociologists and anthropologists have called attention to the fact that the modern urban community tends to create a new structure of social behavior and thought radically different from that which prevailed in a simpler society. The intricate division of labor endows work with a variety of forms and makes the urban labor force a composite of diversified types. These changes in turn give rise to new tastes and values, new manners and life styles, new attitudes toward problems, new expectations, and new concepts of what life ought to be like.[28]

The structure of behavior which results from this transformation finds reflection in the new demands on the social and political institutions of the urban community. Thus we see increased emphasis on educational and training facilities, on cultural and recreational services, on home ownership and better housing, on renewal of the city, and on the elimination of racial and ethnic barriers. And with rising incomes, public goods and activities once considered luxuries have now come to be regarded as indispensable. The metropolitan governmental system, on the other hand, has been slow to react to the modern industrial age, but the pressures which this era generates may in the end give new forms to local government despite deep and inbred resistance.

[28] These effects are discussed in Ralph E. Turner, "The Industrial City: Center of Cultural Change," in Caroline F. Ware (ed.), *The Cultural Approach to History* (New York: Columbia University Press, 1940), pp. 228–242.

Economics as a science is basically concerned with the process by which scarce resources are allocated among competing interests and goals. As public policy-makers, local governmental officials are directly or indirectly involved in this process. Their decisions on educational, recreational, and other types of governmental expenditures are allocational judgments that help to determine the community tone and environment. So also their action on urban renewal projects, mass transit, planning and zoning, and capital improvement projects have important repercussions in the economic sphere. And although ultimate decisions on such matters as business and industrial location will continue to be made by private interests on economic grounds, the actions of local authorities may do much to influence these decisions and to determine the future course of the metropolis.

LOS ANGELES COUNTY COURTHOUSE

5 /
GOVERNMENT
IN THE
METROPOLIS

THE FORMAL OR LEGAL STRUCTURE OF LOCAL GOVERNMENT, ALTHOUGH deemphasized by some political scientists, constitutes a vital facet of the metropolitan scene. The linkages between this structure and other variables such as citizen participation, the distribution of political power, and service levels have become a subject of increasing concern and study. Investigations by researchers cut in two directions. One is the extent to which local political forms are expressions of community values or socioeconomic interests; the other, the extent to which these forms influence value or resource allocations as manifested in public policy outputs. As a recent study pointed out, "The implicit, or at times explicit, causal model in much of the research on municipal reformism has been a simple one: socioeconomic cleavages cause the adoption of particular political forms. A more sophisticated model would include political institutions as one of the factors which produce a given output structure."[1] In terms of the

[1] Robert L. Lineberry and Edmund P. Fowler, "Reformism and Public Policies in American Cities," *American Political Science Review*, LXI (September, 1967), 714.

latter type of inquiry, structure becomes an important variable in explaining how inputs in a community are transformed into public programs.

In the typical metropolis we find a complicated and bewildering pattern of government: many municipalities, a large number of school districts, a variety of nonschool special districts, and one or more counties. These categories of local government differ in many respects—in territorial size, powers, financial authority and resources, structure, and ability to deal with the conditions and perplexities of modern urban life. Taken as a whole, this array of governments determines in large part the quality and capability of the metropolitan political system.

This chapter examines the formal structure and pattern of government in metropolitan areas, looking at the abundance and complexity of the local units, their historical development and adaptability, and their relationship to the state and national government. It also examines the association between structure and political environment. Such an analysis helps in comprehending how the governmental system functions and its capabilities and deficiencies in meeting metropolitan challenges.

GOVERNMENTS IN ABUNDANCE

The governmental pattern of metropolitan areas resembles a crowded bus or subway. Occupying about one-tenth of the land, these areas have a total of 20,703 local governments; this is an average of ninety-one for each complex. The number represents independent units and not simply adjuncts, subordinate agencies, or departments of other governments. Each of them has its own corporate powers, such as the right to sue and to be sued and to obtain and dispose of property, its own officials, its own authority to provide service (and often to enforce regulations), and its own power to raise revenue through taxation or charges. Each of them thus wears the powerful mantle of public authority, including the power of financial exaction from the citizenry and the ability to affect people's lives beneficially or harmfully. Furthermore, since each is a separate unit and legally independent, it is able, if it wishes, to act unilaterally and without concern for the desires of or the effect on the people in neighboring jurisdictions.

Variations

Although supporting on the average a large array of local units, metropolitan areas differ considerably in the complexity of their governmental systems. A limited number have only a few local governments—from five to twenty. Located chiefly in the South, many in this category have recently experienced extensive population growth that has brought metropolitan status to them for the first time. On the other hand, twenty-nine

TABLE 13   SMSAs by Total Number and Average Number of Local Governments, 1967

SMSA Size Group (1960 Population)	Number of SMSAs	Number of Local Governments	Average Number of Local Governments
All SMSAs	227	20,703	91.2
1,000,00 or more	24	7,367	307.0
500,000–1,000,000	32	3,878	121.2
300,000–500,000	30	2,734	91.1
200,000–300,000	40	2,919	73.0
100,000–200,000	74	3,123	42.2
50,000–100,000	27	682	25.3

SOURCE: U.S. Bureau of the Census, *Census of Governments: 1967*, Vol. 1, *Governmental Organization* (Washington: 1968), p. 11.

metropolises, about one of every eight, have 200 or more local units. The most prolific is the Chicago SMSA with a total of 1113. It is followed by the Philadelphia area, 876; Pittsburgh, 704; New York, 551; and the St. Louis area, 474.

The governmental organization of these five areas mirrors a general characteristic of government in the metropolis: as a rule, the greater its population, the larger its number of local units. Also, as Table 13 shows, substantial differences in the number of local governments are present in every succeeding population group of areas, with each increase amounting to one-fourth or more. The widest disparity occurs between the two most populous classes, where the largest has almost three times the average of the next group.

Wide discrepancies are also apparent when certain individual metropolitan areas are compared. Metropolitan Baltimore, one of the largest in the nation with a population of nearly two million, has only twenty-one local governments, thus deviating greatly from the governmental complexity of most large centers. Conversely, the Madison, Wisconsin, area, with about 250,000 residents, has sprouted 88, a larger number than that in the nearby Milwaukee SMSA where the population is almost five times as large. Another important exception is the Portland, Oregon, area; it ranks sixth in number of governments even though it contains less than one million inhabitants.

THE COMPLEXITY OF GOVERNMENT

Part of the complexity of government in metropolitan areas is due to the large number of local units. Special districts and school districts are the major contributors to this profusion; together, they make up almost

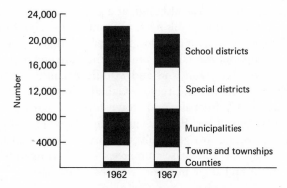

FIGURE 16   **Local Governments in SMSAs by Type, 1962 and 1967. From U.S. Bureau of the Census,** Census of Governments: 1967, **Vol. 1, p. 20.**

60 percent of the total. The former are being created at a rapid pace, however, while the latter are noticeably decreasing (Figure 16). As a result of the continuance of these countertrends, which have been apparent for several decades, special districts recently became the most prevalent local unit in the metropolis. Also, the rate of reduction in school districts has been so rapid in the last few years that the metropolitan total of local units has dropped slightly (Table 14). Municipalities (vari-

TABLE 14   **Number of Local Governments in 227 SMSAs, 1967, and Changes in Number, 1962–1967**

Class of Local Governments	Number in SMSAs, 1967	Percentage of SMSA Total	Increase or Decrease in Number, 1962–1967	Percentage Change in Number, 1962–1967
All local governments	20,703	100.0	−1,114	− 5.1
Special districts	7,049	34.1	896	14.6
School districts	5,018	24.2	−2,054	−29.0
Municipalities	4,977	24.0	74	1.5
Towns and townships	3,255	15.7	− 27	− 0.8
Counties	404	2.0	− 3[a]	− 0.7

[a] The decrease in counties is due entirely to the consolidation of Nashville and David-son County, Tennessee, into a metropolitan government, which is counted for Census statistics as a municipality, and the absorption of two Virginia counties into the independent cities of Chesapeake and Virginia Beach.

SOURCE: U.S. Bureau of the Census, *Census of Governments: 1967,* Vol. 1, *Governmental Organization* (Washington: 1968), p. 11.

ously called cities, villages, incorporated towns, and boroughs) are third in number of local units. They represent about one-fifth of the aggregate and are continuing to increase, although at a greatly reduced rate in recent years. Towns and townships rank next, accounting for about one of every seven units. A major reason for their low incidence is that they were never in common use throughout the United States. They are active in twenty-one states, mainly in the New England and Middle Atlantic regions and certain parts of the North Central region. Called "towns" in New England, New York State, and Wisconsin, and "townships" in many North Central states and in New Jersey and Pennsylvania, their number is dropping very slowly. Counties, which are generally the largest territorial units in the metropolis, are by far the least numerous. They constitute only one-fiftieth of the total and their number is almost stationary.

Small Populations and Areas

A primary contributor to the abundance of local governments in the metropolis is the smallness of many of the units. This characteristic is very evident in many muncipalities, school districts, and special districts, and it is well illustrated by their population and territorial size. About one-half of the municipalities in SMSAs have fewer than 2500 inhabitants and collectively they contain less than 3 percent of the metropolitan popu-

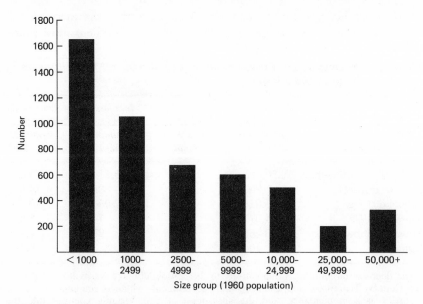

FIGURE 17   **Municipal Governments in SMSAs by Population Size, 1967. From U.S. Bureau of the Census, Census of Governments: 1967, Vol. 1, p. 20.**

lation. Moreover, a large number of these sparsely populated units have territories that encompass less than three square miles and therefore constitute minuscule segments of metropolitan land. Similarly, many school districts in the metropolis are small in terms of the number of people and the area they serve. About one-fifth of them have fewer than 300 students, including more than 200 districts with as few as fifty students and about the same number which do not directly provide public education but in-

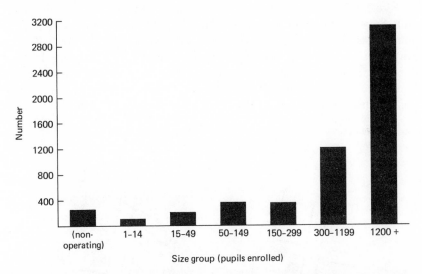

FIGURE 18   Public School Systems in SMSAs by Enrollment Size, 1967. Public school systems consist of both independent school districts and school operations that are dependent agencies of other local or state governments. School districts make up almost 91 percent (5018 of 5529) of the total number of school systems in metropolitan areas. From U.S. Bureau of the Census, Census of Governments: 1967, Vol. 1, p. 20.

stead transport students to the schools of other systems. Many school districts have a very small area; in fact, they sometimes cover less land than is contained within municipalities. And the situation is much the same for numerous special districts. Many have a very small number of residents, less than a hundred in some instances, and an extremely small amount of land, at times as little as a fraction of a square mile.

People frequently think of metropolitan areas as characterized by many forms of giantism. There are, it is true, some giants among their local governments—counties larger in area than certain states, cities of hundreds of thousands or millions of people, of hundreds of square miles of territory, and of annual budgets that range from hundreds of thousands of dollars to billions in New York City, school districts of tens of thousands of students and of areas frequently larger than those of the biggest cities, and special districts that stretch over and beyond entire metropolitan areas. But these big local governments are the exception rather than the rule. Gargantuan governments exist, but standing among them are far more governmental Lilliputians.

Territorial Overlapping

Government in metropolitan areas is also complex because so many units have overlapping boundaries. In most SMSAs a county overlies the boundaries of numerous municipalities. So also in a number of instances, townships spread over municipal limits and represent another layer, a third tier, as it were, of local government. However, the most frequent instances of overlapping jurisdictions are found in school districts and special districts, particularly the latter (Figure 19). No unit of any other

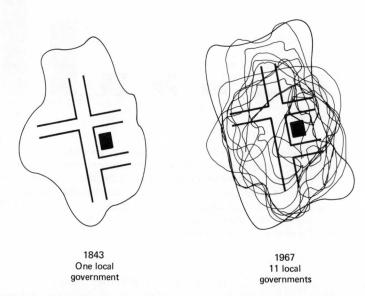

1843
One local
government

1967
11 local
governments

FIGURE 19 **Governmental Change in an Unincorporated, Recently Urbanized Portion of Portland, Oregon, SMSA, 1843–1967. Used by permission of the Portland Metropolitan Study Commission.**

class can have part or all of the same territory as any other government of that class. Thus, two municipalities cannot include any of the same territory, although, as we have seen, a municipality can encompass a portion (or in rare cases even all) of the same territory as a county. This mutual territorial exclusiveness is not the situation with school districts and special districts. A school district providing high school education is frequently superimposed upon one or more school districts furnishing elementary education. Similarly, a number of special districts, sometimes as many as five to eight different functional types, are at times piled upon part or all of the territory of one another and of two or more school districts, a county, a city, and even a township.

Such governmental stacking is repeated in varying degrees in all sections. Since most local governments are small in territorial size, they individually occupy only a minor portion of a metropolitan area. Few of them, most often a county or a special district, encompass the territory of an entire SMSA. In fact, in many metropolitan communities no local government is area-wide. As a result, the governmental pattern of a metropolis typically consists of many adjoining but uneven stacks of overlapping units, with few, if any, local public agencies covering the whole area.

THE ORIGINAL GOVERNMENTAL SYSTEM

The system of local government laid out originally by each state in its constitution and legislation, usually in either the late eighteenth century or the nineteenth century, was fairly simple in design and reasonably understandable. Moreover, each class of local governments in the system was assigned responsibilities wholly or largely unique to it.

Three General Classes

On a national basis, counties, municipalities, and school districts were initially the classes most commonly set up to form the local governmental system of a state. Counties were created to serve two kinds of purposes. They were to aid the state government in carrying out some of its obligations, such as assisting judges of the state court system, conducting elections, and recording legal documents, and they were to provide services to the residents of rural areas, such as building farm roads and keeping the peace. To assure the performance of the former responsibilities, the entire state was usually divided into counties.

In contrast to counties, municipalities were organized to be the suppliers of local services—fire protection, law enforcement, public works, and the like—to the inhabitants of urban settlements. As such, they were to include only a small portion of the territory of a state. School districts, on the other hand, originated as a separate class for a different reason. They were established as independent units mainly because of the strong conviction that public education was so important it should have its own local financing and should be free of the politics of other local governments. (Public schools had been parts of the operations of general local units in colonial America, and today in some states they are not operated or financed by districts but by other governments.) From the early years of statehood, school districts were formed in settled portions where children lived. Such units were kept small in territorial size since youngsters of a "bus- and car-free" society had to travel to school on foot or by horse.

Two Regional Classes

The two important regional exceptions to the commonly established system of local government are the town and the township. The former, most prevalent in New England (and not to be confused with a similarly named type of local government of another class—the town as a type of municipality—existing in a number of other states), originated in colonial days and is still a vigorous government. In the colonial era, settlements in New England, which were called towns, took a compact, small form because the land was densely wooded and represented both a barrier to developing agricultural lands over a large area and a threat to the inhabitants from Indians and animals. Towns grew up around the church, the public meeting place, and the fort or stockade and included the residents' agricultural fields. From the beginning, therefore, these units were natural, real communities, based on social groupings or concentrations of people, conforming to geographical features, and usually containing both urban (initially mostly village centers) and rural territory.

As the population increased and the need for protection declined, other towns were established by dividing old ones or organizing new ones in the recently settled land; eventually towns contained most of the territory of the six New England states. Only occasionally was a heavily populated center detached from a town and organized as a municipality. Boston, Providence, Worcester, Springfield, Bridgeport, and Portland are prominent current examples. Accordingly, as some towns became thickly populated, they took on all the functions handled elsewhere by municipalities. Also, since they included most of the state's territory, towns in New England were assigned many activities carried on by counties in other states. (Counties were established as units of government in New England but were never significant.)

Townships, most evident in the North Central region, generally followed a different and less successful course of development. From their creation, most of them were highly artificial governmental areas, since their original boundaries were marked out in rectangular fashion by federal surveyors while the land was still part of the national domain. Although attempting to imitate New England towns as institutions of local self-government, many townships were doomed to early oblivion, for several reasons: the aforementioned artificiality of their areas; the early and continued widespread practice of separating both large and small urban centers from the authority of townships, thereby sharply diminishing their financial resources; and the dispersed nature of farm settlement in many states that adopted township organization.

In the early years as well as now, the functions of most townships have been restricted in number and minor in nature; many states, in fact, never established them as a class of local governments. Generally, however, townships, once created, have tenaciously withstood efforts to eliminate them. Today, obsolete as most of them are, they continue to perform a few functions and to levy taxes in various metropolitan areas.

Few Nonschool Special Districts

When the states, even those created during the late nineteenth and early twentieth centuries, formulated their original systems of local government, a present-day significant element was conspicuously absent—nonschool special districts. Legal provision certainly seemed to have been made for enough types of local agencies to provide capably for necessary public services. The system, moreover, seemed to be sufficiently adjustable to future needs. Some people may have thought that from time to time unique circumstances might make necessary the occasional formation of a special nonschool unit. But no state foresaw the development of a widespread demand for the legal means of establishing a multitude of such districts, which in total would undertake such a broad range of activities. Scattered uses were made of them before the current century—one, for example, being organized in the Philadelphia area as early as 1790. However, the extensive activation of these districts to the point where they became an important part of the nationwide local governmental system is primarily a phenomenon of the twentieth century, particularly since the 1930s.

EVOLUTION OF THE GOVERNMENTAL PATTERN

A tremendous transformation has occurred in the governmental pattern of most areas as they have proceeded from early urbanization to metropolitanization. At the time of the former, they were sparsely populated, compact, and composed of largely self-contained communities. By the time they had become metropolitan, they were far more densely populated, considerably larger in territorial size, and each of them had developed highly interdependent and interacting parts. In this transitional span, their governmental system changed from a simple and rational arrangement of relatively few units to a complicated and improvised hodgepodge of numerous units (many having considerable functional similarity) and of much governmental pyramiding.

A portrayal of the evolution of the governmental situation from the era of early urbanization to the age of metropolitanization is revealing. What was the governmental pattern in an area like before it became metropolitan? How did it become more complex? What is it like now? Let us take a typical metropolis of today, look at its governmental pattern in earlier years, and then broadly trace what has happened.

Early Urbanization

In its early years, an area that is now metropolitan contained only a few municipalities (or if in New England a few towns or a combination of a few cities and towns). For the most part these units were separated from one another by large expanses of rural land, ten to twenty miles or more in length. Each municipality, embracing a small amount of territory, was in large measure self-sufficient in its economic, social, and governmental activities. All land development of an urban nature was within municipal (or town) limits. A county government overlaid both the rural and urban portions of the area, furnishing certain services to all residents of the county and certain others to the inhabitants of its rural portions. School districts were the most numerous units, as the drive got under way early to have a separate government for each school. If the area was in the North Central region, it also might have townships performing a few functions, predominantly in the rural sections. Other special districts did not exist or were present in only a few instances.

Period of Growing Urbanization

As urbanization began to intensify, the result of scientific and technological gains and population growth, the governmental pattern began to undergo a metamorphosis. For a time, the local governmental system seemed to be keeping pace with the changes. Many municipalities experienced substantial increases in population and enlarged their territorial size by annexing adjoining land to accommodate the growth. Some new municipalities sprang up through use of the incorporation process, but usually they were not numerous. As these annexation and incorporation developments occurred, the amount of space between incorporated places in the area lessened.

During this period, the county may have been divided into two or more counties in response to the demands for certain services at close range. Even in the Rocky Mountain and far western regions where the original counties were usually much larger in territory than in the eastern and midwestern parts of the nation, counties were frequently divided as the population grew. For instance, California, which was admitted as a state in 1850, promptly established twenty-seven counties. Little more than a half century later it had fifty-eight, counting the city-county of San Francisco, a number that has since remained the same. Towns in New England continued to exhibit great durability, partly because they were playing the functional role handled elsewhere by counties. In the North

Central region, many townships were declining in importance because some of their sections had become highly urban and had been annexed to an existing municipality or incorporated as a new municipal unit.

Many new schools were built, causing the creation of numerous school districts in recently developed land and the division of many long established districts into separate and independent operations. An increasing number of special districts sprouted. (Special districts are so called because each of them supplies only one or a very limited number of functions, thus serving a special purpose.) They grew as the older general units failed to be sufficiently adaptable, or as quick and supposedly adequate answers to immediate or deeply rooted problems were sought.

The Metropolitan Age

As an area became metropolitan in population and in such social and economic characteristics as interdependence and specialization, its governmental pattern usually displayed increasing complexity and improvisation.[2] By this time, the pattern bore only slight resemblance to the system as originally conceived in a pre-metropolitan period for nonmetropolitan conditions. Although demonstrating some ability to adjust to changing circumstances, the system had not been sufficiently flexible, nor had it been intelligently reformulated in a conscious and comprehensive manner. Its high degree of rigidity had caused odd-looking patches to be added to the governmental quilt. The lack of an intelligent reformulation had resulted in plugs of adjustment being inserted in the metropolitan wall to avoid successive waves of disasters.

MUNICIPALITIES   With the arrival of the metropolitan age, municipalities greatly increased in number and the boundaries of many of them came to border one another. In brief, this increase was largely the product of policies that deliberately made many state annexation laws more difficult while keeping the incorporation procedures outlandishly easy. As a consequence, long established municipalities often could no longer sufficiently enlarge their territorial limits to encompass all the additional urban population. Concurrently, new municipalities were frequently created, many times at the very borders of the largest city and other major population centers in the area.

The countryside formerly separating cities and villages had become metropolitan in its social and economic characteristics and much of it was carved into a large number of incorporated units.[3] Although metropolitan in nature, not all of this land was within the boundaries of any

---

[2] The principal nongovernmental aspects of metropolitan development are considered in the section on metropolitan characteristics in Chapter 1.

[3] For discussions of incorporation patterns in a recent decade, see Henry J. Schmandt, *The Municipal Incorporation Trend, 1950–1960* (Madison: University of Wisconsin Bureau of Government, 1961) and Richard L. Stauber, *New Cities in America: A Census of Municipal Incorporations in the United States, 1950–1960* (Lawrence: University of Kansas Governmental Research Center, 1965).

municipality. A stiffening of annexation laws often left the residents or property owners of a newly developed section free to incorporate the land as a separate municipality or to leave it unincorporated. And many people made and have stood by the latter choice. As a result, municipal governments do not now contain all urban land and population within their jurisdictions; in fact, about one-fourth of all metropolitan residents currently live in unincorporated territory, much of which is distinctly urbanized. Other local governments—for instance, many counties and special districts—have adjusted or have been established to satisfy the most pressing city-type needs of unincorporated urban residents—and both developments have at times met bitter opposition from municipal officials and inhabitants. Furthermore, some types of local governments, again many counties and special districts and even some townships, have become functionally similar to municipalities, thereby destroying the original concept of a system of local governments in which each class was to serve different purposes. Functional as well as territorial overlapping of local units thus became common in the metropolitan period.

A considerable upsurge in municipal annexation has taken place in the post-World War II years. In large part, however, its usefulness has been confined to the absorption of neighboring unincorporated urban fringe areas, many of which had developed serious service and regulatory deficiencies that have repercussions both locally and elsewhere in the metropolis. In the meantime, many of the largest cities have become substantially or completely hemmed in by other municipalities and have found annexation to be of little or no value. And there have been few instances where two or more municipalities have consolidated or merged into a single unit.

COUNTIES, TOWNS, AND TOWNSHIPS   In the metropolitan age, the number and areas of counties have remained virtually unchanged. Similarly, towns, especially in New England, have shown great staying power, changing little in number or territorial size. In contrast, townships generally have developed into inconsequential units, performing only a few minor functions and often stripped of much of their financial resources through loss of their wealthier sections as a result of incorporation or annexation. Some of them have been eliminated as their importance has declined, but many others still exist, although for no justifiable reason. A countertrend has appeared, however, in the metropolitan areas of a few states where townships have been assigned some urban functions.

SCHOOL AND OTHER DISTRICTS   The lone important simplification of the local governmental pattern of various areas during the metropolitan period has involved school districts. Abandonment of the longtime practice in cities of having as many school districts as schools has contributed substantially to this development. Many small elementary districts have merged, as have many high school districts. This has reduced the number and increased the size of the service areas of the consolidated units.

Also, on frequent occasions a number of elementary districts have merged with a high school district into a unified operation, offering education from kindergarten through the twelfth grade and at times expanding the program through the junior college years.

The extent of school district consolidation in metropolitan areas contrasts sharply with the trend in the case of other types of local government. The magnitude of the movement so far can nevertheless be easily exaggerated since school districts were so numerous until recent years. Also, even though consolidated, school districts frequently continue to have boundaries that differ from those of municipalities. In some instances, this results from the consolidation covering an area larger than that of the municipality in order to bring the residents of unincorporated urban fringe areas into the school system. In other cases, however, the difference in boundaries develops from planned action by professional educators and school board members who apparently fear the eventual merger of school and municipal governments if their boundaries are made coterminous.

Spreading with the swiftness of a brush fire, nonschool special districts are largely the product of the metropolitan era. Most of these districts operating in the metropolis cover only a portion, often merely a tiny fraction, of its territory. They may include only a small amount of unincorporated urban land (a very large number are of this type) or simply the area of a municipality (true of many housing authorities) or a combination of parts or all of certain unincorporated land and a municipality. A relative few encompass the entire SMSA or operate facilities, such as mass transit, airports, or harbors, that are vital to the well-being of the metropolitan residents as well as to many people living elsewhere. Because of the scope of the area they serve, districts of this last group often function as the closest approximations to a metropolitan government. Moreover, unlike any other local units, a limited number of such districts are interstate in territorial jurisdiction.

LOCAL GOVERNMENTAL ADJUSTMENTS
IN THE METROPOLITAN AGE

The previous discussion of the evolution of the governmental pattern from early urbanization to metropolitanization dealt chiefly with the expansion or contraction in the number and territory of the respective local units. But other important adjustments, or the lack of them, have also been in evidence. These include changes in local functions, structure, and procedures.[4]

[4] Public finance, which has also been subject to change in the metropolitan era, is considered in Chapter 10.

Functions

Governments in urban areas have greatly increased their service functions in the metropolitan period. Much of this gain has resulted from intensifying the level of already established services or broadening their scope. Numerous counties, for example, have substantially enlarged their public health efforts to combat communicable diseases, epidemics, and unsanitary practices, and their social welfare programs to provide more assistance to various types of needy people. Large and medium-sized municipalities, in particular, have developed extensive public works systems (including major programs of streets and street lighting, water lines and sanitary sewers, storm drainage, and traffic signals), modernized law enforcement operations, and added fire prevention to fire fighting.[5] School districts have presented vastly expanded curricula. Towns, especially in New England, and certain townships and special districts have augmented their personnel and facilities in following a similar course of action.

In addition to expanding services, many governments have also entered into new activities. Various counties have developed airports, built public hospitals, laid out sewers, installed sewage disposal systems, and established large park and recreation areas. Similarly, many municipalities have initiated airport, hospital, and recreational programs; and some have taken over the operation of mass transit systems and constructed auditoriums and other cultural facilities. A number of school districts have instituted steps toward equalization of educational opportunities for all persons, irrespective of racial or ethnic background. Certain towns and townships have undertaken specific urban-type functions, such as refuse and sewage disposal.[6] Although few special districts have assumed new functions, many new functional types designed to deal with urban needs (fire protection, water supply, and sewage disposal, for instance) have been created.

Governmental functions have undergone other important changes in recent years. While improving and increasing their services to the public, a number of local units have also enlarged their functions by adding various regulatory activities. Municipalities in particular, and counties to a lesser degree, have imposed land-use controls affecting the subdivision of land and the types of purposes for which it may be utilized and have adopted building codes that set standards for structural soundness

[5] Service expansion has not been the pattern of all municipalities in the metropolis. The public activities of many of these units that are small in both population and financial resources are narrow in range and of an elementary level.

[6] Townships in a number of states, however, are largely useless relics of a bygone day; they perform only a few highly restricted services, such as maintaining minor roads and providing some limited aspects of social welfare.

and utility installations. Also, a smaller number of governments have become agents of social change by passing open or fair housing and public accommodations laws.[7]

As has been the case with many other phases of modern society, the functions of governments have moved from a simple to a technical and complex stage in the metropolitan era. They have generally produced living conditions that contrast dramatically with those portrayed by historian Blake McKelvey in describing the activities of the typical city in 1860:

Some basic tasks, such as fire fighting, appealed to the lusty energies of volunteers; others often went by default. . . . Nowhere did [water mains] reach half the residences. . . . Less obvious civic functions were little improved, if at all, over those of the colonial cities . . . law enforcement [generally] retained the characteristics of the volunteer period. Boards of health and similar civic agencies, except in the case of a few school boards, were temporary bodies with at best a small emergency staff. Sanitation was loosely regulated by ordinances adopted impulsively from time to time, but the collection of garbage was generally left to the pigs, which were more numerous in some towns than the human residents. Horses and cows, dogs and cats, chickens and geese were accepted members of the urban community and contributed a bucolic aroma even to the largest [city].[8]

Structure and Procedures

Adjustments in the internal organization and administration of local units have been evident during the metropolitan period, although they have been less extensive than changes in functions. These alterations have occurred most often in municipalities, where efforts have been made to achieve a more integrated structure by reducing the number of elected officials, decreasing the use of administrative boards or eliminating them entirely, and establishing a strong executive. In addition, municipal personnel has grown in professionalization and has increasingly been placed under a merit system.

In many cities the concept of a strong chief executive has supplanted either of two other systems. One is the long discredited but still frequently used weak mayor-council organization, an arrangement which generally means dominance by the council or by independent administrative boards. The other is the commission plan, which features a small governing board whose members serve collectively as the legislature and

[7] Duane Lockard, *Toward Equal Opportunity: A Study of State and Local Antidiscrimination Laws* (New York: Macmillan, 1968), pp. 118, 136.

[8] Blake McKelvey, *The Urbanization of America [1860–1915]* (New Brunswick, N.J.: Rutgers University Press, 1963), p. 13.

individually as heads of the principal departments. This plan experienced considerable popularity—and in some cases overly enthusiastic claims—in the very early decades of the present century, but its use has been constantly declining since 1920. Although offering more integration than the weak mayor-council form, it generally provided inadequate coordination, insufficient internal control, and amateur direction of administration.

The council-manager plan has been the more widely adopted strong executive form and its two major features have been followed without significant deviation by most municipalities. The first is an elected council of small size, which serves as the legislative body. The second is a manager, appointed by the council, who directs and supervises the administrative departments, appoints and removes their heads, prepares the budget for the council's consideration and administers it after adoption, and makes reports and recommendations to the council at its request or on his own initiative. (Unlike school superintendents in many localities, a manager seldom has a contract, and therefore may be removed by the council at any time.) The mayor in a council-manager community may be selected by the council from its own membership or elected by the voters to the position (each is the situation in about half the cities), but usually his only additional authority is to preside at council meetings and to sign certain legal papers.

The city manager idea, first used in Staunton, Virginia, in 1908, received nationwide attention six years later when Dayton, Ohio, became the first sizable city to put the plan into effect. Subsequently the plan had a steady but not spectacular growth until after World War II. At that time the councils in many municipalities were confronted with a lengthy list of deferred services and improvements that had backlogged since the depression and recession years of the 1930s. It became increasingly apparent to them that professional assistance was needed for the tasks at hand. The answer in many cases was adoption of the council-manager form of government. The plan has been especially attractive to small and medium-sized localities, many of them suburbs in the metropolis, but it has not generally caught hold in the large cities. It is in operation in a majority of the municipalities of 25,000 to 250,000, but is used in fewer than one-fifth of the urban centers containing more than 500,000 people.

The council-manager form has been viewed by many upper middle-class whites as an efficient and businesslike replacement for the "political" mayor-council government. This belief implies that the city is similar to a business operation that can function like an administrative machine with few conflicts of interest. Such an implication leads to the conclusion that council-manager governments are best adapted to relatively homogeneous white-collar communities where the political representation of diverse interests is not an important factor. This conclusion is supported in a study of 300 suburban governments by Leo Schnore and Robert Alford who found that the manager form predominated in communities where the residents had above-average incomes.[9]

The strong mayor-council plan is the second form that the modern executive concept has taken. This arrangement is characterized by a mayor who has significant personnel, financial, and general administrative powers and the authority to veto legislative actions of the council. He also possesses the means of being a policy-making and thus political leader as exemplified by his role in enunciating new or extended municipal programs to the council and to the public through the mass media and frequently by his stature in a nationwide political party. The strong mayor-council form has firm footing in many large metropolitan central cities, although there are notable exceptions, such as Los Angeles and Minneapolis, which fall into the weak mayor-council category, and Kansas City and Dallas which have city managers.

Other than occasional outcries in some cities about political machinations, the principal complaint against the strong mayor-council form has been that the chief executive, despite his strength in the policy field, is often uninterested in and therefore neglectful of the administrative side of city business. To obtain the best of both worlds, a number of strong mayor-council municipalities have established a general management position, variously titled city administrator, city administrative officer, and managing director. The post is staffed by a professional administrator appointed by and usually accountable solely to the mayor. His function is to relieve the chief executive of much administrative detail and to leave him free to devote his time to policy formulation and political leadership.

Internal changes also have taken place in a number of metropolitan counties, but they have not generally been as comprehensive as those in municipalities. For one thing, the merit system in many instances has grown sporadically and often only partially. Also, the number of elected officials in most counties has not been reduced substantially, if at all.[10] They still have a long list of such officials, many of whom perform either duties calling for considerable training and skill (the coroner, for instance) or duties of a routine and clerical nature (such as the clerk and the recorder or registrar of deeds). Significantly, however, as new departments have been created, such as health and welfare, the tendency has been to provide for the appointment of directors with professional qualifications. Although this practice does not reduce the large number of elected officeholders, it does place significant functions and a larger

[9] Leo F. Schnore and Robert R. Alford, "Socioeconomic Characteristics of Suburbs," *Administrative Science Quarterly*, 8 (June, 1963), 1–17.

[10] State and regional tabulations of elected county officials are contained in U.S. Bureau of the Census, *Census of Governments: 1967*, Vol. 6, no. 1, *Popularly Elected Officials of State and Local Governments* (Washington: 1968), pp. 18–20.

proportion of county activities under the immediate supervision of persons with relevant training and experience.

Some counties have adopted the idea of a chief executive—either county manager or elected county mayor—but the movement in this direction has not been widespread. County managers total only forty-three, a large proportion of whom are in nonmetropolitan counties. The number of county mayors is smaller, but they are usually found in metropolitan areas. More common than either of these two types is the position customarily titled administrative officer or assistant. This is a central management post of limited authority, with responsibility for such functions as budget preparation and administrative coordination. Although those holding the position are the equivalent of chief administrators, they are much weaker in formal powers than county managers and mayors.[11] About 400 counties—many in metropolitan areas—have such an office.

Changes have been noticeable in other governments, too. In school districts both teaching and administrative personnel have become more professional in training and outlook, and an increasing number of school superintendents, the top administrators in the systems, have emerged as the highest paid of all local public officials and very powerful forces in the metropolis. Various towns and townships and a number of the larger special districts have also turned to professionally trained managers; however, many of these units have remained small, and the only supervision of their operations is provided by part-time boards.

THE STATES AND THE NATION

Over the years the state and national governments have become increasingly active in the metropolis, contributing both constructively and harmfully to its development and having broad effects on its local units. These levels of higher authority are integral parts of the metropolitan governmental system and their significance and impact are vast and large in scale. Some basic facts concerning their relation to the structural and procedural features of the local system will be outlined here.[12]

Local governments are the creatures of the states, which set their ground rules in laws, constitutions, and implementing administrative orders. Through these means, the states have always determined the shape and much of the substance of their local governmental systems. If

---

[11] William H. Cape, *The Emerging Patterns of County Executives* (Lawrence: University of Kansas Governmental Research Center, 1967), pp. 26–29.

[12] State and national governmental activities affecting metropolitan areas are discussed at many other places in this book. On state actions, see particularly Chapters 7, 10, and 11–13; on national efforts, see especially Chapters 7–10, 13.

local units are deficient in territorial size, structure, service and regulatory powers, and financial authority, the responsibility must rest chiefly with the states, primarily with their legislatures.

Although the states generally have been slow to respond adequately to metropolitan needs, some acceleration of concern became apparent in the 1960s.[13] Financial assistance for certain urban programs began to grow, and services provided directly by the states to metropolises increased; the immense state water project in California is a dramatic example of the latter. Recently reapportioned legislatures in various states—Colorado, Michigan, and Virginia, for instance—gave serious consideration to particular metropolitan problems and provided the means of financing solutions to them. However, in the politically controversial area of metropolitan governmental reorganization—with the important exception of school districts—the states continued to evidence no desire to intervene.

Many states have increased their metropolitan consciousness because of another development: growing proportions of their populations live in urban complexes that transcend state lines. The number of interstate metropolitan areas has enlarged to thirty-two and many of them—New York-Northeastern New Jersey, Chicago-Northwestern Indiana, Philadelphia, St. Louis, Washington, Cincinnati, and Kansas City, for example —are among the principal population and economic centers of the nation. Adjacent states having parts of their territory in the same SMSA often have been confronted with the expanding need to establish an instrumentality to deal with mutual difficulties. Consequently, in more and more instances interstate agreements or compacts have been worked out. An outstanding recent use of the device concerned the formation of the Delaware River Basin Commission for the four-state area centering on Philadelphia. The Commission has broad powers in terms of river basin planning and development. Moreover, it is authorized to review (and thereafter disapprove or require modification of) proposals by other agencies that affect the region's water resources—proposals such as those relating to flood protection, recreation, hydroelectric power, and water withdrawals or diversions.[14]

The establishment of state offices of local (or urban or community)

---

[13] For examples of growing state concern about metropolitan affairs, see Council of State Governments, *State Responsibility in Urban Regional Development* (Chicago: 1962); Norman Beckman and Page L. Ingraham, "The States and Urban Areas," *Law and Contemporary Problems,* XXX (Winter, 1965), 76–102; and National Governors' Conference, Committee on State-Urban Relations, *The States and Urban Problems* (Chicago: 1967). Illustrations from individual states are New Jersey County and Municipal Government Study Commission, *Creative Localism: A Prospectus* (Trenton: 1968) and New York Joint Legislative Committee on Metropolitan and Regional Areas Study, *Governing Urban Areas: Realism and Reform* (Albany: 1967).

[14] An interesting case report on the development of this project will be found in Roscoe C. Martin, *Metropolis in Transition* (Washington: U.S. Housing and Home Finance Agency, 1963), chap. X.

affairs is a prominent institutional manifestation of the recently accelerated state interest in metropolitan affairs. Currently operating in twenty-five states, in contrast to only five before 1966, such agencies differ as to their functional scope, although their common basic objective is to assist local governments (and often to aid other local groups such as nonprofit housing, community action, and business job development organizations as well). All provide advisory and technical services and assist the governor in coordinating state activities affecting localities. Most of them undertake planning (in a number of instances they are the state planning agency) or are responsible for administering local planning assistance and coordinating regional planning. Only a minority, however, have direct program responsibilities, usually for urban renewal, housing, and poverty programs. In even fewer cases, they supervise local finances or provide financial aid. As a rule, the newer agencies have the broader responsibilities.[15]

Paul N. Ylvisaker, who heads the New Jersey Department of Community Affairs, has spoken with considerable enthusiasm about this generally new development:

These new state community affairs agencies and the wide range of emerging functions for which they are responsible are strengthening the role of the States in what has been described as the "seamless web" of our federal governmental system. Through grant-seeking, planning, research, program development, assistance in staffing and recruiting, direct operations, and a variety of financial aid . . . they are helping to bring the resources and concerns of the State more directly to bear upon the long-neglected problems of local government.

Nevertheless, at the same time, he has warned that

there is real danger that they [the state governments] will only dabble in community affairs. . . . If [they] pull up short of a full commitment, their involvement may produce a large residue of bad results to go with the good they do.[16]

Legally, the national government, unlike the states, has no direct ties to local governments, yet it is a huge supplier of programs and funds to such units, only some of which are routed through the states.[17] Supported

[15] Information about most of these agencies is contained in Page L. Ingraham, "State Agencies for Local Affairs," *Municipal Year Book: 1968* (Washington: International City Managers' Association, 1968), pp. 37–45, and Council of State Governments, *Summary of Budgets and Functions of State Offices of Community Affairs* (Washington: 1969).

[16] Paul N. Ylvisaker, "The Growing Role of State Government in Local Affairs," *State Government*, XLI (Summer, 1968), 154, 156.

[17] Directories of federal grant programs are now the size of telephone books, as demonstrated by the enlightening publication, Office of the Vice-President, *The Vice-President's Handbook for Local Officials: A Guide to Federal Assistance for Local Governments* (Washington: 1967).

by enormous financial resources, its actions have often been prompted by the neglect or sluggish responses of many states to metropolitan problems and by the growing realization by federal officials of the ever-increasing importance of the metropolis in national elections.

Mass transit, water pollution control, highways, urban renewal, public housing, hospitals, aid to needy persons, airports, river and harbor improvements, and sewage treatment facilities are among the functional programs of the national government having broad repercussions in the urban areas. In addition, nonfunctional programs at the national level have wide metropolitan impact; for example, the mortgage financing policies of federal lending agencies have greatly sped suburban development, while defense contracts with private firms importantly support the economic life of many urban communities. These various programs have directly and indirectly contributed to the proliferation of local units in metropolitan areas. To illustrate, federal stimulation produced independent housing authorities, a type of special district, and federal encouragement of the growth of suburbia through underwriting liberal mortgage arrangements indirectly led to the creation of many new suburban governments.

The two newest cabinet-level departments—Housing and Urban Development in 1965 and Transportation in the following year—are both institutional examples of recognition by the national government of its deep involvement in metropolitan affairs. Their establishment also demonstrated a rising sensitivity to the need for better coordination of federal activities in urban areas. Advocates of these new units stressed this point in gaining support for their formation. The sponsors of the Department of Transportation urged that its organization would mark a historic step toward the development of a coordinated national transportation policy. And in its enabling legislation, HUD was directed to assist the President in achieving maximum coordination of federal urban programs—a difficult objective for this agency to fulfill since so few programs in this field were made its administrative responsibility.

In recent years the national government has devoted more attention to effectuating various kinds of coordination and cooperation that are particularly significant to metropolitan areas. One type has been concerned with producing greater coordination among the more than a dozen federal agencies possessing responsibilities for urban programs. Accordingly, for instance, the Secretary of Housing and Urban Development was authorized in 1966 to convene meetings of the appropriate oficals "to promote cooperation among Federal departments and agencies in achieving consistent policies, practices, and procedures for administration of their programs affecting urban areas."[18]

Another type of endeavor has been to strengthen coordination and

[18] Executive Order 11297.

cooperation between the national government and state and local units. One form of such activity, begun in 1967, provided for consultation with the heads of state and local units, through their nationwide associations, in the development of federal rules, regulations, procedures, and guidelines.[19] A second form involved setting up in 1959 the Advisory Commission on Intergovernmental Relations, a permanent body composed of representatives of the national, state, and local governments and the public at large. This group, which has proved very influential, has been engaged in studying and making recommendations on common problems and promoting legislative and administrative action in support of its conclusions. A third form of this type of effort was the establishment, as an early act of the Nixon administration in 1969, of the Office of Intergovernmental Relations, under the supervision of the Vice-President and headed by a former governor. It combined into a single staff and focal point various concerns for national-state and national-local relations which previously had been divided. The functions of the Office are to:

(a) Serve as the clearinghouse for the prompt handling and solution of federal-state-local problems brought to the attention of the President or Vice-President by executive and legislative officers of state and local governments;

(b) Identify and report to the Vice-President on recurring intergovernmental problems of a federal interdepartmental and interprogram nature;

(c) Explore and report to the Vice-President on ways and means of strengthening the headquarters and interagency relationships of federal field offices as they relate to intergovernmental activities;

(d) Maintain continuing liaison with intergovernmental units in federal departments and agencies and with the staff of the Council for Urban Affairs [created to advise the President on urban policies], and provide the staff of the Council with information and assistance regarding issues arising in federal-state-local relations; and

(e) Review procedures utilized by federal executive agencies for affording state and local officials an opportunity to confer and comment on federal assistance programs and other intergovernmental issues, and propose methods of strengthening such procedures.[20]

A final type of national governmental activity has been to seek better coordination of applications by local units in metropolitan areas for a variety of federal grants. Since mid-1967, a federally-approved area-wide agency must comment on each proposal regarding the extent to which it is consistent with comprehensive planning developed or in the process of development for the metropolis.[21] Conceivably this requirement may

[19] Executive Office of the President, Bureau of the Budget, *Circular No. A-85* (Washington: June 28, 1967).

[20] Executive Order 11455.

[21] Executive Office of the President, Bureau of the Budget, *Circular No. A-82*, rev. (Washington: December 18, 1967).

be a major stimulant to improved interlocal coordination; the technique receives considerable attention in Chapters 9 and 13.

STRUCTURE AND POLITICAL ENVIRONMENT

In discussing structural aspects of government, which we have done in some detail in this chapter, attention should also be given to their environmental setting. Forms of government do not exist in isolation; they operate in and are affected by differing kinds of political environments or cultures. Political scientists Oliver Williams and Charles Adrian have devised one way to view such environments. They have classified cities into four groups according to the primary role exercised by their local governments: (1) promoting economic growth, (2) providing life's amenities, (3) maintaining traditional services only, and (4) arbitrating among conflicting interests.[22] Cities in the first category are dominated by the philosophy that the good community is one that grows. Accordingly, the policies of their governments are directed toward the creation of an image of municipal stability, sound fiscal status, honest government, and friendliness toward business. Those of the second type emphasize the creation and maintenance of a pleasant living environment as the major objective of collective political action. They regard the primary task of local government as one of providing a high level of services designed to increase the comforts of urban living and the attractiveness of the community.

Municipalities in the third category are "caretaker" oriented; that is, they are committed to minimal services and to restriction of the public sector. Their policies are characterized by opposition to planning, zoning, and assumption of new functions by local public agencies. The fourth type considers the role of local government as essentially that of arbitrator among conflicting interests. Emphasis here is placed upon the process rather than the substance of public action. In other words, governments in this category are so structured that they do not act directly in terms of substantive conceptions of the common good but seek to balance diverse interests and pressures in formulating policy.

Determining the community power systems provides another perspective on the various kinds of political environments in which governmental structures or forms exist. Political scientists Robert Agger, Daniel Goldrich, and Bert Swanson have developed a valuable typology by using two variables to produce four categories of power systems.[23] One variable

[22] Oliver P. Williams and Charles R. Adrian, *Four Cities; A Study in Comparative Policy Making* (Philadelphia: University of Pennsylvania Press, 1963), pp. 23–32, chaps. IX–XII.

[23] Robert E. Agger, Daniel Goldrich, and Bert E. Swanson, *The Rulers and the Ruled: Political Power and Impotence in American Communities* (New York: Wiley, 1964), pp. 73–78.

is the extent to which political power is distributed broadly (mass) or narrowly (elite) among the citizenry. The other is the extent to which the ideology of the political leadership is convergent and compatible (and therefore consensual) or divergent and conflicting (and thus competitive). The resulting four power patterns may be characterized as consensual mass, competitive mass, consensual elite, and competitive elite.

By combining these two classifications—the one based on the primary roles of local governments and the other on power systems—fourteen variations in political environment may be delineated (Table 15).[24]

TABLE 15   Types of Political Environments

	Community Growth	Provider of Life's Amenities	Caretaker	Arbitrator
Consensual mass	1	2	3	—[a]
Competitive mass	4	5	6	7
Consensual elite	8	9	10	—[a]
Competitive elite	11	12	13	14

[a] By definition, the arbitrator community is characterized by competition among interests.

What this typology illustrates—and this is our sole purpose in presenting it here—is that the great variety of environmental settings for governmental structures produces a far greater number of governmental forms in terms of actual operations than the few that exist in a formal or legal sense. In short, each governmental type responds to the political environment in which it functions, and in the process its behavior is influenced and shaped by the forces at work in the community. Thus a mayor or a manager in a city characterized by divergent socioeconomic interests and class cleavages is not likely to act in the same fashion as his counterpart in an exclusive and tranquil residential suburb. The aggregation of these governmental forms and environmental settings within the spatial confines of the metropolis results in a complex mosaic, more challenging than understandable.

[24] This combined typology was developed initially to examine the varying roles of city managers. See John C. Bollens and John C. Ries, The City Manager Profession: Myths and Realities (Chicago: Public Administration Service, 1969).

GOVERNMENT IN PERSPECTIVE

As society has expanded, diverse groups have been brought together in the same network of social or community control. Shorn of the simplicity of the manor or the rural village and overrun by hordes of new-comers—refugees of a changing technocracy and social world—the twentieth century metropolis offers a troublesome challenge to the practitioners and reformers or medicine men of local government. The massing of people together in relatively small areas—more than 100,000 to the square mile in New York City's Manhattan—has placed new responsibilities and obligations, new stresses and strains, on their governmental (as well as economic and social) systems. Concentration of human and material resources has opened up many new opportunities to society but at the same time it has aggravated the problem of governmental control and service. The task of housing, feeding, and educating the populace, of minimizing and resolving social conflict, of maintaining order, and of providing indispensable public facilities has increased manyfold. And in the process, different values, varied modes of living, and divergent interests must somehow be accommodated to one another. Governing the metropolis is an exercise in social adjustment as well as an object of public administration.

6 / POWER,
POLITICS, AND PARTICIPATION

SOCIAL SCIENTISTS VIEW THE POLITICAL SYSTEM OF THE METROPOLIS IN
various ways. Some look upon it as a game in which the contestants
compete for the prizes of political action. Others regard it primarily
as a service-providing bureaucracy that seeks to satisfy the public
needs of its consumer citizens. Still others consider it as a process of
interaction among innumerable role-playing actors, institutions, groups,
and individuals. None of these views is exclusive; they merge into each
other with many combinations and permutations. Even though they may
involve basically different theoretical conceptions of the metropolitan
system, the pragmatic question in each instance becomes one of focus
and emphasis. Is attention to be concentrated on the configurations of
power and interest within the community; on the operation of the
bureaucracy; on the roles the various participants play; on the imputed
pathology of the system? Or is the approach to be one of the shotgun
variety in which the elusive target is sprayed with intellectual buckshot
in hopes of hitting the crucial variables?

Regardless of arguments over theory and research methods, one point bears repeated emphasis: a metropolitan political system exists in each of the nation's 230 SMSAs. Although almost always balkanized and without a centralized agency of policy-making and control, this system constitutes a viable pattern of public and private relationships and interactions. Decisions of area-wide concern get made in one fashion or another, services and goods are provided the residents, the rewards of metropolitan life are parcelled out, crises are generally averted and problems solved or mitigated, expansion and development take place. The system in operation demonstrates that the proliferated and diffused pattern of governmental organization in most metropolitan areas is not wholly the result of drift and chance; in important part it is the product of deliberate, conscious decisions and actions by numerous governments, private organizations, and individuals. Whether the combined output of this highly decentralized structure is conducive to the well-being of the total metropolitan community is a question that has provoked bitter debate. Whether the system can indefinitely continue in its present form as the problems of the large urban areas intensify is a further question of importance.

To speak in terms currently popular in the social sciences, we are concerned in this chapter generally with the input side of the metropolitan system. Where and how do demands on the public sector originate? What are the sources of support for these demands? Who are the key influential persons ("the influentials") in the community? How extensive is participation and how democratic the system? These are critical questions since local government is being challenged today as at no time in the past. Caught in the vortex of the social and physical problems which are engulfing urban America, the political system of the metropolis finds itself confronted with a wide range of demands including those by the racial minorities and the poor for a greater share of public power.

THE PATTERN OF INFLUENCE

The political process, whether at the national, state, or local level, involves the translation of public needs and desires into official policy and action. Politics need not be viewed as a game or as "who gets what, when, and how" to appreciate the fact that power and influence play important roles in the making and execution of law. A zoning ordinance or building code is enacted by an elected body of representatives, a formally constituted arm of government. The formulation of such laws does not take place in a political or social incubator. Those who legitimize and administer public policy—councilmen, mayors, commissions, agencies, departments—are subject to various pressures from the many competing groups and individuals in the community. This pressure may be overt at times, as when a group of property owners protests a zoning change or a downtown business association demands better street lighting in the central business district. Often it will not be so apparent, as when the awarding of a liquor license is at stake or a vacancy on an important public commission is to be filled.

The question is sometimes asked: Who really runs the community? To pose the query in this fashion is to imply that some individual or group of influentials stands behind the scene calling the civic signals. In recent years an increasing number of sociologists and political scientists have taken up this question and have sought to determine the pattern of influence or the so-called power structure of local communities. Their approaches and techniques have differed but their objective has been the same: to discover "how things get done" in the urban polity or community. The resultant studies have aimed at identifying the key actors, those who are the leaders and wielders of power and influence, and tracing the roles they play in the making of public and semipublic decisions.

Monolithic or Pluralistic?

The spate of studies about local influentials was touched off by the publication of Floyd Hunter's Community Power Structure: A Study of Decision Makers in 1953.[1] Hunter, a sociologist, sought to identify these persons in Regional City (a pseudonym for Atlanta, Georgia) by first assembling lists of known civic, governmental, and business leaders. These lists were then submitted to a panel of six judges (well-informed individuals active in local civic affairs) who were asked to rate the reputed leaders according to their relative power. From his study, Hunter concluded that key decisions in Regional City are made by a handful of individuals who stand at the top of a stable power hierarchy. Drawn largely from business and industrial circles, these men constitute a strongly entrenched and select group that exercises predominant influence over community policy. With their blessing, projects move ahead; without their express or tacit consent, little of significance can be accomplished. On community-wide issues, policy is channeled through a fluid committee structure down to a lower level bureaucracy where it is executed.

A second study made by Robert Dahl, a political scientist, and reported in his provocatively titled book Who Governs?, employs a different method and reaches different conclusions than Hunter.[2] Underlying Dahl's approach is the assumption that leaders can best be identified and patterns

[1] Chapel Hill: University of North Carolina Press, 1953.
[2] New Haven: Yale University Press, 1961. A third approach, seldom used alone but instead as an adjunct to one of the other two, is the "positional" study. This method searches for the likely power offices in the community's institutional structure. It rests on the assumption that formal position is correlated with power.

of influence best determined by observing and analyzing the resolution of various kinds of community issues. His approach, to put it briefly, is based on the study of power in action rather than on opinions of who the leaders are. Turning his analytical insights on New Haven, Connecticut, Dahl examined sixteen major decisions on redevelopment and public education and on the nominations for mayor in both political parties for seven elections.

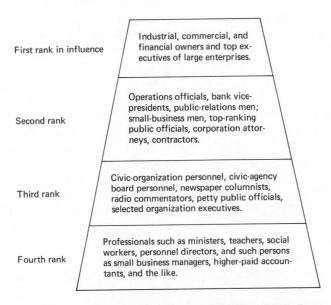

First rank in influence — Industrial, commercial, and financial owners and top executives of large enterprises.

Second rank — Operations officials, bank vice-presidents, public-relations men; small-business men, top-ranking public officials, corporation attorneys, contractors.

Third rank — Civic-organization personnel, civic-agency board personnel, newspaper columnists, radio commentators, petty public officials, selected organization executives.

Fourth rank — Professionals such as ministers, teachers, social workers, personnel directors, and such persons as small business managers, higher-paid accountants, and the like.

FIGURE 20   **Hierarchical Model of Community Power. From Delbert C. Miller, "Decision-Making Cliques in Community Power Structures,"** American Journal of Sociology, **64 (November, 1958), 308. Copyright 1958, University of Chicago Press.**

In contrast to Hunter's monolithic and centralized power structure, Dahl found a pluralistic system in which community power is dispersed and different elites are dominant in different issue-areas. Influence over the course of community affairs is possessed by many individuals in a considerable variety of roles, with each exercising his power only within a fairly limited scope and on certain questions but not others. Thus, if the matter involves urban renewal, one set of participants will control; if it concerns building a new hospital, a different coalition of leaders will dominate. In this pattern, business elites of the type who are said to control Regional City are only one among many influential groups or power clusters. As Dahl states it, "The Economic Notables, far from being a ruling group, are simply one of many groups out of which individuals sporadically emerge to influence the politics and acts of city officials. Almost anything one might say about the influence of the Economic Notables could be said with equal justice about a half dozen other groups in the New Haven community."[3]

Study of Community Power

The period which has elapsed since the publication of Hunter's seminal book has witnessed an outpouring of community power structure studies. It has also witnessed a lengthy, and at times acrimonious, debate between students of community power, with the work of Hunter and Dahl serving as polar models. The findings vary, dependent largely—it would seem—on which model is utilized.[4] Those who follow Hunter and employ the reputational technique have most often discovered an elite group of upper class and economic dominants running the community. A recent example is Carol Thometz's study of Dallas in which she found a highly structured pyramid of power with seven key leaders at the apex and sixty influential figures at the level immediately below.[5] Those who follow the power-in-action model of Dahl, on the other hand, have generally found influence to be widely dispersed among many competing groups. Aaron Wildavsky's analysis of Oberlin, Ohio,[6] and Kent Jennings' study of Atlanta[7] are two of the more recent issue-oriented endeavors, the latter contradicting Hunter's earlier finding of a monolithic elite in that city.

Social scientists working in the community power field have evidenced increasing preference for comparative studies in which several cities or towns are examined and several methodologies employed conjointly. One of the more perceptive of these efforts is Robert Presthus' *Men at the Top*, a study of two small New York towns.[8] Employing both the reputational and decisional techniques, Presthus concluded that the two might best be regarded as complementary rather than competing research strategies, the first useful in revealing potential and "behind-the-scenes" centers of power, the latter valuable in discerning overt power. Another example of the comparative approach is the well-regarded work of Robert Agger and

---

[3] *Ibid.*, p. 72.

[4] See in this connection John Walton, "Substance and Artifact: The Current Status of Research on Community Power Structure," *American Journal of Sociology*, 71 (January, 1966), 430–438. After analyzing a large number of power structure studies, Walton concluded that the disciplinary background of the researcher tends to determine the method of investigation he will use, which in turn tends to determine the image of the power structure that results from the investigation.

[5] *The Decision-Makers: The Power Structure of Dallas* (Dallas: Southern Methodist University Press, 1963).

[6] *Leadership in a Small Town* (Totowa, New Jersey: Bedminster Press, 1964).

[7] *Community Influentials: The Elites of Atlanta* (New York: Free Press, 1964).

[8] New York: Oxford University Press, 1964.

his colleagues, *The Rulers and the Ruled,* in which four communities varying in size from 2000 to 100,000 were examined.[9] The authors utilized a combination of techniques including a sample survey of the citizens to determine their perceptions of influence and leadership. The study concluded that power was broadly distributed in two of the cities and narrowly concentrated in the others.

The predominant majority of the community power structure studies have been conducted in small or medium-sized areas. Relatively few have involved large cities—Atlanta and Dallas are the principal exceptions—and less than a handful have attempted to deal with the metropolis as a whole. One effort in the latter respect was the extensive and systematic study of decision-making in the Syracuse SMSA by sociologist Linton Freeman and his associates.[10] Selecting thirty-nine significant issues that had been resolved over a five-year period, the investigators compiled a leadership pool of those who had been instrumental in reaching the decisions. Patterns of participation were then examined by statistical procedures, and clusters of issues which shared a common core of decision-makers were identified. The results were closer to the findings of Dahl than to those of Hunter. Nowhere did the researchers find evidence of the existence of an old-fashioned monolithic elite. They discovered instead that twenty-nine of the thirty-nine issues were grouped into nine clusters with common participants while the remaining ten showed no identifiable pattern. Not one but many leadership cliques were revealed, with approximately nineteen different groups involved in the decisions selected for study.

The Anatomy of Power

The results of nearly two decades of community power structure studies leave much to be desired. What emerges from them is the impression that there are various legitimate answers to the question "Who Governs?" Different patterns of power appear to exist in different communities under different conditions; but what types exist in what cities under what conditions remains an unanswered question. The Syracuse study concluded that as society increases in scale and complexity, specialized or pluralistic participation becomes necessary as well as desirable. No longer is it possible for one group to make all kinds of decisions covering the whole gamut of community affairs, a situation conceivable when social organization is relatively simple. The tendency in a universe of specialization is for each group to involve itself only in those decisions which are of direct interest to it and in which it has special competence and skills.

[9] New York: Wiley, 1964.
[10] *Metropolitan Decision-Making* (Syracuse: University College, 1962). Also see Warner Bloomberg, Jr. and Morris Sunshine, *Suburban Power Structures and Public Education* (Syracuse: Syracuse University Press, 1963).

If the Syracuse observations are sound, and the evidence points con-
vincingly in this direction, we should expect to find cities, particularly the
larger ones, located at the pluralistic end of the power continuum. As
Banfield noted with respect to Chicago, no one is in a position to survey
the city as a whole and to settle the public issues which arise. It is only
after the pulling and hauling of various views and forces that decisions of
some kind are finally reached.[11] This fragmentation of power becomes
even more manifest when metropolitan areas are considered. Here the
existence of numerous political subdivisions adds a further measure of
decentralization to the decisional structure. Set in a separate social and
economic environment, each of these subcenters of policy-making seeks
to promote its individual values and interests and to guard its autonomy.[12]

If there is a center of influence with regard to local public issues in the
sizable community, it is more likely to be found in the political sector than
among the economic notables. Empirical support for this view is provided
by sociologist Claire Gilbert's analysis of 167 community power structure
studies. Using a data quality-control technique, she concluded from the
studies that while most of the cities ranging from 20,000 to 50,000 in population were dominated by businessmen and other nonpolitical persons, or
coalitions of such persons and elected public officials, most of the large
municipalities were ruled, not by a hidden power elite, but by those who
held formal political office.[13]

Individuals in these latter positions, however, do not govern by fiat;
even the strongest must be highly sensitive to a variety of interests.
Requiring the support of many elements in the community, they cannot
politically afford to limit access to any one group or small coterie of
interests or to alienate any major segment of the community by high-
handed action. Daley in Chicago and Lee in New Haven have the
reputation of being strong mayors, and from all indications they exercise
more influence over the course of community affairs than any private
person or group. Yet as Banfield observed about Chicago, nothing important is done by the mayor or others without first ascertaining what
interests would be affected and without weighing the losses which would
accrue to some against the gains that would accrue to others. And as
Dahl points out about Lee, "The mayor was not at the peak of a pyramid
but rather at the center of intersecting circles. He rarely commanded.
He negotiated, cajoled, reasoned, promised, insisted, demanded, even

[11] Edward C. Banfield, *Political Influence* (New York: Free Press, 1961).

[12] See Robert J. Mowitz and Deil S. Wright, *Profile of a Metropolis* (Detroit:
Wayne State University Press, 1962). After examining in depth ten cases of metropolitan decision-making, the authors note (p. 630): "Our cases have not turned up a
single master decision-maker for the Detroit metropolis in the form of a person,
group, or organization."

[13] "Community Power and Decision-Making: A Quantitative Examination of Previous Research," in Terry N. Clark (ed.), *Community Structure and Decision-Making:
Comparative Analyses* (San Francisco: Chandler, 1968), pp. 139–158.

threatened, but he most needed support from other leaders who simply could not be commanded. Because the mayor could not command, he had to bargain."[14]

Out of the welter of studies and controversy over community power, one interesting area of agreement has emerged. No matter what methodology is employed, and no matter what the size or type of city or town examined, the results invariably show that only a small minority of the citizen body, actually less than one percent, are active participants in the community decision-making process (other than voting on referenda). This fact prompted one observer to remark that where sociologists found monopoly and called it elitism, the political scientists found oligopoly but defined it in more honorific terms as pluralism.[15] What has been at issue, in other words, is not so much the number of decision-makers but whether those in this category constitute a cohesive group or coalition which always or most of the time acts in concert and whose power extends across a range of decisional areas.

To the practitioner and others interested in the operation of the urban polity, the power structure studies and the accompanying academic fray have offered little of use or value. About all they have gained from their observations of these efforts is an ability to embellish their own rhetoric with such terms as "the power structure" and "the establishment." They have found little help in what they consider abstractions about the centralization or fragmentation of power. What is relevant to their concern has to do with immediate and concrete situations; with identifying, for example, those who could be mobilized or activated to support or oppose particular issues. The study of community power is still in its infancy and it is unrealistic to expect definitive answers at this time to a subject of such vast complexity. Fortunately, the methodological battle between the "reputationists" and the "pluralists" shows signs of abating—at least it has been reduced to a cold war—with researchers turning their attention increasingly to large-scale comparative studies of community power arrangements. In doing so, the new thrust is to seek answers not only to the question "Who Governs?" but also to the questions of under what circumstances they govern and with what effects on policy output.

THE FORMAL DECISION-MAKERS

No matter who may be the real wielders of power in a community, decisions on public policy ultimately rest with those who occupy positions of formal authority in the governmental system. Only the city

[14] *Who Governs?*, p. 204.
[15] Robert O. Schulze, Review of *Men at the Top*, *Social Forces*, 43 (October, 1964), 110.

council, for example, can appropriate public funds for a new park or rezone a parcel of land. Only the school board can approve the site for a new school or let the contracts for its construction. (Some decisions require voter ratification by referenda, but the vast bulk of local government business is carried on by the elected and appointed officials.) Individuals or organizations seeking to influence governmental action may be important in the community, but they will be badly handicapped in their efforts unless they have access to the appropriate legal authorities.

Individuals in governmental positions of power range from officials who follow relatively independent courses of conduct to those who are little more than puppets of various interests and from chief executives and councilmen to building inspectors and policemen. All of them are subject, in varying degrees, to various forces and pressures. A councilman dependent for election upon the support of his party committeeman or on campaign funds provided by tavern operators will not be unsympathetic to their interests. Nor is the mayor of an industrial community likely to slight the wishes of his working-class constituency. However, individuals and groups providing electoral support for public officials are normally concerned with only a limited number of issues that are of particular relevance to their own interests. They make no effort to influence the official policy-makers in most items on the local public agenda, thus giving the latter a greater area of freedom than is commonly assumed.

The Governmental Bureaucracy

Political leaders in the government have received considerable attention in discussions of the community power structure of the metropolis, but the governmental bureaucracy usually has been overlooked. This neglect is unwarranted; the professional civil servant has come to play an important role in policy-making as well as execution. By virtue of numbers alone, the bureaucracy constitutes a force in metropolitan life that cannot justifiably be ignored. The pressures for new and expanded services generated by increasing urbanization have swelled the ranks of local governmental employees. At the time of *1967 Census of Governments,* local units, including school districts, had 5.7 million employees (full-time equivalent) on their payrolls, an increase of over 35 percent since the previous census in 1962. Approximately two-thirds of this total worked in SMSAs.

The importance of the local bureaucracy has been augmented not alone by numbers but more significantly by the growing need for expertise in government at the metropolitan level. As functional activities become more dependent on science and technology, political officials find themselves compelled to rely increasingly on the knowledge, specialized skills, and advice of professional administrators. Intuition, common sense, and native shrewdness, the stock-in-trade of the successful politician, are no longer enough. The central city mayor, the urban county executive, or the elected council of a large suburban government cannot afford, politically or otherwise, to formulate programs and determine policies without the assistance of administrative technicians and specialists. Political judgment in the attack on such complex problems as traffic, air and water pollution, juvenile delinquency, crime, and governmental financing must feed on bureaucratic appraisal and know-how. And as amateurs in the many technological aspects of community functioning, political officials find it more and more difficult to challenge policy advice based on specialized knowledge. The expert may be on tap and not on top but the demands of a technological society have increased his influence over political officials. Council-manager governments provide a readily observable illustration of this development. There the city manager, once looked upon as the employee and servant of the elected council, is now—by virtue of his expertise—frequently an influential policy-maker guiding the chosen representatives of the people.

The political and bureaucratic structure of government in urban areas, however, is not a monolithic giant that encompasses all public personnel within its administrative tentacles. Like other interested groups, and like government in the metropolis itself, local officialdom and its accompanying bureaucracy are highly pluralistic. Each unit, whether a school district, municipality, or countywide sewer district, has its own entrenched officials and employees and its own fenced-in area of jurisdiction. The central city mayor, the suburban manager, the school district superintendent, the county health commissioner, and the village police chief all constitute centers of power and influence, and all are contenders in the urban arena. Water departments in the city and county vie with each other to become the metropolitan supplier. A county health department seeks to expand its authority at the expense of municipal agencies. Autonomous sewer districts resist efforts of a metropolitan agency to bring them under its jurisdiction. County and municipal police departments argue over their respective jurisdictional spheres. A central city mayor and a county governing board member or chief executive compete for recognition as the major political figure of the area. In this interplay of forces, each segment or subunit of the structure cultivates clientele relationships and affords points of access to the private influentials of the community. The king has many ears.

THE PARAPOLITICAL STRUCTURE

The democratic dogma assumes an order based on control through the consent of the governed. As long-standing community institutions have been modified or dissolved under the impact of technology and urbanization, the nature of popular control has changed also. The Jacksonian ideology of rule by friends and neighbors has given way to the realities of mass society with its impersonal, large-scale, and bureaucratic institutions. In the process, new participation patterns, a new organizational topography, and new citizen attitudes toward the community and its governmental instrumentalities have evolved.

If, as Durkheim and other social theorists have emphasized, the plural organization of society is a precondition for freedom, it follows that people must be joined together in groups which stand between the isolated individual and the state or government. These groups, which Greer and Orleans refer to collectively as the parapolitical structure of the community, serve as mediating agencies between the individual or family and the institutions of mass society.[16] They permit people of like interests to combine and pool their resources for a wide variety of purposes. Although they are not specifically oriented to politics or public affairs in their major activities (political parties and some civic associations are exceptions), many of them are "politicized," that is, they seek occasionally or often to further their aims through the medium of government. As such, they provide a mechanism for the individual to make his influence felt in community affairs and to be represented meaningfully in the decision-making process. It is no exaggeration to say that these organizations are a precondition for the translation of individual desires into social action.

The congeries of voluntary associations, from garden clubs to labor unions, which form the parapolitical structure of the urban community differ greatly in the number and character of their membership. They also differ markedly in territorial scope, from the strictly neighborhood group to one drawing membership from the entire metropolis and even beyond. Organized around a broad spectrum of interests, their purposes vary from simple social interaction to influencing governmental policy. Since these combinations of individuals form, in effect, subsystems of power which compete and cooperate in the community, they are vital, in Durkheim's terms, to the maintenance of a democratic and pluralistic society. An examination of several major categories of organizational participants at the local and metropolitan level will serve to illustrate the role they play in community affairs.

Business

Businessmen and business-oriented organizations such as the chamber of commerce have long been active in civic affairs. Their resources and

[16] Scott Greer and Peter Orleans, "The Mass Society and the Parapolitical Structure," *American Sociological Review*, 27 (October, 1962), 634–646. See also D. H. Smith, "Importance of Formal Voluntary Organizations for Society," *Sociology and Social Research*, 50 (July, 1966), 483–494.

reputed influence are great and their economic stake in the community substantial. However, as we have already had occasion to observe, the picture is not one of a business elite scheming to direct the course of community action. Their role in local public decisions is more often than not confined to rather passive membership on civic or governmental committees and to more active service in the private welfare sector of the community. The case may be different in a "company-dominated" town or in a small city where the Main Street merchants are in control; but today it is the exception rather than the rule for businessmen to play the role of civic overlords.

To deny the reputed power of the economic notables in the governance of the community is not to imply that they are without influence. As Peter B. Clark, a political scientist and newspaper executive, has observed: "If one looks at the outcomes of local government decisions over long periods of time, one finds that the interests and ends of businessmen taken as a group tend to be served more often than, to take the most contrasting case, the interests and ends of Negroes and Puerto Ricans."[17] Clark argues that the businessman's influence in local affairs is not so much directly exercised as it is anticipated. Rather than being based upon conspiracies or control of wealth, this influence rests upon the usefulness of the economic notable to others, such as political leaders, who seek the prestige and legitimacy which he can lend to their undertaking. In the process of co-opting him to their cause, local governments and civic groups tend to anticipate and, at least to some extent, satisfy his wishes.

CHANGING ROLES OF BUSINESS   Until well into the nineteenth century, the economic notable and the political notable were identical in most American cities. With the ruling elite sharing the same social and economic perspectives, community controversy was minimized and consensus on overall policy readily reached. By the end of the century, however, the situation had changed. As cities grew in size and heterogeneity, demands upon the public sector increased in scope and magnitude. Local governments found it necessary to assume new functions and undertake new services to meet the mounting needs of a rapidly expanding urban society. And as these developments occurred, the demands on local officials became more burdensome while at the same time the stakes of local public office grew more attractive. The stage was now set for a new breed of community leader, the professional politician.

Cooperating closely at first with the economic notables who were gradually withdrawing from active public roles, the new leaders soon established their own independent basis of support. Instead of social position and wealth, their principal resource was the strength of numbers.

[17] "Civic Leadership: The Symbols of Legitimacy." Paper presented at the 1960 annual conference of the American Political Science Association.

Appealing to the rising class of workers, the immigrants and low-income groups, they offered them access to opportunities and rewards that had been denied them under the passing system of oligarchical control. "Machine" politics, the "boss," and the "ward heeler" became the prevalent symbols of local government as the nineteenth century drew to a close. The response of the economic dominants in the large cities—and ultimately of the middle class in general—to the new "working class" politics was withdrawal. One finds an analogue to this in the present-day flight from the central city to suburbia. The exodus in a sense dramatizes what has long been true in most large urban areas: the noninvolvement of the upper and middle classes in the political and civic affairs of the core city.

After relinquishing the political reins, commercial and industrial leaders became content to influence the conduct of government indirectly through various citizen groups and reform leagues. More importantly, they began to play predominant roles in the private welfare sector of the community. Service on boards such as the Community Chest, Red Cross, and hospitals became a substitute for political involvement. Activity of this type served several purposes for the economic notable. It furnished him with a means of satisfying his traditional sense of civic obligation without becoming immersed in local politics. It provided him with a highly prestigious and noncontroversial role in civic affairs. And finally, it enabled him to retain certain responsibilities within control of the private sector of the community that otherwise would have to be assumed by government.

Changes in business organization and styles also contributed to the separation of economic and political power in community affairs. In place of the local proprietors, the family- and home-owned establishments, came the large and impersonal corporate enterprises, frequently branches of national firms or controlled largely by outside capital. Along with them came the modern business elite, the organization men described so graphically by William Whyte of *Fortune* magazine. The new managers and engineers of economic power were not imbued with the sense of personal commitment to the community that had characterized their predecessors. Mobile, subject to frequent transfer from city to city, engrossed with their careers, they were men of limited civic commitment. Their involvement in the affairs of the local community was minimal and generally restricted to the specialized economic interests of their organizations. Communication with governmental officials was rare, with both business and public sectors pursuing their own objectives under an implicit truce of "no intervention" in the other's bailiwick.

Today, the situation is again changing, although the chasm still remains wide. Corporations, increasingly sensitive to their public image and, more significantly, troubled by the racial unrest which has swept through the nation's urban centers, are beginning to assume a more active responsibility to the communities in which their plants are located. "Urban coalitions" are being formed in many cities and metropolitan areas bringing businessmen together with representatives of all sectors of the community, including minority groups, to consider local problems. Insurance companies have pledged $1 billion for mortgage and home improvement loans in core areas. Many firms have modified their employment practices to provide more jobs for nonwhites and a few, such as Xerox, have set up plants in the ghettos and are training blacks to take over the management. In some communities, both North and South, businessmen have exerted pressure on local officials to negotiate with civil rights groups in order to end demonstrations and boycotts. Increasingly also, talk is heard of industry and government joining together to attack certain urban problems such as housing and ghetto reconstruction. It is not so much a sense of civic responsibility—although this is present in many instances—as it is self-interest in an orderly and viable urban environment which is pulling business and industry back into the community arena.

Labor

A popular conception of "who gets what" in American society centers around the triad of "Big Business, Big Labor, and Big Government." The contest in the public arena is pictured as a struggle between the first two giants with the third acting as mediator and controller and, in the eyes of some, as dispenser of lavish favors to those on the "in." This view is not limited to the national and state scenes; even at the local or metropolitan level murmurs are heard about business or labor running the community or being the recipients of political largess. The evidence, as noted previously, offers little to substantiate the mythology of business dominance in community affairs, particularly in the large cities. The case with respect to labor is no different.

In discussing labor's role in community affairs, several observations may be made at the outset. First of all, if unions and business are contesting for power over local civic matters, the struggle is taking place behind the scenes. Seldom do clashes over issues of a noneconomic character stir the community waters. In civic causes, trade union leaders will often be found in the same camp with the business notables assisting a chest or hospital drive, endorsing a bond issue for public improvements, working to establish a cultural center, or supporting an urban redevelopment project. Second, like business, labor is not a monolithic aggregation of power. Differences among and even within unions militate against any effective system of centralized control. Third, union leadership is likely to be most effective in mobilizing support for those issues that the membership considers legitimate concerns of the organization.

The generalization that American unions do not display great interest in local governmental affairs has empirical support. When labor intervenes and uses its strength in the metropolitan arena it usually does so because matters of direct relevance to the economic interests of its members are involved. The construction trade unions, for example, will resist building code changes that threaten to reduce the job potential of their constituents. Or the joint AFL–CIO council will lend its support to public employee unions in disputes over wages and working conditions. Labor leaders will also speak out at times on various non-economic matters of local concern, such as educational and recreational needs, but they will try to avoid the more controversial questions such as racial discrimination in housing and job opportunities. Even though the national leadership of organized labor takes strong stands on issues of equality, the local leadership treads cautiously in this realm. The rank and file of union membership is by no means committed to the abolition of discrimination, particularly in its own house or at its own doorstep. For local union officials to act militantly in issues of this kind presents threats to their continuance as leaders.

Labor's principal access to influence in local affairs is through the elective officials who are concerned with the mass mobilization of numbers. In the large cities, labor is usually found closely allied to the Democratic party; and where partisan elections for local office are held, it normally supports candidates of this political faith. On occasions, the union will line up behind local political leaders to oppose charter reform measures that threaten to diminish the patronage or other perquisites of their allies in government. Their support of "friendly" candidates and their interests gives them access to the governmental structure and entitles them to certain rewards, such as the appointment of labor officials to various local boards and commissions.

Today, organized labor is also attaching increasing importance to participation in activities of private welfare agencies where its guarantee of financial support provides a means of penetration. Union officials are now found on the Community Chest and similar boards and on various civic commissions. Studies indicate, however, that despite its increased representation, labor has not materially altered the goals of these agencies or effectively challenged the controlling power of other groups.[18] Rarely, if ever, is a labor official selected to head the community welfare council or to serve as general chairman of the annual fund drive. These positions remain within control of the economic notables. Indicative also in this connection is the fact that lists of persons of influence within the community, whether compiled on the basis of reputation or participation, seldom include a high percentage of union members.

[18] See, for example, Donald E. Wray, "The Community and Labor-Management Relations," in *Labor-Management Relations in Illini City* (Champaign: University of Illinois Institute of Labor and Industrial Relations, 1953), pp. 7–145.

Beyond the acquisition of these trappings and symbols of civic legitimacy and the occasional intervention in matters of economic concern to its membership, labor still does not occupy a place in the community power structure commensurate with its numbers or economic strength. As a perceptive study of Lansing, Michigan, concluded, "Organized labor's community power lags behind its economic power."[19] The reason for this lag is possibly as Dahl speculates: "If the local union group has had much less influence in political decisions than considerations of sheer numbers might suggest, this is partly because the leaders and members have had no clearcut image of the functions unions should perform in local politics—or even whether unions should have any role in local government at all."[20]

Political Parties

Generalization about the role of political parties in local governmental affairs is no easier than it is in the case of business and labor. Their influence and the degree of their participation vary from community to community. In Chicago and New York it is relatively high, in Cincinnati and Los Angeles, less evident. One important variable in determining the role and activity of parties at the metropolitan and local levels is their formal status in the governmental structure.

In some metropolitan communities, nonpartisan elections prevail throughout the area; in others the central city chooses its local officials on partisan tickets while suburban municipalities utilize nonpartisan ballots; and in still others different combinations are found. In Montgomery County, Ohio, for example, Dayton city officials are selected in nonpartisan elections, and county and township officers in partisan contests.

Form, of course, is not the all-determinative element in assessing the activity and influence of political parties in local elections. Some nonpartisan communities carefully observe the principle in practice and spirit as well as form; in others partisanship merely operates under a nonpartisan label. An extreme instance of the latter is found in Chicago where the highly partisan board of aldermen is selected on nonpartisan tickets. Generally, however, nonpartisan elections impose restraints on the extent of partisan activity and weaken party influence in the conduct of local government.

Where political parties are able to nominate and elect their candidates to municipal and county offices, their stake in local affairs will be greater than when they are excluded from these prizes. As Eugene Lee found in a study of nonpartisanship in California cities, ". . . removal of the

---

[19] William H. Form, "Organized Labor's Place in the Community Power Structure," *Industrial and Labor Relations Review*, XII (July, 1959), 537.
[20] Dahl, *Who Governs?*, p. 254.

party label tends to reduce the stake of the party organization and leaders in the outcome of the local races, and their interest and activity is correspondingly lessened."[21] Yet even in jurisdictions where partisanship prevails, the insignificant amount of patronage that generally remains at the local level diminishes the inducement for intensive involvement by the party leadership. When patronage jobs were available on a large scale, the party could readily utilize these rewards to recruit loyal workers and strengthen its organization for pursuing the more important stakes at the state and national levels. Now, the widespread adoption of merit systems in municipal governments has lessened and in some cases virtually destroyed these opportunities.[22]

Party leaders themselves are far from unanimous in favoring the participation of political parties in local politics. Some feel that local issues have little connection with the policies of the two major parties. Others maintain that parties are too preoccupied on the state and national levels to expend their energies and resources on local affairs. Still others are of the opinion that extensive participation in community affairs offers little payoff while entailing considerable risk. They point out that such activity not only drains off organizational resources but also involves the party uselessly in highly controversial issues. It is one thing, they say, to support civil rights legislation in Washington; it is another matter to be responsible for passing open-occupancy ordinances and anti-discrimination measures in Middletown where the issues strike close to home.

PARTY DIVISIONS AND DECENTRALIZATION   Two additional factors are relevant to a discussion of party influence in metropolitan affairs: the divisions within the parties themselves, and the many separate centers of political power arising from the fragmentation of the local governmental structure. The traditional image of a tight political hierarchy extending from the "boss" to the precinct captain is the exception rather than the rule today. Men like Hubert Humphrey, a political amateur when he was mayor of Minneapolis, were able to achieve local public office without party support and even against the opposition of their parties.[23] Many examples could also be cited of differences over local issues between party officials in the white and Negro wards and between those in and outside the central city.

Governmental balkanization of the metropolis further diminishes the opportunities for political parties to exercise effective control or significant influence in area-wide public affairs. Even where only partisan elections are employed, each municipality has its own political cadre that vies for the rewards of local office. The "politicos" in each of these

21 The Politics of Nonpartisanship (Berkeley and Los Angeles: University of California Press, 1960), p. 176.

22 See Frank J. Sorauf, "The Silent Revolution in Patronage," Public Administration Review, XX (Winter, 1960), 28–34.

23 See, for example, Robert L. Morlan, "City Politics: Free Style," National Municipal Review, XXXVIII (November, 1949), 485–490.

minor strongholds enjoy their own independent basis of operation, their own constituency, and their own interests. To be elected to office they must be attuned to the needs and desires of their individual local electorates; and these needs and desires, as conceived by the residents, do not always correspond to those of the metropolitan area as a whole. Programs that political leaders in the central city or at the county level might like to see adopted for the area may be anathema to inhabitants in the suburban municipalities. Public officials with stakes in the suburbs are unlikely to jeopardize their local interests by supporting the position of the area-wide party organization. It is unlikely also that the party leadership would demand such compliance. More probably the party would avoid taking a stand on such local or metropolitan issues.

The facts of political arithmetic in this fragmented system also discourage greater party participation in metropolitan affairs. Where the two-party system operates as it does in many urban communities with the core city Democratic and the suburbs Republican, the difficulties of area-wide policy formulation are compounded. The favorite strategy in such instances has been one of "live and let live." Political parties have thus exhibited little interest in reforming the governmental structure so as to make centralized decision-making institutionally possible. Amalgamation or even lesser schemes of functional consolidation and federation might either dilute the strength of the core city Democrats or submerge the influence of the suburban Republicans. If, as one observer has speculated, the city of Buffalo were consolidated with Erie County, control over the city would pass from the Democratic to the Republican party. Or if Chicago were combined with Cook County, the Democrats would have a chance of capturing the area-wide government; but why should they take the risk when control of Chicago is a sure thing?[24] The situation is different in some areas, as in Metropolitan Syracuse, where the central city, the suburban municipalities, and the county government are all controlled by the same party. In the Syracuse area the concurrence of party membership has made it possible for a Republican mayor of the central city, who is also Republican county chairman, to bring about certain area-wide decisions such as integration of welfare functions on a county basis. This ability, however, is severely circumscribed, as the Syracuse studies show, and can be exercised only in limited spheres of a relatively noncontroversial nature.[25]

"Change-Oriented" Groups

The organizations thus far discussed aspire to goals that can be achieved largely within the framework of society as it is presently con-

[24] Edward C. Banfield, "The Politics of Metropolitan Area Organization," *Midwest Journal of Political Science*, I (May, 1957), 77–91.
[25] See Roscoe C. Martin, Frank J. Munger, and others, *Decisions in Syracuse* (Bloomington: Indiana University Press, 1961).

stituted. But there are also other associations which are predominantly change-oriented, and which are convinced that their objectives cannot be attained without a restructuring of the existing system. Hence they seek basic modifications in society as a whole or in certain of its institutions. Included in this classification are the civil rights groups such as the National Association for the Advancement of Colored People (NAACP), Congress of Racial Equality (CORE), Student Non-Violent Coordinating Committee (SNCC), Southern Christian Leadership Conference (SCLC), and the many neighborhood and functional groups which have emerged as a byproduct of the War on Poverty. These organizations have assumed new importance during the last decade as the problems of discrimination and inequality have been brought forcefully to public attention.

The extent of activity engaged in by civil rights groups and associations of the poor at the community level often exceeds that of the long established organizations. The names of their leaders are not likely to appear on any list of reputedly influential persons, and the resources they have at their disposal are not great by modern standards. Yet their impact in recent years has been substantial and their ability to precipitate change in limited areas of concern dramatically demonstrated. Their efforts have been aided materially by national legislation and court decisions in the field of civil rights and by the Economic Opportunity Act with its provision for "maximum feasible participation" of the poor in local poverty programs.

The civil rights and poverty groups vary considerably in their philosophy and strategy. They range from those dominated by active militants to those which seek change through the established political and legal channels. Increasingly, however, many of them have turned from the use of traditional interest-group means to approaches and techniques which deviate from the "rules-of-the-game" as they are conceived by the middle class. Tactics running the gamut from peaceful demonstrations to the strategic and selective obstruction of community activities are employed in efforts to wring concessions from the majoritarian society. The theoretical underpinning for the militant posture of many of these associations has been provided by the "social protest" or "conflict" model.[26] This model assumes the existence of a wide cleavage between a class or racial-ethnic minority and a majority which supports or acquiesces in the institutions dominated by the "establishment." Collaboration with existing community agencies will yield little, according to the theory, unless the poor or racial minority confront them from positions of power. Lacking the traditional resources of money and access to the centers of influence, organizations representing the under-

[26] For the pioneering formulation of this model in the United States, see Saul Alinsky, *Reveille for Radicals* (Chicago: University of Chicago Press, 1946).

privileged segments of the society must seek to develop and use every opportunity to

. . . bring latent conflict to the surface, to intensify it, and to aid the poor [and racial minorities] in developing and using whatever power resources can be developed by those who have little money: the capacity to disrupt the community's "peace and tranquillity," to develop bloc voting, to investigate and disclose practices disadvantageous to the poor, to consolidate such economic power as the poor can muster through action such as boycotts, and to obtain from sympathetic supralocal sources of community funds, such as the federal government, conditions to the granting of those funds.[27]

A second model, known as community development, has been employed by some organizations of the poor and racial minorities. This approach assumes that enough capacities for leadership and action are distributed among all communities or subcommunities to make possible the development of effective self-help programs and proposals at the grassroots level. Conflict, the organizational cement of the social protest model, is not sought as a necessary part of the process. In fact, efforts are usually made to avoid conflict until the organization has gained internal strength and self-confidence through completion of initial projects. Collaboration with the established political and social agencies is commonly practiced so that required developmental resources may be channelled into the locality. Eventually projects of substantial scope intended to bring more basic changes in the total community may be undertaken, and an increasingly participative local democracy is continuously sought.[28]

The community development model is more compatible with the American myth of "pulling oneself up by his own bootstraps," and thus arouses less hostility. However, the persistent failure of local political and social institutions to respond adequately to the needs of groups following this approach has led racial minorities and the poor to turn increasingly to the social protest model, with resulting intensification of community conflict. Even organizations such as the Urban League which have long worked within the established structure have been compelled to assume a more militant stance to avoid losing the support of blacks altogether. Despite the backlash it has precipitated among segments of the community majority, militant activism has undoubtedly led to a greater consideration of the interests of racial minorities and the poor by local decision-makers. It has also contributed to the growth of "low-income" power at the community level.

27 Warner Bloomberg, Jr. and Florence W. Rosenstock, "Who Can Activate the Poor?" in Warner Bloomberg, Jr. and Henry J. Schmandt (eds.), *Power, Poverty, and Urban Policy* (Beverly Hills: Sage Publications, 1968), p. 322.

28 Clarence King, *Working with People in Community Action* (New York: Association Press, 1965).

THE INDIVIDUAL AS CIVIC PARTICIPANT

Thus far we have been speaking of groups and organizations and the role they play as collective forces in the local polity. Here we focus attention on the individual and his activities both as a voter and as a member of "politicized" formal organizations. In doing so, we are immediately confronted with what appears to be a contradiction between democratic dogma and practice. Pluralist theory, as we have had occasion to observe, posits a society in which power is widely shared and influenced by an electorate organized into voluntary associations. When we turn to individual behavior, however, we find that local politics and community involvement are not central concerns in the lives of most Americans. As numerous studies indicate, well over one-third of the adult population can be characterized as politically apathetic or passive; another 60 percent play largely spectator roles in the political process; and no more than 5 percent are actively involved.

As long as local government officials and community institutions perform their tasks with reasonable efficiency and without scandal or patent disregard of public needs, most citizens appear content to remain uninvolved. The problem is not so much the relatively low level of participation, undesirable as this may be from the standpoint of civic vitality; the relevant question is whether the system is responsive to the interests of all sectors of the society. If those who participate are randomly distributed throughout the population, such responsiveness is more likely; but if the nonparticipators are disproportionately concentrated in certain socioeconomic categories, the chances of inequitable treatment are increased substantially. For we would assume that those segments of the community which are active and highly organized are in a better position than the inactive and unorganized to make their influence felt in the public sphere. The question of who participates is therefore of critical importance.

Who Votes?

Man is involved in many role relationships: as husband or parent, employer or employee, neighbor or stranger, producer or consumer. In this social matrix of seemingly endless interpersonal relations, the individual is also a political actor and as such a participant in the governance of his community. This participation may take many forms. It may be limited to the occasional act of voting, or it may also entail electioneering, standing for office, and exerting leadership in community affairs.

Social scientist Lester Milbrath has suggested a hierarchy of political involvement ranging from holding public office to exposing oneself to political stimuli (Figure 21). Voting ranks low in this hierarchy since it requires a lesser expenditure of time and energy than acts higher on the scale. Milbrath calls it a "spectator" activity to distinguish it from the more active forms of participation. As he puts it, "The spectators in the stands cheer, transmit messages of advice and encouragment, and, at given periods, vote to decide who has won a particular battle (election)."[29] True as this may be, the act of voting is basic to a democratic system. It provides, moreover, an objective, if not the most relevant,

Holding public and party office

Being a candidate for office

Soliciting political funds

Attending a caucus or a strategy meeting

Becoming an active member in a political party

Contributing time in a political campaign

Attending a political meeting or rally

Making a monetary contribution to a party or candidate

Contacting a public official or a political leader

Wearing a button or putting a sticker on the car

Attempting to talk another into voting a certain way

Initiating a political discussion

Voting

Exposing oneself to political stimuli

Gladiatorial activities

Transitional activities

Spectator activities

Apathetics

FIGURE 21   **Hierarchy of Political Involvement. From Lester Milbrath,** Political Participation, **(Chicago: Rand McNally, 1965), p. 18.**

measurement of general citizen interest in the affairs of the polity. (Milbrath's hierarchy, it should be noted, includes only the traditionally recognized forms of political participation. It does not take account of the increasing amount of "extra-political" activity, such as demonstrations, protests, and sit-ins, which involve many individuals who would be classified as apathetic according to the standard indexes of participation.)

As election statistics graphically demonstrate, many citizens do not

[29] *Political Participation* (Chicago: Rand McNally, 1965), p. 20.

take the trouble to vote regularly. In fact, a conspicuously wide disparity exists between the potential size of the electorate and those who go to the polls. Only 60 to 65 percent of those of voting age participate in presidential elections, and it has been estimated that 17 percent of the electorate has never voted in any national contest. Although data on voting behavior at the local level are much less complete, the evidence reveals a pattern generally similar to that found in national and state elections. Turnout is low, actually far less than in presidential and congressional contests. Seldom do more than 50 percent of the registered voters go to the polls in municipal elections. The more likely figure is 30 percent, and it is not uncommon for the vote to drop to less than one-fourth of the registered electorate, with the usual turnout in school district and other nonmunicipal contests even lower. The percentage of those who never participate in local elections is also larger than that at the national level. Studies in St. Louis and Dayton found that over one-fourth of those eligible to vote in local contests had never done so. They further revealed that almost all who take part in local elections also vote in national contests but that the reverse does not hold true.[30]

The demographic characteristics of local voters and nonvoters follow the same pattern found at the national level.[31] Women tend to vote less than men although the difference is not great and is becoming progressively less so; young people and those individuals over 65 are less likely to go to the polls than the intervening age groups; and those with lower incomes and less formal education are more apt to refrain from electoral participation than individuals of higher social rank. Two additional variables—length of residence and home ownership—are also significant determinatives of community participation patterns. The longer a person lives in the same locality, the greater the likelihood that he will vote in local elections. Similarly, if he owns his home, he is more apt to vote than if he rents his dwelling quarters.

The male-female differential in voting participation is seemingly a result of less interest and less opportunity for involvement in public affairs on the part of women as well as less social pressure on them to vote. In recent years, however, women have so increased their electoral participation that when other factors are held constant, their rate of voting no longer differs greatly from that of men.

The lower rate of voting among young adults undoubtedly grows out of factors associated with their stage in the life cycle. Persons in their twenties and early thirties are often not yet involved in neighborhood and community networks of commitment and responsibility. Geographically

---

[30] John C. Bollens (ed.), *Exploring the Metropolitan Community* (Berkeley and Los Angeles: University of California Press, 1961), p. 182; *Metropolitan Challenge* (Dayton: Metropolitan Community Studies, 1959), p. 231.

[31] For a general analysis of political participation, see Robert E. Lane, *Political Life* (New York: Free Press, 1959).

and occupationally mobile, they are busily engaged in establishing new families, finding their way in new job situations, and meeting mortgage payments. The personal commitments consume their time and energies and channel their interests away from public affairs. Toward the other end of the age continuum, the rate of voting also tends to decline. Persons over 65 begin to find many of their community bonds falling away with the dissolution of their families and the relative isolation of old age. For them, voting and the round of civic participation tend to become more burdensome if not less meaningful.

Several factors help to explain the close relationship between socioeconomic level and voting rate. People with more education, better jobs, and higher income are likely to be knowledgeable about public issues, feel a high sense of personal efficacy in political matters, and have a large personal stake in the outcome of elections. Even if they do not have a sense of responsibility to their community—which they are more likely to have than those of lower socioeconomic rank—they nevertheless feel socially compelled to participate in the electoral process. Social norms in the lower status groups, on the other hand, place less emphasis on political and civic activity.

Both length of residence and home ownership are indicators of commitment to the community and both tend to stimulate participation in its public affairs. The individual who has lived in the same locality for a long time has struck deeper roots than the transient, knows more about the area, and is more likely to have acquired interests that he is anxious to protect. A similar statement may be made about the home owner as against the renter. Investment in a home gives a feeling of greater permanence as well as a vested stake in the neighborhood or community. Empirical findings support these propositions. The Metropolitan Dayton survey, for example, found that the nonvoter in local elections is most likely to be an individual who has lived in his present location less than five years, does not own his home, and has a lower educational level. To the same effect, the St. Louis area study reported that 26 percent more owners than renters voted in local contests. A recent study of four middle-sized cities in Wisconsin generally supports these observations, although length of residence was found to be a less influential factor in determining participation than noted earlier. According to the findings, social status, organization activity, and home ownership are the most important characteristics associated with local political involvement.[32]

Who Belongs?

More than a century ago, Alexis de Tocqueville, the noted French commentator on American mores and institutions, observed that "Ameri-

[32] See Robert R. Alford and Harry M. Scoble, "Sources of Local Political Involvement," *American Political Science Review*, LXII (December, 1968), 1192–1206.

cans of all ages, all conditions, and all dispositions constantly form associations."[33] Historians Charles and Mary Beard, writing in more recent times, commented that the tendency of which de Tocqueville spoke "has now become a general mania."[34] The habit of joining, of organizing human contacts around some cause or activity, is a well recognized feature of our cultural environment. Voluntary associations act as stimuli, arousing their participants to greater involvement in the political life of the larger society. They provide a far-flung although highly decentralized network for mobilizing citizen interest and activity on public issues and problems. Together with the formal structure of local government they constitute an integral part of the community's organizational system. Segmented in their membership and purposes, and frequently in competition with one another, such groupings enlist the allegiances of the citizenry in a variety of causes. In playing this role, they serve as important anchoring points for the political and associational life of the individual.

Although organizational membership is widespread and pervasive, a substantial number of individuals remain outside it. A study based on evidence from national sample surveys reveals that somewhat less than one-half of all adult Americans are members of voluntary associations (other than church-related groups); and of those who are joiners, only a small part have membership in two or more groups.[35] Other studies of individual communities have also found considerable nonparticipation, with the rate varying from one-third to one-half.[36]

Membership in organizations that are primarily interested in or have some substantial concern with local public affairs and community action involves a much lower percentage of the population. Data gathered in national studies show that only 2 percent of the adult citizenry belong to a political club or organization and 31 percent to an association that sometimes takes a stand on such public issues as housing, better government, or school affairs.[37] (This latter figure includes membership in unions, chambers of commerce, and other groups that only occasionally become involved in local civic issues.)

Membership alone, of course, is not a reliable indicator of organiza-

---

[33] *Democracy in America* (New York: Knopf, 1946), Vol. II, p. 106.

[34] *Rise of American Civilization* (New York: Macmillan, 1927), Vol. 2, p. 730.

[35] Charles R. Wright and Herbert H. Hyman, "Voluntary Association Memberships of American Adults: Evidence from National Sample Surveys," *American Sociological Review*, 23 (June, 1958), 284–294.

[36] Sampling of the Detroit area population in the mid-1950s disclosed that 37 percent of the respondents were not members of formal groups. See Morris Axelrod, "Urban Structure and Social Participation," *American Sociological Review*, 21 (February, 1956), 13–18. The Metropolitan Dayton survey similarly found that one-third of the adult residents belonged to no organization, one-fourth to only one, and the remainder to more than one (*Metropolitan Challenge*, p. 227).

[37] Lane, *Political Life*, p. 75.

tional participation. To belong to a formally organized group is one matter, but to play an active and meaningful role in its affairs is another. Many people are members in name only. They belong because it is occupationally necessary or socially desirable for them to do so but they have little inclination (some, in fact, have no capacity) to become involved in organizational activities. If we define the active member as one who attends meetings regularly and who holds office or serves on committees in the organization, the proportion of the citizen body in this category is probably as low as 15 or 20 percent. One study found that among those who belonged to voluntary associations, one-fourth had not attended any meeting during the three months preceding the interview while another one-third indicated that they rarely attended.[38] Thus like voting, active involvement in organizational life is confined to a minority of the population.

When the demographic features of associational membership are examined, a pattern similar to that found in electoral participation emerges. Belonging to formal organizations is closely related to social rank (education, occupation, income), age, and length of residence in the community. Based on a nationwide sample, the Michigan Survey Research Center found that 47 percent of those with grade school education or less belonged to no organization while the comparable figure for those who had attended college was 19 percent. The study also revealed that 60 percent of those in the lower income brackets as against 20 percent in the higher categories were nonjoiners.[39] The same situation prevails in the case of multiple memberships. Findings of the Metropolitan Dayton survey show that about one-fourth of metropolitan residents of lower educational status as against nearly three-fourths of those who had attended college belong to two or more organizations. They also demonstrate that socioeconomic variables bear a close relationship to organizational activism. The college group in the Dayton area was four times as well represented as the lower educational categories among those who attend meetings regularly. And so were individuals in the higher occupational and income levels, thus again indicating the class-linked nature of membership in voluntary associations.

Age is a further determinative factor in organizational affiliation. Membership is highest among individuals between the ages of 35 and 65, with a significantly lower figure for those not yet 35 and a sharp drop among older persons. The heavy involvement of young adults in establishing careers, families, and homes detracts from their participation in the community's organizational life. Later, after they reach retire-

[38] Axelrod, "Urban Structure and Social Participation," pp. 13–18.
[39] Lane, *Political Life*, p. 78. Also see Mirra Komarovsky, "The Voluntary Associations of Urban Dwellers," *American Sociological Review*, 11 (December, 1946), 468–498.

ment, their roles in organizations and civic endeavors become less meaningful and less active. They find, moreover, that with increasing age useful participational roles become less available to them as society turns to more youthful leadership and new ideas.

Length of residence, the third variable found to be related to membership, reflects the degree of local identification and commitment held by the individual citizen. The relationship is a positive one: membership in voluntary associations tends to increase with length of time in the community. The highest rate of both membership and active participation occurs among natives and those residing in the neighborhood for more than twenty years. Less than one-half the newcomers to the Dayton area (those living there no more than five years) belonged to a formal organization of any kind, and less than one-fifth of those who did belong could be classified as active members.

The United States is a nation of families and individuals who often change their place of residence. So widespread is this trait that one of the first questions asked of a new acquaintance is, "Where are you from?" An average of 38 million persons, or about one of every five of the population, change their residence during the course of a single year. For about two-thirds of these, the move does not cross county lines; for more than 4 million, however, it is to another state. Young people in their twenties constitute the most mobile segment of the population, changing their residence four times as frequently as those above forty-five. This geographical mobility is a factor of importance to metropolitan living. Many urban residents do not remain in the same locality long enough to cultivate close ties or to become integrated into the associational web of the community. The constant moving back and forth across the country in search of better jobs or other opportunities, or as a result of corporate policies of transferring personnel, puts a premium, as one sociologist has said, "on the tree which can survive with shallow roots."[40] So also the ceaseless movement from central city to the ring, from suburb to suburb, from the fringe to exurbia (the area beyond the established suburbs), leaves little time for the family to sink its roots into the community soil.

Informal Participation

Individuals participate in community life through informal and primary group relations as well as through voting and membership in voluntary associations. Relatives, friends, and neighbors serve as major anchors and points of interaction in the daily life of most people. As intimate and informal groupings, they provide an important source of the norms and attitudes which the members of a given society share.

[40] Roland Warren, *The Community in America* (Chicago: Rand McNally, 1963), p. 21.

The family gatherings, the discussions with one's fellow workers at the plant or with friends at the poker or bridge table, the conversations over the back fence or around the barbecue pit, all leave their mark on the impressions and views of the participants and all are important channels of communication. The nature and extent of an individual's relation with others in these informal, face-to-face situations inevitably affect his beliefs and his ways of thinking. If, to cite only one example, he enjoys close contact with relatives or friends who are active in civic affairs, this fact will probably be reflected in greater community involvement on his own part. If, on the other hand, those with whom he regularly associates are totally uninterested in local government and local public issues, the odds are that his own community participation will be low.

Prior to 1940, urban sociology tended to emphasize the lack of integration and high degree of social disorganization in the city. Urbanization was looked upon as leading to greater dependence on voluntary associations at the expense of primary groups. Stressing the impersonality of relationships in the metropolis, it saw the formal organization becoming a substitute for the kinship and neighborhood group with a consequent weakening of the integrative fibers of the community. In more recent decades, sociology has become interested in the informal group as a significant factor in the maintenance of the urban system.[41] Researchers have found that while voluntary associations are fundamental to city residents, primary or face-to-face contacts continue to play a vital part in the lives of most urbanites. As sample surveys show, most urban dwellers visit frequently with relatives, neighbors, co-workers, and friends.

Although these primary groups do not appear on any organization chart of the local community, they constitute key building blocks upon which more elaborate social structures are founded. These small units of personal interaction create common interests and values in the community and thereby serve as important unifying devices. This function extends even beyond local government boundaries to embrace the metropolis. When, for example, a suburbanite's close friends or kin live in the central city, each brings to the other a better understanding and appreciation of the linkages and mutual interests between the two sections of the larger community.

Participational Pattern of Negroes

Minority groups have generally facilitated their assimilation into American society through political and social organizations. The one conspicuous failure to achieve integration has occurred in the case of

[41] A. K. Tomeh, "Informal Participation in a Metropolitan Community," *Sociological Quarterly,* 8 (Winter, 1967), 85–102.

the Negro. According to some observers, the low level of electoral and organizational participation of Negroes has contributed to this failure by handicapping them in bringing their demands to bear on the community. Those who hold this viewpoint refer to studies which show that while one-third of the total adult population is politically very inactive, 60 percent of the blacks fall into this category. Other scholars take issue with these figures, pointing out that they fail to take into account the Negro-white variances among comparable socioeconomic groups. When this factor is considered, a different picture emerges. Holding socioeconomic status constant, differences between the electoral participation of whites and blacks (outside the South where extra-legal barriers to Negro voting still exist) are not significant. The fact, however, that Negroes are disproportionately represented in the low educational, occupational, and income categories (where voting rates among both blacks and whites are substantially below the average) creates the impression of lower participation.

The situation with respect to membership and activity in organizations is even more revealing. Negro membership in voluntary associations is considerably higher than that shown for whites as a whole, with the discrepancy more pronounced when blacks are compared to whites of similar socioeconomic levels.[42] The relationship between social class and membership, moreover, is much less pronounced for Negroes. Lower-class blacks are more likely to belong to organizations than whites of similar status while middle- and upper-class whites are more likely to be joiners than their black counterparts. In all cases, Negroes are more likely to participate actively in the associations to which they belong than are whites. Gunnar Myrdal, in offering an explanation for this phenomenon, holds that Negroes compensate for the social deprivation they suffer by intensive organizational participation. In his words, "Negroes are active in associations because they are not allowed to be active in much of the other organized life. Negroes are largely kept out, not only of politics proper, but of more purposive and creative work in trade unions, businessmen's groups, large-scale civic improvement and charity organizations and the like."[43]

When discussing organizational participation, it is necessary to consider not only the number but also the kinds of associations to which individuals belong. Although the findings are not conclusive, evidence indicates that the extensive membership pattern of Negroes has not been useful for representing their special interests. The predominant par-

[42] Nicholas Babchuck and Ralph V. Thompson, "Voluntary Associations of Negroes," *American Sociological Review,* 27 (October, 1962), 647–655; Anthony M. Orum, "A Reappraisal of the Social and Political Participation of Negroes," *American Journal of Sociology,* 72 (July, 1966), 32–46.

[43] *An American Dilemma* (New York: Harper & Row, 1944), p. 952.

ticipation among blacks has been in nonutilitarian organizations such as church-related groups and fraternal clubs. Only in recent years has their membership in such instrumental associations as labor unions showed significant gains. However, church and fraternal organizations in the Negro community are becoming increasingly committed to furthering the social goals of blacks, and in the process are assuming a more utilitarian role. Since organizational participation is itself a learning or socializing process, affording the individual member opportunity to take part in decision-making and to experience power, American communities are likely to witness a growing degree of sophistication on the part of Negroes in making their demands felt through interest group activity. And as this occurs, social protest will pass to effective political action.

PARTICIPATION IN SUBURBIA

What we have been saying about voting and other forms of civic involvement applies to suburbia as well as the central city. Little evidence exists to substantiate the common assumption that the small suburban community stimulates greater citizen activity. A study of electoral participation in forty-five cities in Los Angeles County, California, over a seventeen-year period found little relation between size of municipality and voting turnout. Los Angeles ranked twenty-sixth of the forty-five in the percentage of the qualified electorate who voted in municipal elections while one of the smallest cities had the poorest turnout.[44] A similar study of St. Louis area municipalities found no significant differences in rate of voter participation based on size. Voting turnout in the central city compared favorably and, in fact, exceeded that in over half the ring municipalities.[45] Given the relatively higher social rank of most suburban populations and the relationship between this variable and voting, the findings on electoral participation are even more telling than the figures indicate.

Is the picture any different when we turn to the organizational life of suburbia? If we can take the word of some commentators, the answer is "yes." William H. Whyte, in *The Organization Man*, says of suburban Park Forrest and the amount of civic energy it swallows up, "Every minute from 7 A.M. to 10 P.M. some organization is meeting somewhere."[46] Max Lerner in his observations on American civilization similarly notes

[44] Lawrence W. O'Rourke, *Voting Behavior in Forty-Five Cities of Los Angeles County* (Los Angeles: University of California Bureau of Governmental Research, 1953, p. 104).
[45] Bollens (ed.), *Exploring the Metropolitan Community*, pp. 87–88.
[46] (New York: Doubleday, 1956), p. 317.

that "when people move from the mass city to the more compassable suburb, their participation in club and associational life increases deeply."[47] Another writer sees the new suburbs as "very gregarious communities, in which people wander in and out of one another's houses without invitation and organize themselves into everything from car pools to PTAs and hobby clubs of numerous sorts."[48] In the light of these statements, the findings of the Dayton area survey as set out in Table 16 are of interest. Here we find that suburban residents are more

TABLE 16   **Membership in Organizations, Montgomery County (Dayton), 1959**

Type of Organization	Central City	Suburban Zone
Child-centered	18 percent	30 percent
Fraternal	19	21
Church-centered	21	15
Labor union	15	12
Other work centered	8	12
Community action	12	8
Community service and welfare	10	4
Other (including social and hobby)	14	23

SOURCE: *Metropolitan Challenge*, p. 228.

likely than central city dwellers to belong to child-centered organizations and social and hobby clubs but less inclined to participate in civic-oriented groups. Overall, the differences between the rate of organizational membership in city and suburbs is not great; and when controlled for social rank, it is negligible.

We would expect more suburbanites to belong to child-centered organizations simply because more young families live outside the core city. We would also expect them to belong to more social groupings because of the generally higher social ranking of suburban populations. On the other hand, we would anticipate that a greater proportion of central city residents would· participate in civic-oriented associations because of the broader range of opportunities open to them and the higher significance of public affairs and issues in the metropolitan hub. Moving to suburbia does not transform one's participational and civic habits any more so than it does his political beliefs.[49] The nonjoiner

[47] *America as a Civilization* (New York: Simon and Schuster, 1957), p. 637.

[48] Frederick L. Allen, "The Big Change in Suburbia," *Harper's Magazine*, 208 (June, 1954), 26.

[49] Jerome G. Manis and Leo C. Stine, "Suburban Residence and Political Behavior," *Public Opinion Quarterly*, 22 (Winter, 1958), 483–489.

leaving a home in the central city for an outlying ranch house is likely to remain a nonjoiner just as the migrating Democrat is unlikely to become a Republican.

Myth and Reality

Some observers argue that the low rate of electoral and other formal participation in suburban government is due less to lack of interest than to satisfaction. The average suburbanite, they say, is content with the way his community is being run. He feels, moreover, that access to the governmental structure is open to him at any time he may desire to reach into its official portals. Whether Jones or Smith is mayor makes little difference to him since neither is likely to act contrary to prevailing community norms or disturb the existing order in any substantial way.

Certainly suburbia provides a large body of elected officials—far more per citizen than the central city—who are accessible to the people and ready to listen to their grievances. How meaningful this accessibility may be is another question. The data on local power structures cast doubt on the proposition that the suburban community is an open and free political system. Control of the governmental machinery generally rests in the hands of a small minority. In some cases this may be the local merchants; in others the social notables or prominent citizens who seek assurances that the community will remain a preserve for the privileged; and in still others it may be simply a group that gets psychic enjoyment from the exercise of political power, small-scale as it may be. This concentration of formal power, however, by no means implies that it can be used as its holders desire. Whatever the controlling clique in the local political system, its members are conscious of the fact that they or their surrogates can best retain the trappings of power by offending no group and by disturbing the status quo as little as possible.

Thus, in a negative sense, it is probably true that the exercise of political power in the small suburban community is highly responsive to the citizenry. But this responsiveness is more attuned to the objector than the proposer. The suburban citizen may exercise a more effective veto over governmental action than the central city dweller; but by the same token he is less likely to be successful in pushing for changes or new programs that meet with objections from even a very small minority.

Studies of suburban council meetings emphasize the role of the citizen as objector. The sturdy villagers who appear at the town hall come, with few exceptions, as protestors. Shaken out of their lethargy by a proposed zoning change in the vicinity of their homes, a notice of assessment for costly street improvements, or the erection of an unsightly fence by one of their neighbors, they will descend on the miniature citadel of government with righteous indignation. Only the rare individual goes to learn more about the operations and goals of his local polity or to propose new policies and programs.

It is hardly surprising that reality contradicts the image of the suburban community as a modern Athens where the citizen body is actively engaged in the vital process of self-government. What, after all, is there to stimulate a high level of political participation in such a setting? The majority of suburban municipalities are essentially homogeneous in social composition and have few divisive issues to arouse their residents. Governmental policy-making is confined largely to routine matters of administration and the provision of noncontroversial services. Even competition for public office is usually low, probably because the stakes and potential rewards are not high. (The St. Louis area study found that the smaller the suburb, the less the competition for office.) Suburban man may be well satisfied with his government and believe it closer to him, but he shows no greater civic activity than his core city counterpart. The irony is that few rule in suburbia but many believe they could.

THE "ALIENATED" URBANITE

Despite unprecedented affluence, sizable pockets of discontent exist within American society. For some, this discontent is manifested in what social scientists refer to as "alienation"—a feeling of powerlessness, life dissatisfaction, a rejection of the prevailing distribution of influence within the community. Alienation occurs disproportionately among manual workers, individuals with little formal education, older age groups, and Negroes. It generally results in two forms of civic behavior, withdrawal and protest. Within the lower socioeconomic classes, alienated individuals tend to be apathetic, to refrain from political participation, and to retreat into the little world of their own immediate and personal problems. Among those higher on the social scale, alienation often leads to acute displeasure at being powerless (as they perceive their condition) and to a distrust of persons in positions of influence. When such is the case, political alienation is likely to be translated into a vote of resentment or protest against the "powers that be."[50]

The local political system provides "alienated activists" with an arena for expressing their dissatisfaction. They find little such opportunity in

[50] Wayne E. Thompson and John E. Horton, "Political Alienation as a Force in Political Action," Social Forces, 38 (March, 1960), 190–195; John E. Horton and Wayne E. Thompson, "Powerlessness and Political Negativism: A Study of Defeated Local Referendums," American Journal of Sociology, LXVII (March, 1962), 485–493. See also Murray B. Levin, The Alienated Voter (New York: Holt, Rinehart and Winston, 1960).

national politics since both major parties must accommodate many points of view to secure a winning coalition. Only an extremist, such as George Wallace, appeals to them since his attacks against "the preachers, professors, judges, and newspaper editors" give expression to the resentment they feel against the established institutions. But since the opportunities to vote for a Wallace are not frequent, alienated individuals tend to participate more in local referenda where they feel they can more effectively and directly register their protest than in national elections.[51] Such issues as fluoridation, charter amendments, and school bond elections, in particular, tend to attract an exceptionally large number of individuals predisposed to cast a negative ballot. This phenomenon is also relevant to the cause of metropolitan governmental reorganization. Interviews with a sample of suburban residents in the Nashville, Tennessee, area showed that political alienation was significantly related to an unfavorable attitude and negative vote on the issue of consolidating the city and county governments of that metropolis.[52] Voting against issues of this kind, in other words, is more than the rejection of the particular program; it is, in addition, an expression of general discontent on the part of the politically alienated.

An indifferent attitude toward local government is characteristic of a far broader portion of urban residents than those of low income or the socially estranged. There is, in fact, a tendency among many city dwellers to speak of their local government as if it were something separate and apart from them. It is a common experience to hear an individual refer to his municipal government as some ill-defined "it," "they," or "the city hall." When matters arise which bring him in direct contact with his local unit, he finds the whole process complicated and impersonal. He conceives of himself on one side and something called the city or the bureaucracy on the other. Those with this attitude are generally content to let local government go its way so long as it takes care of the community's normal housekeeping functions in fairly adequate fashion, avoids scandal, and keeps the tax rate within reasonable bounds.

Local government, moreover, means different things to different people. In the more extreme cases, those found most frequently among low-income ethnic and racial groups, the policeman and his night-stick symbolize city government. To the slum landlord trying to milk his property dry, the building and health inspectors are the bureaucracy. To the suburban mother and active PTA member, the local school district constitutes the government. However local government is regarded, seldom is interest in it as a basic community institution high.

[51] K. W. Eckhardt and G. Hendershot, "Transformation of Alienation into Public Opinion," *Sociological Quarterly*, 8 (Autumn, 1967), 459–467.

[52] Edward L. McDill and Jeanne C. Ridley, "Status, Anomia, Political Alienation and Political Participation," *American Journal of Sociology*, LXVIII (September, 1962), 205–213.

Bigness and specialization, two key attributes of metropolitan life, contribute to this general attitude. The first makes direct citizen participation in community affairs difficult. The simple fact of bigness engenders a feeling of personal helplessness in the presence of the leviathan. When a sample of Detroit citizens was asked, "Do you feel that there is anything you can do to improve the way the city is run?" one-half of the respondents said no. Only one in twelve believed that he could exert influence by means of personal criticism or by joining in group action. The authors of the study concluded that "great numbers of Detroit citizens feel helpless and indifferent about changing their city. They have few ideas how things can be made better and little understanding of how they personally can play a part."[53]

Equally important, the high degree of specialization of the metropolis focuses the attention and energies of the residents on their vocational responsibilities and interests to the almost total exclusion of the polity. Life in modern urban society becomes compartmentalized around one's business or work while an individual's leisure hours are devoted mainly to his primary relationship: family, relatives, and friends. Little time or inclination remains for more than occasional and haphazard involvement in civic affairs. Actually, the number of legitimate community concerns has now become so great that individual citizens cannot actively involve themselves with all of them even if they are so inclined.

THE METROPOLITAN NETWORK

Metropolitan residents are caught in the maelstrom of modern society with all its advantages and liabilities. Their reaction to this environment takes many forms: from social conformity to deviance, from aggressive behavior to submissiveness, from community involvement to withdrawal, from commitment to the system to estrangement. Within the borders of the metropolis, amorphous as they may be, individuals vie for the rewards that society has to offer. As businessmen, professionals, skilled craftsmen, or just common laborers, they daily pursue their social and economic objectives in a milieu too complex to understand and too large to conquer. In their role as community citizens these same individuals participate in a political system whose function is to maintain order, provide services, adjust conflicts among its members, and shape an environment conducive to the achievement of human goals.

Society, it is true, is structured in such a way that many of the crucial decisions relating to the local community are made miles away from it: in the halls of Congress, in the offices of federal agencies, in the

[53] Arthur Kornhauser, *Detroit as the People See It* (Detroit: Wayne State University Press, 1952), p. 176.

state highway commissions, at the headquarters of national associations, or in corporate board rooms in the skyscrapers of New York. Despite this movement of power to higher levels, the residual functions of the urban polity involve stakes of great significance to the local citizenry. Where a park is located, how land is zoned, what portion of community resources is allocated for educational purposes are but a few such activities. Of even more importance is the fact that the successful execution of many national policies and programs, whether pertaining to housing, racial discrimination, equality of opportunity, or crime reduction, largely depends upon the actions of local and area-wide governments.

From the standpoint of government and the distribution of political power, the metropolis can best be viewed part by part, subunit by subunit. At the center of the stage is the core city dominating the political scene even though its sphere of governmental control stops at its legal boundaries. In less conspicuous places are the satellite municipalities, nonschool special districts, and, in some states, townships or New England towns, each with its own retinue of court followers. Moving toward the front of the platform in some metropolitan areas is the county government, hoping to be tapped for the role of metropolitan majordomo. Scattered around the stage are the school districts, that of the central city occupying the most important spot. What distinguishes this drama from those of the past is the absence of a script and a director. The actors improvise their lines, establish working relations with each other, and jockey for more favorable positions. None of the participants is quite sure of the theme or objective of the play; they are certain only that the show must go on. Although rivals for attention, they are aware that no one of them is self-sufficient to keep the play moving. They are consequently willing to cooperate among themselves within limited spheres and to observe certain ground rules. Coalitions are formed, often aimed at the leading actor, bargaining is sporadic, understandings are reached. As crises arise, minimal accommodations in roles and positions are made to solve the immediate issue or problem and avert a more serious showdown.

This system of loose control and wide distribution of power is largely a function of the pluralism that characterizes American urban society. Every man may not be king in the metropolis but the numerous power clusters provide him with many opportunities to further his personal aims and protect his vested interests. Unfortunately not all people have the means or capabilities to take advantage of these opportunities so that some profit unduly while others suffer. The critical problem for the metropolitan community, in terms of a democratic system, is to find ways of enlarging participation and more equitably allocating power resources so that all sectors of the society can be fully represented in the public decision-making process.

7 /
THE
SERVICE
CHALLENGE

RIDING ABOUT NEW YORK CITY, THE VISITOR IS INEVITABLY STRUCK WITH AWE and wonder. He is amazed at the bigness, the congestion, the noise, the bustle of activity, the polyglot population. He sees subway and railroad stations packed with commuters, streets jammed with taxi-cabs, buses, trucks, and passenger cars, sidewalks crowded with shop-pers and tourists, and huge office buildings filled with workers. How, he may ask, is government able to manage the mammoth task of ser-vicing this vast complex? How is it able to maintain order, keep traffic moving, dispose of the waste, supply water, and perform the numerous other functions necessary to keep the city operating? As Wallace Sayre and Herbert Kaufman have pointed out in their study of the New York city government:

It takes two billion gallons of pure water a day, removal of four million tons of refuse, thousands of miles of sewers and huge sewage disposal plants, regulation and inspection of food and food handlers and processes, disease control to prevent epidemics, air pollution control to prevent the poisoning of the atmosphere, and a fire-fighting organization capable of handling every kind of blaze from small house fires to immense conflagrations in tenements, sky-scrapers, industrial structures, and the waterfront. The basic physical and biological requirements of urban life are either provided or guaranteed by government.[1]

The New York case is, of course, exceptional. No other American metropolis approaches it in population size, density, or economic importance. Yet the same general problem of providing basic public services is faced by local government in each of the nation's many SMSAs; only the scale is smaller and the degree of intensity less. Growth and change are no respecters of size; they confer their benefits and inflict their penalties on the small metropolises as well as on the giants. But whether in Sacramento, California, or Chicago, Illinois, the service problems which expansion engenders are not so much indicators of weakness in the governmental system as they are evidence of the dynamic forces that are reshaping the urban world.

LOCAL VERSUS AREA-WIDE FUNCTIONS

Before turning to several of the major service problems that confront metropolitan areas, it would be well to note a distinction that is commonly made when discussing governmental reorganization, that between local and area-wide functions. The first are assumed to be those which can be provided separately by the individual municipalities or other units with less than area-wide jurisdiction; the latter those which require administration on a metropolitan basis.[2] The area-wide approach is said to be necessary when the function is of such nature that it transcends individual municipal, and in some cases county, boundaries (such as the control of air and water pollution); or when it would be economically unfeasible for the local units to perform individually (such as the operation of a sewage treatment plant).

It is impossible to draw a clear line of distinction between the two categories, "local" and "area-wide." Most attempts to make the differen-

[1] *Governing New York City* (New York: Russell Sage Foundation, 1960), p. 34.

[2] A report of the Advisory Commission on Intergovernmental Relations employs a threefold classification of urban functions: local, intermediate, and area-wide. The first includes those performed by units whose jurisdiction extends only to a portion of the metropolitan area, such as municipalities, townships, school districts, and small special districts. The second are those administered by a single unit, or a number of local units acting jointly, and having jurisdiction over a substantial part of the area. The third are those performed throughout a metropolitan area by a single unit or a number of local units acting cooperatively. (*Performance of Urban Functions: Local and Areawide,* Washington: 1963, p. 34).

tiation are based more on impression than objective criteria. Virtually all functions performed by the various governments of a metropolis have some impact on the larger area. Poor police protection in one municipality may be detrimental to the neighboring units. Or an inadequate building code in one city or village may adversely affect property values in surrounding areas. Even if we assume that these traditional local functions are performed reasonably well by the individual units, the classification still presents difficulties. Police protection, for example, can normally be handled locally if the municipality is large enough to support a professional department. Yet certain aspects of this function, such as communications, training, central records, and laboratory facilities can often be provided more efficiently and economically on an area-wide basis.

In the case of urban functions of this latter character, how is one to determine the level to which they should be allocated? Should the function itself be divided and appropriate portions assigned to both the local and area-wide units? Or should responsibility for the total function be vested in one or the other level, depending on which aspects—local or area-wide—are predominant? No systematic attempt has been made to resolve these questions either theoretically or empirically. Local government proponents have generally resisted any division of individual functions, fearing that such action would open the door to eventual absorption of the total service by the higher echelon. Supporters of metropolitan reorganization, on the other hand, have preferred the transfer of whole functions, maintaining that confusion and inefficiency would result if portions of the same service were allocated to two different levels. However, in recent years their attitude has tended to shift to the point where many of them have come to accept the notion as feasible.

One of the few attempts to develop a set of standards for judging whether a function should be performed at the local or area-wide level was made by the Advisory Commission on Intergovernmental Relations in one of its many reports.[3] The Commission suggested seven criteria for making this determination:

1. The unit of government responsible for providing a particular service should have territorial jurisdiction large enough to minimize the spillover of benefits or social costs into other jurisdictions.

2. It should be large enough to permit realization of the economies of scale.

[3] A more theoretically oriented attempt to develop criteria for the areal division of governmental powers is contained in Arthur Maass (ed.), *Area and Power: A Theory of Local Government* (New York: Free Press, 1959). For a discussion of service allocation based on the criteria of economy of scale, people-government proximity, and administrative and welfare considerations, see Werner Z. Hirsch, "Local Versus Areawide Urban Government Services," *National Tax Journal*, XVII (December, 1964), 331–339.

3. It should have a geographic area of jurisdiction adequate for effective performance.

4. It should have the legal and administrative ability to perform the service.

5. It should be responsible for a sufficient number of functions so that it provides a forum for resolution of conflicting interests and is able to balance governmental needs and resources.

6. It should be so organized that the performance of its functions remains controllable by and accessible to its residents.

7. It should be able to maximize the conditions and opportunities for active citizen participation while still permitting adequate performance.[4]

We cite these criteria because they illustrate the difficulty of devising operational standards for making an areal distribution of functions. As is evident, the list is a mixture of economic, administrative, and political tests that are not altogether in harmony with each other. The political criteria in the sixth and seventh categories, for example, may run counter to the economic standards in the second and third specifications. The latter may call for a governmental unit of such large size that citizen control and accessibility would be limited and participation discouraged. To arrive at allocational decisions, moreover, each of the factors would have to be weighted since all are not of equal value. But on what basis is the relative importance of each to be determined? It is easy to say that an accommodation must be made between the traditional values commonly associated with local government and the realities of modern urban society; but again, how is such a balance to be struck? A list of criteria, such as that developed by the Advisory Commission, serves a useful purpose in focusing attention on the most patent factors involved in the areal division of powers. It does not, however, provide a pat formula or a quantitative measuring device for making allocational determinations in concrete cases.

The Continuum from Local to Area-Wide Functions

The Advisory Commission, in the same report, used its set of criteria to rank fifteen urban functions on a scale from "most local" to "least local" (Table 17). The ranking is based more on impression than on measurable data and is, as the Commission admits, only a rough approximation of the possible order.

Many analysts of the metropolitan scene would undoubtedly disagree with the ranking of particular functions. To some, public education and libraries would be less local than, say, police or urban renewal, or health more area-wide than parks and recreation. Others would point out that the listing fails to take account of the various aspects of individual functions and their differing degrees of "localism." Refuse

[4] *Performance of Urban Functions: Local and Areawide* (Washington: 1963), pp. 41–60.

collection, for example, is more local than its complementary element of disposal, and the operation of a sewage treatment plant is less local than the maintenance of the lateral sewer lines. What is of interest, here, however, is not the validity of the ranking but the approach which was employed. Instead of starting with the assumption that administrative reorganization is needed and then documenting the problems to justify this conclusion, the Commission focused its attention on the optimum scale of operation for each of the major urban services without reference

TABLE 17   **Rank Order of Urban Functions from Most Local to Least Local**

	Rank	*Function*
Most local	1	Fire protection
	2	Public education
	3	Refuse collection and disposal
	4	Libraries
	5	Police
	6	Health
	7	Urban renewal
	8	Housing
	9	Parks and recreation
	10	Public welfare
	11	Hospitals and medical care facilities
	12	Transportation
Least local	13	Planning
	14	Water supply and sewage disposal
	15	Air pollution control

SOURCE: *Performance of Urban Functions: Local and Areawide*, pp. 9–23.

to governmental structure. By divorcing these two aspects for analytical purposes, such an approach is capable of providing greater insight into the kinds of governmental accommodations that are necessary to keep a metropolitan system functional.

These preliminary observations furnish the general framework and background for our examination of seven major urban services: transportation, water supply, sewage disposal, air pollution, fire protection, police, and parks and recreation. The first four rank high on the area-wide or "less local" end of the scale, the fifth is one of the "most local," and the last two are in the intermediate category. Although this list is by no means exhaustive, it is representative of the range and kind of governmental services that are provided in metropolitan areas. (Other functions including planning, housing, urban renewal, and several organizational aspects of public education are discussed in other chapters.)

TRANSPORTATION

April 1, 1898, marks a memorable occasion in the annals of urban life, for it was on that day that the first recorded sale of an automobile took place: a one-cylinder Winton. Fifteen years later, the age of the rubber-tired motor vehicle began in earnest with the advent of Henry Ford's mass-produced car. By 1920 nine million motor vehicles were registered in the United States; in 1967 the number exceeded ninety-seven million, almost twice as many as there were seventeen years earlier. Approximately 80 percent of all American families now own at least one car and 25 percent more than one (Figure 22). When the automobile was

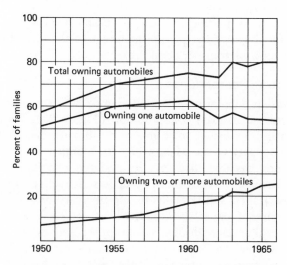

FIGURE 22   **Automobile Ownership, 1950–1966. From** Tomorrow's Transportation: New Systems for the Urban Future, **U.S. Department of Housing and Urban Development, 1968, p. 13.**

first introduced, the hard-surfaced roads in this country, if laid end to end, would not have stretched from New York to Boston. Today, there are 2.8 million miles of such facilities, enough to circle the earth at the equator more than 100 times.

It is sometimes said that the automobile is the cause of most metropolitan problems. Critics charge that it has precipitated urban sprawl, rendered the central city obsolete, destroyed the beauty of the community by generating unsightly expressways, polluted the air with gas fumes, and led to mass congestion. Few would deny the element of truth in these charges. Relying upon the automobile to satisfy most of the travel needs in the metropolis has led to serious consequences. Yet consider the other side of the coin. The transportation of people and goods is basic to the life of the modern urban community, and the motor vehicle has provided a dynamic instrument for fulfilling this need. It has also given man greater freedom of choice in his place of residence and greater mobility to pursue his cultural and recreational goals.

Consider also the role of the motor vehicle in the American economy. Automobile retail sales, including vehicles, accessories, parts, repairs, and gasoline, total more than $67 billion each year, $13 billion in motor vehicle taxes are collected annually, and one of every seven wage earners is employed in some phase of the automotive and transportation industries.[5] The enemy is not the automobile; it is the long-prevalent policy of putting our transportation eggs in one basket by developing facilities for the private motorcar to the virtual exclusion of every other form of transportation.

Trends in Urban Transportation

The increasing popularity of the automobile has been accompanied by a steady decrease in mass transportation (Figure 23). Since 1940, the transit industry, exclusive of commuter railroads, has lost almost 4 billion revenue passengers. Meanwhile, the number of routes of commuter railroads has dwindled greatly, and the remaining service generally has become less frequent and less attractive. Profits of the industry have fallen substantially in recent years despite upward adjustment of fares, financial institutions have shown little inclination to invest new capital in a declining enterprise, and many private lines have either stopped operations or been taken over by public agencies. The cycle has been vicious since lower patronage has led to fare increases and service cutbacks, which in turn have contributed further to rider losses.

Practically all metropolitan areas in the United States, large as well as small, depend wholly on their street systems to accommodate the movement of people. (Only New York, Boston, Chicago, Cleveland and Philadelphia have rapid transit systems utilizing rails. The San Francisco-Oakland area is now building such a system amid persistent and serious financing problems.) Since the street patterns in the older cities were laid out before the automobile age, they are wholly inadequate to meet the demands of modern traffic. Even the "post-auto" communities such as Los Angeles designed their circulation systems apparently

[5] These statistics are from *Automobile Facts and Figures* (Detroit: Automobile Manufacturers Association, 1968).

oblivious to the flood of automobiles that was soon to inundate them.

Since World War II most metropolitan areas have made frantic efforts to enlarge their street and road capacity. In the mad scramble, freeway building became the popular response to congestion. The Los Angeles area alone has more than 500 miles of such facilities, and the story, in lesser degree, has been repeated all over the nation. The free-

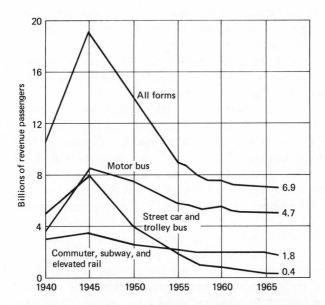

FIGURE 23   **Trends in Revenue Passengers of Urban Public Transportation. From** Tomorrow's Transportation: New Systems for the Urban Future, **U.S. Department of Housing and Urban Development, 1968, p. 10.**

way boom received a boost from the Federal Aid Highway Act of 1956 which provides for the financing of a 41,000-mile interstate network. Presently about two-thirds completed, this total includes 5500 miles of urban expressways that will skirt or penetrate virtually all cities over 50,000 population. With the national government bearing 90 percent of the cost of such roads, there has been little incentive for urban areas to seek alternative solutions to their transportation ills.

A Balanced System

Traffic experts have long pleaded for the development of a balanced transportation system in which mass transit takes its place alongside the private automobile. They point out that it is wholly unrealistic to build costly new expressways but neglect the needs of public transportation. Every additional motor vehicle which appears on the streets during the peak hour traffic periods in the morning and evening requires an increase in the load-carrying capacity of the network as well as additional road maintenance, parking space, and policing. Experience has also demonstrated that new expressways fill to the point of saturation almost from the day they are opened. This outcome is ironic since in creating easier and more rapid driving conditions, the new roads encourage greater use of private vehicles in the work-home trip and thereby further aggravate the congestion problem.

At the present time, the automobile is the primary means of conveyance in urban areas, with no formidable competitor in sight. Only about one-tenth of the nation's labor force travel to their place of employment by public transportation. The battle against the ensuing congestion has been fought chiefly by building more and larger roads and converting more of the community's land area to off-street parking facilities. This strategy, however, has been self-defeating since it has ignored the plight of mass transit. Congestion simply will not be conquered by the cement mixer and the paving roller; it will be eased only by diverting a substantial number of commuters from private automobiles to public conveyance.

Motorists will not be lured away from their self-powered vehicles by advertising campaigns. Unless public transit is upgraded to the point where it can compete with the private automobile in terms of speed and convenience, present trends will not be reversed. This revitalization, as traffic analysts emphasize, cannot take place without decisive public action. Congestion will not improve until urban communities and higher levels of government see fit to devote a far greater share of their energy and resources to the development of mass transportation facilities than they do at the present time. The general resistance of the citizen body to any "subsidization" of public transit has severely handicapped efforts in this direction. Voters have been willing to support huge expenditures for road and freeway construction, but at the same time they have usually insisted that public transit be self-supporting. In doing so they have disregarded the fact that urban transporation—both public and private—is conceptually a single function that, like education, includes large indirect social benefits as well as direct individual benefits.

Recent Developments

The demonstrated inability of local government to deal adequately with the transportation problem is causing the initiative to shift to higher echelons of public authority, particularly to the national level. State governments thus far have done little to assist their metropolitan areas in achieving a balanced system for moving people and goods. It is still the definite exception for states to make certain tax sources or other funds available for improvements in mass transit, such as was done in 1967 by Minnesota with a motor vehicle tax in the Twin Cities area and by New York State with a large bond issue, devoted in part to public transportation. In general, when states take cognizance of the need to bolster mass transportation, they are unwilling to discard the requirement of self-support. The action in 1963 of the Pennsylvania legislature in creating a metropolitan transportation authority to operate an integrated mass transit system for Philadelphia and four nearby counties is typical of this reluctance. No taxing power was granted to the authority and its revenues were restricted to fares and to funds contributed by the participating governments. The policy of barring such transit agencies from tax sources prevents them from making the large-scale capital investment in facilities and equipment that is required if public transportation is to be placed on a competitive basis with the private automobile.

As in the case of housing, urban renewal, and planning, which are discussed in Chapters 8 and 9, the national government is stepping into the breach.[6] In 1961, Congress provided funds for demonstration projects to determine the effects of fare reductions, service improvements, and new equipment on public transportation. Three years later came the passage of the Urban Mass Transportation Act authorizing grants on a matching basis to aid urban areas in financing improved mass transit. The legislation was renewed in 1966, when the Department of Transportation also was established. (However, the administration of federal mass transit programs was not transferred to this new department from the Department of Housing and Urban Development until 1968.) Although so far the total amount of money channeled into federal financial assistance to mass transit has been quite small, these actions serve as official recognition of the crucial role of public transit and the need for governmental aid in this field.

Federal transportation demonstration grants, first made available in 1961 and continued under the later transit legislation, have had considerable effect in various localities. Two of the best known and most successful are the Skokie Swift rail transit project in the Chicago area and the Minibus in Washington, D.C., both of which have apparently become permanent. The former, which was organized by the heavily populated village of Skokie and the Chicago Transit Authority, utilizes a five-mile stretch of abandoned right of way of a discontinued commuter line to pro-

[6] The growing federal involvement in transportation is recounted in detail in George M. Smerk, *Urban Transportation: The Federal Role* (Bloomington: Indiana University Press, 1965) and in his article, "Federal Urban Transport Policy: Here— and Where Do We Go from Here?" *Traffic Quarterly*, XXI (January, 1967), 29–51.

vide a nonstop shuttle service at a scheduled speed of forty-six miles an hour. The response surprised even the most optimistic. The number of riders on opening day was about 4000, more than twice the maximum carried earlier by a railroad company on a less frequent but through service between Chicago and Milwaukee. The current total is about double that of the first day of the Skokie Swift, and trains run at five-minute intervals during peak hours. The Washington Minibus, which is a small vehicle that accommodates eighteen seated passengers and twelve standees, gained immediate popularity because it furnished an easy and economical (presently a ten-cent fare) means of getting around in the widely spread-out downtown area of the nation's capital. Expected to serve 900,000 passengers in the initial twelve months, the patronage was double the planned estimates.

In the Boston area a mass transportation demonstration project led to state action. The legislature created the Massachusetts Bay Transportation Authority to handle mass transit in Boston and seventy-seven neighboring cities and towns and vested it with power to assess the participating communities to make up any operating deficits. It also authorized a $225 million revenue bond issue and a two-cent increase in the state cigarette tax for the support of the new agency. And in a number of centers, including Los Angeles, Nashville, and New York, projects have sought the improvement of transportation service in areas containing many unemployed, poor, or aged persons.

A provision of the amendments of 1966 to the Urban Mass Transportation Act called for the preparation of a program of research, development, and demonstration of new systems of urban transportation. The resulting study identified various problems common to heavily populated areas against which benefits from new systems could be measured:

1. Equality of access to urban opportunity. Present urban transportation tends to immobilize and isolate nondrivers: the poor, the old, the handicapped, the young, and secondary workers in one-car families. It is also a major obstacle for some in seeking and retaining jobs.

2. Quality of service. Public transit service too often is characterized by excessive walking distances to and from stations, poor connections and transfers, infrequent service, unreliability, slow speed and delays, crowding, noise, lack of comfort, and lack of information for the rider's use. Also passengers are too often exposed to dangers to personal safety while awaiting service.

3. Congestion. This condition results in daily loss of time to the traveler. Too often "solutions" are expensive in dollars and landtaking, destroying the environment in the process.

4. Efficient use of equipment and facilities. Increased efficiency and greater economy through better management and organizational techniques—including cost control, scheduling and routing, and experimenta-

tion in marketing and new routes—are needed to satisfy transportation requirements at minimum cost.

5. Efficient use of land. More rational land use made possible by new forms of transportation might help reduce travel demands, aid in substituting communications for transportation, and achieve greater total transportation services for the amounts of land required.

6. Pollution. Air, noise, and esthetic pollution from all current means of urban transportation is far too high, degrading unnecessarily the quality of the environment.

7. Urban development options. Transportation investments can be used creatively in the orderly development of urban complexes. Service should provide for choice in living styles, locations, and modes of transportation.

8. Institutional framework and implementation. An improved framework—legal, financial, governmental, and intergovernmental—is required to eliminate rigidities and anachronisms which prevent the adoption of new technologies and methods. This framework should assist metropolitan planning agencies and enhance interlocal cooperation in solving joint transportation problems.[7]

The study recommended many immediate improvements, some of which are presented here. For buses, it suggested exclusive lanes and metered traffic flow control on freeways, computer-assisted scheduling, and vehicles with propulsion systems other than gasoline or diesel engines. For rail transit, it advocated automatic train identification and monitoring for route allocation, automatic coupling and detaching of cars, and better noise control through improved equipment maintenance and carefully determined acoustical treatment techniques. For automobiles, it supported a rental service of small, low-powered vehicles for short trips and traffic light controls that respond to traffic flow patterns.

According to the report, seven major types of new systems for the longer future could be expected to be technically and economically feasible and to contribute importantly to solving significant urban problems:

1. Dial-a-bus, to be activated on demand by telephone requests, after which a computer will log the calls, origins, destinations, location of its conveyances, and number of passengers, and select and dispatch the vehicles.

2. Personal rapid transit, to be composed of small vehicles, traveling over exclusive rights of way and automatically routed from origin to destination over a network guideway (roadbed) system.

3. Dual-mode vehicle system, to involve small cars which can be individually driven and converted from street travel to travel on automatic guideway networks.

[7] U.S. Department of Housing and Urban Development, *Tomorrow's Transportation: New Systems for the Urban Future* (Washington: 1968), pp. 6–7.

4. Automated dual-mode bus, to consist of a large vehicle system operating on public streets as conventional buses to pick up and unload passengers and functioning on longer high speed runs as fully automated conveyances.

5. Pallet system, to be made up of flatcars or platforms to ferry automobiles, minibuses, or freight automatically on high-speed guideways.

6. Fast intraurban-transit link system, to feature automatically controlled vehicles capable of operating separately or coupling into trains to serve metropolitan travel needs between major urban centers.

7. System for major activity centers (central business districts, large airports, universities, for instance), to include continuously moving sidewalks functioning at improved speeds and small automatically controlled capsules operating at low speeds on tracks above the street level and stopped when turned into a siding.[8]

Transportation Administration

Urban transportation by any meaningful criterion is an area-wide function. The network of roads and mass transit facilities in an urban complex cannot be divided up by local governmental jurisdictions. As origin and destination surveys show, a large portion of the trips that begin in one section of the metropolis terminate in another of its sections, passing through the boundaries of two or more localities in the process. To facilitate this movement, the entire urbanized area must be considered as the geographic base for coordinating the planning and operation of the transportation system.

Several approaches may be taken to the question of governmental jurisdiction in relation to the urban transportation function. The most extreme, and the one preferred by many experts, is an overall regional agency to plan and administer the total system. The Metropolitan St. Louis Survey in recommending an integrated system for that area put the case in this way:

The traffic and transportation problem in St. Louis City-St. Louis County must be attacked on an area-wide basis by correlating expressways, major arteries, feeders, bridges, and parking facilities with an efficient and rapid mass transportation system. This objective can be attained only if a single governmental authority is endowed with power over the planning, construction and maintenance of expressways, principal arteries and major off-street parking facilities, and with control over mass transit facilities.[9]

No such agency presently exists in the United States. A number of area-wide transit authorities have been created but their jurisdiction does not

[8] *Ibid.*, pp. 32–42, 58–77.
[9] *Path of Progress for Metropolitan St. Louis* (University City: 1957), p. 59.

extend to other segments of the transportation network. Since the efficient operation of public transportation is dependent upon many factors that lie outside the control of transit agencies, some means of coordination is essential. Roads, for example, must be designed to feed the rapid transit lines, local authorities must cooperate in facilitating the movement of buses by parking restrictions, lane reservations, and similar measures, and those responsible for land use policies must take into account their effects on the circulatory system.

At the opposite pole from the integrated approach is the now generally prevalent practice of carving up jurisdiction over the total transportation function among the many governments that make up the metropolis. The drawbacks to this method are obvious since the movement of people and goods occurs wholly without reference to the boundaries of these units. However, three developments are tending to neutralize some of the dis-integrative forces in the local governmental pattern. They are widespread acceptance of regional planning organizations, the requirements for continuing comprehensive transportation planning in metropolitan areas as a condition of federal highway aid, and the necessity for transit facilities to fit into officially coordinated transportation systems to qualify for federal assistance.[10] In an era of increased cooperation, transportation planning programs concerning both highways and transit and involving local, state, and national participation have been undertaken recently in most urban complexes. The highway aspects of the study recommendations have generally been at least partially executed through using normally available highway funds. The transit portions, however, have not usually gained implementation, due to the absence of a similar constant source of financing and to the frequent division of ownership.[11]

A middle course between integrated control of transportation and voluntary cooperation is based on the idea that individual functions can be divided and allocated to different levels of public authority. The most prominent example of this practice is found in the Toronto area where the metropolitan government has jurisdiction over the main highways and major arteries while the municipalities retain responsibility for local streets and roads. (On the other hand, mass transit is provided solely by an agency of the Toronto metropolitan government.) Recommendations embodying this concept of dividing functions have occasionally been advocated by metropolitan survey commissions in the United States, but they have met with little favorable response. To a limited degree, however, this arrangement exists in the present system. Generally, the states administer the main trunk highways in their urban areas, the counties in

[10] The existing and potential strengths of comprehensive transportation planning are considered in Norman Beckman, "Impact of the Transportation Planning Process," *Traffic Quarterly*, XX (April, 1966), 160–173.

[11] Automotive Safety Foundation, *Urban Transit Development in Twenty Major Cities* (Washington: 1968), p. 13.

some instances operate the expressways and secondary roads, and the municipalities control the remainder of the streets within their boundaries. The division is wholly inadequate and lacking in coordination, yet the practice furnishes precedent and a possible basis for strengthening the transportation network.

WATER SUPPLY

Urban areas require water for a variety of purposes including human consumption, waste disposal, manufacturing, and recreation. As in the case of our other natural resources, the amount of water consumed has risen steadily. Part of the increase is due to population growth but a substantial portion is attributable to the rise in per capita use, the result of improved living standards that have made such appliances as automatic dishwashers, washing machines, and air conditioners common household items. The concentration of industry in metropolitan areas has also caused urban water needs to soar. Industrial requirements are enormous; the manufacture of a ton of paper, for example, takes 25,000 gallons of water, and that of a ton of rayon fiber 200,000 gallons. In all, the nation's average daily consumption exceeds 300 billion gallons.

The problem is less one of overall shortage than lack of facilities for transporting usable water from where it is to where it is needed. According to reliable estimates, the United States as a whole has ample water to meet its foreseeable needs, but this supply is not uniformly distributed and in some cases it is of poor quality. This latter characteristic is a cause of major concern in the eastern cities where water is fairly abundant. There, intense urban and industrial concentration has caused severe pollution of the rivers and lakes and magnified the task of providing pure water. In the western states where rainfall is substantially below the national average, the problem is one of quantity. Many communities must rely on distant sources for their needed supply. San Francisco's reservoirs are located as far as 150 miles from the city, and Los Angeles and San Diego will be drawing some of their water from as far away as 550 miles upon completion of the Feather River Project, which was underwritten by a huge state bond issue.

Water Administration

The pattern of providing water in metropolitan areas is extremely diversified. In the Sacramento SMSA, for example, there is a large number of both public and private agencies engaged in this task; in the Minneapolis-St. Paul complex, municipal ownership is dominant and there are many separate water systems. In Chicago the central city plant supplies water on contract to approximately 60 suburban communities, a practice followed by other large cities such as Detroit, Cleveland, New York, and San Francisco. Special districts provide another type of water supplier. The *1967 Census of Governments* lists 964 such agencies operating in metropolitan areas. The largest is the Metropolitan Water District of Southern California which serves communities, including Los Angeles and San Diego, in five metropolises.

Most central cities in the metropolis are served by their municipally-owned and operated water systems. Outside the West, supply has seldom been a problem for them since the majority are located on rivers or lakes that provide ready quantities of surface water. The metropolitan suburbs, on the other hand, have been in a less fortunate position. For many of them supply has been a real problem, aggravated by rapid expansion and lack of access to surface water. Individual household wells, the initial source of supply, have long since proved inadequate in all but the yet undeveloped peripheral sections. As experience has shown, to the dismay of many a suburbanite, water tables usually drop and artesian wells become subject to contamination by septic tank seepage as the area is built up. When this happens, the outlying communities are left with two choices: secure their water from the central city plant or establish their own facilities by sinking deep wells to tap underground sources.

Some core cities have offered their suburbs the more drastic alternative of annexation. Both Milwaukee and Los Angeles at one time used water as a weapon to press annexation on fringe areas that did not have the resources to develop their own systems. The more common practice, however, is for the central city to furnish water to its suburbs on a contractual basis. Arrangements for accomplishing this vary widely. In a majority of cases the city sells water wholesale to the neighboring municipalities or water districts and these in turn handle the distribution to the consumers. In other instances, the city provides direct extensions of service to the individual users. Often both methods are employed, as in Seattle where a small proportion of the city's suburban customers are served directly and the remainder through the distribution systems of many water districts and municipalities.

None of these methods has been considered satisfactory by those seeking metropolitan reorganization. As a Senate Committee has pointed out, a serious problem affecting the provision of water in urban areas "stems from difficulties in the field of political structure or organization."[12] Because of these difficulties, most metropolitan studies have tended to favor a unified system for the entire area. The advantages claimed for such a solution include (1) economies of scale, (2) elimination of disputes over water among local units, (3) comprehensive planning for the total sys-

[12] *Water Resource Activities in the United States: Future Water Requirements for Municipal Use* (Washington: 1960), p. 19.

tem, (4) orderly extension of facilities, and (5) more effective conservation of water resources.

Logically, there is no more compulsion for consolidating water administration than for integrating control over other functions such as transportation. The major question is not whether there should be a single supplier; it is whether some institutional means should be established to assure the coordinated planning and development of the overall system and to see that the water needs of all sections of the metropolis receive proper consideration. As one authority has commented:

A plan for a regional system does not necessarily mean that a region has to have a single integrated regional facility. It merely means that all of the alternatives for supplying water or disposing of it have been studied, and that combination adopted which is best suited to the topography and geography of the region, and will most efficiently and economically provide the required service with the least interruption or damage to people, property and resources. The selected combination might very well include several sources of water, several points of waste disposal and several separate systems and operating agencies.[13]

The function of water supply in the metropolis readily lends itself to a division of responsibility. Even if a single regional agency were established, local units could still retain the task of distributing the water to the consumers. The same arrangements could be employed if the central city were the sole supplier. When this latter practice is followed, many objections would be eliminated if the city were compelled to operate as a utility subject to the regulatory powers of the state public service commission. In this way suburban customers would be protected against arbitrary rates or practices by the city, while the latter would have the monopoly rights of a utility and be assured of a reasonable return on its investment.

As a final observation, it should be noted that the problem of water supply often extends beyond the boundaries of individual metropolitan areas. Southern California's struggle with Arizona interests over the use of Colorado River water is one example of the territorial extent of the problem. Chicago's attempt to utilize additional water from Lake Michigan for sewage disposal purposes, an attempt opposed by five Great Lakes states and Canada, is another. Water supply, in other words, is a national—and in a few instances an international—problem. It involves all levels of government and its proper administration requires that local units relate and integrate their water policies and programs with state and national agencies as well as among themselves.

[13] Melvin E. Scheidt, "Water Management Problems in Urban Areas," Paper presented at Residence Course on Urban Planning for Environmental Health, U. S. Public Health Service, Cincinnati (April 3, 1962), pp. 7–8.

SEWAGE DISPOSAL

"Fifty million Americans drink water that does not meet Public Health Service standards," warned a recent task force to the Secretary of Health, Education, and Welfare.[14] These remarks point to the close relationship between the supply of water and the disposal of sewage. No matter how large a quantity of water may be available to a community, inadequate waste disposal can seriously limit its use and affect its quality.

In the past, urban areas devoted considerable effort to supplying their residents and industries with water but paid much less attention to the task of getting rid of the waste. Until well into the present century, it was common practice for cities to dump their sewage untreated into the watercourses that conveniently flowed by their doorsteps and from which they drew their needed water. In fact, as late as 1950 every major city on the Missouri was discharging raw sewage into the river.

The growing pollution of the nation's watercourses prompted the national government to intervene actively in the field after World War II. In 1948, Congress passed the first comprehensive federal legislation on the subject. The measure was designed principally to stimulate state action in establishing effective enforcement programs. When the state follow-up proved disappointing, Congress enacted the Water Pollution Control Act of 1956. As later amended, this measure gives the national government the power to deal with the pollution of all navigable waters in the United States. It authorizes the Secretary of the Interior to call conferences of affected parties in areas where serious pollution problems exist and to initiate court action when satisfactory solutions cannot be worked out. The cooperative approach, although time-consuming, has been successful in eliminating some of the worst sources of pollution; only occasionally has court action been necessary.

Also in 1956, the national government began to make grants to aid in the construction of local sewage treatment facilities. Persistent urban population growth and the obsolescence of an increasing number of existing plants made it difficult for this construction program to make noticeable overall progress at the initial level of grant support. Indeed, in reporting in 1965, a Congressional committee emphasized, ". . . the present backlog of needed facilities remains about the same as it was at the beginning of the program."[15] In the same year a survey by the Conference of State Sanitary Engineers revealed that in excess of 5000 communities with a total population of 33 million needed new, enlarged, or

[14] U.S. Department of Health, Education, and Welfare, Task Force on Environmental Health and Related Problems, *A Strategy for a Livable Environment* (Washington: 1967), p. 13.

[15] U.S. House of Representatives, Committee on Government Operations, *Disposal of Municipal Sewage* (Washington: 1965), p. 2.

improved sewage treatment facilities and another 2500 localities containing 5 million people had no treatment systems despite a need for them.[16] Congress later substantially raised the amount of its financial assistance in an effort to make major inroads into this troublesome and always potentially dangerous problem.

Sewage Disposal Administration

The administrative pattern for the function of waste disposal varies widely. At least five different types of arrangements are in effect in metropolitan areas: (1) municipal operation of both collection and treatment facilities: (2) administration of the total sewerage system in all or most of an urban area by a special district government; (3) operation by a series of special districts, often in combination with municipal systems; (4) various contractual combinations; and (5) municipal operation of the local collection systems and special district management of the disposal facilities.

A majority of central cities fall into the first category, operating all aspects of the sewerage function. Some of the older and larger suburbs likewise maintain their own systems, but most of the smaller suburban communities do not possess adequate resources to warrant construction of treatment plants. Moreover, those that are not located on watercourses have no economical way of discharging their effluent even if they have the financial means to build disposal facilities. The second method, integrated administration for the total metropolis, has not been fully achieved in any major SMSA. In the St. Louis area, for example, a metropolitan sewer district operates all sewerage facilities in the central city and in most of the urbanized portion of St. Louis County, but the remainder of the area is served by a variety of systems. The third approach, a profusion of special sanitary districts, is becoming less popular as costs mount and the disadvantages of maintaining many separate systems become more apparent. The fourth approach, contractual arrangements, is employed with reasonable success in some metropolitan areas such as Detroit where the central city handles sewage from approximately forty suburban communities.

The last arrangement, that of splitting responsibility between local units and a regional agency, has received increasing attention in recent years. Some metropolises, such as Milwaukee with its Metropolitan Sewerage Commission and Chicago with its Metropolitan Sanitary District of Greater Chicago, have long employed this device. Others, such as Seattle, are relative newcomers to the practice. With increasing emphasis by federal and state authorities on pollution control, many suburban communities and even some central cities find themselves faced with the need

[16] Federal Water Pollution Control Administration, *Building for Clean Waters, 1965* (Washington: 1966), p. 9.

for large investments in treatment facilities. Where this is the case, local units are generally more receptive to proposals involving the transfer of responsibility to an overall agency.

The ideal solution to the problem, as many reform advocates suggest, might well be a metropolitan district with jurisdiction over both water supply and waste disposal. Such an agency would be in a position to plan for the coordinated development and expansion of these two highly interrelated functions. However, there is little indication of any serious movement in this direction at the present time. What appears to be evolving in sewage disposal administration is more in the nature of a threefold allocation of responsibilities with (1) the municipal level handling the construction and operation of local sewage collection facilities, (2) the metropolitan level furnishing the major interceptor sewers and the treatment plants, and (3) the state and national governments providing the policy framework for water resource management and stimulating the lower levels to action by minimum water purity standards and financial assistance. Federal intervention in this field has been welcomed by lower governments since national enforcement action can remove incentives for industries to penalize states and local areas that adopt strong water pollution control programs by moving their operations elsewhere. It can also remove some of the political costs to local officials when they support increased expenditures for facilities to correct pollution problems.

AIR POLLUTION

Not only the purity of water but also the purity of air is becoming a matter of increasing metropolitan concern. According to the U. S. Public Health Service, more than 104 million people live in communities troubled by polluted air. The plight of Metropolitan Los Angeles, penned between the mountains and the ocean, is a well-publicized fact, but a number of other large population centers are about as severely affected. A study by the National Center for Air Pollution Control in 1967 determined that the New York, Chicago, and Philadelphia areas had higher pollution levels and eight others, all in the East and Midwest, had levels not significantly lower than that of Los Angeles.[17]

Contamination of the air is one of the prices of an industrialized and motorized civilization. It is estimated that motor vehicles alone daily emit into the air more than one-half million pounds of carbon monoxide, sixty-six million pounds of hydrocarbon, and eight million pounds of nitrogen oxide. There would be little problem if the pollutants were dispersed evenly throughout the atmosphere, but they are concentrated primarily

[17] John T. Middleton, "Air Pollution in 65 Metropolitan Areas," *Nation's Cities,* 5 (August, 1967), 8–11.

in the metropolises that produce them. The physical damages from such contamination—to horticulture, paint on homes, fabrics, and other commodities—are as high as $11 billion annually according to some sources. More important is the possible damage to health. Medical scientists feel that polluted air can aggravate heart conditions and respiratory diseases such as asthma, chronic bronchitis, and lung cancer (Figure 24). About two decades ago, the air pollution problem was regarded as a soiling nuisance composed of smoke. Today, the problem involves a host of gaseous and particle pollutants that are difficult to disperse, and it represents an omnipresent threat to human welfare.

It has been said that there is nothing small about the air pollution problem in the United States except efforts to solve it. The validity of the statement has been lessening in recent years, although the rate of progress still does not equal the magnitude of the difficulty and the per-capita financial support for state, regional, and local efforts remains far below the generally accepted minimum. Between 1961 and 1966, the number of states with air pollution programs more than doubled, to a total of forty, but only nine of these states exercised regulatory powers. Moreover, the general emphasis at this level continued to be on technical assistance to and encouragement of local and regional programs, which increased by more than 50 percent in this same period.[18]

The national government first entered the field in 1955 when Congress authorized the Public Health Service to conduct research and provide technical aid to state and local units. In 1963, Congress approved the Clean Air Act which greatly enlarged the role of federal authorities in pollution control.[19] The measure directed the Department of Health, Education, and Welfare to (1) initiate an expanded national program of research and training on the causes, effects, and prevention of air pollution, (2) award grants-in-aid to state, regional, and local agencies for beginning or broadening action programs, and (3) engage directly in abatement and enforcement activities when the health or welfare of citizens in one state is found to be endangered by air pollution emanating from another state.

Further major action at the national level materialized in 1967 with the passage of the Air Quality Act, which enlarged the basic legislation of four years earlier. The new law authorizes grants to air pollution control agencies for the planning of their programs, expands research support for new and improved methods to prevent and control pollution

[18] U.S. Department of Health, Education, and Welfare, Public Health Service, *Today and Tomorrow in Air Pollution* (Washington: 1967), p. 23; U.S. Department of Health, Education, and Welfare, Public Health Service, *State and Local Programs in Air Pollution Control* (Washington: 1966), pp. 5–7.

[19] An analysis of this legislation is contained in U.S. Department of Health, Education, and Welfare, Public Health Service, *The Federal Air Pollution Program* (Washington: 1967), pp. 7–46.

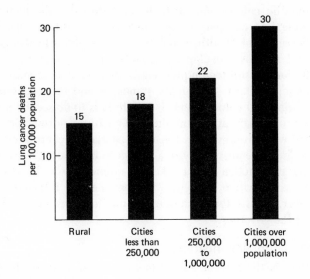

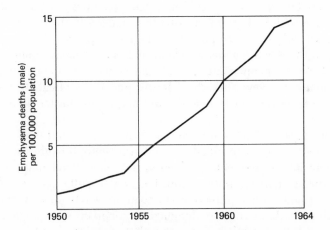

FIGURE 24   **Bigger Cities, More Air Pollution, More Deaths.
From** A Strategy for a Livable Environment,
**U.S. Department of Health, Education, and
Welfare, Task Force on Environmental Health
and Related Problems, 1967.**

resulting from the combustion of fuels, and provides for financial assistance to interstate air quality commissions. In addition, this law instructs the Secretary of Health, Education, and Welfare to designate air quality control regions, develop air quality criteria, and issue recommended pollution control techniques. Each affected state is subsequently expected to adopt suitable air quality standards and an acceptable plan of implementation and enforcement. If a state fails to do so, the Secretary is empowered to prepare and promulgate regulations setting forth standards consistent with his previously released criteria and control techniques. Whenever he finds the air quality in a region to be below the established standards and state action is not taken to enforce them, he may go to court on his own initiative to secure the abatement of interstate air pollution. However, in intrastate situations, he may use the courts only upon the request of the governor.

Air Pollution Control Administration

More so than in the case of other functions, local units are helpless to protect themselves against the failure of their neighbors to control air pollution. It is surprising therefore that until recently so few area-wide agencies were created or designated to administer abatement programs. These agencies, which increased appreciably in number for the first time in the 1960s, take one of several forms. One type, in use in Milwaukee, for instance, is established by transferring the function to the county government. A second is a metropolitan or regional special district, such as operates in the San Francisco-Oakland and Boston areas, among others. A third form is an interstate commission, a mechanism first employed collaboratively by New York, New Jersey, and Connecticut. In many instances, however, city governments continue to administer air pollution programs.

The inadequacy of many state and local programs—and their complete absence in a number of troubled areas—has recently brought the national government into a prominent position in this field. Paralleling the nature of its growing activity in the control of water pollution, the national government now directly intervenes to abate interstate air contamination, but much of its total effort is designed to stimulate state, regional, and local agencies to strengthen their controls and enforcement.

FIRE PROTECTION

Fire protection is an essential function of urban government. An adequately manned and equipped department not only minimizes the loss of life and property from fire hazards but it also substantially reduces insurance costs to the owners of homes, commercial establishments, and factories. The task of protecting a large city against fire is both quantitatively and qualitatively different from that in the small and predominantly residential suburb. Fighting conflagration in a densely settled community of tall office buildings, apartments, factories, and department stores is a highly complex responsibility. Specialized equipment and expertly trained personnel are absolute requirements. These needs are far less in the small suburban village where the houses are farther apart and the tall buildings few or nonexistent. Here, only a pumper or two and less skilled personnel, even volunteers, may be all that is needed to provide an acceptable level of protection.

Each year over 10,000 people perish in fires in the United States, and each year the nation suffers a loss of more than $1.5 billion worth of property from this source. In 1966, property loss from fires reached an all-time high of $1.8 billion. Any substantial reduction in these figures depends less on increasing the efficiency of fire-fighting agencies than on more effective fire prevention activities. It is in the latter that most communities have been deficient. Smaller departments, often staffed at least in part by volunteers, seldom have the qualified personnel to carry out the necessary inspections and to see that the fire code is properly enforced. Larger agencies are often precluded by budgetary limitations from hiring enough inspectors to do the kind of job they feel essential in prevention.

Fire Protection Administration

Of the major functions administered by local government, fire protection is one of the "most local." Spillover effects from the performance of this service are not geographically extensive. Residents in one community receive no direct benefits from the fire protection activities of neighboring municipalities other than those derived from mutual aid pacts or informal understandings of assistance in emergencies. Nor do they suffer any serious disabilities from the failure of adjacent jurisdictions to maintain an adequate level of protection as they do, for instance, in the case of water and air pollution. Although it is true that a fire in one city or village could spread into the surrounding area, the likelihood of this occurring is seldom strong enough to cause any significant expenditures for additional fire-fighting equipment or personnel on the part of other communities.

The pattern of fire protection administration is relatively simple— although varied. Most municipalities maintain their own departments, some with full-time professionals, others solely with volunteers, and still others with a combination of the two. A number of the smaller incorporated communities, and even some of medium size as in California, purchase their fire protection from other cities or the county government or are members of county-governed fire districts. The unincorporated areas are served in a variety of ways: by volunteer departments, special districts, and the county government, and by private companies on a subscription basis. Numerous mutual aid pacts are in existence among communities providing for each party to render assistance to the others upon call. For example, in Erie County, New York, which contains Buffalo, all the towns, cities, and villages participate in a countywide mutual aid fire protection system that is linked by a radio network.

Fire protection is not a critical organizational problem in metropolitan areas. Economies of scale could undoubtedly be realized by consolidation of the smaller departments, and more efficient services could be provided if the training of personnel was standardized and central communications systems created. But these and other deficiencies which now exist hardly call for a radical reorganization of the system, although at times proposals are made to form a metropolitan fire department (usually county-wide) or to merge the fire and police operations of a city into a public safety unit. It is likely that the future will bring greater emphasis on the establishment of minimum area-wide standards and their enforcement by county or state fire marshals. Cooperative efforts by local units to develop a coordinated system of protection will also continue. These measures should upgrade the present system sufficiently to serve at least the basic fire protection needs of the metropolitan community.

POLICE

Police administration, like that of fire protection, is a function related to the safety of the public and is therefore one of the key services provided by local government. The protection of lives and property against law violations is a complex and highly specialized task in a metropolitanized and industrialized society. Crime has become a social problem of front rank with the growth of urban concentrations, the multiplication of wealth, and the development of speedier automobiles and better roads that allow criminals to escape more easily across the boundaries of local jurisdictions. No one actually knows how much crime costs the nation each year, but estimates go as high as $15 billion, not to mention the loss in lives.

The police constitute the most visible public personnel in the community. Of all local agencies, the police department is the only one that has a continuous, around-the-clock presence in all parts of the governmental jurisdiction. Accordingly, its members have more frequent and direct contact with the citizenry than any other public employees. This presence is differently perceived by those they are presumed to serve. In some neighborhoods, their image is that of protectors of a civilized way of life; in others, particularly ghettos, their critics consider them essentially an occupation force.[20] Part of this divergence in attitudes has been precipitated by events of recent years. While seeking to deal with the rising crime rate and the increase in juvenile delinquency among all segments of the society, the police have also had to face civil disorders and community conflicts of serious proportions and deep social significance. In the process of coping with hundreds of riots, near-riots, and other major civil disturbances, they have evoked criticism from some people for alleged brutality, hostility, harassment, and insensitivity and from others for their inability to contain and bring mass violence and disruptions quickly under control.[21]

The police perform in two worlds. One is as the first agency of the criminal justice system where their responsibility is to initiate a criminal action against alleged lawbreakers. The other consists of all phases of police activity not related to apprehension and arrest: preventing crimes, abating nuisances, resolving disputes, controlling traffic, furnishing information, and providing various other miscellaneous services. Although the police spend most of their time in the second of these two worlds, they are geared primarily to work in the first. This is evident in all aspects of their operations, but most importantly in the value system and narrow orientation they bring to the noncriminal matters that make up their second world. However, if the police are to reduce the hostility of various citizens, particularly among minorities, it is mandatory for them to give far more attention to their activity outside of the criminal process, as some agencies have been doing lately.[22]

Spurred by recommendations of the President's Commission on Law Enforcement and Administration of Justice and the availability of federal funds, the number of police departments with police-community relations programs has been gradually increasing. The most frequent kind of program involves working, often through a departmental community relations unit, with citizen groups, chiefly in minority neighborhoods—sending speakers, participating in their sessions, and listening to their grievances.[23] So far the results of this kind of activity have been disappointing, partly because changes in attitude are only achievable over time. There are other important reasons, too, for the general lack of suc-

[20] Many civil rights in relation to the police are discussed in Sidney H. Asch, *Police Authority and the Rights of the Individual* (New York: Arco Publishing, 1967).

[21] W. Eugene Groves, "Police in the Ghetto," *Supplemental Studies for the National Advisory Commission on Civil Disorders* (Washington: 1968), p. 103.

[22] For more details on these points, see Herman Goldstein, "Police Response to Urban Crisis," *Public Administration Review*, XXVIII (September/October, 1968), 417–423. James Q. Wilson, *Varieties of Police Behavior* (Cambridge: Harvard University Press, 1968), particularly Chapter 2, contains an interesting analysis of the police roles of maintaining order and enforcing laws.

[23] President's Commission on Law Enforcement and Administration of Justice, Task Force on Police, *Task Force Report: The Police* (Washington: 1967), pp. 150, 153.

cess, as revealed by Detroit's experience with police-community meetings: minimum participation by ghetto residents, infrequent sessions, lack of involvement by patrolmen, lack of attention to youth programs, and lack of coordination with other city programs.[24]

The police in various localities also have become active in community service efforts, a specific type of police-community relations program. These endeavors differ according to the particular city or town, but include assisting young people with police records to acquire jobs, assigning police officers to antipoverty centers to aid juveniles in obtaining services, assisting them with problems, or referring them to the appropriate welfare and other agencies, and manning store-front offices to receive and transmit grievances against various departments. One of the most innovative is New York City's family crisis intervention program where specially trained officers respond to situations involving marital disputes.[25]

Although some police-community relations programs have registered important accomplishments, many have not done so. Lack of interest at the precinct level, failure to integrate these activities into the departments, and inadequacy of budget support are frequent contributors to the unsatisfactory results. However, a more basic defect, as pointed out by the National Advisory Commission on Civil Disorders, is that many of them "are not community-relations programs but public relations programs, designed to improve the department's image in the community."[26]

Some seasoned observers are convinced that the fundamental problem in police-minority relations does not lie in the nature of formal programs but in a set of values and attitudes and a pattern of behavior operative in many police departments. An articulate spokesman for this viewpoint, Burton Levy, director of the community relations division of the Michigan Civil Rights Commission, has noted:

. . . the police system can be seen as one that is a closed society with its own values, mores, and standards. In urban communities, anti-black is likely to be one of a half-dozen primary and important values. The department recruits a sizable number of people with racist attitudes, socializes them into a system with a strong racist element, and takes the officer who cannot advance and puts him in the ghetto where he has day-to-day contact with the black citizens.[27]

Levy earlier believed that the gulf between the minority community and the police in urban centers could be breached by allocating substantial

[24] *Report of the National Advisory Commission on Civil Disorders* (Washington: 1968), p. 167.
[25] Morton Bard and Bernard Berkowitz, "Training Police as Specialists in Family Crisis Intervention: A Community Psychology Action Program," *Community Mental Health Journal,* 3 (Winter, 1967), 315–317.
[26] *Report,* p. 167.
[27] Burton Levy, "Cops in the Ghetto: A Problem of the Police System," *American Behavioral Scientist,* 11 (March-April, 1968), 33.

funds to various activities, including police recruitment, in-service training in human relations, police-community relations programs, and general upgrading and professionalizing of the police service. However, two additional years of intensive experience with police in all sections of the nation (gained in part as a consultant to the Department of Justice in establishing its nationwide police-community relations program), in combination with the results of other studies and statements by police officers, have led him to reverse his position that these activities alone could produce significant improvements.

Two formidable problems in successfully confronting the issue of "institutional racism," according to Levy, are the information gap and the defensiveness and secrecy of the police. On the former, the leaders of white America have not dealt with the issue of racism in law enforcement as they have with other civil rights problems; on the latter, the professional policemen and the old-line cops stand together against outside review or criticism. Systemic change in police-minority relations will only take place, Levy concludes, when the mayor (or manager) and the police chief are sufficiently committed to it and strong enough to prevail over the police system in their community; moreover, such change will require a political base and a sensitive power structure and, if the white citizenry is politically dominant, a transformation in the belief system of many of its members.

Police Administration

The police function has a long tradition of local autonomy in the United States. Regardless of size or financial resources, virtually every city, town, or village regards itself capable of providing adequate law enforcement within its boundaries. Many thousands of separate police departments exist throughout the country, ranging in size from those with no full-time personnel to the New York City force of about 30,000. In the larger metropolitan areas, the number of individual departments often runs well over one hundred. Within a fifty-mile radius of Chicago, for example, there are approximately 350 locally maintained police forces, and in the five counties surrounding Philadelphia the number exceeds 160.

County governments, through the sheriff's office, usually provide police protection to the rural sections and the urbanized unincorporated areas. A limited number, such as Los Angeles and St. Louis counties, offer police services to the municipalities on a contractual basis. Similar arrangements also exist among cities, but the contractual device is employed nationally far less extensively than it is in fire protection. The same is true with respect to special districts. In contrast to the more than 3600 such agencies utilized for fire protection purposes, special police districts are virtually nonexistent.

The wide diversity among police departments in the typical metropolitan area militates against efficient and uniform law enforcement. This diversity is not simply one of size; it relates to training, equipment, record-keeping, and even attitude as well. Some smaller communities operate with only part-time departments; many employ untrained or partly trained personnel; a majority do not have adequate facilities for crime prevention and detection. Yet each individual department constitutes, in effect, a part of a single system that has as its objective the maintenance of law and order in the metropolis.

Although the police and fire functions are closely related, the spillover effects of the former are substantially greater. Inadequate law enforcement in one community can have important social costs for the remainder of the area. Fires cross corporate boundaries only occasionally but law violators are highly mobile. Police departments throughout an urban area must therefore be trained and equipped to detect and apprehend criminals within their territorial limits no matter where the crimes are committed. This mission requires the close coordination of police activities, an effective communications network, and modernized facilities for record-keeping and identification.

Some authorities maintain that a consolidated department is the only satisfactory answer to the problem of police administration in metropolitan areas. Suggestions of this nature, however, have almost always fallen on deaf ears. Only two American metropolises—Jacksonville and Nashville—have followed this path in recent years and in both instances city-county consolidation of many services was realized simultaneously. There has been some movement lately toward centralization of certain functions such as communications, record-keeping, laboratory facilities, and training. There has also been some feeling that either the state or an area-wide agency such as the county should be authorized to establish and enforce minimum standards for local departments. New York was the first state to take steps in this direction when it enacted legislation in 1961 to require all local police officers to have formal training before assuming the responsibilities of law enforcement.

The middle approach to police administration in SMSAs is illustrated by the recommendation of the Metropolitan St. Louis Survey which called for the county police department in that area to become the agency for correlating the municipal forces and for providing centralized services of the type mentioned above.[28] Proposals of this kind are typical. They rest on the assumption that area-wide needs can be balanced against the claims of local autonomy by dividing the police function in such a way as to satisfy both. Reasonable as this solution may seem, it has met with little favor among suburban departments and progress toward metropolitan police coordination has been far from spectacular.

[28] Path of Progress for Metropolitan St. Louis, pp. 87–88.

As in many other functional areas, the national government has shown increasing concern for the improvement of local law enforcement. Its Omnibus Crime Control and Safe Streets Act of 1968, for example, is an effort to promote coordination in this vital field. The legislation provides for state and general local units to develop collaboratively a comprehensive statewide plan which, among other features, encourages local governments to combine or provide for cooperative arrangements with respect to law enforcement services, facilities, and equipment. Federal grants are made available to states whose plans are approved by the Department of Justice. They range from 50 to 75 percent of the total cost of such programs as recruitment of general law enforcement personnel and training of community service officers in grievance resolution procedures, community patrol efforts, and related activities.

Crime and Local Government

As we have been repeatedly reminded, crime in the United States is rising faster than the rate of population growth. No single causal factor or well-established set of them can explain this increase. Some commentators attribute it to a breakdown in family life, others to the emphasis that modern society places on material goods, and still others to a general weakening of the moral and religious fiber of the nation. Most sociologists subscribe to some form of multiple causation theory, holding that crime is the product of many associated variables that defy simple analysis, citing the fact that maladjustment and disorder are characteristic of rapid social change. They point out that the process of transforming a nation from an agricultural and rural society to an industrial and urban civilization—a development we are now witnessing on a worldwide scale—cannot be accomplished without social costs. One such cost appears to be the increased rate of adult crime and juvenile delinquency.

Obviously, no local government or combination of local units can cope with or treat all the forms of social disorganization or eradicate the basic causes of crime and delinquency. No governmental instrumentality, whether the police department or welfare agency, can eliminate prejudice or the cultural factors that build up vast reservoirs of resentment and frustration by depriving certain groups of the opportunity to participate fully in the society. Nor can it strengthen or assume the role of the family, church, and other institutions which are influential determinants and molders of social behavior. Inadequate and unprofessional law enforcement by municipal and county authorities may contribute to increased crime rates and exacerbate the bitterness among certain segments of the population, but in the final analysis the problem transcends the metropolitan community. Like poverty and racial discrimination, crime and delinquency have their roots in national as well as local conditions.

PARKS AND RECREATION

The rise of recreation as a governmental responsibility in the United States is largely a product of the present century. The opening of the nation's first playground, a large sandpile in front of a children's home in Boston, did not occur until 1885. Some of the larger cities began to develop park systems earlier, more for their aesthetic qualities than their recreational potentialities. New York City acquired Central Park in 1853 but the purchase was condemned by many as an extravagant waste of public funds. Most of the smaller municipalities did not begin to acquire park acreage until after 1900, and a majority of the suburban communities created since World War II have ignored this responsibility altogether. St. Louis City, to cite one example, has over 2800 acres of parkland; this exceeds the area maintained by local governments throughout the remainder of the seven-county SMSA where the population is almost triple that of the city.

The need for parks and outdoor recreational areas has become more imperative as urban populations have multiplied and as leisure time has increased because of the shorter workweek, longer vacations, and earlier retirement (Figure 25). Attendance at state parks exceeds 300 million and at national parks and forests 200 million. Many millions also utilize the 30,000 parks and the more than 150,000 playgrounds under the jurisdiction of local governments. Local public expenditures for this function are now approximately $1 billion a year, but the gap between need and availability of facilities continues to be wide.

Land for park and recreational purposes, once plentiful in and around urban areas, is now in scarce supply. The title of a Department of Interior booklet, "The Race for Inner Space," reflects the urgency of this situation. The nation still has lots of open space but little of it is available where it is needed most. Several states, such as New York, New Jersey, Massachusetts, and Wisconsin, have become active in financially assisting their local units to acquire land while the opportunity still exists. The national government's concern has been expressed in various ways. Examples are the Housing Act of 1961 which authorized federal grants to state and local governments for acquisition of open space land and the extensive reports of the early 1960s by the national Outdoor Recreation Resources Review Commission. They were followed by the Congressional decision in 1963 to have a federal bureau formulate and maintain a comprehensive nationwide outdoor recreation plan,[29] and by the passage in the following year of the Land and Water Conservation Fund Act to

[29] As part of its responsibility for such a plan, the Bureau of Outdoor Recreation in the Department of the Interior has prepared *Federal Outdoor Recreation Programs* (Washington: 1968).

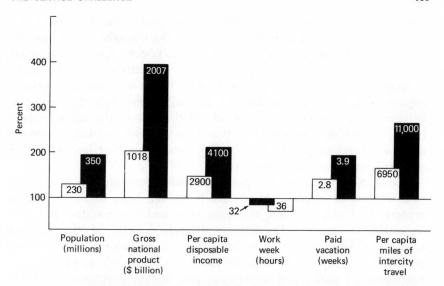

FIGURE 25   **Estimated Changes in Population, Income, Leisure, and Travel in the Years 1976 and 2000 Compared to 1960. The 1960 rate is 100 percent. White bars show change by 1976; black bars, by 2000.** From Outdoor Recreation for America, **Outdoor Recreation Resources Review Commission, 1962, p. 45.**

assist state and local units in acquiring and developing land to meet high priority outdoor recreation needs.

Park and Recreation Administration

All levels of government—local, state, and national—are engaged to one extent or another in providing public recreational facilities. The greatest burden, however, falls on municipalities in urban areas where the day-to-day needs of burgeoning populations must be met. County participation in this function has increased in recent years but is still relatively minor in comparison to that of the incorporated communities.[30] The special district device is also employed for park and recreational purposes to a limited extent; the *1967 Census of Governments* reports 613 such agencies in existence, over one-third of them in the state of Illinois and about one-half in metropolitan areas. State agencies maintain and operate approximately 2700 parks and the national government more than 200 parks and monuments (exclusive of the national forests) with a combined acreage of over 27 million.

The spillover benefits from parks and recreational facilities rank rela-

[30] For an illustration of growing county interest, see the ten community action guides, *Outdoor Recreation* (Washington: 1968), prepared by the National Association of Counties.

tively high among urban functions. A large park, zoo, or public beach invariably attracts many users from outside the immediate governmental jurisdiction in which it is located. Furthermore, open space areas, wherever they are located, enhance the attractiveness of the entire metropolitan complex, give psychic benefits to the residents, and serve an important conservation function by helping to maintain the ecological balance of nature. On the other side of the ledger, the social costs of failing to provide adequate facilities in one densely settled community may be substantial for the surrounding area in terms of lowered health standards and juvenile delinquency.

The administration of the park and recreation function lends itself to a division of responsibilities, largely on the basis of the benefits it confers. One such division, that into local and metropolitan, has been suggested by George D. Butler, research director of the National Recreation Association. Under his proposed breakdown, facilities and services that primarily benefit the local residents, such as playgrounds, neighborhood parks, and supervised recreational programs, would be handled by the municipalities. The larger parks, golf courses, zoos, beaches, and similar facilities serving the entire area would be administered by the county or, where the SMSA is comprised of more than one county, by a special park district.[31] This division might be extended to one additional level, that of the state. A large urbanized population should have available within reasonable distance large tracts of land that are kept in their natural condition for hiking, camping, picnicking, boating, and fishing. These regional parks or reservations, which may serve several metropolitan areas, can most appropriately be administered by the state government.

Little agreement has as yet evolved among the various governments as to their proper roles with respect to parks and recreation. In general, each local unit in a metropolis has its own ideas as to what it should or should not do, and each proceeds on its own way without reference to any overall plan for the area. With the shortage of open space in and around the nation's large urban areas becoming increasingly critical, the fragmented and uncoordinated approach characteristic of existing policy in this field is extremely shortsighted and unrealistic.

The park and recreational problem, along with the other service difficulties that have been considered in this chapter, differ from each other in their functional characteristics, territorial scope, and administrative requirements. Our purpose here has been to call attention to the various dimensions of these problems and to possible avenues of solution. In doing so, we have considered each function as an individual activity separate and apart from the others. In reality, of course, many of the

31 "Recreation Administration in Metropolitan Areas," *Recreation*, LV (September, 1962), 349–351.

problems are interrelated in such a way that a satisfactory solution of one cannot be achieved without action on the others. But whether citizens interested in improving the urban governmental system should concentrate their resources on a single function or strive for a larger or "total" package can only be answered in the light of many considerations. Subsequent chapters will deal with the various overall approaches to metropolitan reorganization and the factors they involve.

8 / SOCIAL AND ECONOMIC DILEMMAS

CONTEMPORARY MIDDLE-AGED AMERICANS HAVE SUCCESSIVELY WITNESSED THE New Deal of the Roosevelt era, the Fair Deal of the Eisenhower period, the New Frontier of the Kennedy days, and more recently the Great Society of the Johnson presidency. Although the rhetoric of promise has far exceeded the attainment, they have seen notable strides made in social legislation and in the enlargement of the opportunity structure for many in the society. At the same time, however, they have also witnessed rank discrimination in housing and employment on the basis of race, civil disturbances and riots, deep internal divisions and even violence over United States military involvement in Vietnam, a growing unrest among the youth, the poor, and the racial minorities, and an intensification of urban problems in general. They have listened to optimistic prophecies but increasingly they have heard warnings that the nation's large cities and metropolises are on the verge of catastrophe and doomed, as Thomas Hobbes' man in the state of nature, to a "poor, nasty, brutish and short life" unless immediate and massive action is taken to redeem them.

196

Current events, the outbreaks of violence in particular, have awakened some concern among the citizenry, but blessed with unprecedented prosperity—as a majority are—they are reluctant to believe that major change is necessary or desirable or that the problems are as bad as portrayed. To many of them, only simplistic solutions—better law enforcement, for example—are required to eliminate the most obvious difficulties. Whether the problems are as alarming as some would have us believe or a natural and inevitable by-product of a technological society is not the question. Problems of major import do exist—no one denies this fact—and they are affecting in important ways the quality and potential of urban life and the environment in which man pursues his daily tasks. The individual who wants to behave like a metropolitan ostrich will find little sand in which to bury his head. Even the most callous city dweller cannot fail to sense the changes that are sweeping over and around him, impinging upon numerous aspects of his life, affecting his activities and goals, and conditioning his behavior.

Problems are an integral part of this environment, the common lot of men everywhere and at all times and the inevitable concomitants of living together. These problems, moreover, are continually changing just as the community itself is constantly, if slowly, evolving into new forms. What constitutes a minor source of irritation today may be a major issue tomorrow. Nothing is more certain than that if we solve one troublesome difficulty, another will soon appear in its stead. Thus we may drain a swamp to get rid of the mosquitos only to find that the water table drops because rain is no longer being absorbed into the earth. Or we may speed up production by automating the factories only to discover that we have an unemployment problem on our hands. Or we may build massive expressways or freeways to move people swiftly in and out of the central business district only to learn that we have created a severe parking crisis. We cannot expect to find the total answer for our rapidly urbanizing communities, for the future is never finished. Nor can we ever expect to have enough resources and enough agreement on goals to make everybody happy. Yet we can and must act vigorously in seeking solutions to our most pressing problems and in correcting the inequities and injustices which exist in the society.

THE WEB OF PROBLEMS

Until the civil disturbances of the mid-1960s came as a rude awakening, most political scientists, planners, and community influentials tended to limit the discussion of metropolitan problems to those of a service nature. Written in large print in their catalogue were such items as water supply, sewage disposal, air pollution, and traffic control. This emphasis on the service role of the metropolis finds expression in the notion that local government is a business institution to be structured and administered like a private corporation. Such being the case, the most important metropolitan task to many people was to organize the bureaucratic machinery so that it could furnish the necessary services in an efficient, economical, and apolitical manner.

Accompanying this preoccupation with service problems was a heavy emphasis on the city as a physical plant. Paul Ylvisaker, then director of the Ford Foundation's public affairs division, called attention to this fact when he said:

Examine the literature on the city and the substance of action programs and you will find them dominated by a concern with physical plant. The going criteria of urban success are the beauty and solvency of the city's real properties, not the condition of the people who flow through them. As a result, the civilizing and ennobling function of the city, mainly its job of turning second-class newcomers into first-class citizens, is downgraded into pious pronouncements and last-place priorities. We despair of our wasting city property, and count the costs of urban renewal in building values. These are nothing compared to the wasting resources of the human beings who get trapped in these aging buildings, and the value of their lost contribution to their own and the world's society.[1]

The problems of service and of physical development are not to be minimized. Nor is the efficient and economical operation of the governmental machinery to be denied as a desirable goal. What is to be avoided, whether by central city or suburban residents, is the tendency to regard such matters as exhausting the list of locally relevant issues or as occupying first priority on the civic agenda. We can put water in the taps, dispose of the waste, develop an outstanding fire department, build countless miles of expressway to accommodate the automobile, and bulldoze the slums, yet leave untouched some of the most critical issues facing the urban complex. What can be done to provide adequate housing and equal opportunities for all members of the metropolitan community? How can racial strife be mitigated and minority groups, particularly the Negro, be assimilated fully into the life of the city and its environs? What changes can be made in the educational system to make it more relevant to the needs of modern urban society?

One might argue that social and economic problems of this nature and magnitude lie outside the sphere of local government and cannot be solved by action at the municipal or metropolitan level. Some of the more conservative would even maintain that their resolution lies primarily in private hands, by business, labor unions, social agencies,

[1] Address to the World Traffic Engineering Conference, Washington, D.C., August 21, 1961.

property owners, and people acting individually and through their voluntary associations. Arguments of this kind are valid up to a point. Obviously, a problem such as poverty or discrimination is national in scope and cannot be effectively dealt with solely by local means. Even the control of crime and delinquency, while basically a community function, is affected by national conditions such as poverty, unemployment, and general societal attitudes.

But whether these problems are "national" or not, their location is principally in the metropolis. Local government cannot possibly escape involvement with them, for they are part and parcel of the community environment. Urban renewal is a case in point. Even though the national government furnishes the lion's share of the money, it is local authorities which must design and initiate the project, resolve the differences among competing interests, and administer the program. The same is true of race relations. Constitutional and statutory provisions at the national and state levels may bar racial segregation in public schools and discrimination in housing and employment, but the full enforcement of these rights will depend upon the active cooperation of local officials and private groups.

Whose Responsibility?

Some myopic defenders of suburbia go so far as to say that the major socioeconomic problems of urban society are problems of the central city, not those of the total metropolitan community. Where but within the boundaries of the core city, they ask, does one find an abundance of racial strife, crime, blighted housing, and welfare recipients? Superficially, their logic may seem sound since they are correct about the prevalent spatial location of these maladies. Although crime and other social problems exist in suburbia, their magnitude and extent are substantially less than in the central city. But why in an interdependent metropolitan community should the responsibility of suburbanites be any less than that of the central city dwellers? Certainly no one would think of contending that residents of higher income neighborhoods within the corporate limits of the city should be exempt from responsibility for its less fortunate districts. What logic then is there in believing that neighborhoods on the other side of a legal line can wash their hands of social disorders in these sections?

Low-income areas are unfortunately a part of every large urban complex. Without the workers that these neighborhoods house, industrial production would be curtailed and the service trades seriously crippled. It was not too long ago, for example, that factories in the northern cities were conducting active recruiting campaigns for low-income southern workers. Automation may be reducing this demand, but it has not stopped the migration of dispossessed rural dwellers, also victims of the new technology, into our urban centers. In fact, it would be difficult to find any industrial community that did not have its concentrations of the poor and underprivileged. These concentrations most often happen to be in the central city simply because it is here that cheap and available housing is located. Were the reverse true, as it is in some smaller metropolitan areas, these groups would be found in the suburban ring. No large community can hope to reap the benefits of industrialization and urbanization and yet escape their less desirable by-products. The suburbanite and the central city resident share responsibility for the total community and its problems. Neither can run fast enough to escape involvement.

In other chapters we deal with various service and organizational difficulties confronting the nation's metropolitan areas. Here we direct our attention to three closely related socioeconomic issues of vital concern to the contemporary urban community: housing and urban renewal, race, and education. Other social and economic problems exist—the observant city dweller can readily make a lengthy compilation of them—but none is more determinative of the peace and well-being of our populous SMSAs than these. Like most major urban problems, all levels of public authority are today involved in their solution, but like the others also, the immediate burden and the consequences of success or failure fall primarily on the governments and citizens of the metropolitan communities themselves.

THE "DETERIORATING" CITY

In 1953, economist Miles Colean wrote a book for the Twentieth Century Fund which he titled *Renewing Our Cities*. The term "urban renewal" caught on and became the symbolic designation for the efforts of public agencies and private groups to eliminate slums and curb the spread of blight in American cities. Urban renewal is not a modern invention; only its technical aspects are. Man has been engaged in the construction and reconstruction of cities since antiquity. Athens, for example, was rebuilt under Pericles, Rome under Augustus, and Paris under Napoleon III, and one might even say with tongue in cheek, New York City under Moses—that is, Robert Moses. Renewal, however, is not always so spectacular or dramatic, yet it is constantly taking place in one fashion or another regardless of whether we are aware of the fact. The city we live in today, if not destroyed or abandoned in the interim, will be completely rebuilt—renewed if you please—for better or worse within the next 100 years.

A city or a metropolitan area is not like frozen sculpture. It is forever undergoing change, being added to and subtracted from, shaped and reshaped like pliable clay, sometimes with deliberate intent, more often without conscious design. The visitor to any major American city today— and many of lesser size, such as New Haven, Connecticut—is invariably amazed at the physical transformations that are taking place. In New York, Chicago, Philadelphia, St. Louis, Detroit—and the list could go on —large sections of the community have been razed. This planned destruction is being followed by rebuilding, in a few cases at a feverish pace, in the others more slowly and even hesitantly.

Governmental efforts at urban renewal in the United States have been subjected to a barrage of criticism in recent years from both conservative and liberal sources. Economists have questioned the economic arguments advanced in behalf of the program, and one of their number has even called for its abolition on the grounds that the private market could eliminate the nation's housing problem and clear its slums at less social cost.[2] Other critics charge that redevelopment authorities have been more responsive to the desires of central business district interests than the housing needs of low-income groups and have thus created new slums by uprooting families from old ones without providing adequate relocation. Still others object to the disruption of "viable" although poor neighborhoods in the name of redevelopment. Joined to these voices of protest are those of individuals and groups who have become alarmed at the "human impact" of renewal projects and the emphasis on physical rehabilitation to the seeming exclusion of social consequences. Finally, increasing resistance has come from those most affected, the residents of the neighborhoods slated for renewal, who rightfully feel they should have a voice in the determination of their fate.

Housing

The extent of substandard housing in metropolitan areas has been the subject of considerable dispute. Martin Anderson, author of the highly controversial *Federal Bulldozer*, uses census data to show that such housing in central cities of over 100,000 declined from 19 percent to 11 percent during the decade of the 1950s and can be expected to drop to 4 percent by 1970.[3] In attacking these findings, a staff member of the National Association of Housing and Redevelopment Officials charged Anderson with distorting the figures by failing to take into account definitional changes and post-census enumerations which reveal that no significant reduction in the amount of substandard dwellings took place over the decade.[4] Other observers point out that while the overall proportion of

[2] Martin Anderson, *The Federal Bulldozer: A Critical Analysis of Urban Renewal, 1949–1962* (Cambridge: The M.I.T. Press, 1964).

[3] "Fiasco of Urban Renewal," *Harvard Business Review*, 43 (January–February, 1965), 6–21.

[4] Robert P. Groberg, "Urban Renewal Realistically Reappraised," *Law and Contemporary Problems*, XXX (Winter, 1965), 212–229.

inadequate units in SMSAs has declined due to the large amount of new suburban construction, at least one-sixth to one-quarter of the population in most of the large central cities is inadequately housed.[5] Regardless of who is right in this numbers game, a great many American families, disproportionately nonwhite, still reside in substandard dwelling units or unsuitable living environments despite the nation's much publicized opulence.

Universally condemned as slums, the areas where most of this housing is located serve as the home of the poor and the deprived, those not integrated into the mainstream of community life because of lack of equal educational and employment opportunities, color barriers, and social problems. Slums, however, are nothing new; they have been with us ever since the middle-class families abandoned the task of rebuilding the original areas of settlement and moved outward in search of better neighborhoods and better homes. Boston, Chicago, New York, San Francisco, St. Louis, and other large communities had their slums long before the wave of southern migrants began to enter the industrial cities of the North and West.

Blight and substandard housing went unrecognized in public policy until the 1930s when interest was generated in a wide range of social legislation. The first efforts of the national government in this field embodied the curious combination of goals—economic pump-priming and social amelioration—that characterized many of the New Deal programs. To stimulate the home building industry and at the same time clear away some of the worst slums, Congress enacted the Housing Act of 1937 authorizing loans and subsidies to local agencies for construction of public housing. The law required cities as a condition of the grant to eliminate dilapidated dwelling units equal in number to those constructed with federal aid. This was a cautious beginning, but the severe housing shortage which followed World War II fanned wider public interest in the problem and led to the passage of the more comprehensive Housing Act of 1949.[6]

In passing the new legislation, Congress made explicit its purpose: "a decent home and a suitable living environment for every American family." To accomplish this objective, two major components were included in the act, one pertaining to slum clearance or renewal, the other to public housing. The first (the famous Title I) provided for grants to

[5] See, for example, William Grigsby, Housing Markets and Public Policy (Philadelphia: University of Pennsylvania Press, 1963).

[6] The history of urban renewal legislation is outlined in Ashley A. Foard and Hilbert Fefferman, "Federal Urban Renewal Legislation," Law and Contemporary Problems, XXV (Autumn, 1960), 635–684. A perceptive analysis of the program is found in Scott Greer, Urban Renewal and American Cities (Indianapolis: Bobbs-Merrill, 1965).

local redevelopment agencies covering two-thirds of the loss involved in acquiring, clearing, and disposing of blighted areas at a marked-down price for public or private purposes; the second authorized aid to localities for the construction of 810,000 low-rent housing units. Despite strong opposition to the latter program, the bill passed largely because the various interests, like the blind men feeling the elephant, made entirely different assumptions about the purpose of the legislation.[7] Welfare groups viewed it as an enlargement of the power to get rid of bad living conditions. Businessmen saw it as a means of bolstering waning property values in central areas. Central city officials looked upon it as a device for bolstering the tax base and luring back some of the expatriates, the consumers and taxpayers of substance who had fled to the greener pastures of suburbia.

Two trends have been discernible in the evolution of the housing and renewal program since the enactment of the 1949 act, one relating to philosophy, the other to emphasis. At the time of its passage, Senator Robert Taft and other sponsors of the bill made it clear that the program should be housing-oriented as distinguished from the betterment of cities and urban life in general. This concept was vigorously questioned by representatives of the planning profession who argued that the major objective should be redevelopment in accord with a general plan for the entire community. In such a plan, slums would be treated as but one important phase of urban blight and housing as but one important segment of renewal. Objections to the housing orientation of the act also came from economic interests and city officials who wanted primary emphasis placed on the reconstruction of blighted business and industrial properties rather than the dwelling needs of the poor.

In reality, subsequent congressional and local action has moved in both of these directions despite the continued reaffirmation of a decent home for every American family as the principal goal of urban renewal. The 1954 revision of the Housing Act, for example, embodied the philosophy of the planners by requiring cities, as a condition of federal aid, to formulate a workable program or plan of action for meeting the overall problems of slums and of community development generally. The 1959 legislation went a step further by authorizing funds for the preparation of long-range community renewal programs (CRP) with respect to all of the urban renewal needs of a city. Along with these modifications, the provision in the original act limiting aid to residential projects only was amended in 1954 to permit 10 percent of federal capital grant funds to be used for nonresidential projects, a proportion that was later tripled. These

[7] See in this connection Catherine Bauer Wurster, "Redevelopment: A Misfit in the Fifties," in Coleman Woodbury (ed.), *The Future of Cities and Urban Redevelopment* (Chicago: University of Chicago Press, 1953), pp. 7–25.

trends are not necessarily undesirable; in fact, the increasing attention to overall planning and the economic base of the community makes sense in terms of general city development. The misfortune is that, amid all of this, the housing needs of low-income families somehow or other became lost in the shuffle.

Urban Renewal

Although the arguments for urban renewal are not necessarily compatible, they reflect the different assumptions on which the program was originally inaugurated. If the principal objective is to bolster the tax base of the community, efforts should be directed toward developing the cleared land at its highest income-producing use. The fate of the people who are to be relocated becomes secondary in this case. If, on the other hand, the primary and overriding purpose is to provide better housing for the low-income and underprivileged classes, the economic argument must give way to the social. In most communities, the former goal has prevailed. Private investors are seldom interested in building low-income housing on renewal sites since the land is too expensive, even with the federal and local write-down.

Whatever the motives of those who have promoted urban renewal, the economic rather than the social or moral appeal has sustained the program. Given this emphasis, it is understandable that the plight of low-income families has not been of high priority in the renewal plans of municipalities. Solving the housing problems of the poor does little to solve the financial problems of the cities while redevelopment for other purposes presumably does. Blighted areas have thus generally been rebuilt for new occupants and not for the slum dwellers themselves. Only a small fraction of the total construction on renewal sites has been devoted to public housing. Most of the new buildings are high-rise apartments for upper-income families. This fact has prompted the charge that the program has actually made housing conditions worse for the poorer residents of cities by destroying more low-cost dwelling units than it has created.

Growing public resistance to large-scale residential demolition has caused the emphasis in urban renewal to shift from wholesale clearance to the rehabilitation and conservation of existing structures and neighborhoods. The underlying philosophy of this approach is to help the residents of affected areas help themselves through a combination of governmental action and private effort. Local governments are to use their powers in upgrading and stabilizing the neighborhood environment through public improvements, creating additional new open space, reducing heavy traffic on residential streets, providing new playgrounds and other recreation facilities, and stepping up enforcement of minimum housing standards and zoning. At the same time individual owners are to be encouraged to improve their property by making liberal government-insured financing available to them.

Rehabilitation and conservation are obviously applicable only in neighborhoods where a majority of the buildings are still structurally sound even though shabby and in need of repairs. They cannot work effectively

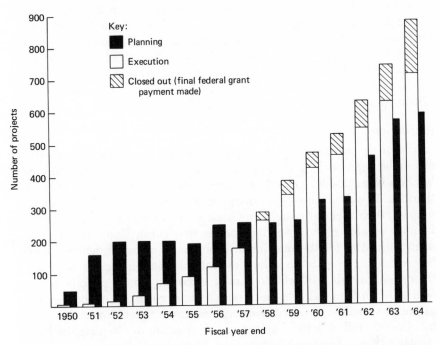

FIGURE 26 Urban Renewal Projects by Status, 1950–1965. From William Slayton, "The Operation and Achievements of the Urban Renewal Program," in James Q. Wilson (ed.), Urban Renewal: The Record and the Controversy, (Cambridge, Mass.: M.I.T. Press, 1966), p. 204. Reprinted by permission of The M.I.T. Press. Copyright 1966 by the Massachusetts Institute of Technology.

in areas where poverty and social disorganization are rampant or where the residents are contemplating flight because of threatened invasion by racial minorities or evicted slum dwellers. More basically, these devices are not the answers to the housing needs of low-income families. For if successful, they raise the price of the property and its rental value in many cases to a point beyond the resources of the poorer members of the community. Rent supplements for the latter in which government pays a portion of the rent can be particularly helpful in bringing rehabilitated housing within the means of this group. Congress enacted such a law in 1965 but the appropriation accompanying it was minuscule. Lack of public support for any form of shelter subsidy to low-income families remains an obstacle to anything beyond token action in this direction.[8]

By the end of 1968, approximately 1550 urban renewal projects in over 1000 communities had been approved for execution by the Department of Housing and Urban Development (HUD) and its predecessor agencies. Less than $3 billion in federal funds had actually been disbursed since the inception of the program in 1949, with another $4.5 billion committed for projects under way or in the planning stage. (The long time-period involved in bringing projects to completion is illustrated in Figure 26.) This is a remarkably small amount for the national government to invest in the redevelopment of cities, particularly in comparison to the $24 billion spent on the lunar program.

Relocation

A strongly criticized aspect of urban renewal has been the relocation of families uprooted by slum clearance projects. For the most part, relocation was initially ignored or not considered a problem by local authorities. It was assumed that many of the displaced would be able to upgrade their shelter through the filtering-down process as higher income families vacated older properties for the new construction in redevelopment sites. And for the remainder, a minimum of public housing could be provided. The question of how relocated families make out in meeting their shelter needs is difficult to answer. According to the periodic reports of the Urban Renewal Administration, a high proportion of them end up in "locally certified standard housing," but these figures are contradicted by several studies which indicate that most move to neighborhoods similar to those from which they were cleared, usually on the fringe of renewal projects. One study in the early 1960s, for example, revealed that roughly 60 percent of the relocated families in the forty-one cities examined were still living in substandard conditions.[9] A Bureau of the Census survey in 1964, on the other hand, lent support to the URA statistics

[8] According to the rent supplement program authorized by the Housing and Urban Development Act of 1965, those eligible are required to pay 25 percent of their income for rent. The difference between this amount and the full market rent for the dwelling unit represents the amount of the supplement. It is well to keep in mind that many of the problems which have plagued public housing generally, such as increasing nonwhite occupancy, site selection, and segregation of low-income families, are also applicable to the rent supplement program. See in this connection Irving H. Welfeld, "Rent Supplements and the Subsidy Dilemma," *Law and Contemporary Problems*, XXXII (Summer, 1967), 465–481.

[9] Harry W. Reynolds, Jr., "Population Displacement in Urban Renewal," *American Journal of Economics and Sociology*, XXII (January, 1963), 113–128. See also Peter Marris, "The Social Implications of Urban Redevelopment," *Journal of the American Institute of Planners*, XXVIII (August, 1962), 180–186; and Alvin L. Schorr, *Slums and Social Insecurity* (Washington: U.S. Government Printing Office, 1963).

by showing that 94 percent of the families displaced during the summer of that year found standard housing. This, however, was a single survey and its findings have also been disputed.[10]

Whatever the validity of these various figures, relocation has been one of the weak features of the renewal program, a fact acknowledged by federal officials.[11] There is general agreement in the studies that those families which have succeeded in moving to better housing have done so at the cost of substantially higher rent.[12] Many of the poor, however, cannot afford such an additional expenditure. If the nation is to assure standard housing for low-income families displaced by renewal projects or living in slums, it must follow one of two paths (or a combination of them). The first is to provide the disadvantaged with sufficient income—in the form of family allowances, minimum income guarantees, rent supplements, or similar aids—to enable them to compete for housing in the private market; the other is to make sufficient public housing available to them. Up to the present the former course (with the exception of the timid beginning in rent subsidization) has been rejected and the latter followed but in a totally inadequate fashion. At the end of 1968, nearly two decades after the passage of the 1949 act, only about 700,000 public housing units were in operation and another 50,000 under construction.

Aside from the question of low income, one need not search far to find the major impediment to relocation. Over 70 percent of the people who have been forced out of their homes by Title I clearance projects have been nonwhites. Racial discrimination has greatly complicated the task of finding satisfactory dwelling units for the displaced blacks in the private market and has significantly curtailed the expansion of public housing.[13] The latter is well demonstrated by the eagerness with which local officials have embraced federally-subsidized housing for the aged, authorized by Congress in 1961, while showing a distinct coolness toward projects for low-income families generally.[14] (In 1968, for example, over

[10] The census survey is reported in Housing and Home Finance Agency, *The Housing of Relocated Families* (Washington: March, 1965). The findings of this survey are questioned by Chester Hartman in a commentary in *Journal of the American Institute of Planners*, XXXI (November, 1965), 340–344.

[11] For example, Robert Weaver, former Secretary of the Department of Housing and Urban Development, frankly acknowledged the weaknesses of the relocation program, pointing out, however, that much of the criticism relates to conditions which the government has moved to correct. See his *Dilemmas of Urban Renewal* (Cambridge: Harvard University Press, 1965).

[12] Nathaniel Lichfield, "Relocation: The Impact on Housing Welfare," *Journal of the American Institute of Planners*, XXVII (August, 1961), 199–203.

[13] For a refutation of the myth that the entrance of Negroes into a neighborhood lowers property values—an obstacle to relocation as well as to the solution of the Negro housing problem generally—see Luigi Laurenti, *Property Values and Race* (Berkeley and Los Angeles: University of California Press, 1960).

[14] For a review of public housing and the controversy over it, see William H. Ledbetter, Jr., "Public Housing: A Social Experiment Seeks Acceptance," *Law and Contemporary Problems*, XXXII (Summer, 1967), 490–527.

100,000 low-rent units for senior citizens were under construction.) As one observer trenchantly explains it: "Housing for the elderly taps the only remaining reservoir of poor people who are also white, orderly, and middle-class in behavior. Neighborhoods which will not tolerate a ten-story tower packed with Negro mothers on AFDC [aid to families with dependent children] might tolerate a tower of sweet but impoverished old folks."[15]

Recent Trends

In signing the 1968 Housing and Urban Redevelopment Act, President Lyndon Johnson called it "the most farsighted, the most comprehensive, the most massive housing program in all American history." The act, obviously a reflection of the concern over the disturbances in many of the nation's cities, reaffirmed the place of housing as the major component in urban redevelopment and gave the highest priority to meeting the shelter needs of the underprivileged. It set a ten-year goal of 6 million new and rehabilitated homes for those in this category (Table 18), specifying that a majority of the units provided in future urban renewal projects for residential purposes must be for low- and moderate-income families.

The act contains a number of interesting features which constitute at

TABLE 18   Ten-Year Goals: Publicly-Assisted Housing, 1969–1978 (in thousands)

Fiscal Year	Total Publicly Assisted Starts and Rehabilitation	Public Rental Housing	Private Rental Housing	Private Home Ownership
1969	300	75	125	100
1970	400	130	140	130
1971	500	190	160	150
1972	550	200	200	150
1973	600	200	250	150
1974	700	200	350	150
1975	700	150	400	150
1976	800	150	450	200
1977	750	100	450	200
1978	700	100	400	200
Total	6,000	1,495	2,925	1,580

SOURCE: Reprinted from the *Journal of Housing*, Vol. 25, Issue no. 7, August, 1968, p. 358, published by the National Association of Housing and Redevelopment Officials, 2500 Virginia Avenue, N.W., Washington, D.C. 20037.

[15] Laurence M. Friedman, "Public Housing and the Poor: An Overview," *California Law Review*, 54 (May, 1966), 654.

least a partial answer to some of the criticism directed at earlier programs. These include: (1) subsidies to reduce mortgage interest rates for lower-income families to assist them in purchasing homes; (2) credit assistance for low- and moderate-income families who do not qualify for FHA mortgage insurance; (3) a relaxation of mortgage insurance requirements for housing in older, declining neighborhoods; (4) grants to local housing agencies to furnish tenant services (such as counseling on household and money management, housekeeping, and child care; and advice as to resources for job training and placement, education, welfare, and health) with preference to be given to programs providing for maximum tenant participation in the development and operation of such services; (5) a bar on the construction of high-rise public housing projects for families with children unless no practical alternative exists; and (6) creation of a government-chartered nonprofit corporation, known as the National Home Ownership Foundation, to assist public and private organizations in initiating, developing, and conducting programs to expand home ownership and housing opportunities for lower-income families.

The 1968 law, in short, embodies several key concepts indicating changes in the direction of federal housing policy. First of all, it enlarges opportunities for the less affluent members of society to own homes by modifying the traditional business-management and banking philosophy which has long dominated such governmental finance agencies as the Federal Housing Administration and the Federal National Mortgage Association. Second, it specifically espouses the concept of citizen involvement initially enunciated in the anti-poverty legislation by making it clear that lower-income families are to be involved as participants as well as recipients in housing assistance programs. Third, it lends further support to the "total approach" philosophy to slum-area needs first embodied in the Model Cities law.[16] Finally, the 1968 act, for the first time in the country's history, makes housing an element of national economic planning, requiring the President to report annually on progress in this field and establishing a National Advisory Commission on Low Income Housing.

As is evident from the multi-faceted and far-ranging provisions of the law, President Johnson's encomium is more than mere administrative rhetoric. What remains in doubt, however, is the extent to which Congress will be willing to implement the legislation by adequate appropriations. The initial action in this regard unfortunately was not very encouraging. Allocations in the 1969 budget were reduced substantially below those called for in the act and funds for several of the key programs, such as

16 The Model Cities Act of 1966 provides for technical and financial assistance to enable communities to carry out comprehensive attacks on the total range of urban problems—social, economic, and physical—in selected disadvantaged areas of the city through coordinated federal, state, local, and private efforts.

rent supplements, interest subsidies, and tenant services, were either drastically cut or eliminated altogether.

Housing, of course, is only one aspect of a much larger picture. Many of the families in blighted or slum areas are plagued by other problems besides poor living quarters. Merely moving the residents of these neighborhoods into better dwelling units will not cure the other social and physical ills which beset them. Much of the disillusionment over public housing has been caused by the failure to recognize that a change in dwelling status does not automatically lead to changes in the attitudes or behavior of low-income families or inculcate them with middle-class values. Some empirical findings, in fact, question the relationship between poor housing and social or physical maladies.[17] Yet whatever this association may be, decent housing is at minimum critical to providing a proper setting for an attack on the other related problems of poverty and deprivation.

THE PROBLEM OF RACE

Many of the most acute social problems of metropolitan areas including housing, poverty, unemployment, and education revolve around the racial question. By virtually every socioeconomic indicator, the wellbeing of urban nonwhites ranks substantially below that of whites. Compared to the latter, they have on the average lower incomes, more substandard dwellings, greater unemployment, less education and training, and more families on welfare. The last two decades have brought material gains to minority people but they have not narrowed significantly the gap between black and white nor eliminated the crippling discrimination based on the color of one's skin.

The Negro—and in lesser numbers the Puerto Rican and Mexican-American—is the latest ethnic migrant to the cities. Earlier groups of ethnic newcomers, such as the Irish, Polish, and Italians, achieved the goals of better housing, improved neighborhoods, adequate schools, and occupational mobility once they had demonstrated adherence to the dominant culture and secured the economic rewards offered by the system. The case has been far different for the Negro. Even when he has succeeded in attaining middle-class status, as a minority of blacks has done, discriminatory practices by the white-dominated society have continued to deny him the acceptance and social recognition to which his income and behavior qualify him. The attitudes and actions of the majoritarian society toward Negroes as a whole have left the nation with

[17] See, for example, Daniel M. Wilner and Rosabelle P. Wakely, "The Effects of Housing on Health and Performance," in Leonard J. Duhl (ed.), *The Urban Condition* (New York: Basic Books, 1963), pp. 215–228.

a legacy of unredressed grievances, bitter frustrations, and deep alienation in the black ghettos of the metropolises. And for a disproportionate number of nonwhites they have created almost insurmountable barriers to the development of individual abilities that would enable them to escape from their inferior status.

Racial Disturbances

The decade spanned by the school desegregation decision of 1954 (*Brown* v. *Board of Education*) and the Civil Rights Act of 1964 was the period in which the legal foundations of racial discrimination were destroyed. As described by Bayard Rustin, a leading Negro intellectual, the civil rights movement is now concerned "not merely with removing the barriers to full opportunities but with achieving the fact of equality."[18] Voting guarantees, school desegregation, fair employment acts, and similar legal remedies, the chief thrust of the movement during the 1950s, do not of and by themselves solve the problems of poor housing, inadequate educational resources, and unemployment or provide the institutional means through which the disadvantaged can develop their potential. Rustin's words were echoed a short time later by President Johnson in his famous Howard University speech of June, 1965.[19] In the President's words, we must seek "not just freedom but opportunity—not just equality as a right and a theory but equality as a fact and a result." This, he said, is the next stage of the battle for civil rights.

Two months later, as if to underscore the President's remarks, a large-scale riot erupted in the Watts area, a predominantly Negro section located largely within the city of Los Angeles, resulting in thirty-four deaths, hundreds of injuries, and $35 million in property damage. The earlier disturbances had been confined largely to the South, but Watts signalled the beginning of a long series of violent disorders in cities in other parts of the nation during the course of the next two years (Table 19). Some observers began to refer to urban communities with large racial concentrations as "tinder-boxes." The riots came as a shock to most white Americans who had assumed that progress was being made in solving the race problem. They also dramatized the inadequacy of the response, in all regions and by all levels of government, to the needs of the racial minorities and the poor. "Tokenism" could no longer serve as a substitute for basic change.

The wave of disorders led President Johnson, in July, 1967, to establish the National Advisory Commission on Civil Disorders with the charge to seek answers to the questions: "What happened? Why did it happen?

[18] "From Protest to Politics: The Future of the Civil Rights Movement," *Commentary*, 39 (February, 1965), 27.

[19] The text of the President's speech and an account of the events surrounding it are found in Lee Rainwater and William L. Yancey, *The Moynihan Report and the Politics of Controversy* (Cambridge: The M.I.T. Press, 1967).

TABLE 19   Disorders by Level and City Population, 1967

Population (in thousands)	Number of Major Disorders	Number of Serious Disorders	Number of Minor Disorders	Total
0–50	1	5	31	37
50–100	0	3	27	30
100–250	0	8	23	31
250–500	5	10	15	30
500–1000	1	4	10	15
Over 1000	1	3	13	17
Total	8	33	119	160

SOURCE: *Report of the National Advisory Commission on Civil Disorders* (Washington: 1968), p. 66.

What can prevent it from happening again and again?" The Commission in its widely-heralded report found racial prejudice ("white racism" as it was termed) essentially responsible for the explosive situation that has been developing in the cities since the end of World War II.[20] Striking a basic theme in its indictment of the majoritarian society, the Commission reminded the nation: "What white Americans have never fully understood—but what the Negro can never forget—is that white society is deeply implicated in the ghetto. White institutions created it, white institutions maintain it, and white society condones it."[21]

The inability on the part of most white Americans to comprehend the nature and depth of Negro grievances is itself an important facet of the racial problem. The following exchange between Senator John McClellan, chairman of a Congressional subcommittee which investigated the riots, and Harvey Judkins, a Negro councilman of Plainfield, New Jersey, illustrates in a disturbing fashion how this lack of comprehension is not confined to the poorly educated white.

CHAIRMAN: You spoke about recreational facilities. I think the record already reflects, and I don't recall exactly, what recreational facilities your city has. What does it have?

MR. JUDKINS: We have several playgrounds.

CHAIRMAN: How many?

[20] The term "racism" has different meanings for different people. Many whites define it in terms of overt, intentional hostility, or the expression of attitudes of superiority toward Negroes. But for many blacks it goes beyond such patent manifestations; to them it means a form of prejudice so ingrained in the feelings of whites that it is often subtle and even unwitting, yet always sensed by the non-white.

[21] *Report of the National Advisory Commission on Civil Disorders* (New York: Bantam Books, 1968), p. 2.

MR. JUDKINS: I would say roughly maybe about 10. . . .

CHAIRMAN: Counsel reminds me there are about 13.

MR. JUDKINS: I could be wrong about three playgrounds.

CHAIRMAN: Of course, I was just trying to get as near the facts as we could. What kind of playgrounds are they? Are they large, small, enough to accommodate substantial groups?

MR. JUDKINS: Some are small. The majority of them are small. We have three major size playgrounds which don't offer too much for, I would say, the age group of 15 to 20 years old. There isn't any type of planned program for the type of youth we are talking about, who were basically involved in the riots that we had.

CHAIRMAN: You have a city of 50,000 population and you have 13 playgrounds, 13 public recreational places. How many more do you think it would take to satisfy them? How many more do they want?

MR. JUDKINS: It is not the point of satisfying anyone, as far as this is concerned. It is the point of a program, I stipulated a program, a planned program.

CHAIRMAN: It wasn't facilities but lack of a program?

MR. JUDKINS: That is correct.

CHAIRMAN: It wasn't inadequate facilities?

MR. JUDKINS: That is correct.

CHAIRMAN: That is what I was trying to determine. I thought they were complaining about facilities. What kind of program did they want?

MR. JUDKINS: A program that offered them some type of athletic opportunities, to maybe let off steam if we want to speak in that term; something constructive.

CHAIRMAN: Was there anything to keep the young people from organizing and having their own ball games and so forth and playing? . . . I never did have anybody plan a baseball game for me when I was young. . . . Is that the reason they gave for this rioting, that there wasn't anybody there to organize and plan recreation for them?

MR. JUDKINS: I said that was one of the reasons. I didn't say it was the primary reason. . . .

CHAIRMAN: What is the other one?

MR. JUDKINS: The other one was the Vietnam situation.

CHAIRMAN: How could they blame the mayor for the Vietnam situation or blame you as a councilman for it? . . . What else was the rioting about?

MR. JUDKINS: The dethroning of Cassius Clay.

CHAIRMAN: Because of Cassius Clay?

MR. JUDKINS: Dethroning him.
CHAIRMAN: Did you have anything to do with that?
MR. JUDKINS: No.
CHAIRMAN: Neither did I.[22]

The ,vast gulf between the perceptions of the racial problem held by whites and Negroes is strikingly evident in their views toward the riots. Studies show that most blacks saw the disorders partly or wholly as spontaneous protests against unfair conditions and economic deprivations. Only a very small percentage defined the disturbances as criminal acts to be suppressed forcibly by the police. A majority of the white population, on the other hand, viewed the riots as criminal or conspiratorial acts precipitated by riffraff, hoodlums, and outside agitators. Numerous surveys have documented the existence of this perceptual gap across a wide range of issues and events. A Harris poll taken in August, 1967, for ex-

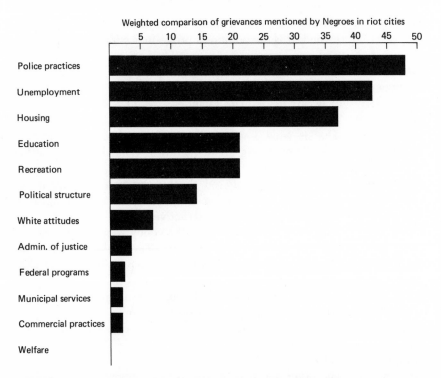

FIGURE 27   **Comparison of Negro Grievances in Riot Cities. From** Report of the National Advisory Commission on Civil Disorders, **U.S. Government Printing Office, 1968, p. 83.**

[22] U.S. Senate, Committee on Governmental Operations, Permanent Subcommittee on Investigations, *Riots, Civil and Criminal Disorders,* part 4 (Washington: 1967), pp. 1080–1085.

ample, revealed that two-thirds of the Negroes attributed the riots to police brutality while whites rejected this proposition by 8 to 1.[23]

Contrary to popular impression, the riots were not the work primarily of criminal types or those lowest on the socioeconomic status scale. Surveys made by the Commission on Civil Disorders disclosed that the typical rioter was a young adult with somewhat more education than the average inner-city black, employed, and a long-time resident of the area. In Detroit, more than two-thirds of the men arrested during the 1967 disorders were fully and gainfully employed. And in Watts, support for the disturbances was found to be as great among the better educated and economically advantaged persons in the riot area as among the poorly educated and economically disadvantaged.[24] These and similar facts run counter to the conventional wisdom concerning the racial problem and show the utter incongruity of the type of questioning observed in the McClellan hearings.

The Racial Paradox

"Our nation is moving toward two societies, one black, one white—separate and unequal." This conclusion of the Commission on Civil Disorders is reinforced by the white "backlash" and the growing separatist movement among the blacks. To most liberals, these latter developments represent critical threats to the goal of a fully integrated society in which whites and blacks live together harmoniously and in which an individual's race is not an important factor in determining public or private action. To others, however, separatism is regarded as the only path to the attainment of this ideal. These divergent views have resulted in two fundamentally different strategies or approaches to the racial problem. On the one hand, a majority of white liberals and older Negro leaders call for the massive upgrading of efforts and programs designed to facilitate integration and improve the socioeconomic status of the disadvantaged. On the other hand, many of the younger black leaders advocate the deferment of integration efforts and the development of "black power." Each course has

[23] On the question of attitudes generally, see William Brink and Louis Harris, *Black and White: A Study of U.S. Racial Attitudes Today* (New York: Simon and Schuster, 1967) and the National Advisory Commission on Civil Disorders, *The Supplemental Studies for the National Advisory Commission on Civil Disorders* (Washington: 1968). The insupportability of the "riffraff" hypothesis is shown in James Geschwinder, "Civil Right Protests and Riots," *Social Science Quarterly*, 49 (December, 1968), 474–484.

[24] Nathan E. Cohen, *Los Angeles Riot Study: Summary and Implications for Policy* (Los Angeles: University of California Institute of Government and Public Affairs, 1967). See also William McCord and John Howard, "Negro Opinion in Three Riot Cities," *American Behavioral Scientist*, 11 (March–April, 1968), 24–27, showing that the better-educated Negroes tended to express greater concern about the speed of integration, claimed to have participated in civil rights activities more often, and condemned police behavior with greater vehemence than those lower on the socioeconomic scale.

different policy and tactical implications although the ultimate objective of each is presumably the same.

Until the mid-1960s, the whole spectrum of civil rights efforts was concentrated on the goal of integration. The strategy was to desegregate the schools, disperse black families in white neighborhoods, end discrimination in employment practices, and improve the social conditions of the nonwhites. As expectations rose but progress toward equality in fact proved distressingly slow, black leaders turned to direct action to speed up the process: sit-ins, demonstrations, rent strikes, economic boycotts, poverty marches, and similar forms of pressure. Integrationists urged the nation to respond to these developments by increasing the rate of material and social advance. The report of the Commission on Civil Disorders is a brief for this position. It calls both for stepping up the pace of programs like Model Cities, the War on Poverty, and manpower training, and for creating strong incentives to facilitate Negro movement out of central city ghettos.

The second and more recent approach to the racial problem rests on the assumption that equality cannot be achieved through integration efforts because of implacable white resistance. As Kenneth Clark describes it: "The hopes of the Negroes that racial equality and democracy could be obtained through legislation, executive action, and negotiation, and through strong alliances with various white liberal groups were supplanted by disillusionment, bitterness and anger which erupted under the cry of 'Black Power'. . . ."[25] Those who advocate black power often have little more in common than the desire to redress the historical pattern of black subordination to white society.[26] The term, in fact, has many meanings ranging from ideological commitment to violence and the creation of a separate black nation within the United States ("black nationalism") to the development of political and economic strength within the ghetto.

The argument for black power, as defined in the latter sense, states that the Negro population must first overcome its feelings of powerlessness and lack of self respect and develop pride in its color and ethnicity before it can function effectively in the larger society. For this purpose, it must have control over decisions which directly affect its members. Implicit here is the creation of some form of neighborhood government and the promotion of "black capitalism" within the confines of the ghetto. These developments would be accompanied by what some refer to as "ghetto enrichment," or attempts to improve dramatically the quality of life for residents of the area.

[25] "The Present Dilemma of the Negro," *Journal of Negro History*, LIII (January, 1968), 5.

[26] See in this connection Martin Kilson, "Black Power: Anatomy of a Paradox," *Harvard Journal of Negro Affairs*, 2 (1968), 30–35.

Defined in this way, black power is difficult to fault since it is based on the proposition that the nonwhite minority must achieve a position of strength through solidarity if it hopes to bargain effectively with the rest of society—the majority is far more likely to make concessions to power than to justice or conscience.[27] It is also hard to deny the justice of the argument for more self-government in areas of the large central city when suburban villages can have their own school systems and police forces. At the same time, however, it is unrealistic to believe that "black capitalism" can successfully compete in a white-controlled economy or that local political and educational institutions can be manned solely by blacks. The wide range of skills and resources necessary for these complex tasks is simply not available in sufficient quantity among the nonwhites.

The manner in which the majoritarian society responds to the separatist movement and the aspirations it represents will do much to determine the fate of the nation's metropolitan areas. Such a response can take several forms. First, the white-dominated institutions of the community, public and private, can resist the movement by insisting on the retention of full control over the formulation and administration of programs in the nonwhite enclaves, thereby seeking to perpetuate the dependency relationship which the blacks desperately and rightfully want to sever. Two, they can use the demand for autonomy as an excuse for abdicating their responsibility to the black community (other than providing financial subsidization) and in this way encourage the maintenance of a segregated society. Or three, they can demonstrate a genuine rather than rhetorical commitment to the philosophy of maximum feasible participation of the disadvantaged by permitting a devolution of limited governmental powers to the neighborhoods and by significantly enlarging the opportunity structure for the nonwhites in such areas as housing, employment, and education so that alternatives would be open to them.

The first two courses would be disastrous since they would further dichotomize urban communities and strengthen the appeal of the black extremists who maintain there is no effective way of "moving the system" short of violence—"patience got us nowhere." (Unfortunately, the record of community response to the needs of the nonwhites shows that the militants have a point here.) The third course offers the only realistic alternative for both whites and blacks. It can succeed, however, only if the latter are permitted to develop the same kind of power base enjoyed by other groups in the society and if the more moderate Negro leaders are afforded the opportunity and means of demonstrating that they can bring about changes in the intolerable conditions of the nonwhite minority. No matter which path is taken, neither the Negro nor white can, in Kenneth Clark's words, "be free of the other."

[27] Martin Duberman, "Black Power in America," *Partisan Review*, XXXV (Winter, 1968), 34–48.

URBAN EDUCATION

The major problem of urban education today is not curriculum or instruction but the challenge of upgrading the educational achievement of the disadvantaged who are concentrated in the nation's metropolitan areas. Since the majority in this category are nonwhite, the racial dimensions of the problem overshadow its other aspects and dominate the debate over solutions. In seventy-five of the most populous cities, for example, three of every four Negro children in the elementary grades now attend schools with enrollments of 90 percent or more black. Moreover, it is estimated that by 1975, assuming current practices and trends continue, 80 percent of all Negro students in the twenty largest cities—which contain nearly one-half the nation's black population—will be attending schools 90 percent to 100 percent nonwhite.

The Brown decision in 1954 outlawed segregation imposed or recognized by law (de jure) but its effect on segregation resulting from residential patterns (de facto) has been negligible. If anything, color lines—and therefore socioeconomic lines—have sharpened significantly, with more pupils today attending totally segregated schools in all regions than at the time of the decision. In the District of Columbia, to cite one instance, 55 percent of the enrollment in the public schools in 1954 was white; today this proportion is less than 10 percent, as most of the white families have either fled to suburbia or placed their children in private or parochial schools.

Equality of Opportunity

After surveying the public school systems of ten major metropolitan areas in 1961, James B. Conant warned: "We are allowing social dynamite to accumulate in our large cities."[28] Citing the high dropout rate and the generally lower levels of educational achievement of slum area youth, he commented that the large differential between funds available to schools in the wealthier suburbs and those in the core cities "jolts one's notion of the meaning of equality of opportunity." Conant's statement strikes at the heart of the urban school issue. As a nation, we are dedicated to the principle of equal opportunity whether in education, housing, employment, or other basic areas of human living. But while there is wide societal acceptance of this goal, there is considerable disagreement over its meaning when it comes to the matter of specific application.

Equality, as the concept relates to public education, may be evaluated in several ways. It may be measured in terms of the community input to the schools, such as expenditures per pupil. Or it may be assessed on the basis of the racial composition of the student body in light of the

[28] *Slums and Suburbs* (New York: McGraw-Hill, 1961), p. 2.

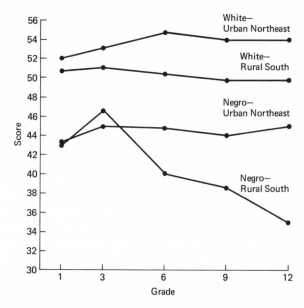

FIGURE 28   **Patterns of Achievement in Verbal Skills at Various Grade Levels by Race and Region. The national mean score at each grade is 50, and the standard deviation is 10. From James Coleman, "The Concept of Equality of Educational Opportunity,"** Harvard Educational Review, **38 (Winter, 1968), 20. Copyright © by President and Fellows of Harvard College.**

Supreme Court's holding that segregated schooling is by its very nature inferior. Or it may be defined in terms of the outputs or effects schools have on their students.[29] On all three of these counts, substantial inequality is found among metropolitan educational systems. Those in the suburbs spend more on the average than their counterparts in the central city; *de facto* racial segregation is the common pattern; and the academic achievement of students in schools of predominantly middle-class composition exceeds by a wide margin that of pupils in lower-income schools.

A striking illustration of inequality in the third sense can be seen in Figure 28. The comparison of achievement in verbal skills by Negro and white students in the urban Northeast shows the two groups beginning far apart in the first grade and remaining about the same distance from each other through the twelfth year. In other words, the gap did not

[29] For a discussion of this question, see James S. Coleman, "The Concept of Equality of Educational Opportunity," *Harvard Educational Review,* 38, (Winter, 1968), 7–22.

narrow; instead, the average Negro pupil was left at about the same level of academic accomplishment relative to whites as existed at the beginning of his school career. The contrast between whites and blacks in the rural South is even sharper. The two groups begin far apart and the distance widens considerably over the years of schooling to the disadvantage of the Negro.

Integration or Separatism?

School integration has been one of the prime targets of civil rights advocates, both black and white, for more than three decades. Following the invalidation of the "separate but equal clause," they turned their attention to the elimination of de facto segregation in urban areas outside the South as well as in southern cities. Since this form of racial and social-class segregation is the normal consequence of providing school facilities as close as possible to the pupil's home (the widely-publicized "neighborhood school" concept), whites have been able to draw on this traditional practice as justification for their resistance to integration. The obstacles to school integration, moreover, have multiplied with the growing concentration of nonwhite minorities in the core cities. Such remedies as the busing of pupils, adopting open enrollment or voluntary transfer policies, redrawing school district boundaries to cut across racial and socioeconomic population lines, and even establishing educational parks (the concentration of a set of schools in a limited spatial area, thus permitting joint use of common facilities) no longer offer meaningful solutions in many of the large urban centers. The only possible way of effecting integration in cities where the nonwhite school population far exceeds that of the whites—Washington, D.C., Newark, Baltimore, and St. Louis are examples—is through a metropolitan-wide plan involving the suburbs. Such a solution is presently beyond the realm of political feasibility.

Just as the years prior to 1954 were devoted to the legal war against de jure segregation and the succeeding decade to attacking the de facto variety, the period since the middle 1960s has been characterized by increasing emphasis on upgrading the quality of Negro schools. This emphasis takes many forms but basically it falls into two categories, one pragmatic, the other philosophical, both of which are prompted by the persistent failure of integration attempts. The first reasons that, given the present strong resistance to integration, efforts should be mobilized and directed toward obtaining the highest quality education for Negro pupils regardless of the racial composition of the school they attend. Stress would be placed on compensatory education (measures designed to overcome shortcomings in the learner) and would include such programs as Project Headstart and Follow Through. This approach, espoused by many of the moderate black leaders, represents a shift in tactics and strategy, not an abandonment of the larger goal of racially integrated schools.

The second category places primary emphasis on the attainment of power and control by Negro and other racial-minority parents over the schools their children attend.[30] Those who support this course argue that families in the deprived neighborhoods have been through the whole range of educational challenges and responses, from desegregation to compensatory schooling, without witnessing significant improvements in either the achievement levels of their children or in the opportunities open to those who graduate. Since, as they have come to conclude, the white-dominated and centralized school bureaucracies are really not interested in improving the educational lot of the disadvantaged minority, the latter should be permitted to operate their own systems. The underlying rationale, an outgrowth of the general philosophy of black power, is that after the nonwhites attain a higher educational level under their own aegis, they will then be in a position to integrate with white society on a basis of parity rather than deficiency.

Decentralization of control over the schools as a solution to the urban educational problem has won some political support although it is regarded with skepticism and even downright hostility by many officials and educators, including administrators and teachers. The first comprehensive decentralization plan for a large city was proposed in 1967 by an advisory panel appointed by Mayor John Lindsay and headed by McGeorge Bundy, president of the Ford Foundation.[31] Under the panel's recommendations, the New York city school system would be reorganized into a federation of 30 to 60 units, each governed by an 11-member board (6 elected by the parents and 5 appointed by the Mayor from a list prepared by the central educational authority). Each of these local boards would be vested with power to hire and fire personnel, make curriculum adaptations, and control its budget (funds would be allocated to it by the central authorities on the basis of a need formula). As is evident, the Bundy plan embodies the principle of community or neighborhood control; it does not, however, go as far as ghetto leaders want because of the Mayor's appointive authority over part of the governing board and the retention of certain veto powers over local decisions by the central board of education. These latter requirements were designed to provide broader perspective in the administration of the community schools and prevent arbitrary localism from jeopardizing the educational goals of the total city. The reorganization proposals, on the other hand,

[30] There is also a third approach known as "parallel systems." It rests on the rationale that if the disadvantaged cannot reform the public education system they should be afforded options to it. One version is to give tuition grants to parents who would then be able to purchase education from competing private schools. In view of the many constitutional, political, fiscal, and philosophical questions involved, this alternative is not likely to receive serious consideration in the foreseeable future.

[31] Mayor's Advisory Panel on Decentralization of the New York City Schools, *Reconnection for Learning: A Community School System for New York City* (New York, 1967).

went much too far in the eyes of the teachers' union which fears a diminution of its powers in a decentralized system and the loss of job security for its white members in black-dominated districts.[32]

The Coleman Report

Equality of Educational Opportunity, known as the Coleman report, appeared at a time (1966) when the thrust of the civil rights movement in the field of education was turning from the quest for racial integration to the establishment of black control over the public schools serving black children.[33] Carried out under a mandate in the Civil Rights Act of 1964 and based on a nationwide statistical survey of integrated and segregated public schools, the report represents the most far-reaching study of educational inequality yet conducted in the United States. Although the findings have been challenged as well as variously interpreted, they have been described by Daniel Moynihan and others as the most powerful social science case for school integration yet made.

According to the study, organizational efforts at educational improvement, such as reduced class size, account for little, if any, of the difference in pupil achievement when other variables are held constant—a finding which casts doubt on the efficacy of special or compensatory programs. The central thesis of the study is essentially a substantiation of the rationale in the Brown decision: the major favorable influence on the academic attainment of minority group students is the presence in the classroom of the more motivated and higher-achieving pupils from more advantaged backgrounds. In the words of the report: "If a minority pupil from a home without much educational strength is put with schoolmates with strong educational backgrounds, his achievement is likely to increase."[34] The question of whether this improvement is an effect of racial or social-class integration is for the most part academic since there are proportionately so few middle-class Negroes that the social integration of black children—and the same would be true for other nonwhite minorities—could not be accomplished without racial desegregation.[35]

The Coleman findings, in short, suggest that the mere improvement of school facilities exercises little independent effect on pupil achievement

---

[32] Several experimental districts have been set up, the one in the Ocean Hill-Brownsville area of New York City being the best known because of the controversy it precipitated between the local governing board and the teachers' union. For an account of this struggle, see Agee Ward, *The Center Forum,* 3 (November 13, 1968), 1–10.

[33] James S. Coleman et al., *Equality of Educational Opportunity* (Washington: 1968).

[34] *Ibid.,* p. 22.

[35] See in this respect David K. Cohen, "Policy for the Public Schools: Compensation and Integration," *Harvard Educational Review,* 38 (Winter, 1968), 114–137; also U.S. Commission on Civil Rights, *Racial Isolation in the Public Schools* (Washington: 1967).

when family background variables are controlled. At the same time, however, the data also lend support to those who argue for community or neighborhood control of the schools. They indicate, for example, that in the case of minority group students a sense of control over one's environment is more highly related to academic accomplishment than any other single variable measured in the study. This suggests the possibility of enhancing achievement by vesting more control over the schools in the parents and pupils in the disadvantaged neighborhoods— a key concept in the black power philosophy. Subsequent analyses of the Coleman data also indicate that the educational attainment levels of Negro children are particularly sensitive to the quality and attitudes of the teaching staffs assigned to them. Presumably local control over the hiring of teachers and administrators (accompanied by adequate financing) could better assure this quality and compatibility.[36] At any rate, the movement for parental control is likely to increase in cities with serious racial problems. In others, the status quo of appointed or elected boards composed of businessmen and professionals may be expected to continue.

Educational Responsibility

When Sputnik I launched the space age in 1957, it set off a barrage of criticism directed against the "weaknesses" of the American educational system and led to major reforms in the teaching of the sciences and mathematics. Were the United States in a similar race with the Soviet Union to eliminate the inequities in educational opportunities, Americans might also be willing to invest similar efforts in bringing about the necessary social changes. As it is, the nation's response to the growing demands for equality in the field of education have been woefully disproportionate to the challenge. This situation is hardly surprising since the sources of inequality are deeply embedded in the structure of metropolitan areas and their school systems. To achieve the goal of equal opportunity would require changes in the distribution of power; and rarely does any group or institution relinquish power without a struggle, as the New York city school controversy demonstrates so dramatically.

Education obviously cannot be treated separately from the problems of housing, welfare, and employment. To raise the academic attainment levels of Negro students but leave them with inappropriate job opportunities and restricted housing choices would only compound the bitterness and frustration which now exist. The attack must come on a broad front and involve the total range of public and private agencies, such as is envisaged in the Model Cities program. The educational system, nevertheless, is an important instrumentality in combatting the critical

[36] Samuel Bowles, "Toward Equality of Educational Opportunity," *Harvard Educational Review*, 38 (Winter, 1968), 89–99.

problems facing urban communities even though many of these difficulties are rooted in poverty and social disadvantage. It cannot absolve itself from this responsibility, as it has sometimes tended to do, by citing the failure of other institutions in the society. The easy answer in school integration, for example, has been to point to the segregated housing patterns as justification for inaction. Yet if the public school establishment is to remain relevant to the needs of the modern metropolitan community, it must deliberately use its skills and resources to promote social change in the interest of equality of opportunity.

THE GOOD LIFE

The growth of the metropolitan economic and social system has brought expanded opportunities for millions of Americans in the form of better jobs, improved educational and cultural facilities, and greater social mobility. At the same time it has also brought problems of far greater magnitude than those experienced by less complex societies. We have discussed some of these difficulties in this chapter and others. We have also observed that burgeoning urbanization and its accompanying features have decreased the self-sufficiency of individual metropolitan areas and made their economy and well-being more dependent than ever before on national and even international events and trends. Whether a particular metropolis thrives can be affected only partially by what its local institutions do or fail to do. Greater forces are at work than the zeal and resources of local leaders and officials. Nevertheless, within these circumscribed limits, achievement of the good life for the city or the metropolis can be fostered or deterred by the spirit and acts of the local citizenry and its public and private agencies.

For some urban dwellers the "good life" or its approximation has become a reality. The goal seems within the grasp of many others. For the economically and culturally deprived whites and a majority of nonwhites, the American dream appears a hollow mockery. Throughout a century in which the Negro enjoyed freedom from legal servitude, equality remained for him little more than a vague dream and an unattainable ideal. All this has been changed with the events of the 1960s. Equality has ceased to be an abstraction for him and has now become directly related to the house in which he lives, to the job opportunities available to him, to the schools where he sends his children, and to the public and private accommodations open to him. He no longer wants just the right to sit anywhere in the same bus or live in the same neighborhood with whites or go to the same school with them, but to own a car and a home and have his children receive quality education.

Nonwhites who were formerly apathetic and resigned to their lot in life have now been drawn into a massive campaign of social action. Embittered by the seeming intransigency of the white-dominated institutions and sparked by a growing sense of pride in their race, American Negroes have turned from the regular channels of democratic decision-making to the strategy of confrontation politics, crisis precipitation, and direct action. The transformation has been traumatic for the officials and administrators who man the urban bureaucratic structures. Accustomed to operate in a basically consensual milieu governed by middle-class norms and practices, they now find their intentions and objectives questioned, their expertise challenged, and their policies resisted by groups traditionally excluded from the power arrangements. Refusing to believe that the script has been changed, they have often reacted in ways which have served to aggravate social tension and unrest. Their ability to adjust to the new urban and metropolitan world is critical for the future.

𝟡 / THE PLANNING CHALLENGE

URBAN OR CITY PLANNING IS NOT A NEW OR NOVEL PUBLIC RESPONSIBILITY. The cities and towns of the world have always made some kind of blueprints for their physical development. Community-building based on clearly determined plans can be found in the cities of ancient Greece and Rome, in the villages of medieval Europe, and in many New England towns. Major l'Enfant's design for the physical pattern and development of our national capital is one of the more outstanding instances of American city planning, but other examples can be found in places like colonial Philadelphia and Salt Lake City. Although planning in these earlier settlements was elementary in the light of modern needs and conditions, its continued development and conscious use would have given us cities of greater beauty and livability today. The tragedy is that urban planning was largely ignored during the past century in the wake of the Industrial Revolution and the craze for land speculation, and in what Coleman Woodbury has referred to as the "intellectual blight of laissez-faire."[1]

[1] Coleman Woodbury (ed.), *The Future of Cities and Urban Redevelopment* (Chicago: University of Chicago Press, 1953), p. 637.

Despite its long, if disregarded, tradition, city planning has only in recent decades become established as a distinct process within the framework of local government. Land decisions in the past were made by private businessmen, realtors, and developers with little or no governmental guidance or control. Only occasionally did public agencies intervene to prevent flagrant abuses. The first municipal planning commission was established in 1907 in Hartford, Connecticut, but several more decades were to pass before land planning with controls could be said to exist. The Detroit experience is typical in this respect. A city charter adopted in 1918 provided for the appointment of a commission charged with preparing a comprehensive plan for the physical development and improvement of the community. For years the agency operated on a shoestring budget and with virtually no staff. Not until 1940 did the city enact a zoning ordinance and not until eight years later did it adopt a master plan. Thus by the time the commission had become established as the recognized agency for guiding Detroit's development, most of the vacant land within the municipality had disappeared and much of the physical layout had been set.

City planning is now an acceptable public function, but not many years back the mere mention of the term was sufficient to conjure up visions of governmental regimentation, creeping socialism, and infringement of private rights. With the course of contemporary events, these fears have largely faded into the background. Like Molière's Monsieur Jourdain who discovered that prose was what he had been speaking all his life, so Americans in recent decades found that planning was what they had been doing all along: in their private lives, their businesses, and even in their governments. In the face of mounting urban pressures, local officials and residents alike have become increasingly cognizant of the social and economic threats implicit in a system which leaves land use expansion and development almost entirely to the decisions of the market and the ingenuity of its participants. The awakened fear of permitting communities to grow like Topsy has given legitimacy and respectability to the planning function and to the professionals who perform it.

Today, the need for planning or controlling community change is no longer seriously questioned. The debate has now shifted to more troublesome issues. What is the relationship between physical and social planning? What institutional mechanisms are most appropriate for performing the function? To what extent should the residents of a neighborhood or community be involved in the process? What is the planner's role in easing racial conflict and facilitating social change? How can effective metropolitan planning be achieved without depriving local residents of a meaningful measure of control over the immediate environment in which they live? The present chapter considers these questions in light of the trends that are evolving in the field of city and metropolitan planning. First, however, it examines the nature of planning as it has traditionally been defined and the principal tools commonly associated with it.

THE TRADITIONAL APPROACH

Urban planning, in the broadest sense, is simply the process of deciding in advance what to do in order to achieve the goals of a community. It is, in short, a method for reaching decisions about what specific objectives are to be pursued and what specific action is to be taken. As such, it provides inputs for the policy choices which involve consideration of the future. Planning for cities, as traditionally understood and practiced, has related to the shaping of the physical environment and the spatial organization of activities within the community. This orientation was explicitly prescribed by the tenets of the profession as the following provision in the constitution of the American Institute of Planners (AIP) illustrates:

Its [the profession's] particular sphere of activity shall be the planning of the unified development of urban communities and their environs and of states, regions, and the nation, as expressed through determination of the comprehensive arrangement of land uses and land occupancy and the regulations thereof.[2]

It was not that planners were unaware of the social realm; the profession, in fact, has always attracted idealists with strong social reform orientations. It was rather their espousal of a theory of environmental determinism—the influence of physical factors over social behavior—which shaped their attitudes and actions. The "city beautiful" movement, for example, rested on the belief that improvement of the physical setting with well-designed homes, playgrounds, and community facilities would drastically reduce social disorganization and pathology.

One might find it surprising that planners relied so heavily on efforts at manipulating the physical environment to affect human behavior rather than seeking to deal with the social factors more directly. Yet in a profession dominated by architects, engineers, and landscape designers, such an approach was probably inevitable. Only in recent years has the simple clarity of the planner's perspective been shaken as empirical research has punctured the myth of environmental determinism. As Melvin Webber notes: "The simple one-to-one cause-and-effect links that

[2] The qualifying clause "as expressed . . . thereof" was deleted by amendment to the constitution in 1967.

once tied houses and neighborhoods to behavior and welfare are coming to be seen as but strands in highly complex webs that, in turn, are woven by the intricate and subtle relations which mark social, psychic, economic, and political systems."[3]

THE TOOLS OF PLANNING

Planning results in blueprints for future development; it recommends courses of action for the achievement of desired goals. This process, as commonly understood, involves four steps or categories of functions: research (Where are we now?); goal formation (Where do we want to go?); plan-making (How do we get there?); and implementation (What means or tools do we employ to effectuate the design?). The first three steps culminate in the formulation of what is known variously as the general plan, master plan, or comprehensive plan. The last group consists of the techniques or tools to carry out such a design, principally zoning, subdivision regulations, and capital improvement programming. Not all cities follow these stages in systematic fashion. Most have a general notion of where they would like to go and on this basis determine their zoning and other developmental decisions. The availability of federal planning (701) grants in recent years has, however, prompted a large number of communities to formulate comprehensive plans. The extent to which the latter actually serve as guidelines for development varies substantially from municipality to municipality. In some they are relegated to the archives, in others conscientiously adhered to; and in most their use lies somewhere between these extremes.

The General Plan

The general plan serves as the overall blueprint for the physical development of the community (Figure 29). It is not, as commonly assumed, a rigid and static physical design attractively presented on a large and colorful chart but a composite of maps, programs, and policy statements that are intended to serve as guides for both public and private action. Its basic components include plans for land use, transportation, and community facilities.[4] The Connecticut statute authorizing municipalities to formulate and adopt a master plan provides a typical legislative definition of the scope of such instruments. Under the terms

[3] "Comprehensive Planning and Social Responsibility," in Bernard J. Frieden and Robert Morris (eds.), *Urban Planning and Social Policy* (New York: Basic Books, 1968), p. 10.

[4] For an incisive treatment of the elements of land use planning see F. Stuart Chapin, Jr., *Urban Land Use Planning*, 2nd ed. (Urbana: University of Illinois Press, 1965).

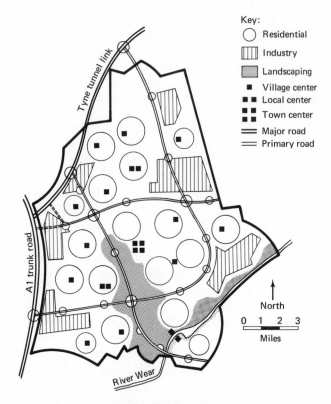

FIGURE 29   **The Master Plan for Washington New Town,
England. From** Journal of the Town Planning
Institute, **77 (February, 1967), 53. Plan pro-
duced by Llewelyn-Davies Weeks Forestier-
Walker & Bor, London.**

of the statute, the plan may include recommendations:

for the most desirable use of land within the municipality for residential, recreational, commercial, industrial, and other purposes; for the most desirable
density of population in the several parts of the municipality; for a system of
principal thoroughfares, parkways, bridges, streets, and other public ways; for
airports, parks, playgrounds, and other public grounds; for general location, relocation and extent of public utilities and terminals, whether publicly or
privately owned, for water, sewerage, light, power, transit, and other purposes;
and for the extent and location of public housing projects.[5]

The master plan as such is not legally binding on anyone. Only those
elements of it which the governmental policy-makers see fit to adopt

[5] General Statutes of Connecticut (1949 revision), title 8, chap. 45.

and incorporate into law through zoning and other implementary means have this effect. The execution or enforcement of the plan, in other words, is strictly a political act. Planners are powerless to effectuate their work except as their proposals are appealing to the policy-makers. They may carefully and arduously prepare a comprehensive plan for community development but unless the mayor and council are willing to employ it as the basis for decisions on land use, space allocations, circulation patterns, and public improvement projects, it will stand merely as a collection of attractive maps and noble statements.

Responsibility in the past for the preparation and adoption of the master plan commonly rested with a semiautonomous agency or commission appointed by the mayor or council. In more recent years the prevalent practice has been to submit the plan to the legislative council of the city for its adoption. As T. J. Kent shows, the general plan has evolved over the last fifty years from a technical guide for a nonpolitical commission to a statement of public policy about the community's physical development enunciated by the local governing body.[6] Such a procedure does not endow the plan with greater legal force but it does increase the likelihood that its provisions will receive greater attention from the policy-makers.

Zoning

Zoning is often regarded as planning; in fact, it serves as a substitute for it in many communities. Some planning obviously is involved in the zoning process, since local policy-makers are designing a pattern for future development when they draw up districts for the various types of land use. However, unless this design is based on a knowledge and evaluation of the many interrelated elements influencing community growth and change, it is likely to be unrealistic as well as dysfunctional. How, for example, could local officials intelligently estimate the amount of land that should be reserved for residential use, or for industrial and commercial purposes, without reference to a host of other factors? Zoning, if it is to be employed rationally, must be related to future needs and trends, community resources and potentialities, the road and utility systems, and demographic characteristics. It must, in short, be grounded on a comprehensive plan that reveals these interconnections and provides perspective for coordinating and harmonizing the numerous pieces of the urban puzzle.

Zoning is commonly defined as the division of a community into districts for the purpose of regulating the use and development of the land and buildings. It is an exercise of the police power directed primarily at the use of private property. It originated in efforts to segregate noxious activities from residential areas and to protect property values by the

[6] *The Urban General Plan* (San Francisco: Chandler, 1964).

similarity of uses in each zone. Frequently zoning was brought into operation as the result of a local emergency. Stuart Chase, the well-known author, relates how zoning came to his town when a small drug-preparation shop opened in a residential area and began emitting an unpleasant smell. He also tells of a similar awakening in a neighboring town when it was suddenly confronted with a project for a large trailer park. In this case, Chase notes, zoning "heretofore held to be un-American by the good people of Hartland was rushed through in an emergency town meeting."[7]

Comprehensive or community-wide zoning is accomplished by means of an ordinance specifying the types of districts and the permissible uses within each type. The boundaries of the various districts are then indicated on an official map which is adopted as part of the zoning ordinance. Three broad categories of zones are customarily established—residential, commercial, and industrial—with each divided into several classifications or grades. In addition to governing the kind of development permitted in each type of district, the zoning ordinance also contains regulations pertaining to the height of buildings, the proportion of the lot that the structure may cover, the setback and side lines, and, in the case of multifamily and business uses, the amount of off-street parking facilities. Once adopted, the ordinance is enforced by the building commissioner who has authority to deny building and occupancy permits for structures not complying with provisions of the zoning law.

Subdivision Regulation

Subdivision regulation, like zoning, is of relatively recent vintage. It grew out of the many problems and abuses, such as disconnected street patterns and lack of essential utilities, that flow from the uncontrolled division of land holdings for developmental purposes. Whereas zoning concerns the type of building and use that may take place on the land, subdivision control is concerned with the manner in which the land is divided and made ready for improvements. Enacted under the police powers of the municipality or other local governmental unit, subdivision regulations specify the standards to be followed by developers in laying out new streets and building lots and the site improvements that they must provide, such as sewers, water mains, and sidewalks. With relatively little raw land remaining in the central city, such regulations are of greater applicability in the expanding suburban communities. However, many states permit their municipalities to exercise subdivision control in the fringe areas outside their boundaries, usually for a distance of three to five miles.[8]

---

[7] "Confessions of a Town Planner," *The Reader's Digest*, 83 (July, 1963), 133–137.

[8] Subdivision regulation is treated in detail in Donald H. Webster, *Urban Planning and Municipal Public Policy* (New York: Harper & Row, 1958), chap. 9.

Capital Improvement Program

Zoning and subdivision regulation are primarily protective functions. They prevent land use development that the community deems undesirable, but of themselves they have no power to effectuate desirable development. This task depends more on private initiative and private resources than on public action. Zoning an area for an industrial park is no assurance that industry will locate there; or redesigning the central business district is no guarantee that the merchants and property owners will make the investments in building construction and alterations necessary to carry out the plan.

One implementary device, which is positive in character and both directly and indirectly contributes to plan execution, is the capital improvement program. This program is simply a planned schedule of public projects designed to meet present and future public needs. As such, it is a key element in carrying out the community master plan and serves two purposes in this connection. First, it provides for the execution of that portion of the plan which calls for public investment, such as the acquisition of park sites or the redesigning of the road network. Second, it influences private investment decisions by the timing and allocation of public expenditures for various programs. Thus a governmental decision to give priority to an urban renewal project in the older section of the city over a program to extend sewer and water mains into an undeveloped area would probably have much to do with the direction of private developmental activity.

A long-range capital improvement program has certain other practical advantages. By revealing the total picture of immediate and future needs, it enables public officials to evaluate these requirements better in relation to other facets of the master plan and to available resources. This procedure reduces the possibility of costly mistakes and permits the establishment of realistic priorities for public facilities. The existence of such a program also affords local officials a degree of protection from political pressures in resolving capital allocations. Although public expenditures, or zoning for that matter, cannot be insulated from politics and the demands of special interests groups, a carefully worked out program and schedule of priorities give public officials a sound basis on which to stand in resisting ill-conceived or untimely action. Without such a program, there is danger that the policy-makers will spread the capital budget over a wide range of projects in efforts to satisfy all interests. When this occurs, needs which should be given priority inevitably suffer.

THE CHANGING CHARACTER OF PLANNING

The classical, simplistic ideals which have marked city planning practice for the last half century have begun to break down under the inexorable pressures of continuous urban growth and the problems it generates. These forces have prompted considerable soul-searching and reassessment on the part of the planning profession and have led to numerous proposals for the modification of existing theory and practices. More specifically, they are reflected in changing concepts about the nature of planning, the tools of the trade, and the position and role of the planner in the governmental process. Each of these warrants examination.

New Perspectives

The most obvious perceptual changes of academics and practitioners in the field during the last decade relate to the nature of planning.[9] Although the new viewpoints have thus far found only limited application, their influence is not to be discounted. Of particular interest is a broadening of the planner's subject matter from its narrow physical base to include matters of an explicitly social nature as well. In the words of one observer: "The idea of city planning as physical planning alone has been riddled with bullets on the streets of Watts and Harlem."[10] No longer is it taken for granted that good urban form or design will automatically enhance the well-being of the people who comprise the community. Instead, planning literature is increasingly stressing the need for careful analyses of the import of physical changes on human beings and the desirability of integrating physical and social planning. It is also emphasizing the necessity for planners to become more fully attuned to the paramount problems of the cities and the needs of their poorer inhabitants and racial minorities.

When discussing this new trend, it is helpful to distinguish between the two general types of planners now functioning in urban communities: physical and social. Those in the former category continue to dominate the city planning departments or commissions, although they are giving increasing attention to the social implications of master plans, zoning ordinances, and the siting of public housing and urban renewal projects. Social planners, on the other hand, are found in a wide range of agencies —public and private—including health and welfare councils, community

[9] Analyses of the new trends are found in Kenneth L. Kraemer, "New Comprehensiveness in City Planning," *Public Administration Review*, XXVIII (July-August, 1968), 382–389; and Richard S. Bolan, "Emerging Views of Planning," *Journal of the American Institute of Planners*, XXXIII (July, 1967), 233–245.

[10] Bertram M. Gross, "The City of Man: A Social Systems Reckoning," in William R. Ewald, Jr. (ed.), *Environment for Man: The Next Fifty Years* (Bloomington: Indiana University Press, 1967), p. 142.

action groups, and neighborhood associations. The problem of coordinating these two forms of planning so as to encompass the full range of a community's social, economic, and physical development remains largely unsolved. Ideally, the goal is to incorporate a genuinely comprehensive social and physical planning process into the structure of local public decision-making. Some efforts are under way in this direction—the Model Cities program is one such attempt—but progress thus far has not been significant.[11]

Historically, as noted earlier, planners regarded their major task as the production of a long-range master or comprehensive plan indicating what the pattern of land use development should be at some distant point in the future and the general means for achieving this result. The assumption is that short-term and day-to-day development decisions can then be measured against this yardstick. This is an eminently rational approach but its execution has encountered numerous difficulties including changes in community goals, failure of predictions about the future, and the problem of taking into account the new values and opportunities which keep coming into the picture. It has also suffered because the political organs of city government generally lack the power or willingness to carry out the provisions of such a plan. As William Wheaton, one of the leading theoreticians in the planning field, has said:

Little of what is called comprehensive city planning today is effective. In older cities it ratifies what the market did before planning and land use controls were established. In suburban and newly developing areas it sanctions what the market will do anyway. One could compare Houston, which has had no planning, with any of a score of cities of comparable size and recency of development, which have had the most advanced planning and find no discernible important differences.[12]

Increasing awareness of these various factors on the part of the profession has caused a shift in planning emphasis from what is referred to as a product-oriented activity to a process- or project-oriented one. Although considerable ambiguity still remains as to the precise meaning of this approach, the general notion is that planning is a continuous process

[11] See in this regard Michael P. Brooks and Michael A. Stegman, "Urban Social Policy, Race, and the Education of Planners," *Journal of the American Institute of Planners*, XXXIV (September, 1968), 275–286; and Harvey S. Perloff, "New Directions in Social Planning," *Journal of the American Institute of Planners*, XXXI (November, 1965), 297–304.

[12] "Metro-Allocation Planning," *Journal of the American Institute of Planners*, XXXIII (March, 1967), 103. Houston is the only large city in the United States which does not have a zoning ordinance. Its planning department, established in 1940, has been concerned mainly with the enforcement of subdivision regulations and the preparation of park and major thoroughfare plans. See Louie Welch, "The Strength of Planning in Houston," *Planning 1967* (Chicago: American Society of Planning Officials, 1967), pp. 253–259.

of moving toward provisional goals rather than the delineation of an ideal or single "best" plan (product) to be attained at some future date. Planning, in other words, is viewed as an ongoing process and the master plan a general expression of and a flexible guide to public policy embodying nonphysical aspects of the city as well as its spatial layout. The new procedure calls for constant evaluation of development policy—pulse-taking, monitoring, testing, feedback—to determine the efficacy of plans and programs as they relate to problem-solving and goal achievement. Anthony Downs explains it in this way:

The . . . process will include specification of goals, development of major strategies for accomplishing those goals, recurrent production of detailed plans within the broader framework of these strategies, and constant adjustment of all these items in response to feedback from the communities affected and the major political and economic interest groups therein.[13]

Some critics reject altogether the notion of a master plan, citing as impediments the inability to predict the future much beyond a few years, the nature of the political system which limits the planner to problem-solving or "opportunity-seizing," the difficulty of determining goals or values which are always in a state of flux, and the practical limits of man's rationality. As one of them has suggested: "Long range definitive design plans encompassing whole urban areas should become an internal office exercise, an envelope for ideas, a model referred to for comparison —replaced by development and redevelopment policies limited both in scale, area and time span."[14]

Not all planners, actually only a small minority, are prepared to reject the basic importance of the master plan as traditionally conceived. Recognizing its limitations and the need for increasing its flexibility and enlarging its horizons beyond the physical, they point to the fact that public investment in such facilities as expressway systems, urban renewal projects, mass transit, and sewers inevitably (and almost unalterably) fix the future shape of a community. When millions and even billions of dollars are committed to such projects (reconstruction of the central business district, for example), a city or metropolitan area is unlikely to disregard their existence in formulating current policy. The hand of the past weighs too heavily on the present. For this reason alone, many planners argue, the necessity of preparing long-range comprehensive plans is imperative.

[13] "The Coming Revolution in City Planning," in Edward C. Banfield (ed.), Urban Government, rev. ed. (New York: Free Press, 1969), p. 602.
[14] Marshall Kaplan, "The Planner, General Planning and the City," Land Economics, XL (August, 1964), 300.

New Tools of Planning

The tools for planning are becoming more diverse and complex as technology and the social sciences make new techniques of research and analysis available. The adding machine and desk calculator are giving way to electronic data processing while scientific methods of prediction and evaluation are replacing intuition and hunch. Systems analysis, involving the formulation and evaluation (through cost-benefit and cost-effectiveness methods) of alternative approaches to a problem, is finding its way into the planning office. Sophisticated efforts are being made, with computer assistance, to show the interrelations between the components of the urban system so that the impact of action taken in respect to one element, such as zoning, can be analyzed in terms of its effects on other parts, such as the roads, schools, and public utilities. The large-scale transportation studies in the major urban areas, using mathematical models to simulate traffic flows under alternative transportation and land use plans, represent the most advanced of these efforts.

Along with the utilization of scientific methods of inquiry and validation, planners are also experimenting with new techniques for moving from diagnosis and prescription to execution. One difficulty with long-range master plans as commonly formulated is their failure (or one might more appropriately say their inability) to specify the detailed courses of action required for their implementation. As a consequence, most policy-makers consider the comprehensive plan too generalized, remote, and unreal to serve their purposes in reaching decisions on present needs and problems. To remedy this gap between the general and the particular, proposals have been made (and adopted in some cases) for the use of short-run development plans, revised and acted upon annually much in the same way that local capital budgets are handled. Such plans, according to one description, indicate "the specific changes in land use programmed for each year, the rate of new growth, the public facilities to be built, the structures to be removed, the private investment required, the extent and sources of public funds to be raised, the tax and other local incentives to encourage private behavior requisite to the plan."[15]

More recently, some planner-scholars, like Henry Fagin, have been advocating the use of what they call a "policy plan," which would consist of a compendium of the separate plans of the various governmental units and subunits relating to any individual development program or proposal. A multicolumn reference format juxtaposing the relevant agencies would be employed for this purpose. Such a format would

[15] Martin Meyerson, "Building the Middle Range Bridge for Comprehensive Planning," *Journal of the American Institute of Planners*, XXII (Spring, 1956), 62.

provide policy expressions by narrative description as well as by maps, tables, and schedules, specifications of annual costs of financing and operations, space and locational requirements, legal steps involved, personnel needs, and interrelated measures. In this way the specific programs of the different public agencies addressed to a particular urban problem or development issue could be integrated (at least conceptually).[16] The Fagin proposal and the other activities mentioned above illustrate the efforts which planners are making to fashion new tools and techniques commensurate with the needs of the modern urban community.

Planning and the Political Process

The role and place of the planner in the local governmental system still remain largely undetermined. Should he be an advisor to the policy agencies of government or a spokesman articulating his professional judgment on what he perceives to be the broad public interests of the community? Should he be an arm of the mayor, the council, or an independent commission? Should he be in a line position, such as the health director and police chief, or in a staff post, such as the budget officer or city attorney? Although the issues implicit in these questions are the subject of considerable debate, certain definite trends in resolving them are emerging.

Historically, the planning function was assigned to a semiautonomous agency or commission appointed by the mayor or council. This body was vested with authority to hire its own professional staff, prepare and adopt a master plan, and hear requests for zoning changes and submit recommendations on them to the council. The location of these duties in an agency outside the regular administrative channels of government was largely the result of reformist zeal. Pressure for planning (or more accurately for zoning) originated with civic improvement groups during the municipal reform era early in the present century. By assigning the responsibility to an independent commission, the reformers hoped to insulate the program from politics and politicians. Since World War II, such commissions—although continuing to prevail in number—have lost favor as many practitioners and scholars urge the integration of the planning function into the regular administrative structure of government. Chicago moved in this direction in 1957 when it reconstituted its planning agency as a full-fledged executive department and retained the commission only as an advisory board to the department. Those who support this approach argue that a strong mayor aided directly by a well-conceived planning program and the necessary staff is in a position

[16] Henry Fagin, "The Evolving Philosophy of Urban Planning," in Leo Schnore and Henry Fagin (eds.), *Urban Research and Policy Planning* (Beverly Hills: Sage Publications, 1967), pp. 309–328.

to accomplish far more than one who is compelled to work indirectly through a semi-independent commission.[17]

The planning profession, as such, has taken no official stand on the question of structure. Apparently lacking general consensus among the members on this subject, it has preferred to let the decision rest in the hands of the individual governmental jurisdictions. In those cases where the function has been placed under the municipal chief executive—and this is now the dominant trend—planners are generally regarded by the mayor (or city manager) as staff aides. When this is the case, they often find themselves immersed in the day-to-day problems confronting the executive and in the particular projects of interest to him. Overall or long-range planning thus tends to become downgraded in the priorities of the staff.[18] At the same time, however, the planner is in a position by virtue of his direct relation to the chief executive to influence policy and further the implementation of planning objectives.

There are obviously risks for the planner in such an arrangement since involvement in governmental policy development inevitably immerses the participant in politics. Most planners, while concerned about the dilemma of "professionalism versus opportunism," have come to recognize the facts of political life both in winning support for their proposals and in acquiring the needed resources to carry them out. It seems clear that, regardless of what formal structural arrangements a locality may choose to utilize, the move is toward the establishment of closer working relationships and ties between the planner and the political officials responsible for policy-making and administration.

PLANNING AND CITIZEN INVOLVEMENT

Planners have been long on the rhetoric of citizen participation—"we must plan with people, not for them"—but exceedingly short in putting this precept into effect. The common practice has been to formulate plans and then simply present them to the people at a public hearing. Citizens in such cases have only the opportunity to react, under very inappropriate circumstances, to proposals about which they have little or no knowledge. Even the workable program requirement of citizen involvement in urban redevelopment has been met largely by the creation of "reactor" committees.

[17] This viewpoint is forcefully expressed in Robert A. Walker, *The Planning Function in Urban Government*, 2nd ed. (Chicago: University of Chicago Press, 1950).

[18] A similar situation, however, exists even where there is a separate planning commission or department. In many such cases as much as 90 percent of the staff's time is taken up with the processing of applications for zoning changes and the supervision of subdivision regulations. The answer to this problem, as many see it, is the establishment of a separate office of zoning administrator to handle these day-to-day matters and free the planners for "planning."

The "participation explosion" of recent years has not left the planning function untouched. Yet the demand for greater involvement comes at a time when the increasing complexity of the public management bureaucracy and the transfer of wider and wider areas of public policy from the realm of politics to that of expertise have made it difficult for the ordinary citizen to comprehend the system and the nature of its outputs. People, as psychological studies indicate, may respond to a situation of this kind either by political apathy and disengagement, or by resort to protest. Increasingly, the latter course is being followed with consequences disturbing to the professional tranquillity of the planners. "Planning with people" is now acquiring new meaning as the professionals are required to ascertain and take into account the values, desires, and demands of the affected neighborhoods and groups in formulating their proposals.

The shift from politics to expertise, as one scholar notes, changes the rules for exercising power since the planning recipients who want to make their views felt—short of resorting to disruptive politics—must now possess the technical resources to confront the bureaucratic establishment. Groups disadvantaged in the traditional political framework, such as the poor, the uneducated, and the racial minority, find themselves further disadvantaged when it comes to dealing with those who speak the language of statistics, diagrams, maps, and computers.[19] To remedy this situation, some authorities in the field have proposed what they call "advocacy planning," or the use of experts by neighborhood organizations and other interest groups to make their case and articulate their needs and desires.

Paul Davidoff, a city planning professor, has been one of the leading formulators and proponents of the advocacy approach. He views it as a way of balancing the demands for increasing centralization of bureaucratic controls against the growing concerns for the requirements of local interests. If citizens are to be included in the planning process, he argues, they must not only be permitted to be heard but must also "be able to become well informed about the underlying reasons for planning proposals, and be able to respond to them in the technical language of professional planners."[20]

According to the concept of advocacy planning suggested by Davidoff and others, planners would be retained by individual groups and organizations to prepare plans for them and to argue for their adoption much as

[19] Lisa Peattie, "Reflections on Advocacy Planning," *Journal of the American Institute of Planners*, XXXIV (March, 1968), 80–88.

[20] "Advocacy and Pluralism in Planning," *Journal of the American Institute of Planners*, XXXI (November, 1965), 332. See also Alan S. Kravitz, "Advocacy and Beyond," in *Planning 1968* (Chicago: American Society of Planning Officials, 1968), pp. 38–51.

a lawyer pleads for his client. Planners serving in this staff capacity would not be responsible to the city government nor have the function of weighing neighborhood needs against community-wide considerations. This would remain the task of the official agencies and policy-makers of the local government. Through the use of advocate planners, citizen groups would not be limited to protesting plans formulated by the city or redevelopment authority but would be in a position to evaluate them and offer alternative proposals for debate and consideration.

Advocacy planning on a limited scale has been experimented with in a number of cities. In Chicago, for example, the Woodlawn Organization formed by Saul Alinsky hired planning consultants to evaluate a proposed urban renewal project and present more acceptable alternatives. Mobilization for Youth in New York City, aided by federal funds, has also utilized this technique in connection with its neighborhood organization work. And in Cambridge, Massachusetts, a nonprofit corporation has been organized to "review and evaluate specific planning proposals which affect low-income communities; to develop planning strategies, physical designs and implementation programs for these communities; and, to act as planning advocate for these communities in order to make public plans reflect their needs."[21]

The advocacy concept has been greeted with less than enthusiasm by a majority of the planning profession. Quite apart from such difficulties as finances, organization, and drawing low-income neighborhoods into the process, many of them question the appropriateness and wisdom of transferring the adversary principle of the legal system to the planning system. As one member of the profession charges: "The natural tendency of the adversary procedure is to harden the lines of thought; to stiffen the obstinacy with which people cling to intellectual positions they might otherwise have abandoned; to embody conflict in institutional forms; to castigate compromisers as cowards; to widen the gaps between ethnic and economic groups. . . . Once permanently attached to the anti-official side, the advocates will have changed themselves from planners into tribunes of the people."[22] One can detect in much of the criticism the attitude that planning is beyond the ken of the common man while the planner is an impartial expert whose judgment about what is best for the community ought not be questioned. Advocacy may not provide a practical answer to the problem of citizen involvement but it at least indicates the direction to be taken in an age when the individual is being overwhelmed by large-scale institutions.

[21] Articles of Organization of Urban Planning Aid, incorporated under General Law 180, State of Massachusetts, June 6, 1966.
[22] Roger Starr, "Advocates or Planners?" *ASPO Newsletter*, 33 (December, 1967), 137–138.

PLANNING THE METROPOLIS

The discussion up to this point has dealt with the subject of planning mainly as it applies to the municipal level of government. This approach was necessary since the development of the metropolis has been determined largely by the planning decisions of the individual local units which comprise it. Metropolitan planning, in fact, was little more than a subject of discourse in this country until after World War II. A few isolated efforts in this direction were made earlier, such as the Regional Plan for New York and Its Environs sponsored by a private foundation in the late 1920s; and some special districts engaged in area-wide planning as it related to their functional concerns. For the most part, however, whatever planning occurred was done by the local units acting individually. The result of this neglect is reflected in a study prepared for a congressional subcommittee by the Joint Center for Urban Studies at the Massachusetts Institute of Technology and Harvard University:

> In the absence of well-developed metropolitan plans, the urban patterns that are emerging today are a random collection of local plans and policies designed to meet local objectives. Yet each community, in seeking an optimum solution to its own problems, does not necessarily work in the interests of the people in the larger metropolitan area. Many suburban towns, for example, have chosen to promote the development of single-family houses on large lots as a means of forestalling costly investments in new utility systems. From their own point of view, these strategies have often been effective. But when large numbers of communities in an area limit their development in this way, the net result has often been to force a vast outward movement of people to the fringes of metropolitan areas, creating a need for new and expensive utility systems in the peripheral communities, and forcing long commuting trips to the central cities. A pattern of development that is economical for many suburbs can be very costly for the metropolitan area and the Nation at large.[23]

Number and Composition

The term *metropolitan* (or *regional*) planning commission is generally applied to public agencies which are set up on a multijurisdictional basis. It includes those serving two or more counties, several municipalities, a combination of counties and municipalities, or a city and county jointly. A survey by the National Municipal League staff in 1962 showed sixty-three such bodies operating in SMSAs.[24] Six years later the Graduate

[23] U.S. Senate Committee on Government Operations, Subcommittee on Intergovernmental Relations, *The Effectiveness of Metropolitan Planning* (Washington: 1964), p. 3.

[24] For an annotated list of these agencies see *National Civic Review*, LI (July, 1962), 384–390. A companion list is found in Housing and Home Finance Agency, *National Survey of Metropolitan Planning* (Washington: 1963).

School of Public Affairs at the State University of New York at Albany listed 351 "metropolitan planning commissions," including county-wide agencies both within and outside standard metropolitan statistical areas.[25] This latter compilation serves to highlight the mounting number of public planning organizations with territorial jurisdiction larger than the municipality. However, a more realistic enumeration of viable area-wide agencies is the list of planning commissions (including councils of governments that perform the planning function) approved by the Bureau of the Budget to review the applications of local units for federal facilities grants. The number of such agencies now totals approximately 175.

The majority of metropolitan planning commissions are established by joint action of local units under state enabling acts. The provisions regarding size and membership are so varied that generalization is difficult. In most cases the participating governments appoint the members; in others the governor names all or a portion of them; and in still others different combinations of selection methods are employed. The Southeastern Wisconsin Regional Planning Commission, for example, has a membership of 21, including 7 appointed by the county boards and 14 by the governor; the Metropolitan Area Planning Council in the Boston SMSA consists of 127 members: one representative from each of the 96 municipalities in the area, 21 gubernatorial appointees, and 10 ex-officio members from important state and city agencies; and the Metropolitan Washington Council of Governments, the officially designated planning unit for that region, is composed of 47 members, including officials of the cities and counties and representatives of Congress and the states of Maryland and Virginia.

The composition of such bodies also varies widely, as these examples indicate. The most common practice is to limit membership to the municipalities and counties but a growing number include representatives from other units, such as school and nonschool special districts, port and housing authorities, and federal and state agencies. About 40 percent of the commissions serve areas coterminous with the SMSA while the remainder have territorial jurisdiction either of greater or less geographical scope. A few cross state lines, such as the permanent committee on regional planning set up by the governors of Delaware, New Jersey, and Pennsylvania.

The operating budgets of metropolitan commissions have increased almost three-fold since 1963, with the total now exceeding $50 million annually. Only a minority of the agencies, however, possess the power to levy taxes or make compulsory assessments on the member governments. Most must rely on voluntary contributions from their constituent units and on grants-in-aid. Thus far the burden of support has been borne

[25] *1968 Survey of Metropolitan Planning*, pp. 15–26.

largely by the national government, with funds from municipal and county sources next in importance and state contributions last.

Nature of Metropolitan Planning

Like its counterpart at the municipal level, metropolitan planning has concerned itself almost exclusively with the physical aspects of the region. As Table 20 shows, land use and transportation studies predom-

TABLE 20   **Types of Studies Conducted, Metropolitan Planning Commissions, by Region, 1968**

Type	Total	Northeast	South	Midwest	West
Land use	123	37	37	34	15
Transportation	114	33	36	31	14
Water resources	63	27	16	14	6
Air pollution	31	9	12	6	4
Community facilities	83	24	27	24	8
Recreation	11	2	3	5	1
Open space	19	8	4	4	3

SOURCE: *1968 Survey of Metropolitan Planning*, p. 8.

inate with community facilities and water resource analysis next in line. This substantive limitation was stipulated by most state enabling laws and (until 1967) by the legislative and administrative guidelines of the "701" program which equated "comprehensive planning" with "physical planning." It was also explicitly expressed in various background and policy papers issued by the American Institute of Planners, such as the following:

The metropolitan planning agency should seek the development of a unified plan for land use, density and design, the provision and correlation of public facilities, services and utilities, and the preservation of open space and wise use of natural resources. It should strive to coordinate local planning, both public and private, with planning at the metropolitan level; similarly, the metropolitan plan should be coordinated with state and national plans—particularly those affecting transportation, public facilities and natural resource programs and functions that are metropolitan in scope. To this purpose, there should be a legal requirement that the agency review the content, conformity or compatibility of all proposals affecting the metropolitan area.

. . . The metropolitan planning agency should seek establishment and acceptance of goals, both long-range and immediate, for the metropolitan area's physical development (with due regard to economic and social factors). These goals should be the basis for the formulation of the comprehensive metropolitan area plan—and that plan, in turn, should serve as a framework within which may be coordinated the comprehensive plans of municipalities, counties and other units of government in the metropolitan area.[26]

As the AIP memorandum makes clear, metropolitan planning is supplementary to local planning and not a substitute for it. The purpose of the comprehensive area-wide plan, as generally understood, is to provide a broad framework within which local units can plan for their own growth and expansion. It therefore deals primarily with functional elements of metropolitan significance, such as the transportation network, conservation of natural resources, open space, economic potential, water pollution, drainage and flood control, and general patterns of land use. To take an example, if local officials are provided with a plan for developing the major arterial system of the region, they presumably are in a better position to plan their own road network and land use to fit into the overall scheme.

The memorandum also emphasizes that a metropolitan planning agency is basically a coordinating mechanism. Because its territorial jurisdiction usually includes many autonomous local units, it must operate in working partnership with them and the relevant agencies of the state and national governments. In this capacity, it serves as a sort of catalyst or broker seeking to relate the activities of all the affected public agencies in integrated efforts to achieve area-wide planning objectives. Again using the road system as an example, many governmental units are involved in the process of locating a major metropolitan throughway: the federal Bureau of Public Roads, the state highway commission, the county, and various municipalities. A metropolitan agency with a carefully prepared plan for regional development is conceivably in a position to bring about a consensus among the parties that will be in the best interests of the total area.

One notable trend, paralleling the similar development at the municipal level, has emerged since the AIP statement was drafted in 1962: the efforts to expand the scope of metropolitan planning beyond the physical realm.[27] The push in this direction has come from the national government. For example, the Bureau of the Budget in 1967 formulated a "physical-economic-human resources" definition of comprehensive planning as part of its official guidelines for federal support of multijurisdictional planning activity. And in the same year, "701" assistance was broadened by adding governmental services and human resource development to the program's original physical-planning mission. Although these require-

[26] American Institute of Planners, The Role of Metropolitan Planning (Chicago: 1962), pp. 4–5.

[27] For a discussion of this trend see Willard B. Hansen, "Metropolitan Planning and the New Comprehensiveness," Journal of the American Institute of Planners, XXXIV (September, 1968), 295–302.

ments have not made their impact felt in any dramatic fashion, they are compelling area-wide planning agencies to give increasing if reluctant attention to the social dimensions and needs of the metropolis.

Structural Relation to Local Units

The formal relationship of metropolitan planning bodies to the local units varies widely. At one end of the continuum are the few remaining agencies which are established and financed by private organizations and groups. Those in this category have no official standing but seek to interest the citizenry and local governments in metropolitan-wide planning through research, preparation of land use plans, economic analyses, and publicity concerning the problems of the area. At the other end are several agencies which are constituent parts of a general metropolitan or area-wide government in much the same way that city plan commissions are component units of their municipal governments. Between these two extremes are the great majority of metropolitan or regional planning bodies with varied degrees of relationship to their local units.

Private planning organizations, such as the New York Regional Plan Association, have played a useful role in stimulating interest in area-wide planning and in performing a function that government has been slow in assuming. However, they cannot, nor do they claim to, serve as substitutes for officially constituted metropolitan planning bodies. As private groups with only advice and expertise to offer, they are severely handicapped in seeking to influence public policy. Lacking official status and divorced completely from the governmental structure, they are unable to relate their planning closely to the operations of the public agencies involved or participate in the decision-making process of these units except as outsiders. With the current move to public planning bodies at the metropolitan level, the future of the privately-supported organizations (in those instances where they manage to survive) is likely to be limited to problem-raising and technical criticism, a sort of planner-advocate-at-large role.

The most desirable arrangement for metropolitan planning exists in those few instances where the responsible agency is an integral part of an area-wide government. In such cases the function can more easily be tied into the programs and decision-making processes of an ongoing public body with implementing powers. Such a situation is found in Toronto where the metropolitan planning board is a component unit of a government possessing jurisdiction over an impressive range of area-wide functions. It also exists in the Miami, Florida, SMSA (Dade County) where the county government serves as the area-wide instrumentality and in the new consolidated governments of Nashville-Davidson County (Tennessee) and Jacksonville-Duval County (Florida).

A somewhat more common arrangement in use is the joint city-county planning body. One of the strongest agencies of this type is the Tulsa Metropolitan Area Planning Commission formed in 1953 to take over the planning functions of the city of Tulsa and Tulsa County. The commission's area of jurisdiction includes the central city, a five-mile perimeter around it, and the unincorporated sections of the county. Because of its structural relationship to the two major operating governments of the area, the commission is in a strategic position to function effectively as a metropolitan planning agency. In other communities where joint city-county planning is in operation, this relationship is generally not as close. The more usual arrangement is for both governments to retain their separate commissions but employ a single professional staff. Although not as effective as consolidation of the commissions themselves, this system does offer the opportunity for coordinating the respective planning programs through use of the same staff.

The last decade has witnessed a large increase in the number of metropoltan or regional commissions serving a multiplicity of governments throughout an urban complex. Precipitated largely by the requirements of the various federal assistance programs and by sizable financial support under the "701" provisions, many SMSAs have turned to this type of agency. Unlike the city planning commission or department, metropolitan bodies, with few exceptions, are not attached to a corresponding political entity. This detachment leaves them with only the power of education and persuasion to secure implementation of their plans. The Northeastern Illinois Planning Commission is a prominent example of this type. Within its area of 3700 square miles in the Chicago SMSA are 250 municipalities and over 950 other units of government. To relate to this number of public bodies and attempt to coordinate their planning activities in matters of regional concern is a herculean task. As Paul Oppermann, the former executive director of the commission, has observed: "A critical difference becomes visible here between the conditions of city planning and metropolitan planning. In the city or village, the whole governs while the parts advise, petition, and seek to amend. At the metropolitan scale, the situation is reversed, and the parts govern while the viewpoint of the whole is . . . recommended to units of government."[28]

Some observers maintain that the development of area-wide planning will act as a stimulus to cooperative action by local units as the realities of metropolitan problems are brought into focus and as a framework is provided for joint action. Others are inclined to argue that metropolitan planning commissions will remain impotent in the absence of area-wide government.[29] Certain recent developments, however, are increasing the potential strength of such bodies and providing them with means

[28] "Five Years of Metropolitan Planning: A Special Report," *Inland Architect* (April, 1963).
[29] These various points of view are presented in Joseph F. Zimmerman, "The Planning Riddle," *National Civic Review*, LVIII (April, 1968), 189–194.

to influence planning decisions of overall concern. The most important trends in this direction are the federal steps aimed at increasing the action relatedness of these agencies. Of particular significance is the stipulation in the Demonstration Cities and Metropolitan Development Act of 1966 that all applications by local units for federal grants and loans for specific projects, including airports, highways, hospitals, sewerage and water supply facilities, and open space acquisition, must be submitted for review to an area-wide agency responsible for metropolitan planning. Since an increasing proportion of major development funds for urban areas is likely to come from the national government, the latter's insistence that local units conform to metropolitan plans could supply an important implementing weapon. This resource would be further strengthened if the states would follow the federal lead and place similar restrictions on their grant-in-aid programs.

Another development of importance in this regard is the creation of area-wide councils of governments (COGs) which, in the view of some observers, constitute incipient political entities corresponding to the jurisdictional area of metropolitan planning agencies.[30] In some cases, these agencies, such as the Association of Bay Area Governments (San Francisco-Oakland) and the Puget Sound Council of Governments, included the planning function among their original responsibilities. Others, such as the Metropolitan Council of the Twin Cities Area (Minneapolis-St. Paul) and the Metropolitan Washington Council of Governments, replaced already existent area-wide planning agencies. And still others, such as the Metropolitan Atlanta Council of Governments, exist alongside previously established metropolitan planning commissions. The planning function under all of these arrangements remains advisory but the COGs provide a means of attaching it more closely to the operating governments of the area.[31] Whether this consensual-type approach will be sufficient to meet metropolitan needs is, of course, an unanswered question. It could be, as one writer speculates, that the national government may at some point in the future decide to write off these various experiments in regional advisory planning as attempts to run a race on crutches and propose more powerful measures.[32]

[30] Councils of Governments are discussed in Chapter 13.

[31] Federal policy is becoming increasingly insistent on the integration of planning with decision-making. The Demonstration Cities and Metropoltan Development Act, for example, specifies that the metropolitan reviewing agency for facilities grants shall, "to the greatest extent possible," be "composed of or responsible to the elected officials of a unit of area-wide government or of the units of general local government within whose jurisdiction such agency is authorized to engage in such planning."

[32] Melvin R. Levin, "Planners and Metropolitan Planning," *Journal of the American Institute of Planners*, XXXIII (March, 1967), 81.

THE PLANNING OUTLOOK

Charles Abrams, chairman of the Division of Urban Planning at Columbia University, in commenting on planning education, recalled that one could have made a passable lecturer thirty years ago with a knowledge of architecture, garden cities, zoning, and a smattering of information on housing and transportation. Now, however, the field has widened to embrace racial and social problems, politics, sociology and anthropology, land economics, systems analysis, and many other areas of knowledge.[33] And Victor Gruen once remarked that the planners who had often taken refuge in an allegedly value-free application of techniques to achieve goals set by others have now been shoved willy-nilly into the ideological arena. Increasingly they are being asked whom they are planning for, whose values they are advocating, whose interests they are serving, and what they are doing about the critical social issues of the day. In such a milieu there is no return to the simple measurable problems of traffic flow, population densities, and open space ratios. The contemporary demands are large for a field which, in Abrams' words, "is just about where physics was at the time of Newton."

The picture on the nontechnical or political side of the coin is similarly mixed. Planning, whether at the local or metropolitan level, involves proposals and commitments that pertain to an indefinite future. People find it much easier to act when they are confronted with a self-evident problem or when a decision is forced on them by the pressure of circumstances. At the same time, they are less ready to commit themselves to community plans that may involve present self-sacrifices on their part in return for some projected future benefit. Planning, for this reason, requires the strong support of political leaders who are in a position to articulate community needs and goals and rally public support. It is precisely in this respect that metropolitan planning is seriously handicapped. Since the governmental or institutional pattern in most urban complexes is not conducive to the emergence of political leaders who consider the general good of the whole area as their primary responsibility, the task of guiding metropolitan growth is relegated to numerous locally-based officials with locally-oriented allegiances.

Coupled with the general lack of public appreciation for long-range goals and the absence of metropolitan political leadership, the possibility of meaningful area-wide planning is further impaired by the near-feudal isolationism and internecine rivalry that exist among the various governmental units which make up the metropolis. The picture would indeed be bleak were it not that the pressures of contemporary events are forcing

[33] "Present Labor Pains in Planning Education," *ASPO Newsletter*, 34 (January, 1968), 1–2.

even the most provincial officials to be less intransigent in their opposition to certain forms of action at the metropolitan level. Steps thus far taken in this direction have been reluctant rather than enthusiastic, timid rather than bold. What is important, however, is that progress is being made. Metropolitan areas are creating planning commissions, preparing comprehensive land use and transportation plans, and setting up area-wide councils of governments. These developments may fall far short of the demands of the modern urban era, but in typical American fashion adjustment will be made as the people and their elected representatives are brought face-to-face with immediate and concrete needs. If this in-cremental process persists, the less sanguine would say, metropolitan areas will be confronted with future problems that will be staggering by today's standards.

10 / THE FISCAL CRISIS

FINANCE IS ONE OF THE MOST CRITICAL ASPECTS OF THE METROPOLITAN "problem." What can be done to meet the rising costs of local government? Where can new revenues be obtained? How can public services be financed on a basis equitable to all residents of the metropolitan community? What kind of taxes will be least harmful to urban economic activity? How should fiscal responsibility be divided between the levels of government? Answers to questions of this nature do not come easily. The era of population explosion and the expanding metropolis is not without its social costs in the form of new problems and aggravations of already existing ones. It is an era that places mammoth burdens on governmental agencies and public facilities and calls for ever expanding services to meet the needs which it generates. It is a period, moreover, in which demands on the local treasury have been further intensified because of greater service wants—the consequence of higher standards of living—and the necessity to devote more attention to the long-slighted needs of the less affluent members of the community—the result of their rising expectations and newly-awakened power.

THE FISCAL DILEMMA

Some observers contend that public finance, not governmental structure, is the nub of the metropolitan problem. They argue that given sufficient funds and equitable distribution, most of the difficulties, whether traffic, blight, or pollution, can be overcome without major changes in the existing governmental pattern. Others agree on the importance of the fiscal problem but maintain that it is precisely the lack of adequate administrative machinery which gives rise to much of the trouble. They point to the numerous local units competing for the tax dollar, the wide range of fiscal capacity among local jurisdictions, and the difficulty of relating benefits and taxes when public activities extend across corporate boundaries as they do in the metropolis. Both positions have a measure of validity. Certainly the most thoroughgoing reorganization of the governmental structure will not in itself assure better schools, more parks, improved transportation facilities, or the elimination of blight. The new structure, as that of the old, would still be confronted with the problem of securing sufficient revenue to finance the rapidly growing needs of an urban populace. On the other hand, a rational reordering of the machinery would make possible the mobilizing of an area's resources more effectively and help to reduce some of the inequities which now exist in the system.

Neither of these views, however, strikes at the heart of the fiscal problem. Although the bulk of the nation's wealth is concentrated in the SMSAs, the control of these areas over their financial fate is severely circumscribed. In the first place, local units must rely on a far less productive tax system than either the national or state governments since the latter two levels have virtually preempted such major revenue sources as the income and sales taxes. Second, even if constitutional and statutory restrictions on the taxing powers of local governments were removed, these units would still be unable to take full advantage of the authority because of the risk of driving out persons and industry beyond their boundaries. Third, and most important of all, neither resources nor needs are evenly distributed among territorial jurisdictions within the same economic community, so that frequently those with the most serious public wants have the least means to meet them.

Economists commonly refer to three major fiscal functions of a democratic government: stabilization of the economy, allocation of resources, and redistribution of income.[1] The first rests exclusively with the national or central government and is pursued through policies which seek to maintain a high level of resource utilization and a stable monetary

[1] Richard A. Musgrave, *The Theory of Public Finance* (New York: McGraw-Hill, 1959), chap. 1.

system. The second is largely a function of the local units which, in the main, determine the priorities and the proportions of the public budget to be allocated to the various collective goods and services such as education, police protection, and sewerage facilities. The third, income redistribution, is the primary responsibility of the national government and, to a lesser extent, the states and localities. This function is undertaken principally through the use of taxes and transfer payments designed to eliminate some of the worst inequalities in the distribution of wealth which inevitably occur in an economically competitive society. Thus incomes are taxed on the basis of ability to pay and a portion of the proceeds assigned to the deprived in the form of welfare payments, housing subsidies, medical services, and the like.

Redistributive aspects of fiscal policy are present at the local level, although on a much smaller scale. In the larger cities, for example, wealthier neighborhoods where tax revenues are high help to pay for education and other services in the poorer sections where tax receipts are low. Exercise of this function locally is possible only when both the well-to-do and the poor reside within the same political jurisdiction. But when numerous governmental units serve the metropolitan community, as is usually the case, no one of them has extensive redistributive capacity. The problem is especially acute in the large SMSAs of the East and North where the central cities are fiscally overburdened by the heavy concentration of low-income residents and the continuing exodus of high-paying taxpayers.

THE GROWING PUBLIC SECTOR

Despite the nation's unprecedented prosperity, governments in many metropolitan areas are confronted with serious financial difficulties. For the older central cities, the problem is one of shrinking tax bases in the face of expanding health, welfare, safety, compensatory education, and housing needs. For the developing communities in the urban ring, the problem—despite their growing fiscal capacity—is one of increasing requirements for schools, water, and other public facilities. Governmental spending at all levels has soared astronomically since World War II in efforts to cope with the needs of the society. In 1942 national, state, and local agencies spent a total of $45.5 billion; twenty-five years later the amount exceeded $250 billion. On a per capita basis, total state and local expenditures alone almost doubled (from $279 to $539) during the ten-year period from 1957 to 1967.[2]

Aggregate revenue or expenditure statistics, of course, tell only one

[2] See Alan K. Campbell, "Most Dynamic Sector," *National Civic Review,* LIII (February, 1964), 74–82.

side of the story. The increases registered in recent decades have been accompanied by rising standards of living, vastly accelerated productivity, higher personal income, expanding demand for public goods and services, and greater capacity to pay the bill. The growth in dollar volume also in part reflects the price inflation of the last several decades. As in every sector of the economy, wages of governmental employees have risen and the cost of materials consumed by public agencies has soared upward.

A more realistic picture of governmental fiscal behavior is obtained when spending is related to such measures of wealth as the gross national product (total national output of goods and services valued at market price) and disposable personal income (that left for the individual to spend or save after payment of taxes). When this is done, the increases in governmental costs appear less startling. From 1957 to 1967, the GNP jumped from $440 billion to $785 billion, a rise of 78 percent, and disposable personal income from $312 billion to $545 billion, an increase of 75 percent. The picture is even more revealing when service charges and fees are excluded and taxes only are computed as a percent of total personal income. Measured in this way, the aggregate tax burden of the nation has remained virtually unchanged since 1957.[3] As Table 21

TABLE 21   Taxes as Percent of Total Personal Income, 1957 and 1967

Governmental Level	1957	1967
Local	4.1%	4.7%
State	4.2	5.0
Federal	20.0	18.4
Total	28.3%	28.1%

SOURCE: U.S. Bureau of the Census, *1957 Census of Governments*, Vol. III, no. 5 and *Governmental Finances in 1966–67; Statistical Abstract of the United States, 1958* and *Statistical Abstract of the United States, 1968.*

shows, the federal proportion has decreased slightly while the state and local shares have risen. These figures demonstrate that no massive diversion of income or capital to public purposes is taking place, whether at the local, state, or national level.

[3] An earlier analysis showing that the increase in taxes corresponded almost exactly with the rise in the nation's income from 1952 to 1962 is presented in Reuben A. Zubrow, "Recent Trends and Developments in Municipal Finance," *Public Management*, XLV (November, 1963), 247–254.

Although these facts run counter to the folklore of governmental spend-ing, they do not eliminate the financial headaches of local units or ease their hard-pressed budgets. Nor do they negate the fact that the ex-penditures of local governments are going up at a much faster rate than the natural increase in the yield of currently used sources of local revenue. Thus, while the ability to pay for services exists when viewed in relation to the rising economic status of most Americans, the task of finding equitable and persuasive ways of drawing upon this capability still remains.

REVENUE PATTERNS

National, state, and local governments are in a very real sense com-petitors for the tax dollar. Each level has found it necessary to draw more heavily on existing revenue sources and to impose new levies to meet enlarged responsibilities. In this competitive system, a rough division of revenue sources has developed between the three jurisdictional tiers. The bulk of federal funds is derived from income taxes on individuals and corporations; states rely heavily on sales and gross receipt taxes; and, since the turn of the present century, the general property tax has been acknowledged as the almost exclusive domain of local government. Com-petition for tax resources, moreover, is not confined to the interplay be-tween the three levels of government; it occurs with even greater intensity among overlapping local units within urban areas. The county govern-ment, municipality, school district, and other autonomous special dis-tricts draw on the same taxpayer, and all rely on the property levy in varying degrees for a portion of their revenue.

General Property Tax

The general property levy has provided the historical base of support for local governments since colonial times. Next to federal income and excise taxes it has been the most productive source of public revenue in the American system. In fact, as late as 1932 it was contributing more than all other federal, state, and local taxes combined. Prior to that time it was providing almost three-fourths of the general revenue of local governments (Figure 30). Its relative importance has declined in recent decades due to the substantial boost in state and federal aid to localities and to the utilization of other forms of taxation. Today, the property levy finances only about 43 percent of the aggregate budget of local governments, although in absolute or dollar terms its yield has continued to mount: from $18 billion in 1962 to $26 billion in 1967, an increase of approximately $40 for each man, woman, and child in the country.

Considerable variation exists among the major urban areas in the extent

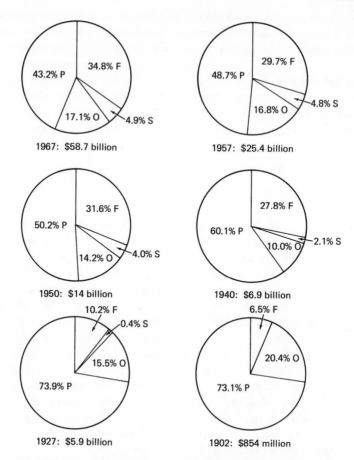

FIGURE 30   **General Revenue Sources of Local Government,
1902–1967. P is property tax, F is federal and
state aid, S is sales and income taxes, and O is
other taxes and charges. From** Guiding Metropolitan Growth, **Committee for Economic Development,
1960: U.S. Bureau of the Census,** 1957 Census of
Governments, **Vol. III, no. 4, and** Governmental
Finances in 1966–1967.

of their dependence on the property levy. In states where local taxes
other than property are virtually non-existent, in New England for example, SMSAs rely on this source for 80 to 90 percent of their locally
raised revenue. By contrast, in SMSAs where income taxes are widely
used by local units, such as Cincinnati and Pittsburgh, the property levy
proportion is only about 60 percent. Similarly, in the metropolitan areas in
Illinois and California where local sales taxes are in effect, the range is

from 65 to 70 percent.[4] In general, the property tax finances a significantly smaller portion of public services in the central cities of the larger SMSAs than in the outlying jurisdictions because of the more extensive use of other revenue sources by the former. When computed on a per capita basis, however, property tax collections in most of the large core municipalities are equal to or greater than those in the suburbs—which is another way of saying that tax burdens in the central cities are usually heavier than in the ring communities.[5]

Not all types of local units, as Figure 31 shows, rely equally on the

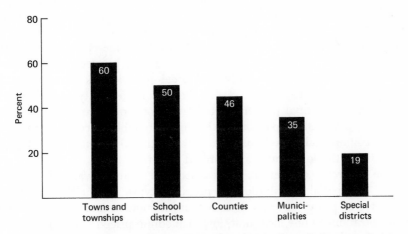

FIGURE 31   Property Tax as Percent of Total General Revenue by Type of Local Unit, 1962. From U.S. Bureau of the Census, Census of Governments: 1962, Vol. 4, nos. 1, 2, 3.

property tax. Towns and townships are the most dependent, and special districts the least; the latter obtain the bulk of their income from utility and service charges. School districts receive virtually all their locally-derived funds from the property tax and practically all of the remainder from state aid. Municipalities, as a result of their success in tapping other sources, now draw only about 35 percent of their operating revenue from property taxation. County governments, like school districts, depend on the property levy for almost one-half their total funds and on state aid for a substantial portion of the remainder. Since the property tax is

---

[4] Dick Netzer, *Impact of the Property Tax: Its Economic Implications for Urban Problems* (Washington: U.S. Congress, Joint Economic Committee, 1968), pp. 8–12.

[5] This situation is extensively treated in Advisory Commission on Intergovernmental Relations, *Fiscal Balance in the American Federal System: Metropolitan Fiscal Disparities*, Vol. 2 (Washington: October, 1967).

commonly utilized by all types of local units, those which overlap each other in territorial jurisdiction look to the same property owner for much of their support. The urban dweller therefore must customarily pay the traditional municipal, county, and school district levies and, in addition, property taxes assessed by such other local agencies as fire protection and sewer districts.

PROPERTY TAX BASE Because of the heavy local reliance on the general property tax, the base for this levy is an important measure of a community's financial ability to support its services.[6] Property subject to the tax in the United States was officially assessed at $507 billion in 1967, over 70 percent of which was located in metropolitan areas.[7] Approximately four-fifths of the total consisted of assessments on real estate and the remainder on personalty. Nonfarm residences accounted for 60 percent of the real estate valuation and commercial and industrial establishments, 25 percent. The balance or mix between these various uses is important to the individual local jurisdictions since the ratio between service demands and tax receipts for each type differs substantially. Residential property, except that of more than average value, normally pays only a portion of the costs of public services it receives, while commercial and industrial uses contribute as much as two to three times the local outlays generated by them.[8]

The different cost-benefit ratios associated with the various land uses make the spatial distribution of property types within the metropolis a matter of prime concern. It is not uncommon to find large industrial concentrations in one local unit, low or medium priced homes in another, and luxury housing in a third. When this pattern prevails, fiscal resources and public needs are poorly correlated. The lower income unit with little or no industrial property finds itself hard pressed to pay for its municipal, school, and other local needs while its two neighboring communities are able to enjoy higher levels of service with less tax effort.[9] The result is

[6] The general property tax is primarily a levy on real estate (land, buildings, and other permanent improvements) and on tangible personal property such as household goods, motor vehicles, and business inventories.

[7] The relationship between assessed value and market or sales price varies considerably from jurisdiction to jurisdiction. For the nation as a whole the level of assessment averages about one-third of market value.

[8] See in this connection W. N. Leonard and W. F. Clarke, *Does Industry Pay its Way?* (Hempstead, New York: Hofstra College Bureau of Business and Community Research, 1956). For an analysis of the net fiscal effect of an industry on school districts when indirect costs such as those related to the education of the workers' children are taken into account, refer to Werner Z. Hirsch, "Fiscal Impact of Industrialization on Local Schools," *The Review of Economics and Statistics,* XLVI (May, 1964), 191–199.

[9] Robert Wood cites the case of a Bergen County municipality with an assessed valuation of $5.5 million per student. This wealthy industrial enclave draws its manpower from the surrounding municipalities which house the workers and educate their

unevenness in the quality of the area's public services and in educational opportunities for its children. In suburban St. Louis, for example, the school district with the highest assessed valuation per capita was found to spend five times more per pupil than the district with the least fiscal capacity; yet residents of the latter were paying a higher tax rate for school purposes than those of the former.[10]

From the standpoint of tax base, the well-balanced municipality is one which has a mix of residential and nonresidential properties. So also the well-balanced metropolis is one which contains a similar blend of land uses. In the latter case, however, it would be no more possible or even desirable for each autonomous unit in the area to embody this mix than it would be for each neighborhood of the central city to do so. Yet an effort to achieve this very end takes place within the metropolitan community as each local government seeks to attract the kind of development that will produce more in tax revenues than it costs in public services. What generally happens—the St. Louis case just cited provides a good illustration—is that communities with the wealthier taxable capacity spend more on public services than their less affluent neighbors, but not as much as their superior tax base would permit. Consequently, the rich communities often have lower tax rates than the poorer units. This inversion has two deleterious effects. It encourages economic activity to locate in low-tax jurisdictions with the effect at times of distorting overall metropolitan development patterns; and it encourages communities to plan their land use for fiscal advantages rather than on the basis of broader considerations.[11]

The general property tax has been the subject of severe criticism. It has been condemned as regressive (not based on ability to pay), difficult to administer fairly, and a deterrent to central city development. However justified these criticisms may be, the tax does exist, it produces large revenues, the economy has long been adjusted to it, it is not as regressive as some levies such as the sales tax, and it has shown surprising elasticity (the responsiveness of its base to changes in GNP). Moreover, the scarcity of satisfactory alternatives will alone assure its dominance as a prime source of local government revenue for some time to come. The problem is not its abolition but the correction of its administrative defects and the more equitable distribution of its benefits.

---

children but which derive no direct tax benefits from the concentration of the high-yield property. *1400 Governments* (Cambridge: Harvard University Press, 1961), p. 55.

[10] *Background for Action* (University City: Metropolitan St. Louis Survey, 1957), pp. 61–63.

[11] These points are elaborated upon in Dick Netzer, *Economics of the Property Tax* (Washington: Brookings Institution, 1966), pp. 125–130.

Some reduction of its relative role in the financing of urban public services is also called for in many communities.

Nonproperty Taxes

Rising costs and mounting public needs in the nation's urban areas following World War II made continued heavy reliance on the property tax infeasible as well as politically unacceptable. Fear of repercussions on the local economy together with the mounting dissatisfaction of property owners sent public officials scurrying about for new revenue lodes. Two alternatives were open to them: one, to attempt to have a larger proportion of local expenditures financed (or certain services assumed) by higher levels of government which do not use the property levy; or two, to seek out new local sources of income. Both of these paths have been pursued in recent decades. State and federal aids to municipalities, counties, and school districts have been significantly increased and a broad array of nonproperty taxes imposed at the local level, including those on utility and business gross receipts, gasoline and motor fuel, motor vehicles, cigarettes, alcoholic beverages, income, and retail sales.[12] Only the last two named types of taxes have been of major consequence and their use has been restricted mainly to the large central cities.

MUNICIPAL INCOME TAX   The municipal income tax, sometimes referred to as an earnings or payroll tax, is utilized in six states by twenty cities of over 100,000 population (including New York, Philadelphia, Pittsburgh, Detroit, Cleveland, St. Louis, and Baltimore) and by more than 150 smaller communities. Although it does not account for a large proportion of total municipal tax collections (slightly over 2 percent in 1967), it does provide significant amounts of revenue for those cities in which it is employed. In New York City alone, receipts from the levy are in excess of $400 million. The tax has usually been introduced under conditions of severe financial distress. However, it has acted more as a substitutive than supplemental source of revenue and, in particular, has taken some of the pressure off the general property levy.[13]

The local income tax rate is relatively low, in no case more than 2 percent on the gross earnings of individuals and on net profits of businesses and professions. As commonly employed, it taxes residents for all income earned regardless of source and nonresidents for that portion of their income earned within the municipality. Central cities are attracted to this device because it is less likely than local sales and business taxes to encourage migration of economic activity outside their boundaries.

[12] A discussion of local nonproperty taxes will be found in David Davies, "Financing Urban Functions and Services," *Law and Contemporary Problems*, 30 (Winter, 1965), 127–161.

[13] Elizabeth Deran, "Tax Structure in Cities Using the Income Tax," *National Tax Journal*, XXI (June, 1968), 147–152.

More importantly, it provides them with a means of reaching suburban-ites or urban fringe dwellers who derive their income within the core boundaries. They defend this "extra-territorial" aspect of the tax on the grounds of equity, contending that it enables them to recoup some of the added costs of the services and facilities which they must furnish to the nonresident working population.

The suburban commuter clearly adds to the operational and capital costs of the central city. His presence during the workday requires the city to provide more road and parking space, public utilities, police protection, and similar services than would otherwise be necessary to accommodate its resident population. But the costs and benefits are not one-way streets. The commuter-worker spends money in the shops, restaurants, and entertainment spots of the central city, and these ex-penditures are reflected in increased tax returns for the municipality. He also helps man the business and industrial enterprises that enrich the core municipality's tax base while at the same time relieving the city of the costly burden of educating his children.[14] In saying this, however, it is important to keep in mind that the central city carries a disproportionate burden in housing the less affluent members of the metropolitan community—the poor, the elderly, the unskilled—a fact that conventional cost-benefit analyses do not take into account.

LOCAL SALES TAX   Another innovation of the post-World War II years, the local sales tax, is employed by approximately 2000 local govern-ments in thirteen states. Total nationwide receipts from this source ($1.3 billion in 1967) exceed those of any of the other nonproperty levies. California and Illinois, the biggest users of this revenue producer, contain four-fifths of all local sales-tax jurisdictions in the United States (over 300 in the former and 1300 in the latter). In most instances, the local levy is added to the state sales tax and collected by the state for the municipality or county (counties also utilize this tax in California and Illinois). Local sales taxes have the advantage of revenue produc-tivity, relative ease and low cost of administration, and a means of tapping nonresidents who otherwise would not contribute to the mu-nicipality's coffers.

Like most nonproperty levies, the local sales tax is not without its drawbacks when employed in metropolitan areas. The most obvious is that merchants in a sales-tax municipality may be penalized if resi-dents can avoid the levy by shopping in an adjacent city or town. Some of the deficiencies of this and other nonproperty taxes would be eliminated if they were imposed by a metropolitan-wide unit, since

[14] To what extent subsidization, if any, takes place has not been conclusively dem-onstrated. See Julius Margolis, "Municipal Fiscal Structure in a Metropolitan Region," *Journal of Political Economy*, 65 (June, 1957), 225–236; and James M. Banovetz, *Governmental Cost Burdens and Service Benefits in the Twin Cities Metropolitan Area* (Minneapolis: University of Minnesota Public Administration Center, 1965).

in this way all individuals and businesses in the area would be uniformly reached. Other defects, however, would remain, such as the regressiveness of many of these taxes and their general nuisance to the citizen. The "hand-to-mouth" operations which have characterized metropolitan area financing in recent decades have given little consideration to long-range effects and objectives, or even to the relations among the various types of levies and their impact on different segments of the population. In this setting, the search for new revenue sources has been more in the nature of frantic improvisation than a constructive approach to a sound fiscal system.

Service Charges

In addition to taxes, local governments derive a portion of their income from fees, permits, and user charges of various kinds. The most important of these nontax revenues in terms of total dollars are utility or service charges which are collected in return for specified services supplied to the consumers. These charges are based on the measurable benefits received. The citizen consumer who is furnished with a specific service by his local government pays for it just as he would if the supplier were a private agency. The provision of water by a municipality or special district is a case in point. The consumer is billed for the amount of water he uses, that is, for the benefit he receives. In this way, a householder will pay less than the florist or the factory owner whose water needs are greater. The same principle has been applied in many jurisdictions to sewage disposal, garbage collection, and other services.

If viewed as taxes, such charges would be classified as regressive, but so also would electricity, telephone service, and other commodities purchased in the private market place. As economists point out, each local government competes for available resources with every other public activity as well as with the private sector of the economy. Where services and goods are bought by individuals, each consumer takes part in the decision-making process of allocating his resources by determining what service or product and how much of it he will buy. In brief, he is able to choose that combination of goods and services which, within the constraints of his income, will give him maximum satisfaction. On the other hand, where purchases are made by groups—as in the case of most local public services—decisions as to how much to spend and for what purposes are political judgments that are reflected in the budgets of the various governmental units.

The market mechanism obviously cannot be applied to all local public services since some of them, such as education and welfare, are designed to meet social rather than private needs; and for others, such as water pollution control and police protection, the connection between individual benefits and costs is less evident. The resort to user charges instead of general taxation is therefore limited. However, the case for employing them is strong when (1) the product or service would be significantly wasted if it had a zero price, such as unmetered water; (2) it yields direct and measurable benefits to individuals or families; and (3) the cost of collecting the charge is not excessive. When these factors are present, financing can take place in the same way as the output of public utilities—by user charges which are like prices—rather than through general taxes.[15]

Room undoubtedly exists for greater exploitation of this revenue potential in connection with services that do not have significant income redistribution as a major objective. For one thing, the device can be employed to reach those who live in one political jurisdiction and who benefit from but escape payment for services furnished them by some other unit. For another, charges or prices on certain public services can be used as a means of social control. Economist Wilbur Thompson suggests, for example, that a sophisticated manipulation of tolls, parking fees, and licenses could be resorted to by a community for the purpose of promoting certain forms of urban transportation and discouraging others.[16] Finally, the more extensive employment of user charges would reserve existing local taxes for the support of those public services that cannot be handled in a fashion analogous to the market place.

State and Federal Aid

Starting in the early 1930s, the jurisdictions with superior fiscal capacities, the state and national governments, have slowly but steadily assumed a larger share of the financing of programs formerly regarded as local responsibilities. Each important step in this direction has been associated predominantly with redistributive functions. Most public welfare costs, for example, have been assumed by the higher echelons through grants-in-aid, direct national social insurance, and, more recently, antipoverty programs. In 1942, local units received a total of $1.8 billion in state and federal aid; by 1967, this figure had increased to over $22 billion, enough to provide more than one-third of the total general revenue of local governments.[17]

Increased state and federal aid is an obvious route toward reduced reliance on the property levy. As a result of this assistance (and the assumption of certain functions by these higher levels), nearly one-half

[15] The case for greater use of service charges is made in Garth L. Mangum, "The Benefit Principle," *Municipal Finance*, XXIV (February, 1962), 125–136.

[16] *A Preface to Urban Economics* (Baltimore: Johns Hopkins Press, 1965), pp. 280–286.

[17] Grants by the national government directly to local units constitute only a slight proportion of total local revenue (about 3 percent in 1967). Most federal funds are channeled through the state governments and hence are included in the aid figures of the latter.

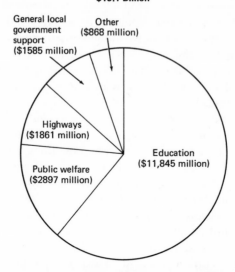

$19.1 Billion

General local
government   Other
support   ($868 million)
($1585 million)

Highways
($1861 million)

Public welfare
($2897 million)

Education
($11,845 million)

FIGURE 32   **State Payments to Local
Governments by Function,
1967. The portion labeled
Other consists of $116 mil-
lion for hospitals, $185 mil-
lion for health, and $567
million for miscellaneous
functions. From U.S. Bureau
of the Census, 1967 Census
of Governments, Vol. 6, no.
4, p. 7.**

the potential property tax burden in education, highways, public welfare, and health and hospitals has been shifted upward. Experts in
public finance, such as Dick Netzer, argue for further movement in this
direction in at least two areas: education and poverty-linked services. In
the case of the first, as they point out, only a small portion of the eventual
benefits from education is recaptured within the confines of individual
school districts because of the high mobility of the population. In the
matter of the second, state and federal financing of services related to
poverty (which is concentrated mainly in the core municipalities) would
alleviate the central city-suburban disparities and the regressivity problem of taxing the poor for services to the poor.[18]

Neither state nor local officials are opposed in principle to federal

---

[18] Netzer, *Impact of the Property Tax: Its Economic Implications for Urban
Problems,* pp. 36–37.

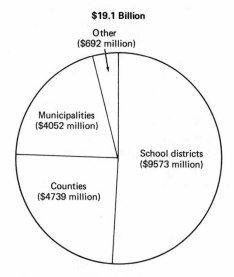

$19.1 Billion

Other
($692 million)

Municipalities
($4052 million)

School districts
($9573 million)

Counties
($4739 million)

FIGURE 33   **State Payments to Local Governments by Type of Government, 1967. The portion labeled Other consists of $588 million for townships and $104 million for special districts. From U.S. Bureau of the Census, 1967 Census of Governments, Vol. 6, no. 4, p. 7.**

grants-in-aid; on the contrary, most of them would like to see the amounts enlarged. The states, however, prefer block grants with no restrictions on their use (such as proposed in the Heller Plan under which the national government would distribute annually to the states an amount equal to a specified percentage of the individual income tax base). They would also like to have all federal aid, including that for local purposes, channeled through them, a procedure vigorously opposed by the large central cities. Grants-in-aid for specified purposes are most useful to the extent that Congress wishes to use monetary incentives to promote the accomplishment of particular national goals.[19] Block

[19] Several studies show that federal aid is not merely substitutive for state and local revenue but has the effect of stimulating expenditures on those functions to which it is directed. See Jack W. Osman, "The Dual Impact of Federal Aid on State and Local Government Expenditures," *National Tax Journal*, XIX (December, 1966), 362–372; and David L. Smith, "The Response of State and Local Governments to Federal Grants," *National Tax Journal*, XXI (September, 1968), 349–357. A conflicting view is contained in Thomas Pogue and L. G. Sgontz, "The Effects of Grants-in-Aid on State-Local Spending," *National Tax Journal*, XXI (June, 1968), 190–199.

grants, on the other hand, are best suited to the objective of increasing and equalizing the general fiscal capacity of the states.[20]

State aid takes the form of either grants for the support of particular services such as education and welfare, or of specified shares of state-collected taxes on such items as motor fuel, liquor, cigarettes, and income. The first, which provides by far the larger portion of state financial assistance, is usually distributed with reference to some measure of local need: for education, school age population or enrollment; for welfare, number of cases or estimated expenditures; for highways, miles of road or number of vehicles. In education particularly, the grant formulas commonly aim at some degree of equalization between the relatively poor and more prosperous local districts or units.

Under the second type of monetary aid, the state imposes and collects the tax and then returns a portion of it to the local unit. Since these levies are actually local taxes with the state acting as collecting agency, the recipients are generally allowed to use the revenues for whatever legal purposes they see fit. This shared tax device has the effect of substituting the greater taxing capacity of the state for the inferior capacity of the smaller units. It also helps local officials meet their growing revenue needs without incurring the political risks involved in raising or levying additional local taxes.

Grants-in-aid have been the subject of criticism, some of it merited but much without foundation. One of the most frequently heard objections is that the device constitutes a threat to local self-government and responsibility. This danger, however, is more mythical than real. As one student of public finance has remarked: "There seems to exist, all too commonly, a kind of implicit assumption among those who talk about intergovernmental relations, that the purposes of policy-makers at different levels of government are diametrically opposed to each other, that they have goals which are incompatible, that the larger unit invariably plots the destruction of the smaller. It seems that, on the other hand, a decent respect for the dangers of centralization might well exist along with a willingness to use central authority where the nature of the problem to be solved is moving beyond the unaided capacity of the smaller units."[21]

There are two other criticisms of intergovernmental aid which have more basis in fact. The first is the patchwork system of grants-in-aid. Developed through the years as the result of many *ad hoc* political decisions and governed by no coherent or consistent philosophy, the

[20] See Lester Thuron, "Theory of Grants in Aid," *National Tax Journal*, XXI (September, 1968), 373–377.

[21] Carey C. Thompson, "Financing Government in Metropolitan Areas," *Proceedings of the Texas Conference on Metropolitan Problems* (Austin: University of Texas Institute of Public Affairs, 1958), pp. 33–34.

pattern of fiscal assistance to local subdivisions is unduly complicated and in many cases inequitable. The second criticism, applicable mainly to state-shared taxes, is that such assistance often bears little relation to need. Since shared taxes are generally returned to the local jurisdiction where they originate, wealthy communities receive an added boost to their already sufficient resources while the poorer units derive proportionately less than their greater needs call for. Neither of these objections indicates defects that are irremediable, although their correction may be politically difficult. The patchwork nature of grants could be cured by overhauling the system and setting it up on a more rational basis. Similarly, the imbalance occasioned by state-shared taxes could be overcome by returning the local portion to an area-wide government, such as the county, rather than to the individual units. In this way the money would be pooled for use throughout the metropolis on the basis of need.

EXPENDITURE PATTERNS

Local units within a metropolis serve up different packages of public programs. At one extreme is the government of the small dormitory suburb which operates with part-time personnel, relies on volunteers instead of professional firefighters, avoids installing curbs and sidewalks, and provides no parks or recreation facilities. At the other end of the spectrum is the central city government with its broad range of services encompassing everything from tiny-tot play areas to hospitals and museums. The same differences, perhaps not as extreme, prevail among school districts. Beyond meeting the minimum requirements of the state department of education, local districts vary widely in their educational offerings and facilities. One may provide courses in music, art, and specialized types of vocational training, employ school psychologists and nurses, conduct extensive recreational programs, and furnish bus transportation to the pupils. Another may offer none of these services but limit itself to a "skin and bones" or 3 Rs educational program.

Current Expenditures

In examining the output side of the local public budget, it is helpful to distinguish between two broad categories of expenditures: current operations and capital outlays. The first refers to the cost of running the various departments and agencies and providing services to the citizen consumers; the second includes appropriations for the acquisition or construction of public buildings, roads, parks, sewers, and other facilities and for the purchase of major items of equipment. In 1967, local units spent a total of approximately $60 billion for general governmental purposes and over $6 billion for the development and operation of publicly-owned utilities such as water, electric, and transit systems. The latter item relates to revenue-producing facilities that are generally self-sustaining.

The percentages in Figure 34 show the average distribution of current expenditures in the thirty-eight most populous SMSAs in the United

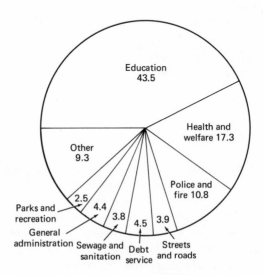

FIGURE 34 **Percentage Distribution, by Function, of Current Expenditures of Local Governments in Large SMSAs, 1966. From U.S. Bureau of the Census,** Local Government Finances in Selected Metropolitan Areas, 1965–1966.

States during fiscal 1966. Education, as we might anticipate, dominates the spending pattern. Well over 40 percent of the total operational outlay of all local units combined is devoted to this function. Health and welfare is a poor second with slightly over 17 percent, and police and fire protection third with about 11 percent. These proportions tend to vary with population size: the larger the area, the greater the percentage of the budget spent on such functions as health and welfare, police and fire protection, waste disposal, and parks. In the smaller communities, on the other hand, expenditures are spread out over a more limited range of services with educational allocations running, in some instances, as high as 65 percent of total current outlays.[22] The extensive analysis of local fiscal patterns made by Alan Campbell and Seymour Sacks shows that educational spending per capita is similar on the average in metropolitan and nonmetropolitan areas, but in the former, police, fire, and sewer expenditures are twice as great, sanitation, parks, and recreation three times larger, and housing, urban renewal, and airports five times more.[23]

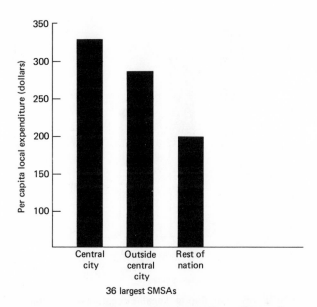

FIGURE 35   **Local Governmental Expenditure Comparisons, 36 Most Populous SMSAs and Rest of Nation, 1965. From Advisory Commission on Intergovernmental Relations,** Fiscal Balance in the American Federal System, **Vol. 2, 1967, p. 63.**

During recent decades, outlays of central city residents in the large SMSAs have exceeded those of suburban and nonmetropolitan dwellers. In 1965, for example, local government expenditures per capita within the core municipalities of the most populous metropolises were on the average 21 percent higher than in the ring communities and almost two-thirds above those for the rest of the nation (Figure 35). This differential

[22] See in this connection, Henry J. Schmandt and G. Ross Stephens, "Local Government Expenditure Patterns in the United States," Land Economics, XXXIX (November, 1963), 397–406.

[23] Metropolitan America: Fiscal Patterns and Governmental Systems (New York: Free Press, 1967), pp. 75–76.

is reflected in the tax burden of central city residents which, as a proportion of income, is more than one-third higher than that in the outlying areas.

What is significant to note in this connection is that higher spending for services other than education account for the variance. As Figure 36 shows, per capita educational expenditures in the large central

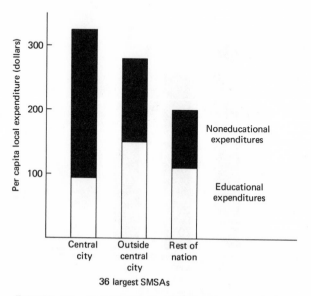

FIGURE 36   **Per Capita Local Educational and Noneducational Expenditures, 36 Largest SMSAs and the Rest of the Nation, 1965. From Advisory Commission on Intergovernmental Relations,** Fiscal Balance in the American Federal System, **Vol. 2, 1967, p. 72.**

cities were actually less (by about $42) than in their suburbs while noneducational outlays were almost double. The city of San Francisco, to cite a typical example, with one-fourth the population of the SMSA, spends well over one-third the area's total output for police protection and 31 percent for welfare, but only 14 percent for education. Similarly, New York City, with 70 percent of the metropolitan population, records four-fifths of the area's total police costs, nine-tenths of its welfare budget, and only one-third of its educational outlays. In other words, the huge requirements of the large central cities for safety and welfare functions allow less than an adequate margin for education. To quote the Advisory Commission on Intergovernmental Relations, "This is a perverse expenditure pattern if it be true, as we believe it to be, that children from underprivileged families require a greater educational outlay to compensate for the educational deficiencies of their home environment."[24]

Capital Outlays

Urban growth affects not only operating expenditures but it also compels local governments to invest heavily in the enlargement of their physical plants. Along with the demand for more teachers, policemen, firemen, sanitarians, engineers, and other workers, expansion is accompanied by the need for additional classrooms, police and fire stations, hospitals, roads, sewers, and parks. In 1967 local expenditures for these latter (capital) items, including publicly-owned utilities, totaled almost $13 billion, over one-third more than in 1962. The largest share, one-third, went into educational facilities, with locally operated utilities next and streets and roads third (Table 22).

TABLE 22   **Local Governmental Expenditures for Capital Outlay, 1967 (in millions of dollars)**

Function	Amount	Percent of Total
Education	$4,313	33.3
Streets and roads	1,888	14.5
Local utilities	2,044	15.8
Health and hospitals	299	2.3
Sewerage	1,093	8.4
Housing and urban renewal	966	7.5
Parks, recreation, natural resources	664	5.1
Airports and harbors	361	2.8
All other	1,334	10.3
Total	$12,962	100.0

SOURCE: U. S. Bureau of the Census, *Governmental Finances in 1966–67* (Washington: 1968).

Both central city and suburban units in the metropolis have large-scale capital requirements but, as noted earlier, they have different emphases. For the core municipality, the major physical needs are those relating primarily to the renewal of social capital: redevelopment of

[24] *Fiscal Balance in the American Federal System: Metropolitan Fiscal Disparities,* Vol. 2, p. 65.

blighted neighborhoods, replacement of obsolescent and worn-out public structures and utilities, and modernization of the transportation system. For the suburbs, the basic problem is the provision of new social capital in the form of school buildings and libraries, streets and roads, water and sewer mains, and park and recreational lands.

Expansion and renewal are both costly processes, but capital investment in the suburbs has generally exceeded that in the central city since World War II. In the Philadelphia and Washington, D.C., SMSAs,

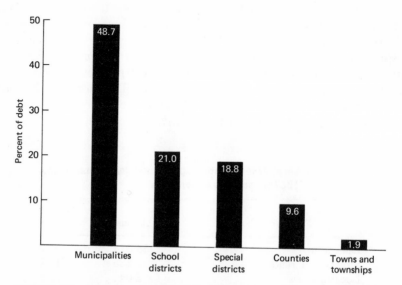

FIGURE 37   **Percent of Outstanding Debt of Local Units in Large SMSAs by Type of Government, 1965–1966. From U.S. Bureau of the Census,** Local Government Finances in Selected Metropolitan Areas, 1965–1966.

for example, almost two-thirds of the total capital outlay in 1966 was made by suburban units. Computed in per capita terms, however, both the city of Philadelphia and the District of Columbia spent more for capital improvements than their ring communities ($46 as against $45 in the former, and $102 to $87 in the latter). The significant difference, as in the case of operating expenditures, is attributable to the educational sector. Here the city of Philadelphia spent $6.60 per person for capital outlays in education as contrasted to an average of $15.50 for the area as a whole. The comparable figures for the District of Columbia were $20 and $35, respectively.

The capital indebtedness of state and local governments combined has been growing at a rate in excess of 6 percent annually while the national debt has been increasing by less than 2 percent. On a per capita basis, the accumulated debt of the two lower levels in 1967 was $544 for every person in the country, while the similar figure for the national government was $1649. During the ten-year period from 1957 to 1967, the outstanding long-term obligations of local units more than doubled (from $37.3 billion to $76.4 billion). Outlays for education headed the list, followed by those for publicly-operated utilities, sewerage facilities, housing and urban renewal, and street and road construction. The principal debtors are the local governments in the thirty-six largest SMSAs. These units are responsible for over one-half the total outstanding obligations of public agencies below the state level. About 65 percent of total local indebtedness is represented by general obligation bonds, the remainder by revenue or nonguaranteed issues.[25]

DETERMINANTS OF FISCAL BEHAVIOR

The expenditure patterns of American local governments are characterized by variances of considerable range both among and within metropolitan areas. These differences are not confined to those between central city and suburbs; they also exist between core municipalities and among ring communities. For example, total per capita expenditures by local governments in the New Orleans SMSA in 1966 were $157 while in the New York metropolitan area they were $395. Part of this differential is due to the assignment of expenditure responsibilities between state and local units, particularly in the field of public welfare. Where the latter is financed out of municipal funds, as in New York, local spending will be appreciably higher than in other areas where this function is a state responsibility. However, even when the factor of assignability is taken into account, substantial differences still remain. These can readily be observed among suburban communities within the same SMSA where variances of 50 percent or more among the individual units are not uncommon.

The last two decades have witnessed a large outpouring of statistical analyses seeking to explain the determinants of local fiscal behavior. These efforts have been designed to identify the factors which cause spending levels to be what they are and the variables which cause them to change. Such knowledge is essential for predictive purposes and, equally important, as guidelines for normative decisions by public

---

[25] General obligation bonds are backed by the full credit and tax resources of the local unit while revenue bonds are paid out of the proceeds of some self-liquidating project, such as a water supply system or parking garage.

policy-makers. Unfortunately, no definitive explanations have thus far emerged. Disagreements among the researchers over methodology and data interpretation continue to obscure the picture. In addition, the inability of statistical techniques to take account of the "non-quantitative" factors in the political decision-making process serves as a further barrier to full explanation.

Research in this general area has tended to concentrate on a limited number of independent variables as explanatory of local public expenditures (the dependent variable). These include per capita or median family income, degree of urbanization, population size, density, and state and federal aid.[26] Others, such as the proportion of the SMSA population residing in the central city, age of community, property value, and ethnic characteristics, have also been employed. Several of the conclusions drawn from recent studies are summarized here as illustrative of the factors which influence local fiscal behavior.

1. Availability of resources—the wealth of a community, in other words—whether measured in terms of income or property valuations, is the most important single determinant of local public spending. As several researchers have found, the greater the per capita income differential between localities, the greater the variance in service expenditures, particularly for education.

2. State grants-in-aid show a positive relationship to local spending levels. By increasing the funds available to local governments, these aids not only enhance the ability of a community to provide services but also stimulate it to greater fiscal effort on its own part.

3. The greater proportion the central city population represents of the SMSA total, the smaller the expenditure differential between the core municipality and its outside area. Researchers usually attribute this relationship to suburban exploitation of the central city, but the causal factors have yet to be demonstrated empirically.

4. The Campbell and Sacks study found that the above three variables —income, state aid, central city-suburban population ratio—have a combined explanatory power of 0.639; that is, they account for approximately 64 percent of the variance in per capita expenditures by urban communities.[27]

5. The common impression is that size is the most important determinant of local public expenditures: the larger a unit is the more it

[26] Examples of such investigations are Glenn W. Fisher, "Determinants of State and Local Government Expenditures: A Preliminary Analysis," *National Tax Journal,* XIV (December, 1961), 349–355; Seymour Sacks and Robert Harris, "The Determinants of State and Local Government Expenditures and Intergovernmental Flow of Funds," *National Tax Journal,* XVII (March, 1964), 75–85; and Woo Sik Kee, "City-Suburban Differentials in Local Government Fiscal Effort," *National Tax Journal,* XXI (June, 1968), 183–189.

[27] *Metropolitan America: Fiscal Patterns and Governmental Systems,* pp. 163–164.

will spend per person.[28] Earlier studies gave some support for this conclusion, as did Bureau of the Census figures which showed that cities in the higher population classes spend on the average more per capita than those in the lower categories.[29] More recent research, while acknowledging the generally higher spending levels of the larger governments, casts considerable doubt on the assumption that population size is the major determinant of this phenomenon.[30] As economist Harvey Brazer concluded after a systematic and statistically rigorous study of city expenditures in the United States: "There is little, if any, demonstrable positive relationship between the population size of cities and their levels of expenditure per capita when other independent variables are taken into account and the sample studied is a large one. Assertions to the contrary have typically been based upon simple correlation analysis or observations of data for broad groups of cities. Careful study of such groups discloses the fact, however, that variations in the mean level of per capita expenditures between groups is not significantly greater than that within groups."[31]

Not surprisingly, the major thrust of these various findings is that local government expenditure levels are in large part reflections of the resources available to a community. High spending patterns are associated with superior fiscal capacity and low with correspondingly smaller assets. On this basis we would expect lower per capita spending in the southern states where industrial development has been slow and where median family income is proportionately less than it is in the remainder of the nation. Similarly, we would expect higher spending levels in the larger metropolitan areas since it is there that the greatest wealth is concentrated and personal and corporate income highest.

THE QUEST FOR SOLUTIONS

To a considerable extent, as economist Lyle Fitch has observed, the American system of local finance still operates as though the various

[28] Central city and suburban partisans frequently engage in verbal controversy over this question. The former contend that suburban units are generally uneconomical and inefficient because of their small size while the latter maintain that there are diseconomies of scale in the larger governments. The argument obscures many factors of a more relevant nature but it has received wide publicity.

[29] See, for instance, Mabel L. Walker, *Municipal Expenditures* (Baltimore: Johns Hopkins University Press, 1930), where the conclusion is reached (p. 117) that "per capita costs of government increase rapidly as the population increases."

[30] Stanley Scott and Edward L. Feder, *Factors Associated with Variations in Municipal Expenditure Levels* (Berkeley: University of California Bureau of Public Administration, 1957).

[31] *City Expenditures in the United States* (New York: National Bureau of Economic Research, 1959), p. 66.

activities of the urban polity were concentrated in one governmental jurisdiction.[32] It blatantly ignores the fact that political splintering has arbitrarily divided up the tax resources of metropolitan areas and has left some units with insufficient capacity to provide needed services. Under a single government, the spatial differentiation of economic activities and wealth does not affect an area's financial structure; in a governmentally divided metropolis, this differentiation normally results in an uneven distribution of tax capabilities among the individual entities.

The present system also disregards the spillover effects which result from the extension of activities across jurisdictional lines and which make it virtually impossible to relate benefits and taxes. A high quality of police protection in one unit will be reflected in a lower incidence of crime in an adjacent community; efficient sewage treatment by one jurisdiction will benefit its downstream neighbors; a first-rate school system in one district will enhance the economic potentialities of the total urban complex. Obviously each unit will be both the source and beneficiary (or victim) of such spillovers, but it is highly unlikely that the scales will be balanced for each.

This brings us to the question of how the inequities and weaknesses in the metropolitan fiscal system can be resolved or mitigated short of political consolidation. Three broad approaches to this problem, all of them based on the principle of expanding the taxing jurisdiction, have been used in varying degrees: (1) superimposing new operating agencies on the existing governmental structure; (2) shifting responsibilities or functions to units of broader territorial scope; and (3) redistributing tax resources.

The first approach is represented by the familiar device of the special district, both school and nonschool. We have already noted that a single government in urban areas would eliminate the inequities resulting from spillovers and uneven distribution of taxable capacity. Similar results may be achieved on a lesser scale when individual services are administered by special districts. By permitting the pooling of area resources for carrying out certain functions, these units help reduce the effects of territorial differentiation in wealth. The special school district for handicapped children in St. Louis County, Missouri, illustrates this point. Invested with power to levy a countywide property tax to support its activities, the district is able to draw on the wealth of the area to serve handicapped children regardless of their place of residence in the county. In this way, those who live in the poorer districts where lack of funds would prevent such services are able to benefit from the tax resources of the larger community.

[32] "Metropolitan Financial Problems," *Annals of the American Academy of Political and Social Science*, 314 (November, 1957), 67.

The second method, transfer of functions to a larger unit of government, has the same effect. If responsibility for such items as public health and hospitals is assumed by the county, or if welfare programs are administered directly by the state, the problem of logistics—getting the service distributed where it is most needed—is solved. In other words, there is a close positive association between the equitable fulfillment of needs and the proportion of the local service package that is handled by area-wide units. The more services of a local nature are administered by the county, area-wide special districts, or the state government, the less territorial variance will exist in the system between need and fiscal ability.

The third device, redistribution of tax funds, offers another means of overcoming the uneven spatial distribution of metropolitan resources. State grants-in-aid that are based on need serve this purpose to a limited extent. A more direct method is for the county or a metropolitan taxing agency to collect and distribute funds to the local units according to some equalization formula. The Toronto area follows this practice in the case of education. The metropolitan government, through an area-wide school board, subsidizes the local school districts by direct grants designed to provide an equivalent standard of education for each child. The Toronto arrangement permits the retention of local school districts but, by tapping the resources of the total area, assures each of sufficient funds to maintain a comparable level of education.

These various approaches are not mutually exclusive. All three may be, and occasionally are, utilized in efforts to resolve the fiscal difficulties that plague metropolitan areas. They provide no total solution but only partial remedies. Nor are they without their serious disadvantages and dangers. One might argue, for example, that the creation of special districts only compounds the difficulties of administering metropolitan public affairs, or that the redistribution of tax funds permits the continued existence of local units which should not survive as autonomous entities. Or he might point out that the devices mentioned here depend largely on local tax sources and these, as we have had occasion to see, are limited essentially to the property levy and a few lesser means of support.

THE INTERGOVERNMENTAL ROAD

Financing local government is a major facet of the metropolitan problem. By means of taxes and other revenue-producing methods, local units seek to maintain an orderly and efficient environment in which people can live comfortably and business and industry flourish. The execution of this task is impeded to the extent that funds are insufficient or resources unevenly distributed throughout the total community. Fiscal responsibility for meeting urban and metropolitan needs does not, however, rest solely on the shoulders of local agencies. With few exceptions, domestic public functions have become the shared responsibility of several governmental levels. Indeed, when the source of financing is taken into account, there is hardly a functional area—even among those traditionally considered local such as elementary and secondary education—in which federal, state, and local governments do not participate.[33]

The upward shift of fiscal obligation for urban-oriented programs is inevitable if crisis is to be averted. Only if jurisdictions with superior financial capabilities assume a larger share of the local budget can the mounting needs of the nation's metropolitan areas be met. Moreover, it is only in this way that a solution can be found to the problem of moderating the gross inequalities created by the widely different fiscal abilities of local units within the same urban complex. For given the governmentally divided nature of the metropolis, attempts to resolve this dilemma at the metropolitan level merely add to its ramifications since local units invariably resort to protective devices that tend to generate more, rather than less, inequity. They carry on interlocal economic warfare through competitive underassessment; they help to create tax havens for concentrations of industry; and small suburban communities engage in protective planning and zoning which often is a deterrent to the well-balanced development of the larger urban community. The Advisory Commission on Intergovernmental Relations eloquently put the case for enlarged activity by all public levels in this field when it recently said:

Regardless of actions taken by the public sector to control riots, regardless of actions taken by the private sector to protect or increase economic investment and opportunity, and regardless of efforts by private and public enterprise together in combating poverty and disease among low-income residents of central cities or depressed suburban areas, state, local and Federal legislative action is necessary and urgent to bring fiscal needs and resources of our urban governments into better balance.[34]

---

[33] On this matter, see Advisory Commission on Intergovernmental Relations, *Fiscal Balance in the American Federal System*, Vol. 1 (Washington: October, 1967), pp. 73–74.

[34] *Ibid.*, Vol. 2, p. 7.

11 /
THE ONE-GOVERNMENT APPROACH

THE IDEA OF A SINGLE GOVERNMENT FOR AN ENTIRE METROPOLITAN AREA has long intrigued many urban scholars and persons influential in civic affairs. They see such a structure as a more efficient, economical, and effective means of handling public affairs and functions. They also see it as a way of allocating public financial resources on the basis of needs of the various territorial parts of the area, thereby eliminating the great disparities between resources and needs that commonly prevail in a metropolis of many local units. These claims are vigorously contested by opponents of the one-government concept who argue in terms of loss of local control, decreased citizen access to public officials and employees, reduced attention to local services, and the greater efficiency of other area-wide approaches short of complete unification.

Activities to implement the one-government goal have taken several principal forms and have experienced varying degrees of success. In most instances these efforts have related either to municipalities alone or in combination with counties or to school districts. Interest in other types of unification has existed, but supporting activity has been intermittent and unproductive. Discussion about combining school districts with municipalities or counties has been held from time to time, mostly by scholars and consultants, but despite this talk the schools remain strongholds of governmental separatism. Similarly, the merging of counties and the combining of townships have also been urged, with little tangible result. The same is true of nonschool special districts. Despite proposals to consolidate them with one another and with general local units, particularly counties, the trend toward proliferation continues.

Although pronouncements for large-scale consolidation have emerged sporadically during the present century, two major pleas directed to national audiences recently came in close order. In 1966, the Committee for Economic Development, a private research group of prominent businessmen and educators, recommended a reduction of at least 80 percent in the number of the nation's local governments. It also specifically advocated, among other things, consolidation of the approximately 2700 nonmetropolitan counties into not more than 500 units and the use of city-county consolidation and greatly strengthened counties as area-wide governments in metropolitan situations.[1] Two years later, the National Commission on Urban Problems, headed by former Senator Paul H. Douglas, suggested the use of financial incentives for consolidation. Under the Commission's proposal a percentage of the federal individual income tax revenue would be earmarked for this purpose. Major municipalities and urban county governments (those of both types containing at least 50,000 inhabitants) would be eligible to share directly in these funds. The plan was designed deliberately to favor general-purpose local governments that "are sufficiently large in population to give some prospect of viability as urban units."[2]

MUNICIPAL EXPANSION:
THE HALCYON AND DORMANT YEARS

The single-government approach centering on municipalities has involved three techniques: absorption of nearby unincorporated land (annexation); merger of municipalities (municipal consolidation); and

---

[1] Committee for Economic Development, Research and Policy Committee, *Modernizing Local Government to Secure a Balanced Federalism* (New York: 1966), pp. 17, 44–47. For a defense against criticisms of this report, see Robert F. Steadman, "Oh, Ye of Little Faith," *National Civic Review*, LVI (November, 1967), 562–567. A commentary by John A. Rehfuss on the Steadman article appears in *National Civic Review*, LVII (January, 1968), 6–7.

[2] National Commission on Urban Problems, *Final Report*, Part IV (Washington: 1968), pp. 5–9, 5–14, 5–15.

merger of one or more municipal governments with the county government (city-county consolidation). The first of these has been the most common means of changing governmental boundaries in urban areas.[3]

The Pre-1900 Period

State governments from the beginning have acknowledged the necessity of setting up means for the creation and enlargement of municipalities. In doing so they recognized that what became urban, in the sense of a concentration of people, should also become municipal—that is, possess the type of local government capable of satisfying the service and regulatory needs of population centers. This rationale for accommodating urban growth was generally accepted until the turn of the present century. Its acceptability, however, rested primarily on the fact that the early urban settlements were generally distant from each other. Consequently, as an area became urban it was incorporated as a municipality; and as growth spread beyond the original boundaries into the surrounding countryside, the newly populated land was usually annexed to the existing municipal government—an action deemed to be a logical and natural extension of the original city. In some instances, consolidation took place when two municipalities through growth eventually became contiguous to each other.

In the era before 1900, the expansion of municipal boundaries largely kept pace with population growth. Boundary extensions frequently enabled an originally small and usually isolated municipality to become large in population and territory. Today, these units comprise the central cities of many metropolises. Without annexation, few large central cities would have developed. Instead, clusters of numerous small municipalities, none constituting a governmental, economic, and social hub for the larger community, would exist in most metropolitan areas.

The pre-1900 annexation movement had three prominent characteristics: many municipalities absorbed much territory; the land annexed was not extensively urbanized at the time of absorption; and on occasion annexation was used simultaneously with another area reorganization approach, such as municipal consolidation or the separation of a city from a county. A conspicuous example of the last named is St. Louis, which in 1876 more than tripled its area through annexation at the same time it detached itself from St. Louis County.[4]

[3] Some state laws speak of the annexation of one municipality by another. In this book, for purposes of clarity, the term "municipal annexation" is used to refer only to the absorption of unincorporated territory and the term "municipal consolidation" refers to the absorption of one municipality by another or the combining of two or more municipalities to create a new unit.

[4] R. D. McKenzie, *The Metropolitan Community* (New York: McGraw-Hill, 1933), pp. 191–198, 336–337, and Richard Bigger and James D. Kitchen, *How the Cities Grew* (Los Angeles: University of California Bureau of Governmental Research, 1952), pp. 143–151, describe the early annexation activities of a number of cities.

The Time of Decline

The nature of municipal annexation changed quickly and decidedly around the turn of the century, and from then until the end of World War II its usage was infrequent and generally of minor significance. During this time, annexations decreased in number, in total territory absorbed, and in the average size of the annexed areas. The total amount of territory absorbed, for example, in the decade of the 1920s was substantially smaller than in the 1890s. By the 1930s, only a handful of municipalities were completing annexations, mostly of minuscule size. Only a few cities—most prominently Detroit and Los Angeles— made sizable annexations between 1900 and 1945 (Figure 38).

Municipal consolidation was even less active and less consequential than annexation during these years. Again, as in annexation, there were occasional exceptions, almost always fostered by extraordinary circumstances. Los Angeles, for example, using its control of the area's major water supply as an enticement, was able to persuade a number of municipalities to consolidate with it. In general, however, the device was almost completely abandoned.

The Changing Conditions

The precipitous decrease in annexation and the near demise of municipal consolidation were directly related to the pronounced urban and metropolitan growth of this period. Technological improvements, such as the automobile, greatly facilitated the expansion of urbanization over more and more land and converted many people into commuters traveling many miles to their work locations. As these newly urbanized sectors outside the old established large municipalities gained in population, their residents established their own municipal governments or at least avoided becoming parts of those already in existence. Formerly many small but old municipalities had been fairly or completely isolated from the big city, but now they often found themselves to be its neighbors as a result of the big city's annexations of the nineteenth century. In the early 1900s, therefore, many new urban concentrations and most small neighboring municipalities developed stiff resistance to absorption through annexation or consolidation. The halcyon years of governmental assimilation by large cities of adjacent unincorporated urban areas and nearby small incorporated places had come to an end.

For opposition to the one-government concept to be effective, it was necessary to get state legislatures to make municipal annexation and consolidation difficult to use successfully. In many states this objective was accomplished, with a coalition of suburban and rural legislators usually the decisive force. Annexation procedures were made extremely complex by giving the property owners or voters in the unincorporated territory

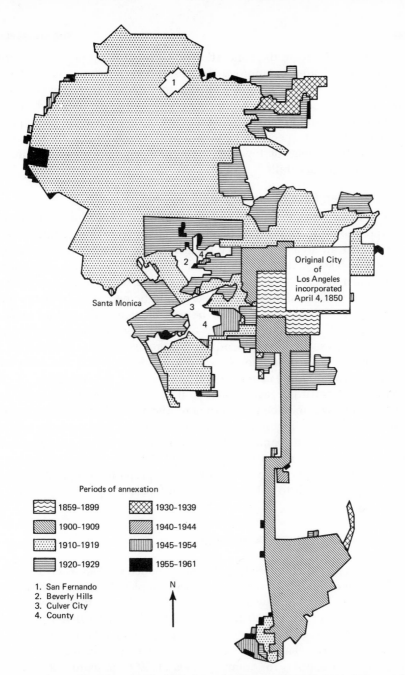

Periods of annexation

1859–1899		1930–1939	
1900–1909		1940–1944	
1910–1919		1945–1954	
1920–1929		1955–1961	

1. San Fernando
2. Beverly Hills
3. Culver City
4. County

N

Original City
of
Los Angeles
incorporated
April 4, 1850

Santa Monica

FIGURE 38 **Annexations to the City of Los Angeles by Time Periods. Only a small amount of land has been annexed since 1961. From Winston W. Crouch and Beatrice Dinerman,** Southern California Metropolis **(Berkeley and Los Angeles: University of California Press, 1963), p. 161. Reprinted by permission of The Regents of the University of California.**

the sole right to begin the annexation or by requiring a popular majority in the affected area to approve the absorption. Similarly, general consolidation laws were commonly altered to stipulate that separate voter majorities (sometimes two-thirds majorities) had to be obtained in both municipalities. And in the declining number of states that still used special legislation to effect specific annexations and consolidations, the suburban representatives alone or together with rural legislators were ordinarily able to defeat such bills.

The Continued Ease of Incorporating

In contrast to annexation and consolidation procedures, municipal incorporation provisions remained extremely lax. They continued to specify that an area with a very small number of residents—commonly only 100 to 500—could incorporate and thus establish a municipal government. Then as now, most states did not have a set of legal standards to be applied in determining when areas should be permitted to incorporate and whether they should annex or be consolidated with existing municipalities. Greatly stiffening the terms of annexation and consolidation but retaining excessively liberal incorporation provisions naturally resulted in extensive use of incorporation as a technique for avoiding the other two processes. Annexation, moreover, related only to the acquiring of unincorporated territory; consequently, if a small amount of land was incorporated as a municipal government, the annexation process, regardless of its liberal or highly restrictive nature, could no longer be applied to this area. In like manner, use of incorporation in an area generally meant that two incorporated places could not be consolidated unless a majority of the voters in both approved the proposition separately. Such consent was difficult to obtain and seldom forthcoming.

THE ANNEXATION RENAISSANCE

The long period of annexation dormancy ended in 1945 when 152 cities in the 5000 or more population category completed annexations, a total greatly exceeding the prewar level of the 1930s. And in the following two years the number passed 250 and neared 300. This renewed vigor, thought by some analysts to be merely a postwar spurt to relieve a backlog of postponed actions, has proved to be of considerable longtime strength. In 1967, for example, 787 municipalities of 5000 or more residents annexed additional territory, a number almost five times as great as in 1945. Although part of the increase is due to the rise in the number of cities in this size category, the bulk of the gain is attributable to the much greater proportionate use of the annexation device. In addition, the total amount of land annexed by cities of this population size has become considerable. The total in 1967—the lowest year in the last ten—was 392 square miles, almost three times as much as that of 1948.[5] Basically, this resurgence may be traced to two interrelated factors: the continuance of metropolitan growth and the general lack of public acceptance of comprehensive governmental reorganization in urban areas.

Much of the annexation activity since the end of World War II has taken place in SMSAs, with a number of central cities and suburbs em-

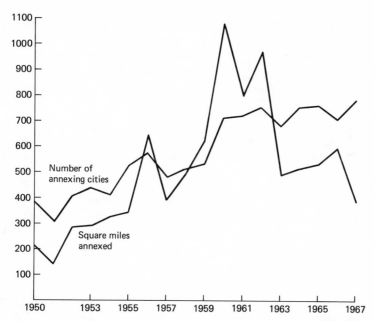

FIGURE 39   **Number of Annexing Municipalities of 5000 or More Population and Amount of Territory Annexed, 1950–1967. From** Municipal Year Book: 1968, **International City Managers' Association, 1968, p. 31.**

ploying the device. In the overwhelming number of instances, however, the amount of land involved has been small—less, in fact, than one-half square mile. What is even more irritating is that difficult annexation laws have made it necessary for the initiating governments to proceed through an intricate legal procedure to obtain a tiny amount of territory.

For the nation's most populous cities—those containing not fewer than 100,000 people—annexation has had limited general utility during this

[5] John C. Bollens, "Metropolitan and Fringe Area Developments in 1967," *Municipal Year Book: 1968* (Washington: International City Managers' Association, 1968), p. 31.

renaissance. In the postwar years some of these concentrations have remained unchanged in areal extent, while many others have gained only a few square miles. One reason for this situation is that annexation is legally unusable, or nearly so, for a number of major urban centers which are fully or largely hemmed in by other municipalities. (Minneapolis is an example of complete encirclement.) Another is that many annexation laws continue to favor owners and residents of unincorporated land, who often do not wish their area to become part of a city, particu-

TABLE 23   The Leaders in Annexation, 1950–1967, Among Cities with Populations of 100,000 or More

City	1969 Estimated Population (in Thousands)	Land Area (Square Miles)		1950–1967 Increase
		1950	1967	
Oklahoma City, Okla.	380	50.8	649.7	598.9
Houston, Tex.	1165	160.0	452.9	292.9
Kansas City, Mo.	555	80.6	316.0	235.4
Phoenix, Ariz.	515	17.1	246.7	229.6
San Diego, Calif.	680	99.4	307.2	207.8
Dallas, Tex.	815	112.0	295.3	183.3
Tulsa, Okla.	325	30.4	175.2	144.8
Mobile, Ala.	215	25.4	152.9	127.5
San Antonio, Tex.	695	69.5	182.1	112.6
Fort Worth, Tex.	355	93.7	197.6	103.9
San Jose, Calif.	425	17.0	116.5	99.5
El Paso, Tex.	315	25.6	117.5	91.9
Atlanta, Ga.	515	36.9	128.4	91.5
Columbus, Ohio	535	39.4	114.1	74.7
Newport News, Va.	138	4.2	75.0	70.8[a]
Tucson, Ariz.	240	9.5	75.9	66.4
Tampa, Fla.	295	19.0	85.0	66.0
Lubbock, Tex.	162	17.0	75.0	58.0
Knoxville, Tenn.	187	24.0	77.0	53.0
Milwaukee, Wis.	750	50.0	95.8	45.8
Charlotte, N. C.	264	30.0	71.0	41.0
Amarillo, Tex.	154	20.9	60.3	39.4
Beaumont, Tex.	125	31.4	70.8	39.4
Greensboro, N. C.	138	18.2	51.8	33.6

[a] This increase in area resulted from the consolidation of the cities of Newport News and Warwick. Consolidated city-counties, such as Jacksonville, are not included.

SOURCES: Population estimates were prepared by Rand McNally & Company, Chicago, for use in its *Commercial Atlas and Marketing Guide* (100th edition, 1969) and are included here through the courtesy of that publisher. (Copyright by Rand McNally & Company.) The official land area data were supplied by the cities to the Bureau of the Census and the International City Managers' Association.

larly a heavily populated one. A third reason is that some large cities are uninterested in annexation, either viewing it as an unsatisfactory or too costly means of meeting metropolitan needs or concentrating their attention instead on problems present within their existing boundaries.

The Exceptions: Large Annexations

Sizable annexations have not been entirely unknown in this period dominated by small land absorptions. In fact, a limited but still impressive number of municipalities have acquired large amounts of territory. Since 1950, for example, of a total of 148 cities containing an estimated 1965 population of at least 100,000, nine have added not less than 100 square miles, while another fifteen have gained between 30 and 100 square miles (Table 23). Annexation of unincorporated land accounted for virtually all the territorial expansion by these units. Newport News, the only major exception, grew by means of municipal consolidation with the city of Warwick in 1958.

Some of these cities have made highly spectacular use of annexation. Oklahoma City has had the most dramatic activity, one of almost incredible scope, and undertaken, according to its officials, as the only feasible method by which proper and orderly development of the area

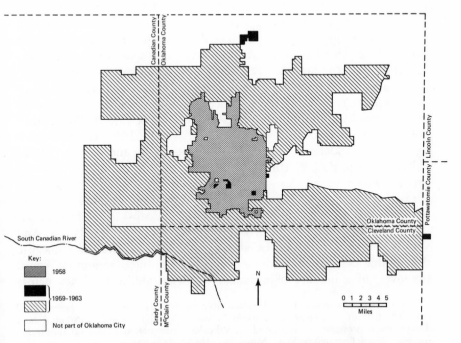

FIGURE 40   The Growth of Oklahoma City, 1959–1963. Data compiled by Thomas M. Ballentine, unpublished thesis, University of Oklahoma, 1964.

could be assured. Fairly large in territory (about 50 square miles) but only moderate in population (about a quarter of a million) at the start of the 1950s, Oklahoma City annexed 270 square miles in the following ten years, an area larger than that of Chicago, the nation's second most populous municipality. Oklahoma's capital continued its torrid pace into the 1960s, more than doubling its territorial size, until it now includes territory in several counties and contains almost 650 square miles (Figure 40); it was easily the largest city in area in the United States until Jacksonville and Duval County consolidated in 1967 as the city of Jacksonville with 760 square miles. As a result of large-scale annexation, Houston, Kansas City, and San Diego also have surpassed the geographic size of New York City, still by far the nation's largest population center. In similar fashion, Dallas has moved on to encompass more land than Chicago, while Phoenix has changed from a small municipality into a territorial giant.

The Favorable Factors

Recent large land acquisitions through annexation have taken place chiefly under conditions not generally present in metropolitan areas. Most cities involved in these actions have been aided by favorable annexation laws.[6] Equally as important, they were bordered by substantial unincorporated territory and thus had room for expansion. As to the first factor, most large annexations have been completed under one of four procedures that preclude the outlying area from vetoing the action: (1) an ordinance enacted by the council of the annexing city; (2) a favorable vote by the electorate of the initiating city; (3) a special act of the state legislature; and (4) an order by a court after reviewing the proposal.

The relation of these four procedures to major land acquisitions is readily apparent from considering a few examples. Oklahoma City's unrivaled annexation accomplishments were realized by means of ordinances passed by its city council, as were the large gains by Tulsa, the other leading center in Oklahoma. The huge absorptions by the Texas cities of Dallas, El Paso, Fort Worth, Houston, and San Antonio also were made through council action. Kansas City, Missouri, grew in area through the affirmative responses of its voters who have the right to pass on annexation proposals presented as charter amendments. Most of the land added to Atlanta was obtained by a single act of the state legislature. And Norfolk, Virginia, increased by almost twenty-two square miles because of favorable determinations by a specially constituted annexation court. Moreover, in a number of instances the legal ability to annex across

[6] An analysis of central city annexation activity in urbanized areas between 1950 and 1960 that finds a clear relationship between liberal laws and substantial land absorptions is presented in Raymond H. Wheeler, "Annexation Law and Annexation Success," *Land Economics*, XLI (November, 1965), 354–360.

county lines (which is not permissible in some states) enabled the municipalities to accomplish such large-sized absorptions of land.

The existence of considerable unincorporated territory adjacent to the
annexing city, the second factor important to large land acquisitions, has
been basic to the successful use of these laws. The presence of liberal or
equitable processes would have been meaningless to the principal users
of annexation if they had been surrounded by other incorporated places.
Under such circumstances expansion would have had to follow the stipula-
tions of municipal consolidation laws, which virtually always require the
separate and seldom forthcoming consent of the neighboring municipality.
Thus, to cite several examples, Oklahoma City, Phoenix, Tulsa, Houston,
and Dallas were located next to ample unincorporated land when they
launched their annexation drives. This condition had vanished long before mid-century in many other metropolises where the major cities became engulfed in a veritable sea of municipalities.

Since the highly fortuitous combination of these two circumstances has
generally been necessary in the postwar years to accomplish large annexations, such expansions have been mostly confined to metropolitan areas
of small or medium size, such as Oklahoma City, Phoenix, Columbus, San
Antonio, Charlotte, and Amarillo. In contrast, ten of the twelve most
populous cities in the nation have annexed little or no land since 1950.
(Milwaukee and Chicago are the exceptions, absorbing 45.8 and 19.5
square miles, respectively.) In fact, half of them had acquired all or
virtually all of their present territory by 1900. Some large annexations,
however, have materialized in SMSAs that have undergone rapid population growth in the postwar years, including Houston, Dallas, San Diego,
Atlanta, and Kansas City (Missouri), all located in heavily populated
metropolitan areas which currently have more than one million inhabitants. (Due partly to annexation, Houston, between 1950 and 1960,
rose from fourteenth position to become the seventh most populous city
in the United States.)

Large annexations in booming metropolises have a more important
consequence than merely increasing the territorial size of the central city.
In some of these SMSAs annexation has been used early and compre-
hensively enough so that the areas contain far fewer municipalities than
most of their older counterparts. The latter generally completed annexations earlier and at a much slower pace, in part because urbanization of
land then materialized much less rapidly. Thus some metropolises of
medium size at present, such as Phoenix, are likely to become heavily
populated but still remain relatively uncluttered in terms of number of
municipalities because of their sizable land absorptions. A few examples
demonstrate the possible long-range importance of some of the recent
large annexations. In 1967, the San Diego SMSA had 14 municipalities;
the Phoenix area, 18; and Metropolitan San Antonio, 21. The situation in

many of the older large metropolises was distinctly different; for instance, the Cleveland SMSA had 90 municipalities; St. Louis, 169; and Chicago, 250. The variations are pronounced even when the comparisons are made of metropolises of the same population class. The Cleveland area has more than six times as many municipalities as Metropolitan San Diego, even though both are very heavily populated complexes, in the 1 million to 3 million category.

Annexation as a Metropolitan Device

Although of dramatic scope, large annexations in recent years have not proved to be an adequate governmental instrument for dealing with metropolitan-wide services and problems. They have brought an appreciable portion of land within the jurisdiction of a single municipal unit in the metropolis, thus guaranteeing a unified governmental operation in the entire territory occupied by that city. They also have greatly simplified the existing governmental system in at least parts of the metropolis by eradicating numerous nonschool special districts that had operated in the formerly unincorporated sections. On the other hand, such absorptions have at times produced defensive incorporations, thereby contributing to the proliferation of municipalities.

Large annexations do not represent a metropolitan-wide device, falling short in two important ways. First, they have taken place in urban areas already containing a considerable number of municipalities (and frequently many special districts and one or more county governments as well). Second, cities that have utilized this device in a large-scale way still embrace merely a portion, most often a relatively small part, of the total metropolitan area.[7] Some SMSAs where large annexations have recently occurred are obviously less complicated governmentally than some longer established metropolises, but generally the difference is one of degree of complexity rather than its absence or presence. The San Diego, Phoenix, and San Antonio areas contain fewer municipalities than many of their older counterparts, but the number nonetheless ranges between fourteen and twenty-one.

Before 1900, annexation was repeatedly used to keep all of the urban area within the boundaries of one municipal government; since 1945 not a single use of annexation has produced a similar result. The latter has

---

[7] Annexation nevertheless has been used on an extensive basis in a variety of situations in the last few decades. For example, it has been utilized (1) after the rejection of a more comprehensive plan (Knoxville, 1960), (2) as a stimulant to prompt acceptance of a comprehensive proposal (Nashville, 1960), and (3) as a corollary to implementation of another approach, as in the attachment of considerable land to the city of Baton Rouge in 1949 when a modified city-county consolidation plan became operative in Baton Rouge city and parish (county), and as in the addition of 82 square miles to Atlanta in 1951 when a redistribution of functions between the city and the county was made.

inevitably been the situation, even under the most favorable conditions, largely because (1) metropolitanization has spread rapidly over a widening area, thereby encompassing numerous formerly isolated municipalities, (2) unincorporated communities located in the path of metropolitan expansion have often incorporated to avert absorption, (3) many of the recent major annexations have been completed in SMSAs that already have considerable governmental complexity, and (4) regardless of the total amount of territory annexed by any city in recent years, its current boundaries fall far short of being congruent with the territorial limits of the metropolis.

Despite the inability of annexation, even when employed on a large scale, to provide an area-wide approach to services and problems, it nevertheless continues to be a significant device for dealing with certain difficulties in the metropolis. And in all likelihood this will remain true so long as there are unincorporated urban areas in SMSAs, a probable situation in most of them for some time to come. Even the installation of various area-wide approaches to problems—such as extensive cooperation among existing units, the conversion of the county into an urban unit, and the establishment of metropolitan districts—does not eliminate the existence of unincorporated urban territory and the problems it engenders.

ANNEXATION AND THE URBAN FRINGE

The magnitude of urban fringe areas and their difficulties, though frequently underestimated or ignored, contribute some troublesome conditions in the metropolis.[8] First, many of these areas are large in population and territory. Second, most of them are entirely or predominantly residential, rather than commercial or industrial, and thus often tend to possess limited financial resources. Third, their residents frequently prefer to choose services cafeteria-style—that is, to select a few that meet their most pressing needs from whatever sources that are willing to provide them, whether a private company, a special district, the county, or even the adjoining city. Fourth, many such areas are seriously deficient in some or even all basic urban-type services and regulatory activities— water supply, garbage collection, streets, sewerage, fire protection, police protection, parks and recreation facilities, zoning controls, and subdivision regulations—which may be detrimental to both their residents and city inhabitants.

[8] An unincorporated area adjacent to a municipality is often called the urban fringe because it has undergone urban development, has urban needs, and borders but is not part of a city. John C. Bollens, *Urban Fringe Areas: Zoning, Subdivision Regulations, and Municipal Services* (Chicago: International City Managers' Association, September, 1960). A summary will be found in "Urban Fringe Areas—A Persistent Problem," *Public Management*, XLII (October, 1960), 218–221.

Resistance to Annexation

On the surface, annexation seems a relatively simple method of meeting the deficiencies of the urban fringe. By absorbing such land, a city can usually supply services and regulations sufficient to eliminate the inadequacies. But operationally the process is not as simple as it may seem since, as noted earlier, the authority to start an annexation action or to vote separately on the proposition, or both, usually rests with the outlying sector. The urban fringe frequently takes advantage of these provisions to oppose annexation. It may not want to pay city taxes, even though the city tax rate is sometimes lower than the combined rate of special districts operating in the unincorporated section. It may not want to have the city's subdivision and zoning regulations applied to its area.[9] It may conclude that it is already receiving a sufficient number of services, a judgment which may be tenuous. It may fear that it will not have a potent voice in local affairs, but instead will be dominated by people who currently control the city government. It may want to remain "countryfied," to escape being inside a city by remaining semirural as long as possible, even though it already has, or is fast developing, urban needs. Also, as political scientist Thomas Dye has shown, annexation is less likely to occur when the urbanized area containing both the municipality and the fringe is an old settlement, strong socioeconomic differences exist between the city and the unincorporated section, and the form of city government is other than the council-manager system.[10]

The continued unincorporated status of fringe areas is not always attributable to their obstinancy or shortsightedness. The devil's role is sometimes played by the cities. On a number of occasions when a municipality has had the controlling position in a locally-determined annexation question, it has absorbed only the financially attractive portions of adjacent territory. By completing leap-frog annexations, it has bypassed those sections that would cost far more to serve than they would return in revenue. Yet these are often the sections most in need of municipal services, regulations, and corrective actions and the chief sources of the problems affecting both the city and the fringe.

[9] A law (Ch. 73) passed in Washington State in 1967 deals innovatively with this sensitive sphere. It provides for the organization of a community municipal corporation in an unincorporated area that annexes to a city (as well as in a smaller city consolidating with a larger one). The corporation's governing body, which includes residents of the area, may disapprove the adoption of that part of a comprehensive city plan applying to its section and may reject any ordinance or resolution pertaining to land, building, or structures within its territory. The corporation exists initially for four years and may be continued beyond that period by approval of the area's voters.

[10] Thomas R. Dye, "Urban Political Integration: Conditions Associated with Annexation in American Cities," *Midwest Journal of Political Science,* VIII (November, 1964), 446. Professor Dye's work pertains to annexation activity by central cities in 213 urbanized areas between 1950 and 1960.

The use of annexation in fringe situations is further lessened, in fact often eliminated, by the availability of easy incorporation processes, which are still common although becoming less numerous. In most states an unincorporated area of relatively few residents can block annexation by deciding to proceed with incorporation as a separate municipality. When fringe areas of low financial resources and many deficiencies become separate municipalities, their problems remain and may even increase in time. At the other extreme, when wealthy but unincorporated areas adjoining a municipality incorporate, they are able to capitalize on all the benefits of the adjacent city but escape any share of its burdens.

Municipal Expansion: Different Approaches

Midway in the twentieth century it seemed as if the urban fringe problem would generally continue to be approached more on the basis of counteracting maneuvers by cities and adjacent unincorporated areas than on rational considerations. During the first half of this century, Virginia was the only state to adopt and use a distinctly improved process for adjusting municipal boundaries. In 1904, its legislature provided for judicial determination of annexation and consolidation proposals (the latter limited to city-town or intertown mergers). It also prescribed standards, although in the very general terms of "the necessity for and the expediency of" the proposal, to be followed by a special court of law, composed of three circuit court judges and specifically organized to consider a particular boundary adjustment proposition.[11]

The Virginia procedure of determination by an impartial body rather than by either a city or a fringe has received wide acclaim both inside and outside the state. A limited amount of criticism has developed over two specific features—the use of circuit court judges instead of persons possessing special technical competence and the review body's lack of jurisdiction over proposed incorporations. However, virtually all observers have vigorously supported the basic idea of the plan, namely, the vesting of power to decide annexation and municipal consolidation issues in an impartial body with authority to sift the evidence and approve, modify, or deny the proposals on the basis of prescribed standards and relevant facts.[12] Despite the long-time praise of the Virginia procedure,

[11] A detailed consideration of the judicial determination process in Virginia is given in Chester W. Bain, *Annexation in Virginia: The Use of the Judicial Process for Readjusting City-County Boundaries* (Charlottesville: University Press of Virginia, 1966).

[12] A factor complicating the use of the procedure in Virginia, but nonexistent in other states, is the legal detachment of cities, but not towns, from counties (city-county separation). A town may change to city status upon reaching a population of 5000; it thereby becomes politically and administratively independent of the county, except for sharing a circuit court until the city grows to 10,000 inhabitants. Territory awarded to a city by an annexation court ceases to be part of the adjoining county; in time, through a number of such actions, only a "rump" county without

it was many years before even its basic concept was transplanted to and placed in general use in any other state.

Breakthroughs in methods of dealing with urban fringe areas (and to a lesser extent, with various small municipalities that are uneconomic and functionally inept) came on two fronts around 1960: one involving restrictions on incorporation, the other review of incorporation and annexation proposals and the establishment of standards for evaluating them. These changes, constituting substantial and encouraging departures from the long-established haphazard practices, are still exceptions; up to now they have been adopted by only a small number of states.[13]

The first change relates to prohibiting the creation of additional incorporated places in the vicinity of existing municipal governments or severely curbing their establishment. Arizona, Georgia, Idaho, Nebraska, New Mexico, North Carolina, Ohio, and Wyoming all have passed state legislation of this nature, appropriately termed "anti-incorporation" laws. The acts differ in particulars, but they all contain the significant idea of creating around a municipality a buffer zone in which further incorporations cannot take place under any circumstances or only if the existing municipality consents to the proposed incorporation or refuses to annex the territory when the latter makes such a request. (Frequently the zone is larger for the more populous municipalities.)

The Arizona anti-incorporation law is typical. No territory within three miles of the boundary of a city or town of less than 5000 population or within six miles of the official limits of a more populous municipal government may incorporate as a separate municipality, unless one of two conditions develops. One, the governing body of the nearby municipal government adopts a resolution approving the proposed incorporation. Two, the municipality does not respond affirmatively to a petition for annexation from an unincorporated fringe area. Texas has adopted a similar, but stronger law which stipulates that a city may regulate the subdivision of land in the peripheral zone. This provision endows the municipality with extraterritorial power to prevent undesirable physical developments in the unincorporated area.

Several aspects of this anti-incorporation approach deserve explanation. First, its value is limited to the present and the future; none of the laws has a retroactive effect. Any municipalities already located in such a zone continue to function as separate governments unless the regular legal channels of municipal consolidation are successfully employed. These

---

the financial resources necessary to be a viable government may remain, although an annexation court may decide it is too large to be annexed. Chester W. Bain, *"A Body Incorporate:" The Evolution of City-County Separation in Virginia* (Charlottesville: University Press of Virginia, 1967), provides a careful treatment of the subject.

[13] Annexation laws continue to show great diversity. A valuable compilation is contained in National League of Cities, *Adjusting Municipal Boundaries: Law and Practice* (Washington: 1966).

laws, therefore, are preventive rather than remedial; their objective is to stop the further proliferation of municipal governments, not to reduce the existing total through consolidations. Second, only some of the anti-incorporation laws place any requirement on municipalities to annex part or all of the "frozen" unincorporated territory, and those that do require annexation only when the fringe is the initiator. At that time, the municipality must annex or allow incorporation to proceed. Third, the anti-incorporation technique so far has not generally taken hold in states having the heaviest concentrations of population in metropolitan or urban areas. Fourth and finally, the anti-incorporation plan, if supported by adequate annexation procedures, may do much in particular states to eliminate unincorporated fringe areas and their problems.[14] However, the process established by the plan favors the municipalities and therefore it does not work impartially or necessarily equitably.

Review and Standards

The second breakthrough, which is a more comprehensive and more impartial process than the anti-incorporation approach, has two basic elements: review of proposed incorporations and annexations (and in two states, proposed municipal consolidations as well) by an administrative agency or official endowed with quasi-judicial powers; and the use of standards for evaluating and making determinations about the proposal. Alaska, California, Michigan, Minnesota, Nevada, New Mexico, Washington, and Wisconsin have enacted laws of this type. This change is similar in some important respects to the Virginia practice started in 1904. Both feature a disinterested party making a determination about a boundary question in the light of specified criteria. However, while in Virginia a few members of the regular judiciary are specially convened to consider a particular matter, in the other states the review and determination are made by agencies or officials possessing quasi-judicial powers and having regular and continuing responsibilities along these lines.[15]

Although differing in certain major ways, the process of review and determination in the various states has common characteristics. A commission is the usual form of organization; it may be entirely or largely a state agency, a mixed state-local body, or a strictly local group. The review and determination procedure generally applies throughout an entire state, but it is often exercised by agencies with countywide jurisdiction. When the practice is less than statewide, it may pertain exclusively to either the most populous counties, as in Washington, or to all except the most populated one, which is the case in Nevada.

[14] The Texas law, for one, recognizes that fringes tend to re-emerge beyond municipal boundaries despite the extension of the city limits through municipal annexation. The legislation specifies that the no-incorporation zone expands outward as the city increases territorially.

[15] Ad hoc commissions also may function in New Mexico, where they have been seldom used, and in the less populous Washington counties.

Both municipal incorporations and annexations are commonly within the purview of the reviewing agency or official, although the authority is limited to annexation in Nevada and New Mexico and to incorporation in Michigan. The Alaska and Minnesota commissions also can consider municipal consolidations, the latter only in metropolitan areas. The California commissions have no jurisdiction over consolidations, but they can review the proposed formation of nonschool special districts and their territorial expansion. (In New Mexico a special commission in each county handles such district questions.) The process of review normally involves approval or disapproval of a proposal. Disapproval terminates its progress (in some instances it may be reactivated after a specified period of time), while approval is generally a screening action allowing the matter to proceed to a popular vote. In some states the commission may modify or attach conditions to a proposal before sanctioning it.

The review procedure includes standards that must be applied to each proposition before a decision is reached. These tend to be in the nature of broad guidelines permitting the commission wide discretion. For instance, the commission in Michigan must consider three sets of factors. The first consists of total population and density, land area and uses, assessed valuation, topographical features, and the past and probable future urban growth. The second relates to the need for organized community services, the present cost and adequacy of and probable future needs for public services, and the anticipated cost and benefits of the proposal. The third is concerned with the general effects of the proposed action upon the entire community and its relationship to any existing local or regional land use plans.

Review of proposed new local governments and boundary changes by a disinterested party is an important departure from the irrationality of the older practices. The use of the concept is growing, no state adopting the procedure has later relinquished it, and the overall evaluation is favorable, although in some states the authority has not been vigorously employed.[16] Moreover, the impact of review commissions may go far beyond merely a determination on an immediate question of a boundary change. In one state, for instance, their activity has prompted the establishment of city expansion zones, simplification of governmental structure in urban complexes, prevention of scattered and speculative development, cooperation among governments in working out problems, and studies of long-term governmental needs.[17] The late acceptance of the review idea in the

[16] Ronald C. Cease, A Report on State and Provincial Boundary Review Boards (Portland, Oregon: Portland Metropolitan Study Commission, 1968), pp. 32–39.

[17] California Intergovernmental Council on Urban Growth, Report on a Statewide Survey of Local Agency Formation Commissions (Sacramento: 1966), p. 7. For an analysis of conflicting viewpoints over certain features of these agencies, see John Goldbach, "Local Formation Commissions: California's Struggle over Municipal Incorporations," Public Administration Review, XXV (September, 1965), 213–220.

metropolitan age and the severe limitations usually placed on the agency —inability to initiate proposals, exclusion of municipal consolidations from its jurisdiction, and lack of authority to put its affirmative decisions into effect—may be lamented by some observers. Nevertheless, if properly implemented, the device can still be significant in view of the expected continuance of metropolitan and urban population growth.

CITY-COUNTY CONSOLIDATION

City-county consolidation, a broader one-government approach than either municipal annexation or municipal consolidation, has been a subject of discussion and debate for many years. The process usually consists of the complete or substantial merger of a county government with the principal city or all municipalities in the county. Variations of this common pattern also occur; on some occasions more than one county government is involved or school districts or other special units are included in the consolidation proposal.[18]

Despite widespread consideration, this type of governmental reorganization has seldom been put into operation. Indeed, it is functioning in only eight metropolitan areas, exclusive of a few in Virginia where special circumstances prevail.[19] Four of them—New Orleans (1813), Boston (1821), Philadelphia (1854), and New York (1898)—antedate the twentieth century, and until well into the 1950s such consolidation was generally regarded as a matter of historical record. "Often proposed, never adopted" might well have been its theme during this time. In recent years, however, the system has been installed in the Baton Rouge, Nashville, and Jacksonville areas.

[18] Distinct from, but often confused with, city-county consolidation is another process of area adjustment, city-county separation. The latter features the detachment of a municipality, sometimes after its territorial enlargement, from the remainder of the county. The separated government then performs both municipal and county functions, although not necessarily all of the latter. Adding to public confusion over the two processes is the legal identification of some separated cities, Denver and San Francisco for example, as city-counties. City-county separation is an act of withdrawal and is therefore not a metropolitan approach. Except in Virginia, where separation applies to every city, all other separations occurred many years ago: Baltimore (1851), San Francisco (1856), St. Louis (1876), and Denver (1902).

[19] One of the eight is Honolulu, which acquired its city-county consolidated status by act of the territorial legislature of Hawaii in 1907; the system was retained when statehood was gained in 1959. City-county consolidations that have been accomplished in some Virginia metropolises are excluded from the discussion here because they are the product of the unique practice in that state which removes land annexed by a city from the jurisdiction of the county. Also see footnote 24 of this chapter.

An Historical Overview

Two common threads run through the four city-county consolidations of the pre–1900 era: all were accomplished by state legislative acts, not by approval of the local voters; and all originally were not complete mergers since a remnant county government continued to operate apart from the consolidated government. The New Orleans and Boston reorganizations each involved only one county (called parish in Louisiana) and one city; the Philadelphia and New York actions, on the other hand, merged many local governments and also brought public education into the new system. The New York plan was the only one of an intercounty nature, the city's boundaries being extended to embrace four counties, one of which (New York County) was later divided into two counties. This reorganization also was unique in retaining local areas, which were designated as boroughs, and granting them several administrative functions (minor public works, for instance) and membership on the Board of Estimate, a major policy agency of the consolidated government.[20] These early city-county consolidations stand as notable governmental changes, particularly since each of the major affected cities is the hub of a highly important metropolis. The New York reorganization is especially impressive because even in 1898 the city was preeminent among American urban centers in population and financial importance.

The period from 1900 to the end of World War II was characterized by considerable interest in city-county consolidation and by its supporters' inability to secure its adoption in any metropolis in an American state. In these years of metropolitan growth, suburbanites developed stronger resistance to the absorption of their communities into a unified government. Arguments that consolidation would result in greater efficiency, economy, and equity and would establish a government capable of dealing with area-wide problems left them unpersuaded. Instead they continued to insist on local autonomy, which enabled them to control local zoning and local financial resources. Many also expressed fear that they would not have sufficient access to officials in a larger and possibly more remote government.

In this setting of substantial opposition, the advocates of city-county consolidation waged totally unsuccessful battles in many metropolises up to 1945. Besides local resistance, their efforts were also impeded by formidable legal barriers. Many states added municipal home rule provisions to their constitutions, thus prohibiting their legislative bodies from passing laws that would effect city-county consolidation. Even in states where the legislatures still had this authority, they were disinclined to use it, often because of the opposition of rural and suburban forces. Thus,

[20] New York, however, is not an example of a two-level or federal governmental system since the boroughs have no legislative powers.

the avenue used in the four consolidations completed in the nineteenth century—state legislative action—was sealed off.

To achieve consolidation, two legal hurdles had to be overcome: (1) passage of a state constitutional amendment or legislative enabling act authorizing metropolitan areas to adopt city-county consolidation, and (2) approval of the proposal by the local voters, usually by two separate majorities: the central city and the rest of the county. Most consolidation efforts in the 1900–1945 period fell before the first hurdle, as in the Birmingham, Boston, Cleveland, Kansas City (Missouri), Louisville, Milwaukee, Portland (Oregon), and Seattle areas. Only three city-county proposals reached the stage of local voter scrutiny and all were defeated: St. Louis–St. Louis County; Macon–Bibb County, Georgia; and Jacksonville–Duval County.

Success in Baton Rouge

In view of this background of unproductive efforts, city-county consolidation by Baton Rouge and East Baton Rouge Parish (County) in 1947 came as a surprise. A combination of highly favorable factors, however, greatly aided this accomplishment. First, it was easy to get constitutional amendments of strictly local application on the ballot in Louisiana unless the local legislative delegation opposed them. In this case, legislators from the Baton Rouge area had little knowledge of the import of the proposed amendment to permit a county home rule charter to be written for that area. Not realizing the effect the proposal could have on the local political organization and desiring to please the local industries which favored the amendment, they recommended its submission to the state electorate.[21]

Second, unlike the people in many other states, Louisiana voters are accustomed to repeatedly amending their state constitution. Accordingly, it was not extraordinary when the amendment was approved by a margin of almost four to one in 1946. Third, the charter board specified in the amendment was made up of representatives of a number of organizations, including the president of the state university, who could not be controlled by the local political machine. Six of the nine votes on the board were therefore consistently cast in favor of city-county consolidation and improved governmental structure and processes. Fourth, the plan of government written into the charter needed only a single parish-wide majority to be adopted. It acquired that majority in 1947 by the narrow margin of 307 votes of approximately 14,000 cast, with only about one-third of the electorate participating.

The Baton Rouge-East Baton Rouge Parish plan, which went into effect in January, 1949, involved only partial consolidation; it provided for re-

[21] Thomas H. Reed, "Progress in Metropolitan Integration," *Public Administration Review,* IX (Winter, 1949), 8.

tention of both the city and parish governments. It also continued the existence of two small municipalities, but prohibited them from further territorial expansion. A prominent innovation of the plan was the interlocking of the city and parish governments. The seven members of the city council and two other persons elected from the rural area constitute the parish council. The mayor-president, who serves as the chief administrator of both governments, presides over both councils, but has no vote, and is elected on a parish-wide basis. He appoints the finance director, personnel administrator, public works director, and purchasing agent, all of whom serve both the city and the parish. He also selects the police and fire chiefs, who function only in the city. The parish council appoints the attorney, clerk, and treasurer, who are both city and parish officials. The city and the parish share equally in the cost of operating the finance department. Thus, the two governments are integrated at many key points, although there are separate governing bodies and separate budgets and accounting for city and parish funds and a number of officials and boards continue to have independent status.

A second innovation of the Baton Rouge plan was the establishment of taxing and service zones throughout the consolidated area. The parish was divided into three types of zones or areas: urban, industrial, and rural. Under the charter, the boundaries of Baton Rouge were extended to the limits of the urban area, thus increasing the territory of the city from about six square miles to thirty square miles and its population from about 35,000 to more than 100,000. The city government provides police and fire protection, garbage and refuse collection and disposal, street lighting, traffic regulation, sewerage, and inspectional services in the urban area, which is subject to both city and parish taxes. (Uniform parish taxes are also levied in the rural zone and the two industrial zones.)

Bridges, highways, streets, sidewalks, and airports are provided on a parish-wide basis by the public works department, which serves both the city and the parish, and are financed by parish taxes. City-type services needed in the industrial areas are provided by the industries at their own expense. The rural zone cannot receive city-type services (except the services of the sheriff's department) unless special taxing districts are established there by the parish council to pay for them. Built-up, adjacent portions of the rural zone can be annexed to the urban area with the consent of a majority of the owners of the affected property and the city council. No further incorporations can take place in the parish. The idea of creating tax and service differentials on the basis of differing needs and land use development gave an important degree of flexibility to the city-county approach that had previously been lacking.

The Quickened Tempo

Interest in city-county consolidation accelerated in the 1950s and early 1960s. During this time, consolidation proposals were submitted to a local vote in numerous metropolises and were rejected (Table 24). With the exception of the St. Louis area, all such attempts were concerned with medium- and small-sized metropolises, predominantly in the South. Practically all of them required dual majorities—one in the principal city, the other in the remainder of the county. In most of them, the proposition obtained the necessary majority in the former, but failed to do so in the outlying territory. However, the plan did not acquire either majority in the Memphis and Columbus, Georgia, areas. This may indicate a growing resistance to consolidation by central cities, long the main sources of sup-

TABLE 24 Voter Defeats of City-County Consolidation Since 1950[a]

Year	Area
1950	Newport News–Warwick County–Elizabeth City County, Virginia
1953	Miami–Dade County, Florida
1958	Nashville–Davidson County, Tennessee
1959	Albuquerque–Bernalillo County, New Mexico
	Knoxville–Knox County, Tennessee
1960	Macon–Bibb County, Georgia
1961	Durham–Durham County, North Carolina
	Richmond–Henrico County, Virginia
1962	Columbus–Muscogee County, Georgia
	Memphis–Shelby County, Tennessee
	St. Louis–St. Louis County, Missouri
1964	Chattanooga–Hamilton County, Tennessee
1967	Tampa–Hillsborough County, Florida

[a] Similar proposals were defeated earlier in two of these areas: St. Louis–St. Louis County and Macon–Bibb County.

port for the idea.[22] In addition, most consolidation plans provided for the creation of taxing and service zones (usually a county-wide general services zone and an urban zone) in the consolidated city-county.

Victory in Nashville

The fifteen-year drought of city-county consolidation successes ended in 1962 in the Nashville-Davidson County area where a similar plan had been rejected by the suburban voters only four years before. The proposal, requiring dual majorities, received almost as large a proportion of

[22] Unlike a similar reorganization proposal of 1926 which required dual local approval, the St. Louis area consolidation effort of 1962 was attempted by means of a state constitutional amendment. The proposal lost by three-to-one in the state, by six-to-five in St. Louis, and by almost four-to-one in St. Louis County. The election results represent another example of opposition by a central city to the idea of complete city-county merger.

affirmative votes in the outlying areas as in the core city.[23] At the time of the consolidation, the area contained 527 square miles and approximately 415,000 inhabitants.

A prominent feature of the consolidation is the two-district (or zone) arrangement. One part is an expandable urban services district, consisting initially of only the city of Nashville. The other is a general services district covering the entire county, including the central city, in which all residents receive and pay for area-wide services. Six suburban municipalities, which in total contained only 16,000 residents at the time of the merger, remain outside the urban services district but are included in the general services district and are therefore subject to the jurisdiction of the metropolitan government for area-wide functions and controls.

Functions carried out by the metropolitan government only in the urban services district (which pays for them) include fire protection, intensified police protection, sewage disposal, water supply, and street lighting and street cleaning. Functions performed by the metropolitan government and financed on an area-wide basis, that is, in the general services district, include schools, public health, police, courts, public welfare, public housing, urban renewal, streets and roads, traffic, transit, library, refuse disposal, and electrical, building, plumbing, and housing codes. An elective metropolitan county mayor and an elected forty-one member metropolitan county council, six chosen at large (including the council's presiding officer, the vice-mayor, who appoints all council committees but votes only to break a tie) and thirty-five from single-member districts, are major organizational features. The mayor, who is full time, has considerable authority. He appoints the heads of all departments, except the assessor and two minor officials who are separately elected, and he selects, with council confirmation, the members of practically all boards, including the school board.

The Newest Adoption

The most recent city-county consolidation, that of Jacksonville and Duval County, materialized in 1967, when voters throughout the county voiced their approval by a margin of almost two-to-one. Four small municipalities totaling about 20,000 inhabitants were given the right of separate vote on the proposition by the state legislature, and all decided against being included. They now receive from the consolidated government the services formerly provided to them by the county. The new government, officially named the City of Jacksonville, has more than a half million people and a land area of 760 square miles.

---

[23] Nashville's annexation of approximately fifty square miles between the two consolidation efforts was a decisive factor in the success of the second attempt. A discussion of the various reasons for the change of attitude by many suburbanites (as well as the mayor of the central city) is contained in Chapter 14.

The consolidated area is divided into a general services district and an urban services district.[24] In the former, which contains the total territory, the new government supplies such services as airports, electricity, fire protection, health, hospitals, police protection, recreation and parks, schools, streets and highways, and welfare—all financed by area-wide funds. In the latter, which consists initially of the former city of Jacksonville, the new unit furnishes water, sewerage, street lighting and cleaning, and garbage and refuse collection, for which an additional charge is made. This district may be enlarged by action of the new government's council as the need for these peculiarly urban-type services spreads to other sections of the area.

The consolidated government is a mayor-council system characterized by a fair degree of administrative integration. The independently elected mayor, who may not serve more than two consecutive four-year terms and receives a full-time salary, appoints many of the department heads, subject to council confirmation, and selects a chief administrative officer. The council is composed of five members elected at large and fourteen chosen from single-member districts. The sheriff, tax assessor, tax collector, and supervisor of elections are separately elected, as are the members of the civil service and school boards. (Some of these officials not only retained their elective status but also gained increased powers under the consolidation. The sheriff, for instance, has become the chief law enforcement officer throughout the area.)

The Latest Consolidations: Some Observations

The three most recent city-county consolidations—Baton Rouge, Nashville, and Jacksonville—are similar in a number of ways. Each included a single county and a single city. Each occurred in the South in a growing, but still not heavily populated area that had few local governments. Each excluded small municipalities. All three have service and tax differential zones. All have an independently elected chief executive in-

[24] Most of the features of the consolidated arrangement are described in Local Government Study Commission of Duval County, *Blueprint for Improvement* (Jacksonville: 1966). Some of the proposed provisions, however, were changed by the state legislature before the official charter was submitted to the county electorate. The ninth city-county merger of metropolitan consequence (the third in eight years) took place too late for detailed analysis in this chapter. In 1969, in an action unprecedented in any state in the present century, the Indiana legislature passed a law consolidating Indianapolis and Marion County. No local popular vote was involved, and the reorganization went into full effect in 1970. Resembling in some respects the Nashville and Jacksonville models, the legislation required the unification initially of only certain city and county functions, including roads, transportation, and public works, but provided options for additional functional mergers in the future. With the exception of three small urban centers, the unified government has jurisdiction throughout the county, which has 402 square miles and almost 800,000 inhabitants. Its principal officers are a mayor and a council of twenty-nine members.

vested with considerable authority. All render a number of major services on an area-wide basis.

The Nashville and Jacksonville consolidations resemble one another in further respects, too. Each constitutes a complete merger, the full unification of city and county governments, whereas in Baton Rouge the city and parish governments remain separate legal entities although interlaced. Each was realized after an earlier rejection of the same type of reform and, at its installation, each had a population of about a half million. Each decided upon a large governing board, composed of at-large and district members, with the latter being the decided majority. Both supply many of the same functions throughout their entire areas, including education, public welfare, public health, and streets and highways, and most of the same services in their urban services districts: water supply, sewage disposal, and street lighting and cleaning.

The Baton Rouge-East Baton Rouge consolidation initially encountered considerable animosity.[25] Many people brought into the territorially enlarged city of Baton Rouge under the plan had voted against the proposal. Also, the inclusion of their property within the city removed its first $2000 of assessed valuation from exemption for purposes of municipal taxation. Compelled to pay new taxes, they generally felt that municipal services and improvements should be furnished immediately, but the increased tax revenue was based on a low rate of assessment and was insufficient for this purpose.

Almost immediately after the plan became operative in January, 1949, opposition groups unsuccessfully sought major changes in the reorganization. For four years more litigation developed over local governmental operations than had occurred previously in the entire history of the parish. The plan of reform seemed at the point of disaster in 1950 when a bond issue for public improvements was thoroughly defeated and opponents called the reorganization a hopeless instrument of government. Spurred into action, the city council levied a one percent sales tax, and within two years public services were extended to the whole urban area, a minimum capital improvement program was accomplished, and public confidence in the new governmental arrangement was restored. Since then the continued existence of the reform has never been in doubt.

Two of the most important attainments have been the adoption of comprehensive zoning and subdivision regulations throughout the parish. Building codes and a minimum housing ordinance have been adopted, along with major street, drainage, and sewerage programs. Some shortcomings, however, persist under this partial consolidation: the two law enforcement agencies have overlapping jurisdictions, separate civil ser-

[25] E. Gordon Kean, Jr., "East Baton Rouge Parish," in National Association of Counties, *Guide to County Organization and Management* (Washington: 1968), pp. 31–35.

vice systems operate for the fire and police departments, and certain offices, which remain independent under the state constitution, cannot be effectively controlled by local government in the parish.

An official study committee has been organized every four years since the reform in the Baton Rouge area went into effect. Changes, most of them minor in nature, have been recommended and generally accepted either by the voters as charter amendments or by council or administrative action. The first review group, a particularly prestigious body, held extensive public hearings and discussions and greatly increased citizen understanding of the reorganization.[26] Each study committee has lauded the consolidation, speaking of the charter under which the government operates as well-suited to the area and as a flexible framework capable of meeting future needs.

In the Nashville-Davidson County area, some impressive results are evident. The accomplishments ranked most important by many people are the upgrading and racial integration of the public schools and the removal of many inequities which existed in the former two-system arrangement, including general financial support, teachers' salaries, and educational programs. Open space for future park needs has been purchased in the county's outer portions, thereby stopping the long-established practice of losing suitable sites to residential development. Park, school, and road personnel have worked together effectively to acquire land for coordinated development in support of all three purposes. A massive sewer construction program has moved forward ahead of schedule, and branch libraries are serving the areas outside the old city of Nashville (the urban services district) for the first time.

General changes are also apparent, according to Daniel R. Grant, an experienced observer and participant in metropolitan affairs.[27] The fixing of responsibility for local public performance has been greatly simplified by doing away with the bickering and the absence of clearly-defined accountability of the previously separate city and county governments. Much duplication of activities has been erased and some economies in operations realized. Specialization and professionalization of public employees have been developed. Various city-county inequities, in addition to those in schools, have been removed by shifting a number of services to a countywide tax base. Also, in Professor Grant's judgment, accessibility of government to the people has not decreased under the consolidated system.

26 William C. Havard, Jr., and Floyd L. Corty, Rural-Urban Consolidation: The Merger of Governments in the Baton Rouge Area (Baton Rouge: Louisiana State University Press, 1964), p. 42.

27 Daniel R. Grant, "A Comparison of Predictions and Experience with Nashville 'Metro'," Urban Affairs Quarterly, 1 (September, 1965), 38–42, 47–48. Also useful is C. Beverly Briley, "Nashville-Davidson County," in National Association of Counties, Guide to County Organization and Management, pp. 22–28.

City-county consolidation has obviously not worked a miracle in Nashville and Davidson County. Some overly exuberant supporters of the reform sold it as all things to all people, thus laying the basis for disappointment by some individuals and groups. It has not been possible to wipe out in quick order a heavy longtime backlog of unsatisfactorily met needs, although, as has been indicated, progress has been made along a number of lines. Available financial resources, regardless of the form of governmental organization, simply make the early attainment of such a goal infeasible. As service additions and expansions have been made, in part because the consolidation has stimulated rising public expectations, taxes have gone up. The metropolitan police department, which has freed itself of the old city department's reputation for graft and corruption, continues to face charges of brutality and insensitivity in race relations. Acrimonious racial controversies have developed over the building of an urban renewal project, the construction of an interstate highway through a Negro section, and the employment of the National Guard to control racial disturbances. Such actions have subjected the metropolitan mayor to criticism by some Negro leaders as being too negative to the interests and aspirations of the nonwhites. The charge has also been made that the consolidated government has diluted Negro political power. At the same time, other people have expressed optimism about race relations, noting in particular that the selection of Nashville under the Model Cities program—due partly to the area's unique governmental system and its mayor's national prominence—may make it possible to improve such relations. A key question is whether the black and white communities have become so polarized by controversies as to negate the possible catalyst role of this new program in mobilizing community resources to produce vast improvements in depressed areas.[28]

The Jacksonville consolidation, the newest of the three mergers, has experienced difficulties, despite the provision in the charter for a seven-month period of orderly transition from the old system to the new. A number of the outgoing officials put various obstacles in the path of the new government. For example, the old county commission voted to turn over the regulation of many small franchised water companies located outside the former city of Jacksonville to the state utilities commission, thereby subjecting the users to much higher rates under the latter's automatic formulas. This compelled the consolidated government to request the area's state legislative delegation to introduce a special act to undo this action and thus return regulation to local control, pending deter-

[28] Daniel R. Grant, "Governing the Metropolis," *County Reorganization Advisory Service of the National Association of Counties,* no. 7 (October, 1968), pp. 3–4. Recent but not yet published research by Professor Grant has involved interviews with panels of "most knowledgeable" observers in three reorganized areas—Nashville, Miami, and Toronto—to determine their perceptions of the political and administrative effects of these reforms.

mination of how the new government can supply water and sewerage services in the affected sections. Similarly, the old city council voted large salary increases to the firemen to take effect immediately before the consolidated unit went into operation, an action financially embarrassing to the new government. Opponents also filed a law suit challenging the constitutionality of the merger in an attempt to nullify the entire reorganization. However, a ruling by a circuit court that upheld the legality of the consolidation was sustained unanimously by the state supreme court.

The first mayor of the merged city-county, who was unopposed for the position, had an impeccable record as a judge and is widely respected. He appointed highly qualified administrators and has worked diligently with the budget director on developing a rational financial plan. A recreational program has been advanced, a minimum housing code adopted and strictly enforced, and a study begun on extending water and sewer services beyond the old city limits. In addition, since the consolidation, the area has gained its first large industry in many years.[29]

SCHOOL DISTRICT CONSOLIDATION

The substantial amount of school district consolidation (or reorganization or redistricting, as many professional educators prefer to call it) in the last several decades stands in marked contrast to the handful of city-county and municipal consolidations realized during the same period. School districts continued their longtime trend of rapid proliferation until the early 1930s; by 1932, they had reached the staggering total of approximately 127,000, constituting almost three-fourths of all governmental units. Since then, a steady decrease has taken place, with the rate of consolidation accelerating considerably since the end of World War II. By 1967, the number had dropped to 21,782, which is less than one-fifth of the total of thirty-five years before; such units now make up only about one-fourth of all governments.

School district consolidations have been common in many metropolises, but they have been occurring there at a slower pace than in nonmetropolitan sections and have involved suburban schools almost exclusively.[30] Granting the existence of a superabundance of school districts when the

[29] Based largely on information provided by Dr. Gladys M. Kammerer, Director, Public Administration Clearing Service and Professor of Political Science, University of Florida. Dr. Kammerer and her associates are studying the consolidation efforts in the Jacksonville and Tampa areas.

[30] For differing attitudes of central city and suburban residents and officials toward a single metropolitan school district, see Basil G. Zimmer and Amos H. Hawley, *Resistance to Reorganization of School Districts and Government in Metropolitan Areas* (Providence: Brown University, 1966), pp. 293–316.

movement got under way, this development represents the first large-scale use of consolidation in the nation's history. And it has been occurring at a time when municipalities and nonschool special districts are continuing to grow in number.

Two factors stand out as contributing most to the success of the school district consolidation movement. One has been acknowledgement by many state legislatures of the need to foster such reorganization, a recognition prompted by the spiraling proportion of school support obtained from the states since the 1930s. The other has been the increased advocacy of the device by many professional educators and lay leaders who are convinced of the relationship between this kind of reform and higher quality education.

State legislatures have used two means to prompt school district consolidations. They have made major changes in the school reorganization laws, which had required local initiation of a proposal and usually majority consent of the voters in each affected district. They also have made financial grants available to districts that merge, thus supplying an adequate incentive, an enticing carrot on the end of a stick.

The consolidation legislation has taken various forms, some quite drastic. In a number of instances, existing county boards of education or specially constituted county school reorganization committees have been empowered to order a merger without a local popular vote. In others the law has specified that on a certain date all school districts (or all of a specific kind) would be combined into one district. In still other states, the legislation has called for study and recommendations in each county by the county board of education or a special countywide committee, approval or disapproval of the plans by the state board of education, the state school superintendent, or a special state commission, and submission of the proposals to the voters in the affected districts. Many laws of this type, called the comprehensive-planned-permissive approach, do not require majority consent of the voters of each affected district for the proposal to pass. For example, a number of them simply require a single, overall majority in the area of the proposed district, a far easier requirement to meet. (Many consolidations, it should be pointed out, have involved the simultaneous merger of more than two school districts.)[31]

Professional and lay leadership in school district reorganization has been exhibited in several ways. Strong support has been given to the passage of new state consolidation laws, often including the providing of

[31] A more detailed analysis of the techniques of school district consolidation will be found in John C. Bollens, *Special District Governments in the United States* (Berkeley and Los Angeles: University of California Press, 1957), pp. 197–227. The factors working to the advantage of school district reorganization as opposed to consolidation of general governments are discussed in National Commission on Urban Problems, *Final Report*, Part IV, pp. 1–36 to 1–39.

financial incentives. Professional educators, working through their state associations, have been particularly effective in this regard. Both the professionals and private leaders have taken on major roles in implementing the legislation through activities in regular and special state and county education agencies. In brief, the certainty of public officials (state legislators and educators in this case), of private leaders, and of seemingly a fairly large segment of the general public that school district consolidations produce better service and more economic use of public funds largely accounts for the widespread acceptance of this type of merger. The lack of a comparable conviction by similar elements, on the other hand, helps to explain the slow rate of municipal and city-county consolidations.

NEIGHBORHOOD DECENTRALIZATION: COUNTERPOISE TO BIGNESS

The idea of using neighborhoods as centers for public services, citizen-government communication, and public decision-making has gained considerable prominence in recent years. Such a concept, which is concerned with decentralizing activities and power in big cities through structural arrangements, is a counterbalance to that of metropolitan government. Interestingly, some of the leading exponents of area-wide government for the metropolis are also advocates of the regeneration of neighborhoods as governmental areas in large municipalities. The Committee for Economic Development and the National Commission on Urban Problems, mentioned earlier in this chapter, are illustrations. The CED has suggested the possibility of forming neighborhood districts in big cities for the purposes of clarifying neighborhood needs and proposing solutions to them. The national commission similarly has noted that such cities should have manageable decentralized areas since "the psychological distance from the neighborhood to City Hall has grown from blocks, to miles, to light-years. With decreasing communication and sense of identification by the low-income resident with his government have come first apathy, then disaffection, and now—insurrection."[32]

The suggestions for decentralization differ greatly and are often presented in very generalized terms. One is to establish little city halls or neighborhood centers from which certain services would be supplied and more direct means of communication between government and neighborhood residents made available. A second is to place a trained individual

[32] Committee for Economic Development, *Modernizing Local Government*, p. 47; National Commission on Urban Problems, *Final Report*, Part IV, p. 2–1. It should be pointed out that declining communication and identification in large urban centers are not confined to low-income people.

in the neighborhood, employed by the city government but preferably indigenous to the area, to serve as a communication link between the locality and the city and other governments and to take care of citizen complaints and requests. A variation of this suggestion is to have neighborhood action task forces, consisting of officials and local leaders and community representatives, organized for largely the same purposes. Another approach concerns decision-making. In its milder form, it involves the creation of neighborhood advisory councils that would send their conclusions about local issues and goals to the central authorities. In its stronger form, which is based on the aim of local community control, neighborhood boards would have final decision-making authority over particular activities. Such an arrangement, often referred to as "participatory democracy," is being most widely sought in public education, where efforts and actions are under way (beginning with the McGeorge Bundy report for New York City) to delegate decisions on such matters as budgets, curriculum, personnel, and pupil assignment to neighborhood school administrators or to newly established community school boards.[33]

Without doubt, many big city governments (and big school and other local governments as well) need to be made more sensitive and humanized in the face of large-scale and growing bureaucratization. It is hoped that the techniques of decentralization will produce improvements in this direction. However, a basic question concerning local community control is how extensive it may be without unduly jeopardizing the ability of the city government to achieve the goals and well-being of the larger community.

THE ONE-GOVERNMENT APPROACH:
THE FUTURE

The expected continuance of urban and metropolitan growth seemingly assures the continued annexation of unincorporated land by many municipalities. In general, the device will be employed in metropolitan areas, particularly to eliminate urban fringe problems, but it will not be used as a means of creating a metropolitan government. The prevalence of in-

[33] Various decentralization suggestions are contained in Advisory Commission on Intergovernmental Relations, *ACIR State Legislative Program: New Proposals for 1969* (Washington: 1968), p. 803–1; *Report of the National Advisory Commission on Civil Disorders* (New York: Bantam Books, 1968), p. 297; Milton Kotler, "Two Essays on the Neighborhood Corporation," in U.S. Congress, Joint Economic Committee, Subcommittee on Urban Affairs, *Urban America: Goals and Problems* (Washington: 1967), pp. 170–191; Milton Kotler, *Neighborhood Government: The Local Foundations of Political Life* (Indianapolis: Bobbs-Merrill, 1969); and Mayor's Advisory Panel on Decentralization of the New York City Schools, *Reconnection for Learning: A Community School System for New York City* (New York: 1967), Parts II-IV. Also see the symposium on alienation, decentralization, and participation in *Public Administration Review*, XXIX (January-February, 1969), 3–63, particularly the introductory article by Herbert Kaufman.

corporated places in most metropolises precludes annexation on a scale that would be necessary to produce such a government. The recent establishment in a few states of annexation-incorporation review commissions furnishes hope that these boundary questions will be decided more rationally than in the past and with proper attention to their probable effects on the entire metropolis. If these commissions carry out their responsibilities impartially, their powers will probably be increased to include the authority at least to initiate proposals and conceivably to effectuate annexations and incorporations without a local popular vote. In time some commissions may be granted the power to order the consolidation of very small, financially poor municipalities.

In the immediate decades ahead, it is very unlikely that local boundary commissions will be permitted to order city-county consolidations, although some school reorganization agencies have such power. There is a growing feeling that a number of functions in the metropolis are of an area-wide nature (and therefore in some instances should be handled by an area-wide government), but there is also a strong belief, often valid, that various functions are not of this nature and therefore can best be performed by local governments smaller in territory than the total metropolitan area. There may be too many local governments in the metropolis, but this does not necessarily mean they should all be replaced by a single government performing both metropolitan and local services. As a consequence, city-county consolidations almost certainly will continue to be confined chiefly to small and medium-sized metropolises that are not governmentally complex. Most, if not all, of those that materialize will encompass both urban and rural land and will feature tax and service zones. Furthermore, city-county consolidation is almost always a one-county concept, both in legal authorizations and proposals, but more and more SMSAs are becoming intercounty, even interstate.

Conversely, school district consolidation will persist. Public officials and private leaders are caught in the swirl of growing school enrollments and costs and of dealing with a government performing a single but crucial function, thus excluding the possibility, as in the case of municipalities, of establishing an area-wide government to assume some but not all of their activities. They therefore will probably move ahead with the merger of more school districts. Support is increasing in various states, however, for area-wide financial equalization as an alternative to school district merger.

In general, the one-government approach to area-wide problems has passed its heyday, although it will retain its vigor in many situations concerning only part of the metropolis; the latter is apparent in both municipal annexation and school district consolidation. But in terms of the entire metropolitan area, the one-government approach is almost certain to be bypassed usually in favor of other techniques.

12 / THE TWO-LEVEL APPROACH

THE SERIOUSNESS OF AREA-WIDE PROBLEMS HAS GENERATED MANY PROPOSALS for the governmental restructuring of the metropolis. One approach, as we have seen, involves political unification, through either consolidation or annexation. But many who believe reorganization is necessary are convinced, for various reasons, that the one-government remedy is too drastic a response to the need. The solution which some of them offer is based on the concept of local federalism, an approach that has received increased advocacy and use. Under this plan, area-wide functions—one or many—are allotted to area-wide governments while local functions remain with local units, thus creating a metropolitan-local, two-tier system.

The two-level arrangement takes various forms. The first is the metropolitan district, a governmental unit usually encompassing a substantial part or all of the metropolis but generally authorized to perform only one function or a few closely related activities of a metropolitan nature. The second is the comprehensive urban county plan, which calls for the simultaneous transfer of selected functions from municipalities (and at times from other local units) to the county government. The third is federation, which features the establishment of a new area-wide government (customarily replacing the existing county government if the metropolis covers only one county) that is assigned numerous responsibilities. In brief, the two-level arrangement in its varied forms represents a halfway house between the extremes of very drastic and very moderate techniques of attacking metropolitan problems. It seeks to preserve much of the existing governmental system of the metropolis while making only those modifications deemed necessary to combat serious area-wide difficulties.

METROPOLITAN DISTRICTS

Metropolitan district governments represent the mildest version of the two-level approach if considered in terms of their functional nature. However, in respect to their territorial scope, they generally include the entire metropolis or a major part of it, such as the central city and the heavily populated suburbs.[1] Some even extend far beyond the confines of the SMSA and are in fact regional governments. Yet even when this is the case, such districts are usually limited to a single service or a very small number of activities. Thus, although their jurisdiction is area-wide and they are often the only metropolitan units in existence in many localities, district governments are essentially governments of strictly limited purpose.

Metropolitan districts are now common in urban areas. Although a few were established before the present century (one in the Philadelphia area as early as 1790), they are chiefly a post-World War I development that has accelerated in the years since 1945. Approximately 100 districts of this type are now in operation. They are active in about one-fourth of the SMSAs and are particularly prevalent in the larger metropolises of at least 500,000 population, many of which have more than one such

[1] A few metropolitan districts (some building and operating bridges, for instance) do not have defined areas or they have within their official boundaries only the small amount of land on which their facilities have been constructed. Comprehensive analyses of metropolitan districts will be found in John C. Bollens, *Special District Governments in the United States* (Berkeley and Los Angeles: University of California Press, 1957) and Max A. Pock, *Independent Special Districts: A Solution to the Metropolitan Area Problem* (Ann Arbor: University of Michigan Law School Legislative Research Center, 1962). For observations about such governments in five eastern states, see Robert G. Smith, *Public Authorities, Special Districts and Local Government* (Washington: National Association of Counties Research Foundation, 1964).

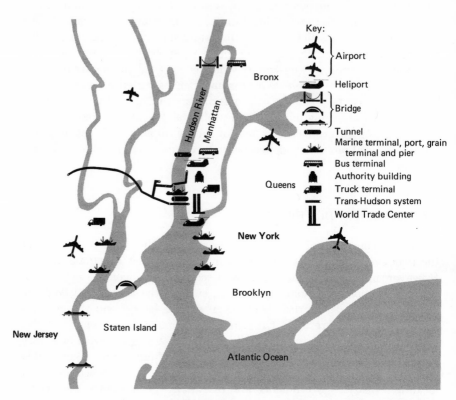

FIGURE 41   **Facilities of the Port of New York Authority. From** Port of New York
Authority 1967 Annual Report.

government. Found in all sections of the nation, they are most numerous
in California, Ohio, and Texas.[2]

Many Functions and Accomplishments

Taken altogether, metropolitan districts perform a wide range of service
activities. Providing port facilities and sewage disposal are easily the most
frequent functions, followed by airports, mass transit, parks, public housing, and water supply. Others less common are air and water pollution
control, bridge construction and maintenance, electricity, flood control,
hospital facilities and care, and libraries. Still others include insect pest
control, public health, transport terminal facilities, and tunnel construction and maintenance. Strangely enough, however, certain functions con-

[2] Many district governments other than those of metropolitan character exist in
SMSAs, mainly school and urban fringe units. Also, metropolitan districts are governments and should not be confused with state and municipal authorities and
dependent districts that are adjuncts of state and local governments.

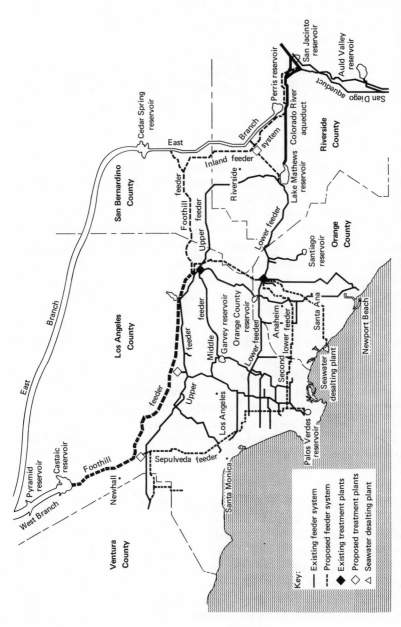

FIGURE 42   **Existing and Proposed Distribution System of the Metropolitan Water District of Southern California.
From** Metropolitan Water District of Southern California, Twenty–Ninth Annual Report, **1967, p. 98.**

sidered by some people to be definitely area-wide in character—law enforcement in particular—are not provided by any metropolitan districts.

The record of accomplishment of metropolitan district governments
is impressive, despite their functional restrictiveness. In total, they have
done much to satisfy or alleviate some of the most pressing area-wide
needs of the SMSAs they serve. A sampling of their significant activities,
often unrecognized as district operations by most of the citizenry where
they function, is illuminating. The Port of New York Authority runs airports, port facilities, bridges, tunnels, and bus, motor truck, and railroad
freight terminals, and other facilities (Figure 41). The Chicago Transit
Authority and the Bi-State Development Agency (St. Louis area) operate
mass transit systems and the latter also owns port facilities; the Cleveland
Metropolitan Park District, the Huron-Clinton Metropolitan Authority
(Detroit area) and the East Bay Regional Park District (San Francisco
Bay area) provide regional parks; and the Metropolitan Sanitary District
of Greater Chicago, the Metropolitan St. Louis Sewer District, and the
Municipality of Metropolitan Seattle (a district government) handle sewage disposal. The Metropolitan Water District of Southern California is
the wholesale supplier of water (after transporting it hundreds of miles
from the Colorado River) to a large number of cities and other water
agencies in six southern California counties (Figure 42). And the Bay
Area Rapid Transit District (San Francisco Bay area) is constructing
an extensive rapid transit system, the first completely new dual-rail
facility established in the nation in about fifty years.

The magnitude of their finances and personnel gives even greater significance to metropolitan districts and offers a strong reason why these
big governments should receive close and continuing public attention. The
Port of New York Authority, for instance, has more long-term outstanding
debt than each of eighteen state governments, and the Chicago Transit
Authority surpasses seventeen states in number of employees.

Facilitating Factors

The widespread use of the metropolitan district device as a reform
mechanism has been facilitated by several factors. One is its moderate
character as exemplified by the usual single-function restriction. Another
is that most such districts are not given the power to tax or are severely
limited as to the amount of tax they can levy. A large number must rely
wholly or mainly on service charges, tolls, and rents and on revenue
bonds whose principal and interest must be paid from operating funds.
Although such limited financial authority makes these districts more
palatable to taxpayers, it restricts the kinds of activities in which they
can successfully engage. Certain area-wide problems such as air pollution
control cannot be handled on a profit-making basis; consequently, such

difficulties will remain outside the orbit of metropolitan agencies that lack the taxing power or have only minor access to it.

Another factor promoting the spread of metropolitan districts is the liberal nature of most legal provisions authorizing their formation. Many of these units have been established under state laws requiring only a single area-wide popular majority, a process uncommon to most other reorganization methods. Many others have been created without any popular vote at all, a procedure used only once in the current century in connection with federation, comprehensive urban county, and city-county consolidation proposals. Districts in this latter group have been formed by special acts of state legislatures (the air pollution control and rapid transit districts in the San Francisco Bay area are examples), state legislation providing a nonvoter means of activation (the metropolitan park district in the Cleveland area), and interstate compacts (the Port of New York Authority and the Delaware River Basin Commission).

Frequent Remoteness from Public

Metropolitan districts have registered important attainments, but they have also drawn much condemnation. One of the strongest criticisms is the remoteness of many of them from the influence and control of the residents of the areas they serve. This remoteness takes various forms: the authority of the directors to issue bonds on their own judgment without submitting the proposals to voter approval; annexations of territory through state legislative action, thus bypassing the consent of residents within either the existing district or the area to be attached; and the indirect method of selecting the governing boards. All three elements are present in a number of metropolitan districts established under interstate compacts. The governing body can float bonds after its own unilateral decision. The district boundaries can be enlarged by amending the interstate compact. The governing body consists of appointed or ex officio members.

The composition of many district governing bodies also makes adequate accountability to their constituencies extremely difficult, if not impossible. Two illustrations will point up the difficulty. The governor appoints three of the seven members of the Chicago Transit Authority with the consent of the state senate and the mayor of Chicago; one of these three must reside outside Chicago. The mayor appoints the other four members with the approval of the city council and the governor. In the St. Louis area, the central city mayor with the sanction of the judges of the circuit court in the city appoints three members of the governing body of the Metropolitan St. Louis Sewer District and the county supervisor, the elected executive of St. Louis County, selects the other three members with the approval of the local district judges. In both of these cases, the district

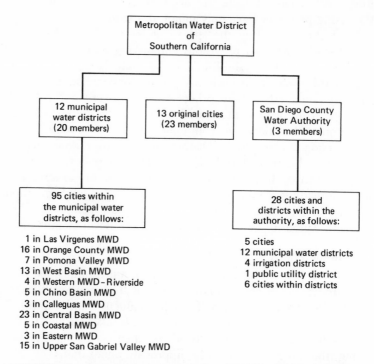

FIGURE 43   **Organization and Board of Directors of the Metro-politan Water District of Southern California. The governing board of the Metropolitan Water District consists of forty-six members distributed among the municipal water districts, the cities, and the San Diego Water Authority as shown. From** Twenty–Ninth Annual Report, **1967, pp. xvi–xvii, xxxiii.**

board is at least one step removed from the public and the divided method of appointment leaves the members without direct responsibility to any one public official or elected body. (Figure 43 presents another example.)

Constituent-Unit Principle of Representation

The constituent-unit principle of representation for metropolitan districts—meaning that members of the governing body are appointed by, and often from, the governing boards of the cities and counties located within the district—has received growing support and use in recent years.[3] There are three major reasons why interest in this method has

[3] For further discussion of the constituent-unit idea, see Arthur W. Bromage, *Political Representation in Metropolitan Agencies* (Ann Arbor: University of Michigan Institute of Public Administration, 1962).

been expanding. One is the irrationality of the system of board representation used in many instances and the desire to avoid a similar practice as additional districts are established. (The constituent-unit principle has been confined to new district legislation; it has not been used to change the method of composition of any existing agencies.) Another is the opposition to making the governing bodies of new units of this type popularly elected, thereby adding to the load of an already overburdened electorate. And the third is the desire to link metropolitan districts more closely to the cities and counties they overlie. Such interlocking assures greater intergovernmental cooperation and coordinated planning, and places the cities and counties in a position to control these agencies.

This factor of control has been very influential in fostering acceptance of the constituent-unit idea. Cities and counties, realizing the probability of new metropolitan districts being created, have often made effective use of the old political maxim, "If you can't beat them, join them." By successfully advocating the installation of the constituent-unit system of representation, they not only assure themselves of a direct association with these governments but also acquire means of controlling them.

The constituent-unit principle has taken various forms. In the Municipality of Metropolitan Seattle, extensive use is made of local and county officials with the amount of representation divided about equally between the central city and the rest of the county. The twenty-member governing body is composed of the mayor and the nine councilmen of Seattle, two county commissioners, the mayors or councilmen of the five largest municipalities other than the central city, a mayor or a councilman from one of the remaining nine municipalities (selected by ballot by their mayors), a representative of the unincorporated areas appointed by the county commissioners, and a chairman, who is a private citizen, chosen by the other members.

The Bay Area Air Pollution Control District (Metropolitan San Francisco), which currently is active in six counties, has a governing body of twelve members, two from each county, all public officials. One member of each pair is a county supervisor, chosen by the county board of supervisors. The other is a mayor or a councilman of a city chosen by a selection committee, composed of the mayors of all the cities within the county. The San Francisco Bay Area Rapid Transit District, which also employs the constituent-unit principle, follows a similar formula except that the more populous county areas are entitled to a larger number of representatives.

Although the constituent-unit principle represents a more logical system of selecting district governing boards than do other methods of appointment, it is doubtful that it affords sufficient accountability to the metropolitan electorate. At most, it offers indirect, remote, and cumbersome public control. It is particularly indirect when private citizens, instead of public officials, are chosen as board members. Moreover, when local officials constitute such boards the process of public control is subject to inconsistencies. These members are elected to city or county offices in campaigns that rarely if ever are concerned with the affairs of the district. Nevertheless, if the voters become dissatisfied with the performance of these officials as district board members, they can recall them from the city and county offices (in those states where recall is permitted) or they can defeat them if they make bids for re-election. Doing so, however, means disregarding or playing down the records of these officials in the positions to which they were elected—records that may be satisfactory or superior—and focusing on their subsequently obtained, tangential responsibilities relating to the district. Another peculiarity of concurrent office holding is that some officials spend less time on the activities of the positions to which they have been elected than on those of the district governing boards to which they have been appointed.[4]

So long as each metropolitan district performs only a single function or at most a few (and those recently created continue to fall within this general pattern), the element of representation will be beyond rational solution. Election of district governing board members furnishes a direct means of popular control, but as these agencies proliferate in number such control becomes increasingly ineffective. Conversely, the constituent-unit method of representation avoids increasing the number of elected officials but provides circuitous channels of accountability.

Some supporters of the constituent-unit system recognize the problem of public accountability inherent in this method. They admit that, as a district becomes multipurpose in the functions it performs, direct election of some or all members of the governing body may be preferable. Racial and ethnic minorities have expressed concern about the constituent-unit system in terms of both adequate public control and sufficient representation of the cross section of groups in the metropolis. Another factor has also entered the picture in this regard. Although recent judicial application of the principle of equal representation to the apportionment of local governing bodies does not yet extend to metropolitan districts employing the constituent-unit concept, it may in the future. At present the court rule applies only to units with general governmental powers, which elect their representatives from single-member areas. However, the United States Supreme Court has strongly suggested that representational schemes which are permitted to deviate from the one-man, one-vote principle should not be allowed to minimize or cancel out the voting strength of particular racial or political elements of the voting population.

[4] Stanley Scott and Willis Culver, *Metropolitan Agencies and Concurrent Office-Holding: A Survey of Selected Districts and Authorities* (Berkeley: University of California Bureau of Public Administration, April, 1961), Legislative Problems no. 7, pp. 12–13.

Advocacy of Multipurpose Districts

In addition to criticism of their frequent remoteness from public control, metropolitan districts have been widely condemned because of their generally restricted functional nature. This limited-purpose approach has resulted in a fragmentary and usually uncoordinated attack on area-wide problems. It has also produced an even more complicated and confusing pattern of government, and by dealing with a few acute problems, it has on occasion lulled metropolitan residents into the false belief that no major area-wide service difficulties exist. As a consequence of their functional restrictiveness, interest and efforts to make these agencies multipurpose governments—authorized to undertake a considerable range of different types of area-wide functions—have been growing in recent years.

Scattered advocacy of the metropolitan multipurpose district idea, and even isolated adoptions of legal provisions permitting its implementation, are not recent developments. The California legislature passed the Municipal Utility District Act in 1921, providing that any district organized under the legislation could furnish light, water, power, heat, transportation, telephone service, sewerage, and refuse and garbage disposal; and an investigator of district governments urged nationwide utilization of the multipurpose district idea as long ago as 1936.[5] Major support for the concept, however, has come in the last fifteen years, particularly through the circulation of draft bills by the national Advisory Commission on Intergovernmental Relations and the Council of State Governments to state legislators and other major public officials.

Implementing the Multipurpose District Idea

The metropolitan multipurpose district idea can materialize in three ways: through endowing existing metropolitan special districts with more functions, through consolidating those in existence, and through enacting new legal provisions of broad functional scope to be used by districts formed in the future. There is no substantial evidence that the first is likely to take place in the years immediately ahead. Districts of limited purpose have shown little or no desire to take on additional functions. The vast majority have been content to perform their one service or few closely related activities. When local residents have urged them to seek a broader functional authorization, they customarily have turned aside the request by suggesting that another district be set up. The interested persons, wanting a service and not feeling strongly about which particular agency provides it, organize still another special district, even though it might seem logical to them that the activity be assigned to an already

---

[5] California Statutes, 1925, p. 245 ff.; Ralph F. Fuchs, "Regional Agencies for Metropolitan Areas," *Washington University Law Quarterly*, 22 (December, 1936), 64–78.

existing unit. This is accomplished under an available statute or under a new bill submitted by a state legislator on their behalf. State legislatures are usually very willing to accommodate requests for new laws of this type. By complying with such proposals, they please individuals and groups wanting a specific service and at the same time escape making enemies of those who are opposed to any significant enlargement of the powers of existing metropolitan districts.

The built-in positions of influence of persons in control of existing special districts makes merger of these agencies into multipurpose governments unlikely.[6] Advocates of the constituent-unit system of representation are hopeful that in time the interlocking type of governing board membership will promote the consolidation of such bodies. They cannot point to any evidence of such a trend, however. For example, in the San Francisco Bay area, where the constituent-unit principle is used most extensively, metropolitan special districts have shown no serious inclination toward consolidation. A recent study of that region, however, suggests that considerable integration of certain metropolitan functions might be attained short of merging various districts. One way of doing this would be to establish a metropolitan coordinating or umbrella agency (district) to determine overall area-wide goals, review proposed projects of other units having intercommunity effects, and stop those in conflict with the agreed-upon regional objectives.[7]

Slow Progress

The most current interest in implementing the multipurpose idea centers on the passage and the effective use of state laws, state constitutional provisions, and interstate compacts authorizing new districts to perform numerous diversified functions. Although this method of gaining implementation of the idea strikes many people as untidy, if not unsound, since it does not build on and seek to improve existing metropolitan districts, it has become the most discussed approach. Supporters point out that if this method receives thorough use, its potential is great in many SMSAs that still have few, if any, metropolitan special districts. But so far effective use has not been made of the new legal provisions of this type that have been enacted nor has widespread acceptance by state

[6] Other ways exist to reduce the number of metropolitan special districts, such as converting them into dependent entities of the state and county governments. Numerous metropolitan districts are not independent governments but adjuncts of counties; however, they have been dependent agencies since their inauguration. Strong resistance, based on the desire for area-wide operations to be controlled by the metropolitan public, exists to transforming independent metropolitan districts into agencies dependent on the state government.

[7] Stanley Scott and John C. Bollens, *Governing a Metropolitan Region: The San Francisco Bay Area* (Berkeley: University of California Institute of Governmental Studies, 1968), pp. 36–37, 76–79. The umbrella concept was made operative in the Minneapolis-St. Paul area recently.

legislatures and metropolitan voters of such proposals been realized. Regarding the former, no area-wide district operating under a broad multipurpose grant has fully utilized its powers. For example, the East Bay Municipal Utility District (in the San Francisco Bay area), which was organized in 1923, performed only the function of water supply until the late 1940s when it added sewage disposal. Interest by its governing body in undertaking any of the numerous other functions included in its broad grant of powers has never developed, despite periodic public advocacy. This agency's record is typical of the relatively few metropolitan districts that are legally permitted to undertake a broad, diversified series of activities; potentially multipurpose, they continue in practice to provide simply one function or very few.[8]

State legislatures have generally been reluctant to enact metropolitan multipurpose district laws; and when passed the statutes have usually been substantially circumscribed. A few years ago, for instance, both an interim committee of the California legislature and a commission appointed by the governor of that state recommended the passage of new multipurpose district laws that differed in functional powers and governing board composition from the much earlier and narrowly used municipal utility district act. In neither case did positive legislative action follow. Also the much publicized Metropolitan Municipal Corporations bill enacted by the Washington state legislature in 1957 (permitting the creation of multipurpose districts to handle a maximum of six area-wide functions: sewage disposal, water supply, public transportation, garbage disposal, parks and parkways, and comprehensive planning) was restricted in two important particulars. First, the functions to be undertaken by the district were required to be named in the ballot proposal (instead of allowing such decisions to rest with the agency's governing board) and the proposal had to receive dual majorities in the central city and in the rest of the metropolitan area. Second, any functions not specified in the initial proposal could be carried out by the district only by gaining the consent of the voters, in this instance on a single overall majority basis.

The experience of Metropolitan Seattle with this multipurpose law is revealing. In March, 1958, a proposal to create a district to perform three of the six functions—sewage disposal, public transportation, and comprehensive planning—received an overwhelming overall majority vote but failed to obtain the required majority outside Seattle. In September of the same year, a proposition to establish a district limited to sewage disposal was approved, receiving the more decisive majority outside Seattle where the sewage problem was worse. In 1962 and again six years later, the district, legally named the Municipality of Metropolitan Seattle (nomenclature that surely will not aid the public to distinguish different

[8] The Port of New York Authority carries on many activities, but they are all within the single functional field of transportation.

types of governmental units), tried to add public transportation as its second function; but the proposal failed to acquire the necessary popular majority. Thus, the widely heralded Seattle district remains as most such agencies: multipurpose in potential but single-purpose in operation.

Another method of implementing the multipurpose district idea—placing the authorization in the state constitution and permitting a locally-appointed charter commission to determine what functions should be assigned to such an agency—has also proved ineffective. Such a procedure, applicable to St. Louis and St. Louis County, was written into the new Missouri constitution of 1945. The first use of the constitutional section in 1954 resulted in the acceptance by dual majorities of a single-purpose district for sewage disposal. Although the district charter provided for assumption of other functions with the consent of the voters, no effort has ever been made to broaden the agency's activities. The following year, a second use of the constitutional authorization produced a proposal to organize another single-purpose district, to operate a transit system, but the measure was soundly defeated in both the city and the county. Four years later, a third utilization of the authorization resulted in a proposed multipurpose district to handle such area-wide functions as the metropolitan road system, master development planning, sewage disposal (by absorbing the previously established metropolitan sewer district), and civil defense. The plan was resoundingly defeated by a two-to-one count in the city and a three-to-one margin in the county. As in the case of Metropolitan Seattle, the St. Louis area continues to employ multipurpose enabling provisions in a single-purpose manner.

COMPREHENSIVE URBAN COUNTY PLAN

The comprehensive urban county plan, a second major variation of the two-level approach, involves the simultaneous reallocation of various functions from all municipalities (and sometimes other local units) to a county, thereby transforming the latter into a metropolitan government. The functional shifts are comprehensive in scope and occur at the same time, usually through local adoption of a charter.[9] The plan may also involve the allocation of functions to the county not previously possessed by any local governments in the area. Through reassignment of powers and possibly new grants of authority, a county thus assumes functions deemed to be of an area-wide nature while municipalities and other local units remain in existence to perform local services.

[9] The combination of two characteristics of this plan—comprehensiveness and simultaneity—differentiates this method of reorganization from other forms of the urban county development, which are discussed in Chapter 13.

The basic geographical fact that many metropolitan areas lie within the boundaries of a single county enhances the appeal of this plan. However, the concept is attractive even in various intercounty metropolises where the majority of the residents and the most serious aspects of their problems are found in the central county. The plan is also appealing in that, unlike the metropolitan district and federation methods of reform, it does not require the creation of still another unit of government in an already fragmented system. These factors have made the comprehensive urban county plan the decided choice of many people who favor some type of two-level arrangement. During the past two decades, they have succeeded in advancing their objective to various stages—a package of recommendations, an official proposal submitted to the voters, and public acceptance of the idea. However, they have also encountered numerous difficulties along the way so that in only one locality (Metropolitan Miami) has the concept become a reality.

Stumbling Blocks to Implementation

Recent efforts on behalf of the comprehensive urban county plan in four areas—Cleveland, Dayton, Houston, and Pittsburgh—reveal, in combination, five formidable obstacles to utilizing the concept.[10] First, in many states legal authorization to use the idea does not exist and may be obtained only by amending the state constitution. Second, substantial agreement is present that a structurally integrated county government, one capable of efficiently performing its functional responsibilities, must be an essential part of any such plan. Although some improvements in the organization and processes of many county governments have developed in recent decades, few counties in the metropolis have undergone the thorough reorganization advocated by most proponents of the comprehensive urban county idea. Without doubt, the sweeping nature of the structural renovation presumed to be a basic condition of converting the county into a metropolitan government is a strong deterrent to securing the necessary legal authorization. Numerous incumbent county officials see such authorization as an opening threat to their continuance in office and naturally work quietly or openly against it.

Determining the criteria to be employed in constituting the governing body of the restructured county is a third source of difficulty. In 1968, the United States Supreme Court, in *Avery v. Midland County*, enunci-

---

10 Promotion of the antithesis of the comprehensive urban county plan is not unknown. The most prominent example is the Plan of Improvement for Atlanta and Fulton County, enacted by the Georgia legislature in 1951. In addition to annexing eighty-two square miles to Atlanta and establishing a procedure involving judicial determination for future annexations, the plan provided for the reallocation of functions between the city and the county and largely excluded the latter from performing municipal functions.

ated an important and helpful guideline for formulating county representational arrangements: The populations of single-member areas from which representatives are elected must be substantially equal. This decision eradicates the long-time controversy over rural dominance of many county governing boards which refused to reapportion themselves or did so to the disadvantage of the urban sections. It may also lead to greater public receptivity of the comprehensive urban county plan since the governing bodies will have increased urban representation.[11] Reapportionment, however, does not eliminate the sensitive task of setting the exact location of the lines to be drawn to establish the election areas. Accordingly, in comprehensive urban county proposals, the representational boundaries decided upon may importantly affect what sections of the county, and in certain instances what political party, will have control of the greatly strengthened county government.

Answers are needed to many questions about representation when such a plan is being prepared. Should all governing board members be nominated and elected at large or by districts (wards), or should a combination of the at-large and district methods be used? What about the size of the governing board and the length of the terms of office? And, when local option permits, should the elections be partisan or nonpartisan? Not unexpectedly some element of the composition of the governing body may be decisive to the voters' decision about the entire plan.

A fourth major difficulty concerns the activities to be assigned to the county government. In developing such a proposal, judgments must be made about what functions to reassign and how many of them to reallocate at the inception of the plan. In other words, what compelling problems need to be handled on an area-wide basis and what degree of change will be acceptable to the electorate? If the transfer of merely a few functions to the county is proposed in the belief that a conservative approach will be welcomed by the voters, the electorate may decide the proposal is inconsequential and turn it down. If on the other hand, the transfer of a considerable number of functions is offered, the voters, often led by disgruntled city officials, may decide the plan is too revolutionary. Furthermore, the decision to include a particular activity may be decisive to approval or rejection. The formulators of such a plan therefore have to strike a balance between the too moderate and the overly drastic redistribution of responsibilities; and an accurate judgment on this matter is not easy. For instance, the commission that wrote the unsuccessful Cuyahoga County charter of 1959 decided to propose a far-reaching reallocation of functions. This decision generated the opposition of the

[11] For speculations about a number of effects of county reapportionment, see Daniel R. Grant and Robert E. McArthur, " 'One Man-One Vote' and County Government: Rural, Urban and Metropolitan Implications," *George Washington Law Review*, 36 (May, 1968), 760–777.

influential mayor of Cleveland, who had no desire to see certain important activities and assets of his city taken away.

A final difficulty, which is more than an occasional point of harassment to implementation of the comprehensive urban county plan, is the inadequacy of the financial powers of many county governments. Heavily dependent on the property levy and often faced with constitutional tax limitations, many counties lack the financial means to assume the functional responsibilities called for in this approach. The seriousness of these restrictions to the successful working of such a plan has been frequently acknowledged. Here, for example, are the strong conclusions about a basic phase of the problem reached by the staff of Metropolitan Community Studies in its recommendations report on the Dayton area:

The 10-mill limitation was adopted by state constitutional amendment in 1933 during a period of depression and low prices. Under its terms, the total or combined property tax rate that can be levied by all local units and the state government without a special vote of the electorate cannot exceed 10 mills or $10 per $1,000 of assessed valuation. Home rule municipalities, such as Dayton, may provide for higher millage rates in their charters.

The absurdity of this limitation is apparent. Operating costs in every local school district alone require more than the 10-mill rate. In fact, the total tax levy in virtually all of the urbanized portion of Montgomery County is at least three times this limit. The restriction imposes a severe handicap on the local units, particularly the school districts and the county government, since it compels them to appeal constantly to the electorate for even basic operating funds. If the powers of the county government are enlarged, the millage limitation would constitute a serious impediment to the execution of its new responsibilities.

Unfortunately, removal or modification of the 10-mill limitation can be accomplished only by constitutional amendment. . . .[12]

METROPOLITAN MIAMI:
COMPREHENSIVE URBAN COUNTY GOVERNMENT

When its charter went into effect in July, 1957, Dade County (Miami) became the first metropolis in the United States to put the comprehensive urban county plan into operation. Two barriers to this type of dual-level approach, which so far have proved insurmountable elsewhere, had to be overcome. They were state constitutional authorization to draft a county charter featuring such a plan and local voter approval of the document.

The state legislative delegation from Dade County, operating under astute leadership, successfully guided a proposed constitutional home

[12] *Dayton Journal Herald*, special supplement, January 16, 1960.

rule amendment for its county through the legislative session of 1955.[13]
The proposal, which authorized the preparation of a plan of governmental
reorganization for the Miami area, was decisively approved by the
statewide electorate in the following year. In 1957, the charter, which had
been prepared by a board appointed by the governor, barely gained
the required single countywide majority (44,404 to 42,620). With only
about one-fourth of the county's registered voters participating in the
special election, a heavy supportive majority in the city of Miami brought
victory for the proposition.

County Functions and Organization

The new charter provided for a powerful and structurally integrated
county government, officially designated as Metropolitan Dade County,
and for the continuance of the existing twenty-six (later twenty-seven)
municipalities, nineteen of which had fewer than 10,000 people. The
county government, encompassing 2054 square miles, was authorized to
construct expressways, regulate traffic, and own and operate mass transit
systems and transportation terminals; maintain central records, training,
and communication for fire and police protection; provide hospitals and
uniform health and welfare programs; furnish parks and recreational areas;
establish and administer housing, urban renewal, flood and beach erosion
control, air pollution control, and drainage programs; regulate or own
various public utilities (under certain limitations); and promote the area's
economy. It was also authorized both to prepare and to enforce comprehensive plans for the development of the county, thus gaining a grant
of authority of potentially great significance that is seldom even proposed
for a metropolitan government. On related fronts, it was permitted to
adopt and enforce zoning and business regulations and uniform building
and related technical codes throughout its territory.

The county government was also empowered to set reasonable minimum service standards for all governmental units in the county to meet
and to take over an activity if there was failure to comply with these
criteria. Additional municipalities can be created only upon the authorization of the county governing body and after affirmative majority approval
by the voters in the proposed incorporation. However, no municipality

[13] Following voter defeat of city-county consolidation in 1953, the city of Miami
created a study group, the Metropolitan Miami Municipal Board, which employed
Public Administration Service, a consulting firm, to prepare a report on local government in Metropolitan Miami. Some important conclusions of that report (*The
Government of Metropolitan Miami*) are discussed later in this chapter under federation. The county's legislative delegation objected to the study board's recommendation to eliminate the existing county government. The constitutional amendment
introduced by the county's delegation and passed by the legislature stipulated that
the board of county commissioners would be the governing body of the new metropolitan government, thus transforming this reorganization proposal from the federation approach to that of the comprehensive urban county.

existing at the time of the charter's adoption can be abolished except by majority consent of its electors. The sanction of the county governing board must be gained before annexation of land to municipalities is completed. Finally, the board may establish and govern special districts and finance district services and facilities by charges made within such areas.

The charter also brought on a thorough revamping of county governmental organization and processes. It specified that the county commissioners, elected on a nonpartisan ballot, were to constitute the legislative and governing body with power to appoint and remove a county manager. Administrative operations were brought under the manager's jurisdiction, a far cry from the supplanted rambling structure. The charter abolished the elective status of the assessor, tax collector, surveyor, purchasing agent, and supervisor of voter registration, and made the holders of these offices appointees of the manager. It also conferred authority on the county board to eliminate the election of the sheriff and constables, a power that the board subsequently exercised.

The five county commissioners in office at the time the charter went into effect were continued in those positions under a provision of the charter. Since their four-year terms had just begun in the previous year they constituted the entire membership of the board until 1958. In that year, other original provisions of the charter relating to the governing board became operative; they called for one commissioner to be elected at large from each of five districts, one to be elected from each of these districts by the district voters only, and one to be elected from each city containing an official population of at least 60,000. When these charter sections first became applicable, the governing board consisted of eleven members, as Miami was then the only municipality to qualify under the 60,000 population rule. After the federal census of 1960, the board's size increased to thirteen since both Hialeah and Miami Beach then exceeded 60,000 people. (As noted later, the composition and size of the commission were changed in 1963 by charter amendment.)

The new metropolitan government (Metro) in Dade County has encountered major opposition, mainly during its initial seven years when it was subjected to continuing harassment by various municipal officials and former county officeholders. Hundreds of law suits, for example, were filed against it, with some not reaching final settlement for years.[14] Certain of these actions resulted from the hasty and drastic manner in which the board of county commissioners immediately moved ahead on a number of highly sensitive subjects. Others, however, were deliberate efforts to torment the new government.

Another form of attack employed by the opponents were the attempts

[14] Joseph Metzger, "Metro and Its Judicial History," *University of Miami Law Review*, XV (Spring, 1961), 283–293, considers a number of cases.

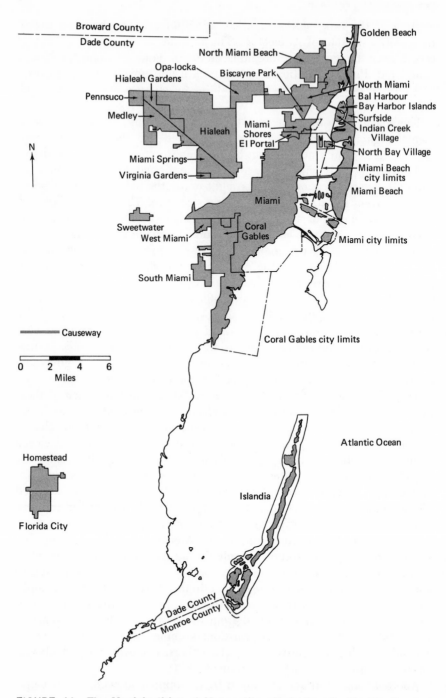

Broward County
Dade County

Golden Beach

North Miami Beach

Opa-locka
Hialeah Gardens
Biscayne Park
Pennsuco
North Miami
Bal Harbour
Bay Harbor Islands
Medley
Surfside
Indian Creek
Village
Miami
Shores
El Portal
Hialeah
North Bay Village
Miami Springs
Virginia Gardens
Miami Beach
city limits
Miami Beach

N

Miami

Sweetwater
West Miami
Coral
Gables
Miami city limits

South Miami

Coral Gables city limits

Causeway

0   2   4   6
Miles

Atlantic Ocean

Homestead

Islandia

Florida City

Dade County
Monroe County

FIGURE 44   **The Municipalities of Metropolitan Dade County, Florida. Courtesy Metropolitan Dade County Planning Department.**

to secure adoption of anti-metro charter amendments, which were presented in both large and small packages. Two endeavors of the former type were made. The first, launched only a few months after the charter became operative, would have stripped the county government of all its charter powers except tax assessment and collection and permission to set reasonable minimum standards for service performance. The second, which came four years later in 1961, was even more radical. It provided for taking away from the county its area-wide functions, replacing the council-manager system with the commission form, restoring the elective status of the sheriff and the assessor, and reducing the county commission to five members. Both of these proposals were defeated.

The small packages of proposed amendments fell into three categories. The first was to return the positions of assessor and sheriff to elective status. The assessor proposition was turned down three times; the measure for the sheriff was rejected twice, then adopted by a margin of about 2000 votes in 1963, and subsequently overturned three years later. The second group was to return individual functions to the municipalities or to make certain activities independent of the metropolitan county government. The unsuccessful efforts to restore the traffic courts to the cities and to establish an independent port authority are illustrations. The third kind was to place restrictions on the county manager, as exemplified by the adopted amendments to require county governing board approval of the manager's appointment of department heads and of his administrative orders to create or merge departments.

The efforts of the anti-reform forces have been plentiful and for a time seemingly unending. In total, however, all these endeavors have largely represented only much sound and fury. They have produced very little change in the metropolitan government as originally constituted.

The tenure of the county manager has been another unsettling factor for the Metropolitan Dade County plan, at least in its early stage. The first two incumbents in the position each lasted less than three and one-half years. Hired as the initial manager by a closely divided vote in July, 1957, O. W. Campbell, then holding a comparable post in San Diego, never knew when the pivot man on the governing board (the Commission) might shift sides and bring on his removal. But even after this body was increased in size, the stability of the manager's tenure did not improve. Accusations about its members' interference with administration and their obstructionist tactics and counter contentions by the Commission and the manager that the other party had failed to assume leadership were made. Finally, in February, 1961, the Commission, with only one dissenting vote, dismissed Campbell.

Campbell's successor was Irving G. McNayr, then city manager of

Columbia, South Carolina, and formerly manager of Montgomery County, Maryland. He took over the position on May 1, 1961, and immediately sought to reassure municipal officials of the county's intention to cooperate fully with them. Prompted by the unfavorable public reaction to the reassessment program required by the charter (all property in the county was to be reassessed by 1961), McNayr recommended an amendment to postpone this requirement. The change, approved by the voters, was considered to be a deciding factor in the defeat of the second big package amendment later that year. But the basic problem still remained since Florida law required assessment at cash value and that in Dade County was only at about 50 percent of such value. When the court in July, 1964, ordered the doubling of all assessments to comply with the law, the resulting public uproar precipitated the firing of McNayr by unanimous vote. Although there had been increasing signs of tension between him and the Commission newly elected in 1964 the immediate cause of his dismissal stemmed from the assessment fiasco.

The current incumbent is Porter W. Homer, also a former city manager, who has served in the top appointed executive position since May, 1965, a longer period than either of his predecessors. Terming himself "a professional nonpartisan," Homer has been a quiet, hard worker who has avoided the limelight. He has moved cautiously after thoroughly planning his actions and considering all the political contingencies. Unlike the previous managers, however, he has kept the governing board members informed about his proposals and appraised of plans before making them public. Sometimes criticized for his slowness, he nevertheless has made progress on many projects that had been stalled and has settled a number of severe controversies. He has made some enemies, in part because of his advocacy of consolidation of municipal-county police operations and of fire protection responsibilities, but no attempt has been made to oust him from office. Homer, in brief, has exhibited staying power and has brought to the managership a degree of stability that was unknown earlier.[15]

County Governmental Activities

Since its inception, the Metropolitan Dade County government has registered accomplishments in terms of both its organization and processes and its functional activities. Some of its principal actions are summarized here to indicate the range and direction of its efforts:

1. Integration of a formerly haphazard administrative organization, installation of modern management practices by standardizing procedures and developing a full battery of auxiliary services such as data processing, records handling, and internal auditing, and staffing the departments with competent professionals

[15] "Three Managers Gave Metro Present Image," *Miami Herald,* October 22, 1967.

2. Completion and adopting of a countywide general land use plan

3. Adoption of stringent regulations to control air and water pollution

4. Establishment of uniform, countywide traffic laws, with all violators being tried in the metropolitan court

5. Assumption of the tax assessment and collection functions from all the cities after a reassessment of its own rolls

6. Enactment of a uniform subdivision ordinance to control the development of vacant land both inside and outside of the municipalities

7. Establishment of a community relations board to work on easing racial tensions

8. Coordination of youth services

9. Creation of a department of housing and urban development, thus bringing together agencies that deal with urban renewal, prevention of neighborhood blight, and housing for low-income persons

10. Purchase of four bus lines as the nucleus for an area-wide system.

Problems and Challenges

Finance and leadership are two vexing and persistent problems in Dade County. The constitutional county home rule amendment furnished the means of creating a metropolitan government but it did not confer additional taxing powers on that new unit. In essence, the county government has had to utilize its pre-reorganization tax structure to finance new and improved area-wide services as well as municipal-type services to the hundreds of thousands of residents in the unincorporated areas. In 1967, however, it obtained important financial aid when the state legislature revised its gas tax distribution formula. Moreover, as the research of political scientist Parris Glendening shows, Dade County has increased its share of state funds since 1957 at a greater rate than other urban counties in Florida and has fared even better in its fiscal relations with the national government.[16] Nevertheless, these are only relative gains and the Metropolitan Dade County government continues to have serious financial difficulties.

Lack of sufficient leadership, including an absence of aggressive civic organizations and strong political leaders both inside and outside the metropolitan government, has been a long-standing complaint. Various people attribute an important part of the problem to the manager form

[16] Parris N. Glendening, "The Metropolitan Dade County Government: An Examination of Reform," Unpublished Ph.D. dissertation, Florida State University, Tallahassee, 1967. Professor Glendening also demonstrates in his dissertation how the claims of proponents about probable effects of the Dade County reform on the electoral system, such as increased citizen participation, have generally been erroneous, whereas those about the impact on the governmental system, such as greater efficiency, have usually proved to be valid. For an analysis of the electoral assertions, see the same author's, "Metropolitan Dade County: A Test of the Local Government Reform Model." Paper presented at the 1968 annual meeting of the American Political Science Association.

of government. (Dade County is the only general metropolitan unit to use this plan.) Some of these individuals and groups have unsuccessfully sought to supplant it with a strong mayor-council system.[17] Others have advocated retention but modification of the original manager arrangement. In 1963 certain adherents of the latter type prevailed, when a potentially significant charter amendment was approved. It provided for a county governing commission of nine members, eight elected county-wide with district residence requirements (on the premise that such elections would bring a greater area-wide perspective to this body) and one elected as mayor and serving as permanent board chairman. Many supporters of this amendment believed that simply by independently electing an official and designating him as mayor would produce at least part of the needed political leadership. Such, however, has not been the case. The mayor is merely the first among equals: he is just another commissioner who serves as the ceremonial head of Metropolitan Dade County. Political scientist Edward Sofen, who has observed local reform developments since their inauguration, is convinced that the mayor must possess specific powers, such as delivering state of the city addresses and appointing various boards and citizen committees, if he is to exert leadership.[18] For the present, the problem of political leadership remains unsolved.

Although finance and leadership persist as shortcomings, the overriding uncertainty about the two-level arrangement in Dade County centers on the municipalities. For one thing, the municipal level includes a number of incorporated places that may never be viable units capable of performing a variety of local services. An even more important factor contributing to the insecurity of the system has been the slow development of effective working relationships between the county and the cities. In 1962, the county manager noted, "Municipal cooperation to date in developing area-wide services has occurred only rarely, and every bit of progress by Metro has been made despite, rather than in concert with, municipal officials."[19] Four years later, the Dade County state legislative delegation uttered a similar lament: The problem of city-county relationships is crucial to the success of this reform approach. Moreover, the legislators pointed out, the existence of this difficulty is unfortunate as "there are more than enough problems crying out for a solution in Dade County to fully and fruitfully occupy both Metropolitan Dade County and any city willing and able to provide meaningful services for the

[17] One such attempt is described in Thomas J. Wood, "Dade Commission Dismisses Manager," National Civic Review, LIII (October, 1964), 498–499.

[18] Edward Sofen, The Miami Metropolitan Experiment, rev. ed. (Garden City N.Y.: Anchor Books, 1966), pp. 253–255. Professor Sofen's recommendations parallel the practice in San Diego, which is a council-manager city. Also see by the same author, "Quest for Leadership," National Civic Review, LVII (July, 1968), 346–351.

[19] Irving G. McNayr, "Recommendations for Unified Government in Dade County," (A Report of the County Manager to the Board of County Commissioners, Miami, September 25, 1962), p. 7.

foreseeable future."[20] A recent development may represent a significant breakthrough on this problem, however. A joint liaison committee composed of members of the County Commission and the Dade League of Municipalities has been set up and has reached agreement on such matters of mutual interest as a countywide minimum fire code, simplified annexation procedures, and increased coordination of police records and communication.

The permanency of the two-level arrangement in Metropolitan Miami is still in doubt. It is clear, however, that a "federal-type" system can operate properly only if its two vital elements, the county and the cities, work together. Any governmental structure involving a division of interlocking powers depends upon a high degree of cooperation for success. A period of greater maturity seems to be under way for this reform in Dade County, and the increased liaison that has been established between the two levels is an encouraging sign.

FEDERATION

Federation, the third variation of the two-level approach, involves the creation of a new area-wide government of intercounty or one-county territorial scope. The new unit, usually designated as the metropolitan government, carries out area-wide responsibilities. The municipal units continue to exist, perform local functions for which the metropolitan agency is not responsible, and retain their governing boards. Under some federation plans the municipalities are territorially enlarged by adding adjoining unincorporated land and are renamed "boroughs." Another feature of all federation plans proposed in the United States is local representation, generally from the municipal or borough areas, on the metropolitan governing board.

Similarity Between Federation and Other Two-Level Variations

Federation has considerable similarity to the comprehensive urban county and metropolitan multipurpose district arrangements. In fact, virtually indistinguishable federation and comprehensive urban county plans can be developed for a one-county SMSA. In such cases, the principal difference is that the former calls for replacing the existing county government and its incumbent officeholders by the new metropolitan agency, whereas the latter retains the county government as the area-wide unit. At first glance, this seems a broad distinction, but it need not be so.

Utilization of the county government under the comprehensive urban

---

[20] Dade County Legislative Delegation, *Review of Governmental Problems in Metropolitan Dade County* (Miami: 1966), p. 7. This report cites finance and leadership as the two other principal difficulties.

county plan is generally predicated upon substantial reorganization of its structure. Such renovation entails the conversion of many elective positions to the appointment method of selection. It also often includes the immediate or eventual reconstitution of the county governing body and in some cases the nomination or election of the board members from local areas. When reorganization encompasses all these changes, the difference between one-county federation and the comprehensive urban county arrangement is minor at most. (The enlargement of municipalities as called for in some federation proposals might be the only important point of variation.) Of course, these two types of reform do differ importantly in terms of an intercounty metropolitan area; there only federation is usable.

Federation and the metropolitan multipurpose district can likewise be very similar. Since either can be used in both intercounty and one-county situations, the inclusion of municipal boundary enlargements in some federation proposals is often the only major distinction. This stipulation is unknown to the metropolitan multipurpose district concept.

Major Federation Attempts: Similarities and Differences

Although federation has been discussed in generalized terms in many metropolitan areas in the United States, much in the manner of fashionable conversation, few serious efforts have been made to formulate specific plans and to obtain their adoption. The sparse record consists of:

1. State legislative refusal to submit federation proposals to the Boston area voters in 1896 and 1931

2. Popular defeats of propositions in Alameda County (Oakland) and Allegheny County (Pittsburgh) in 1921 and 1929, respectively

3. Lengthy discussions and a privately-prepared plan in San Francisco-San Mateo County in the late 1920s and early 1930s[21]

4. Electoral disapproval in 1930 of a state constitutional amendment specifying certain provisions to be inserted in a federation charter to be drafted for St. Louis City and St. Louis County

5. Revived interest in Alameda and Allegheny counties in the 1930s

6. Preparation of a federation plan for Metropolitan Miami in 1955 by a professional consulting firm for an official study group; the proposal, however, was converted into a comprehensive urban county system before adoption.

Subsequent support for federation has virtually disappeared in the United States, despite the not uncommon belief that it is a logical form of governmental organization for a number of SMSAs. Oddly enough, in the 1950s, at the very time interest in this approach practically vanished

[21] The Alameda County and the San Francisco-San Mateo County federation activities are reviewed in detail in John C. Bollens, *The Problem of Government in the San Francisco Bay Region* (Ann Arbor: University Microfilms, 1964), chap. IV.

in this nation, it grew in neighboring Canada to the point of adoption in the major metropolis of Toronto, and subsequently in other metropolitan aggregations.

Federation plans prepared for areas in various states possess common characteristics as well as differing features. A brief consideration of them illustrates some principal obstacles to adopting this type of reform and some complexities inherent in this two-level system, such as the allocation of functions.

As for the first similarity, the federation efforts in the United States, with the exception of those concerned with Metropolitan Boston, had to obtain state constitutional authorization before they could proceed to the stage of official formulation. This step proved to be an impossible hurdle in the St. Louis and Miami areas. Second, all federation plans (other than the three Boston area proposals which were presented as legislative bills) took the form of charters, drafted by locally elected boards. (The only exception was the Pittsburgh area charter which was prepared by a commission appointed by the governor.) In both these characteristics, therefore, most federation proposals have been similar to comprehensive urban county plans but unlike metropolitan special districts which have usually been authorized (and even created in some instances) through the much easier process of state legislation.

A third characteristic of federation efforts has been the requirement of local popular approval for adoption (again the Boston area proposals have been the sole exceptions). Frequently multiple majorities have been required—majorities so numerous as to make such consent a virtual impossibility for any type of proposal, even consent for motherhood, as one wag has suggested, let alone a complex and politically sensitive matter such as federation. Three illustrations show the difficulty of the approval requirement: a majority in each of the ten cities in Alameda County; a countywide majority and a two-thirds majority in each of a majority of the municipalities in Allegheny County; a majority in San Francisco, in San Mateo County, and in each of the municipalities in San Mateo County. Federation plans have usually had to acquire more majorities than the comprehensive urban county proposals, a surprising circumstance in view of the comparable nature of the two approaches. (In the case of the comprehensive urban county plan in Dade County only a single area-wide majority was necessary, a stipulation identical to that required to form many metropolitan special districts.) In fact, the voting requirements to put some city-county consolidation plans into effect—a single countywide vote in the Jacksonville area and dual majorities in Metropolitan Nashville, for example—are far simpler than those applied to most federation propositions, surely an illogical situation since city-county consolidation is far more drastic in its effects.

A further common characteristic of proposed federations has been the method of constituting the metropolitan governing board. Exclusive of most of the Boston area proposals, all other federations called for direct election of all governing body members and for the nomination or election (or both) of some or all of the members from areas smaller than the entire territory of the metropolitan government. This matter of board composition has proved to be as controversial an issue in federation attempts as in comprehensive urban county endeavors.

Proposed federations have also exhibited dissimilar characteristics. In terms of area, for instance, the Alameda, Allegheny, and Dade proposals were cast in a one-county context, while the Boston, San Francisco, and St. Louis plans extended beyond a single county. Those for the Boston area concerned one entire county and parts of three others; the San Francisco proposition involved a city-county and a county; and the St. Louis effort related to a city (not situated within county boundaries) and a county.

In terms of allocation of functions, pronounced differences are also apparent. Should the metropolitan government or the municipalities have enumerated powers, or should the powers of both levels be specified? All three possibilities have been proposed. In the Alameda and San Francisco-San Mateo County plans, the powers to be exercised by the municipal governments or boroughs were enumerated. In contrast, the Allegheny County charter and the Boston area bills listed the functions of the metropolitan government. In the Dade County federation plan approved by the countywide study group, the powers of both levels of government were specified. One of the most imaginative elements of the Dade County plan was the division of many functions between the metropolitan and municipal levels rather than the assignment of all phases of a function to one or the other level. Thus, for instance, refuse collection in municipalities was to be a municipal responsibility while refuse disposal throughout the county was to be handled by the metropolitan government.[22]

Another functional difference in federation proposals involves the magnitude of the responsibilities assigned to the metropolitan unit, a point often of considerable contention. Since area-wide problems are not identical in all SMSAs and since certain advocates of federation take a conservative viewpoint and others a drastic one, some differences can be expected. But the diversity has been extremely broad. In both the Alameda County and San Francisco-San Mateo County plans, the powers enumerated for the municipal governments or boroughs were relatively few in number, thus endowing the metropolitan level in both instances

---

[22] Further details about the proposed division of many services into metropolitan and local aspects in the Dade County federation will be found in Public Administration Service, *The Government of Metropolitan Miami* (Chicago: 1954), pp. 89–90.

with sweeping authority. On the other hand, in Allegheny County and Metropolitan Boston, where the proposed federations gave the metropolitan unit enumerated powers and the municipalities residual duties, the functional distribution would have made the former less powerful than its counterparts in the Alameda County and San Francisco area plans. The proposed federation for Dade County established still another pattern of distributing functions, with the metropolitan unit assigned very few in their entirety but allotted certain aspects of many others.

METROPOLITAN TORONTO: FEDERATION IN ACTION

Metropolitan Toronto, Canada's second most populous urban area, succeeded where various metropolises in the United States failed. Federation came into being in this area in April, 1953, when the governing body of the new unit was organized, and became fully operative in January, 1954. Exactly thirteen years later, the reform arrangement simultaneously underwent a number of major changes, chiefly of an organizational nature.

Forces Leading to Adoption

A combination of three forces was largely responsible for realization of the federation idea: the criticalness of certain financial and service problems, the recommendations of an impartial board, and the receptivity of the Ontario provincial (state) legislature.[23] After World War II, the needs of a number of localities began to outdistance their financial resources, thus causing their tax rates to rise rapidly and making it impossible to borrow money at reasonable interest rates. These fiscal shortcomings, coupled with the inability of the communities to work out adequate solutions through interlocal agreements, caused serious service deficiencies, most notably in education, water supply, and sewage disposal.

The time was propitious for governmental reorganization, but much disagreement existed over what course of action should be followed. The crucial factor in resolving these differences was the existence of the Ontario Municipal Board. A province-appointed quasi-judicial and administrative agency, it exercises control over aspects of local governmental finance and, upon application by one or more municipalities, can order boundary adjustments permitted under existing provincial legislation.

---

[23] Federation acts for two other Canadian metropolitan areas, Montreal and Winnipeg, were subsequently passed by the Quebec and Manitoba provincial legislatures in 1959 and 1960, respectively, but the area-wide units there were given far fewer powers than the Toronto counterpart.

During 1950 and 1951 the Board held many months of hearings on separate but related requests by two municipalities for different types of metropolitan governmental change.

In 1953, about eighteen months after taking the matters under advisement, the Board announced its denial of the applications, but stated that it felt obliged to "assume the responsibility of presenting its own proposals for the organization of a suitable form of metropolitan government in the Toronto area . . . [largely because the present applicants] have clearly established the urgent need for some major reform of the existing system. . . ."[24] Accordingly, it submitted a plan of federation for the thirteen municipalities in the metropolis to the provincial premier. At his direction a bill, largely following the Board's suggestions, was introduced in the provincial legislature and promptly enacted. Passage of the bill marked the first large-scale metropolitan governmental restructuring in Canadian history. (Neither an impartial agency nor broad legislative authority, it should be noted, has been present in any of the federation efforts in the United States.)

The First Thirteen Years

The Metropolitan Toronto federation, as originally designed, embodied several major features. First, it established an area-wide government, the Municipality of Metropolitan Toronto, encompassing the territory of all thirteen contiguous municipalities (a total of 241 square miles, containing at the plan's inception about 1,200,000 residents), to perform functions deemed essential to the entire metropolis. Second, it provided for the continued existence of the city of Toronto and of the twelve suburbs (the latter now separated from York County), to carry out functions not assigned to the metropolitan government. And third, it gave representation on the metropolitan governing body to each municipality.

The plan set up a strong area-wide government, one endowed with a broad range of powers relating to many functions—assessment of property, water supply, sewage disposal, arterial roads, transit, health and welfare services, administration of justice, metropolitan parks, public housing and redevelopment, and planning. In 1957 its authority was enlarged to include law enforcement, air pollution control, civil defense, and most aspects of licensing. (All of these powers were retained by the metropolitan government when the federation entered its second stage in 1967.)

From the outset certain responsibilities in a number of functional fields were assigned to the area-wide unit and others remained with the mu-

[24] Ontario Municipal Board, *Decisions and Recommendations of the Board* (Toronto: January 20, 1953), p. 42. This publication is also known as the Cumming Report (after the board chairman, Lorne Cumming).

nicipalities. In some instances of shared functions—water and sewerage, for example—the metropolitan government took on the role of wholesaler. It has responsibility for construction and maintenance of pumping stations, treatment plants, trunk mains, and reservoirs in supplying water. It sells water at a wholesale rate to the municipalities, which own the local distribution system and supply water to consumers at locally-determined retail prices. Similarly, it constructs and maintains trunk sewer mains and treatment plants and disposes of sewage from municipalities at wholesale rates. The latter in turn operate the local sewage collection systems.

In other instances, the sharing of a function was devised on a different basis, that of making the metropolitan unit a financial overseer. For example, in the field of education (until 1967) the metropolitan government, on the advice of an independent metropolitan school board, determined the amounts of funds to be approved for the purchase of school sites and the construction of buildings, and issued bonds for such purposes against its own credit. Also, the area-wide school board increased the degree of equalization of educational opportunities by making uniform per-pupil payments to local school boards to provide a minimum floor. However, eleven locally-elected school boards operated the public elementary and secondary schools and levied a local tax to provide funds beyond those received from the metropolitan unit and the province. (In 1967, the metropolitan school construction and equalization powers were greatly increased and the authority of local school boards to impose local school taxes was severely reduced.)

In still other instances of shared functions, the Municipality of Metropolitan Toronto was assigned various aspects of a service on the basis of a definite area-wide need. It was, for example, made responsible for building and maintaining a system of arterial highways (but not local streets) and developing and operating large metropolitan parks (but not local parks).

The metropolitan government also was given the power to appoint the members of the Toronto Transit Commission, which consolidated all existing systems and became the area's exclusive supplier of public transportation. It was further authorized to undertake public housing and redevelopment projects; provide a courthouse, jail, and juvenile and family court; and assess property at a uniform rate throughout the area for use in both metropolitan and local tax levies. Finally, the new government was empowered to adopt an area-wide general plan, which would be controlling in the municipalities after the approval of a provincial minister (first the minister of planning and development, now the minister of municipal affairs).

Until 1967 the Toronto federation provided for equal representation on the Metropolitan Council, the area-wide governing body, between the central city and the suburbs (both had twelve members) and among the suburbs (regardless of population size, each had a single member). All these individuals had to be elected officials of the constituent municipalities; their terms on the Council were originally for one year but were increased to two years in 1956. A chairman, designated as the new government's executive officer, could be selected from within or outside the Council's membership; accordingly, its total initially could be either twenty-four or twenty-five. The provincial premier made the first appointment to the chairmanship and the Council made all subsequent ones, with the chairman's term being the same as that of the other members of the governing body.

The Changes of 1967

The major changes that went into effect in January, 1967, as the result of provincial legislation in the preceding year, pertain in substantial part to the local tier in the two-level system and to the size and representational base of the metropolitan legislature.[25] As to the local level, the thirteen municipalities were consolidated into six municipal governments, composed of the city of Toronto and five boroughs. The boundaries of the central city and three boroughs were extended through mergers of two to four units. The limits of the two other boroughs were unaltered; they had been the most populous suburban governments under the original federation (Figure 45). Also, the eleven school boards were consolidated into six, with their territories being made identical to those of the six municipalities.

The size of the Metropolitan Council was increased to thirty-two, or thirty-three if its chairman were chosen by the board from outside its membership. (During the lifetime of the federation, there have been only two chairmen, both former local officials selected from outside.) The enlarged city of Toronto was allocated twelve members, the same number as it had previously, and each suburban borough was allotted between two and six members. The new formula thus appreciably increases the proportion of representation from the outlying areas. As before, all members, except the chairman, must be elected officials of the participating local units.

The reapportionment provisions for borough representation on the Metropolitan Council were based on the 1964 population of the newly enlarged city of Toronto, divided by twelve. Therefore, at the time this change was instituted, each member of the Council represented approx-

[25] Before the legislation, a royal commission, consisting of a single commissioner, H. Carl Goldenberg of Montreal, made a two-year study of the existing federation. Its recommendations, which were partly adhered to by the provincial legislature, are contained in *Report of the Royal Commission on Metropolitan Toronto* (Toronto: 1965).

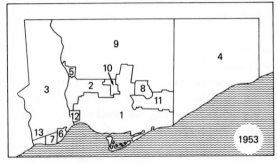

Key:

1. City of Toronto
2. Township of York
3. Township of Etobicoke
4. Township of Scarborough
5. Town of Weston
6. Town of Mimico
7. Town of New Toronto
8. Town of Leaside
9. Township of North York
10. Village of Forest Hill
11. Township of East York
12. Village of Swansea
13. Village of Long Branch

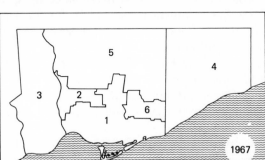

Key:

1. City of Toronto
2. Borough of York
3. Borough of Etobicoke
4. Borough of Scarborough
5. Borough of North York
6. Borough of East York

FIGURE 45   The Municipality of Metropolitan Toronto and Its Member Municipalities, 1953 and 1967. From Metropolitan Toronto 1967,
Municipality of Metropolitan Toronto, p. 3.

imately 60,000 people, thereby implementing the principle of equality
of representation according to population. In addition, the new representational formula was made subject to periodic review by the provincial
government, the first to occur between seven and nine years after its
installation.

These alterations in the metropolitan governing body emanated from
persistent dissatisfaction with the original arrangements. From the
beginning, most of the criticism centered on the allotment of one seat
to each suburban government, irrespective of its population. At the
inception of the federation plan, some suburbs had more than ten times
the population of others, and these disparities became even greater
with the passage of time. Controversy over the equal division of representation between the central city and the suburbs was not present at
the outset. Toronto, which then had almost three-fifths of the population,
was deliberately underrepresented in the initial stage to avoid the possibility of its domination of the metropolitan government. Opposition
to Toronto's proportion of the total representation developed as the

suburbs surpassed the core municipality in number of people; when the reform went into effect the latter had only about 40 percent of the area's population.

The most important functional alterations of 1967 took place in the field of education. After reviewing and modifying as necessary the local school operating budgets, the metropolitan school board now provides the required funds through an area-wide tax. This procedure eliminates the earlier disparities in educational financing and makes it possible to furnish an equivalent standard of education for every student in the metropolis. The local school boards may obtain limited additional money only for special purposes through a local tax levy. In a related field, the metropolitan government now has complete responsibility for financing school construction; it has assumed all existing local school capital indebtedness and is obligated for all new debt.

The other significant functional transfer in this same year involved the allotment to the area-wide government of all public welfare services. Previously the local units had carried out certain welfare activities, including general assistance, day care nurseries, and support of nursing homes.

Other changes also became operative in 1967. The terms of office of the chairman and other members of the Metropolitan Council were lengthened from two to three years. Its executive committee was increased to eleven members, made up of the chairman, five representatives from Toronto, and five from the suburbs; previously it had had five members and then seven. This powerful committee is responsible for preparing the annual budget, awarding contracts, nominating all heads and chief deputies of departments, and proposing policies. As before, a two-thirds vote of the Metropolitan Council is necessary to overrule the executive committee on contract awards and personnel nominations.

Amid these various major and minor changes of 1967, two prominent aspects of the federation remained the same. No powers vested in the area-wide unit were given over to the local governments, and the territorial boundaries of the former were not expanded. However, the total impact of the alterations undoubtedly represents a strengthening of the metropolitan tier and a further integration of the system.

Gains and Limitations

The greatest progress of the Toronto area federation had been registered in dealing with certain highly critical needs of the pre-reform period, particularly those relating to education, water supply, and sewage disposal. Many new school buildings and additions have been completed, and the capacities of water supply and sewage disposal facilities have been greatly enlarged. An extensive program of expressway construction has been undertaken, and mass transit has progressed through subway and bus-line extensions. In addition, a regional park system has been established and public housing and homes for the aged erected. Unified law enforcement has helped to produce a reduced crime rate and increased clearance of crimes. The equalization ability of the area-wide school unit has improved public education. Also, the metropolitan government has obtained a triple "A" credit rating in Canada and a double "A" rating in New York City, the highest classification a foreign corporation can receive in the United States. The savings on interest charges of many millions of dollars has been one of the consequences of this excellent financial standing.[26]

As political scientist Harold Kaplan has pointed out, the metropolitan federation was a necessary but not sufficient cause of these achievements. One important contributor has been the powerful role played by both chairmen of the Metropolitan Council—Frederick A. Gardiner, a former suburban mayor who served for more than eight years, and William R. Allen, a former Toronto city official. In their capacity as chairman, first Gardiner and now Allen have worked with the Council's executive committee to secure approval of their policy proposals, since committee-sanctioned propositions have been difficult to overturn in the legislature. They have also followed the practice of securing agreement among department heads on policy matters before their transmittal to the Council. In other words, they have operated as the vital middleman between the metropolitan councilors and the department heads, who have seldom interacted directly with one another. Other factors contributing to the accomplishments have been the low-pressure politics of the metropolis, the weak involvement of interest groups in area-wide issues, the lack of structuring of the Metropolitan Council by factions or parties, and the general willingness of the Council members to go along with the chairman. The last named factor has been due to the emphasis of Canadian political culture on deference to individuals in positions of authority as well as the time-consuming involvement of metropolitan councilors in the affairs of their own municipalities.[27]

The accomplishments of the Toronto area metropolitan government have been far less significant in what Frank Smallwood, also a political scientist, has called "the softer, more socially-oriented issue areas where results are usually less tangible and more controversial."[28] Writing in

[26] Various accomplishments are recounted in Municipality of Metropolitan Toronto, *Metropolitan Toronto, 1953–1963: A Decade of Progress* (Toronto: 1963), and later annual reports.

[27] Harold Kaplan, "Metro Toronto: Forming a Policy-Formation Process," in Edward C. Banfield (ed.), *Urban Government: A Reader in Administration and Politics*, rev. ed. (New York: The Free Press, 1969), pp. 623–625. Also see Harold Kaplan, *Urban Political Systems: A Functional Analysis of Metro Toronto* (New York: Columbia University Press, 1967).

[28] Frank Smallwood, *Metro Toronto: A Decade Later* (Toronto: Bureau of Municipal Research, 1963), p. 35.

1968, five years after Smallwood's appraisal, Kaplan decried the lack of substantial gains in many of the same fields, including health and welfare, urban renewal, and "all the social problems resulting from the assimilation of a large immigrant population."[29]

The metropolitan government concept is firmly established in Metropolitan Toronto. There is no interest in returning to the highly fragmented arrangement that existed before 1953; this is true even among the many suburbs which so strongly opposed consolidation at that time. Instead, the changes that have emerged have been in the direction of more comprehensive reform, as witness the additional functions assigned to the metropolitan unit and the reduction in the number of municipalities by more than one-half. It may be asked whether these two developments foretell the eventual evolution of the federation into a complete consolidation, even though the substantial changes of 1967 were a reaffirmation of support for the former.

The matter of governmental reorganization will undoubtedly remain on the civic agenda of Metropolitan Toronto for some time to come. Debate will continue to revolve around such questions as the division of powers between the area-wide and local levels of government and the respective merits of federation and consolidation.[30] The situation could not be otherwise, as no governmental system can be considered final in a dynamic and rapidly changing urban community.

THE TWO-LEVEL APPROACH: THE FUTURE

The various comprehensive forms of the two-level approach—the metropolitan multipurpose district, the comprehensive urban county plan, and federation—will continue to be appealing to reformers, at least on a theoretical basis, because these devices grant only certain functions to a metropolitan unit and generally have the members of its governing body chosen from local areas. But these very elements which make this approach appealing will remain major obstacles to gaining acceptance for any of its variations. Once the decision has been reached to construct a two-level arrangement, it is very difficult to reach consensus on what functions should be vested in the upper or metropolitan level and how its governing board should be constituted. Whatever determination is made on these two matters, considerable dissatisfaction almost inevitably emerges.

[29] Kaplan, "Metro Toronto: Forming a Policy-Formation Process," p. 626.

[30] Some consolidation adherents argue their case in part on the premise that the Ontario Municipal Board, in drawing up its proposals in 1953, regarded federation as a short and immediate step to consolidation. Actually that body said, "The board is convinced that the local governments will always have a vital role in the general scheme of metropolitan government." Ontario Municipal Board, *Decisions and Recommendations of the Board* (Toronto: January 20, 1953), p. 45.

Neither of these troublesome issues haunts metropolitan special districts; each is assigned only one function (or a very few) and generally little thought is given and little concern is expressed about the composition of their governing boards, even when the districts are of an interstate nature. Moreover, each such agency has usually been created to deal with a particular problem, one on which a considerable portion of the citizenry wants action; it thus has built-in public support, a favorable factor that has customarily been lacking in efforts on behalf of the more thorough forms of the two-level approach. In addition, the metropolitan special district has great territorial flexibility (some districts are the only interstate metropolitan governments in existence) and its establishment does not cause a major upheaval in the governmental system. It is also conceivable that some metropolitan special districts may in the future serve as a metropolitan coordinating (umbrella) agency, scrutinizing proposals of other units which have area-wide impact and halting those which are inconsistent with regional goals. For all these reasons, the district approach seems likely to grow in use.

On the other hand, there is at present no substantial evidence foretelling the probability that metropolitan special districts will evolve into or will be replaced by multipurpose districts. In fact, as the multipurpose district concept has become more widely advocated and understood, opposition to it has increased, even to the point of successfully blocking the passage of enabling legislation to permit its use. Such a unit poses a threat to the powers of established governments, including previously created metropolitan special districts, all of which have proprietary interests in avoiding extensive changes.

Next to the metropolitan special district, the comprehensive urban county plan seems the most likely prospect among the two-level arrangements for expanded use in the future. It has a distinct advantage over other multipurpose two-level forms since it uses an existing governmental unit instead of creating a new one. The advantage can be deceptive, however, since employment of the plan generally calls for substantial structural and functional (and often financial) renovation of the county government. In the past the strength of the county bureaucracy in opposing major structural change, a strength enhanced by the fact that county organization is often imbedded in the state constitution, has been such as to block the drive for adoption of the comprehensive urban county plan in practically all cases. No important signs of change on this matter are present; consequently there is little prospect of extensive adoption of this idea in the near future. The much more likely prospect is that a considerable number of county governments in metropolitan areas, many of which still embrace only a single county, will gradually become more important through piecemeal transfers of functions and contractual relationships involving municipalities.

Federation conceivably may be proposed and actually adopted in a limited number of urban areas. Like the metropolitan multipurpose district, however, it is confronted by a lack of public knowledge and enthusiasm, the latter emanating in part from the fact that use of this device produces still another government. Furthermore, in some instances creation of a federation system would result in elimination of the county government, an action that would encounter strong opposition, particularly from county officials and their supporters. Finally, as in the case of the other comprehensive types of the two-level approach, federation faces strong competition from three already widely used alternatives: the metropolitan special district, the gradually evolving county government, and interlocal cooperation.

13 / THE COOPERATIVE APPROACH

THE FRAGMENTED GOVERNMENTAL STRUCTURE OF THE METROPOLIS HAS demonstrated considerable adaptive capacity in the face of rapid urban change. Leaving aside the question of whether its replacement by a more integrated pattern would better enhance the quality of public services and areal development, the system has managed to survive with only occasional threats to its existence. This fact should lead us, as political scientist Robert Warren has suggested, to place greater priority on such matters as how the governmental systems of individual metropolitan areas evolve, how they are maintained when confronted by changing demands, what values they satisfy, and what factors tend to stimulate or inhibit incremental organizational changes in them.[1]

In this chapter we examine what has been—and will probably continue to be—one of the important means of sustaining the multinucleated

[1] Robert O. Warren, *Government in Metropolitan Regions: A Reappraisal of Fractionated Political Organization* (Davis: University of California Institute of Government Affairs, 1966), pp. 1–4.

pattern of the metropolitan complex: interlocal cooperation. With the continued growth of intercommunity needs and problems in the metropolitan
age, cooperation among local governments has greatly increased in
efforts to meet the challenges of adequate services and facilities. Although neither a recent innovation nor one used exclusively in the
metropolis, the marked upsurge in interlocal cooperation since World
War II has occurred mainly in the major population complexes. Indeed,
the cooperative method is now primarily and most importantly a metropolitan trend.

Interlocal cooperation is a broad term and takes many implementing
forms. At one extreme are informal, verbal understandings, often called
"gentlemen's agreements" which involve such elementary matters as the
exchange of information by administrators or technicians of two local
governments operating in the same substantive field, for example, public
health. At the other end of the range are formal, written agreements
among a sizable number of local units that decide jointly to build and
operate a major facility, such as a sewage treatment plant. Without in
any sense downgrading the importance of informal arrangements, which
often reduce the abrasions of metropolitan living and help the system
function without major disaster, we will focus our attention here on
two types of formal interlocal cooperation: one relating to specific
functions or services, the other to a more general mechanism for reaching consensus on area-wide issues and policies.

The first type is composed of three kinds of formal agreements, in
which: (1) a single government performs a service or provides a facility
for one or more other local units, (2) two or more local governments
perform a function jointly or operate a facility on a joint basis, and (3)
two or more local governments assist or supply mutual aid to one another
in emergency situations, such as a large fire or a serious riot. The second
type of cooperation consists of the formation and operation of metropolitan councils, permanent associations of governments that are convened
regularly to discuss and try to reach agreement on solutions to common
difficulties and needs.

An increasing number of individuals and organizations, especially
those made up of local public officials, are strong adherents of the
cooperative device. Its greatest attraction to them is that it provides a
process for dealing with needs and problems on a voluntary basis and a
means of retaining local determination and control. Moreover, its advocates view the cooperative approach as an effective countermove to
demands for the creation of powerful metropolitan governments that
would substantially reduce the authority of existing local units and
possibly eliminate many of them. Supporters also look upon it as contributing to increased efficiency and lower cost since this process makes it
unnecessary for each local government to hire its own personnel and

construct its own facilities for each service for which it has a legal responsibility. Far from everyone, however, agrees to the wisdom of the cooperative approach. Its most vigorous detractors consider it to be a weak palliative incapable of handling the total major area-wide difficulties of the metropolis.

THE GROWTH OF COOPERATION

Many factors have prompted the rapid spread of interlocal governmental cooperation to the point where many thousands of agreements on services and facilities are now in operation in metropolitan areas.[2] For one thing, the mutual needs and difficulties of communities have become more numerous as urban expansion has persisted, and the cooperative approach is a method of dealing with such problems. In some instances, too, cooperation has been employed deliberately as an alternative to other means; thus, in a number of areas the threat of establishing a metropolitan government has served as a whiplash in speeding the growth of interlocal cooperation. In other instances, the method has been utilized as a last resort—one employed, at least extensively, only after other types of reform have been suggested and turned down by the local voters.

An important common difference between the cooperative method and alternative approaches has also facilitated the expansion of the voluntary principle. In general, cooperative agreements are negotiated by administrators of the respective local governments and go into effect after their governing bodies pass the necessary ordinances or resolutions. In contrast, alternative approaches generally become operative only after they have surmounted the often difficult hurdle of obtaining the sanction of the local voters. Unquestionably, cooperative arrangements, often accomplished without general public awareness that they exist, are subject to a much easier adoption procedure.

The Role of Counties

Changes in county governments have also been a big contributor to the increased popularity of interlocal cooperation. Many counties in metropolitan areas, in response to public needs not otherwise being met, have widened their span of functions and become providers of important urban services. In addition, a number of them have improved their organizational structures and operational procedures and have thereby

[2] Detailed treatments of the cooperative movement are presented in W. Brooke Graves, *Interlocal Cooperation: The History and Background of Intergovernmental Agreements* (Washington: National Association of Counties Research Foundation, 1962) and in his book, *American Intergovernmental Relations: Their Origins, Historical Developments, and Current Status* (New York: Scribner, 1964).

generated increased confidence in their ability to carry out contractual agreements efficiently and effectively. As a result of these two developments, they have become increasingly active participants in cooperative arrangements.[3]

More Authorizations and Advocacy

More and more states have enacted laws making cooperation legally possible. A wide variety of such enabling legislation has been adopted since World War II—an amount far exceeding the prewar quantity. The constitutions of the two newest states, Hawaii and Alaska, illustrate this strong trend. Although these documents are noted for their brevity and concentration on the essentials of state and local government, the device of interlocal cooperation had become of sufficient importance by the time they were written to warrant the inclusion of permissive provisions relating to it.

A final contributor to the growth of the cooperative approach has been the support it has received from national, state, and local organizations composed entirely or partly of state or local officials. Both the national Advisory Commission on Intergovernmental Relations, a permanent bipartisan body created by Congress in 1959, and the Council of State Governments, the official spokesman for all fifty states, have advocated use of interlocal cooperation and have prepared draft legislation on the subject for the consideration of state legislatures. In addition, the National League of Cities (formerly the American Municipal Association) and the National Association of Counties have been vigorous supporters of cooperation, particularly the metropolitan council movement, and various state leagues of cities have also been active adherents.[4]

INTERLOCAL AGREEMENTS: SCOPE AND CHARACTERISTICS

In terms of its total use in metropolitan areas, the cooperative method embraces an exceedingly broad sweep of local services and facilities and involves every type of local government. Some of the important functions included are airports, building inspection, civil defense, con-

[3] Research by John E. Stoner has disclosed a high degree of association between the metropolitanism of Indiana counties (here defined as location in a metropolitan area) and their incidence of interlocal cooperation. U. S. Department of Agriculture, Economic Research Service, *Interlocal Governmental Cooperation: A Study of Five States* (Washington: 1967), pp. 21, 26.

[4] See, for example, *1968 State Legislative Program of the Advisory Commission on Intergovernmental Relations* (Washington: 1967), pp. 499–511; Council of State Governments, *Program of Suggested State Legislation: 1957* (Chicago: 1956), pp. 95–97; and American Municipal Association and National Association of Counties, *Voluntary City-County Regional Cooperation: A Collection of Exhibits* (Washington: 1963).

struction and operation of public buildings (including not only the headquarters of governments but also auditoriums, automatic data processing, hospitals, libraries, memorials, and stadiums), correctional and detention facilities, election services, fire protection, flood control, public health activities, and hospital services. Others include law enforcement (particularly communications and identification), library services, parks and recreation, personnel services, planning, purchasing, refuse disposal, road construction and maintenance, sewage disposal and treatment, tax assessment and collection, public welfare activities, and water supply. Especially numerous are arrangements relating to libraries, personnel services, public health, public welfare, purchasing, and tax assessment and collection. Many of the functions furnished under cooperative agreements are direct services to the public. Others, such as personnel examinations, purchasing, tax collection and assessment, and data processing, are services provided to government to enable it to operate more efficiently or economically.

Municipalities are by far the most numerous participants in interlocal agreements. They have many such arrangements with one another as well as a substantial number with other types of local units, especially counties. The latter, in fact, are becoming increasing users of the cooperative method, largely on a county-municipal rather than an intercounty basis. School districts, too, are more frequently entering into various arrangements with one another and with municipalities. School-municipal agreements on recreational and library services, for instance, are growing markedly. In New England, many towns are active in intertown and town-city endeavors. Townships and nonschool special districts are the least frequent participants in cooperative enterprises, largely because their narrow scope of functions makes them less likely prospects for such activity.

One Function, Two Governments

Some common characteristics of interlocal cooperative agreements on services and facilities can be delineated despite the great diversity of such arrangements. First, most consist of agreements between two governments concerning a single activity. For instance, a city and a county may sign a contract specifying that the latter will collect the city's taxes on a fee basis. Or a number of municipalities in the metropolis may want the county government to perform this function for them; again, a separate contract for only one activity is negotiated between each interested city and the county. Thus where interlocal cooperation is used extensively there will be a plethora of contractual arrangements, encompassing in total many local governments and many services and facilities, with the vast majority of agreements, however, relating to only two governments and one specific function. The limited nature of most individual interlocal arrangements should be remembered before one is overawed by the number of cooperative efforts. The significance of the device can be properly gauged only if the quantity is related to its piecemeal or fragmented character.

Service Orientation and Time Factors

Second, most interlocal agreements pertain to services rather than facilities. Cooperative arrangements have been completed for the building of civic centers, hospitals, and other public buildings, and for the construction of water and sewage disposal plants, roads, and bridges; but they are the exception rather than the rule. Agreements concerned with services (such as public health, libraries, and protective activities) are much more numerous. Interlocal cooperation, in other words, has a predominantly service orientation.

Third, these agreements are not necessarily permanent. In fact, they contain one or more time factors, thus emphasizing their possible temporary nature. For example, either party can terminate such a contract. A common provision is that an agreement may be abrogated at the beginning of a new fiscal year by written notification given at least two months before the proposed date of termination. (The situation is similar in those fewer cases where an agreement involves a number of governments; the withdrawal of any one unit may make the contract unworkable for the others.) Also, many contracts provide that they are effective for only a specified period of years after which there must be mutual consent for their renewal. At this time the financial terms of the agreement may be renegotiated and, unless the terms are satisfactory to the participants, the contract will terminate. However, many agreements in practice have had a long life, particularly those relating to facilities in cases where a withdrawing government would immediately have to invest in the construction of a replacement.

Many interlocal cooperative agreements represent a type of functional consolidation characterized by voluntarism and possible temporariness. This kind of consolidation contrasts with two other types: the first based on state laws that require the transfer of functions from one kind of local government to another (say the transfer of public health services from all municipalities in an area to the county government); the second involving the abdication of a function by one government to another (for example, the relinquishment of the health services of a big city to the county government for economy or other reasons). The former kind of consolidation is mandatory and both types are permanent. Thus they differ basically from the agreements dealt with in this chapter.

Frequent Standby Arrangements

A fourth characteristic of interlocal agreements is that many of them are standby arrangements. They are operative only when certain conditions come into existence and they continue only so long as these conditions are present. Known as mutual aid pacts, such commitments are activated only when fire, disturbance, or other local emergency cannot be adequately handled by the personnel and equipment of the affected contracting party. The extent of the aid furnished is determined by the supplying government, which may at any time, and solely at its own discretion, withdraw the aid.

One factor prompting the execution of many mutual aid pacts is the question of legal liability when a government participates in activities beyond its boundaries in the absence of appropriate agreements. Such contracts providing for the operation of a government outside its normal jurisdictional limits protect it while rendering emergency aid from damage suits, loss of personnel rights to its employees, and loss of workmen's compensation rights. As a report of the Cleveland Metropolitan Services Commission notes:

> The principal purpose of the "mutual aid" agreement would appear to be *legal* rather than *operational* [operational in the sense of providing systematic coordination of an activity]. It is believed to reduce possible legal problems *in the event* that a department should respond to external calls. (One has reason to believe that law officers have been influential in persuading municipalities to adopt such agreements, with this end in view.)[5]

Although mutual aid pacts commonly specify that they do not relieve the parties from the obligation of providing adequate protective services within their respective boundaries, some of the participants do not comply with these requirements. The key element of such pacts is reciprocity, and some small cities having mutual aid agreements with an adjacent large city know the latter will immediately come to their assistance if a major fire or other serious emergency occurs within their borders. As a consequence, numerous small cities that do not or cannot finance adequate protective services improperly rely on mutual aid to compensate for the deficiency. This unjustifiable use of the device contributes to the continuance of inadequate fire and police departments in various metropolitan areas.[6]

Specific and General State Laws

A fifth and final characteristic of interlocal agreements is that a majority of them are based on specific state legislative authorizations,

[5] Matthew Holden, Jr., *Inter-Governmental Agreements in the Cleveland Metropolitan Area* (Cleveland: Cleveland Metropolitan Services Commission, 1958), pp. 19–20.

[6] For evidence of this effect on fire service in Metropolitan Los Angeles, see Frank P. Sherwood, "Legislative and Administrative Powers for Intergovernmental Cooperation for Metropolitan Affairs in California," in Governor's Commission on Metropolitan Area Problems, *Metropolitan California* (Sacramento: 1961), p. 95.

each allowing cooperation in simply one particular field. The tendency has been for lawmaking bodies to respond in a highly restricted or unifunctional way to individual needs as they arise. The amount of enabling legislation has thus proliferated as the demands for cooperative authorizations for an increasing number of services and facilities have been heeded.

In recent years, two types of deviations from this highly restricted approach have been gaining increased acceptance, both involving the concept of a general interlocal cooperation act. In the one, the legislature lists a number of services and facilities that can be subject to cooperative arrangements. In the other, it authorizes a general permission of either narrow or broad scope without making any specific enumeration. The narrow form provides that any power within the authority of each of the contracting governments can be exercised jointly by them or by one government for the other. The broad grant specifies that any power possessed by one of the contracting governments can be employed jointly by them or by one of them on behalf of the other. Although in a legal sense the latter form of general legislation seemingly endows contracting governments with a wider range of action, in practice there has been no significant difference in the purposes for which the two types have been used.

COOPERATION IN METROPOLITAN PHILADELPHIA

The nature and the direction of the movement involving interlocal cooperative agreements can be more fully perceived by considering the use of this approach in two specific metropolitan areas: Philadelphia and Los Angeles. In the former the device has been the subject of three thorough research studies; in the latter it has received its most extensive employment.

Prominent features of the interlocal cooperative development in the Philadelphia area, revealed by two inquiries, are the widespread use of agreements, the large number of participating governments, and the frequency of cooperation among suburbs (rather than central city-suburban contracts). The first survey, which considered eight counties, discovered that 427 local units had entered into a total of 756 agreements. More than three-fifths of the cities, boroughs, and townships and about three-fifths of the school districts were participants.[7] A similar study, made seven years later but limited to five counties, disclosed a

[7] Jephtha J. Carrell, "Inter-Jurisdictional Agreements as an Integrating Device in Metropolitan Philadelphia," Unpublished Ph. D. dissertation, University of Pennsylvania, 1953; a summary is contained in "Learning to Work Together," *National Municipal Review*, XLIV (November, 1954), 526–533.

continuation of the high level of cooperative activity. It further found the greatest amount of participation by densely populated suburbs which most commonly entered into agreements with one another and a high concentration of cooperative relations in law enforcement, fire protection, education, and sewage disposal.[8]

The third and most recent investigation, also concerned with five counties, focused on determining the impact of community differentiation (in socioeconomic terms) on the willingness or tendency of local units to cooperate. The study was particularly interested in determining if some types of suburbs enter into intergovernmental arrangements more than others. It was hypothesized that (1) high social-rank municipalities are more prone to cooperate than those of lower status; and (2) for functions affecting life styles, such as education and planning, communities will seek relations with other units of similar social characteristics as opposed to those of different status. To test these hypotheses, attention was given to three kinds of agreements—school, sewage disposal, and police radio; the first of these services directly affects the life-styles of communities, the second has little to do with them, and the third has no such impact at all. The municipalities examined were characterized in terms of social rank (based on the population attributes of education and occupation) and wealth.

The findings of the study are revealing. School cooperation tends to develop between governments of similar social rank and financial resources. Sewage agreements also occur more frequently between units of comparable social status and, where a range of choice exists, this factor appears more important than the taxable resources of the respective municipalities. Although, as the authors of the study point out, school and sewerage systems have far different social and cultural connotations, both involve expensive capital facilities and protracted negotiations among local officials. Apparently the latter prefer to deal with their counterparts who are socially similar to themselves. In the case of police-radio agreements, on the other hand, socioeconomic distance between municipalities appears to have no apparent effect on contractual patterns. Such cooperation does not relate to life styles, it involves only modest sums of money, and it is of concern primarily to technicians. The researchers sum up their findings in these words:

> Social and economic distance between municipalities [including school districts] influences cooperative activities involving life-styles and large capital investments. However, differences in social rank appear to be more significant than inequalities of resources. . . . Generally, given a choice as to the selec-

[8] George S. Blair, *Interjurisdictional Agreements in Southeastern Pennsylvania* (Philadelphia: University of Pennsylvania Institute of Local and State Government, 1960).

tion of partners to an agreement, cooperation occurs among municipalities with similar social rank and tax resources, in that order. Where agreements are necessary for the performance of a particular function, and little choice with respect to social rank is available, the resources of prospective partners become the prime consideration. This scale of values is not operative for some minor cooperative activities [police-radio agreements, for instance] with but slight social and financial impact.[9]

COOPERATION IN LOS ANGELES COUNTY

The most extensive use of cooperative agreements in the nation has taken place in Los Angeles County. Although a number of intermunicipal arrangements exist there, most agreements involve the county government as the provider of services to municipalities.[10] Because of this role, Los Angeles County represents a highly prominent illustration of the urban county development, and one that has attracted considerable attention, if not extensive emulation, elsewhere in the country.

Five Forms of the Urban County Development

The designation, "urban county development," is so widely used and embraces so many kinds of actions that it requires further explanation. The term is applied to five types of practices, one or more of which are utilized by several hundred counties in the United States. First, it is used to refer to an increase in the number and levels of services which a county provides to unincorporated areas within its boundaries. Thus it can mean, for instance, that the manpower and equipment of the sheriff's department have been augmented to the point where the county furnishes extensive law enforcement in unincorporated urban areas. In fact, the level of protective service supplied by some counties

[9] Oliver P. Williams, Harold Herman, Charles S. Liebman, and Thomas R. Dye, *Suburban Differences and Metropolitan Policies: A Philadelphia Story* (Philadelphia: University of Pennsylvania Press, 1965), p. 264. A later analysis by Williams distinguishes between life-style services and system-maintenance services, such as water and sewer functions, indicating that attempts to centralize administration of the latter generate less resistance than in the case of the former. See "Life Style Values and Political Decentralization in Metropolitan Areas," *Southwestern Social Science Quarterly,* 48 (December, 1967), 299–310. For a research design on charting the frequency of functional agreements by various governments and correlating their ranking with social, political, and demographic factors, see James V. Toscano, "Transaction Flow Analysis in Metropolitan Areas: Some Preliminary Explorations," in Philip E. Jacob and James V. Toscano (eds.), *The Integration of Political Communities* (Philadelphia: J. B. Lippincott, 1964), pp. 111–114.

[10] Interlocal cooperation is common throughout California, which has more than 5000 city-county and intercity agreements in effect. Several significant case studies are included in League of California Cities, *Inter-Municipal Cooperation Through Contractual Agreements* (Berkeley and Los Angeles: 1963). For examples from another state, see New York Office of Local Government, *Local Government Cooperation: Uses-Procedures-Case Studies* (Albany: 1963), pp. 24–33.

in heavily populated unincorporated sections approximates, and sometimes exceeds, that offered by small municipal governments within their
own city limits. This urban type of law enforcement stands in decided
contrast to the county's traditional role as supplier of a modest level of
police protection in rural areas only.

A second use of the designation pertains to the transfer of a function,
usually under mandatory state law, from cities to counties so that the
latter may carry out the urban-type activity on a countywide basis. An
example is state legislation that requires transferring to counties the responsibility for checking the accuracy of meters on taxicabs, rented cars
and trucks, and private ambulances.

A third use of the term relates to the intensification of a long-established
function or the assumption of a new one by the county government
throughout the entire county. Recreational programs, regional parks, and
libraries are frequent examples. A fourth refers to the completion of cooperative agreements under which a county provides services to municipalities. And a fifth and final use pertains to the conversion of a county
government into a metropolitan unit through the installation of a comprehensive plan of governmental reorganization that simultaneously
reallocates many urban functions from all cities in a county to the
county government.[11]

Los Angeles County as an Urban County

The government of Los Angeles County is a leading representative
of the urban county development in terms of the first four types of
practices. As for the first of them—the provision of urban-type services
to residents of densely settled unincorporated areas—Los Angeles County
supplies high levels of such services as law enforcement, streets, and
traffic signals to its many residents who live in such sections. For instance, the county sheriff's department is the fifth largest police operation
in the nation and is widely recognized as a first-class law enforcement
agency. Indeed, the urban services rendered by the county (and to a
lesser extent by some other county governments in the state as well)
were at such a high level in the 1950s that a bitter controversy developed.
The cities claimed that since their inhabitants were paying both city
and county taxes they were being forced to subsidize services extended
by the county to residents of built-up unincorporated sections.[12] The

[11] The fifth use of the term is in operation only in Dade County (Miami), Florida,
which is discussed in Chapter 12. For a consideration of the different forms of the
urban county development, see Victor Jones, "Urban and Metropolitan Counties,"
Municipal Year Book: 1962 (Chicago: International City Managers' Association,
1962), pp. 57–66, and his earlier similar article in the *Municipal Year Book: 1954*,
pp. 133–147.

[12] California Legislature, *Final Report of the Assembly Interim Committee on
Municipal and County Government Covering Fringe Area Problems in the State of
California* (Sacramento: 1953).

controversy has subsided in recent years, in part because many areas incorporated and contracted for urban-type services from the county government, and in part because the latter cut back on some services to unincorporated urban areas. However, occasionally some city officials still get agitated about the matter, which they continue to regard as inequitable. And it is a fact that some communities remain unincorporated largely because of the urban services they can obtain from the county government out of general county tax funds.

The second practice—transferring functions from cities to the county by action of the state legislature—is illustrated by a state law that forces the county government to take custody of city prisoners booked on drunk charges. This law compelled the county to lease the drunk farm of the city of Los Angeles, add 125 officers to the sheriff's department, and spend an additional $2.5 million annually. Noteworthy illustrations of the third practice—a county government intensifying an old function or taking on a new one on a countywide basis—are the ownership and operation by Los Angeles County of a considerable number of parks and the administration of extensive, diversified recreational programs.[13]

Los Angeles County as a Contractor

The wide use of any one of these three practices would qualify Los Angeles County for recognition as an urban county, but its most notable attribute in this regard is the provision of services to municipalities under cooperative agreements. It has approximately 1600 such agreements, involving all seventy-seven municipalities within its borders, with the number of services furnished to them ranging from seven in one city to forty-five in another.

The provision of some types of services to municipalities is universal, or virtually so. The county supplies election administration for all cities, the housing of prisoners and the enforcement of state health laws for all except one, tax assessment and collection for all but two, and the enforcement of city health ordinances for all except three. The county provides various other services to at least one-half of the cities: animal control, emergency ambulance, prosecution of violations of city ordinances, subdivision final map check, inspection of mobile homes and trailer parks, and library. Many others are rendered to at least one-third of the cities, including hospitalization of city prisoners, building inspection, engineering, industrial waste regulation, weed abatement, rodent control, law enforcement, and fire protection. In total, fifty-eight types of services are available to cities through the county, mostly by means of contracts but also occasionally through special county taxing areas

[13] The urban county development in Los Angeles County is also discussed in Winston W. Crouch and Beatrice Dinerman, *Southern California Metropolis* (Berkeley and Los Angeles: University of California Press, 1963), chap. 7, and pp. 222–225.

(county-administered districts). And the number offered continues to grow; in the last several years, radar equipment maintenance, tree planting and maintenance, parcel map checking, and helicopter patrol for crime prevention and detection have been added.

Establishment of the Lakewood Plan

The catalyst to the rapid growth in recent years of county-city service agreements was the establishment in 1954 of the Lakewood Plan (or as cities other than Lakewood operating under the same arrangement and the county government prefer to call it, the contract cities or contract services plan). Under this system a municipality receives a sizable package of municipal services—virtually all of them in some instances—from the county government under contracts and through county-administered districts (for fire protection and library services, for example). The Lakewood Plan was the product of a combination of factors: passage by the state legislature of a uniform local retail sales and use tax that made it financially attractive for areas to incorporate as municipalities, the controversy over whether city residents were subsidizing urban services supplied certain unincorporated areas by the county government, and the continued rapid growth of the county's population, particularly in some of its unincorporated sections. Other important factors were the existence of highly respected county departments already staffed and equipped to furnish municipal services and the willingness of county officials to think through the idea of a package of services (at least partly because of the fear of some department heads that the size of their operations would be reduced as burgeoning unincorporated sections found it necessary to incorporate or annex to a municipality). A final significant influence was the desire of built-up unincorporated sectors to escape annexation by incorporating (and thus being vested with local control, especially of land use)—but at the same time avoiding the necessity of large capital investments for facilities like police and fire stations and for recruiting a corps of city employees.

The Lakewood Plan: Differences and Characteristics

The Lakewood Plan differs in several important respects from the earlier city-county service agreements. It entails the purchase of a package of services instead of individual services on a piecemeal basis. It includes for the first time county law enforcement and fire protection to cities; previously the sheriff's department did not enter into contracts with municipalities, and newly incorporated areas withdrew from county-administered fire districts. Use of the plan has been confined entirely to communities incorporated since Lakewood became a city in 1954— that is, to municipalities not already having long-established departments of their own.

The Lakewood Plan system is in operation in all but two of the thirty-two municipalities that have been created since 1954. These communities range greatly in population size, from small to moderately large. At the time of incorporating, Lakewood had approximately 60,000 inhabitants (now almost 90,000) and immediately became the fifteenth most populous city in the state. Several others also have populations of nearly 100,000, while at the other extreme a number have fewer than 10,000 residents.

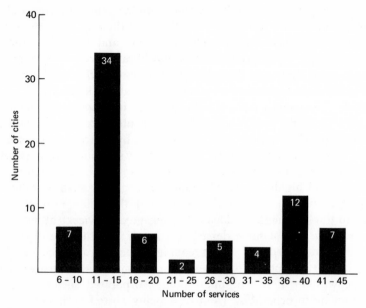

FIGURE 46   **Number of Municipal Services Provided to Cities by the Los Angeles County Government. Data provided by the County–City Coordinator's Office, County of Los Angeles, 1969.**

Although the package of services idea is central to the Lakewood Plan, cities operating under the system do not all purchase the same package from the county. The common practice has been for the newly incorporated cities to buy at the outset virtually all the municipal services they need. Over a period of time, however, a number of them have terminated some contracts and withdrawn from particular county-administered districts. Such action was usually taken after they had determined that they could perform certain services more economically than the county government, or when they decided to undertake some functions on their own for such nonfinancial reasons as preference

Service

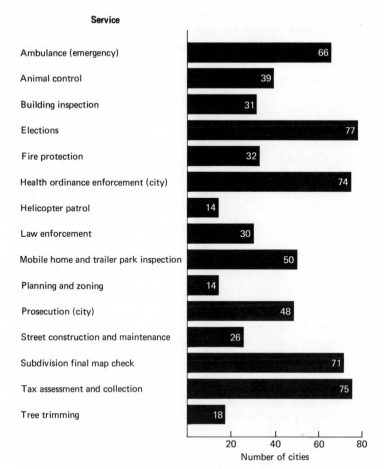

FIGURE 47   **Selected Types of Municipal Services Provided to
Cities by the Los Angeles County Government. Data
provided by the County–City Coordinator's Office,
County of Los Angeles, 1969.**

by community residents. (The county's contract rates must be set at
full cost—the direct costs for the number of units of each service rendered and a share of the county's general administrative or overhead
expenses; the rates are subject to revision annually to reflect changes in
the factors making up the charges, such as pay scales.) The contents of
the service package thus vary according to a community's decisions as
to what it initially needs from the county and what subsequent changes
should be made in the original arrangements.

While the Lakewood Plan has flourished, the number of agreements between the county and older, pre-Lakewood cities (often called "old-line" or "traditional" cities) has also grown. The latter have become increasingly interested in obtaining specialized services such as sewer maintenance, storm drain design, traffic signal maintenance, and traffic striping and marking. At present, about one-third of the total number of agreements are with the older cities.

A Viewpoint About Cooperation

L. S. Hollinger, the chief administrative officer of Los Angeles County, has made some interesting judgments about the value and probable future course of development of the cooperative agreement device from the vantage point of that government's many years of experience. Providing county services to cities on a contract basis, he has pointed out,

. . . demands a forward-looking, "urbanized" county government willing and able to provide adequate municipal-type services at reasonable costs and with acceptable responsiveness.

. . . has worked successfully and has provided a vehicle for functional consolidation without the need for political consolidation.

. . . has improved the organization and service of county operations.

. . . has provided a laboratory in government, which is enabling us to determine those particular elements of governmental activity that can best be provided by the county and those that can best be provided by each city. Thus, a process almost akin to natural selection in the life sciences is taking place and will result (we are confident) in the establishment of the logical role of both the city and the county in a highly urban area.[14]

METROPOLITAN COUNCILS OF GOVERNMENTS

The metropolitan or regional council of governments (COG) is the newest form of institutionalized cooperation in the metropolis. Employed for the first time in the 1950s in only a few areas but more recently adopted in a great many, the council idea has evoked a varied response. Some regard it as a logical device for achieving integrated metropolitan development in a politically fragmented system; others look upon it as a toothless tiger or—even worse—a protector of the inadequate status quo; and still others consider it a step toward the achievement of some form of metropolitan government.

[14] L. S. Hollinger, "The Lakewood Plan," in National Association of Counties, *Guide to County Organization and Management* (Washington: 1968), p. 58. For other observations about the Lakewood Plan, see Crouch and Dinerman, *Southern California Metropolis*, pp. 201–205, 222–225; and Richard M. Cion, "Accommodation Par Excellence: The Lakewood Plan," in Michael N. Danielson, *Metropolitan Politics: A Reader* (Boston: Little, Brown, 1966), pp. 272–280.

Called a "new political animal" by *Nation's Business,* a metropolitan council is a voluntary association of governments (customarily general local units only) designed to provide an area-wide mechanism for key officials to study, discuss, and determine how best to deal with common problems. This mechanism is not a government, as it has no mandatory financing and enforcement authority. Instead, it is a continuing agency to furnish research, plans, advice, recommendations, and coordination. The legal basis for its organization is either a specific state enabling law, a general state interlocal agreement act, or nonprofit corporation legislation.

Development of the Movement

The use of the COG idea originated in 1954 with the establishment of the Supervisors Inter-County Committee in the Detroit area; its inception thus trailed by many years the inauguration of a number of other metropolitan approaches of a more drastic nature. Even after its introduction the concept did not promptly catch hold on an extensive basis, despite its simplicity and moderateness and the widespread praise and support given to it, especially by national organizations of local officials. New councils—in such widely separated urban complexes as Washington, Atlanta, San Francisco, and Seattle—were subsequently created but by 1965 only nine were in operation in metropolitan areas. These pioneering councils all came into being for one or both of two reasons: a belief that collaborative governmental decisions were necessary to deal with area-wide problems; and a fear that local units were about to lose power to proposed metropolitan governments. The early organizations of this type were few in number and trouble-laden; according to one analysis, "all of them suffered from uncertainties, inexperience in metropolitan cooperation, and lack of adequate financial resources."[15]

A great transformation has taken place in the COG development since 1965. The number of such councils has multiplied until at present approximately 100 of them are in existence, chiefly in metropolitan areas. (Some metropolitan planning commissions of pre-1965 vintage have been converted into COGs, as noted in Chapter 9.) This numerical increase has been accompanied by programmatic expansion. Two federal stimulants largely prompted these developments. In 1965 the federal housing legislation was amended to make COGs eligible (section 701) to receive grants, paying up to two-thirds of the cost, of various activities, including studies, data collection, and regional plans and programs, and of expenses concerned with general administration and staffing professional, technical, and clerical positions. In the following year the

[15] Royce Hanson, *Metropolitan Councils of Governments* (Washington: Advisory Commission on Intergovernmental Relations, 1966), iv.

Demonstration (Model) Cities and Metropolitan Development Act, in section 204, stipulated that after June 30, 1967, all federal grant and loan applications for many types of projects, mainly in the public works field, must be submitted for review to an area-wide agency that performs metropolitan or regional planning for the area in which the assistance is to be used. Councils of governments were one such agency authorized to carry out this review function. These two legislative acts sped the formation of COGs and broadened the activities of those already in existence.

Another important action supportive of COGs occurred in 1967 when the National Service to Regional Councils obtained its own staff and offices and greatly enlarged its program. This development was made possible by grants from the Department of Housing and Urban Development and the Ford Foundation. The Service had been organized five years earlier by the National League of Cities and the National Association of Counties to encourage the formation of councils and strengthen their operations, but strong financial support had been lacking until these outside sources of aid became available. The current activities of the National Service include: (1) clearinghouse for information on the organization, programs, and progress of regional councils, (2) consultation with local officials to assist councils in their development and with specific questions and problems, (3) information on federal programs and their effects on regional activities and conversely alerting federal and state agencies to the needs of regional councils, and (4) evaluation of such councils and local government structures as they are developing in order to understand and improve techniques of intergovernmental cooperation and communication. The agency serves both COGs and other types of regional agencies such as metropolitan planning commissions, transportation study groups, and economic development districts.

Membership and Activities

Typically the members of a COG are cities and counties, although occasionally other local governments (including school and other special districts), the state government, and even private citizens designated by civic organizations may be included.[16] The governing board representatives normally are elected officials. The council's structure, particularly when the organization's membership is large, often consists of a general assembly (legally the policy-making body but actually the ratifying unit) and an executive committee. The latter handles most of the business and its actions are seldom reversed by the assembly. The former, consisting of all the representatives, meets once or twice a year, whereas the executive committee, usually composed of officials

[16] Joseph F. Zimmerman, "Metropolitan Ecumenism: The Road to the Promised Land?" *Journal of Urban Law*, 44 (Spring, 1967), 439, 443–444.

from the major city and each county with representation from the smaller municipalities determined by an agreed-upon formula, convenes monthly or oftener. (Appointed administrators, while not serving in the general assembly or on the executive committee, are frequently members of technical study groups.)

The procedure, as originally employed in most cases, of permitting each member government, regardless of population size, to have one vote in the general assembly (or on the regular governing board if the combination of a general assembly and an executive committee is not employed) has recently been undergoing revision or reconsideration. This action has resulted in part from court cases calling for a population basis of representation in general local governments. Even though COGs do not qualify as such governments they foresee that this standard might be applied to them as their importance as metropolitan instrumentalities grows. Revision or reconsideration has also resulted from the expressed convictions of minority-group spokesmen who fear the complete absence of representation in COGs unless the one-man, one-vote principle is followed.

Membership in metropolitan councils is voluntary; governments join of their own volition and withdraw as they wish. The degree of voluntarism has shrunk, however, with respect to those COGs responsible for reviewing various types of federal grant applications. Since the review requirement extends to nonmembers as well as members, the former will be without a voice in either their own or other applications which may concern them so long as they remain outside the council.

Metropolitan councils have generally undertaken studies of specific regional needs, most often pertaining to physical facilities. Some have engaged in the preparation of comprehensive land use and transportation plans. Various of them have sponsored training programs for officials and employees of member governments, entered into joint purchasing programs, and engaged in lobbying at the local, state, and national levels. So far few of them have paid more than passing attention to social problems and issues, but a number are giving consideration to placing such items on their agendas, largely as a result of requests by member governments of low socioeconomic status and by minority groups.

A number of COGs have been serving as the review agency to comment on federal grant requests. A report on the first six months' experience of COGs and other area-wide agencies functioning in this review capacity shows that only thirty-eight of more than 1000 applications submitted for such scrutiny were returned to the applying jurisdictions with critical comments.[17] This low rate of criticism is due principally to two factors: (1) the ability of some review agencies to

[17] Executive Office of the President, Bureau of the Budget, *Section 204—The First Six Months* (Washington: April, 1968), p. 5.

obtain modifications of applications through informal consultations before their official submission and (2) the frequent absence of a general area plan (many are being prepared but are not yet finished) that may be used as a guide in judging the soundness of projects proposed by individual governments.

Implementation, Financing, and Staffing

Metropolitan councils have no authority to carry out their decisions on area-wide issues. Their judgments are simply recommendations. To effectuate them, the representatives of the various member units of a COG must succeed in convincing their local governing bodies to carry out the proposals of the metropolitan organization. Subsequent supportive action by at least the principal local units must be attained (since each usually has authority in only part of a metropolis) if a COG decision is to be put into operation. Such an attainment is no easy accomplishment, particularly in instances where a proposal appears disadvantageous to them.

None of the councils has the power to levy taxes. Dues from member governments constitute their major local source of finances, and they are most frequently calculated on the basis of population, assessed valuation, or a flat rate. In some instances a combination of bases is employed, such as a mixture of population and assessed valuation, the largest units paying according to population and the others paying a flat rate, or the largest units paying a fixed percentage and the remainder paying according to population or assessed valuation.[18] In addition, more than half of the COGs have received federal grants for planning and other types of studies and for general administrative and staff support;[19] and in a few states, like Texas, the state government has made financial aid available.

The staff size of COGs varies tremendously. A number of them, due to limited budgets, have developed no professional staff structure beyond the executive director. At the other extreme, some have sizable staffs composed of an executive director, his deputy, planners, general and specialized key researchers and assistants, and secretarial and clerical personnel. For instance, the Washington Council of Governments has thirty-eight professionals and thirty-five clerical workers. Many executive directors are recruited from the ranks of city managers and municipal and regional planners.

[18] National Service to Regional Councils, *Summary of Questionnaires to Staff Directors of Regional Councils* (Washington: 1968), p. 5.
[19] International City Managers' Association, *Councils of Governments* (Washington: September, 1968), Management Information Service Report No. 296, p. 7.

THE COOPERATIVE APPROACH: THE FUTURE

The cooperative approach, as exemplified by both service agreements and metropolitan councils, is in a period of rapid growth that is characterized generally by sympathetic feelings toward the device. Expanding as a defense against more thorough methods, already discussed in the previous two chapters, and as a means of securing some integration in view of the general resistance to comprehensive approaches, cooperation is being promoted by a variety of individuals and organizations. Furthermore, a favorable image of cooperation has been fostered by making it a leading topic at local, state, and national conferences of governmental representatives and private citizens.

What is surprising about the cooperative technique is not that it has been receiving greatly increased use lately, but that its expansion did not come much earlier. Certainly it would be logical to expect that the most moderate method of attacking problems—one based on voluntary agreement and no major disturbance of existing governments in the metropolis—would have received widespread use when serious interlocal problems were initially developing extensively in the first third of the current century. But such was not the case. Equally astonishing is the fact that service agreements are still not in common use in most metropolitan areas. Even the mildest form of cooperation—mutual aid in emergencies—is not universally employed. For example, a tragedy in recent years in a southern California community, where a call about a drowning was rejected by a city rescue squad two minutes away from the scene because the home was a few feet outside the city limits, brought to light the complete absence of intermunicipal emergency aid agreements in that area covering such situations.

The piecemeal nature of service agreements—each normally concerned with only two governments and one service or facility—means that the device would have to be used extensively in order to produce an area-wide approach to needs and problems. Although a growing amount of interlocal contracting is taking place, it is only in rare instances that the total use of the method in relation to any function constitutes an area-wide solution to a difficulty. (Two significant exceptions are the multigovernmental sewage disposal agreements in effect in the Phoenix and San Diego metropolitan areas under which the central cities serve most or all the communities.) Even in Los Angeles County, where the greatest number of contracts involving a single government (the county) are in operation, the cooperative method has emerged in only a very few noncontroversial functions as an area-wide approach. The nationwide metropolitan pattern, therefore, is one of a limited number of governments reaching agreement about individual functions. The common result is a patchwork of agreements, usually relating to long-standing noncontroversial matters, and a lack of an overall design and system.

The severest limitation on interlocal agreements is found in their financial nature. In the overwhelming number of instances, they involve the provision of services for an exchange of money. But a number of local units in most metropolitan areas do not have the financial resources to contract and pay for certain services even when they are available on this basis. As the Cleveland Metropolitan Services Commission well stated the case in its final report:

. . . Since, for example, a contract assumes an exchange of values between the parties involved, this presumes that the receiver of the services has the financial means to make the required payment. A major part of the metropolitan service problem, however, arises as a result of service inadequacies in communities where there are insufficient resources for the task. An intergovernmental contract cannot very easily meet this type of difficulty.[20]

Because of the compensation requirement, service contracts generally will continue to be of restricted value. It is true that the use of such agreements would grow if more state laws (California, for instance, has one in the health field) were passed which required counties to perform certain services for cities at the request of the latter and without additional charge to them. The political controversy that would be generated by such legislative proposals and the probable confinement of such state-imposed service request arrangements to activities which counties already performed in unincorporated areas or as agents of the state (and thus have existing departments and personnel to handle) make it improbable that service agreements will increase significantly by this route.

The prospect is that at least in the years immediately ahead interlocal service agreements will continue to grow in number, mainly because of the rising pressure to deal with certain needs and problems and the lack of general appeal of more comprehensive methods. But it also appears likely that such agreements will remain ineffective for dealing with area-wide needs. Moreover, there seems to be little probability that many county governments soon will take on the role of major contract supplier as performed most prominently by the Los Angeles County government. Not very many of them are ready in terms of personnel, equipment, facilities, and programs to undertake this assignment.

The future for metropolitan councils, the other type of cooperation considered in this chapter, may be more promising. Two developments

[20] Cleveland Metropolitan Services Commission, *Prologue to Progress* (Cleveland: 1959), pp. 40–41.

in particular make this possible. First, the number and significance of contacts between local governments in a metropolitan area and the state and national governments are increasing and with them the realization is growing on the part of local officials of the need for a unified spokesman. The metropolitan council, which is multigovernmental in membership and outlook, can fill this area-wide role. Second, the state and national governments are becoming increasingly metropolis-conscious in preferring to deal with one organization and in attempting to foster a greater amount of interlocal coordination. Federal financial support to COGs (as well as to planning agencies of large geographical scope) and federal action in establishing a grant review procedure by an area-wide instrumentality illustrate such thinking. To an important degree, the national government is counting on metropolitan councils and regional planning organizations to bring about significant achievements.

A word of caution should be interjected at this point, however. Metropolitan councils are voluntary and advisory; thus governments can join and abandon them at will and council decisions are simply wishful thinking unless at least the major local governments in an area want to follow the recommendations. It therefore takes much continuing co-operation by many local governments, which may have quite divergent aspirations and interests, to make the council idea a success.

Councils of governments represent too new a metropolitan technique to make it possible to evaluate the movement with much precision, but the device has already generated sharply divided judgments about its usefulness. Although general agreement exists that COGs have produced increased intergovernmental communication and regional awareness, adherents of the idea feel this will lead to consensus and action while its detractors believe that talk will be the end result. Accordingly, on the one hand, COGs are seen as offering "one of the most productive means of translating plans into action for many of America's metropolitan areas," but on the other they are appraised as suffering "all the disadvantages of the United Nations approach to the solution of world problems."[21] (Conceivably, of course, both evaluations may be accurate, depending upon which particular councils are being included in the generalization.)

Royce Hanson, president of the Washington Center for Metropolitan Studies, summarized the trends to be watched for as this form of coopera-tive action develops:

In those areas where a functioning council of governments has been es-tablished . . . a new system of regional politics is emerging, or is likely to

---

[21] Zimmerman, "Metropolitan Ecumenism: The Road to the Promised Land?", pp. 454, 451.

emerge. If the federal government will back the legislative intent of section 204 [review of various federal grant applications by an area-wide agency], the councils of governments will become at the very least, a new arena for inter-governmental negotiations or program trade-offs among the various jurisdictions. The result could be a new regional politics based on negotiable programs, rather than a politics of functional isolation and technical monopoly exercised by autonomous agencies generating their own information and programs. If this occurs, and there is reason to believe that it can, we may see the emergence of political leaders with new kinds of skills in metropolitan diplomacy obtaining previously unreachable prizes for their local constituents.[22]

[22] Royce Hanson, "Councils of Governments and the Demise of Service Regionalism," (Speech, American Society for Public Administration Conference, Boston, March 29, 1968), pp. 6–7. Three articles dealing with different aspects of COGs—the job of executive director, the evolution of the organization, and the future of the movement—are featured in *Public Management,* 51 (January, 1969), 5–15.

14 /
THE POLITICS OF REFORM

THE POST-WORLD WAR II PERIOD HAS WITNESSED A RASH OF ATTEMPTS IN the United States (and in other nations as well) to adapt the political structure of metropolitan areas to contemporary needs. These efforts have ranged from simple tinkerings with internal administrative mechanisms to the creation of unified area-wide governments. The record of reform accomplishment has not been impressive; to some critics it has been dismally poor. What has emerged from the reorganization campaigns, however, is a greater awareness of the complexity of the problem and a reaction to the time-worn nostrums. As Luther Gulick, long a close observer of the metropolitan scene, described the change in perspective:

The answer is not as easy and simple as most American reformers thought as recently as five or ten years ago. When we first faced the problem of urban explosion it was natural to seek a solution of emerging governmental difficulties through the direct application of simple measures such as annexation

373

of the suburbs, consolidation, public utility extensions, and the simple direct
enlargement of the boundaries of the local general government. Where this
approach encountered difficulties, we turned to "authorities" and other special
districts and created state commissions without much thought as to where
this might lead us. Thus we met what we thought were simple problems with
simple, direct answers.[1]

The metropolitan problem, as traditionally formulated, was one of
relating sound engineering and administrative solutions to such matters
as sewage disposal, water supply, traffic congestion, and land use.
Economy and efficiency became the bywords of the reform movement, and
reshaping of the local bureaucratic machinery its avowed objective.
This seeming obsession with structural reorganization caused the proponents of change to deemphasize the metropolitan community as a
social and political system and to regard it merely as an administrative
mechanism for providing services. It was only gradually that the reformers came to view reorganization as a highly charged political question rather than an exercise in management efficiency.

Every proposal for redesigning the governmental pattern of an urban
area—whether in minimal fashion through cooperative devices or in more
fundamental ways, such as consolidation or the comprehensive urban
county plan—must at some point meet the test of political acceptability,
a test provided in some cases by popular referendum and in others by
the legislative bodies of the units involved. The very fact that the question is political requires it to be approached in a political manner and
not as a civic crusade for a new music hall or sports arena. Changes in
the governmental structure involve alterations in the division of power,
rewards, and labors. These changes may, and often do, jeopardize the
positions of local officials and employees, threaten the protective controls exercised by suburban units, affect the representation of different
constituencies, and modify the impact of taxes and services on various
groups. It is naive to expect a reorganization proposal to have such
overwhelming logic from the standpoint of efficiency or equity that
it can avoid attacks from those who perceive it as a threat to their interests.

BARRIERS TO CHANGE

Scott Greer, in his brief but incisive analysis of metropolitan civic
life, lists three groups of interrelated impediments to governmental restructuring: (1) the underlying cultural norms of Americans concern-

[1] *The Metropolitan Problem and American Ideas* (New York: Knopf, 1962),
p. 119.

ing local government; (2) the resulting legal-constitutional arrangements; and (3) the political-governmental system built upon them.[2] These relate, in one way or another, to the ideology and theory on which the American urban polity is based and to the attitudinal and value patterns of its citizenry.

The norms that have helped shape our system of local government are derivatives of Jeffersonian and Jacksonian ideologies. From Jefferson we inherited the "grass-roots" concept of government and the distrust of those who exercise the powers of office. His ideas on local government were always couched in terms of the small community of educated yeomen rather than the large city with its teeming populace. To him, the New England town with its meetings of all the citizenry was "the wisest invention ever devised by the wit of man for the perfect exercise of self-government and for its preservation." Jacksonians, too, stressed the "sacred right" of local self-rule, but unlike their aristocratic predecessors, they welcomed the urban masses to share in the function of government. Public office was opened to all on the premise that any citizen of normal intelligence could satisfactorily manage the affairs of his city or county. Rotation in office, popular election of numerous officials, and the spoils system became standard features of local government during the second half of the nineteenth century.

The municipal reform movement, at the turn of the present century, was a repudiation of Jacksonian practices but not of its grass-roots ideology. To combat the corruption of city politics, the reformers offered the short ballot, professional management, nonpartisan elections, and the initiative, referendum, and recall, which exposed the governmental system to the direct action or veto of the voter. The inherent right of the community to govern itself free from undue interference by the state legislature, a right implicit in both Jeffersonian and Jacksonian theory, was also institutionalized during this period by state constitutional and statutory provisions relating to municipal "home rule." These enactments supplemented the earlier guarantees of local self-determination, which included generous incorporation laws for the indiscriminate creation of municipalities. They were also accompanied by difficult annexation requirements permitting intransigent groups of fringe area dwellers to remain outside the corporate citadel and by legal conditions making it virtually impossible to consolidate or eliminate existing governmental units. So deeply entrenched in American folklore are the norms which these measures purport to safeguard that those who attempt to alter the system must be prepared to face charges of removing government from the people, infringing on basic human rights, and destroying local self-rule.

[2] *Governing the Metropolis* (New York: Wiley, 1962), pp. 124–125.

The political-governmental pattern that has evolved at the local level, grounded as it is on these norms and beliefs, stands as a formidable obstacle to change. Cloaked in the protective mantle of statutory and constitutional legitimacy and defended by the entrenched bureaucracy, the system has managed to maintain itself without submitting to major surgery. Any alteration of significance is viewed as a threat to the "establishment" and its retinue of followers. Few incumbent officeholders or others who benefit from existing arrangements are willing to gamble on possible gains that a reordered structure might bring them. Similarly, those who aspire to the rewards of local public office are willing to play the game within the existing system and according to its rules. The local "establishment," moreover, holds a strategic weapon for defending its stronghold against attack. Unlike the reformers who have no ready-made machine for mobilizing support, it has access to political cadres and mass-based organizations that serve as important reference points for voters.

It would be wholly erroneous, however, to assume that metropolitan reorganization represents a battle between the enlightened and un-selfish on one side and the ignorant and self-seeking on the other. The tendency of many reformers, and even some academic writers, to con-ceptualize the issue in these simple and moralistic terms has handicapped the movement by divorcing it from reality. It has also impeded under-standing the forces and factors which are brought into play when gov-ernmental changes are sought. Reorganization involves not only jobs and rewards but, more importantly, value differences among groups and individuals in the metropolitan complex. As we observed in the preceding chapter, urban dwellers are particularly sensitive to any arrangements, even those of a cooperative nature, which might diminish their control over public services and regulatory devices related to the maintenance of their life styles. In this light, the notion that voter re-jection of seemingly rational proposals for metropolitan restructuring is due to ignorance or misunderstanding requires considerable qualifi-cation.

WHO GETS INVOLVED

In a large-scale society, individuals acting alone are handicapped in affecting collective behavior. It is primarily through organizational membership that they enlarge their opportunities and resources to in-fluence social action. Hence, the question of who gets involved in metropolitan reform efforts pertains less to the individual actors than to the groups or associations of which they are a part. To answer the question, it is necessary to ascertain what kinds of organizations become active either as proponents or opponents, and why they become involved. We need not throw our net wide in this inquiry since the active participants in metropolitan reform campaigns have constituted a relatively minor segment of the organized populace.

Although there are exceptions, the lineup of key supporters and adversaries has been strikingly similar from area to area. Among the groups usually favoring change are alliances of top businessmen, central city chambers of commerce, civic or good government associations, such as the League of Women Voters, and the metropolitan press. Commonly in the ranks of the opposition are suburban officials and employees, suburban newspapers, farmers, and right-wing organizations, such as the John Birch Society. Central city and county government officials are found in both camps, depending on the nature of the proposal and local peculiarities. The same may be said of the political parties and labor unions although the tendency is for them to avoid active participation.

The Initiators

Much of the impetus for metropolitan reorganization has come from the top business leadership of the area acting through either the central city chamber of commerce or more exclusive organizations. The prime movers in the Dade County restructuring, for example, were the *Miami Herald* and the central city businessmen who were unhappy with rising taxes. In Cleveland, the economic notables provided the initiative for the urban county plan presented to the voters in 1959; in Nashville, the chamber of commerce was instrumental in securing the enabling legislation to permit the drafting of a city-county consolidation charter; and in Jacksonville, Florida, it was also the chamber of commerce, disturbed by inefficient government and the slow rate of the area's growth, that spearheaded the consolidation movement.

Variations from the common pattern do take place, as in the 1959 metropolitan district effort in St. Louis where the original impetus came from a young and politically ambitious central city alderman (now mayor), A. J. Cervantes, who was looking for a "live" issue to promote his candidacy for president of the city council. In his words:

It had all started when I tried to get three councilmen each from the City and County together to do something about traffic problems. A reporter told me about this constitutional possibility, and I started the move for a new City-County charter. I called a meeting at Medart's Restaurant in April of 1955. I got the labor guys, the politicians, the Teamsters, and others out, and we formed the Citizens Committee for City-County Consolidation. The Teamsters helped out, and we got out our petitions.[3]

[3] Quoted in Scott Greer, *Metropolitics: A Study of Political Culture* (New York: Wiley, 1963), p. 38.

However, exceptions such as this are rare and serve only to emphasize the fact that the reform initiative or push has come predominately from the nonpolitical sectors of the community and from groups without mass-based support.

Civic and Business Organizations

The civic groups which have evidenced a concern with the governmental structure and processes of the metropolis are, in a sense, heirs of the municipal reform spirit and philosophy of the early 1900s. They began to turn their attention to the larger community as central cities became better governed and the critical urban problems outgrew individual corporate boundaries. Gradually, over the years, metropolitan reorganization came to occupy the place on the civic agenda that municipal reform held earlier.

The interests of the social and economic influentials were channeled into the metropolitan reform field largely by the professionals who staff the key civic organizations, by concerned political scientists, and by the promptings of the National Municipal League, the patriarch of the good government groups. Few of the notables who support such movements are motivated by prospects of personal gain. Some feel that reorganization will result in a better business and industrial climate, but most act out of a sense of *noblesse oblige*. As persons of civic reputation and stature, they have a feeling of responsibility for the well-being and governance of the area. Metropolitan reform provides them with a respected outlet for meeting this obligation. However, the role, as they see it, does not necessarily imply personal involvement; more often, it means legitimizing the issue as worthy of community support. The actual task of carrying the campaign forward is generally left to the professional staffs and younger aspirants in the group, to public relations hirelings, and to the workhorse civic organizations such as the League of Women Voters.

One element of the business community, the downtown interests, has a more personal stake in metropolitan reorganization. Concerned with the economic position of the central business district, many merchants and property owners feel that area-wide governmental change may in some way aid the center by giving it greater prominence in a reconstituted polity. In the Miami area, the downtown groups pushed vigorously for metropolitan government, seeing in it a means of relieving the tax pressure on property in the core city by spreading the base over a larger area. Central city or metropolitan chambers of commerce serve as the organizational mechanism for articulating and executing the support of these interests.

Aside from the nebulous prospect of direct economic gain for their members, chambers of commerce are ideologically disposed to regard such movements with favor. The "booster" spirit which permeates their operations finds expression in the gospel of "a bigger and better community." Most of the groups see metropolitan restructuring as a symbolic aid in promoting the image of a progressive community, one distinguished by civic vitality and modernized government. Typical was the plea in the Dade County charter campaign: "Give Miami a chance to be a big city." This view of metropolitan aggrandizement through governmental integration is not shared by the suburban chambers of commerce and the local merchants they represent. To them, reorganization means a loss or diminution of their influence over the public affairs of the suburbs in which they operate.

The Press

The daily newspapers in the central city are usually staunch advocates of metropolitan reform, although on a few occasions, as in the Jacksonville-Duval County consolidation, their close relationship to the city political machine may lead them to take an opposing position. Their role has been primarily one of lending editorial and news support to reform efforts or of prodding the civic elite into action.[4] As organs with an area-wide audience and outlook, they are attracted to metropolitan reorganization as an appropriate cause for their crusading zeal. And by championing the vision of the larger community, they can fulfill their role expectations as "integrative" symbols of the metropolis.

In contrast to the large dailies, the suburban community press is almost always opposed to major change in the existing system. Long characterized by bias against the central city and an equally strong anti-metropolitan press attitude, the suburban papers find area-wide reorganization measures useful targets. By picturing such proposals as the products of central city politicians or of "undesirable" elements seeking to invade suburbia, they can pose as protectors of small-community virtues. Metropolitan reorganization gives them an opportunity to launch a "safe" crusade of the type they can rarely afford on local issues for fear of alienating some of their readership. As locally based and locally oriented instrumentalities dependent on the business advertising of the village merchants and the subscriptions of residents in their limited area, they feel a personal stake in keeping the existing governmental system intact. The fiction of small community autonomy is a strong legitimizer for their

---

[4] Occasionally, as in the Dade County charter campaign in 1957, the newspapers play a more direct role. There the associate editor of the *Miami Herald* was a key strategist and major participant in the movement. Since the mass-based organizations, such as political parties and labor unions, are relatively weak in that area, Miami newspapers enjoy considerable influence as a referent for voters on local public issues. On this point, see Thomas J. Wood, "Dade County: Unbossed, Erratically Led," *Annals of the American Academy of Political and Social Science,* 353 (May, 1964), 64–71.

existence. Any movement which threatens to undermine this fiction or lessen the importance of the suburban governments is a cause for battle.

The Local Bureaucracy

Wherever a "going system" of local government exists, we can expect it to react against radical transformation. If it did not, it could hardly be called a system. We can thus generalize that incumbent officeholders will usually be found in the camp of the opposition. There are, of course, many exceptions, some of them significant. The city manager of Miami, the county engineer of Cuyahoga County, the president of the St. Louis Board of Aldermen, the mayors of Nashville and Memphis, all supported metropolitan reorganization efforts in their areas. In each instance, however, the incumbent could see in the proposed reform an opportunity to extend his sphere of control or obtain other rewards. The Nashville mayor, for example, supported the first city-county consolidation effort in 1959 when he was regarded as the most likely choice for the proposed new office of metropolitan chief executive, but he strongly opposed the successful 1962 movement at a time when he had become the target of intense political opposition because of Nashville's vigorous annexation policy.[5]

In the past, central city officials generally supported total merger, viewing such action as an enlargement of the municipality's boundaries and hence an enhancement of its political powers. Conversely, they usually reacted in a negative fashion when lesser remedies were proposed, such as federation or multipurpose metropolitan districts, which would reduce the powers of the core municipality. The Cleveland mayor's action in opposing the 1959 charter referendum on a comprehensive urban county plan was typical; he took this position purportedly because several important facilities, such as the water works and airport, would be taken out of city control. His two department heads who had the most to lose in the way of functions and powers were the most effective campaigners among the opposition.[6]

Today, the tendency is for even central city officials and political leaders to oppose merger. This solution now involves the risk that con-

[5] The Nashville experience is analyzed in David A. Booth, *Metropolitics: The Nashville Consolidation* (East Lansing: Michigan State University Institute for Community Development and Service, 1963); Daniel R. Grant, "Metropolitics and Professional Political Leadership: The Case of Nashville," *Annals of the American Academy of Political and Social Science*, 353 (May, 1964), 72–83; and Brett W. Hawkins, *Nashville Metro: The Politics of City-County Consolidation* (Nashville: Vanderbilt University Press, 1966).

[6] The background of the Cleveland charter attempt is described in James A. Norton, *The Metro Experience* (Cleveland: The Press of Western Reserve University, 1963). Also see Matthew Holden, Jr., "Decision-Making on a Metropolitan Governmental Proposal," in Scott Greer, Dennis McElrath, David Minar, and Peter Orleans (eds.), *The New Urbanization* (New York: St. Martin's Press, 1968), pp. 315–338.

trol may shift to the periphery where the suburban population of many SMSAs is rapidly approaching or exceeding that of the core. The 1962 merger attempt in St. Louis elicited such a political response, with the Democratic city committee going on record against the proposal by a vote of fifty-three to one and the board of aldermen by twenty-one to three. The likelihood of this kind of reaction is greatest in areas where the politics of the central city is predominantly Democratic and that of the suburbs Republican.

Suburban officialdom stands solidly against any major restructuring of the existing system. Only an occasional mayor of an upper socioeconomic community will support a metropolitan multipurpose district or other reform measure short of consolidation. Not uncommonly suburban officials express their willingness to have "true" metropolitan functions handled on a unified basis. Such a function, as they conceive it, is one which they badly need but cannot perform for themselves because of cost. Water supply and sewage disposal are two common examples. In such cases, officials of the affected communities will usually acquiesce in the assumption of the service by the county government or the creation of a metropolitan single-purpose district to handle it. This kind of area-wide administration finds acceptance because it involves little or no loss of power for the local units and wards off the possible danger of more drastic changes by taking care of the most immediate and troublesome deficiencies.

Other Actors

Political parties are at times found among the participants in the reform drama but their involvement has seldom been great. In relatively few of the campaigns during the last decade have they taken an official stand on a reorganization proposal. Party regulars at the ward, township, and state legislative district levels in some instances have utilized the organizational machinery in their bailiwicks to mobilize support or opposition, usually the latter, but the extensiveness of these activities has varied from area to area. Individual political leaders have also taken public positions on the issue, but few have used their political "muscle" to influence the outcome. Neither the reorganization issue nor the potential rewards of an altered system seem to provide sufficient motivation for this kind of commitment. Moreover, the insignificant amount of patronage at the municipal level and the widespread use of nonpartisan elections contribute to this result by dampening party interest in local governmental affairs. Ironically, these two major accomplishments of municipal reformers now seriously impede the efforts of the metropolitan reformers.

Organized labor is frequently found among the participants in reorganization campaigns, but the degree of its involvement ranges only from token endorsement or opposition to moderate activity. Like the political parties, labor does not consider its stake in the outcome sufficiently great to warrant substantial expenditures of its resources. Its position and the extent of its activity in each case will be dictated largely by the possible effects of the proposed restructuring on existing political arrangements and coalitions. If the influence of those officials or political groups with which it has established working relationships will be expanded by the change, labor is likely to favor the movement; if the interests of these groups is threatened, it will probably join the opposition. In neither case, however, is it likely to make large-scale commitments of energy and resources.

TABLE 25   **Anti-Reorganization Vote by Negroes in Duval (Jacksonville) and Hillsborough (Tampa) Counties, 1967**

Precincts by Percent Negro	Duval		Hillsborough	
	CITY	SUBURBS	CITY	SUBURBS
Less than 5%	31.8%	38.4%	56.4%	89.6%
5–24	42.1	41.3	71.8	91.0
25–49	37.5	58.8	79.6	95.8
50–94	42.4	52.0	84.2	—
95–100	41.5	35.3	89.8	89.5

SOURCE: Adapted from P. N. Glendening and J. W. White, "Local Government Reorganization Referenda in Florida: An Acceptance and a Rejection," *Florida State University Governmental Research Bulletin*, 5 (March, 1968), 3.

The Negroes are another group that has become of increasing importance in reorganization issues. For the most part, Negro political leaders look with disfavor on efforts to reorder the system. Their base of operation and strength lies in the central city. An area-wide government poses a threat to their hard-won and long-in-coming major political influence by joining the predominantly white electorate of suburbia to that of the core municipality. It is not surprising, therefore, that both the comprehensive urban county charter in Cleveland and the multipurpose district plan in St. Louis drew heavy opposition from the nonwhite wards. In fact, the heavy opposition in the Negro districts of Cleveland, where 70 percent of the vote was negative, contributed importantly to the proposal's defeat.[7] The campaigns in 1967 for city-county consolidation

[7] A statistical study of the vote on metropolitan reform issues in Cleveland over a period of years revealed that the attitude of Negroes toward area-wide reorganization became more negative as their political strength increased in the central city. See Richard A. Watson and John H. Romani, "Metropolitan Government for Metropolitan Cleveland: An Analysis of the Voting Record," *Midwest Journal of Political Science*, V (November, 1961), 365–390.

in two Florida areas, Jacksonville-Duval County and Tampa-Hillsborough County, further illustrate this point. In the former, a majority of the Negroes supported the proposed charter which called for 14 of the 19 members on the new council to be chosen by districts instead of the existing system of election-at-large employed in both the city and county; in the latter, blacks voted solidly (almost 9 to 1) against a plan under which all 13 seats (8 with district residency requirements) on the consolidated governing body were to be filled by countywide elections (Table 25).

THE ISSUES

As with the lineup of participants, the issues in metropolitan reorganization campaigns have followed a common pattern. Proponents of change have almost invariably rested their case on grounds of efficiency and economy. Aiming their fire at overlapping jurisdictions, governmental fragmentation, confusion of responsibility, outmoded administrative structures, and uncoordinated growth, they have consistently emphasized the theme that problems which are metropolitan in scope and impact demand handling by an agency with area-wide authority. In their campaigns they have stressed the general advantages to be gained from reorganization: improved services, more efficient administration, coordinated planning, more equitable distribution of costs and benefits, and better representation. Supporters of the St. Louis district plan in 1959, for example, pointed to the inability of individual local governments to cope with area-wide problems, such as traffic and transportation; the stifling effects of the existing system on the economic progress of the area, and the need for overall guidance and direction in planning the total community.[8]

The opponents of metropolitan restructuring have similarly capitalized on common themes. Two of their most effective arguments have been higher taxes and the destruction of grass-roots government. Adversaries of consolidation in Nashville, Memphis, Tampa, and elsewhere contended that the change would result in tax increases, bigger government, and the loss of individual rights. Other frequently advanced arguments run along these lines: the objectives of the plan could be fulfilled by less drastic changes within the existing governmental framework; the proposal is unconstitutional and would involve the new unit in extended and costly litigation; and the present system is performing adequately.

Those pressing for change are normally at a disadvantage in answering the arguments of the opposition. The difficulties which the metropolis

[8] The St. Louis effort is examined in Henry J. Schmandt, Paul G. Steinbicker, and George D. Wendel, *Metropolitan Reform in St. Louis* (New York: Holt, Rinehart and Winston, 1961); and Greer, *Metropolitics: A Study of Political Culture.*

faces are not easily comprehensible. Because of this complexity neither the problems nor the possible remedies can be articulated in simple and readily understandable terms. To the charge of higher taxes, the reformers can only respond that reorganization will result in better services. To the plea "keep government close to the people," they can only speak of the more desirable environment and brighter future the proposed change will presumably assure. To the challenge, "show the people why the system which has served them for so long should be discarded," the proponents can only reply with generalized and vague statements about efficiency, orderly growth, and future dangers, or with arguments so complex that their significance often escapes the average citizen. As one Cleveland official remarked in telling of the advantage he had in fighting the proposed comprehensive urban county charter, "I'd say to them, 'Say, what's wrong with the present situation? You've got a good government. What's wrong? Show me.' "[9]

The Political Dimension

The municipal reformers of the early 1900s had simplified the issue of governmental reorganization for the voters by attacking corruption and machine politics, and effectively utilizing the battle cry of "throw the rascals out." Charges of this nature have much less relevance today with the demise of machine politics in most cities, the professionalization of the local civil service, and the use of competitive bidding for contracts. Yet it is interesting to note that in each of the three major reorganization successes since 1950—Miami-Dade County, Nashville-Davidson County, and Jacksonville-Duval County—the issue of corruption or machine politics played a part.

Miami city politics, at the time of the 1957 charter movement, had been marked by considerable in-fighting among council members and by recurring charges of corruption. In particular, the police department had been under fire for its alleged failure to enforce the laws against gambling and other forms of vice. In contrast, the county government was generally well regarded and free from any taint of corruption. These circumstances enabled proponents to juxtapose the "good" county against the "evil" city government.[10]

In Nashville, several events, fortuitous to the 1962 consolidation proposal, occurred after the defeat of the first effort four years earlier. Following the initial rejection of the merger charter, the city of Nashville took two steps that were deeply resented by suburban residents. First, it adopted a ten dollar "green sticker" tax on automobiles to be paid by

[9] Quoted in Greer, *Metropolitics: A Study of Political Culture*, p. 16.
[10] The Miami reorganization movement is documented in Edward Sofen, *The Miami Metropolitan Experiment* (Bloomington: Indiana University Press, 1963). Also see Ross C. Beiler and Thomas J. Wood, "Metropolitan Politics of Miami," (Paper delivered at annual meeting of Southern Political Science Association, Gatlinburg, Tennessee, November 7, 1958).

all city residents and all other persons whose automobiles used city streets during more than thirty days a year. Second, taking advantage of the strong annexation powers granted by the Tennessee legislature in 1955, the city moved quickly to more than triple its territorial size. Without a vote in the affected sections, it annexed seven square miles of largely industrial land in 1958, soon after the consolidation referendum, and forty-two square miles of residential area with over 82,000 residents in 1960 (Figure 48). Among other effects, the two annexations drastically reduced the road tax revenue of the county government and created serious financial difficulties for the schools which remained outside the city.

These moves by the city administration resulted in the organization of

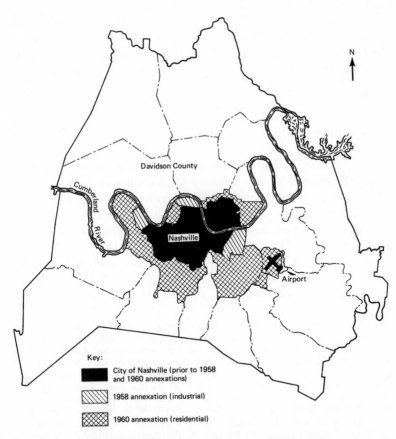

FIGURE 48   **Former City Limits of Nashville and Annexations of 1958 and 1960. Adapted from David A. Booth,** Metropolitics: The Nashville Consolidation, **Institute for Community Development and Service, Michigan State University, 1963, p. 74.**

another charter commission and the presentation of a second consolidation plan to the voters. The Nashville mayor, Ben West, knowing that a victory for the charter forces would be a serious blow to his political career, brought the full weight of his organization into the fray. City employees were mobilized for the fight and police and firemen, as well as school teachers, were used to distribute anticonsolidation literature. These activities enabled the *Tennessean,* one of the two metropolitan dailies in the area, to hit hard at the "city machine" theme and, in the process, reiterate earlier charges of "police corruption" and poor law enforcement.

The Jacksonville-Duval merger in 1967 took place at a time when the local political machine was seriously discredited by exposures of corruption among city and county officeholders. News telecasts of irregularities in purchasing practices and other governmental activities had led to a grand jury investigation and the indictment of eleven officials on various charges, including bribery. How important the corruption issue was in determining the outcome of the referendum in this or the other cases is a matter of speculation. But as two of the consolidation leaders in the Nashville movement observed, it is necessary to wage a "political" rather than a "community project" campaign in order to win, and such a campaign demands a "devil."[11]

VOTER RESPONSE

Citizen apathy is a factor frequently cited as a major impediment to metropolitan reform. As the Advisory Commission on Intergovernmental Relations, after surveying eighteen major reorganization plans submitted to popular referendum between 1950 and 1961, flatly stated: "Proposals for governmental reorganization in metropolitan areas have faced a largely apathetic public."[12] The commission found that in fourteen of these cases less than 30 percent of the voting-age population bothered to cast their ballot on the issue (Table 26). However, as the study further demonstrates, the eighteen efforts offer no evidence that increased activity at the

---

[11] Hawkins, *Nashville Metro: The Politics of City-County Consolidation,* p. 80. One observer, in contrasting the two Nashville efforts, noted that in the second campaign: "It was as if the professionals and the politicians had taken over from the amateurs and do-gooders." Booth, *Metropolitics: The Nashville Consolidation,* p. 85. The highly political nature of metropolitan reorganization is also illustrated by the city-county consolidation now taking place in Indianapolis and Marion County. There the merger was accomplished by act of the Republican-dominated state legislature at the urging of the Republican mayor of Indianapolis, the first of his party to occupy the office since 1955. The consolidation will enhance the opportunity for continued Republican control because of the party's traditional strength outside the central city.

[12] *Factors Affecting Voter Reaction to Governmental Reorganization in Metropolitan Areas* (Washington: May, 1962), p. 24.

polls necessarily assures adoption of a proposal; some of the plans obtained a favorable majority with a rather limited turnout of voters, and some lost in spite of a relatively high percentage of participation. Referenda which have taken place since the commission study continue to show the same mixed pattern. For instance, 40 percent of the registered voters cast ballots in the successful Nashville consolidation of 1962 while 53 percent participated in the defeated Memphis-Shelby County merger the same year. (Registered voters, of course, constitute a somewhat smaller base than voting-age population.)

TABLE 26   Referendum Vote as Percent of Voting-Age Population in Eighteen Metropolitan Reorganization Elections

Percent Voting	Number of Referenda
40–45	2
35–39	0
30–34	2
25–29	5
20–24	4
15–19	3
10–14	2

SOURCE: Advisory Commission on Intergovernmental Relations, *Factors Affecting Voter Reactions to Governmental Reorganization in Metropolitan Areas* (Washington: May, 1962), p. 71.

Some observers have speculated that a small turnout is advantageous to reorganization elections since persons of higher social rank are more likely to participate and since they tend to favor change. This, however, is a dubious assumption as the above figures indicate. The Miami survey, in like vein, found no important difference between the high- and low-status precincts in voter turnout on the charter issue. A similar finding was made in St. Louis where the proportion of those who voted on the district plan did not differ significantly among the various social ranks. One explanation for this deviation from the general pattern of voting behavior is found in the more intensive organizational activity displayed by opponents at the grassroots level. This activity, coupled with lack of concern by many people in the higher socioeconomic categories, leads to a disproportionate turnout of lower-status voters in reorganization elections.

Whatever the validity of these observations, one should not place too great significance on voter apathy in reorganization matters. Local elections in general, and issue referenda in particular, seldom draw high percentages of the citizenry to the polls. As numerous studies reveal, the turnout at municipal and school district elections is consistently below that for national and state contests. The indifference to reform measures (as to other local referenda questions) is due in some instances to the absence of a really critical situation to be remedied; in others, it results from a failure to recognize a problem of serious consequence; and in still others, it prevails because the proposed change is not perceived by the individual as relevant to his interests or concerns.

TABLE 27   Citizen Evaluation of Local Governmental Services, Cleveland Metropolitan Area, 1958

Service	Percent Completely Satisfied	Percent Partly Satisfied	Percent Not at All Satisfied	Percent No Opinion
Water service	90	6	2	2
Fire protection	89	7	1	3
Public health	72	13	4	11
Police protection	70	22	7	1
School	67	22	6	5
Sewer services	64	17	13	6
Public welfare	61	15	5	19
Main thoroughfares	55	27	14	4
Bus and transit	40	24	28	8

SOURCE: James A. Norton, *The Metro Experience* (Cleveland: The Press of Western Reserve University, 1963), p. 61.

Another important reason for the apparent indifference toward major structural change is that many urban dwellers are fairly well satisfied with their local governments and the services they are dispensing. Surveys in both St. Louis and Dayton showed that residents in those areas had no strong criticism of any of their governments and few complaints about services.[13] In St. Louis, only one unit among the 149 was considered to be performing poorly by as many as 10 percent of the residents—and ironi-

[13] John C. Bollens (ed.), *Exploring the Metropolitan Community* (Berkeley and Los Angeles: University of California Press, 1961), pp. 188–190; and *Metropolitan Challenge* (Dayton: Metropolitan Community Studies, 1959), pp. 241–251. Similar findings were made in a study of suburban governments in the Philadelphia area. See Charles E. Gilbert, *Governing the Suburbs* (Bloomington: Indiana University Press, 1967), pp. 272–275.

cally, this was the sewer district, an area-wide agency. In Dayton, only about one of each ten persons felt that his local government was performing inefficiently or was unresponsive to the people. Less than one-half the residents had even registered a complaint or even felt like complaining about a local governmental service. Almost 60 percent could name no more than one service with which they were dissatisfied. Similar results were obtained in a group of Wisconsin communities. Only a relatively small number (less than 20 percent) of the citizens said that their local governments were inefficient or the performance of their public officials poor.[14] The story was the same in Cleveland, as Table 27 clearly demonstrates. These are relevant findings since, as Hawkins' Nashville study indicates, support for reorganization is greater among voters dissatisfied with services than among those satisfied.[15] Whether the recent disturbances in many cities will affect these attitudes is a question that must await further study.

Voter Ignorance

A second factor often pointed to as an obstacle to area-wide restructuring is the unfamiliarity of many citizens with metropolitan issues. The authors of a study of voter attitudes in the Flint (Michigan) SMSA, for example, concluded that resistance to governmental unification rests largely upon ignorance of local government and what to expect from it.[16] A sampling of residents in Cuyahoga County several weeks before the charter election in 1959 revealed that one of every three persons did not remember reading or hearing anything about the proposed new document despite the extensive publicity that had been given to it. More than three-fourths of the people could not name a single reason advanced for or against the charter.[17] Similarly, a survey in the St. Louis area after the 1959 metropolitan district referendum showed in convincing terms that the voters knew little about the issue and those who were involved in the campaign. In 40 percent of the cases, leaders mentioned by the interviewees as supporters of the plan were publicly on record as opposed to it.[18]

Transmitting to the electorate the complex issues inherent in governmental reorganization of the metropolis is an extremely difficult, if not impossible, task. Change of this type does not ordinarily give rise to the

---

[14] Henry J. Schmandt and William Standing, *Citizen Images of the Fox River Valley* (Madison: University of Wisconsin Survey Research Laboratory, 1962), p. 13.

[15] *Nashville Metro: The Politics of City-County Consolidation*, p. 109.

[16] Amos H. Hawley and Basil G. Zimmer, "Resistance to Unification in a Metropolitan Community," in Morris Janowitz (ed.), *Community Political Systems* (New York: Free Press, 1961), pp. 173–174.

[17] Greer, *Metropolitics: A Study of Political Culture*, p. 189.

[18] *Ibid*, p. 101.

use of effective and attention-capturing symbols. Thus, as Greer describes the recent campaigns, they proceeded behind a massive facade of logical argument:

> Seldom have so many thorny problems, involving theoretical and empirical unknowns, been aired on the front page of the daily papers. Seldom have so many businessmen, lawyers, elected officials, politicians, administrators, and League ladies taken public stands on abstract and difficult issues. Seldom have so few worked so hard and succeeded in confusing so many.[19]

Caught in a crossfire of conflicting and abstract arguments, and with the groups to which he normally looks for guidance on public issues silent or only slightly involved, the average voter is frequently confused and uncertain in reorganization elections.

The evidence does indicate that voters who support metropolitan reform tend to be drawn from the upper socioeconomic categories. In the Miami SMSA, the precincts highest on the social scale favored the charter most strongly while those at the bottom gave it the least support. The Nashville and St. Louis findings were the same: the higher the level of an individual's education and income, the more likely he was to be favorably disposed toward the proposed change. We would normally expect the better-educated voter to be more familiar with the issues and more likely to be persuaded by the rationality of reformist arguments. However, a survey of Nashville area voters after the successful charter election found only partial support for the assumption that lack of knowledge is an impediment to reorganization. As the author speculated, ignorance is manipulable and can go either way.[20]

Other Factors

Socioeconomic status is by no means the only relevant variable in explaining voter response to reorganization proposals.[21] According to one analysis, the combined effect of income, education, and occupation accounts for less than half the variation in the voting.[22] What is also of importance is the nature of the proposed change and the place of residence of the elector. Central city dwellers of high social rank are more likely than their suburban counterparts to support a plan calling for complete consolidation. The same is generally true of lower-income city

[19] *Ibid,* p. 193.

[20] Hawkins, *Nashville Metro: The Politics of City-County Consolidation,* p. 217.

[21] For example, interviews with a sample of suburban residents in Nashville showed that political alienation was significantly related to an unfavorable attitude and negative vote on the consolidation issue. See J. E. Horton and W. E. Thompson, "Powerlessness and Political Negativism: A Study of Defeated Local Referendums," *American Journal of Sociology,* LXVIII (March, 1962), 485–493.

[22] Watson and Romani, "Metropolitan Government for Metropolitan Cleveland," pp. 382–385.

residents (holding race constant) as compared to suburbanites in the same status category. The St. Louis merger attempt, for example, lost by only a slight margin in the central city but was rejected by over four to one in the outlying area. Upper-income suburbs that had supported the earlier and more moderate district proposal voted heavily against a plan which would have destroyed the political autonomy of their communities. The findings in an attitudinal survey of fringe area dwellers in the Grand Rapids (Michigan) SMSA run in the same direction. There the desire for better services play only a slight role in determining the position of suburbanites toward integration. Proposals involving loss of identity were predominantly less popular than others. As the author concluded, the desire to maintain local autonomy persuades fringe residents to tolerate more inefficiency and waste than many civic reformers deem desirable.[23]

THE POLITICS OF COOPERATION

The discussion thus far has dealt only with the politics of reorganization proposals that almost always must be submitted to the electorate. But politics, although not as visible or intense, are also involved in the efforts of local governments to adapt to changing urban needs through cooperative devices, which require no popular vote. Social distance, for example, is essentially a political factor which influences the choice of partners in joint ventures. As we observed earlier (Chapter 13), communities tend to enter into agreements with their status equivalents more than with those of dissimilar characteristics.[24] They also assiduously avoid contractual commitments in matters of life-style significance. As a recent study in the Detroit area shows, cooperation among municipalities rarely occurs for functions with social implications, such as zoning, planning, housing, and urban renewal.[25] Nor does it take place in instances where the arrangement would result in a redistribution of resources.

The initiative for interlocal cooperation comes primarily from four sources: citizen groups; businessmen, including developers and real estate interests; federal and stage agencies; and local officials and administrators

[23] Charles Press, "Efficiency and Economy Arguments for Metropolitan Reorganization," *Public Opinion Quarterly*, XXVIII (Winter, 1963), 584–594.

[24] The assumption that social class differences between central city and suburbs constitute a major barrier to integrative measures is questioned in a recent statistical analysis of forty-two metropolitan referenda. The data suggest that as life style differences (based on social rank and familism) increasingly favor the suburbs, there is an increasing tendency for voters in these areas to support some type of political integration, even consolidation. See Brett W. Hawkins, "Fringe-City Life-Style Distance and Fringe Support of Political Integration," *American Journal of Sociology*, LXXIV (November, 1968), 248–255. These results, however, run counter to the overwhelming bulk of available evidence.

[25] Vincent L. Marando, "Inter-Local Cooperation in a Metropolitan Area," *Urban Affairs Quarterly*, IV (December, 1968), 185–200.

—most often the last. The move may be prompted by dissatisfaction with a particular service; by the fiscal or jurisdictional inability of a unit to provide unilaterally a needed function or build a necessary facility; by the intent of local authorities to head off pressures for governmental reorganization; or by the desire of elected policy-makers or the professional administrators to achieve more efficient and economical operation of specific activities. Occasionally, but not often, a local public official will see political or career opportunities in championing the cooperative cause. A Detroit city councilman was the moving force behind the creation of the Supervisors Inter-County Committee, the nation's first COG; and in Salem, Oregon, the city manager was instrumental in establishing the widely-publicized Mid-Willamette Valley Council of Governments.

Unlike reorganization movements, which generate conflict among the affected groups and interests, interlocal cooperation is normally the result of careful negotiation and a meeting of the minds on the part of all concerned. This process can best be conceptualized in terms of a bargaining model in which each of the parties seeks to advance its interests at the least cost to itself. The politics involved are largely of a consensual nature and the strategies employed are similar to those utilized in economic transactions. Also unlike metropolitan reform efforts, which usually encompass more than one function or entail the loss of local control over a service (as in functional consolidation), cooperative arrangements relate predominantly to only one field of concern and involve no relinquishment of power. This focus on a single substantive area limits the actors who take part in the endeavor. Aside from the "good government" groups that traditionally support all efficiency and economy movements, a cooperative effort will activate only those elites and others who happen to be interested or have a stake in the specific subject of negotiation. Thus if the proposal is for the establishment of a common data-processing center, the only concerned parties will likely be the department heads and officials of the individual governmental units; or if the plan relates to the joint operation of a hospital facility, the major participants, other than local officials, will be the medical society and interested physicians. By narrowing the field of actors in this way, trade-offs of benefits and costs are more easily negotiated and settlement reached.

In proportion to the countless opportunities for meaningful joint undertakings among local governments, the number which are in effect is remarkably small. This situation is at least partially attributable to political factors. Suburban units are reluctant to enter into contracts with the central city, even when it is to their advantage to do so, for fear of establishing ties or a dependency relationship that might jeopardize their autonomous status. Central cities, in turn, are often unwilling to extend services, such as water, to the outlying communities so as not to strengthen the latter's ability to compete for industry. Even among themselves, suburban communities are more inclined to develop their own bureaucratic establishments for reasons of power and prestige than they are to become committed to joint control devices. Local department heads and employees, particularly in units where the degree of professionalization is not high, tend to perceive such arrangements as threats to their position and status, and hence they provide little initiative or support for extensive cooperation.

Federal and state pressures aimed at the coordination of local programs and activities on an area-wide basis may in time radically alter the politics of cooperation. As these pressures intensify—which they are almost certain to do—local units will be compelled to engage in considerably more bargaining with each other than is presently the case. And in the process of competing for federal and state largess, as well as in attempting to shape regional plans to their liking, they will be forced to engage in coalition formation to advance what they regard as their interests. Such activities will in all probability strengthen rather than weaken the viability of the metropolitan governmental system.

THE PATH OF REORGANIZATION

Ratification of the comprehensive urban county charter by the voters of the Miami, Florida, area in May, 1957, was widely heralded as a major breakthrough for the cause of metropolitan reform. The victory bolstered the hopes of reorganization proponents throughout the United States, leading many to believe that American urban areas were standing on the threshold of significant governmental change. These hopes, however, proved to be short-lived. Out of the numerous reform efforts that developed after the Miami success, only two have borne fruit: those in the Nashville and Jacksonville areas. In both of these cases, moreover, special circumstances contributed to the success. Few suburban units existed in either county, there was considerable grassroots dissatisfaction with the activities of the local political machine, and the campaigns revolved around essentially political issues, which gave proponents the opportunity to utilize the age-old battle cry of "throw the rascals out." More importantly, many interests and groups, usually hostile or indifferent to change, could see concrete gains for themselves in a reconstituted structure. The circumstances, in brief, permitted the advocates to translate a comprehensive and complex plan of governmental reorganization into terms which were meaningful in the political vocabulary of local or neighborhood affairs.

Despite the unanswered questions and the variance in research results, the experience of metropolitan reform efforts permit certain general observations. At the least, they indicate that the position of individuals and community groups—and the intensity of their support or opposition—is determined largely by (1) the conditions which give rise to particular plans; (2) the kind of changes which are being sought; and (3) the possible effect of the proposals on their respective interests. Plans involving area-wide consolidation, for example, are likely to mobilize a different set of actors than those which relate to the establishment of a council of governments. Or a recommendation for the creation of a special district to handle sewage disposal is likely to activate different groups than a move to transfer property assessment powers from the municipalities to the county government.

Redesigning the metropolitan political structure almost invariably involves incompatible values and needs. The objectives commonly advanced for altering the system include operational efficiency and economy, effectiveness, equity, responsiveness, representativeness, and citizen access to the policy-makers and administrators. Those who argue for change usually contend that their proposals will advance all of these goals. Efficient government, they say, is more responsive to popular will, and representativeness results in a more equitable distribution of costs and benefits and permits greater access. The relationships, however, are not that clear. Suggested reforms may, and frequently do, promote one value at the expense of another. Efficiency and economy, for example, may be furthered by the creation of a governmental unit of such large size that citizen control would be limited and popular participation discouraged. Or the type of representation (for instance, at large instead of by district) may increase overall effectiveness but deny meaningful access to minority groups. The same dilemma exists with respect to needs. The kind and size of organization which may be best for area-wide administration may be dysfunctional for the management of conflict or the protection of valid neighborhood interests.

With different interests and incompatible values at stake whenever changes in an existing system are attempted, proposals to gain the support of one group often incur the antagonism of another. The ideal approach is to design a reorganization plan that involves what social scientists refer to as a non-zero-sum game (one in which the gains for one contestant do not mean a loss for the others). Such a situation, according to two observers, existed in the Jacksonville consolidation. As they described it:

A non-zero-sum game was perceived in Duval County. The central city voters gained the expanded tax base and the modernized government needed for an expansion of desired services. The white suburbs gained an assurance of political control over the city in which they must work and play. The Negroes gained a degree of political influence and representation. No major group perceived an important loss for itself.[26]

The opportunity to engage in such a game is not always available. Yet it represents the most promising strategy to pursue if reorganization is to be considered in pragmatic rather than rationalistic terms.

There is always danger that changes in governmental structure made for purposes of efficiency may have consequences for substantive issues or interests in the community. An analogous example of this possibility occurred recently in a federal district court where the split verdict (the question of liability is determined before the jury is reconvened to hear testimony on the extent of damages) was inaugurated to save time. The device proved successful for this purpose but the procedure was accompanied by a substantial increase in the proportion of verdicts for defendants on the question of liability.[27] Whether this represented a more equitable allocation of justice is not known. What the experiment did demonstrate, however, is the danger of appraising structural or procedural changes in public agencies merely by efficiency or economy tests. A major weakness of the metropolitan reorganization movement is precisely that it has fallen into this trap.

It may seem anomalous to some that the governmental organization of the metropolis should move in a direction opposite to other major segments of the society. While the local polity has become more fragmented, business, labor, and other associations have been able, by means of increasing organizational scale, to achieve a measure of control over their environment that is apparently denied the metropolitan community. Yet local government to many urban dwellers represents a protection for values they perceive threatened by the growing scale of society and the forces it generates. They are consequently less disturbed by the imputed "irrationality" of the existing system than they are fearful of what the consequences of radically changing it might be.

[26] P. N. Glendening and J. W. White, "Local Government Reorganization Referenda in Florida: An Acceptance and a Rejection," *Florida State University Governmental Research Bulletin*, 5 (March, 1968), 4. This analysis lends support to the view of some observers that the suburbs will turn to metropolitan consolidation to prevent Negro control over the core municipality. However, there is little indication of this development elsewhere. If anything, suburbanites have retreated farther behind their protective walls as the nonwhite population in the central cities has increased.

[27] Hans Zeisel and Thomas Callahan, "Split Trials and Time Saving: A Statistical Analysis," *Harvard Law Review*, 76 (June, 1963), 1606–1625.

15 / THE METROPOLITAN WORLD

ALONG WITH THE CONQUEST OF SPACE AND THE RISING EXPECTATIONS OF mankind, one of the most striking aspects of the modern era is the steady increase in the proportion of the world's population residing in urban areas. Today over 20 percent of the earth's inhabitants live in cities of 20,000 or more. In 1800 this figure was only 2 percent; by the year 2000 it is expected to be almost 50 percent. Human history has a long time span but intensive urbanization is a modern phenomenon, beginning in the advanced countries within the past 100 years and in the developing nations more recently. Before 1850 no society could be described as predominantly urbanized, and by 1900 only Great Britain could be so regarded.[1] Now all the industrial states fall into this category and many of the less developed nations are moving steadily in this direction.

The most spectacular manifestations of urban growth are found in the

[1] Kingsley Davis, "The Urbanization of the Human Population," *Scientific American*, 213 (September, 1965), 41–54. Davis is careful to distinguish between urbanization (the proportion of the total population concentrated in urban settlements) and urban growth (the increase in the number of city residents).

TABLE 28   Great Cities of the World, 1950–1965

Area	1950	1965	Increase (Percent)
World	858	1,374	60.1
North America	140	169	20.7
Latin America	44	125	184.0
Europe (exclusive of Russia)	264	308	16.6
Asia (exclusive of Russia)	263	481	82.8
Russia	100	220	120.0
Oceania	10	12	20.0
Africa	37	59	59.4

SOURCE: United Nations Statistical Office, Department of Economic and Social Affairs, *Demographic Yearbook, 1950* (New York: 1950) and Kingsley Davis, "The Urbanization of the Human Population," *Scientific American,* 213 (September, 1965), 45.

large aggregations of people that dot the face of every continent. A century ago there were only five urban areas with a million or more population; today this number exceeds sixty. Between 1950 and 1965, the "great cities" (a term applied to urban concentrations of at least 100,000 population) grew in number from 858 to 1374 (Table 28). The increase

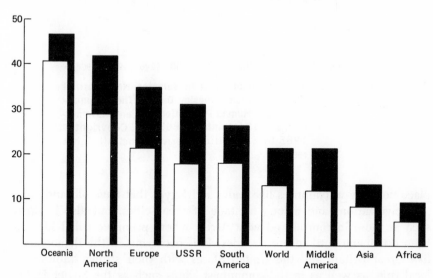

FIGURE 49   Percentage of Population Living in Urban Areas. The black bar shows the percentage of people living in urban areas of 20,000 and over; the white bar, the percentage in urban areas of 100,000 and over. From *Population Bulletin,* 16 (September, 1960), 120.

was worldwide, with the sharpest rise occurring in Latin America and the least in Europe (exclusive of the Soviet Union).

Metropolitan growth, apart from its spatial and geographical dimensions, is not confined to any particular type of nation or civilization. The rate of increase may be radically different but the trend is the same whether in the old and highly industrialized states of Western Europe or in the new and predominantly rural nations of Africa. It is taking

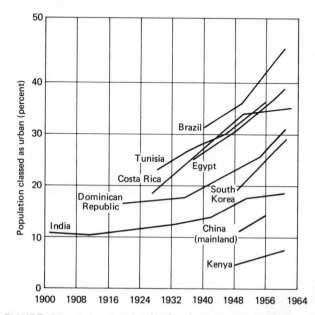

FIGURE 50   Rate of Urbanization in Selected Nonindustrial Countries. From Kingsley Davis, "The Urbanization of the Human Population," Scientific American, 213 (September, 1965), 47. Copyright © 1965 by Scientific American, Inc. All rights reserved.

place not only in countries like India and Egypt that have old and complex civilizations and a long heritage of great cities, but also in areas such as those in central and west Africa where primitive tribal life has been dominant until recent decades. It is occurring in the democracies like Great Britain and the United States with their strong tradition of local rule, as well as in the communist states such as the Soviet Union and China where centralized control is exercised over all governmental levels and all aspects of development.

The pattern of urbanization varies from nation to nation. In some countries, the tendency is to concentrate in one or two large centers.

Egypt is one example, with migration from the rural sections favoring the largest city, Cairo, while bypassing those of moderate and small size. Bangkok in Thailand, Manila in the Philippines, Accra in Ghana, Santiago in Chile, and Lima in Peru are other illustrations of the same phenomenon. Where this trend is evident, the largest city in most instances is also the national capital. Known as a "primate city" (one surpassingly large compared to all others in a country), such an area is the major locus of power and the receptacle of a nation's highest talent and its major investment funds. Whether this concentration works to the disadvantage of other sections of the country is a subject of concern to development specialists and policy-makers.

THE POPULATION EXPLOSION

Behind the phenomenon of urbanization is the fantastic rise in the world's population. From the beginning of the present century to mid-1967, the number of terrestrial inhabitants doubled to a total of 3.4 billion; and if the present rate continues, this figure will again double by the year 2006. The net growth (excess of births over deaths) now approximates 180,000 persons each day, a rate of increase twice what it was before 1940. The swiftest growth has shifted from the advanced countries of Europe and North America to the developing regions of the world.[2] Latin America heads the list with an annual rate of increase of 2.9 percent, followed by Africa with 2.5 percent and Asia with 2 percent. (The comparable figure for Europe is less than 1 percent and for North America 1.3 percent). Three-fourths of the world's people presently live in what are commonly known as the underdeveloped or developing areas and, given the existing growth trends, this proportion will jump to four-fifths by the end of the century.

The unprecedented rise in population during recent decades has been made possible by the advances in medical science with its inoculations and antibiotics and by the extension of health services to wide sections of the globe. Birth rates in the developing countries remain high, ranging from 40 to 45 per 1000 population as contrasted to 15 to 25 in the industrialized states. More importantly, however, this high fertility ratio has been accompanied by a dramatic decline in the death rates, dropping to levels of 15 to 20 per 1000 population in the less developed countries and to 10 or below in the most advanced areas.

Unlike the evolution of the industrialized nations of the West where the number of rural dwellers declined in absolute as well as relative

[2] See Homer Hoyt, *World Urbanization* (Washington: Urban Land Institute, 1962). Also, International Urban Research Center, *The World's Metropolitan Areas* (Berkeley and Los Angeles; University of California Press, 1959).

terms, population growth in the economically underdeveloped states is occurring in both city and countryside. Thus in some countries, such as India, the increase in the proportion of city dwellers when expressed as a percentage of the total population has been slow due to the rapid growth of the rural populace. Generally, however, the increase in the urban areas has been running well ahead of that outside them. In Latin America, where the population doubled between 1930 and 1960, the twenty-two largest cities more than tripled in size. Colombia's five major metropolitan areas, for example, have been averaging annual growth rates of 6 percent while the nation's population as a whole has been gaining 3 percent. These differentials are not due to a higher rate of natural increase in the cities—in fact, birth rates among rural dwellers are invariably higher than among urban residents—but to the incessant and large-scale migration from farm and village to city and metropolis. This lemming-like flow has contributed in major degree to the astounding growth of such centers as Mexico City where the population has multiplied almost sixfold during the last forty years. One of the largest population shifts has taken place in Communist China where it is estimated that 20 million people migrated from rural to urban areas between 1949 and 1956.

Industrialization

The emergence of large cities and the urbanization of extensive sectors of the earth's inhabitants has been closely associated with industrialization and economic growth. With some exceptions, the most highly developed nations are also the most intensely urbanized.[3] Although the world had known cities long before the Industrial Revolution, those which existed were based primarily on commerce and governmental administration.[4] As a consequence, no more than a small portion of the total population of even the most progressive countries could be supported in urban settlements. It was only with the discovery of the steam engine and other forms of power-producing devices that man was freed from dependence on his own energy and enabled to build the factories and mills which have revolutionized society.

The Industrial Revolution led to a rising demand for workers in the cities while technological advances in agriculture simultaneously created surplus labor on the farms. Since the middle of the nineteenth century, economic development in the West has consisted largely in moving farmers or peasants from low-productivity agriculture to urban occupations of much higher output. This transfer has served the dual

[3] See, for example, Jack P. Gibbs and Leo Schnore, "Metropolitan Growth: An International Study," *American Journal of Sociology,* LXVI (September, 1960), 160–170.

[4] Gideon Sjoberg, *The Preindustrial City* (New York: Free Press, 1960).

purpose of reducing population pressure on the land and permitting agrarian improvement through consolidation and mechanization. These advances in turn have opened the doors to a metropolitan civilization.

The story is radically different in the developing nations of the present. Unlike the West where the industrial boom generated the capital needed to build economies which could provide jobs, the pace of urbanization in the low-income countries has been outrunning the rate of industrialization. As a result, the rapid movement of people from the rural areas to the cities has not been accompanied by a corresponding rise in employment opportunity. This imbalance has generated high rates of urban unemployment and encouraged the creation of marginal or low-productivity jobs. Hence, in many instances, the flow cityward is more the result of "push" factors (gross overcrowding of the rural population, dire poverty, too little opportunity for securing land that can be worked to produce a living) than of the "pull" of the urban community. In Latin America, for example, the rapidity of urbanization reflects the "expulsion" of the farm population as much as the attraction of job opportunities in the cities.

Those countries which have experienced the fastest population increase in recent decades have been least able to bring about a significant transfer of their growing labor force into the industrial urban sector. They have also been least able to provide the physical and social infrastructure—housing, education, utilities, transportation—necessary to absorb the migrant streams. The slums, shantytowns, and squatter settlements which lie at the outskirts of the large cities and penetrate their interiors along the river banks, railroad tracks, broad gullies, hillsides, and deteriorated portions of the core stand as mute testimony to this failure. It is estimated that in Africa only 50 percent of the urban dwellers live in housing that could be considered minimally adequate, while the comparable figure for Asia and Latin America is 60 percent.[5] For many of the developing nations, the great internal migration means simply the transfer of rural poverty to the cities where it becomes more concentrated and conspicuous.

SOCIAL ORGANIZATION

Urbanization signifies more than the concentration of vast numbers of people in limited geographical space; it also signals profound changes in the social structure and organization of society. The transfer of countless millions of human beings from rural settings to the cities has revolutionized the social world of mankind. Disruption of the older patterns

[5] See in this connection, Charles Abrams, *Man's Struggle for Shelter in an Urbanizing World* (Cambridge: M.I.T. Press, 1964).

of work and production associated with agriculture and handicraft has diminished the traditional security afforded by the extended family or tribe and placed large parts of the earth's population at the vagaries of the labor market. The response to these changes and their accompanying problems has varied from culture to culture and from one stage of industrialization to another.

The type of social structure and organization required to develop and maintain a system of mass production utilizing inanimate sources of power is radically different from that needed in a simple agrarian society or even in the earlier "urban" economies where the worker participated in nearly every phase of the manufacture of an article.[6] Industrialization necessitates a high degree of specialization and a complex division of labor. It requires the accumulation of capital as well as the development of technical skills and managerial entrepreneurship. These resources evolved in the Western states over the course of a century or more, but they are in low supply in the emerging nations. The latter, moreover, do not have the time leeway that the West had. Faced with explosive population growth and the rising expectations of their people, they opt for "instant" industrialization to raise their economic output and ease their critical problems.

The social organization related to urbanization is largely of Western origin. Its chief characteristics are: (1) disintegration of the extended family; (2) expansion and bureaucratization of nonfamily institutions such as the industrial corporation, local government, and public welfare agencies; (3) a multiplication of social and economic roles; (4) creation of numerous formal or voluntary associations corresponding to the occupational, professional, social, political, and religious interests of the citizen body; and (5) rapid social mobility in a system that promotes social change and bases class stratification on competitive achievement rather than on birth or prescriptive rights.[7] These elements are common in the mature industrial states; in many of the developing countries they are only beginning to evolve.

The absorption of the newcomer into urban life is a problem of social organization common to most contemporary cities. In the West, the rural migrant comes into a highly organized structure that is equipped with formal agencies and voluntary associations designed to facilitate his entry. He usually has at his disposal—although the degree of adequacy varies considerably—educational and training programs, social services, housing assistance, and welfare aid. In the developing regions of the world, on the other hand, the structures for easing his entry into urban life are still in an early stage of formation. For example, in the West

[6] Gideon Sjoberg, "The Preindustrial City," *American Journal of Sociology*, LX (March, 1955), 438–445.

[7] Sylvia F. Fava (ed.), *Urbanism in World Perspective: A Reader* (New York: Crowell, 1968), pp. 273–280.

African cities, extended family and kinship ties serve as substitutes for public welfare programs in helping migrants to meet their economic, housing, legal, and recreational needs.[8] And in Latin America the new-comer is frequently related to sources of urban patronage through in-formal and noninstitutional structures of "clientage arrangements." Few voluntary associations cut across kinship or tribal groups. Labor unions are the major exception, but they are mainly of benefit to the employed, not to the vast number of those without jobs.

COMPARATIVE URBAN STUDIES

Although the study of comparative politics can be traced as far back as Aristotle, the emphasis has been on national systems and on Western experiences. Since World War II, however, increasing attention has been given to the emerging nations and their political, social, and administra-tive institutions. The primary focus thus far has been on the develop-ment of theoretical frameworks and methodological tools to clarify the similarities and differences between political systems and to demonstrate the relationships among key variables.[9] Only a limited amount of empiri-cal investigation has been carried out under the various schema. As one social scientist has observed: "We are very long on theory and still pov-erty stricken as far as research findings are concerned."[10]

International comparative studies of urban problems and of metro-politan political and social systems are even less advanced. Research in this field has understandably been limited in scope and geographic cover-age; and the literature, while growing, is still too sparse for meaningful generalization. Moreover, aside from the question of resources, formid-able obstacles stand in the way of large-scale comparative inquiries into community systems. Not only does the stage of national development differ widely among the regions of the world, but there is also an endless variety of local cultures, customs, and institutions—both among and within countries—which must be taken into consideration. Although these difficulties are not insurmountable, they presage slow progress in research of this character.

What we shall do here by way of illustration is to present a broad

[8] Peter C. W. Gutkind, "The Poor in Urban Africa," in Warner Bloomberg, Jr., and Henry J. Schmandt (eds.), *Power, Poverty, and Urban Policy* (Beverly Hills: Sage Publications, 1968), pp. 355–396.

[9] See, for example, David Apter, *The Politics of Modernization* (Chicago: Uni-versity of Chicago Press, 1965); Gabriel A. Almond and G. B. Powell, Jr., *Compara-tive Politics: A Developmental Approach* (Boston: Little, Brown, 1966); and Fred W. Riggs, *Administration in Developing Countries: The Theory of Prismatic Society* (Boston: Houghton Mifflin, 1964).

[10] Joseph LaPalombara, "Alternative Strategies for Developing Administrative Capabilities in Emerging Nations," *CAG Occasional Papers* (November, 1965), p. 59.

overview of local government and its responses to urban growth in various regions of the world. For this purpose we have chosen to concentrate on four specific urban centers: London, Ibadan, Tokyo, and São Paulo. The first represents a mature Western metropolis; the second, an indigenous but expanding African community; the third, a highly industrialized complex in Asia; and the last, a rapidly growing Latin American city. Set in different cultures and varying widely in their social, economic, and political structures, each of these metropolitan concentrations faces the same relentless pressures of urbanization.

LONDON

Known as a nation of townspeople, England has been highly urbanized for many decades. Its present density of 790 persons per square mile is exceeded by only one other major European country, the Netherlands. The urban population first surpassed that in the rural areas around 1850. By the end of the nineteenth century, three-fourths of the people lived in cities and towns. Since 1939, when the number of urbanites reached 80 percent of the total population, there has been little change in the proportion. However, the long prevalent pattern of migration from farm to town has given way to the movement from one urban area to another, particularly from the older industrial centers of the north to London and other cities in the southeast. Today, over 40 percent of the population is concentrated in London and five other smaller metropolitan areas.

Physical and Demographic Characteristics

The metropolis of London dominates British life. As the political and cultural capital of the nation, the center of its commerce, and the headquarters of its major financial institutions, London exercises an enormous gravitational pull on the rest of the country. It is for all intents and purposes a primate city in the sense that it towers over all aspects of British life, a situation quite unlike the United States model where the major metropolises compete with each other for positions of national influence. Someone once remarked that to create an approximate American equivalent of London, we would have to merge New York, Washington, and Chicago into one overwhelmingly dominant metropolis which would make all other urban centers in the country appear provincial.

The physical dimensions of London can best be described in terms of a series of concentric rings (Figure 51). At the center is the ancient city, "a small island of obstinate medieval structure," which contains but one square mile of territory and a nighttime population of less than 5000. The traditional city and the surrounding area of about ten square miles constitute the densely developed core of the metropolis. Here about 275,000 people reside but over 1.5 million work. Outside this shell is the inner ring of suburbs extending out to the pre-1964 limits of London County. Consisting largely of small and closely spaced homes, this area represents the physical growth of the urban complex before electric railways and automobiles allowed the suburbs to sprawl. Within this ring is an additional population of 1.5 million and a land area of slightly over 100 square miles. The next ring includes suburban development between the two world wars and extends out to the Green Belt, a circle of land varying in width from five to fifteen miles and containing over 35,000 acres

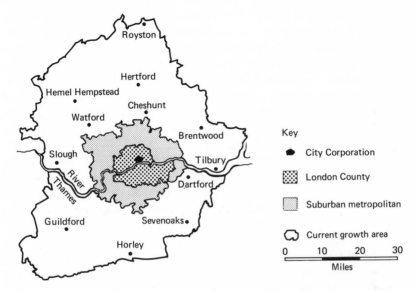

FIGURE 51   **Greater London Area. From Frank Smallwood,** Greater London: The Politics of Metropolitan Reform **(Indianapolis: Bobbs-Merrill, 1965), p. 50. Copyright 1965 by Bobbs-Merrill Co.**

of open space. All of the territory within this belt (723 square miles with a population of 8.2 million) is known officially as the Greater London conurbation.

Beyond the Green Belt is the area of present expansion intended to handle the spillover from the inner rings. It is here that the New Towns, the uniquely English solution to the problem of metropolitan growth, are located. Designed as self-contained communities of finite size (with a target population of 80,000 to 100,000), they have proved attractive to industry as well as residents. Since 1950, the area beyond the Green Belt has increased in population by over 1 million while the planned program of the British government to reduce density and congestion in the center has resulted in a net loss of 165,000 within the conurbation. By the early 1960s, however, the resident population level inside the belt had become stabilized.[11]

Planning for urban growth began early in Great Britain. Before the concept was discussed in other than a few American municipalities, Parliament passed a town planning act in 1909, the same year that the University of Liverpool inaugurated the first formal program in city planning offered by an academic institution. British planning has been strongly influenced by the "garden-city" movement as it found expression in the work of Ebenezer Howard and his followers. They proposed that the large urban centers, such as London, be decentralized by establishing and developing small satellite towns in the outlying reaches of the region. London planners have followed this general concept. Even before World War I, the London County Council had taken steps to effect a redistribution of the population by a program of slum clearance and the construction of new housing outside the central area. The program was accelerated in the 1940s as a result of the war damage which necessitated the rebuilding of large sections of the core. It was also aided by the wartime evacuation which reduced the population of the county of London from four million in 1939 to 2.5 million at the end of 1944.

Starting in the 1900s, various "advisory" plans were drafted for the London area, some commissioned by the national government, others by local authorities and private organizations. Probably the most influential has been the Greater London Plan of 1944, which was prepared under an appointment from the Minister of Works and Planning. The plan called for a continuation of decentralization by moving out large numbers of people and their related employment from central London to new towns in the outer ring and for the establishment of a metropolitan greenbelt encircling the built-up urbanized area of the conurbation. Drafters of the plan regarded the latter as a strategic device for halting the continued spread of suburban growth. As they conceived it, such a belt, aided by the creation of self-sufficient new towns in the outer region and the barring of new industrial development in the interior, would serve as a barrier to the further enlargement of the London commuting zone.[12]

Many of the provisions of the Greater London Plan have been followed in principle, including redistribution of population, creation of the greenbelt, and the channeling of new industry into the outer zone. But the forces of growth and change have proved too strong to permit the degree of decentralization envisaged by the planners. Like the borough of Manhattan in New York City, the heart of postwar London has served as a powerful attraction for the location of new office sites, an attraction

---

[11] For an account of London's growth see Peter Hall, *The World Cities* (New York: McGraw-Hill, 1966), pp. 30–58.

[12] Daniel R. Mandelker, *Green Belts and Urban Growth* (Madison: University of Wisconsin Press, 1962).

too great to be overcome by the public planners. As a result, the central area gained approximately 260,000 jobs, mostly of white-collar or clerical nature, during the 1952-1961 census period. Thus while a reduction in the area's resident population was accomplished by the redistribution plans, the problem of traffic and congestion in central London has increased as more than 1.3 million persons commute to the core each weekday. Well over 200,000 of this number come from beyond the Green Belt, making the twenty- to forty-mile journey on express trains, like their New York counterparts. As one scholar has observed, the Greater London planning experience provides an object lesson in the relentless forces of growth. It demonstrates that containment is extremely difficult even when implemented by controls far more powerful than those available to public authorities in the United States.[13]

The British experience with controlled growth in the large metropolitan agglomerations has been paralleled in other European nations. France, for example, by 1965 had abandoned plans for halting the physical growth of Paris (in the preceding five-year period, authorities had granted permits to build 25,000 homes outside the limits fixed in the 1960 plan) and had rejected the principle of the greenbelt with its ring of new towns. The revised plans instead call for an axial pattern of growth by developing gigantic new nodes of employment, urban facilities, and housing at selected points in the suburban zone, with the ultimate objective of creating a new type of polycentric metropolis. Even in the Soviet Union, the inexorable pressures of economics have hindered efforts to limit growth in the national capital. By 1960, the population target fixed for Moscow in the 1935 General Plan of Reconstruction had already been exceeded by well over 1 million. Plans for the capital area resemble those for London, with a greenbelt ringing the city at a radius of about eleven miles from the center. Interestingly, however, continued pressure for the construction of individual summer *dachas* in the belt area illustrates that the influence of private interests in land development is not confined to the capitalist countries.

Governmental Pattern

Prior to 1964, the governmental structure of the London conurbation consisted of 118 local units including six counties and three county boroughs (larger cities detached from counties). In addition, the area was overlayed with 16 special-purpose authorities such as the Metropolitan Police Commission (responsible to the Home Secretary in the national cabinet), the Metropolitan Water Board, and the London Transport Executive. The picture, in other words, was not unlike that in any large metropolis in the United States.

During the 1950s there was increasing feeling on the part of many

[13] Donald L. Foley, *Controlling London's Growth, Planning the Great Wen* (Berkeley and Los Angeles: University of California Press, 1963), p. 157.

analysts and observers of the London scene that either the existing system
of local government had to be revitalized and modernized or the national
government had to impose greater centralized controls. Although not as
diffused as in the typical American metropolitan area where planning
and zoning powers are exercised by dozens of independent units without
supervision by a higher authority, the local governmental setup in the
London area was the subject of considerable criticism. William A. Robson,
the distinguished British political scientist, called it "obsolete," and others
charged that it was failing to meet many of the essential public needs of
the conurbation in an adequate and effective manner.

In 1960, a Royal Commission appointed for the specific purpose of
examining the local government system in the Greater London area
recommended a major reorganization of the existing structure including
the replacement of the medley of local units within roughly the limits of
the Green Belt by a directly-elected Greater London Council and fifty-
two boroughs.[14] The proposals met a cool reception from local officials
and also aroused the opposition of the Labour party which feared that
it could not control the larger metropolitan government as it did the
London County Council. Labour's greatest strength was in the central
core and the less wealthy inner suburbs while the Conservative party drew
its principal support from the more affluent areas outside London County.

Since the national government was under the control of the Conservatives, official reception of the proposals was favorable; and a bill
to effectuate them was shortly thereafter introduced in Parliament.
Labour immediately accused the Conservatives of trying to use the reorganization program as a means of securing political control over
London's government. Other groups, including teachers' organizations
and borough officials, also entered the fray to protect their interests. In
the interplay which followed, the Government dropped a number of
Conservative-controlled areas in the outer suburbs from the plan and
made certain other concessions to placate opposition forces.[15]

The bill, as finally passed in 1963, provided for a two-tier government
consisting of the Greater London Council as the overall authority, and
thirty-two boroughs and the ancient city as the constituent units. The
reconstituted structure encompasses an area of 620 square miles and almost 8 million people. As specified in the Act, the new metropolitan
council is charged with carrying out a survey of Greater London and the
preparation of a general development plan, including policy with respect

[14] For a discussion of the recommendations, see L. J. Sharpe, "The Report of the
Royal Commission on Local Government," *Public Administration,* 39 (Spring, 1961),
73–92; and William A. Robson, *The World's Greatest Metropolis: Planning and
Government in Greater London* (Pittsburgh: University of Pittsburgh, Institute of
Local Government, 1963).

[15] Frank Smallwood, *Greater London: The Politics of Metropolitan Reform*
(Indianapolis: Bobbs-Merrill, 1965).

to land use. Each borough is required to formulate a redevelopment plan for its own area embodying the relevant features of the metropolitan plan. The metropolitan council is also vested with responsibility for traffic management throughout the area, main roads, trunk line sewers and sewage disposal facilities, major cultural and recreational facilities, refuse disposal, fire protection, and civil defense. All remaining local governmental functions including education (except in central London where the school system is administered by a special committee of the metropolitan council) are borough responsibilities.

The London experience poses the dilemma that the architects of metropolitan reorganization face. Although the plan is far-reaching and its territorial coverage large, it still falls short of constituting an answer to the problem of governmental structure *vis-à-vis* urban growth. That the adopted arrangements will bring more efficient and effective local government and greater control over land use and physical development within the territorial boundaries of the new council is probably correct. That they will provide a solution to the more crucial problem of guiding and controlling the continued outward expansion of the metropolis is another matter. For even though the areal jurisdiction of the Greater London Council is now very extensive, it still lacks control over the outer ring where much of the new development is taking place.

IBADAN

Africa, with a population of about 300 million, is the least urbanized of the world's continents; far less than 10 percent of the people live in communities of 5000 or more. However, the strong tendency toward urbanization is one of the outstanding characteristics of its present-day life. Virtually the entire continent is in a state of rapid transition. Colonialism, with a few exceptions, has been brought to a speedy and often abrupt termination (at the end of World War II only four independent states existed; today there are approximately forty); industrialization is taking place at an accelerated pace; and the cities are experiencing continued migration and swift growth. As in the more advanced countries, the urbanizing trends in Africa have brought with them overcrowding and slum conditions in the population centers, important social and cultural changes, the formation of new types of associations connected with occupations, cults, and recreational activities, and the progressive disintegration of wider kinship groups and family stability.

Africa is a continent of many faces. At the far south is the wealthy and industrialized Republic of South Africa with well-established social and political institutions and with control firmly in the hands of its white minority. North of the Sahara are countries with ancient civilizations such as Egypt and the kingdom of Ethiopia. Below the desert are the new and predominantly Negroid nations of the continent, the recently liberated colonies of the European powers. This vast mosaic is interlaced with a multiplicity of customs, languages, religions, ethnic backgrounds, and political institutions that defy generalization. Rapid transition and the thrust of modernization have intensified the problem of nation-building and in the process have precipitated civil wars and military takeovers. Yet from these travails, a continent of tremendous potential is emerging.

The problems of governmental reconstruction facing the new African nations are monumental. Sweeping away the foundations of a colonial structure, forging a national identity, and adapting traditional political institutions to the needs of an emerging urban society have everywhere produced difficulties. At the local level, the process of change has required the transfer of authority from tribal councils to new elective assemblies and the creation of native administrative systems to replace the body of professional civil servants utilized by colonial powers. The shortage of educated and skilled personnel among the native population contributes to the difficulty of building up an efficient local bureaucracy. In addition, the influx of migrants into the towns often overstrains the labor market and the local economy, not to mention public facilities, and thus helps to create restlessness and insecurity.

Nigeria, in the western part of the continent, is considered to be one of the most promising of the emerging nations, although it has been plagued by severe intertribal strife in recent years. With 22 percent of its 55 million people living in cities of 5000 or more, it enjoys the highest degree of urbanization among the new major African states. It has a federal form of government with twelve states.[16] The capital of the western state is Ibadan, located inland seventy miles northeast of Lagos, the national capital.

Physical and Demographic Features

Ibadan, with a population estimated at more than 1 million, is one of the two largest Negro metropolises in Africa (Lagos is the other). As a political subdivision of a country which only recently achieved statehood (1960), it is in the throes of adapting its governmental structure and social institutions to the needs of independence as well as rapid growth. Its industry, although expanding, is still predominantly oriented toward

[16] Until mid-1968, Nigeria was divided into four regions: North, East, West, and Midwest. These were then converted into twelve states by the military government which has ruled the country since 1964. The change was purportedly made to satisfy the demands of the diverse ethnic or tribal interests for greater autonomy. The decree establishing the states endowed them with virtually the same powers as the former regions. The western region was least affected by the new arrangements; only the national capital area (Lagos) was detached and converted into a separate state.

the processing of agricultural crops from the surrounding countryside; hence it is representative of the more traditional "urbanism" characteristic of many indigenous African communities.

Although the majority of African towns owe their origin in large measure to foreign initiative, Ibadan is an outstanding example of a town founded by the indigenous peoples. It originated as a small forest settlement or war encampment of the Yoruba tribe around 1821, and by the time formal British control was established over western Nigeria in the late nineteenth century, the population of the town was well over 100,000. Under colonial administration the influx of newcomers was accelerated as wider trade relations and better communications (including the construction of a railroad from the coastal city of Lagos) were developed. The successful cultivation of cocoa, which began early in the present century, converted the Ibadan area into a rich agricultural district and increased the city's importance as a service and trading center. In 1948 the University of Ibadan was established by the national government and more recently large-scale industries of a European type have been introduced into the city.

The core or oldest part of the city, known as "Old Ibadan," extends out from the town hall (Mapo) and the market place (Figure 52). Density is remarkably high (as many as thirty houses and 250 residents to the

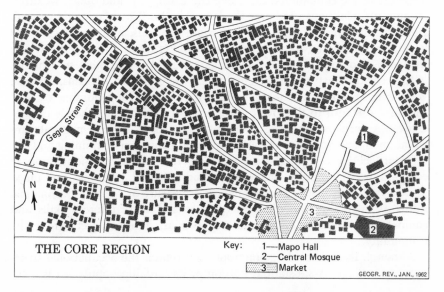

THE CORE REGION   Key: 1—Mapo Hall
                                       2—Central Mosque
                                       3 Market
                                                        GEOGR. REV., JAN., 1962

FIGURE 52   **The Core Region of Ibadan. From Akin Mabogunje, "The Growth of Residential Districts in Ibadan,"** Geographical Review, **52 (January, 1962), 66. Copyright 1962 by the American Geographical Society of New York.**

acre in some sections), open space is negligible, roads are few, and access to many of the dwellings is by means of footpaths. Virtually all the houses are constructed of mud and are roofed with corrugated iron. Sanitary facilities are lacking and the water supply is obtained from communal taps. More than a third of the city's inhabitants are concentrated in this area.

The inner core with its large market and town hall was at one time the economic heart of the city. However, with the arrival of the railway at the turn of the present century, the town began to attract numerous European economic institutions such as department stores, banks, trading firms, specialized shops, and motor garages, as well as the colonial administrative agencies. Since land for these various activities could not be found in the congested core of the city, they located at the periphery, thus creating a large commercial section, the equivalent of the American downtown or central business district. This development caused the economic center of gravity to shift from the core to the suburban ring. It also made further expansion of the old town impractical and lessened economic incentive to redevelop the now obsolescent areas in the inner city.[17] One might speculate what the fate of American CBDs and their surrounding areas would have been had the commercial center of the metropolis been shifted to an outer location early in the twentieth century.

The suburban areas surrounding the inner city house the more affluent members of the community, including the Europeans and other "wealthy" immigrants who began to enter Ibadan after the British assumed control. Here the housing is better, the lots more spacious, and the density far lower. Today, the newcomers who are flocking into the city settle where their means permit. The poor and uneducated Africans must seek homes in the crowded districts of the core, while the educated Africans, or those with some means, settle in the suburbs. (The growing number of non-Africans also turn to the lower-density residential neighborhoods of suburbia.) A surprisingly large proportion of recent African migrants are young men and women who have had some education or training and are therefore better equipped than many of the indigenous population to compete in the rapidly changing society. Spatial patterns, not unexpectedly of course, have become almost a measure of social and economic status as migrants from different cultures and with different skills and competencies tend to congregate together in different sections of the community.

Although Ibadan is a large metropolis, it retains the occupational structure of a village. A substantial portion of its working population is com-

[17] For a description of Ibadan, see N. C. Mitchel, "Yoruba Towns," in K. M. Barbour and R. M. Prothero (eds.), *Essays on African Population* (London: Routledge and Kegan Paul, 1961), pp. 279–301; and A. L. Mabogunje, *Yoruba Towns* (Ibadan, Nigeria: Ibadan University Press, 1962).

posed of artisans (such as weavers, dyers, and iron-workers) and farmers who cultivate the cocoa, cotton, and corn fields in the surrounding agricultural belt. Many of the latter, in fact, spend part of the year in one of the numerous villages in the outlying areas. This close association between the urban and rural bases serves to preserve traditional ties and institutions within a metropolitan setting. The situation differs from that in many African cities where conditions induce rural males to migrate as individual workers but discourage them from settling with their families. In such circumstances, the integration of these men into the industrial urban environment is only partial at best because their most important personal ties and loyalties are in the tribal village, not the city.[18]

Governmental Pattern

Local administration in Africa during the colonial period followed essentially two models: the English pattern of "indirect rule" through native authorities, and the French system of direct and centralized control through their own civil servants.[19] In Nigeria, a prime example of the former practice, the British utilized traditional chiefs and their councils as the machinery of local control while they focused their major change efforts on the central institutions of the society. In this way they sought to effect modernization at the national level for purposes of economic development without significantly altering the basic social and cultural orientations of the broader strata of the population. As one scholar has described the policy: "On the one hand, attempts were made to establish broad, modern, administrative, political, and economic settings, while on the other hand, these changes were to be limited and based on relatively unchanged local and tribal groups and on traditional attitudes and loyalties."[20]

In the post–World War II period, the British moved to replace the system of indirect rule by a more democratic form of local self-government which would better prepare the native population for independence. Local councils were reorganized to include both elected representatives and, to make the transition less drastic, traditional chiefs. Following the English system, these bodies were designed to be both legislative and executive in character. The formal center of British local government has historically been the council, whether at the municipal or county level;

[18] See in this connection, Kenneth Little, *Some Contemporary Trends in African Urbanization* (Evanston: Northwestern University Press, 1966). For an analysis of the Ibadan political system, see George Jenkins, "An Informal Political Economy," in Jeffrey Butler and A. A. Castagno (eds.), *Boston University Papers on Africa* (New York: Praeger, 1967), pp. 166–187.

[19] L. Gray Cowan, *Local Government in West Africa* (New York: Columbia University Press, 1958).

[20] S. N. Eisenstadt, *Modernization: Protest and Change* (Englewood Cliffs, N.J.: Prentice-Hall, 1966), p. 110.

it not only formulates policy but directly manages the work of the administrative staff—the permanent career employees—through its committees. It also chooses the mayor who serves as the presiding officer and as the ceremonial head of the municipality but not as an administrative officer. These features embody the traditional British policy of spreading responsibility widely among elected representatives.

With the advent of independence and the conclusion of colonial rule, Britain's former African territories continued the efforts to reproduce the English system of local government. But the adoption by one country of the political institutions of another is no simple task. The difficulties are compounded when the two countries are as different in tradition, culture, and stage of political development as Great Britain and Nigeria. The English system of local government, for example, makes demands of a kind that can seldom be met in the new African nations. It presupposes, among other factors, the existence of a cadre of politically and administratively knowledgeable individuals who can serve as councillors, a complement of trained civil servants, and a reasonably educated body of voters. It also presupposes willingness on the part of the council to recruit qualified personnel for its staff, to protect them from dismissal for political reasons, and to entrust them with administrative discretion.

As in federal systems generally, local government in Nigeria is a responsibility of the state governments. In the western state, the organization and authority of the local units are spelled out in the Local Government Act of 1953. This act establishes two tiers of councils, municipal and district, the latter usually encompassing the city or town and the surrounding rural territory. The Ibadan district council, for example, has within its jurisdiction the area covered by the city of Ibadan and six rural divisions. Its responsibilities include schools, police, and jails, while the lower-tier governing bodies handle such relatively minor fields as markets, playgrounds, parks, and local cultural facilities. Both tiers have broader formal powers but they are limited in exercising them by their heavy dependence on the national and state governments for grants-in-aid (the major tax sources are preempted by these higher levels of authority) and for the undertaking of major capital improvements. They are also circumscribed in their activities by the close supervision which the State Ministry of Local Government exercises over them. Ministerial approval is required in such matters as senior administrative appointments, the letting of all but minor contracts, and the adoption of budgets and local by-laws.

Party politics occupies a prominent role in the local governing process. Elections to the councils are partisan and usually revolve around national issues. Matters of local concern such as schools, roads, and water supply are seldom raised in the campaigns. Partisan politics also enters the picture through the controls exercised by state officials over local authorities. Political patronage and favoritism are hardly surprising in a system of this nature. The more fundamental question, however, is whether a large measure of autonomy can be granted to local units in the emerging countries or whether, in the national interest, strong centralized controls over local development plans and capital expenditures are required. In the eyes of one observer, the solution toward which Western Nigeria has been slowly working is to "leave the 'neutral areas,' in which peoples' local loyalties reside, untouched; to give them as much to do as possible; but not to give them powers and duties in connection with the major services on which the progress of Nigeria as a nation depends."[21]

TOKYO

Asia, the largest of the continents, contains almost three-fifths of the world's inhabitants (1.8 billion) and more than one-third of its land surface. Its population is growing rapidly, the result of continuing high fertility rates and a sharp reduction in mortality. The people of Asia are still predominantly village-dwelling agrarians, yet the continent has more large cities and a greater total urban population than either Europe or the United States. The number of cities of 100,000 or more jumped from 263 in 1950 to 481 in 1965, and the number of metropolitan areas with more than 1 million residents is approaching fifty. The continent embraces a wide diversity of countries with different cultures, languages, religions, and economic systems. Its governmental forms range from absolute monarchies and communist regimes to nominal republics and parliamentary democracies. If any common threads can be identified in this complex panorama, they relate to the high significance of kinship networks and the prominent role played by religion in determining the philosophical, and often the legal, basis of political and social institutions.

Of the Asian countries, Japan has been the first to reach Western levels of urbanization and the first to approach Western standards of living. The world's fourth ranking industrial power, Japan is already in an advanced stage of urbanization. More than three-fifths of its approximately 100 million people live in cities, and the proportion is steadily increasing. Density is high, 660 persons to the square mile, with 45 percent of the inhabitants living on less than 1 percent of the country's total land area. Unlike most nations in the developing regions, Japan's birth rate is low (the government actively promotes birth control and family planning) and its rate of industrial growth phenomenal.

Japan represents a case of urbanization that has been accompanied by parallel developments in industrialization and technological innova-

[21] Ronald Wraith, *Local Government in West Africa* (New York: Praeger, 1964), pp. 87–88.

tions. It also represents a case where these developments have left largely unchanged the underlying bases of preindustrial social relationships. Factory organization has proceeded along lines compatible with the traditional Japanese values of group loyalty and cohesion and the emphasis on the duties of individuals as distinct from their rights. Workers customarily spend their entire careers in a single firm. Their recruitment into the productive group is based on personal qualities, decision-making is a function of the group rather than the individual, and close involvement of the company in the personal and nonbusiness activities of the worker is an accepted practice. As a result, the factory or firm is relatively undifferentiated from other traditional types of groups in the society. According to one scholar:

> . . . the very success of the Japanese experience with industrialization may well have been a function of the fact that, far from undergoing a total revolution in social structure or social relationships, the hard core of Japan's system of social relationships remained intact, allowing an orderly transition to industrialization continuous with her earlier social forms.[22]

This approach to industrialization has been particularly effective in the case of the rural migrants versed in the elaborate system of obligations spun by kinship and friendship ties in the villages. It has been less effective for the young urban-reared and educated Japanese who have been schooled in a more modern pattern of relationships.

Administratively, Japan consists of two tiers below the central government: provinces (called prefectures) and municipalities. Each of the forty-six provinces into which the country is divided is governed by a popularly elected council and an elected chief executive. Before World War II, local government was rigidly controlled by national authorities; in 1947, the governmental system was decentralized and local units given a large measure of autonomy. Since the end of the United States military occupation in 1952, the trend has again been toward greater centralization, especially at the provincial level. During the 1950s a program of urban amalgamation was undertaken to increase municipal efficiency, with the national government offering financial inducements to communities that would agree to merge. Under the program, the number of cities and towns was reduced from 9622 to 3475.

Physical and Demographic Characteristics

Tokyo, the capital of Japan, is the largest urban concentration in Asia and one of the most intensely crowded cities of the world. Like Egypt's

---

[22] James C. Abegglen, *The Japanese Factory: Aspects of Its Social Organization* (New York: Free Press, 1958), pp. 134–135. The conclusions here are drawn from this study.

legendary bird, the phoenix, Tokyo has risen from its ashes twice in the space of two generations. It was destroyed by an earthquake followed by a tidal wave and fires in 1923; and in World War II large portions of it were leveled by Allied fire bombs. Today it is a teeming, congested, and expanding metropolis, the political, cultural, financial, and industrial center of Japanese life. Its rate of population increase is one of the highest among the world's large metropolitan areas. Since the middle 1950s, it has been growing by an average of 275,000 persons annually, with three-fourths of this gain representing net migration from the rest of Japan. Tokyo's size, as we have seen in the case of London and other large agglomerations, presents a problem of definition. The old city or ward area contains 8.3 million people; the area of the Tokyo Metropolitan Government which has jurisdiction over the old city and the adjacent suburbs includes well over 10.5 million; and the urban conurbation which extends thirty miles out from the center encompasses more than 14 million.

Like the typical large American metropolis, Tokyo is experiencing severe growing pains. Schools are overcrowded, the street system is wholly inadequate, public facilities and services are badly overburdened, and the suburban development continues to sprawl farther out. As late as 1962, 1.6 million households were without sewerage facilities and had to rely on nightmen to collect the excreta. Traffic congestion rivals that anywhere in the world, and the transportation system is stretched far beyond its capacity, so much so that "pushers" are employed to pack the commuting trains during rush hours. And because of the critical housing shortage, many of the new migrants to the city are forced to begin their urban lives in the crowded slum districts where shelter is provided by hovels of rusty sheet metal and old packing crates. The government is moving to correct these deficiencies—large housing programs are under way, the subway system is being extended, expressways are being constructed and sewers laid—but these efforts to improve the physical infrastructure of the metropolis can scarcely run fast enough to keep up with the rapid population increase.

Plans to cope with expansion formulated by the National Capital Regional Development Commission, a body appointed by the central government, are modeled after the Greater London plan. They call for the curbing of growth at the center by restricting major factory building (despite this limitation, however, an average of 80,000 new jobs are being created each year in small plants and in enlargements of existing factories), and for the preservation of a greenbelt around the presently built-up area.[23] Hospitals, universities, and other institutions, and airports and cemeteries will be located in this setting of forests and farmlands. Beyond

[23] For a description of the physical development of Tokyo, see Hall, *The World Cities*, pp. 217–233.

the greenbelt, a necklace of satellite towns is to be developed. These are not to be bedroom suburbs but communities with industry and other sources of employment. To facilitate this development, the central government assures local authorities of necessary funds to build home sites and public facilities. It also makes funds available to private entrepreneurs for constructing railways and factories in these areas.[24]

Governmental Pattern

Metropolitan Tokyo, an area of approximately 1600 square miles, includes 23 wards, 11 cities, 3 counties, and several small offshore islands. The principal governing body is the Tokyo Metropolitan Government which has general jurisdiction over the entire area and which serves both as a local unit of self-government and as an administrative arm (a province) of the national government. It consists of a popularly elected governor or chief administrator and a metropolitan assembly of 120 members elected from 36 districts on the basis of population. Each of the cities also has an elected council and administrator.

The Tokyo wards are not electoral districts as city wards are in the United States but local governing units with an elected council and a head or chief administrator selected by the council with the consent of the governor. There is no separate overall government for the wards other than the Tokyo Metropolitan Government whose jurisdiction extends over a far larger territorial area. Following World War II, the wards were vested with strong self-governing powers equal to those of the ordinary city, but since then a considerable diminution of home rule has taken place.

The wards, as the cities and towns, are authorized to deal with local matters prescribed in the Local Autonomy Law or delegated to them by the governor. These include such functions as the operation of small parks and playgrounds, libraries, community centers, and street lighting. The wards also enjoy a limited power of taxation as prescribed by metropolitan ordinances. Generally their administrative powers are less than the other local units in the Tokyo area since the Metropolitan Government is responsible for certain services in the wards—refuse collection for one —that the other authorities provide for themselves. All powers and activities of the wards and towns are subject to the governor's supervision and his authority to coordinate relations among the various local units.

The Tokyo Metropolitan Government performs a wide range of functions, including health and sanitation, major parks, roads, parking facilities, water supply, sewage disposal, fire protection, and public housing. Police protection is also an area-wide function under the general super-

[24] For a more extended description of these developments, see An Administrative Perspective of Tokyo (Tokyo: The Tokyo Metropolitan Government, 1963).

vision of the Tokyo government. However, the superintendent general of the metropolitan police department is appointed by national authorities, and he and other top officials of the department are treated as national public service personnel. Education is a dual responsibility of the two levels of government. Primary and junior high schools are operated by locally-appointed boards of education in each of the municipalities and wards, with senior high and special schools provided by the metropolitan unit.

As can be seen from this summary, local government in the Tokyo area is basically a two-level system with some services handled exclusively by the upper tier or Metropolitan Government, some relegated to the lower or municipalities and wards, and others jointly administered. What distinguishes this system from the American practice of local federalism is the high degree of control exercised by the upper tier over the local units and their activities. In this respect, the Japanese approach to local government in metropolitan areas more closely resembles that of the British.

The Tokyo experience, like London's, indicates that even where various overall controls exist, the problem of government in rapidly expanding metropolitan areas is far from solved. A consultative body to the governor of Toyko pointed this out in a report submitted in 1962. It noted, among other things, that (1) the task of providing public facilities and other services for a city growing as rapidly as the Japanese capital is so voluminous as to overtax the administrative structure badly; (2) no effective system of coordinating the activities of the many local units has yet been devised; and (3) with population spillover into adjacent provinces, it has become difficult for the Tokyo Metropolitan Government to deal with its administrative affairs effectively without some institutionalized system of cooperation with neighboring prefectures.

These difficulties have led some Japanese scholars and statesmen to propose a larger role for the national government in metropolitan affairs. It has been suggested, for example, that a new agency under national control be established to take over responsibility for certain metropolitan functions, particularly the construction of public facilities and the formulation of development plans. As the following quotation shows, the Tokyo government was no more receptive to this suggestion than local authorities in Great Britain or the United States would have been:

Even if it is an admitted fact that the administration of the metropolitan area now carried on by the Tokyo Metropolitan Government is still far from perfect, its cause may be attributed to a lack of a centrally and locally coordinated plan and to the central government's various financial restrictions upon metropolitan administration. It is no wonder that the central government should make studies in the metropolitan system, but such ideas from some authoritative sources as tramping upon home rule are reckless and unconstitutional.[25]

SÃO PAULO

Latin America, the huge land area lying south of the Rio Grande, contains twenty-three independent countries and more than 250 million people. Although still predominantly agricultural, its rate of urbanization in recent decades has outstripped that of most other regions. As late as 1930, Buenos Aires was Latin America's only city with more than 1 million population; today there are ten such aggregations, four of them— Buenos Aires, Mexico City, Rio de Janeiro, and São Paulo—ranking among the twenty largest metropolises in the world. In 1950, 39 percent of the people of this area lived in urban places of 2000 or more; by the end of the 1960s this figure had passed 50 percent.[26]

Unlike the wide cultural diversity in Africa or Asia, the nations of Latin America enjoy certain common linkages. Ninety percent of the people, for example, are Roman Catholic, and Spanish is the official language in eighteen of the countries. Economically, however, their stage of development and their problems are closer to those of Africa and Asia than to the Western states. Poverty is extensive although the extreme degree found in Indonesia or India is not as widely encountered. The flow of population to the cities has been badly out of proportion to the opportunity for industrial employment, and the birth rate remains high in both urban and rural areas. The ratio of employment in the service sector to that in manufacturing is high, a measure of affluence in the industrial nations but an index of poverty in the developing countries. In the latter, the service category is heavily weighted toward petty commerce and street vending, low-paying domestic work, and transitional chores. Much of it actually represents underemployment or disguised employment, undertaken simply because of the unavailability of industrial jobs.

One of the most visible social hallmarks of the Latin American metropolis are the shantytowns or slums which serve as homes for millions of the urban poor. Known by a variety of names—*favellas* in Brazil, *ranchos* in Venezuela, *villas miserias* in Argentina, *barriadas* in Peru, *jacales* in Mexico—these marginal communities differ greatly among themselves in terms of organization, morale, and internal cultural integra-

[25] *Ibid.*, p. 8.

[26] The factors associated with population growth are treated in Glenn H. Beyer (ed.), *The Urban Explosion in Latin America* (Ithaca: Cornell University Press, 1967). An excellent survey of Latin American urbanization is contained in Richard M. Morse, "Recent Research on Latin American Urbanization," *Latin American Research Review*, I (Fall, 1965), 35–74.

tion. They range from those where social disorganization is great to those which exhibit a high potential for inventive accommodation to urban life.[27] Some are the product of squatter invasions in which groups of families organize to move in on vacant land before the police have time to intervene. Some are devoid of public services or facilities and their dwellings are built of waste materials. Others are settlements in which the residents construct their own housing with technical assistance and materials furnished by government agencies. Compared to these self-help projects, governmental programs to construct housing for the urban poor are relatively minuscule.

Brazil is by far the largest of the South American republics in both population (estimated at 85 million in 1966) and territorial size (3.2 million square miles, an area almost equal to that of the United States). Governmentally, it is a federal system in form but essentially centralist in operation, particularly since the military takeover in 1964. It is composed of twenty-one states, five federal territories, and the federal district containing the new capital, Brasilia. In contrast to most other Latin American nations, Brazil is not a primate-city country. It not only includes the giant metropolises of Rio and São Paulo but it also has five other cities with populations exceeding 500,000.

Physical and Demographic Characteristics

São Paulo, 200 air miles southwest of Rio de Janeiro, is the most industrialized center—"the Chicago of Latin America," as some call it. Within its confines are over 27,000 plants and factories employing 600,000 workers, or about one-third of Brazil's entire industrial labor force. Its economic base, as is apparent from these figures, is more typical of the large metropolises in Europe and the United States than of those in the developing countries. The city celebrated the 400th anniversary of its founding in 1954, but until the latter part of the nineteenth century it was a quiet and unassuming town of 25,000. Today, it is a bustling and rapidly growing metropolis with a population of approximately 5 million (8 million in the Greater São Paulo area). It is served by a modern airport, 28 daily newspapers, 18 radio stations, and 5 television stations, and by such cultural facilities as 3 universities, 16 legitimate theatres, and an excellent symphony orchestra.

The colonial pattern of the city is still discernible and its features continue to influence development. At the core is the historic "triangle," the community's economic and bureaucratic center, where the private and governmental office buildings, hotels, shops and department stores, theatres, and the many banks and financial institutions (São Paulo is also the "Wall Street" of Brazil) are located. The residential neighborhoods near

[27] See William Mangin, "Poverty and Politics in Cities of Latin America," in Bloomberg and Schmandt (eds.), *Power, Poverty, and Urban Policy*, pp. 397–434.

the core, formerly the quarters of the aristocrats, have become favorite points for middle-class penetration. Only the construction of centrally located luxury apartments has prevented the total flight of the élite to the garden sites of suburbia. Growth outward from the core has been concentric and has occurred at immense speed without zoning regulations or comprehensive land use plans.[28]

Outside the central city proper but within the governmental boundaries of the municipality are a host of suburban nuclei of various types, ranging from modern industrial aggregations to rural settlements lacking electricity and piped water. In one section are concentrations that include the plants of such prominent United States firms as General Motors and Firestone. In another are residential sub-communities of middle- and lower-class families. Squatter settlements or *favellas* are also found around the periphery but they are far less extensive than in other Latin American cities, including Rio. Still farther out, in locations with desirable topographical features such as beaches and hills, are the residential enclaves of the new upper-middle class.

People and goods in São Paulo are moved over a road network dominated by a loop-and-spoke system of broad radial and circumferential avenues. As in the typical metropolis in the United States, people converge on the core or central business district from all directions. The city has a good public transit system but the demands placed on it are too great to handle this volume of traffic with facility. Moreover, the street and parking system is wholly inadequate to accommodate the area's growing automobile population. The result is intense congestion in and around the core.

Despite gestures by local authorities to encourage decentralization of central business district activities, the core of the metropolis retains a strong pull on commercial and civic functions and on office building use. Some large department stores are invading the suburbs and a few radial streets offer retail shops and service establishments at a distance from the "triangle," but these developments have in no way detracted from the prominence of the city center. Tall skyscrapers continue to rise within its confines and large luxury apartments continue to be constructed on its periphery. Fortunately, the industrial suburbs provide a degree of decentralization for the area that helps to spread peak-hour traffic loads and affords some relief, however small, to the problem of congestion.

Governmental Pattern

Local government in Brazil has an apparent simplicity that contrasts sharply to the pattern in the United States. Each of the twenty-one states is subdivided into municipalities (*municipios*) which constitute the basic

[28] The historical development of São Paulo is described in Richard M. Morse, *From Community to Metropolis* (Gainesville: University of Florida Press, 1958).

unit of local rule. These entities vary tremendously in size, the smallest encompassing less than a square mile and the largest, in the Amazon region, more than 110,000 square miles. (The *municipio* of São Paulo covers 700 square miles of territory.) Brazilian municipalities are more comparable to an American county than to a city or town since they include suburban settlements, rural villages, and agricultural land as well as the urban center or city. Unlike the American county, however, the Brazilian municipality does not share governmental responsibility with any other local entity. Instead, it enjoys jurisdiction over the entire area with no separately incorporated towns and villages or other autonomous units to challenge its authority.[29]

The municipalities are territorially divided into districts (*distritos*), which are primarily administrative units or branch offices of the municipal government. Suburbs have no administrative or political significance although they constitute very definite social areas in large communities such as São Paulo and Rio de Janeiro. They are also functionally specialized subnuclei, as we have seen in São Paulo, with industrial and residential settlements scattered over the landscape. All they lack to make them analogous to the ring communities of metropolises in the United States are separate governments.

Brazilian municipalities have the strong mayor-council form of government. The council, which may not exceed twenty-one members according to the 1967 Constitution, is elected by a system of proportional representation. It exercises no administrative functions but has power to legislate on all matters of purely local interest. The mayor (*prefeito*) is popularly elected except in municipalities which are state, federal, or territorial capitals. In the case of the state capitals such as São Paulo, he is appointed by the governor and in the other instances by the president of the republic.

Since municipalities in Brazil, like those in Africa, collect only a small part of the total monies available for public services and capital improvements, they must rely on state and federal grants and on the direct financing and administration of certain functions by these higher levels. This reliance has encouraged the political subservience of local units to the upper echelons of public authority, a subservience evident in the importance that municipal officials place on maintaining favorable political relations with leaders at these tiers.[30] The mayor is the key figure in this process. As the local political major-domo, he is the principal spokesman, the "chief beggar," for his community in the state and federal capitols. In the eyes of the electorate, his ability to establish

[29] For a study of Brazilian local government, see Frank P. Sherwood, *Institutionalizing the Grass Roots in Brazil* (San Francisco: Chandler, 1967).

[30] See L. Donald Carr, "Brazilian Local Self-Government: Myth or Reality?" *Western Political Quarterly*, 13 (December, 1960), 1043–1055.

productive relations with the governor or president outweighs all other qualifications.

Formally, the municipalities possess a broad range of powers, but in practice the exercise of these prerogatives has been greatly restricted by the failure of the state and national governments to provide the localities with sufficient taxing authority or the resources to meet their responsibilities. Operating relations between the levels of government, moreover, are not clearly defined, with some functions such as education being performed by both state and municipal agencies. As a United Nations report observed, Brazil is an example of a dual structure in which both center and locality perform services independently.[31] It is also true that the upper tiers intervene in local affairs far more in Brazil than in the United States. Federal intervention, in particular, has increased significantly since the military "revolution" of 1964. All of these factors combine to place substantial limitations on local autonomy.

Another, although lesser, reason for the inability of local units to exercise their full panoply of powers is territorial instability. In many municipalities there has been a tendency to elevate the subunits or districts to municipal status, thus introducing an element of governmental fragmentation into what is otherwise a simplistic pattern of organization. The tendency has been particularly strong in the outlying suburban and rural sections where residents feel their needs are given short shrift by the city-dominated administration. This development is interesting to American observers of metropolitan political institutions because of its implications for governmental consolidation. Most importantly, it suggests that there are limits to the territorial size of a local unit for responsible policy-making and administration. Making the units larger still leaves the problem of how to provide government which can both equitably and effectively serve the needs of diverse populations.

São Paulo occupies a more favored position than most municipalities in the Brazilian local governmental system, due largely to its economic status. Because of its degree of industrialization, its resources are substantial and its standard of living high compared to other communities in the country. The median per capita income of its residents is about three times that of the entire nation. These factors make the city less dependent financially on the state and national governments and enable it to exercise a greater degree of control over its local affairs.

Public services and facilities in São Paulo are among the best in Latin America. Utilities, recreation areas, transportation arteries, hospital and social welfare services, sanitation, and the primary and secondary school system are well developed despite persistent material and administrative deficiencies. There are, of course, chronic problems, a common feature of

[31] *Decentralization for National and Local Development* (New York: United Nations Technical Assistance Programme, 1962), p. 10.

metropolitan areas everywhere. Water distribution, for example, has not kept pace with population growth; inadequate land use planning and control have permitted the indiscriminate intermingling of commercial, industrial, and residential zones; and park and playground facilities are inadequate. Many of São Paulo's difficulties are, of course, attributable to its rapid growth, and no amount of governmental resources or foresight could have coped fully with this development.

METROPOLITAN COMMUNITIES IN A WORLD SETTING

No thorough consideration of the metropolis in time and space can overlook either its social and economic facets or its governmental institutions. The informal means of social control which once regulated the communal affairs of primitive settlements have given way to the more formal methods of modern society. As the populations of cities and metropolitan areas have grown in size and heterogeneity, larger and more complex governmental organizations have evolved as instruments of control and direction. Historically, it has been the emergence of local government that has weakened the bonds of familial or tribal social organization and marked the transference of local loyalties to the broader community.

The patterns of local government that have emerged and are still evolving show great diversity, not only between countries but within individual nations as well. To a large extent these patterns and the manner in which their formal and informal structures function are conditioned by the culture of the country and its subparts. We have had occasion to note this relationship in the case of Nigeria where British institutions and practices have been modified under the pressures of local tradition. The same phenomenon is observable elsewhere where the governmental forms imposed by colonial powers have been reshaped or modified in the crucible of local culture.

The basic tasks of urban government are everywhere the same, whether in the cities of Nigeria and Brazil or those in Great Britain and the United States. Throughout the world, metropolitan communities and their governmental systems are being subjected to heavy strains and incessant demands. The responses to these forces have varied from nation to nation. At one extreme, local units have tended to abdicate or to be divested of their responsibilities and become mere administrative arms of the state or national governments. At the other end of the continuum, too great an emphasis on local autonomy has hindered the development of effective public mechanisms for meeting the problems and needs of an increasingly urbanized and technological society.

Despite the great variations, however, there is universally a manifest trend toward the development of a meaningful role for local government within the framework of national goals and policies. This trend is evident even in political systems at opposite poles. Monolithic structures, such as Yugoslavia and the Soviet Union, have moved in the direction of enlarging the role and autonomy of their local subdivisions, while pluralist systems, such as the United States, have increasingly expanded centralized controls over local operations either by direct fiat or by means of financial inducements. The pressures for such controls are greatest in the less-industrialized nations where an integrated thrust in development activity by all levels of public authority is an imperative. But while countries in the latter category are becoming aware of the desirability of giving greater leeway to local initiative, the mature states are beginning to realize the necessity of placing some restrictions on local autonomy and discretion in the interest of preserving a livable urban environment.

16 /
THE
IMAGE
OF THE
FUTURE

ANTHROPOLOGIST MARGARET MEAD, WITH HER UNIQUE CAPACITY FOR expression, has described the urban transformation in these words:

The whole concept of cities has changed in the last two centuries. Once they were walled, to keep out the wild—the bandits, bears, beasts. Now we put a wall around the natural world to keep the human beings out and protect the wild. People who are starving—physically and intellectually—in rural areas, crowd into the cities to find work and, hopefully, a better life for their children. The rural areas are drained of talent—the best people leave for more opportunities and stimulation of the cities.[1]

As the final third of the twentieth century moves on, the process of change persists. Although the rate of urbanization has slowed down in the industrially advanced countries of the world (but not in the developing nations), the absolute growth of metropolitan population continues.

[1] *Los Angeles Times,* February 13, 1966.

Cities are forced to break out of their old bounds and invade the "open country" in their quest for lebensraum. Ring upon ring of suburbs continue to be added to what were once single and relatively compact communities. Census figures on population, density, and area—we need not repeat them here—present a picture of massive change and astonishing growth. The "exploding metropolis" is more than a figure of speech.

Demographic and spatial statistics, however, do not tell the whole story. They document the increase in volume and scale of urban society but they do not reveal how this growth has altered the traditional concept of the city or how it has required twentieth-century man to think of his metropolitan habitat in new terms. They indicate changes in crime rates, welfare assistance, and school enrollment, but they give us little feel for the wide range of problems and issues—social, economic, physical, governmental, political—that confront the community. They enumerate the increase in water usage, waste disposal, recreation, and automobile ownership, but they fail to disclose how these developments have drastically modified the nature of urban problems and the kinds of approaches necessary to cope with them. They show the increasing variety of economic activities and the growing degree of specialization, but they tell us little about the social and political consequences of such changes or their effects on human values and goals. These facets of the metropolis can be understood only by going beyond the impersonal figures of the statistician, important as they are for objective analysis, to the insights of the scientist, the social critic, the artist, and the philosopher.

Living in an urbanized society, modern man experiences mixed emotions as he contemplates the metropolitan scene and ponders its meaning and import. He is struck with the vigor and force of the system and with the impressive achievements in metropolitan community-building. He observes a broadbacked and boisterous land of "tense, turbulent cities, with fingers of power reaching into space." Everywhere in urban areas he sees evidence of technological miracles, industrial might, and intense human activity. Impressive office buildings, factories, and apartments are being constructed, slums are being cleared, expressways are carving huge paths through dense settlements, and civic monuments are rising in tribute to the new metropolitan age. The picture is one of bold strokes and bright paint, perhaps gaudy and in poor taste, but exuding strength and vitality.

Strong as man's pride and wonder at this scene may be, gnawing doubts keep entering his mind. He is disturbed at the tension and unrest in the cities and the sporadic outbreaks of violence which have struck many urban areas in recent years. He is troubled by the warning of the National Commission on Civil Disorders that the nation is rapidly moving toward two societies, "one black, one white—separate and unequal."

He is not happy about the growing pollution of the atmosphere and the rivers and streams, the increasing traffic congestion, and the rising crime rate. If he is in an inquiring and philosophical mood, he will ponder over many questions. What future is in store for the metropolis? What changes are likely to take place in its form and structure and in its demographic patterns? Can urban peace be maintained and social change directed into constructive channels? Is it possible to maintain viable democratic institutions at the local level in a large-scale society? How can the urban social and political system be structured to meet modern challenges?

The answers to these and related questions do not come easily, if at all; the world of the metropolis is too complex for pat replies. Only diligent and imaginative research, careful analysis, and well-formulated theory can provide reasonably sound propositions that give some understanding of urban phenomena. True, without Cassandra's gift of prophecy, we can only speculate about the shape of events to come. Yet our efforts to look into the metropolitan future, if based on the experience of the past and on the emerging trends of the present, can be productive. To those who are concerned with the quality and livability of metropolitan living, recognition of the forces that are shaping our urban environment is critically essential. For unless we are prepared and willing to capitalize on our knowledge of these forces to guide change in the direction most likely to further human goals and aspirations, we can only rely on fate, luck, and drift to fashion the metropolis of tomorrow.

THE EXISTING SYSTEM

Many processes are at work indicating that modifications in the future character and role of the metropolis will inevitably take place, whether by rational design or not. The forces for change are relentless; they will not be stayed by indifference or inactivity. Technological advances, new life styles, increasing citizen expectations, and the general pressures of growth are but a few of the factors that must be accommodated. Most aspects of the metropolitan system, including its social organization, land use patterns, and functional distribution of economic activities, have undergone substantial modification during the present century. Of the key elements, only the governmental pattern has been able to avoid major alteration. Administrative improvements have been made, contractual arrangements among local units have multiplied, new expedients such as special districts have been employed, and considerable school district consolidation has taken place, but basically the system remains as it was before large-scale urbanization. Lack of serious crisis in the existing governmental structure and the strong forces for continuing the present pattern of balkanization are important factors contributing to this result.

It would be difficult today to find an American metropolis in which the governmental system is in imminent danger of breakdown. The riots and civil disturbances have revealed weak points in its armor and have given us "a moment of truth," but they have not seriously challenged its existence. The basic public service needs of most metropolitan residents, whether in an area of 100,000 or 10 million people, are being provided for in one fashion or another. Lives and property are being protected, goods and people transported, sewage and garbage disposed of, water supplied, and general order maintained. Somehow, in spite of the political and administrative fragmentation, governmental activities manage to be coordinated and policies harmonized at least well enough to keep the system functioning.

The fact that catastrophe has been avoided does not by any means imply that all is well. It is not enough for local government in a metropolitan complex merely to prevent service crises or meet the minimal expectations of the majority. It must also be sensitive to the needs of the disadvantaged minority and take steps to bring those in this category into the community decision-making process. And if it is to realize the potentialities of urban existence which large-scale society promises, it must not only assure orderly growth and aid in fashioning a pleasant, stimulating, and vigorous living environment, but it must also seek to mitigate social conflict and enlarge the opportunity structure for all segments of the society. The likelihood is slim, however, that urban man will move to reshape the present system in any drastic way so long as it continues to function in a manner considered at least tolerable by the majority. Instead, he will continue to tinker with the machinery to get rid of the worst annoyances, preferring to put up with the devils he knows rather than take chances with those he does not know.

As political scientist Norton Long reminds us, metropolitan areas are going concerns and hence can be expected to react vigorously to attempts at major alteration. For if the existing system of local government could be easily changed, "it would be intolerably unstable." And if no powerful interests were vested in the status quo, "the existing order would have so little allegiance, it could scarcely run, much less endure."[2]

Previous chapters have called attention to some of the elements hostile to governmental reorganization: the established bureaucracy, the favored tax position of various units, central city-suburban antagonisms, political differences among sections of the area, and the general lack of community bonds. Another strong factor favoring the retention of the present system, according to Robert Wood, is the opportunity a governmentally fragmented structure affords for social segregation. Modern suburbs may use their political boundaries "to differentiate the character of their residents from their neighbors," and their governmental powers—zoning, residential

[2] *The Polity* (Chicago: Rand NcNally, 1962), p. 161.

covenants, taxation, selective industrial development—"to promote conscious segregation." From the variety of classes, occupations, income levels, races, and creeds in the metropolis, "a municipality may isolate the particular variant it prefers and concentrate on one type of the metropolitan man."[3] In this way socially homogeneous subcommunities with protective armor can be maintained within the larger complex.

EMERGING TRENDS

Each metropolitan community faces important policy decisions in seeking to determine its future. It cannot avoid questions of how it shall organize governmentally, how it shall develop economically and physically, and how it shall deal with social issues. Nor can it disregard the processes by which it evolves over a period of time or the day-to-day interaction that takes place within its territorial confines. It must, in short, be conditioned to accept change and to make the policy choices that will guide this change in the direction most conducive to the well-being of the total community.

In making an assessment of the metropolitan future, certain emerging trends must be kept in mind. Four of the more significant are: (1) the rise of the megalopolis; (2) the movement of decision-making powers to higher echelons of public and private authority; (3) the emphasis on cooperative devices as an alternative to formal restructuring of the governmental pattern; and (4) the growing demands of minority groups and the disadvantaged for a greater voice in community decisions that affect them.

The Megalopolis

More than 2000 years ago, a group of Greek settlers founded a new community in the Peloponnesus which they called *Megalopolis*, to express their hope that it would become the largest of the Hellenic city-states. In subsequent centuries, the word's dictionary definition as a "very large city" was largely forgotten. Recently, however, it has reappeared in the vocabulary as a result of the writings of geographer Jean Gottmann, who used the term to designate the cluster of metropolitan areas in the northeastern part of the United States. Gottmann's description of this section of the nation portrays its amazing character:

An almost continuous system of deeply interwoven urban and suburban areas, with a total population of about 37 million people in 1960, has been erected along the Northeastern Atlantic seaboard. It straddles state boundaries,

[3] "Metropolitan Government, 1975: An Extrapolation of Trends," *American Political Science Review*, LII (March, 1958), 117.

stretches across wide estuaries and bays, and encompasses many regional differences. . . . Crowded within its limits is an extremely distinguished population. It is, *on the average,* the richest, best educated, best housed, and best serviced group of similar size (i.e., in the 25-to-40-million-people range) in the world. . . . It is true that many of its sections have seen pretty rural landscapes replaced by ugly industrial agglomerations or drab and monstrous residential developments; it is true that in many parts of Megalopolis the air is not clean any more, the noise is disturbing day and night, the water is not as pure as one would wish, and transportation at times becomes a nightmare.[4]

Along similar lines, political scientist Charlton Chute had a few years earlier employed the term "urban region" to designate an area in which two or more SMSAs adjoin each other. Identifying nineteen such regions, Chute argued that the historic concept of a metropolitan area as a core city surrounded by suburbs is no longer adequate for analytical purposes. It is now necessary, he stated, to take into account the interrelationships between neighboring SMSAs and to study clusters of such areas as closely as we do clusters of cities and other urban groups.[5]

The trend toward megalopolis in certain sections of the country makes it imperative to think of new devices for coordinating those activities and handling those problems which transcend individual metropolitan areas. In some instances, this may involve cooperative arrangements between metropolitan governmental organizations, such as COGs. In other cases, it may necessitate joint action by the affected states to establish mechanisms for coping with a difficulty or administering a function. And in still others, it may require assumption of the responsibility by the national government. One implication, however, is clear in the continuing development of megalopolitan forms of urban settlement. The better the individual SMSAs are equipped organizationally—either through area-wide governments or viable COGs—to negotiate with each other, the less likely are they to forfeit powers to higher levels of public authority.

The Upward Shift of Power

Metropolitan areas develop and take their particular form as the result of countless decisions by both public and private agencies. These decisions are controlled by various criteria including market facts, professional standards, and community attitudes and values.[6] Governmental policies at the metropolitan level can influence these developments, but the extent of such influence is limited. A decision by local public officials

[4] *Megalopolis* (New York: Twentieth Century Fund, 1961), pp. 7, 15.

[5] "Today's Urban Regions," *National Municipal Review,* XLV (June, 1956), 274–280.

[6] See William L. C. Wheaton, "Public and Private Agencies of Change in Urban Expansion," in Melvin M. Webber and others (eds.), *Explorations in Urban Structure* (Philadelphia: University of Pennsylvania Press, 1964), pp. 154–196.

to encourage industrial growth can have real meaning only if economic factors are favorable to such expansion. Or a decision to undertake a major program of public works can be realistic only if the existing or potential resources of the community are sufficient to warrant such expenditures and the voters are willing to support them.

When government acts, moreover, it must do so within an environmental framework shaped by the cumulative past policies and actions of public agencies and private organizations. Local authorities, for example, may consider it desirable to relegate the central business district to a lesser role, but earlier investment decisions relative to buildings, transportation arteries, and public utilities may compel them to take the opposite tack and promote additional investment in the area to protect what already exists. Or past policies of the planning commission and city council may have resulted in the establishment of land use patterns that severely circumscribe the extent to which future changes in the physical design and ecology of the city can be accomplished.

In addition to these limitations, the ability of individual metropolitan communities to control their own destiny has been steadily diminished by the increase in scale of the urban world. Policies which at one time were determined largely at the local level are now dependent upon the decisions of agencies outside the community. As one observer has appropriately noted, "The discrepancy in organizational scale between local government and the nature of large-scale society results in a movement of power upward, to organizational centers outside the control of the local polity. Such organizations wield power that is area-wide in scope and consequences."[7] Some commentators even go so far as to say that local government has become little more than a "delivery system" for national policies and products.

The growing extent of federal participation and involvement at the local level can be seen in the many grant-in-aid programs now in operation. The national government is presently administering more than fifty separate programs of financial assistance to urban communities, the predominant majority of which has been authorized since 1950. Since such grants usually impose requirements and restrictions as a condition of assistance, the impact of national policy determinations on local and metropolitan operations has been substantial. This development is a far cry from the statement contained in a municipal government text at the turn of the present century which noted: "Nothing need be said about the federal government since it has no connection with city affairs."

The upward shift of power is by no means confined to government; the same phenomenon is occurring in the private sector with similar effects on the metropolis. The rapid disappearance of the family-owned enterprise (which traditionally has had a strong personal commitment to

[7] Scott Greer, *The Emerging City* (New York: Free Press, 1962), p. 162.

the local community) and its displacement by the national corporation with headquarters in one city and branches in many others has caused drastic shifts in the spatial location of power. Many investment decisions which at one time were made locally are now determined at the main offices of the absentee owners who have no emotional attachment to the affected communities. These decisions may have important implications for the development or functioning of individual metropolitan areas, but the latter have no voice in their formulation.

The "Cooperative" Emphasis

Early efforts at reform of the governmental pattern of the metropolis sought to achieve its complete integration by extending the boundaries of the central city through annexation or consolidation. The underlying rationale for this approach was expressed by such veteran political scientists as Chester C. Maxey and William Bennett Munro who stoutly maintained that as an organic and economic unit the metropolitan community demanded a unified government. Although recognizing the case for local rule, they saw little reason for granting political autonomy to what they regarded as neighborhoods or sections of a single community. In their view, the necessary concessions to local sentiment could be made in other ways, such as by the creation of administrative subdistricts within the larger complex.

By 1930, governmental integration had been largely abandoned as the proposed general solution. In its place, various remedies based on the principle of "local federalism" began to make their appearance. In the first comprehensive work on the governance of metropolitan areas published in this country, Paul Studenski gave expression to the new approach when he wrote that "a form of government must be found that will foster the development of a vigorous metropolitan consciousness in the entire area, promote proper standards of service throughout, preserve and cultivate a healthy consciousness of locality in the constituent parts, and secure the proper treatment of purely local as distinguished from metropolitan affairs."[8] This view was repeatedly echoed in the survey-type studies of individual metropolitan areas which appeared during the 1950s.

The decade of the 1960s was marked by increased emphasis on the cooperative approach as reorganization plans involving the federal or two-tier device continued to meet with no greater success than their predecessors. A Rockefeller Foundation study of 1958 advanced the currently popular theme when it said of urban problems: "Cooperation among existing governmental units, under existing authority, can often go far to meet these problems, and this, rather than the creation of new

[8] *The Government of Metropolitan Areas in the United States* (New York: National Municipal League, 1930), p. 41.

layers of government, may be the most effective means of coping with metropolitan growth."[9] Some exceptions to this trend, however, have appeared in more recent years, particularly in the medium-sized SMSAs, where attempts at city-county consolidation have met with success in the Nashville, Jacksonville, and Indianapolis areas. Although it is doubtful that these reformist victories are a harbinger of things to come, they do indicate a residue of dissatisfaction with existing governmental structures and mechanisms.

The cooperative approach is officially acknowledged by the national government as an acceptable means of coordinating interlocal activity. Whether the principal mechanism for putting this approach into execution—the council of governments—can provide the answer to the organizational problem of the metropolis remains to be seen. On the basis of past experience with intergovernmental cooperation among local units, the prognosis would not be very encouraging. However, there are presently several factors in the picture which make it appear somewhat more promising.

First, it seems clear that the national government is going to bring increasing pressure on local units to effect greater administrative and policy coordination in matters affecting the development and functioning of the total metropolitan aggregation. The requirement for review of community facilities applications by an area-wide agency is but one step in this direction. Others are likely to follow, such as a stipulation that COGs determine the priorities for the allocation of federal facilities grants among the local units. As this trend evolves, such bodies will be forced into a more active political role; and some of them may even evolve into metropolitan or regional governments.

Second, local officials will sooner or later come to realize that, in view of the upward movement of power, they must mobilize in self-defense if they are to retain a voice in critical decisions affecting their communities. For if local jurisdictions lack the organizational means of reaching agreement on common issues, they will be at a distinct disadvantage in bargaining with state and national agencies.

Third, the problems of adequate housing, equality of opportunity in employment and education, racial discrimination, and other major urban difficulties have become nationalized to the point where federal policy can be expected to become more deeply involved in promoting their solution. The overriding question here is how long the national government will be willing to go along with the cooperative approach if local units fail to show substantial progress in coordinating their own efforts relative to these problems.

[9] *Prospect for America: The Rockefeller Panel Reports* (Garden City, N.Y.: Doubleday, 1961), p. 304.

Decentralization

As power aggregates, it tends to generate counterpressures for decentralization. This phenomenon has been witnessed in the industrial world where the movement is one of increasing concentration of broad policy-making functions at the upper level but an expansion of administrative discretion and decisional authority at the lower echelons. Similar tendencies are beginning to appear in the metropolitan political sphere with the increased pressures for an area-wide concentration of power on one hand and the demand for greater neighborhood autonomy on the other. Although the latter move is currently manifested most intensely in the black sections of the core city, it is present elsewhere in less conspicuous form.

Just as the federal requirements for comprehensive planning and area-wide review stimulated the creation of COGs, so the "maximum feasible participation" phrase in the Economic Opportunity Act of 1964 became a major rallying point for those seeking to decentralize local political power and enlarge the participatory base of community decision-making. Although these diverse tendencies might at first glance appear contradictory, they may well presage the future evolutionary development of the urban governmental structure. By moving toward a metropolitan or regional government with jurisdiction over the principal maintenance functions of the area, the devolution of certain "life-style" powers to the neighborhood becomes possible and even highly desirable. This type of decentralization may win increasing favor if, as some authorities maintain, neighborhood control over public decisions directly affecting the daily life of its members is conducive to the maintenance of social peace.

THE PRESENT AND FUTURE

The metropolis is not suffering from lack of criticism on the part of either idealists or hard-headed realists. Some observers, like Lewis Mumford, are appalled by what they see. To him the modern metropolis is an accumulation of people accommodating themselves "to an environment without adequate natural or cultural resources: People who do without pure air, who do without sound sleep, who do without a cheerful garden or playing space, who do without the very sight of the sky and the sunlight, who do without free motion, spontaneous play, or a robust sexual life."[10] Others, such as economist John Kenneth Galbraith, are indignant at what they consider an unbalanced emphasis on private wants

[10] *The Culture of Cities* (New York: Harcourt, Brace & World, 1938), p. 249.

to the neglect of urban and other public needs. In Galbraith's words:

The family which takes its mauve and cerise, air-conditioned, power-steered, and power-braked automobile out for a tour passes through cities that are badly paved, made hideous by litter, blighted buildings, billboards, and posts for wires that should long since have been put underground. They pass on into a countryside that has been rendered largely invisible by commercial art. . . . They picnic on exquisitely packaged food from a portable icebox by a polluted stream and go on to spend the night at a park which is a menace to public health and morals.[11]

And still others, such as newspaperman Mitchell Gordon, are overwhelmed by the magnitude of the problems. As he describes the situation:

An observer of the sprawling urban scene today might be compelled to concede that the superficial monotony of physical similarity must be the least important of all the ailments of the squatting modern metropolitan region whose air grows fouler and more dangerous by the day, whose water is threatened increasingly by pollution, whose mobility is undermined by accumulations of vehicles and withering transit, whose educational system reels under a growing variety of economic, social, and national emergencies, and whose entire pattern is assuming an ominous shape and sociological form, with well-to-do whites in their suburban cities ringing poverty-ridden minority groups widening at the core.[12]

Much of the earlier criticism of the metropolis was directed against its physical characteristics and problems, such as appearance, land use development, the service infrastructure, and air and water pollution. However, the riots and civil disturbances during the latter half of the 1960s gave new visibility to its social ills and prompted a flurry of critical comment and analysis. As John Gardner, former secretary of the federal Department of Health, Education and Welfare and now president of the national Urban Coalition, noted in a recent speech, city halls in many metropolitan areas "are out of touch with the suburbs, black people are out of touch with white people, business and labor do not get along, and the youth have no communication with adults. These cities are not communities. They are encampments of strangers."[13]

Not all urban experts agree with these forebodings. Planner Roger Starr, for example, while admitting the presence of serious problems, charges the critics with talking to the city like a nagging wife addressing her drinking husband. In his view these critics are suffering from a myopia that prevents them from seeing the progress which has resulted

[11] *The Affluent Society* (Boston: Houghton Mifflin, 1958), p. 253.
[12] *Sick Cities: Psychology and Pathology of American Urban Life* (New York: Macmillan, 1963), pp. 339–340.
[13] Speech at Town Hall, Los Angeles, September 12, 1968.

from activities in both the public and private sectors.[14] Starr reflects the feelings of many embattled local officials who find their life increasingly complicated by the emerging challenges in the society and the emphasis on new forms of citizen participation and involvement. Highly skeptical of this latter development, and objecting to the theory that the views of those most affected by a public proposal are entitled to special consideration, he longs for the restoration of the party machines which freed the politician from complete dependence on the goodwill of his constituents.

Although none of the nation's metropolitan areas is on the verge of catastrophe, they may be courting future chaos by their present course. They are continuing to grow in size and wealth, if not in beauty and orderliness. Their dynamism shows no signs of abating even though the traffic may be moving more slowly and the air becoming more polluted. But as even their most ardent defenders would have to admit, the metropolises are surviving despite their great problems and not because significant strides are being made in finding solutions to them.

Physical Design

A few years ago a Boston public official gave this capsule description of his city's core area: "The average building in downtown Boston is 75 to 100 years old. Our downtown streets are winding cow pastures. Traffic is so chaotic that an expressway we just built which was to have been adequate for nearly a decade was filled to capacity on the rush hour almost as soon as it was opened. It would cost us $2 billion to get the city core back into shape again and then we couldn't begin to show results for a good ten years."[15] The Boston picture is not atypical; it is duplicated in varying degrees in most of the nation's large SMSAs and even in many of its smaller urban communities. The spread of blight, particularly in the older metropolises, continues to outrun the clearing of dilapidated structures and the upgrading of neighborhoods despite the redevelopment efforts of the last two decades. Indiscriminate use of the bulldozer, moreover, coupled with the failure of the cities to provide housing within the means of the dispossessed, has in more recent years generated intense opposition among affected residents to large-scale clearance projects.

Considering the present situation and the ceaseless pressure of urban expansion several questions come to mind. Are we not likely to witness a major transformation in the physical shape or design of the metropolis in the foreseeable future? Is it not possible that the present pattern of development will be modified so as to divert growth into satellite communities separated from the main metropolitan center by open space

[14] Roger Starr, *The Living End: The City and Its Critics* (New York: Coward-McCann, 1966), p. 23.

[15] Quoted in Gordon, *Sick Cities*, p. 318.

and greenbelts? Or will most Americans soon be living, as some writers predict, in a dozen or so vast "super" or "strip" cities, which are really not cities but great sprawling complexes covering hundreds and even thousands of square miles. No one, of course, can answer these questions with assurance. Events such as a nuclear war or new technological break-throughs in transportation and communication could result in drastic alterations in the present urban pattern. So also might a change in the life styles of the average American family. But discounting the unex-pected, we see no indications on the immediate horizon of a major shift from current trends. Changes, some of substantial significance, will un-doubtedly occur, but most of them will likely be adjustments in existing arrangements rather than a radical departure from them.

We can certainly expect more coordinated land use planning and a higher degree of control over development in the coming years. The pressures which are building up are too great to be disregarded. Met-ropolitan dwellers, for example, are showing signs of greater awareness of the need for rational physical planning. State governments are begin-ning to take a closer look at the development of their urban regions. The national government is steadily adding to its requirements for long-range and coordinated planning on an area-wide basis as a condition of aid. Regional planning agencies are multiplying in number either as separate bodies or integral parts of councils of governments. Finally, hundreds of local communities (with the assistance of federal "701" grants) have prepared or are in the process of formulating comprehensive land use plans. The outcome of this fermentation is yet to be seen but it is encour-aging that far more planning is going on in our metropolitan and urban areas today than at any time in the past. The task ahead is to see that this planning is properly coordinated and translated into concrete results. If we cannot achieve the "city beautiful" we can at least improve con-siderably upon the present situation.

Social Pattern

Observers of the contemporary metropolitan scene have often expressed fear that the central city will become increasingly the home of low-income workers and nonwhites while the suburbs will continue to attract the middle- and upper-income whites. Some, however, are quick to point out that a simple social dichotomy between the core city and its periphery does not now exist and is unlikely to do so in the future. The suburban portion of the metropolis, contrary to the common stereotype, does not constitute a socially homogeneous settlement but a mosaic of subcom-munities segregated by income and classes. There are working-class suburbs as well as fenced-off islands of the well-to-do; industrial as well as residential satellites; blighted as well as carefully maintained and manicured fringe-area villages. This pattern could mean, as Coleman

Woodbury suggests, that "socially and psychologically, both the metropolitan and suburban bodies politic will remain split up into groups and classes unable to communicate effectively, mutually suspicious, incapable of defining their common interests or of cooperating to realize them."[16] Or, conversely, it could be conducive to social peace by giving each group and class the means of controlling its life style functions as it sees fit within a larger framework of common policies and direction. For the latter to occur, however, would require a greater centralization of authority over area-wide requirements and the enlargement of opportunities for the now disadvantaged groups to share in the rewards of such a system.

As in the case of its physical design, there is little reason to believe that the social structure of the metropolis will undergo major modification in the near future. The pattern will likely continue to evolve along present lines with the central city shouldering a disproportionate share of responsibility for the economically and culturally deprived segments of the populace, and the suburbs continuing to attract a large proportion of white families in the lower-middle to upper income range. However, the revolution in race relations now taking place will inevitably lead to a substantial increase in nonwhite penetration across the core city border. To lessen the possibilities of conflict, this dispersal is likely to be furthered by the development (with the aid of federal subsidies and incentives) of new communities in the outer reaches of the metropolis for lower-income families. The expansion of expressways, the construction of mass transit facilities, and the continuing deconcentration of industry will make these sections more accessible and appropriate for settlement by such groups. Decentralization of activities throughout the area will also go on, with cultural facilities, such as little theaters and music halls, making their appearance at various points in the suburban complex along with the commercial and industrial enterprises.

In looking ahead, several emerging developments pertinent to the social structure of metropolitan communities deserve notice. Although their potential impact remains to be determined, they cannot be ignored in speculations about the future. First, the continuous upward movement of urban dwellers in socioeconomic rank, accompanied by expanded income redistributive policies on the part of the national government (such as the negative income tax, rent supplements, and greater social security benefits), will give a higher proportion of the metropolitan population more freedom of choice in housing, life style, and place of residence. Second, the programs to eliminate poverty, along with the steady rise in income levels for all segments of the urban complex, will increase the percentage of citizens with a perceived stake in the community. This

[16] "Suburbanization and Suburbia," *American Journal of Public Health,* 45 (January, 1955), 9.

fact, in turn, should be conducive to a greater degree of social order and less tension.

Third, accelerated progress is likely to be made in improving the housing supply and living conditions of the metropolitan core through new or expanded federal programs, such as mortage interest subsidization for low-income families and model cities. The latter is of particular interest since it is designed to upgrade the quality of blighted neighborhoods or sections by making available to them a combination of physical, social, and economic remedies. These efforts should help to slow the exodus of middle-class families from the central city and attract back some of the expatriates. Fourth, the most intense period of farm-to-city migration now appears to be ending, with much of the surplus population of the rural areas drained off. With this slowdown, the burden on the central city of accommodating large numbers of poverty-stricken and unskilled newcomers will be lightened.

The social structure of the metropolis, in brief, exhibits both encouraging and disturbing trends. The growing affluence of the total society, the rising level of education, and the upward mobility of an increasing proportion of urban residents constitute elements of strength in the system. At the same time, the slow progress in eliminating racial discrimination, the far-from-adequate efforts to upgrade the disadvantaged members of the community, and the increasing polarization of American society between blacks and whites serve warning on the future.

Economic Structure

The economic structure of the metropolis has undergone substantial modification in the present century. Continued growth in size has been accompanied by increasing specialization and industrial diversification. It has also been accompanied by major changes in the location of commercial and industrial enterprises. At one time, not too many decades ago, economic activities were overwhelmingly concentrated in the core city. Today, the situation is strikingly different. Decentralization which began early in this century has created an entirely new pattern. Retail trade has followed the population movement outward. Suburban industrial parks have developed along the new circumferential highways and at other strategic points on the periphery. Office buildings have appeared in large suburban communities, and warehouse and distribution centers have become common sights along the outlying arteries.

The forces which are generating the spatial diffusion of homes, factories, and shopping centers are not likely to diminish in the future. Manufacturing and wholesaling enterprises will continue to respond to obsolescence and changing technological requirements by looking for new quarters. The outward movement of people will continue to be accompanied by the outward movement of jobs, stores, and service establishments. These developments have caused some analysts to regard the future of the core city, and more particularly its downtown area, with a high degree of pessimism. Certainly many central cities will decline in importance as manufacturing centers in relation to the suburban hinterlands. So also will they experience a diminishing share of the total retail market as the proportion of suburbanites in the metropolitan population increases. In many cases these will be absolute losses, a result already observed in some of the large SMSAs where the number of jobs and total retail sales in the core municipalities declined significantly during the 1950s and 1960s.

Despite these trends, the central city is likely to remain a viable economic unit. The tremendous amount of fixed capital, public and private, invested in existing facilities makes it highly improbable that this section of the metropolis will be abandoned to the vagaries of fate. Although it may not capture as high a proportion of the area's economic activity as it has in the past, redevelopment of its physical plant and changes in its functional role should reverse the downward trend. The central business district will become more reliant for its economic existence upon office activity; cleared areas will provide room for certain types of commercial and light industrial enterprises; new housing construction, much of it in the form of middle- and upper-income apartments, will provide a ready clientele for the shops, restaurants, and theaters; and the assumption of a greater portion of the city's welfare costs by higher echelons of government will lessen the tax strain on the local economy.

Many factors, such as industrial structure, population size, and geographical location, influence the income pattern and performance of a metropolitan economy. These variables, however, are subject to national forces which are the primary determinants of the economic base and growth rates of individual SMSAs. Although the local response to these external forces is also important, the circumscriptions on the ability of urban areas to control their own economic destiny are many. But regardless of what direction the future economy of the nation will take, the lion's share of its output will continue to be located in the metropolises. This also means that the struggle for greater equity in the distribution of benefits will continue to be most manifest at this level. Pressures will be intensified to modify the revenue and expenditure patterns of local governments so as to reflect a closer congruence between resources and needs. These changes will not come easily or without struggle, but they are inevitable in the face of the new found activism of the disadvantaged and the increasing intervention of the national government.

Governmental System

Mark Twain once said: "Thunder is good, thunder is impressive, but it is lightning that does the work." The movement in recent decades to redesign the metropolitan governmental system has been characterized by much thunder, but lightning has struck only occasionally, as in the case of several city-county consolidations. This record is not surprising, for as that shrewd observer of politics, Niccolo Machiavelli, observed long ago: "There is nothing more difficult to carry out, nor more doubtful of success, nor more dangerous to handle than to initiate a new order of things."[17] Yet if it is unrealistic to expect a wave of reorganization successes during the next decade, it would be equally shortsighted to assume that no significant changes will take place.

The current emphasis is on interlocal cooperation as the answer to the existing and emerging public needs of metropolitan areas. This form of institutional response can evolve in one of several ways. It may prove, as its proponents claim, that voluntary cooperation of sufficient magnitude to serve the requirements of large urban communities is possible without further centralization of power. It may fall into disuse because of the inability of local units to reach agreement on crucial issues. It may lead to the conversion of COGs into general purpose metropolitan governments. Or it may result in a strengthening of such councils by endowing them with certain policy-making and administrative powers. Present indications point to the last of these alternatives as the most likely course the movement will follow in the near future.

Along with the development of cooperative mechanisms, we will probably see single-county SMSAs make greater use of the county government as the area-wide instrumentality and, in cases where few incorporated municipalities are involved, city-county consolidation. Special districts will remain popular for functions, such as water supply, sewage disposal, air pollution control, and transit, which require administrative areas larger than the county. The tendency to employ approaches with incremental impact on local governmental systems will continue to be most evident, but significant exceptions can be anticipated.

In the immediate years ahead the need will become more intense for a metropolitan governmental system capable of striking a balance between the particularizing and centralizing forces in the urban complex. The two-tier or federal plan in its various forms is designed to accommodate both of these forces. It acknowledges the pressures of localism by seeking to preserve a meaningful sphere of activity at the submetropolitan level and to provide a symbolic anchoring post for community identification and civic participation. At the same time, it recognizes the centripetal forces by fashioning an institutional framework for the exercise of leadership and policy-formulation in matters of area-wide concern.

Although comprehensive forms of the two-level system have recently evoked little support in American metropolises, it is possible that interest in this device may be reactivated, particularly in SMSAs where the black

[17] *The Prince*, Everyman's Edition (London: J. M. Dent and Sons, 1958), p. 29.

population is gaining control of the central city. It is conceivable in such circumstances that both core city blacks and suburban whites would be willing to support a federated system. This is possibly so of the former because such a solution would relieve them of fiscal responsibility for certain expensive systems maintenance functions, such as sewerage facilities and transportation, over which there is minimal race-related conflict. It seems probable of the latter because a metropolitan authority would enable the white majority in the area to retain some measure of jurisdiction over the central city while escaping involvement with its day-to-day governance.

It is not crucial to the shaping of a satisfactory urban environment, contrary to the insistence of the earlier reformers, whether a metropolitan area has a unified fire protection force or a host of smaller departments, or whether water is supplied by one special district, refuse disposal by another, and mass transit by a third. Such a fragmented service pattern does raise problems of coordination and efficiency, but these drawbacks do not necessarily render the system dysfunctional. Telephone, gas, and electric utilities, for example, have been able to respond to metropolitan needs effectively even though they operate as separate entities. What is important, however, is that there be some established means of formulating policies of area-wide import, coordinating and guiding overall development, and giving the metropolitan electorate a voice in the critical issues which affect the total complex. What is important also is that the institutional mechanisms created to accomplish these purposes do not deprive the subcommunities of a meaningful sphere of control over those matters which directly affect their neighborhoods and life styles. Gargantua and Grassroots need not be dichotomous alternatives. Whether the COGs (or strengthened county governments) can adequately play the larger role remains to be seen. If they prove incapable of doing so, we can expect growing pressure for more formidable change.

THE GOOD METROPOLIS

Urban man is so immersed in his personal pursuits and day-to-day problems that, like the Muckraker in *The Pilgrim's Progress,* he does not raise his head to see the broader vision of the good community. The full potential of the modern metropolis escapes his thought as the difficulties and maladies which plague urban living capture his attention. Traffic congestion and overcrowded schools have meaning for him, as do physical blight and crime in the streets. He is unhappy about the racial disturbances, the student protests, and the rising tax rates. But he does not as yet perceive any of these developments as seriously interfering with the attainment of his individual goals. Nor have they disturbed him to the point where he is ready to take action to reconstruct the system rather than merely search for scapegoats on whom to vent his indignation. Perhaps, as political scientist York Willbern has expressed it:

. . . the great sprawling urban areas of this country fall short not so much in their achievement of the goals and ambitions of their residents, as in the degree to which they achieve or fail to achieve the speculative constructs of the intellectuals who concern themselves with the matter. The disparity is not between the metropolis as it is and the metropolis as its residents wish it; the disparity is between the existing metropolis and the City of God of the planners and the dreamers.[18]

But as Bloody Mary in *South Pacific* exclaimed, "You can't make a dream come true without first having a dream." It is the function of those who have caught the vision of a better city and metropolis— planners, philosophers, poets, novelists, social critics—to provide the dream. It is the function of political, civic, and organizational leaders to seize upon those aspects of the vision which are in the realm of possibility, to define them in concrete terms, and to present them to the people for debate and consideration.

The system of local government in a metropolitan area exists to assure order and supply public services. Beyond these basic tasks, it exists to nurture civic life and to foster the values of a free and democratic society. It serves this higher role to the extent that it is able to fashion an environment suitable for the expression and development of human potentialities and for the personal growth of its individual members. Government is by no means the sole or possibly even the most important instrumentality for promoting men's goals. This is a task for which all community institutions share responsibility. The special role of the governmental system is to provide an appropriate framework within which the energy and resources of the community can be mobilized and directed at improving the quality of urban life. Pessimistic as the outlook may seem to some, the good metropolis is more than a figment of utopian fancy. Its achievement is within the capabilities and resources of modern man. The choice of the future is his to make.

[18] *The Withering Away of the City* (University: University of Alabama Press, 1963), p. 47.

A COMMENTARY ON BIBLIOGRAPHY

OUR PURPOSE IN PRESENTING THIS BIBLIOGRAPHICAL ESSAY IS TO COMMENT briefly on important literature about the metropolis that is not generally mentioned elsewhere in this book. As a rule, therefore, the commentary supplements rather than duplicates the extensive footnote citations in the text. To keep it within manageable proportions and increase its usefulness, we have made a representative sampling of significant materials, largely of recent origin, and have organized them under a number of major categories. Except in a few instances, single articles from periodicals have been excluded.

Three extensive compilations of references on metropolitan affairs with emphasis on governmental aspects are Government Affairs Foundation, *Metropolitan Communities: A Bibliography* (Chicago: Public Administration Service, 1956); Government Affairs Foundation and University of California (Berkeley) Bureau of Public Administration, *Metropolitan Communities: A Bibliography, Supplement: 1955–1957* (Chicago: Public Administration Service, 1960), prepared by Victor Jones and Barbara J. Hudson; and *Metropolitan Communities: A Bibliography, Supplement: 1958–1964* (Chicago: Public Administration Service, 1967), compiled by Barbara J. Hudson and Robert H. McDonald. Briefer general bibliographies are Barbara J. Hudson, "The City in America,"

American Review, II (May, 1962), 142–160, and U.S. Senate Committee on Government Operations, Subcommittee on Intergovernmental Relations, *Metropolitan America* (Washington: 1964). *Bibliographia,* issued periodically by the International Union of Local Authorities, The Hague, Netherlands, is a listing of current publications on urban-related subjects.

Various enumerations conducted by the U.S. Bureau of the Census constitute nationwide sources of data. The most relevant here are the *Census of Population* and the *Census of Housing,* which are released decennially; and the *Census of Governments,* the *Census of Manufactures,* and the *Census of Business,* which are available every five years. *County and City Data Book,* published at irregular intervals, is a convenient collection of selected information from these and other census reports. The Bureau also prepares various intercensal publications, such as *Current Population Reports: Special Studies,* some of which pertain to metropolitan areas.

Other basic general sources are *Metropolitan Area Digest* and *Metropolitan Area Annual,* both published by the Graduate School of Public Affairs, State University of New York, Albany; the sections titled "Metropolitan Areas," "County Government," and "Citizen Action" in the *National Civic Review,* issued monthly by the National Municipal League, New York; and articles and tables relating to metropolitan complexes in the *Municipal Year Book,* published by the International City Management Association, Washington. All three publications have bibliographies. Items of urban interest as well as bibliographic references are also found in such periodicals as *Urban Affairs Quarterly* (Beverly Hills: Sage Publications), *Nation's Cities* (Washington: National League of Cities), *American County Government* (Washington: National Association of Counties), *Public Management* (Washington: International City Management Association), *Studies in Comparative Local Government* (The Hague: International Union of Local Authorities), and *Urban Studies* (Glasgow: University of Glasgow). *Urban Affairs Reporter* (three loose-leaf volumes), a service of Commerce Clearing House, furnishes up-to-date information on all federal programs in the United States affecting local and state governments.

The status of research on urbanism and metropolitanism and suggestions about further lines of investigation have been receiving increased attention. Examples are Stephen B. Sweeney and George S. Blair (eds.), *Metropolitan Analysis: Important Elements of Study and Action* (Philadelphia: University of Pennsylvania Press, 1958); Coleman Woodbury, *A Framework for Urban Studies: An Analysis of Urban-Metropolitan Development and Research Needs* (Washington: Highway Research Board, October, 1959); and Raymond Vernon and others, *The Myth and Reality of Our Urban Problems* (Cambridge: Harvard University Press, 1962). Additional illustrations are Roscoe C. Martin and Douglas Price, *The Metropolis and Its Problems* (1960); Stanley Scott, Ronald R. Royce, and Robert L. Brown, *Two Notes on Metropolitan Research* (1961); and Harvey E. Brazer, Scott Greer, and York Willbern, *Metropolitan Issues: Social, Governmental, Fiscal* (1962), edited by Guthrie S. Birkhead (all three monographs published by the Maxwell Graduate School of Citizenship and Public Affairs, Syracuse University, Syracuse); and the *Urban Affairs Annual Review,* issued since 1967 by Sage Publications.

Important critiques also have appeared in article form: Allan R. Richards, "Local Government Research: A Partial Evaluation," *Public Administration Review*, XIV (Autumn, 1954), 271–277; Robert Daland, "Political Science and the Study of Urbanism," *American Political Science Review*, LI (June, 1957), 491–507; Lawrence Herson, "The Lost World of Municipal Government," *American Political Science Review*, LI (June, 1957), 330–345; William Anderson's rejoinder to Professor Herson, "Municipal Government: No Lost World," *American Political Science Review*, LI (September, 1957), 776–783; and N. Paul Friesema, "The Metropolis and the Maze of Local Government," *Urban Affairs Quarterly*, II (December, 1966), 68–90. Abstracts of ongoing research are contained in *Quarterly Digest of Urban and Regional Research*, published by the University of Illinois Press, Urbana. *Urban Research News*, a bi-weekly newsletter of Sage Publications, reports on current developments of interest to urban specialists. An overview of urban research, including its problems and prospects, is presented in a collection of essays by social scientists from several disciplines in Philip M. Hauser and Leo F. Schnore (eds.), *The Study of Urbanization* (New York: Wiley, 1965).

The pioneering broad analyses of metropolitan developments were Paul Studenski, *The Government of Metropolitan Areas in the United States* (New York: National Municipal League, 1930); Victor Jones, *Metropolitan Government* (Chicago: University of Chicago Press, 1942); and R. D. McKenzie, *The Metropolitan Community* (New York: McGraw-Hill, 1933). The Studenski and Jones volumes concentrated on governmental phases; the McKenzie book gave some attention to governmental matters and to certain economic considerations but it emphasized social trends. Professor Jones elaborated upon specific portions of his earlier study in Part IV of Coleman Woodbury (ed.), *The Future of Cities and Urban Redevelopment* (Chicago: University of Chicago Press, 1953).

Many readers containing collections of articles and other materials on urban and metropolitan issues have appeared in recent years. Included are Edward C. Banfield (ed.), *Urban Government*, rev. ed. (New York: Free Press, 1969); Phillip B. Coulter (ed.), *Politics of Metropolitan Areas* (New York: Thomas Y. Crowell, 1967); Michael N. Danielson (ed.), *Metropolitan Politics* (Boston: Little, Brown, 1966); Thomas R. Dye and Brett W. Hawkins (eds.), *Politics in the Metropolis: A Reader in Conflict and Cooperation* (Columbus: Merrill, 1967); and H. Wentworth Eldredge (ed.), *Taming Megalopolis*, 2 vols. (Garden City, N.Y.: Anchor Books, Doubleday, 1967). Other readers are C. E. Elias, Jr., James Gillies, and Svend Riemer (eds.), *Metropolis: Values in Conflict* (Belmont, Calif.: Wadsworth, 1964); Jeffrey K. Hadden, Louis H. Masotti, and Calvin J. Larson (eds.), *Metropolis in Crisis: Social and Political Perspectives* (Itasca, Ill.: Peacock, 1967); Werner Z. Hirsch (ed.), *Urban Life and Form* (New York: Holt, Rinehart and Winston, 1963); H. R. Mahood and Edward L. Angus (eds.), *Urban Politics and Problems* (New York: Scribner, 1969); Alan Shank (ed.), *Political Power and the Urban Crisis* (Boston: Holbrook, 1969); Oliver P. Williams and Charles Press (eds.), *Democracy in Urban America*, 2nd ed. (Chicago: Rand McNally, 1969); and Joseph F. Zimmerman (ed.), *Government of the Metropolis* (New York: Holt, Rinehart and Winston, 1968).

Among the broad studies of recent origin are Scott Greer, *The Emerging City: Myth and Reality* (New York: Free Press, 1962), and his shorter *Governing the Metropolis* (New York: Wiley, 1962); and Webb S. Fiser, *Mastery of the Metropolis* (Englewood Cliffs, N.J.: Prentice-Hall, 1962). General treatments published as entire numbers of periodicals include "A Symposium on Metropolitan Regionalism: Developing Governmental Concepts," *University of Pennsylvania Law Review* (February, 1957); Martin Myerson, Barbara Terrett, and Paul Ylvisaker (eds.), "Metropolis in Ferment," *Annals of the American Academy of Political and Social Science* (November, 1957); Thomas P. Peardon (ed.), "The Urban Problems," *Proceedings of the Academy of Political Science* (May, 1960); Lloyd Rodwin and Kevin Lynch (eds.), "The Future Metropolis," *Daedalus* (Winter, 1961); Robert B. Mitchell (ed.), "Urban Revival: Goals and Standards," *Annals of the American Academy of Political and Social Science* (March, 1964); and "Cities," published first in the September, 1965, issue of *Scientific American* and later released in the same year as a book by Knopf. A monograph of a similar nature is Stephen B. Sweeney and James C. Charlesworth (eds.), *Governing Urban Society: New Scientific Approaches* (Philadelphia: American Academy of Political and Social Science, 1967). *Building the American City* (Washington: 1969), the final report of the National Commission on Urban Problems (the Douglas Commission), is an analysis of many difficulties and deficiencies, with particular reference to housing and physical development.

Also of broad scope are the reports of the national Advisory Commission on Intergovernmental Relations (such as *Urban and Rural America: Policies for Future Growth*); the publications of the Committee for Economic Development (for instance, *Guiding Metropolitan Growth* and Robert C. Wood's *Metropolis Against Itself*); the monographs on legal problems in metropolitan areas issued by the University of Michigan Law School Legislative Research Center (*Planning and Zoning in the United States, Interstate Metropolitan Areas*, and others); and the New York Metropolitan Region Study, which although primarily oriented toward economic factors includes social studies (Oscar Handlin's *The Newcomers*) and governmental evaluations (Robert C. Wood's *1400 Governments*). The summary volume in the New York series is Raymond Vernon, *Metropolis: 1985*, published originally in 1960 by Harvard University Press, Cambridge, and issued in paperback in 1963 by Doubleday, Garden City, New York.

The suburban question is treated generally in Robert C. Wood, *Suburbia: Its People and Their Politics* (Boston: Houghton Mifflin, 1959); William A. Dobriner, *Class in Suburbia* (Englewood Cliffs, N.J.: Prentice-Hall, 1963); Humphrey Carver, *Cities in the Suburbs* (Toronto: University of Toronto Press, 1962); Scott Donaldson, *The Suburban Myth* (New York: Columbia University Press, 1969); and S. D. Clark, *The Suburban Society* (Toronto: University of Toronto Press, 1966). Studies of particular suburban areas include Charles E. Gilbert, *Governing the Suburbs* (Bloomington: University of Indiana Press, 1967); John R. Seeley, R. A. Sims, and E. W. Loosely, *Crestwood Heights: The Culture of Suburban Life* (New York: Basic Books, 1956); Bennet M. Berger, *Working-Class Suburb: A Study of Auto Workers in Suburbia* (Berkeley and Los Angeles: University of California Press, 1960);

Sam Bass Warner, Jr., *Street Car Suburbs: The Process of Growth in Boston, 1870–1900* (Cambridge: M.I.T. Press and Harvard University Press, 1962); and Herbert J. Gans, *The Levittowners* (New York: Pantheon Books, 1967).

The historical approach to urbanism is represented by such works as Gideon Sjoberg, *The Preindustrial City* (New York: Free Press, 1960); Lewis Mumford, *The City in History* (New York: Harcourt, Brace & World, 1961); Oscar Handlin and John Burchard (eds.), *The Historian and the City* (Cambridge: The M.I.T. Press and Harvard University Press, 1963); Blake McKelvey, *The Urbanization of America, 1860–1915* (New Brunswick, N.J.: Rutgers University Press, 1963), and his *The Emergence of Metropolitan America, 1915–1966* (New Brunswick, N.J.: Rutgers University Press, 1968); Charles N. Glaab, *The American City: A Documentary History* (Homewood, Ill.: Dorsey Press, 1963); Wilson Smith (ed.), *Cities of Our Past and Present* (New York: Wiley, 1964); Charles N. Glaab and Theodore A. Brown, *A History of Urban America* (New York: Macmillan, 1967); and Constance M. Green, *The Rise of Urban America* (New York: Harper & Row, 1965). A collection of essays by British historians is contained in H. J. Dyos (ed.), *The Study of Urban History* (New York: St. Martin's Press, 1968). An historical presentation of political and legal theory as applied to local government is found in Anwar Syed, *The Political Theory of American Local Government* (New York: Random House, 1966). The history of cities is traced in E. A. Gutkind's monumental work, *International History of City Development*, published by Free Press, New York, which has now reached four volumes. Scholarly histories of specific cities include Bayrd Still, *Milwaukee: The History of a City* (Madison: The State Historical Society of Wisconsin, 1948); Blake McKelvey's three-volume study of Rochester, New York, published by Harvard University Press, 1945–1956; and A. Theodore Brown, *The History of Kansas City to 1870* (Columbia: University of Missouri Press, 1964). An important contribution to the study of urban political history is Lyle W. Dorsett, *The Pendergast Machine* (New York: Oxford University Press, 1968).

Urban social dimensions are discussed in a wide variety of works including Otis Dudley Duncan and Albert J. Reiss, Jr., *Social Characteristics of Urban and Rural Communities* (New York: Wiley, 1956); Alvin Boskoff, *The Sociology of Urban Regions* (New York: Appleton-Century-Crofts, 1962); James M. Beshers, *Urban Social Structure* (New York: Free Press, 1962); Stanley Lieberson, *Ethnic Patterns in American Cities* (New York: Free Press, 1963); Herbert J. Gans, *The Urban Villagers* (New York: Free Press, 1962); Leo F. Schnore, *The Urban Scene: Human Ecology and Demography* (New York: Free Press, 1965); and George A. Theodorson (ed.), *Studies in Human Ecology* (New York: Harper & Row, 1961). Amos H. Hawley, *The Changing Shape of Metropolitan America: Deconcentration Since 1920* (New York: Free Press, 1956), analyzes patterns of population growth and change. Maurice R. Stein, *The Eclipse of Community* (Princeton: Princeton University Press, 1960), is a review of the sociological community studies written over the preceding thirty-five years.

Social problems in general are examined in Robert A. Dentler, *Major American Social Problems* (Chicago: Rand McNally, 1967); Bernard Rosenberg, Israel Gerner, and F. W. Howton, *Mass Society in Crisis: Social Problems and*

Social Pathology (New York: Macmillan, 1964); Robert C. Weaver, *The Urban Complex* (Garden City, N.Y.: Doubleday, 1964); and *Converging Social Trends and Emerging Social Problems* (Washington: U.S. Department of Health, Education, and Welfare, 1964).

The recent intensification of the racial problem in American cities is reflected in a wide variety of works such as Kenneth B. Clark, *Dark Ghetto: Dilemmas of Social Power* (New York: Harper & Row, 1965); Charles E. Silberman, *Crisis in Black and White* (New York: Vintage Books, 1964); Franklin E. Frazier, *The Negro Family in the United States* (Chicago: University of Chicago Press, 1966), and James Farmer, *Freedom When?* (New York: Random House, 1966). Among the important books expressing ideological positions by black leaders are Malcolm X, *The Autobiography of Malcolm X* (New York: Grove Press, 1964); Stokely Carmichael and Charles V. Hamilton, *Black Power: The Politics of Liberation in America* (New York: Vintage Books, 1967); Eldridge Cleaver, *Soul on Ice* (New York: McGraw-Hill, 1968); and H. Rap Brown, *Die Nigger Die!* (New York: Dial Press, 1969).

The riots and disturbances have received extensive treatment in the literature including Robert H. Connery (ed.), "Urban Riots: Violent Social Change," *Proceedings of the Academy of Political Science*, (July, 1968), and Louis H. Masotti and Don R. Bowen (eds.), *Riots and Rebellion: Civil Violence in the Urban Community* (Beverly Hills: Sage Publications, 1968). Senate hearings on this problem are reported in U.S. Senate, *Riots, Civil and Criminal Disorders*, Hearings before the Permanent Subcommittee on Investigation of the Committee on Government Operations (1968). Accounts of particular riots include Frank Besag, *Anatomy of a Riot: Buffalo 1967* (Buffalo: University of Buffalo Press, 1967); Robert Conot, *Rivers of Blood, Years of Darkness* (New York: Bantam Books, 1967); Jerry Cohen and W. S. Murphy, *Burn, Baby, Burn! The Watts Riots* (New York: Avon Books, 1966); Tom Hayden, *Rebellion in Newark* (New York: Random House, 1967); and Robert Shogan and Tom Craig, *The Detroit Race Riot: A Study in Violence* (Philadelphia: Chilton, 1964). A more general analysis is Paul Jacobs, *Prelude to Riot: A View of Urban America from the Bottom* (New York: Random House, 1968).

Since Michael Harrington wrote his seminal book, *The Other America: Poverty in the United States* (New York: Macmillan, 1962), a vast literature on poverty in urban areas has accumulated. Examples are Oscar Ornati, *Poverty Amid Affluence* (New York: Twentieth Century Fund, 1966); Thomas Gladwin, *Poverty U.S.A.* (Boston: Little, Brown, 1967); Edward C. Budd (ed.), *Inequality and Poverty* (New York: Norton, 1967); Burton Weisbrod (ed.), *The Economics of Poverty: An American Paradox* (Englewood Cliffs, N. J.: Prentice-Hall, 1966); Jeremy Seabrook, *The Underprivileged* (London: Longmans, Green, 1967); Charles A. Valentine, *Culture and Poverty: Critique and Counter-Proposals* (Chicago: University of Chicago Press, 1968); and Leonard Freedman, *The Politics of Poverty* (New York: Holt, Rinehart and Winston, 1969). The second volume of the Urban Affairs Annual Reviews, *Power, Poverty, and Urban Policy*, edited by Warner Bloomberg, Jr., and Henry J. Schmandt (Beverly Hills: Sage Publications, 1968), contains a collection of essays devoted to this topic by specialists from various disciplines. An excellent analysis of the difficulties involved in efforts to effect social change is Peter

Marris and Martin Rein, *Dilemmas of Social Reform: Poverty and Community Action in the United States* (New York: Atherton, 1967).

The problem of educating the urban disadvantaged has received increasing research attention. Among recent works in this area are Robert J. Havighurst, *Education in Metropolitan Areas* (Boston: Allyn and Bacon, 1966); Robert A. Dentler and Mary E. Warshauer, *Big City Dropouts and Illiterates* (New York: Praeger, 1968); Marilyn Gittell and T. Edward Hollander, *Six Urban School Districts: A Comparative Study of Institutional Response* (New York: Praeger, 1968); Marilyn Gittell (ed.), *Educating an Urban Population* (Beverly Hills: Sage Publications, 1967); Benjamin S. Bloom, Allison Davis, and Robert Hess, *Compensatory Education for Cultural Deprivation* (New York: Holt, Rinehart and Winston, 1965). A special issue of the *Harvard Educational Review*, entitled "Equal Educational Opportunity," (Winter, 1968) is devoted to an analysis of the racial problem and urban education. Other studies on the same topic include Robert A. Dentler, Bernard Mackler, and Mary E. Warshauer (eds.), *The Urban R's: Race Relations as the Problem in Urban Education* (New York: Praeger, 1967); Roscoe Hill and Malcolm Feeley (eds.), *Affirmative School Integration: Efforts to Overcome de facto Segregation in Urban Schools* (Beverly Hills: Sage Publications, 1969); T. Bentley Edwards and Frederick M. Wirt, *School Desegregation in the North* (San Francisco: Chandler, 1968); and Robert L. Crain, *The Politics of School Desegregation* (Chicago: Aldine, 1968). Robert J. Havighurst (ed.), *Metropolitanism: Its Challenge to Education* (Chicago: University of Chicago Press, 1968), is a wide-ranging presentation of urban education by scholars from many disciplines. The problem of school redistricting is considered in Basil G. Zimmer and Amos H. Hawley, *Metropolitan Area Schools: Resistance to District Reorganization* (Beverly Hills: Sage Publications, 1968).

The economic aspects of metropolitan communities are treated in such studies as Gunnar Alexandersson, *The Industrial Structure of American Cities* (Lincoln: University of Nebraska Press, 1956); John Rannells, *The Core of the City: A Pilot Study of Changing Land Uses in Central Business Districts* (New York: Columbia University Press, 1956); Otis Dudley Duncan and others, *Metropolis and Region* (Baltimore: Johns Hopkins Press, 1960); Ruth L. Mace, *Industry and City Government* (Chapel Hill: University of North Carolina Institute of Government, 1960); Donald J. Bogue and Calvin L. Beale, *The Economic Areas of the United States* (New York: Free Press, 1961); Richard B. Andrews, *Urban Growth and Development* (New York: Simmons-Boardman, 1962); F. Stuart Chapin, Jr., and Shirley F. Weiss (eds.), *Urban Growth Dynamics in a Regional Cluster of Cities* (New York: Wiley, 1962); Benjamin Chinitz (ed.), *City and Suburb: The Economics of Metropolitan Growth* (Englewood Cliffs, N. J.: Prentice-Hall, 1964); and Harvey S. Perloff and Lowdon Wingo, Jr., (eds.), *Issues in Urban Economics* (Baltimore: Johns Hopkins Press, 1968). The nature and purpose of economic base studies are examined in Charles M. Tiebout, *The Community Economic Base Study* (New York: Committee for Economic Development, 1962). Economic analyses of individual metropolises include John L. O'Donnell and others, *Economic and Population Base Study of the Lansing Tri-County Area* (East Lansing: Michigan State University Bureau of Business and Economic Research, 1960); the excellent four-volume study of the Pittsburgh region, directed by Edgar M. Hoover and published by the University of Pittsburgh Press in 1963 and 1964; and James L. Green, *Metropolitan Economic Republics: A Case Study in Regional Economic Growth* (Athens: University of Georgia Press, 1965), which focuses on the Atlanta area.

Considerable research dealing with redevelopment in urban areas has emerged. The two volumes edited by Coleman Woodbury, the first entitled *The Future of Cities and Urban Redevelopment*, and the second, *Urban Redevelopment: Problems and Practices* (Chicago: University of Chicago Press, 1953), represent the pioneering comprehensive treatment in this field. Other works in this substantive area include Jewel Bellush and Murray Hausknecht (eds.), *Urban Renewal: People, Politics and Planning* (Garden City, N.Y.: Doubleday, 1967); Reuel Hamdahl, *Urban Renewal* (Washington: Scarecrow Press, 1959); Miles L. Colean, *Renewing Our Cities* (New York: Twentieth Century Fund, 1953); George S. Duggar (ed.), *The New Renewal* (Berkeley: University of California Bureau of Public Administration, 1961); Thomas F. Johnson, James R. Morris, and Joseph G. Butts, *Renewing America's Cities* (Washington: Institute for Social Science Research, 1962); Kurt W. Back, *Slums, Projects, and People* (Durham: Duke University Press, 1962); and Bernard J. Frieden, *The Future of Old Neighborhoods* (Cambridge: M.I.T. Press, 1964). The story of urban renewal in the Hyde Park-Kenwood section of Chicago is recounted in Julia Abrahamson, *A Neighborhood Finds Itself* (New York: Harper & Row, 1959). Redevelopment trends abroad are discussed in Leo Grebler, *Urban Renewal in European Countries* (Philadelphia: University of Pennsylvania Press, 1964). The politics of redevelopment is treated in Peter H. Rossi and Robert A. Dentler, *The Politics of Urban Renewal: The Chicago Findings* (New York: Free Press, 1961), and Harold Kaplan, *Urban Renewal Politics: Slum Clearance in Newark* (New York: Columbia University Press, 1963).

The closely related topic of housing has also received considerable attention from scholars. Significant publications include Martin Meyerson, Barbara Terrett, and William L. C. Wheaton, *Housing, People, and Cities* (New York: McGraw-Hill, 1962); Louis Winnick, *American Housing and Its Use* (New York: Wiley, 1957); Edward C. Banfield and Morton Grodzins, *Government and Housing in Metropolitan Areas* (New York: McGraw-Hill, 1958); R. M. Fisher, *Twenty Years of Public Housing* (New York: Harper & Row, 1959); Lawrence M. Friedman, *Government and Slum Housing: A Century of Frustration* (Chicago: Rand McNally, 1968); Glenn H. Beyer, *Housing and Society* (New York: Macmillan, 1965); and William L. C. Wheaton, Grace Milgram, and Margy E. Meyerson (eds.), *Urban Housing* (New York: Free Press, 1966).

General writings on major geographical aspects are Harold M. Mayer and Clyde F. Kohn (eds.), *Readings in Urban Geography* (Chicago: University of Chicago Press, 1959); Jacqueline Beaujeu-Garnier and Georges Chabot, *Urban Geography* (New York: Wiley, 1967); Robert Dickinson, *City and Region: A Geographical Integration* (London: Routledge and Kegan Paul, 1964); Arthur E. Smailes, *The Geography of Towns*, 5th ed. (London: Hutchinson, 1966); and Jean Gottmann and Robert A. Harper (eds.), *Metropolis on the Move: Geographers Look at Urban Sprawl* (New York: Wiley, 1967). A geographical study of an individual metropolis is James E. Vance, Jr., *Geog-*

raphy and Urban Evolution in the San Francisco Bay Area (Berkeley: University of California Institute of Governmental Studies, 1964).

There have been numerous studies of decision-making, power structures, and leadership in urban settings. A series of essays on these topics is contained in Darwin Cartwright (ed.), *Studies in Social Power* (Ann Arbor: University of Michigan Press, 1959); Charles Adrian (ed.), *Social Science and Community Action* (East Lansing: Michigan State University Institute for Community Development and Services, 1960); Morris Janowitz (ed.), *Community Political Systems* (New York: Free Press, 1961); William V. D'Antonio and Howard J. Ehrlich (eds.), *Power and Democracy in America* (South Bend: University of Notre Dame Press, 1961); and Bert E. Swanson (ed.), *Current Trends in Comparative Community Studies* (Kansas City, Mo.: Community Studies, Inc., 1962). Other relevant publications are Martin Meyerson and Edward C. Banfield, *Politics, Planning, and the Public Interest* (New York: Free Press, 1957); James Q. Wilson, *Negro Politics* (New York: Free Press, 1960); and Edward C. Banfield and James Q. Wilson, *City Politics* (Cambridge: Harvard University Press and M.I.T. Press, 1963). General analyses of community power are found in Arnold M. Rose, *The Power Structure* (New York: Oxford University Press, 1967); Terry N. Clark (ed.), *Community Structure and Decision-Making* (San Francisco: Chandler, 1968); Willis D. Hawley and Frederick M. Wirt (eds.), *The Search for Community Power* (Englewood Cliffs, N.J.: Prentice-Hall, 1968); Linton C. Freeman, *Patterns of Local Community Leadership* (Indianapolis: Bobbs-Merrill, 1968); and Morris Davis and Marvin G. Weinbaum, *Metropolitan Decision Processes* (Chicago: Rand McNally, 1969).

Studies of community power and decision-making in individual communities include Roscoe C. Martin, Frank J. Munger, and others, *Decisions in Syracuse* (Bloomington: Indiana University Press, 1961); Carol E. Thometz, *The Decision-Makers: The Power Structure of Dallas* (Dallas: Southern Methodist University, 1963); M. Kent Jennings, *Community Influentials: The Elites of Atlanta* (New York: Free Press, 1964); and Aaron Wildavsky, *Leadership in a Small Town* (Totowa, N.J.: Bedminster Press, 1964). Useful reviews of the research literature concerned with decision-making, power, and leadership are Wendell Bell, Richard J. Hill, and Charles R. Wright, *Public Leadership* (San Francisco: Chandler, 1961), and Charles Press, *Main Street Politics: Policy-Making at the Local Level* (East Lansing: Michigan State University Institute for Community Development and Services, 1962).

Studies of voting and other forms of political participation at the local level are widely scattered in articles, monographs, and sample survey reports. Robert E. Lane, *Political Life* (New York: Free Press, 1959), presents a comprehensive summary of the findings of such studies. Specialized works on this subject include Lawrence W. O'Rourke, *Voting Behavior in the Forty-Five Cities of Los Angeles County* (Los Angeles: University of California Bureau of Governmental Research, 1953); Richard A. Watson, *The Politics of Urban Change* (Kansas City, Mo.: Community Studies, Inc., 1963), which focuses on political participation in an urban redevelopment area; Alvin Boskoff and Harmon Zeigler, *Voting Patterns in a Local Election* (Philadelphia: Lippincott, 1964); Robert Alford, *Bureaucracy and Participation* (Chicago: Rand McNally, 1969); and

J. Clarence Davies, *Neighborhood Groups and Urban Renewal* (New York: Columbia University Press, 1966). A recent review of the literature in this field is found in Dale R. Marshall, "Who Participates in What? A Bibliographical Essay on Individual Participation in Urban Areas," *Urban Affairs Quarterly*, IV (December, 1968), 201–223. Studies of participation and involvement by the disadvantaged in political activities and programs are still confined largely to the journal literature; examples are Frances Piven, "Participation of Residents in Neighborhood Community Action Programs," *Social Work*, 11 (January, 1966), 73–80, and Arthur B. Shostak, "Promoting Participation of the Poor: Philadelphia's Anti-Poverty Program," *Social Work*, 11 (January, 1966), 64–72. Among the few treatments of the subject in book form are Ralph M. Kramer, *Participation of the Poor: Comparative Studies in the War on Poverty* (Englewood Cliffs, N. J.: Prentice-Hall, 1969), and Hans B. C. Spiegel (ed.), *Citizen Participation in Urban Development* (Washington: NTL Institute for Applied Behavioral Science, 1968).

The physical planning of urban and metropolitan communities is discussed in Harland Bartholomew, *Land Uses in American Cities* (Cambridge: Harvard University Press, 1955); Arthur B. Gallion, *The Urban Pattern*, 2nd ed. (Princeton: Van Nostrand, 1963); T. J. Kent, Jr., *The Urban General Plan* (San Francisco: Chandler, 1964); Melvin R. Levin, *Community and Regional Planning: Issues in Public Policy* (New York: Praeger, 1969); and Maynard M. Hufschmidt (ed.), *Regional Planning: Challenge and Prospect* (New York: Praeger, 1969). Harvey S. Perloff (ed.), *Planning and the Urban Community* (Pittsburgh: University of Pittsburgh Press, 1961), is a collection of insightful essays on city planning and urbanism. Various aspects of zoning and land use control are covered in Charles M. Haar, *Land Use Planning* (Boston: Little, Brown, 1959); John Delafons, *Land Use Controls in the United States* (Cambridge: Harvard University and Massachusetts Institute of Technology Joint Center for Urban Studies, 1962); Sidney M. Willhelm, *Urban Zoning and Land Use Theory* (New York: Free Press, 1962); Daniel R. Mandelker, *Managing Our Urban Environment* (Indianapolis: Bobbs-Merrill, 1966); and Richard F. Babcock, *The Zoning Game: Municipal Practices and Policies* (Madison: University of Wisconsin Press, 1966). Works that focus on the new town concept include Erika Spiegel, *New Towns In Israel* (New York: Praeger, 1967); Clarence S. Stein, *Toward New Towns for America* (New York: Reinhold, 1957); and Frederic J. Osborn and Arnold Whittick, *The New Towns: The Answer to Megalopolis* (New York: McGraw-Hill, 1963). The objectives of planning are treated philosophically in Lawrence Haworth, *The Good City* (Bloomington: Indiana University Press, 1963).

A classic critique of urban planning in the utopian tradition is Percival and Paul Goodman, *Communitas*, 2nd ed. (New York: Vintage Books, 1960). The politics of planning and zoning are considered in S. J. Makielski, Jr., *The Politics of Zoning* (New York: Columbia University Press, 1966); Alan A. Altshuler, *The City Planning Process* (Ithaca: Cornell University Press, 1965); Francine F. Rabinovitz, *City Planning and Politics* (New York: Atherton, 1969); and David C. Ranney, *Planning and Politics in the Metropolis* (Columbus: Merrill, 1969). The social aspects of planning are treated in Herbert J. Gans, *People and Plans* (New York: Basic Books, 1968), and Bernard J. Frieden and Robert

Morris (eds.), *Urban Planning and Social Policy* (New York: Basic Books, 1968). John W. Reps, *The Making of Urban America* (Princeton: Princeton University Press, 1965), is a detailed history of city planning in the United States. So also is Mel Scott, *American City Planning Since 1890* (Berkeley and Los Angeles: University of California Press, 1969). Bibliographical material on planning is contained in the *ASPO Newsletter,* published by the American Society of Planning Officials, and the *Journal of the American Institute of Planners.*

The architecture of American cities is considered from an historical perspective in John Burchard and Albert Bush-Brown, *The Architecture of America* (Boston: Little, Brown, 1961), and James Marston Fitch, *American Building,* 2nd ed. (Boston: Houghton Mifflin, 1966). The aesthetic and design aspects of cities are treated in Frank Lloyd Wright, *The Living City* (New York: Random House, 1958); Paul Zucker, *Town and Square* (New York: Columbia University Press, 1959); Gordon Cullen, *Townscape* (New York: Reinhold, 1961); Ian Nairn, *The American Landscape* (New York: Random House, 1965); Paul D. Spreiregen, *Urban Design: The Architecture of Towns and Cities* (New York: McGraw-Hill, 1965); Louis G. Redstone, *Art in Architecture* (New York: McGraw-Hill, 1968); Thomas A. Reiner, *The Place of the Ideal Community in Urban Planning* (Philadelphia: University of Pennsylvania Press, 1963); Christopher Tunnard, *American Skyline* (New York: New American Library, 1956); and Christopher Tunnard, *The Modern American City* (Princeton: Van Nostrand, 1968). George Braziller, New York, is publishing an illustrated series entitled *Planning and Cities,* edited by George Collins, which explores major epochs in the form and design of cities and the ordering of man's environment.

Financing government in the metropolis has been the subject of various studies. Papers covering a wide range of metropolitan fiscal problems are contained in *Financing Metropolitan Government* (Princeton: Tax Institute, Inc., 1955). Several reports of the Advisory Commission on Intergovernmental Relations are pertinent, including *Local Nonproperty Taxes and the Coordinating Role of the State* (1961); *Intergovernmental Cooperation in Tax Administration* (1961); *Measures of State and Local Fiscal Capacity and Tax Effort* (1962); and *State and Local Finances, Significant Features, 1966 to 1969* (1968). An example of a fiscal analysis of a particular metropolitan area is Seymour Sacks and William F. Hellmuth, Jr., *Financing Government in a Metropolitan Area: The Cleveland Experience* (New York: Free Press, 1961). Specialized studies in this field include R. A. Sigafoos, *The Municipal Income Tax* (Chicago: Public Administration Service, 1955); H. F. Alderfer and R. L. Funk, *Municipal Non-Property Taxes* (Chicago: Municipal Finance Officers Association, 1956); Harvey S. Perloff and Richard P. Nathan (eds.), *Revenue Sharing and the Cities* (Baltimore: Johns Hopkins Press, 1968); John F. Due, *Sales Taxation* (Urbana: University of Illinois Press, 1957); Harvey E. Brazer, *City Expenditures in the United States* (New York: National Bureau of Economic Research, 1959); and Raymond J. Green, *The Impact of the Central Business District on the Municipal Budget* (Washington: Urban Land Institute, 1962). The latest works dealing with urban finance include Selma J. Mushkin, *Property Taxes: The 1970 Outlook* (Chicago: Council of State Governments, 1965); Juan de Torres, *Financing Local Government* (New York: In-

,dustrial Conference Board, 1967); Deil S. Wright, *Federal Grants-in-Aid: Perspectives and Alternatives* (Washington: American Enterprise Institute for Public Policy Research, 1968); Arthur D. Lynn, Jr., (ed.), *The Property Tax and Its Administration* (Madison: University of Wisconsin Press, 1969); and James A. Maxwell, *Financing State and Local Governments*, rev. ed. (Washington: Brookings Institution, 1969). A study of local fiscal policy-making is Donald Gerwin, *Budgeting Public Funds: The Decision Process in an Urban School District* (Madison: University of Wisconsin Press, 1969).

Governmental organization, services, and reform receive general treatment in John C. Bollens, *The States and the Metropolitan Problem* (Chicago: Council of State Governments, 1956); *Special District Governments in the United States* (Berkeley and Los Angeles: University of California Press, 1957) by the same author; Roscoe C. Martin, *Metropolis in Transition* (Washington: U.S. Housing and Home Finance Agency, 1963); Luther H. Gulick, *The Metropolitan Problem and American Ideas* (New York: Knopf, 1962); and Robert G. Smith, *Public Authorities, Special Districts and Local Government* (Washington: National Association of Counties Research Foundation, 1964), which is a five-state inquiry. John C. Bollens, in association with John R. Bayes and Kathryn L. Utter, *American County Government* (Beverly Hills: Sage Publications, 1969), contains extensive annotations on general and statewide studies of counties. A further useful source of information about another type of government is Benjamin Novak, *Selected Bibliography on Special Districts and Authorities* (Washington: U.S. Department of Agriculture Economic Research Service, 1968).

General books and monographs focusing on specific service problems include Marshall I. Goodman (ed.), *Controlling Pollution* (Englewood Cliffs, N.J.: Prentice-Hall, 1967); Lewis Herber, *Crisis in Our Cities* (Englewood Cliffs, N.J.: Prentice-Hall, 1965), which deals largely with air and water pollution; James Q. Wilson, *Varieties of Police Behavior* (Cambridge: Harvard University Press, 1968); James Q. Wilson (ed.), *The Metropolitan Enigma*, rev. ed. (Cambridge: Harvard University Press, 1968), which contains chapters on transportation, pollution, and crime; and Public Administration Service, *Regional Law Enforcement* (Chicago: 1969). A great many publications have been issued about one particular metropolitan difficulty—transportation. Several prominent examples are Wilfred Owen, *The Metropolitan Transportation Problem*, rev. ed. (Washington: Brookings Institution, 1966); J. R. Meyer, J. F. Kain and M. Wohl, *The Urban Transportation Problem* (Cambridge: Harvard University Press, 1965); George M. Smerk, *Urban Transportation: The Federal Role* (Bloomington: Indiana University Press, 1965); and Michael N. Danielson, *Federal–Metropolitan Politics and the Commuter Crisis* (New York: Columbia University Press, 1963). Two analyses of environmental issues are William R. Ewald (ed.), *Environment for Man: The Next Fifty Years* (Bloomington: Indiana University Press, 1967), and Orris C. Herfindahl and Allen V. Kneese, *Quality of the Environment* (Baltimore: Johns Hopkins Press, 1965).

Numerous studies relating to governmental organization, services, and reform have been made of individual metropolitan areas, many of which are summarized in Government Affairs Foundation, *Metropolitan Surveys: A Digest*

(Chicago: Public Administration Service, 1958). This work also includes a helpful introductory essay by Daniel R. Grant. Listings of later analyses are contained in the annual issues of *Metropolitan Surveys*, prepared by the Graduate School of Public Affairs, State University of New York at Albany. Most individual studies have been published in small editions by the sponsoring agencies and are not generally available. Among the exceptions are Leverett S. Lyon (ed.), *Governmental Problems in the Chicago Metropolitan Area* (Chicago: University of Chicago Press, 1957); John C. Bollens (ed.), *Exploring the Metropolitan Community* (Berkeley and Los Angeles: University of California Press, 1961), which pertains to the St. Louis area; and Stanley Scott and John C. Bollens, *Governing a Metropolitan Region: The San Francisco Bay Area* (Berkeley: University of California Institute of Governmental Studies, 1968). A history and political analysis of a council of governments is Joan B. Aron, *The Quest for Regional Cooperation: A Study of the New York Regional Council* (Berkeley and Los Angeles: University of California Press, 1969).

The politics of attempts to reorganize the governmental system of particular metropolitan areas has received considerable scrutiny. The published results include Christian L. Larsen and others, *Growth and Government in Sacramento* (Bloomington: Indiana University Press, 1965); Henry J. Schmandt, *The Milwaukee Metropolitan Study Commission* (Bloomington: Indiana University Press, 1965); and Richard Martin, *Consolidation: Jacksonville-Duval County* (Jacksonville: Crawford Publishing, 1968). Frank S. Sengstock and others, *Consolidation: Building a Bridge Between City and Suburb* (Worcester: Heffernan Press, 1964) analyzes the 1962 consolidation attempt in the St. Louis area. The essays in Part III of Norton E. Long, *The Polity* (Chicago: Rand McNally, 1962), edited by Charles Press, are also relevant to the politics of reorganization.

Prominent illustrations of writings on intergovernmental relations and the mounting influence of the national and state governments in the metropolis include Frederic N. Cleaveland (ed.), *Congress and Urban Problems* (Washington: Brookings Institution, 1969); Robert H. Connery and Richard H. Leach, *The Federal Government and Metropolitan Areas* (Cambridge: Harvard University Press, 1960); Lee S. Greene, Malcolm E. Jewell, and Daniel R. Grant, *The States and the Metropolis* (University: University of Alabama Press, 1969); W. Brooke Graves, *American Intergovernmental Relations* (New York: Scribner, 1964); *Impact of Federal Urban Development Programs on Local Government Organization and Planning* (Washington: 1964), issued by the Subcommittee on Intergovernmental Relations of the U.S. Senate Committee on Government Operations; and *State Legislative Program of the Advisory Commission on Intergovernmental Relations* (Washington: annually). Others are three publications by the Council of State Governments, *State Responsibility in Urban Regional Development* (Chicago: 1962); *Report of the Committee on State-Urban Relations* (Chicago: 1968); and *Suggested State Legislation* (Chicago: annually); National Governors' Conference, *The States and Urban Problems* (Chicago: 1967); U.S. Senate, Committee on Government Operations, Subcommittee on Executive Reorganization, *Federal Role in Urban Affairs* (Washington: 1966); and Advisory Commission on Intergovernmental Relations, *Metropolitan America: Challenge to Federalism* (Washington: 1966).

Daniel J. Elazar, *American Federalism: A View From the States* (New York: Thomas Y. Crowell, 1966), presents the states as pivotal parts of the federal system, while Roscoe C. Martin, *The Cities and the Federal System* (New York: Atherton, 1965), examines federal-municipal relations. Harold Herman, *New York State and the Metropolitan Problem* (Philadelphia: University of Pennsylvania Press, 1963), is an analysis of state-local relations in one state. Among the superior state-local studies prepared by official state agencies are New Jersey County and Municipal Government Study Commission, *Creative Localism: A Prospectus* (Trenton: 1968), and New York Joint Committee on Metropolitan and Regional Areas, *Governing Urban Areas: Realism and Reform* (Albany: 1967).

The literature pertaining to metropolitan communities in a world setting is diversified and extensive. The United Nations and its various agencies and the International Union of Local Authorities at The Hague, Netherlands, are rich sources for both bibliographies and specialized studies. Valuable bibliographical compilations are Robert Lorenz, Paul Meadows, and Warner Bloomberg, Jr., *A World of Cities*, published by the Center for Overseas Operations and Research, Maxwell Graduate School of Citizenship and Public Affairs, Syracuse University, in 1964; William Bicker, David Brown, Herbert Malakoff, and William J. Gore, *Comparative Urban Development: An Annotated Bibliography*, issued by the Comparative Administration Group, American Society for Public Administration, Washington, in 1965; Harold F. Alderfer and Lewis M. Stevens, *A Bibliography of African Government, 1950–1964* (Lincoln University, Pa.: Department of Political Science, n.d.); and Francine F. Rabinovitz, Felicity M. Trueblood, and Charles J. Savio, *Latin-American Political Systems in an Urban Setting* (Gainesville: University of Florida Center for Latin-American Studies, 1967). Ruth P. Simms, *Urbanization in West Africa* (Evanston: Northwestern University Press, 1965), contains an analytical review of current literature in that section of the world.

General aspects of urbanization outside the United States are dealt with in Philip M. Hauser (ed.), *Urbanization in Asia and the Far East* (Calcutta: UNESCO Research Centre, 1958); Philip M. Hauser (ed.), *Urbanization in Latin America* (Paris: UNESCO, 1961); Gerald Breese, *Urbanization in Newly Developing Countries* (Englewood Cliffs, N.J.: Prentice-Hall, 1966); and Peter Hall, *The World Cities* (New York: McGraw-Hill, 1966). Recent collections of essays and other material in this field are Sylvia F. Fava (ed.), *Urbanism in World Perspective* (New York: Thomas Y. Crowell, 1968); Gerald Breese (ed.), *Readings on Urbanization* (Englewood Cliffs, N.J.: Prentice-Hall, 1968); and Glenn H. Beyer (ed.), *The Urban Explosion in Latin America* (Ithaca: Cornell University Press, 1967).

Studies of the government and administration of thirteen major foreign cities (Calcutta, Casablanca, Davao, Karachi, Lagos, Leningrad, Lima, Lodz, Paris, Stockholm, Toronto, Valencia, and Zagreb) by the Institute of Public Administration, New York, are being published in the Praeger Special Studies Series. An overview of the individual studies is Annmarie Hauck Walsh, *The Urban Challenge to Government: An International Comparison of Thirteen Cities* (New York: Praeger, 1969). Other works that consider local government on a world basis are William A. Robson (ed.), *Great Cities of the World:*

Their Government, Politics and Planning, rev. ed. (New York: Macmillan, 1957); Samuel Humes and Eileen Martin, *The Structure of Local Governments Throughout the World* (The Hague: Martinus Nijhoff, 1961); and Harold F. Alderfer, *Local Government in Developing Countries* (New York: McGraw-Hill, 1964). Eleven comparative papers, written by scholars from a number of countries and prepared for the Centennial Study and Training Programme on Metropolitan Problems, Bureau of Municipal Research, Toronto (1967), are concerned with finance, intergovernmental relations, planning, and various services.

Other publications covering specific areas of the world include Ronald Wraith, *Local Government in West Africa* (New York: Praeger, 1964); Fred G. Burke, *Local Government and Politics in Uganda* (Syracuse: Syracuse University Press, 1964); J. K. Nsarkoh, *Local Government in Ghana* (Accra: Ghana University Press, 1964); Kurt Steiner, *Local Government in Japan* (Stanford: Stanford University Press, 1965); and several chapters in Robert T. Daland (ed.), *Comparative Urban Research: The Administration and Politics of Cities* (Beverly Hills: Sage Publications, 1969). Recent studies with a sociological emphasis are illustrated by Takeo Yazaki, *The Japanese City* (Tokyo: Japan Publications Trading Co., 1963); Pierre L. Van Den Berghe, *Caneville: The Social Structure of a South African Town* (Middletown, Conn.: Wesleyan University Press, 1963); and Andrew H. Whiteford, *Two Cities of Latin America* (Garden City, N.Y.: Doubleday, 1964).

INDEXES

INDEX OF NAMES

☐ This is an index of personal names. The names of places and organizations appear in the Index of Subjects. The letter "n" after a page number indicates that the reference is in a footnote.

Abegglen, James C., 416 n.
Abrams, Charles, 249, 401 n.
Abrahamson, Julia, 454
Adrian, Charles, 123, 455
Agger, Robert, 123, 130
Alderfer, Harold F., 457, 460, 461
Alexandersson, Gunnar, 453
Alford, Robert R., 30 n., 116, 117 n., 149 n., 455
Alinsky, Saul, 144 n., 241
Allen, Frederick L., 156 n.,
Allen, William R., 345
Almond, Gabriel A., 44 n., 403 n.
Altschuler, Alan A., 456
Anderson, Martin, 201
Anderson, William, 449
Andrews, Richard B., 453
Angus, Edward L., 449
Apter, David E., 44 n., 403 n.
Aron, Joan B., 459
Asch, Sidney H., 187 n.
Augustus, 200
Axelrod, Morris, 150 n., 151 n.

Babchuck, Nicholas, 154 n.
Babcock, Richard F., 456
Back, Kurt W., 454
Bain, Chester W., 293 n., 294 n.
Baker, John A., 20 n.
Ballentine, Thomas M., 287
Banfield, Edward C., 132, 143 n., 236 n., 345 n., 449, 454, 455
Banovetz, James M., 261 n.
Barbour, K. M., 412 n.
Bard, Morton, 188 n.
Bartholomew, Harland, 456
Bayes, John R., 458

Beale, Calvin L., 453
Beard, Charles, 150
Beard, Mary, 150
Beaujeu-Garnier, Jacqueline, 454
Beckman, Norman, 119 n.
Beiler, Ross C., 384 n.
Bell, Wendell, 54 n., 455
Bellush, Jewel, 454
Berger, Bennet M., 450
Berkowitz, Bernard, 188 n.
Besag, Frank, 452
Beshers, James M., 451
Beyer, Glenn H., 420 n., 454, 460
Bicker, William, 460
Bigger, Richard, 281 n.
Bilbija, Zarko G., 82 n.
Birkhead, Guthrie S., 448
Blair, George S., 357 n., 448
Bloom, Benjamin S., 453
Bloomberg, Warner, Jr., 131 n., 145 n., 403 n., 421 n., 452, 460
Blumenfeld, Hans, 81
Bogue, Donald J., 453
Bolan, Richard S., 234 n.
Bollens, John C., 56 n., 124 n., 148 n., 155 n., 285 n., 291 n., 308 n., 313 n., 322 n., 336 n., 388 n., 458, 459
Bonjean, Charles M., 77 n.
Booth, David A., 380 n., 386 n.
Borgatta, Edgar F., 48 n., 77, 78
Boskoff, Alvin, 451, 455
Bowen, Don R., 452
Bowles, Samuel, 223 n.
Branch, Melville C., 33 n.
Brazer, Harvey, 275, 448, 457
Brazer, Marjorie Cahn, 60 n.
Braziller, George, 457

Breese, Gerald, 460
Briley, C. Beverly, 305 n.
Brink, William, 215 n.
Bromage, Arthur W., 318 n.
Brooks, Michael P., 235 n.
Brown, A. Theodore, 451
Brown, David, 460
Brown, H. Rap, 452
Brown, Robert L., 448
Browning, Harley L., 77 n.
Buchanan, James M., 36 n.
Budd, Edward C., 452
Bundy, McGeorge, 221, 310
Burchard, John, 11 n., 26, 451, 457
Burgess, Ernest W., 48 n.
Burke, Fred G., 461
Bush-Brown, Albert, 457
Butler, George D., 194
Butler, Jeffrey, 413 n.
Butts, Joseph G., 454

Callahan, Thomas, 395 n.
Campbell, Alan, 253 n., 269, 274
Campbell, O. W., 331
Cape, William H., 118 n.
Carmichael, Stokely, 452
Carr, L. Donald, 423 n.
Carrell, Jephtha J., 356 n.
Carter, Lewis F., 77 n.
Cartwright, Darwin, 455
Carver, Humphrey, 450
Castagno, A. A., 413 n.
Cease, Ronald C., 296 n.
Cervantes, A. J., 377
Chabot, Georges, 454
Chapin, F. Stuart, Jr., 229 n., 453
Charlesworth, James C., 43 n., 450
Chase, Stuart, 232
Chinitz, Benjamin, 73 n., 80 n., 86 n., 453
Chute, Charlton, 432
Cion, Richard M., 364 n.
Clark, Kenneth, 216, 217, 452
Clark, Peter, 137
Clark, S. D., 450
Clark, Terry N., 132 n., 455
Clarke, W. F., 258 n.

Clay, Cassius, 213
Cleaveland, Frederic N., 459
Cleaver, Eldridge, 452
Cohen, David K., 222 n.
Cohen, Jerry, 452
Cohen, Nathan E., 215 n.
Colean, Miles L., 200, 454
Coleman, James S., 44 n., 219, 222, 223
Collins, George, 457
Collver, Andrew, 74 n.
Conant, James B., 218
Connery, Robert H., 452, 459
Conot, Robert, 452
Corty, Floyd L., 305 n.
Coulter, Philip B., 449
Cowan, L. Gray, 413 n.
Craig, Tom, 452
Crain, Robert L., 453
Crouch, Winston W., 283, 360 n., 364 n.
Cullen, Gordon, 457
Culver, Willis, 320 n.

Dahl, Robert, 128, 129, 130, 131, 132, 141
Daland, Robert T., 29 n., 449, 461
Daley, Richard, 132
Danielson, Michael N., 364 n., 449, 458
D'Antonio, William V., 455
Davidoff, Paul, 240
Davies, David, 260 n.
Davies, J. Clarence, 456
Davis, Allison, 453
Davis, Kingsley, 396 n., 397
Davis, Morris, 455
Delafons, John, 456
Dentler, Robert A., 451, 453, 454
Deran, Elizabeth, 260 n.
Dickenson, Robert, 454
Diebold, John, 43 n.
Dinerman, Beatrice, 283, 360 n., 364 n.
Dobriner, William A., 450
Donaldson, Scott, 450
Dorsett, Lyle W., 451

Douglass, Paul H., 280
Downs, Anthony, 36 n., 236
Duberman, Martin, 217 n.
Due, John F., 457
Duggar, George S., 454
Duhl, Leonard J., 210 n.
Duncan, Otis Dudley, 31, 451, 453
Durkheim, Emile, 136
Dyckman, John, 31
Dye, Thomas R., 29 n., 30 n., 53 n.,
    292, 358 n., 449
Dyos, H. J., 451

Easton, David, 41 n., 43, 45 n.
Eckhardt, K. W., 159 n.
Edwards, R. Bentley, 453
Ehrlich, Howard J., 455
Eisenhower, Dwight D., 196
Eisenstadt, S. N., 413 n.
Elazar, Daniel J., 460
Eldredge, H. Wentworth, 449
Elias, C. E., Jr., 449
Ewald, William R., 234 n., 458

Fagin, Henry, 238
Farmer, James, 452
Fava, Sylvia F., 402 n., 460
Feder, Edward L., 275 n.
Feeley, Malcolm, 453
Fefferman, Hilbert, 202 n.
Field, John, 30 n.
Fiser, Webb S., 450
Fisher, Glenn W., 274 n.
Fisher, R. M., 454
Fitch, James Marston, 457
Fitch, Lyle, 275
Foard, Ashley A., 202 n.
Foley, Donald L., 407 n.
Ford, Henry, 167
Form, William H., 141 n.
Forstall, Richard L., 74
Fowler, Edmund P., 30 n., 100 n.
Frazier, Franklin E., 452
Freeman, Linton, 131, 455
Freedman, Leonard 452
Frieden, Bernard J., 229 n., 454, 456
Friedman, Lawrence M., 208 n., 454

Friesema, H. Paul, 29 n., 449
Fuchs, Ralph F., 321 n.
Funk, R. L., 457

Galbraith, John Kenneth, 436
Gallion, Arthur B., 456
Gans, Herbert J., 31, 451, 456
Gardiner, Frederick, 345
Gardner, John, 437
Gerner, Israel, 451
Gerwin, Donald, 458
Geschwinder, James, 215 n.
Gibbs, Jack P., 400 n.
Gilbert, Charles E., 388 n., 450
Gilbert, Claire, 132
Gillen, Paul Bates, 76 n.
Gillies, James, 449
Gittell, Marilyn, 453
Glaab, Charles N., 451
Gladwin, Thomas, 452
Glendening, Parris N., 333, 382, 395 n.
Goldbach, John, 296 n.
Goldenberg, H. Carl, 342 n.
Goldrich, Daniel, 123
Goldstein, Herman, 187 n.
Goodman, Marshall L., 458
Goodman, Paul, 456
Goodman, Percival, 456
Goodnow, Frank J., 6
Gordon, Mitchell, 437, 438 n.
Gore, William J., 460
Gottmann, Jean, 11, 31 n., 431, 454
Grant, Daniel R., 305, 306 n., 326,
    380 n., 459
Graves, W. Brooke, 351 n., 459
Grebler, Leo, 454
Green, Constance M., 451
Green, James L., 40, 454
Green, Raymond J., 457
Greene, Lee S., 459
Greer, Scott, 7, 31 n., 136, 202 n.,
    374, 377 n., 380 n., 383 n., 384 n.,
    389 n., 390, 433 n., 448, 450
Grigsby, William, 202 n.
Groberg, Robert P., 201 n.
Grodzins, Morton, 454
Gross, Bertram M., 234 n.

Groves, W. Eugene, 187 n.
Gruen, Victor, 96, 249
Gulick, Luther, 373, 458
Gutkind, E. A., 451
Gutkind, Peter, 403 n.
Gutman, Robert, 40

Haar, Charles M., 456
Haas, Ernst B., 34 n.
Hadden, Jeffrey K., 48 n., 77, 78, 449
Hall, Peter, 406 n., 417 n., 460
Hamdahl, Reuel, 454
Hamilton, Charles V., 452
Handlin, Oscar, 11, 450, 451
Hansen, Willard B., 245 n.
Hanson, Royce, 365 n., 371, 372 n.
Harper, Robert A., 454
Harrington, Michael, 452
Harris, Britton, 8
Harris, Chauncy D., 73, 74
Harris, Louis, 214, 215 n.
Harris, Robert, 274 n.
Hartman, Chester, 207 n.
Hauser, Philip M., 29 n., 31 n., 449, 460
Hausknecht, Murray, 454
Havard, William C., 305 n.
Havighurst, Robert J., 453
Hawkins, Brett W., 380 n., 386 n., 389, 390 n., 391 n., 449
Hawley, Amos H., 50, 307 n., 389 n., 451, 453
Hawley, Willis D., 455
Haworth, Lawrence, 456
Hayden, Tom, 452
Heller, Walter, 265
Hellmuth, William F., Jr., 457
Hendershot, G., 159 n.
Herber, Lewis, 458
Herfindahl, Orris C., 458
Herman, Harold, 53 n., 358 n., 460
Herson, Lawrence, 449
Hess, Robert, 453
Hirsch, Werner Z., 31, 164 n., 258 n., 449
Hill, Herbert, 70 n.
Hill, Richard J., 455

Hill, Roscoe, 453
Hobbes, Thomas, 196
Holden, Matthew, Jr., 33, 34, 35, 355 n., 380 n.
Hollander, T. Edward, 453
Hollinger, L. S., 364
Homer, Porter W., 332
Hoover, Edgar M., 80 n., 96 n., 454
Horton, John E., 158 n., 390 n.
Howard, John, 215 n.
Howton, F. W., 451
Hoyt, Homer, 49 n., 399
Hudson, Barbara J., 447
Hufschmidt, Maynard M., 456
Humes, Samuel, 461
Humphrey, Hubert, 142
Hunter, Floyd, 128, 129, 130, 131
Hyman, Herbert, H., 150 n.

Ingraham, Page L., 119 n., 120 n.

Jackson, Andrew, 136, 375
Jacob, Philip E., 33 n., 358 n.
Jacobs, Paul, 452
Janowitz, Morris, 389 n., 455
Jefferson, Thomas, 375
Jenkins, George, 413 n.
Jennings, M. Kent, 130, 455
Jewell, Malcolm E., 459
Johnson, Lyndon B., 196, 208, 209, 211
Johnson, Thomas F., 454
Jonassen, Christen, 77, 78
Jones, Victor, 17, 33, 74, 359 n., 447, 449
Judkins, Harvey, 212, 213, 214

Kain, J. F., 458
Kammerer, Gladys M., 307 n.
Kaplan, Harold, 44, 345, 346, 454
Kaplan, Marshall, 236 n.
Kaufman, Herbert, 35, 39, 162, 310 n.
Kean, E. Gordon, Jr., 304 n.
Kee, Woo Sik, 274 n.
Kennedy, John F., 196
Kent, T. J., Jr., 231, 456
Kilson, Martin, 216 n.

King, Clarence, 145 n.
Kitchen, James D., 281 n.
Kneedler, Grace, 74
Kneese, Allen V., 458
Kohn, Clyde F., 454
Komarovsky, Mirra, 151 n.
Kornhauser, Arthur, 160 n.
Kotler, Milton, 310 n.
Kraemer, Kenneth L., 234 n.
Kramer, Ralph M., 456
Kravitz, Alan S., 240 n.

Lane, Robert E., 148 n., 150 n., 151 n., 455
LaPalombara, Joseph, 403 n.
Larsen, Christian L., 459
Larson, Calvin J., 449
Laurenti, Luigi, 207 n.
Leach, Richard H., 459
Ledbetter, William H., Jr., 207 n.
Lee, Eugene, 141
Lee, Richard, 132
L'Enfant, Pierre Charles, 226
Leonard, W. N., 258 n.
Lerner, Max, 155
Levin, Melvin R., 248 n., 456
Levin, Murray B., 158 n.
Levy, Burton, 188, 189
Lewis, Sinclair, 47
Lichfield, Nathaniel, 207 n.
Lieberson, Stanley, 451
Liebman, Charles S., 53 n., 358 n.
Lindsay, John, 221
Lineberry, Robert L., 30 n., 100 n.
Little, Kenneth, 413 n.
Lockard, Duane, 115 n.
Long, Norton E., 38 n., 39, 40, 430, 459
Loosely, E. W., 450
Lorenz, Robert, 460
Lynch, Kevin, 26 n., 28 n., 450
Lynd, Helen M., 29
Lynd, Robert S., 29
Lynn, Arthur D., Jr., 458
Lyon, Leverett S., 459

Maass, Arthur, 164 n.

Mabogunje, Akin L., 411, 412 n.
McArthur, Robert E., 326 n.
Mace, Ruth L., 453
Machiavelli, Niccolo, 433
Mackler, Bernard, 453
McClellan, John L., 212, 213, 214, 215
McCord, William, 215 n.
McDill, Edward L., 159 n.
McDonald, Robert H., 447
McElrath, Dennis, 380 n.
McKelvey, Blake, 115, 451
McKenzie, R. D., 8, 16 n., 85, 281 n., 449
McNayr, Irving G., 331, 332, 334 n.
Mahood, H. R., 449
Malakoff, Herbert, 460
Malcolm X, 452
Malielski, S. J., 456
Mandelker, Daniel R., 406 n., 456
Mangin, William, 421 n.
Mangum, Garth L., 263 n.
Manis, Jerome G., 156 n.
Marando, Vincent L., 391 n.
Margolis, Julius, 261 n.
Marris, Peter, 206 n., 453
Marshall, Dale R., 456
Martin, Eileen, 461
Martin, Richard, 459
Martin, Roscoe C., 119 n., 143 n., 448, 455, 458, 460
Masotti, Louis H., 449, 452
Maxey, Chester C., 7, 434
Maxwell, James A., 458
Mayer, Harold M., 31, 454
Mead, Margaret, 427
Meadows, Paul, 460
Metzger, Joseph, 329 n.
Meyer, J. R., 458
Meyerson, Margy E., 454
Meyerson, Martin, 237 n., 450, 454, 455
Middleton, John T., 181 n.
Milbrath, Lester, 146, 147
Milgram, Grace, 454
Miller, Delbert C., 129
Miller, John, 5
Minar, David, 380 n.

Mitchell, N. C., 412 n.
Mitchell, Robert B., 450
Molière, Jean Baptiste (Poquelin), 227
Morlan, Robert L., 142 n.
Morris, James R., 454
Morris, Robert, 229 n., 457
Morse, Richard M., 420 n., 422 n.
Moses, Robert, 200
Mowitz, Robert J., 132 n.
Moynihan, Daniel, 222
Mumford, Lewis, 10 n., 436, 451
Munger, Frank J., 143 n., 455
Munro, William Bennett, 434
Murphy, Raymond E., 76
Murphy, W. S., 452
Musgrave, Richard A., 252 n.
Mushkin, Selma J., 457
Myrdal, Gunnar, 154

Nairn, Ian, 457
Napoleon III, 200
Nathan, Richard P., 457
Netzer, Dick, 257 n., 259 n., 264
Newton, Isaac, 249
Norton, James A., 380 n., 388
Novak, Benjamin, 458
Nsarkoh, J. K., 461

O'Donnell, John L., 453
Ogburn, W. F., 73
Opperman, Paul, 247
Orleans, Peter, 136, 380 n.
Ornati, Oscar, 452
O'Rourke, Lawrence W., 155 n., 455
Orum, Anthony M., 154 n.
Osborn, Frederic J., 456
Osman, Jack W., 265 n.
Ostrom, Vincent, 36 n., 41 n.
Owen, Wilfred, 458

Park, Robert E., 29
Parsons, Talcott, 43
Peardon, Thomas P., 450
Peattie, Lisa, 240 n.
Pericles, 200

Perloff, Harvey S., 235 n., 453, 456, 457
Pfouts, Ralph W., 83 n.
Pickard, Jerome P., 11 n.
Piven, Frances, 456
Pock, Max A., 313 n.
Pogue, Thomas, 265 n.
Polsby, Nelson W., 29 n.
Powell, G. B., Jr., 403 n.
Press, Charles, 391 n., 449, 455, 459
Presthus, Robert, 130
Price, Douglas, 448
Prothero, R. M., 412 n.

Rabinovitz, Francine F., 456, 460
Rainwater, Lee, 211 n.
Ramo, Simon, 42 n.
Rannells, John, 453
Ranney, David C., 456
Rapoport, Anatol, 41 n.
Redstone, Louis G., 457
Reed, Thomas H., 299 n.
Rehfuss, John A., 280 n.
Rein, Martin, 453
Reiner, Thomas A., 457
Reiss, Albert J., Jr., 451
Reps, John W., 457
Reynolds, Harry W., 206 n.
Richards, Alan R., 29 n., 449
Ridley, Jeanne C., 159 n.
Riemer, Svend, 449
Ries, John C., 124 n.
Riggs, Fred W., 44 n., 403 n.
Robson, William A., 4, 408, 460
Rodwin, Lloyd, 26 n., 450
Romani, John H., 382 n., 390 n.
Roosevelt, Franklin D., 196
Rose, Arnold M., 455
Rosenberg, Bernard, 451
Rosenstock, Florence W., 145 n.
Rossi, Peter H., 454
Royce, Ronald R., 448
Rustin, Bayard, 211

Sacks, Seymour, 269, 274, 457
Sandburg, Carl, 27
Savio, Charles J., 460

Sayre, Wallace S., 29 n., 35, 39, 162
Scheidt, Melvin E., 178 n.
Schmandt, Henry J., 29 n., 111 n., 145 n., 269 n., 383 n., 389 n., 403 n., 421 n., 452, 459
Schnore, Leo F., 15 n., 29 n., 30 n., 31, 53, 57, 58, 59, 62 n., 116, 117 n., 238 n., 449, 451
Schorr, Alvin L., 206 n.
Schulze, Robert O., 133 n.
Scoble, Harry M., 149 n.
Scott, Mel, 457
Scott, Stanley, 275 n., 320 n., 322 n., 448, 459
Seabrook, Jeremy, 452
Seeley, John R., 450
Sengstock, Frank S., 459
Sgontz, L. G., 265 n.
Shank, Alan, 449
Sharp, Harry, 62 n.
Sharpe, L. J., 408 n.
Sherwood, Frank P., 355 n., 423 n.
Shevky, Eshref, 54 n.
Shogan, Robert, 452
Shostak, Arthur B., 456
Sigafoos, R. A., 457
Silberman, Charles E., 452
Simms, Ruth P., 460
Sims, R. A., 450
Sjoberg, Gideon, 400 n., 402 n., 451
Smailes, Arthur E., 454
Smallwood, Frank, 345, 346, 405, 408 n.
Smerk, George M., 171 n., 458
Smith, D. H., 136 n.
Smith, David L., 265 n.
Smith, Paul A., 40 n.
Smith, Robert G., 313 n., 458
Smith, T. V., 48 n.
Smith, Wilson, 451
Sofen, Edward, 334, 384 n.
Solomon, Ezra, 82 n.
Sorauf, Frank J., 142 n.
Spiegel, Erika, 456
Spiegel, Hans B. C., 456
Spreiregen, Paul D., 457
Standing, William, 389 n.

Starr, Roger, 241 n., 347, 437 n.
Stauber, Richard L., 111 n.
Steadman, Robert F., 280 n.
Stefaniak, N. J., 14 n.
Stegman, Michael A., 235 n.
Stein, Clarence S., 456
Stein, Gertrude, 11
Stein, Maurice R., 451
Steinbicker, Paul G., 383 n.
Steiner, Kurt, 461
Stephens, G. Ross, 269 n.
Stevens, Lewis M., 460
Still, Bayrd, 451
Stine, Leo C., 156 n.
Stoner, John E., 352 n.
Strauss, Anselm, 28
Studenski, Paul, 434, 449
Sunshine, Morris, 131 n.
Swanson, Bert E., 123, 455
Sweeney, Stephen B., 43 n., 448, 450
Syed, Anwar, 451

Taeuber, Alma F., 63, 64
Taeuber, Karl E., 63, 64
Taft, Robert, 203
Terrett, Barbara, 450, 454
Theodorson, George A., 451
Thomitz, Carol, 130, 455
Thompson, Carey C., 266 n.
Thompson, Ralph V., 154 n.
Thompson, Wayne E., 158 n., 390 n.
Thompson, Wilbur R., 31, 37, 72 n., 79 263
Thuron, Lester, 266 n.
Tiebout, Charles M., 36 n., 41 n., 84 n., 453
Tocqueville, Alexis de, 149, 150
Tomeh, A. A., 153 n.
Torres, Juan de, 457
Toscano, James V., 33 n., 358 n.
Tower, W. D., 73
Trueblood, Felicity M., 460
Tullock, Gordon, 36 n.
Tunnard, Christopher, 457
Turner, Ralph E., 98 n.
Twain, Mark, 442

Utter, Kathryn L., 458

Valentine, Charles A., 452
Van Ben Berghe, Pierre L., 461
Vance, James E., 454
Vernon, Raymond, 95, 96 n., 448, 450

Wakely, Rosabelle P., 210 n.
Walker, Mabel L., 275 n.
Walker, Robert A., 239 n.
Wallace, George, 159
Walsh, Annmarie Hauck, 460
Walton, John, 130 n.
Ward, Agee, 222 n.
Ware, Caroline F., 98 n.
Warner, Sam Bass, Jr., 451
Warren, Robert, 36 n., 41 n., 44, 349
Warren, Roland, 152 n.
Warshauer, Mary E., 453
Watson, Richard A., 382 n., 390 n., 455
Watt, Harold R., 43 n.
Weaver, Robert, 207 n., 452
Webber, Melvin, 228, 432 n.
Weber, Arnold R., 86 n., 97 n.
Webster, Donald H., 232 n.
Weinbaum, Marvin G., 455
Weisbrod, Burton, 452
Weiss, Shirley F., 453
Welch, Louie, 235 n.
Welfeld, Irving H., 206 n.
Wendel, George D., 383 n.
West, Ben, 386
Wheaton, William L. C., 31, 235, 432 n., 454
Wheeler, Raymond H., 288 n.
White, J. W., 382, 395 n.
White, Leonard D., 48 n.
Whiteford, Andrew H., 461
Whittick, Arnold, 456
Whyte, William H., 138, 155

Wildavsky, Aaron, 130, 455
Willbern, York, 445, 448
Willhelm, Sidney M., 456
Williams, Oliver P., 53 n., 123, 358 n., 449
Wilner, Daniel M., 210 n.
Wilson, James Q., 187 n., 205, 455, 458
Wingo, Lowdon, 453
Winnick, Louis, 454
Wirt, Frederick M., 453, 455
Wiseman, H. V., 41 n.
Wohl, M., 458
Wolfinger, Raymond, 30 n.
Wood, Robert C., 258 n., 430, 450
Wood, Thomas J., 334 n., 379 n., 384 n.
Woodbury, Coleman, 203 n., 226, 439, 448, 449, 454
Wraith, Ronald, 415 n., 461
Wray, Donald E., 140 n.
Wright, Charles R., 150 n., 455
Wright, Deil S., 132 n., 458
Wright, Frank Lloyd, 93, 94, 457
Wurster, Catherine Bauer, 203 n.

Yancey, William L., 211 n.
Yazaki, Takeo, 461
Ylvisaker, Paul, 120, 198, 450
Young, Oran R., 41 n.
Young, Roland, 7

Zeigler, Harmon, 455
Zeisel, Hans, 395 n.
Zikmund, Joseph, 53 n.
Zimmer, Basil G., 307 n., 389 n., 453
Zimmerman, Joseph F., 247 n., 366 n., 371 n., 449
Zubrow, Reuben A., 254 n.
Zucker, Paul, 457

INDEX OF SUBJECTS

Access to government, in suburbs, 156–158

Advisory Commission on Intergovernmental Relations, 59–60, 122, 278, 321, 352, 450, 457, 459; effort to delineate local and area-wide functions, 163 n., 164–165, 166

Advocacy planning, 240–242

Africa: number of metropolitan areas in, 397; governmental reorganization in, 410

Age: and voting, 148–149; and membership in formal organizations, 151–152

Age composition of population, 67–69; social and political significance of, 67

Air pollution, 181–184; physical damage of, 181–182; methods of controlling, 184

Air Quality Act of 1967, 182, 184

Alaska, no metropolitan areas in, 20

Alienation, 158–160

American Institute of Planners, 244–245

American Society of Planning Officials, 457

American Society for Public Administration, 460

Annexation, 280–297; declining usefulness of, 15; and water supply, 177; pre-1900 characteristics of, 281; rationale of, 281; definition of, 281 n.; decreasing use of, 282; changes in legal requirements for, 282, 284; resurgence of, 284–291; not an area-wide approach, 290–291; and unincorporated urban areas, 291–292; resistance to, 292; establishment of review process for, 295–296

Areas: of municipalities in metropolitan areas, 105; of school districts, 105; of special districts, 105

Asia, number of metropolitan areas in, 397

Atlanta, leadership in, 128, 130

Atlanta SMSA, antithesis of comprehensive urban county plan in, 325 n.

Automation, 199

Automobile: effect on community spatial pattern, 72; rapidly expanded use of, 167; role in the economy, 168; as part of balanced transportation system, 170; and air pollution, 181

Baltimore, declining proportion of white population in, 63, 64

Baltimore SMSA, number of local governments in, 102

Baton Rouge (La.), city-county consolidation involving, 299–300, 303–304, 305

Black capitalism, 217

Black nationalism, 216

Black power, 215, 216–217

Blacks. See Negroes

Blight, 65

Boroughs, 298

Boroughs (incorporated). See Municipalities

Boston SMSA: loss of manufacturing employment by central city in, 92; mass transit in, 168, 172; air pollution control in, 184

Budget, Bureau of the: metropolitan definition established by, 2–3; designation of standard consolidated areas, 21 n.

Buffalo (N.Y.), strength of Democratic Party in, 143

Buffalo–Niagara Falls–Fort Erie international metropolitan area, 23

Business, and civic affairs, 136–139

Business organizations: changes in, 138; and governmental reorganization, 378–379

Businesses, small, 95–96

California: number of metropolitan areas in 21; local sales taxes in, 261

California (Berkeley), University of, Bureau of Public Administration, 447

Capital improvement program, as tool of planning, 233

Caucasians. See White population

Census, Bureau of the, 275; initial recognition of metropolitan areas, 6; recognition of metropolitan development by, 17, 19; major publications of, 448

Central business district: controversy over, 90–91; unique features of, 94; advantages of, 94–97; future of, 96–97, 442

Central cities: commutation area as element of metropolitanism, 8; reliance on suburbs, 9; general socioeconomic comparisons with suburbs, 51–52, 57–60; social rank in, 54–57; segregation in, 54–57; urbanization in, 54–57; income in, 57–58; education in, 57–58; occupations in, 57–58; concentration of nonwhite population in, 62–63; declining proportion of white population in, 63; decline in population, 66; unemployment in, 86; losses in manufacturing employment, 92; losses in retail trade sales, 92–93; losses in retail employment, 93; civic organizations in, 156; infrequent water problem in, 177; attractiveness of municipal income taxes to, 260–261; extensive capital outlays in, 271–272; development through annexation, 281; general limited usefulness of

annexation to, 285–286; growing opposition to city-county consolidation in, 301; and governmental cooperation, 392–393; continued viability as economic units, 442

Centralization, as element of metropolitanism, 14

Change-oriented groups, 143–145

Chicago: predominant ethnic group in, 61; leadership in, 132; businessmen in civic affairs, 137; nonpartisan elections in, 141; political party activity in, 141; strength of Democratic Party in, 143

Chicago–Northwestern Indiana Standard Consolidated Area, 21 n., 24, 25

Chicago SMSA: population of, 21; loss of manufacturing employment by central city in, 92; number of local governments in, 102; mass transit in, 168, 171–172; air pollution in, 181; law enforcement agencies in, 189

Chicago Transit Authority, 171

Chief administrative officer, in counties, 118

Child-centered organizations, in suburbs, 156

Choices, variety of: as metropolitan attraction, 26; in municipal-services market model, 36–37

Cincinnati, political party activity in, 141

Cities: characteristics in preindustrial era of, 10; economic classification by regions, 74. See also Municipalities

Cities, state leagues of, 352

City administrative officer, use in strong mayor-council municipalities, 117

City-county consolidation: alienation as factor in defeating, 159; definition of, 281; nature of, 297; pre-1900 adoptions of, 297–298; obstacles to, 298–299; recent adoptions

City-county consolidation (*Continued*) of, 299–300, 301–307; recent rejections of, 301

City-county separation, characteristics of, 297 n.

City government. *See* Municipalities

City planning: recent establishment as distinct process, 277; disagreement over independence of, 281. *See also* Planning

Civic affairs: and business, 136–139; and labor, 139–141; and political parties, 141–143

Civic organizations: in central cities, 156; and governmental reorganization, 378

Civil disorders, 211–212, 214–215

Civil disturbances. *See* Riots

Civil rights groups, 144–145

Civil rights movement, 216

Classification. *See* Typologies

Clean Air Act of 1964, 182

Cleveland: declining proportion of white population in, 63, 64; decline in population, 66

Cleveland SMSA: population growth in, 66; mass transit in, 168

Commission government, 115–116

Committee for Economic Development, 280, 309, 450

Community: many meanings of, 7; combining two definitions for metropolitan use, 7–8

Community Chest, 138, 140

Community development approach, 145

Comparative shopping, 94–95

Comparative urban studies, 403–404

Competition for public office, in suburbs, 158

Comprehensive urban county plan: features of, 324; appeal of, 325; attempts to adopt, 325–327; in operation in Dade County (Fla.), 327–335

Concentric zones, as type of urban development, 48–49

Confrontation industries, 95

Confrontation politics, 225

Conservation, housing, 204, 205

Consolidation. *See* City-county consolidation; Municipal consolidation; School district consolidation

Cook County (Ill.), strength of Democratic Party in, 143

Coordination, need for institutional means to effect, 444

Core cities. *See* Central cities

Council-manager government: growth of, 116; and socially homogeneous cities, 116–117; characteristics of, 116; organization of, 116–117; influence of expert in, 135. *See also* County managers; Town managers

Councils of governments, 248, 350, 435, 443; contrasting views about, 364, 371; origin of, 365; growth of, 365–366; membership and activities, 366–368; financing, 368; staff of, 368; the future of, 370–372

Council of State Governments, 321, 352, 459

Counties: proportion of metropolitan local governmental total, 103, 104; governmental functional changes in, 114; governmental organization changes in, 118; and air pollution control, 184; and property taxes, 257; and state aid, 265; consolidation of, 280; consolidation with school districts, 280; structural reorganization and comprehensive urban county development, 325; as contributors to governmental cooperation, 351–352; as participants in governmental agreements, 353, 370

County managers, 118

County mayors, 118

County reapportionment, 325–326

Corruption, and governmental reorganization, 384, 386

Crime: costs of, 186; causes of increase in, 191

Crisis precipitation, 225

Dade County (Fla.): comprehensive urban county plan in operation in, 327–335; as an urban county, 359 n. *See also* Miami SMSA

Dallas, sizable amount of land annexed by, 286, 288

Dayton SMSA: input-output economic analysis of, 84–85; nonvoting in, 149; membership in formal groups in, 150 n.

Debt, local governmental: by type of unit, 272; rapid rise in, 272–273

Decentralization: as element of metropolitanism, 10–15; characteristic of both large and small urban places, 14–15; as related to technology, 16; at neighborhood level, 309–310

Decision-making, locational shift of power in, 432–434. *See also* Leadership

Delaware River Basin Commission, 119; based on interstate compact, 317

Democratic Party, and labor, 140

Demonstration Cities and Metropolitan Development Act of 1966, 248, 366

Dependent agencies, 314 n., 322 n.

Deterioration, city, 200–210

Detroit: predominant ethnic group in, 61; declining proportion of white population in, 63, 64; decline in population, 66; riot in, 215; annexations by, 282

Detroit SMSA: population of, 21; population growth in, 66; loss of manufacturing employment by central city in, 92; leadership in, 132 n.; membership in formal groups in, 150 n.; sewage disposal in, 180

Detroit–Windsor international metropolitan area, 23

District of Columbia, part of metropolitan area, 20

Downtown area. *See* Central business district

Durable goods manufacturing, in selected SMSAs, 83

Dwelling units, single family, as factor in urbanization index, 54

Earnings taxes, municipal, 250–261

Economic activities, decentralization of, 441–442

Economic classification of cities, by region, 74

Economic interdependence: as factor in metropolitan definition, 8; as element of metropolitanism, 9–10, 16

Economic model, 36–39

Economic power, separation from political power, 137–139

Economic structure: relation to governmental system, 97–99; future developments in, 441–442

Economy: growth determinants of, 79–80; role of automobile in, 168

Education, 166; as factor in social rank index, 54; in central cities, 57–58; in suburbs, 57–58; and voting, 149; segregation in, 218; unequal opportunity in, 218–220; obstacles to racial integration in, 220; upgrading quality of, 220; decentralization of, 221–222; and the Coleman report, 222–223; relation to other problems, 223–224; and property taxes, 258–259

Elections, participation in, 147–148. *See also* Nonpartisan elections; Partisan elections; Voting

El Paso–Ciudad Juarez international metropolitan area, 23

Employment: base of, 82–83; in economic sectors in selected SMSAs, 82–83

Enrollment, of school systems in metropolitan areas, 105

Erie County (N.Y.), strength of Republican Party in, 143

Ethnic colonies, 61

Ethnicity, as index of social area analysis, 54

Europe, number of metropolitan areas in, 397

Expenditures, governmental, increase in, 253–254

Expenditures, local governmental: for publicly owned utilities, 268; for current operations, 268; patterns of, 267–273; for capital outlays, 271–273; determinants of, 273–275

Expressways, 66; growth of, 169

Feather River Project, 176

Federal aid, 263–267, 433

Federal Aid Highway Act of 1956, 169

Federal concept of governmental reorganization. See Comprehensive urban county plan; Federation; Metropolitan districts; Two-level approach to governmental reorganization

Federal government. See National government

Federation: similarities to comprehensive urban county plan and metropolitan multipurpose districts, 335–336; major attempts to adopt, 336–339; in operation in Montreal (Quebec, Canada) and Winnipeg (Manitoba, Canada) areas, 339 n.; in operation in Toronto (Ontario, Canada) area, 339–346

Fees, governmental, 262

Fertility ratio, as factor in urbanization index, 54

Finance, local governmental, and governmental fragmentation, 276

Financial aid. See Federal aid; State aid

Fire losses, 185

Fire prevention, deficiencies in, 185

Fire protection, 166; needs for differing levels of, 185; administration of, 185–186

Fiscal capacity, as a determinant of local governmental expenditures, 274, 275

Fiscal functions of democratic government, 252–253

Ford Foundation, 366

Foreign-born whites, number in United States, 61

Formal decision-makers, 133–135

Freeways. See Expressways

Functional consolidation, three types of, 354

Functionalism, 43–45

Games model, 39–40

Garden-city movement, 406

General plan, components of, 229–230

Ghetto, 212

Government, access to, 156–158. See also Local government; National Government; State government

Government Affairs Foundation, 447, 458

Governmental agreements, 429; types of, 350; scope of, 352–353; characteristics of, 352–356; types of state laws authorizing, 356; and community differentiation, 357–358; in Los Angeles County, 358–364; as evolutionary means of functional allocation, 364; restrictions on, 369–370. See also Councils of governments; Functional consolidation; Governmental contracts; Governmental cooperation

Governmental bureaucracy: and political power, 134–135; and governmental reorganization, 380–381

Governmental contracts: for sewage disposal, 180; for fire protection, 185; for law enforcement, 189

Governmental cooperation, 443; forms of, 350; factors contributing to growth of, 351–352; and councils of governments, 364–368; the future of, 369–372; politics of, 391–393; increased emphasis on, 434–435

Governmental decentralization, 436

Governmental employees, percentage

Governmental employees (*Continued*) of employed labor force in selected SMSAs, 83

Governmental fragmentation: as element of metropolitanism, 15; effect on political parties, 142–143; and local governmental finance, 276

Governmental functions: changes in metropolitan age, 114–115; local and areawide, 163–166

Governmental officials, and political power, 133–135

Governmental organization: changes in metropolitan age, 115–118; and water problems, 177–178

Governmental overlapping, 106–107

Governmental reorganization: premises of, 374; barriers to, 374–376; and existing political-governmental pattern, 376; initiators of, 377–378; and civic and business organizations, 378–379; and newspapers, 379–380; and governmental bureaucracy, 380–381; and political parties, 381; and labor unions, 381–382; and Negroes, 382–383; issues in, 383–386; voter reaction to, 386–391; in London area, 408–409; in Africa, 410; forces hostile to, 430; changing emphasis in, 434–435. *See also* Annexation; City-county consolidation; City-county separation; Comprehensive urban county plan; Functional consolidation; Governmental agreements; Governmental contracts; Governmental cooperation; Metropolitan districts; Municipal consolidation; School district consolidation; Transfers of governmental functions

Governmental services, increased demand for, 98

Governmental specialists, influence of, 134–135

Governmental structure: interrelation with other variables, 100–101; relation to political environment, 123–124

Governmental system: relation to economic structure, 97–99; no breakdown in, 429–430; future developments in, 442–444; purposes of, 445. *See also* Local government; Local governmental system; National government; State government

Grass-roots concept of government, 375

Greater London Plan of 1944, 406

Health. *See* Public health

Health, Education, and Welfare, Department of, 182

Highways. *See* Expressways

Home ownership, and voting, 149

Hospitals, 166

Housing, 166; limited public amount of, 207; for aged, 207–208

Housing Act of 1937, 202

Housing Act of 1949, different views of objectives of, 203

Housing and Urban Development Act of 1965, 206 n.

Housing and Urban Redevelopment Act of 1968, 208–209

Housing and Urban Development, Department of, 121, 366

Houston, sizable amount of land annexed by, 286, 288

Ibadan (Nigeria) area: physical and demographic features of, 410–413; governmental pattern of, 413–415

Illinois, local sales taxes in, 261

Immigration: changing ethnic nature of, 60; volume of, 60

Income: in central cities, 57–58; in suburbs, 57–58; and voting, 149

Income, median family, in SMSA by region, 88–90

Income taxes, municipal, 260–261

Incorporation. *See* Municipal incorporation

Indianapolis SMSA, city-county consolidation in, 303 n.

Industrial location, effects of transportation improvements on, 14

Industrial Revolution, 14

Industrialization: changes resulting from, 71–72; and worldwide urbanization, 400–401

Industries: basic, 80–82; nonbasic, 80–82; confrontation, 95

Initiative, referendum, and recall, 375

Input-output analysis, 45–46, 83–85

Integration, racial, 216, 220

Intergovernmental Relations, Office of, 122

Intergovernmental relations. See Advisory Commission on Intergovernmental Relations; Senate Committee on Government Operations

Interior, Department of the, 192

International City Management (Managers') Association, 448

International relations model, 33–35

International Union of Local Authorities, 448, 460

Interstate compacts, 184, 317

Interstate metropolitan areas, 23, 24, 25, 119

Investment decisions, 434

Jacksonian ideology, 375

Jacksonville, city-county consolidation involving, 302–303, 303–304, 306–307

Jacksonville SMSA: law enforcement in, 190; metropolitan planning in, 246

Jeffersonian ideology, 375

Johnstown (Pa.) SMSA, small proportion of population in central city of, 22

Journey to work, as element of metropolitanism, 8

Kansas City (Mo.), sizable amount of land annexed by, 286, 288

Kerner Commission. See National Advisory Commission on Civil Disorders

Labor: and civic affairs, 139–141; and the Democratic Party, 140

Labor force, 85–90; in four major economic sectors in selected SMSAs, 82–83

Labor unions, and governmental reorganization, 381–382

Lakewood Plan: originated from combination of factors, 361; characteristics of, 361–363

Land and Water Conservation Fund Act of 1964, 192–193

Land use: patterns of, 48–51; and property taxes, 258–259. See also Planning; Zoning

Laredo–Nuevo Laredo international metropolitan area, 23

Las Vegas SMSA, rapid population growth in, 21

Latin America, number of metropolitan areas in, 397

Law enforcement, 166; public perceptions of, 186–187; major types of activities, 187; police-community relations programs, 187–188; and minority groups, 187–189; diversity of, 189–190; administration of, 189–191; spillover effects of, 190

Leadership, 127–133; in school district consolidation, 308–309

Legislative reapportionment. See County reapportionment

Libraries, 166

Local autonomy. See Municipal home rule

Local federalism, 434. See also Two-level approach to governmental reorganization

Local government: number of units in metropolitan areas, 101–102; variations in number of units of, 102; percentages by types in metropolitan areas, 102–104; original system of, 107–109; evolution of, 109–113; meanings to different groups, 159; and social disorganization, 191; relation to metropolitan planning

Local government (*Continued*)
  agencies, 246–248; norms that shape, 375–376; in London area, 407–409; in Nigeria, 414–415; in Tokyo area, 418; in São Paulo area, 422–424; implication of megalopolis for, 432. *See also* Counties; Municipalities; New England towns; Towns; Townships; School districts; Special districts

Local governmental system: impact of states on, 118–119; impact of national government on, 120–123. *See also* Governmental system

London area: physical and demographic characteristics of, 404–407; governmental pattern of, 407–409

Los Angeles: predominant ethnic group in, 61; political party activity in, 141; water supply of, 176; riot in, 211, 215; municipal consolidation involving, 282; use of annexation by, 282, 283

Los Angeles County (Calif.): voting in, 155; law enforcement in, 189; governmental agreements in, 358–364; as an urban county, 359–361

Los Angeles–Long Beach SMSA: population of, 21; loss of manufacturing employment by central city in, 92; expressways in, 169; air pollution in, 181; fire protection in, 355 n.

Low-income areas, residents of, 199–200

Machine politics, and governmental reorganization, 384–386

Madison (Wis.) SMSA, number of local governments in, 102

Manufacturing employment, losses by central cities of, 92

Market mechanism, and local public services, 262–263

Mass transit: decline of, 168; as part of balanced transportation system, 169–170; subsidy of, 170; aid by

national government, 171–174; recommended changes in, 173

Massachusetts, number of metropolitan areas in, 21

Massachusetts Bay Transportation Authority, 172

Master plan. *See* General plan

Mayor-council government, 115, 117

Megalopolis: characteristics of, 11, 431–432; implications for local government, 432

Merger. *See* City-county consolidation; Municipal consolidation; School district consolidation

Merit system, county, 117

Metropolitan age: governmental system in, 111–113; local governmental adjustments in, 113–118

Metropolitan councils. *See* Councils of governments

Metropolitan districts: territorial scope of, 313; mostly of recent origin, 313; functions of, 314, 316; accomplishments of, 316; factors prompting growth of, 316–317; frequent remoteness from public of, 317–318; governing board composition of, 318; use of constituent-unit principle of representation in, 318–320; proposed expansion to multipurpose basis, 321–324; as umbrella agency, 322

Metropolitan multipurpose districts, 321–324

Metropolitan planning: number and composition of agencies of, 242–244; nature of, 244–246; relation to local governments, 246–248; increased strength of, 247–248; agencies as reviewers of federal grant applications, 248; and councils of governments, 365

Metropolitan reform. *See* Governmental reorganization

Metropolitan research: periods of, 28–31; input-output approach, 45–46;

Metropolitan research (*Continued*)
systems analysis approach, 40–43; functional approach, 43–45

Metropolitan St. Louis Survey, transportation recommendations, 174

Metropolitan Sanitary District of Greater Chicago, 180

Metropolitan Water District of Southern California, 177

Mexican-Americans, as part of white population, 62 n.

Mexicans, migration of, 62

Miami SMSA: labor force employment in certain economic activities, 83; metropolitan planning in, 246; comprehensive urban county plan in operation in, 327–335; politics of governmental reorganization campaign in, 384. *See also* Dade County (Fla.)

Michigan, number of metropolitan areas in, 21

Michigan, University of: Survey Research Center, 151; Law School Legislative Research Center, 450

Migration, characteristics of, 62–63

Milwaukee, predominant ethnic group in, 61

Milwaukee County (Wis.), increased flexibility of industrial location in, 14

Milwaukee Metropolitan Sewerage Commission, 180

Milwaukee SMSA, air pollution control in, 184

Minneapolis, predominant ethnic group in, 61

Minneapolis–St. Paul SMSA, provision of water in, 176

Minibus, 171, 172

Minor civil divisions, definition of, 3

Minority groups: as factor in segregation index, 54; and law enforcement, 187–189

Mobility, 152

Model Cities Act of 1966, 209 n., 223

Models: definitions of, 32; international relations type, 33–35; economic type, 36–39; municipal-services market type, 36–39; games type, 39–40; the future of, 46

Mortgage financing, 121

Multicentered pattern, as type of urban development, 50–51

Municipal consolidation: definition of, 281 n.; decline in, 282; changes in legal requirements for, 284; establishment of review process for, 296

Municipal home rule, 375

Municipal incorporation: liberal legal requirements for, 284; as a block to annexation, 293; legal restrictions on, 294–295; establishment of review process for, 295–296

Municipal reform movement, elements of, 375

Municipalities: annexation by, 15; proportion of metropolitan local governmental total, 103–104; in metropolitan areas, by population size, 104; areas of, 105; governmental organizational changes in, 115–117; forms of government in, 115–117; typologies of, 123–124; and air pollution control, 184; and property taxes, 257; and state aid, 265; consolidation with school districts, 280; use of annexation by, 280–297; number completing annexations since 1950, 285; functions in Toronto area federation, 340–341; as participants in governmental agreements, 353

Municipality of Metropolitan Toronto: functions of, 340–341, 344; member municipalities of, 340, 342; governing board of, 341–344; progress of, 344–345; criticisms of, 345–346

Municipal-services market model, 36–39

Mutual aid pacts, 369; and legal liability, 355; and inadequate services, 355

Nashville, city-county consolidation involving, 301–302, 303–304, 305–306

Nashville SMSA: law enforcement in,

Nashville SMSA (*Continued*) 190; metropolitan planning in, 246; politics of governmental reorganization campaigns in, 384–386

National Advisory Commission on Civil Disorders, 211–212, 215; and law-enforcement community-relations programs, 188

National Association of Counties, 352, 366, 448

National Association of Housing and Redevelopment Officials, 201

National Center for Air Pollution Control, 181

National Commission on Urban Problems, 280, 309

National government: adjustments in the metropolitan age, 120–123; and highway construction, 169; and mass transit, 171–174; and water pollution control, 179, 180; and sewage disposal, 179–180; and air pollution control, 182, 184; and law enforcement, 191; and parks and recreation, 192–193; and metropolitan review of federal grant applications, 248; and fiscal inequities, 278; increasing metropolitan consciousness of, 371; and governmental cooperation, 393; and planning, 439

National Governors' Conference, 459

National League of Cities, 352, 366

National Municipal League, 242, 378, 448, 449

National Recreation Association, 194

National Resources Committee, 73

National Service to Regional Councils, 366

Negroes: as factor in segregation index, 54; migration of, 62–63; as proportion of nonwhite population, 62 n.; segregation of, 63–66; unemployment in central cities, 86; median family income in SMSAs, 90; participation by, 153–155; grievances in riot cities, 214; and governmental reorganization, 382–383. See

also Black power; Minority groups; Nonwhite population; Race; Race relations; Racial disturbances; Segregation

Neighborhood decentralization, 309–310

New England (U.S.), metropolitan definition in, 3 n.

New England towns, as participants in governmental agreements, 353

New Haven, leadership in, 128–129, 130

New Jersey County and Municipal Government Study Commission, 460

New towns, 405

New York (Albany), State University of, Graduate School of Public Affairs, 448, 460

New York City: daily commuting to, 9; relations with neighboring local governments, 35; migration of Puerto Ricans to, 62; population density of Manhattan section of, 125; political party activity in, 141; governmental tasks in, 162–163; police department in, 189; school decentralization in, 221–222; boroughs in, 298

New York Joint Committee on Metropolitan and Regional Areas, 460

New York Metropolitan Region Study, 450

New York–Northeastern New Jersey Standard Consolidated Area, 21, 21 n., 24, 25

New York Regional Plan Association, 246

New York SMSA: recognition of metropolitan nature of, 6; population of, 21; labor-force employment in certain economic activities, 82–83; loss of manufacturing employment by central city in, 92; number of local governments in, 102; mass transit in, 168; air pollution in, 181

Newspapers, and governmental reorganization, 379–380

Nigeria, local government in, 414–415

Nondurable goods manufacturing, in selected SMSAs, 83

Nonpartisan elections, 141, 375

Nonproperty taxes, types of, 260–262

Nonschool special districts. *See* Special districts

Nonwhite population: in South, 62; growth in metropolitan areas, 62; Negro proportion of, 62 n.; Bureau of the Census definition of, 62 n.; concentration in central cities, 62–63; proportion in suburbs, 63

North America, number of metropolitan areas in, 397

North Central (U.S.): foreign-born whites in, 61; median family income, 90

Northeast (U.S.): foreign-born whites in, 61; metropolitan nonwhite population growth, 62; median family income in, 90

Occupations, 85–88; as factor in social rank index, 54; in central cities, 57–58; in suburbs, 57–58

Oceania, number of metropolitan areas in, 397

Ohio, number of metropolitan areas in, 21

Oklahoma City, sizable amount of land annexed by, 286, 287–288

Omnibus Crime Control and Safe Streets Act of 1968, 191

One-government concept: support for, 279; opposition to, 279; forms of, 279–280, 280–281; future of, 310–311

Organization, municipal, 115–117

Parking, 170

Parks, 166, 192–195

Participation: by voting, 146–149; in formal groups, 150–152; in informal groups, 152–153; by Negroes, 153–155; in suburbs, 155–157; in planning, 239–241

Partisan elections, 141, 142–143

Payroll taxes, municipal, 260–261

Pennsylvania, number of metropolitan areas in, 21

Permits, governmental, 262

Personal-services employment, in selected SMSAs, 83

Philadelphia SMSA: labor force employment in certain economic activities, 82–83; loss of manufacturing employment by central city in, 92; loss of retail employment by central city in, 93; number of local governments in, 102; mass transit in, 168; new transportation authority in, 171; air pollution in, 181; law enforcement agencies in, 189; heavy suburban capital outlays in, 272; governmental agreements in, 356–358

Phoenix, sizable amount of land annexed by, 286, 288

Phoenix SMSA, sewage disposal agreement in, 369

Physical design, 438–439

Pittsburgh SMSA: labor-force employment in certain economic activities, 82–83; loss of manufacturing employment by central city in, 92; number of local governments in, 102

Planning, 166; for comprehensive transportation, 175; and water supply, 178; growing acceptance of, 227; traditional approach, 228–229; tools of, 229–233; changing character of, 234–238; new tools of, 237–238; role and place in local government, 238–239; and citizen participation, 239–241; in metropolitan areas, 242–249; outlook for, 249–250; in London area, 408–409; in Tokyo area, 417–418. *See also* City planning; Metropolitan planning

Plants, small, 95–96

Police. *See* Law enforcement

Political alienation. *See* Alienation

Political environment, relation to governmental structure, 123–124

Political parties: and civic affairs, 141–143; effect of governmental fragmentation, 142–143; and governmental reorganization, 381

Political power: and governmental officials, 133–135; and governmental bureaucracy, 134–135; separation from economic power, 137–139

Political system, complexity of, 160–161

Politics, local, attitudes of political parties toward, 142. See also Civic affairs

Population: size as element of metropolitanism, 8–9; total metropolitan, 19; metropolitan proportion by regions, 20; range by individual SMSAs, 21; rate of change in individual SMSAs, 21; central-city–suburban proportions of, 22; metropolitan density, 23; decline in certain central cities, 66; growth in certain SMSAs, 66; social and political significance of age composition of, 67; age composition of, 67–69; of municipalities in metropolitan areas, 104–105; of special districts, 105; density in New York City's Manhattan, 125; and local governmental expenditures, 274–275

Portland (Ore.) SMSA, number of local governments in, 102

Poverty groups, 144–145

President's Commission on Law Enforcement and Administration of Justice, 187

Primary groups: nature of activities, 152–153; as unifying forces, 153

Problems, service, preoccupation with, 197–198

Problems, socioeconomic, some key issues in, 198

Property taxes, 255–260; amount of, 255; productivity of, 255; use by various local governments of, 257;

base for, 258–259; and education, 258–259; and land use, 258–259; criticisms of, 259–260

Public accountability: of metropolitan districts, 317–318; and constituent-unit principle of representation, 319–320

Public Administration Service, 328 n.

Public health, 166

Public Health Service, 181, 182

Public housing. See Housing

Public welfare. See Social welfare

Puerto Ricans, migration of, 62

Puerto Rico, metropolitan areas in, 20

Quasi-market situation, relation to municipal-services market model, 36–37

Race, problem of, 210–218

Race relations, local government involvement in, 199

Racial disturbances, 211–215

Racism, 212, 212 n.

Reapportionment, county, 325–326

Recreation, 192–195. See also Parks

Red Cross, 138

Redevelopment. See Urban renewal

Reform. See Governmental reorganization

Refuse disposal, 166

Regional planning agencies. See Metropolitan planning

Rehabilitation, housing, 204, 205

Relocation of displaced families, 206–208

Rent supplements, 205–206, 440

Representation: constituent-unit principle of, 318–320; in metropolitan districts, 318–320

Research formulation. See Models

Residence, length of: and voting, 149; and membership in formal organizations, 152

Residential covenants, 430–431

Retail employment, losses by central cities, 93

Retail trade sales, losses by central cities, 92–93

Revenue, local governmental, patterns of, 255–267

Riots, 211–212, 214–215, 430

Rockefeller Foundation, 434

Rural areas, renewal of, 19–20

Russia. *See* Soviet Union

Sacramento SMSA: labor-force employment in certain economic activities, 83; provision of water in, 176

St. Louis: predominant ethnic group in, 61; declining proportion of white population in, 63, 64; decline in population, 66; growth through annexation, 281

St. Louis County (Mo.): law enforcement in, 189; special school district in, 276

St. Louis SMSA: social geography of, 54–57; population growth in, 66; loss of manufacturing employment by central city in, 92; number of local governments in, 102; higher electoral participation of home owners in, 149; voting in, 155; sewage disposal in, 180

Sales taxes, local, 261–262

San Antonio SMSA, large proportion of population in central city of, 22

San Diego, water supply of, 176

San Diego SMSA, sewage disposal agreement in, 369

San Diego–Tijuana international metropolitan area, 23

San Francisco: predominant ethnic group in, 61; water supply of, 176

San Francisco–Oakland SMSA: loss of manufacturing employment by central city in, 92; mass transit in, 168; air pollution control in, 184

São Paulo (Brazil) area: physical and demographic characteristics of, 421–422; governmental pattern of, 422–423

School district consolidation, 112–113, 280, 307–309, 429

School district reorganization. *See* School district consolidation

School districts: proportion of metropolitan local governmental total, 102–103; enrollments of, 105; proportion of public school system total in metropolitan areas, 105; areas of, 105; frequent territorial overlapping by, 106–107; and property taxes, 257; indirect costs of industry to, 258 n.; and state aid, 265; and financial inequities, 276; consolidation with municipalities and counties, 280; as participants in governmental agreements, 353

School superintendents, contracts for, 116

Sector pattern, as type of urban development, 49–50

Segregation: as index of social area analysis, 54; in suburbs, 54–57; in central cities, 54–57; of Negroes, 63–66; suburban techniques to support, 430–431

Senate Committee on Government Operations: Subcommittee on Intergovernmental Relations, 448; Subcommittee on Investigation, 452; Subcommittee on Executive Reorganization, 459

Separatism, racial, 215, 217

Service charges by local governments, 262–263

Service problems: local and area-wide, 163–166; interrelatedness of, 194–195; preoccupation with, 197–198

Sewage disposal, 166, 179–181; relation to water supply, 179; administration of, 180–181

Sex, and voting, 148

Shared taxes, 266

Shopping, specialized and comparative, 94–95

Short ballot, 375

Small businesses, 95–96

Small plants, 95–96

Social area analysis, three indexes of, 53–54

Social disorganization, and local government, 191

Social interdependence: as factor in metropolitan definition, 8; as element of metropolitanism, 9–10, 16; and urbanization, 401–403

Social planners, 234–235

Social protest, 145

Social rank: as index of social area analysis, 54; in suburbs, 54–57; in central cities, 54–57; and membership in formal organizations, 151

Social structure: complexity of, 47–48; future evolution of, 440–441

Social welfare, 166

Socioeconomic characteristics, and voting, 148–149

Socioeconomic problems. See Problems, socioeconomic

South (U.S.): foreign-born whites in, 61; nonwhite population in, 62; metropolitan nonwhite population in, 62; median family income in, 90

Soviet Union, number of metropolitan areas in, 397

Special districts, 429, 443; proportion of metropolitan local governmental total, 102–103; areas of, 105; population of, 105; frequent territorial overlapping by, 106–107; and mass transit, 171; and sewage disposal, 180; and air pollution control, 184; and parks and recreation, 194; and property taxes, 257; and financial inequities, 276; as participants in governmental agreements, 353. See also Metropolitan districts; Metropolitan multipurpose districts

Specialization: as factor in metropolitan definition, 8; as element of metropolitanism, 15–16

Specialized shopping, 94–95

Spillover effects, 276

Standard Metropolitan Statistical Areas

(SMSAs). See place names of individual areas

Star-shaped pattern, as type of urban development, 50

State aid, 263–267

State governments: adjustments in the metropolitan age, 118–120; and mass transit, 172; air pollution control efforts by, 182; and parks and recreation, 192; and fiscal inequities, 278; and municipal incorporation, 281; and annexation, 281; and school district consolidation, 308; as contributors to governmental cooperation, 352; increasing metropolitan consciousness of, 371; and governmental cooperation, 393

State offices of local affairs, 119–120

Strip cities, 438

Structural-functionalism. See Functionalism

Subdivision regulations, as tool of planning, 232

Suburbs: reliance on other parts of metropolis, 9; types of, 16; general socioeconomic comparisons with central cities, 51–52, 57–60; segregation in, 54–57; urbanization in, 54–57; social rank in, 54–57; occupations in, 57–58; income in, 57–58; education in, 57–58; proportion of nonwhite population in, 63; participation in, 155–157; child-centered organizations in, 156; access to government in, 156–158; image and reality of participation in, 157–158; residents' role in council meetings, 157–158; competition for public office in, 158; frequent water problem in, 177; responsibility for socioeconomic problems, 199; extensive capital outlays in, 271, 272; and governmental cooperation, 392, 393; segregation techniques of, 430–431

Super cities, 438

Syracuse SMSA: leadership in, 131;

Syracuse SMSA (*Continued*)
strength of Republican Party in, 143
Syracuse University, Maxwell Graduate School of Citizenship and Public Affairs, 448
Systems analysis, 40–43, 237

Tax differential zones, 300, 301, 311
Tax redistribution, and financial inequities, 277
Taxes, in relation to measures of wealth, 254
Technology: as related to decentralization, 16; effects on community spatial pattern, 72
Territorial overlapping by governments in metropolitan areas, 106–107
Territory: metropolitan expansion of, 10–15; metropolitan total, 22; metropolitan interstate, 23, 24, 25; metropolitan intracounty, 23; metropolitan intercounty, 23; metropolitan international, 23; amount annexed by municipalities since 1950, 285
Texas, number of metropolitan areas in, 21
Theory formulation. *See* Models
Tokyo (Japan) area: physical and demographic characteristics of, 416–418; governmental pattern of, 418–420
Tokyo Metropolitan Government, 417; features of, 418–419
Toronto (Ontario, Canada) area: metropolitan planning in, 246; federation in operation in, 339–346; metropolitan school board in, 341, 344; progress under federation in, 344–345; criticisms of federation in, 345–346; general acceptance of metropolitan government in, 346. *See also* Municipality of Metropolitan Toronto
Toronto Bureau of Municipal Research, 461
Toronto Transit Commission, 341
Town managers, 118

Towns (incorporated). *See* Municipalities
Towns in New England. *See* New England towns
Towns and townships: proportion of metropolitan local-governmental total, 103–104; and property taxes, 257
Townships: and property taxes, 257; consolidation of, 280; as participants in governmental agreements, 353
Transfer of governmental functions, 360; and financial inequities, 277. *See also* Functional consolidation
Transportation, 166, 167–176; effects on metropolitanism, 14; effect on industrial location, 14; trends in, 168–169; balanced system of, 169–170; recent developments in, 170–174; demonstration grants, 171–172; administration of, 174–176; comprehensive planning for, 175. *See also* Mass transit
Transportation, Department of, 121
Tulsa SMSA, metropolitan planning in, 247
Twentieth Century Fund, 200
Two-level approach to governmental reorganization: types of, 312–313; need for cooperation in, 334–335; future of, 346–348; an effort to balance different forces, 443
Typologies, 73–78; municipality's primary role, 123; community power systems, 123–124

Umbrella agency, as role of metropolitan district, 322
Unemployment, 86
Unincorporated territory, proportion of metropolitan residents living in, 112
Unincorporated urban areas, and annexation, 291–292
Urban, definition of, 17 n.
Urban coalitions, 139, 437
Urban county development, forms of,

Urban county development (*Continued*) 358–359. *See also* Comprehensive urban county plan

Urban field, concept of, 5–6

Urban fringes. *See* Unincorporated urban areas

Urban Land Institute, metropolitan projections, 11, 13

Urban League, 145

Urban Mass Transportation Act of 1964, 171, 172

Urban renewal, 66, 166, 204–206; local government involvement in, 199; meaning of, 200; unending process, 200–201; and the New Deal, 202; different views of objectives of, 203, 204

Urbanization: growth of, 17–20; growth by states, 18; as index of social area analysis, 54; in suburbs, 54–57; in central cities, 54–57; early, governmental systems during, 110; growing, governmental system during, 110–111; worldwide, 396–399; and industrialization, 400–401; and social organization, 401–403; mixed feelings about, 428–429

Urbanized area, definition of, 4 n.

User charges, governmental, 262

Utilities, publicly owned, local governmental expenditures for, 268

Values, changes in, 98

Vermont, no metropolitan areas in, 20

Villages. *See* Municipalities

Virginia: annexation procedure in, 293–294; city-county separation in, 293 n.

Voluntary associations: membership in, 150–152; active participation in, 151; and socioeconomic characteristics of members, 151–152

Voters, and governmental reorganization, 386–391

Voting, and socioeconomic characteristics, 148–149; in local elections, 148

Washington (D.C.): declining proportion of white population in, 63, 64; decline in population, 66

Washington (D.C.) SMSA: population growth in, 66; labor-force employment in certain economic activities, 83; gain in manufacturing employment by central city in, 92; mass transit in, 172; heavy suburban capital outlays in, 272

Water pollution control, 179–180. *See also* Water supply

Water Pollution Control Act of 1956, 179

Water supply, 166, 176–178; uneven distribution of, 176; administration of, 176–178; poor quality of, 176; division of responsibility, 178; relation to sewage disposal, 179. *See also* Water pollution control

Watts (Los Angeles), 211, 215

West (U.S.): foreign-born whites in, 61; median family income in, 90

White population, declining proportion in central cities, 64

Women, employed, as factor in urbanization index, 54

World: increasing urbanization and metropolitization of, 396–399; number of metropolitan areas in, 397; population growth in, 399–401

Wyoming, no metropolitan areas in, 20

Zoning, as tool of planning, 231–232

71 72 73 7 6 5 4

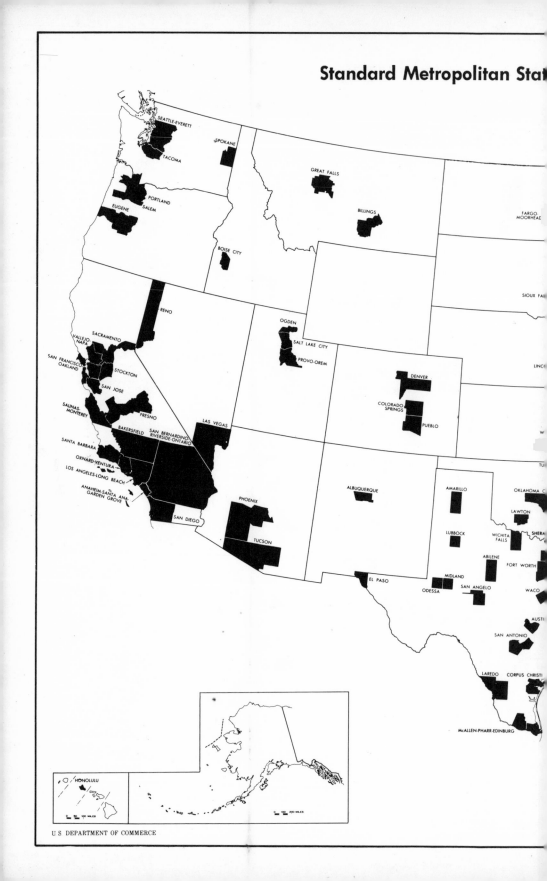

Standard Metropolitan Stat